ANGLO-CHURCH ARCHITECTURE & STONE SCULPTURE

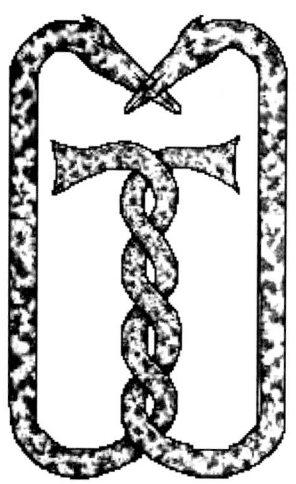

To Frederita with best wishes

GUY POINTS

Guy [signature]
29/8/2023

ANGLO-SAXON CHURCH ARCHITECTURE & STONE SCULPTURE

First Published in Great Britain in 2023 by the author as
RIHTSPELL PUBLISHING
© Guy Points 2023
ISBN 978-0-9930339-6-4

The right of Guy Points to be identified as the author of this work has been asserted in accordance with the Copyright, Designs and Patents Act 1988.

All rights reserved. No part of this publication may be reproduced, stored in a retrievable system, or transmitted, in any form, or by any means, electronic, mechanical, photocopying, recording or otherwise, without the prior written permission of the author and copyright owner.

"IN THE PURSUIT OF CONSISTENT EXACTITUDE"

By the same Author:
A Gazetteer of Anglo-Saxon & Anglo-Scandinavian Sites: Cambridgeshire & Northamptonshire (2017)
A New Church Guide: St Peter's Church, Monkwearmouth, Sunderland, SR6 ODV (2016)
A Gazetteer of Anglo-Saxon & Anglo-Scandinavian Sites: Lincolnshire (2016)
A Gazetteer of Anglo-Saxon, Anglo-Scandinavian & Hiberno-Norse Sites: Cumbria, Dumfriesshire & Wigtownshire ((2016)
An Introduction to Anglo-Saxon Church Architecture & Anglo-Saxon & Anglo-Scandinavian Stone Sculpture (2015), (Reprinted 2018)
The Combined Anglo-Saxon Chronicles: A Ready-Reference Abridged Chronology (2013)
A Gazetteer of Anglo-Saxon & Viking Sites: County Durham & Northumberland (2012)
Yorkshire: A Gazetteer of Anglo-Saxon & Viking Sites (2007)
A Concise Guide to Historic Northumberland and Tyne & Wear (1987)
A Concise Guide to Historic Shetland (1984)
A Concise Guide to Historic Orkney (1981)

Marketed and Distributed by:
Oxbow Books Limited
The Old Music Hall
106-108 Cowley Road
Oxford
OX4 1JE
www.oxbowbooks.com

Printed by Binfield Print & Design
www.binfieldprint.com

PREFACE

This book is for the reader who wishes to learn more about Anglo-Saxon church architecture and Anglo-Saxon and Anglo-Scandinavian stone sculpture. Intended for the student and non-specialist alike, as well as those who already have some knowledge of the subjects covered, it bridges the divide between an academic approach and that of the interested general public. All the places mentioned in the text have been personally visited by the author with most visited on several occasions. All the illustrations and photographs are provided by the author.

The content has three objectives.

First, to identify Anglo-Saxon church architectural features and Anglo-Saxon stone sculpture.

Second, to provide illustrative and photographic examples so that the reader will be able more readily to recognise Anglo-Saxon church architectural features and stone sculpture.

Third, to provide a gazetteer of recommended exemplar churches and museums displaying Anglo-Saxon church architectural features and stone sculpture.

This book includes in Part 1 a Glossary providing an explanation of the technical terms used. In Part 4 there is an alphabetical index of recommended churches and museums identifying the pages and their accompanying photographs where they are referred to in the text.

NOTE: This book expands and builds on the "An Introduction to Anglo-Saxon Church Architecture & Anglo-Saxon & Anglo-Scandinavian Stone Sculpture" by Guy Points first published in 2015 and reprinted in 2018. It takes account of further research and comments received. The number of "Recommended Churches and Museums" rather than "recommended sites" has been increased from 127 to 183.

AUTHOR'S NOTE OF THANKS

With thanks to all the Church and Museum Authorities, English Heritage, Historic Scotland, and in particular the Parochial Church Councils, clergy, churchwardens, guides and key-holders, and museum curators and their staff for facilitating my many visits over the years.

CONTENTS

PAGE

Part 1 - BACKGROUND INFORMATION - PAGE 9

Glossary	10
Who were the Anglo-Saxons?	30
Who were the Vikings?	31
The Hiberno-Norse	32
The Celtic and Roman Church Practices, and the Synod of Whitby	33
Suggested Reading	34

Part 2 - ANGLO-SAXON CHURCHES - PAGE 35

Anglo-Saxon Churches   37
Plans of Anglo-Saxon Churches   39
Two-Cell Church; Church with Tower; Cruciform Church; Monastic Church.
Construction of Anglo-Saxon Churches   45
1. Walling   47
2. Plinths - External Walling   51
3. Quoining   52
   Side Alternate Quoining; Face Alternate Quoining; Long and Short Quoining; Long and Short Quoining - Sussex Variation.
4. Archways   57
   Arched Heads of Archways; Imposts of Archways; Jambs of Archways; Jambs of Archways with Shafts; Jambs of Archways with Shafts - Capitals; Jambs of Archways with Shafts - Bases; Plinths of Archways; Escomb Jambs; Archways in Porches; Tower Archways; Tower-Naves and their Archways; Arcades of Interlocking Archways in the North and South Walls of the Nave; Archways in a Central Crossing in a Cruciform Church; Nave and Chancel Archways providing access into a separate Central Area; Chancel Archways.
5. Doorways   89
   Round-Headed Doorways; Round-Headed Doorways with Arched Heads constructed with Voussoirs; Round-Headed Doorways with Arched Heads constructed with Voussoirs: also with Angle-Shafts, Strip-Work and Hood-Moulding; Round-Headed Doorways with Arched Heads cut out of a Monolithic Lintel; Flat-Headed Doorways; Triangular (Gable)-Headed Doorways; Heads of Doorways: Arched Heads constructed with Voussoirs; Heads of Doorways: Arched Heads constructed with Rubble, Flints and Reused Roman Stonework; Heads of Doorways: Arched Heads cut out of a lintel; Heads of Doorways: Flat-Headed Doorways; Heads of Doorways: Triangular (Gable)-Headed Doorways; Imposts of Doorways; Jambs of Doorways; Sills of Doorways; Doorways below Ground Floor Level; Doorways at Ground Floor Level; Doorways at First Floor Level; Doorways at Second Floor Level.
6. Windows   108
   Single-Splayed Windows; Double-Splayed Windows; Arched Heads cut out of a square lintel; Arched Heads cut out of a lintel externally and constructed with voussoirs internally; Arched Heads constructed with voussoirs both externally and internally; Arched Heads shaped from a single stone; Arched Heads constructed with rubble, flints and reused Roman stonework; Heads of Flat-Headed Windows; Heads of Triangular (Gable)-Headed Windows; Jambs of Windows; Sills of Windows; Typical Windows; Circular Windows; Key-Hole Windows; Windows with a single stone slab inserted within the frame formed by the arched head, jambs and sill; Windows with an external frame; Windows with a protruding external frame; Evidence of Window Shutters and Window Frames; Blocked and Incomplete Windows; Double Windows; Round-Headed Triple-Opening; Triangular-Headed Double-Opening; Triangular Openings.
7. Belfry-Openings   139
   Single Belfry-Openings; Double Belfry-Openings; Arched Heads cut out of a square lintel; Arched Heads constructed with voussoirs; Arched Heads constructed with rubble, flints and reused Roman stonework; Heads of Flat-Headed Belfry-Openings; Heads of Triangular (Gable)-Headed Belfry-Openings; Hood-Moulding accompanying heads of Belfry-Openings; Imposts of Double Belfry-Openings; Jambs of Single

	PAGE

and Double Belfry-Openings; Mid-Wall Shafts of Double Belfry-Openings; Through-Stone Slabs of Double Belfry-Openings; Sills of both Single and Double Belfry-Openings; Sound-Holes; Typical Single Belfry-Openings; Single Belfry-Openings in Pairs; Atypical example of a Pair of Single Belfry-Openings; Unique example of Quintuple Belfry-Openings; Typical Double Belfry-Openings; Double Belfry-Openings with Hood-Moulding, Strip-Work and Sound-Holes; Double Belfry-Openings with arched heads cut out of the same single lintel; Double Belfry-Openings constructed in different stages of the tower indicating possible different building periods; Flat-Headed Double Belfry-Opening.

8. Balusters and Baluster-Shafts — 167
9. String-Courses — 169
10. Pilaster-Strips, Pilaster-Buttresses, Hood-Moulding and Strip-Work — 172
    Pilaster-Strips and Hood-Moulding Externally; Pilaster-Strips and Hood-Moulding Internally; Pilaster-Buttresses.
11. Stairways — 179
12. Porticus — 185
13. Galleries — 191
14. Use of Rooms in Towers — 192
15. Crypts — 195
16. Roofs — 208
17. Church Seating and Other Furnishing — 211

Part 3 – ANGLO-SAXON & ANGLO-SCANDINAVIAN STONE SCULPTURE - PAGE 215

Anglo-Saxon and Anglo-Scandinavian Decoration — 217
1. Moulding — 217
   Flat-Moulding; Grooved-Moulding; Roll-Moulding; Cable-Moulding; Baluster-Shaft Moulding; Beaded-Moulding; Chevron-Moulding; Pellet-Moulding.
2. Designs and Patterns — 221
   Plait-Work and Interlace Designs including: "Stopped" Plait-Work, Basket-Plait Design; Knot-Work Design including Triquetra-Knot Designs; Ring-Twist Design or Ring-Chain Design including Free-Ring Design, Como-Braid Design; Ring-Knot Design. Other Designs including: Cheque-Board Design, Herringbone Design, Meander-Pattern Design or Key-Pattern Design, Pellet-Design. Decorative Fillers. Plant Designs including Plant-Scroll Design, Bush-Scroll, Vine-Scroll or Tree-Scroll Designs; Inhabited Plant-Scroll, Inhabited Bush-Scroll, Inhabited Tree-Scroll and Inhabited Vine-Scroll Designs; Palmette-Design. Scroll Design and Spiral-Scroll Design; Stepped-Pattern Design; Zig-Zag Design; Designs incorporating Creatures, Beasts, Birds, Serpents and Humans; Designs involving the representation of Christ, Crucifixion Scenes and the Virgin Mary and Christ-Child; Designs depicting Angels and Scenes from Biblical Stories; Designs depicting Priests and Monks; Designs depicting Secular Figures; Designs Depicting figures and scenes from Norse Mythology; Designs depicting Hunting Scenes; Designs depicting Warriors.
3. Crosses — 250
4. Surviving Complete Crosses — 250
5. Surviving Parts and Fragments of Crosses — 253
6. Cross-Heads — 255
   Free-Arm Cross-Heads; Billet-Head Cross-Heads; Hammer-Head Cross-Heads; Ring-Head Cross-Heads or Wheel-Head Cross-Heads; Plate or Plate-Ring Cross-Heads; Disc-Head Cross-Heads.
7. Cross-Shafts — 263
   Angular Cross-Shafts including those with collars; Cross-Shafts combining Circular and Angular Shapes including those with collars; Circular "Column" Cross-Shafts.
8. Cross-Bases — 273
9. Grave-Markers — 276
   Grave-Markers; Pillar-Stones; Name-Stones; Grave-Memorials.

		PAGE
10.	Grave-Covers and Grave-Slabs	279
	Grave-Covers and Grave-Slabs; Grave-Covers decorated with "Bull's Head;" "Hogback" Grave-Covers.	
11.	Sarcophagi	289
12.	Shrine Chests	292
13.	Wall Friezes	295
14.	Wall Panels	299
15.	Fonts	304
16.	Sundials	307

Part 4 - RECOMMENDED EXEMPLAR CHURCHES AND MUSEUMS - PAGE 313

Access to Churches 315

Alphabetically listed and numbered recommended exemplar churches and museums with summarised information of architectural features, and/or stone sculpture 317

Index to Churches and Museums identified in the text 432

PART I

BACKGROUND INFORMATION

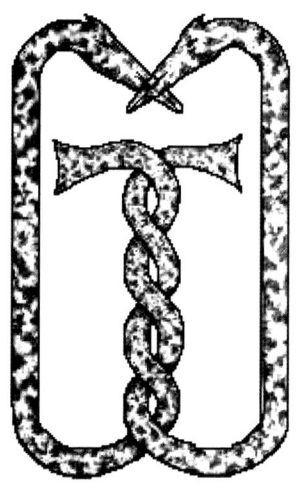

GLOSSARY

ABACUS – A flat slab forming the top of a capital.
ADDORSED - Two figures or features placed symmetrically back-to-back.
AFFRONTED – Two figures or features placed symmetrically with their bodies facing and their heads turned back away from each other.
AISLE – Part of the church running alongside parallel to the nave, choir or transepts usually separated from the nave, choir or transepts by vertical pillars or columns or archways. Also a central passageway in the nave, choir or transepts.
ALCOVE – A vaulted How.
ALTAR – A table made of wood or stone usually situated at the eastern end of the chancel, or the nave; also at the eastern end of side chapels. Altars are consecrated for the purpose of the celebration of the Eucharist (the sacrament of the Lord's Supper, the Communion).
AMBULATORY – An open or enclosed walkway surrounding an apse or crypt; often intended to allow pilgrims to view relics or a shrine; it may also be used for processional purposes. See **RING-CRYPT**.
ANGLE-SHAFT – A vertical, half-round, three-quarter-round, or completely round, shaft in a recess – the angle - on one or both faces of the jambs (not on the opposing walls fronting the central void) of an archway or doorway. Often with distinctive moulded or sculptured shaped capitals and bases.
ANIMALS – Representations of animals on stonework was often not life-like and for this reason this book uses the term "beasts" for larger animals, "creatures" for smaller animals and "serpents" for snake-like creatures. Birds can sometimes be identified by species, but where this is not possible, they are described as "bird-like". Where depicted creatures, beasts, birds and serpents may be shown with stylised, curving and/or entwined bodies, necks and legs, sometimes immersed in vegetation or in geometrical designs.
ANNEXES – Most commonly a pair of square structures usually describes as "porticus" (see **PORTICUS**) abutting the north and south sides of a western porch/tower and the west wall of the nave; their remaining two walls face outwards. Such a combination of two annexes or porticus and a porch/tower are often referred to as a "narthex" – see **NARTHEX**. Annexes or porticus can also be identified singularly abutting the west end of the nave (where no porch or tower exists) and abutting the side walls of the chancel.
ANTIPHON/ANTIPHONAL – A verse or series of short sentences said or sung in plainsong (see **PLAINSONG**) response to the priest officiating at a church service.
APSE/APSIDAL - A semi-circular termination of the chancel or chapel(s) at the eastern end of the church.
ARCADE – A series of freestanding interlinking archways in a row at regular intervals. Often used to separate and provide access between a nave and an aisle. See **BLIND ARCADING**.
ARCHWAY - Curved, structural, stonework over a void intended to support the weight of the wall above comprising an arched head, imposts, jambs including shafts, and often a supporting plinth. They may be accompanied by decorative architectural features and some of their individual features may be moulded or sculptured. See **CHANCEL ARCHWAY** and **TOWER ARCHWAY**.
ARCHITRAVE – A collective name for the features of stonework - lintel, jambs, mouldings - which surround an opening, doorway or window.
ASHLAR – Stonework prepared and trimmed with a finished surface, carefully "dressed", comprising smooth-faced similarly sized square or rectangular blocks laid with fine mortared joints in regular courses.
AUMBRY – A recess or cupboard within a wall specifically to hold sacred vessels.
BALUSTER – A turned, usually short vertical pillar, sometimes with a bulbous centre and at other times with a plain cylindrical shape. Often with spaced raised bands and spaced

grooves. Some examples may also have distinct capitals and bases. They were often used as the central support in a double-window or belfry-opening. They were also used as decorative supporting features in coping, balustrades and altar surrounds. Often referred to as "baluster-shafts".

BALUSTRADE - A series of balusters/baluster-shafts supporting a handrail.

BAND - A strip or length of either flat or thin material used to hold things together or bind around an object. Also commonly used for a strip or length of stonework providing a vertical and horizontal border to enclose decoration within a panel, or to separate one decorative panel from another, or to separate decoration within an individual panel. Moulding is often described as a "band(s) of moulding" when used as decorative features in architecture and to define borders and panels in stone sculpture.

BAPTISTERY - An area for baptism designed to include the font. Often near the usual or main entrance to the church near the west end; occasionally at the east end of the south aisle or in the south transept.

BARREL-VAULTED - A building or room with a roof which is semi-circular in section sometimes within a ribbed framework. See **VAULT/VAULTING**.

BAS RELIEF - Shallow moulding or sculpture in wood or stone where a figure, less than half its true proportion, protrudes from the background.

BASE - The bottom or foot of a shaft, pillar or column, or pilaster-strip which may be moulded or sculptured.

BASILICA - A building commonly used by the Romans for public assemblies and as a court of justice. It comprised a large, tall, rectangular hall with a semi-circular apse at one end. The central hall had a clerestory above and was flanked on each long side by a row of colonnades or arcades which provided access into lower side aisles. Churches were often built on a plan similar to that of a basilica. See the adjacent illustration – for key to plan see Page 39.

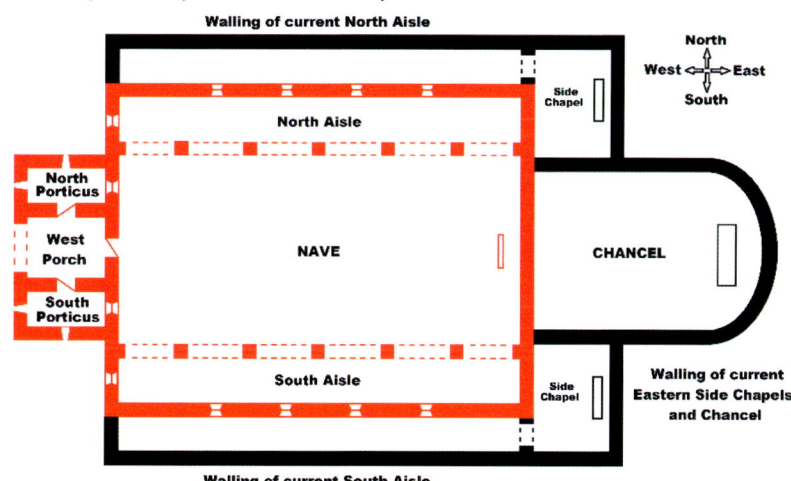

BASKET-PLAIT DESIGN - A variation of plait-work design representing the appearance of plaited wickerwork used in basket ware.

BATTLEMENT - An indented parapet at the top of a wall often used as a decorative feature. The original purpose was as a fortified feature so that archers could shoot through the indentations between the projecting protective solid sections of masonry.

BAY - An opening in a wall often divided by vertical pillars, columns or archways; they may also contain windows. A bay may also be one part of a blind arcade of round-headed or triangular headed pilaster-strips decorating the walls of church both internally and externally.

BEASTS - See **ANIMALS**.

BELFRY - The stage of the tower where the bells are hung, usually the highest stage.

BELL-COTE - An ornamental structure designed to house one or two church bells usually on

the roof of a church.
BEVELLED - A sloping edge or surface greater than a right angle.
BILLET - The additional small circular plate or roll of stonework identifiable at the junctures of the arms of some free-arm crosses. Also a design consisting of raised cylindrical or rectangular blocks placed at regular intervals; sometimes described as "chequer-board".
BIRDS - See **ANIMALS**.
BLIND ARCADING - An arcade of round-headed or triangular-headed pilaster-strips may be used to decorate the exterior or interior face of walling - individually divided into, and comprising, a row of "bays". The arcade of pilaster-strips protrude from the face of the wall. The intervening stonework between the jambs of each of the bays is flush with the face of the adjoining walling and constructed with similar stonework resulting in what is termed "blind arcading" - there is no void between the jambs. These blind arcades were purely a decorative rather than a functional feature. Occasionally, one of the bays the arcade may contain a window, doorway or belfry-opening.
BLOCKED - The description attached to a doorway, archway or window, where it is no longer open and used for its original purpose and where stonework of some description has been inserted to fill in the former void.
BORRE DESIGN - A design distinguished by a symmetrical pattern with concentric circles held together by bands. Beasts with distinctive heads, gripping paws, knot-work and ring-chain work motifs were typical. In use from the mid-9th century to the late-10th century. Named after the designs on artefacts found in a rich ship burial in Borre, Norway.
BOSS - A square or round projecting area of stonework often found in the centre of Cross-Heads which can vary in height considerably. A boss may also be an incised circle in the centre of a cross-head with no depth or height. (Bosses were also used to cover the intersections of the ribs in a vaulted ceiling.)
BRACKET - A small projecting block of stonework or woodwork used as a support e.g. the beam of a roof or an arch.
BRICK - A block of clay that has been kneaded, moulded and hardened to form a definite size and shape (usually rectangular).
BUSH-SCROLL DESIGN - See **PLANT-SCROLL DESIGN**.
BUTTRESS - A distinctive section of stonework or brickwork supporting or projecting from a wall intended to provide extra strength to the structure of the wall.
CABLE-PATTERN DESIGN AND CABLE-MOULDING - A design depicting a series of distinctive thick diagonal lines in relief which take on a distended curved shape.
CAME(S)/CALME(S) - A strip of lead with a groove on each side which holds window glass in place to facilitate a design.
CANOPY - A projection, a hood, over a doorway, niche, statue, altar or pulpit.
CAPITAL - The head or the top part of a shaft, pillar or column; also the head of pilaster-strips. Usually square or rectangular at the top and circular or polygonal at the bottom to fit the shaft, pillar, or column below. They may be chamfered, chamfered to form an inverted triangular shape, or shaped to form a square top with the bottom shaped like an inverted cone, or bell or bulbous-shaped, or shaped to form a spiral-scroll (volute). Capitals can also be decorated with foliate or interlace designs. See **CUSHION-CAPITAL**.
CASTELLATED - A feature decorated with battlements.
CATHEDRAL - The principal church of a diocese, containing the "cathedra" or throne of a bishop - the chair of office.
CEILING - An under covering or lining of a roof or of one of the floors of a room or building which conceals timbers, plaster, etc.
CELL - A small chamber or room or a church subsidiary to (usually) a monastery.
CELTIC DESIGN - Like Anglo-Saxon design, this may be summarised as including interlace, knot-work, scrolls, spirals, key-patterns, lettering, zoomorphic, plant forms, beasts,

creatures and human figures. There is great difficulty in distinguishing Celtic designs from Anglo-Saxon designs since there was considerable cross-fertilisation of ideas.

CELTS - The Celts were the indigenous peoples who retained or acquired land in the western areas of present-day Scotland, Cumbria, the Isle of Man, Wales, and Cornwall. Also the indigenous peoples of Ireland, Brittany and other regions of Europe. Many spoke what might be described as an early form of Welsh. Many accepted Christianity during the fourth and fifth centuries.

CELTIC OR IRISH CHRISTIAN SETTLEMENTS - The Celtic or Irish tradition of Christian community layout comprised a church, groups of circular huts for monks who lived in hermit-like cells, all within an oval enclosure surrounded by an earth bank and ditch. All the buildings were made of wood, wattle and daub and thatch. The church was the only substantial structure. Sometimes wooden preaching crosses may have been erected instead of churches. In England structural evidence of these settlements is lacking, but later, church-centred oval churchyards, may indicate their footprint.

CHAMBER - An enclosed space forming a sub-division of a particular part of a church; a private room used for a variety of purposes.

CHAMFER - A design feature where a square edge or corner has been cut off to provide a surface with a sloping edge which may be angled or part concave and described as a "hollow-chamfer" - see **HOLLOW-CHAMFER**.

CHANCEL - The east end of the church beyond the nave where usually the main altar is located. The part of the church intended for use by the clergy and the choir.

CHANCEL ARCHWAY - An archway providing internal access between: the east end of the nave and the west end of the chancel; the east side of a central crossing and the west end of the chancel; the east end of a central chamber and the west end of the chancel.

CHANTRY CHAPEL - A separate chapel within or attached to a church specifically for saying Mass for the soul(s) of the dead.

CHAPEL - A place of worship usually dependent on, or subordinate to, a church: a subdivision of a larger church containing its own altar.

CHEQUER-BOARD DESIGN - A distinctive pattern representing squares flush with the surface of the stonework alternating with hollow squares below the surface - similar to a chequer or chess board in plan.

CHEVRON-DESIGN - A distinctive pattern comprising a series of "V" shapes, one under another, in an upright, curving, or inverted sequence.

CHI-RHO - A descriptive term applied to the representation of the first two letters (XP) of the word in Greek for Christ, ΧΡΙΣ(C) ΤΟΣ(C). The "X" and the "P" can be depicted in different combinations.

CHOIR - The part of the church, cathedral, or monastery, where services are sung by an organised body of singers ("the choir").

CLERESTORY - The upper (top) storey walls of the nave or chancel pierced by windows.

CLERGY - Persons who have been ordained to conduct religious services in a Christian church: a collective term for such people.

COLONNADES - A series of columns placed at regular intervals.

COLUMN - A vertical cylindrical or slightly tapering section of stonework greater in length than in circumference. Usually with a capital and base.

COMO-BRAID - A term sometimes used where individual rings in two parallel rows of a ring-twist design were linked together by "S"-shaped loops.

CONFRONTING - A description used to indicate that the decoration on stonework or woodwork includes at least two (the usual number) figures of saints, humans or beasts or creatures, standing or meeting face to face with both heads and bodies facing each other.

CONGREGATION - A gathering of usually lay people into a single body or assembly. Sometimes members of the clergy may be in the congregation and sometimes the

congregation may exclusively consist of the clergy.
CONSECRATION - The act of making a solemn dedication for a sacred or religious purpose.
CONSECRATION CROSS - Painted or carved crosses on the fabric of the church indicating the place(s) where the walls were touched with holy oil during the consecration of the church.
COPING - The course of masonry or brickwork covering the top of a wall which slopes in a downward direction to throw off rain. It is also used as an adjective (coped) to describe the shape of an artefact such as a shrine or grave-cover.
CORBEL - A block of stone or wood projecting from the face of a wall to provide support to a beam or other weight.
CORNICE - A projected horizontal moulded feature at the very top of a building or immediately below the ceiling in a room.
COURSE - A continuous row or layer of stones, brick or timber at a similar height in a wall.
CRAMP-HOLE - An identifiable open-ended mortise cut into the centre of an edge of a piece of stonework indicative of Roman construction methods. To firmly secure two pieces of stonework together the Romans cut out open-ended mortises into the centre of the edges of their adjacent sides. The mortises were filled with molten lead, and, whilst still liquid, a bar of bronze, iron or lead was inserted to secure the two stones together. A distinctive characteristic of some Roman stonework and often identifiable in Roman stonework reused in Anglo-Saxon churches. Anglo-Saxon builders mostly reused these stones individually and whilst the bar of bronze, iron or lead is missing the open-ended mortise can still be identified. See adjacent illustration below which is a cross-section of a cramp-hole: continuous solid lines indicate exposed stonework, dashed lines indicate hidden stonework, and hatched lines indicate where stonework has been cut in two to show cramp-hole.

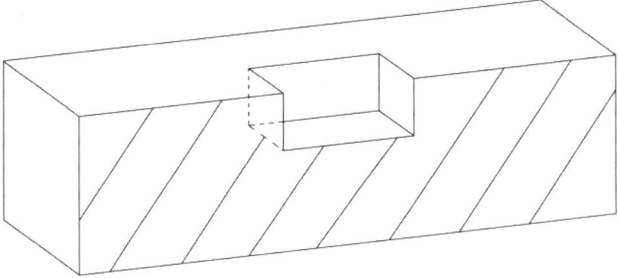

CREATURES - See **ANIMALS**.
CROSS - The standard Latin cross comprises a horizontal line placed across a vertical line. The representation of a cross signifies a sacred mark or symbol. A generic term used to describe a cross-head with its attached cross-shaft; sometimes with its cross-base.
CROSS-BASE - A section of ground or floor-standing stonework specifically designed to support a cross-shaft in a vertical position. Examples vary in height, width, depth, shape and decoration.
CROSS DESIGN - A design depicting the shape of a cross.
CROSS-HEAD - A section of stonework or a design with four arms connected to a common centre. Examples vary in height, width, depth, shape and decoration.
CROSS-SHAFT - A narrow, shaped, free-standing, vertical section of stonework usually tapering in height from the ground upwards; they support a cross-head. Cross-Shafts are often four-sided angular vertical sections of stonework which usually comprise two wider faces and two narrow sides. Alternatively cross-shafts can be circular in shape. Some examples may have a circular lower half and an angular upper half with the join between the two shapes separated by distinctive pendulous swag(s), and/or, by distinctive collar(s). Whether angular or circular or hybrid examples, cross-shafts vary in height, width and depth and decoration.
CROSSING - The central area in a cruciform church forming the junction of the nave, chancel and transepts.
CRUCIFIX - An image depicting Christ on the Cross.

CRUCIFORM - The ground plan of a church shaped in the form of a cross.
CRYPT - An underground vaulted chamber usually provided to house burials, shrines or relics.
CUSHION-CAPITAL - A capital formed by a cube whose lower horizontal edges have been shaped as semi-circles to fit a shaft below.
DECORATED - Where it is possible to identify an artefact or section of stonework that has been decorated with some design.
DECORATED GOTHIC PERIOD STYLE OF ARCHITECTURE - See "GOTHIC PERIOD" STYLE OF ARCHITECTURE".
DESIGN - A combination of details that together go to make up a decorative form of art.
DIOCESE - The district under the pastoral care of a bishop.
DISC-HEAD CROSS-HEAD - Disc-Head Cross-Heads are usually identified by their large circumference and lack of depth. Often a band of moulding around the edges continues around and highlights the "eyelets" between the junctions of the arms. The "eyelets" can surround voids, a sunken section of stonework, or a very large round pellet-like feature. Disc-Head Cross-Heads have similarities in design with Plate or Plate-Ring Cross-Heads.
DOORFRAME - A structure providing the skeleton for hanging a door.
DOUBLE BELFRY-OPENINGS - These openings are found in the chamber of a tower housing the church bells. The openings comprise two lights (openings) which are cut straight through the wall, without being recessed from the face of the walling. In the centre of the thickness of the wall the two lights are separated from each other by a narrow "mid-wall" shaft which may be formed by a baluster-shaft, or by a section of stonework which is cylindrical, rectangular, or bulbous in shape.
DOUBLE-ENDED FREE-ARM CROSS - A description used where two free-arm crosses share different ends of the same long, lower, vertical arm of a free-arm cross. Most often found on grave-covers. See **FREE-ARM CROSS**.
DOUBLE-SPLAYED WINDOWS - These have their narrowest aperture close to the centre of the wall. The opening widens both outwards towards the external face of the wall and inwards towards the internal face of the wall.
DOUBLE-WINDOWS - Two windows are cut straight through the wall, without being recessed from the face of the walling. In the centre of the thickness of the wall the two windows are separated from each other by a narrow "mid-wall" shaft which may be formed by a baluster-shaft, or by a section of stonework which is cylindrical, rectangular, or bulbous in shape.
DRESSED - Stonework whose surface(s) have been prepared or worked on with an implement by craftsmen. Such a description can be applied to individual stones, to sections of walling, and to entire walls. It can also apply to stonework which has been specifically incorporated or added for decorative purposes.
EAVES - The projecting edge of a roof that overhangs the sidewalls of a structure.
EARLY ENGLISH GOTHIC STYLE PERIOD OF ARCHITECTURE - See "GOTHIC PERIOD" STYLE OF ARCHITECTURE.
ESCOMB JAMBS - A description applied to jambs where the construction technique is similar to that employed in the jambs supporting the chancel archway in the Anglo-Saxon church at Escomb, County Durham. On each side of the central void the opposing faces of the two jambs, large, vertical "upright" stones display one of their tall wide faces which alternate with horizontal "flat" stones displaying one of their narrow long sides. See Page 68, Escomb Jambs.
FACE(S) - The two widest and opposite sides of a section of stonework, including cross-heads and cross-shafts. It can also often be used to describe (usually) the front of a building.
FACE ALTERNATE QUOINING - This is where quoins are laid alternately so that on one wall one quoin displays horizontally one long side with above another quoin displaying one short side horizontally, whilst on the adjoining walling the same quoins display a horizontal short side with above a horizontal long side. The quoins are laid horizontally lying flat on their

faces – hence the name "Face Alternate".
FACING STONES – Individually of a self-evident difference in terms of size and finish to the stonework used in the adjoining walling. Facing stones varied in size and shape and were roughly-dressed but not to the uniformity of size, shape and as careful dressed (see **DRESSED**) as ashlar (see **ASHLAR**) although there are a few examples where ashlar stonework was used. They were used on the exposed surfaces of jambs of internal and external archways, doorways, windows and belfry-openings. They may be constructed in a similar fashion to Escomb jambs (see **ESCOMB JAMBS**) or side alternate quoining (see **SIDE ALTERNATE QUOINING**) – some examples may include megalithic stonework.
FETTERED – A description applied to where the main object – usually a creature, beast or serpent – is ensnared by ribbon-like strands which are not part of its body.
FILLERS – Decoration within a panel on stonework may include fillers placed in spaces that otherwise would be empty. Often taking the form of a single or group of pellets, they may also be a triskele, or simply an elongated or round shape with no particular definition.
FINIAL – An architectural decoration on a church, often in the shape of a cross, placed on the apex of a roof or gable, or on each corner of a tower. It is also used to describe decorative features at the apex of woodwork or stonework e.g. pew ends.
FLAG/FLAGSTONES – A flat slab of any fine-grained rock which can be split into flagstones and used as floor-stones or paving-stones.
FLINT – A sedimentary rock formed on chalk sea beds containing organisms such as sponges. A hard stone found in roundish nodules. Usually greyish in colour and covered with a white incrustation. Flints are usually "knapped" (split) and when available used in the construction of Anglo-Saxon churches.
FOLIATE – Decoration which represents a leaf.
FONT – A bowl for holding the consecrated water used for baptisms.
FREE-ARM CROSS – The stonework comprises a representation of a standard Latin cross. The horizontal arms are supported by a centrally-placed vertical arm. Some examples have a long lower vertical arm and are described as a "long-stemmed free-arm cross". See **DOUBLE-ENDED FREE-ARM CROSS**.
FREE-RINGS – A term used where a single "ring", or a pair of connected rings, have been incorporated into a design – often in an interlace design.
FRIEZE – A band of painted or sculptured decoration set into the surface of a wall.
GABLE – The vertical end of the wall at the end of a ridged roof, from the level of the eaves to the summit, often triangular in shape.
GALLERY – An additional storey usually at first floor level.
GEORGIAN PERIOD STYLE OF ARCHITECTURE – This term is applied to churches built between 1715 and 1837. Typically these churches were built in the "classical" style based on Ancient Greek and Roman styles of architecture.
GESSO – A preparation of finely-ground chalk base made up into a paste-like plaster of Paris used for certain types of painting.
GNOMON – An axial pillar, rod, or pin, in the centre of sundials which by its shadow indicates the time of day. When missing, the central hole into which it was inserted remains.
"GOTHIC PERIOD" STYLE OF ARCHITECTURE – This was typified by tall, narrow pointed arches, vaulted roofs, buttresses, large windows and spires. It is often divided into three often overlapping phases:
1. **Early English Gothic Period** – This description is applied to architectural features dating circa 1180 to 1275. These features were typified by tall and narrow "lancet" archways and windows terminating in a pointed head.
2. **Decorated Gothic Period** – This description is applied to architectural features dating circa 1275 to 1380. These features were typified by tracery (ornamental stonework separating the glass) in the upper part of the window. Latterly window heads became

more curving but still terminated in a point although less pronounced than before. Columns became taller and vaulting became more intricate.
3. **Perpendicular Gothic Period** – This description is applied to architectural features dating circa 1380 to 1520. These features were typified by even taller arches and larger windows with more complex tracery and stained glass.

GRAVE-MARKERS - A generic definition including Pillow-Stones, Name-Stones, Grave-Memorials, Grave-Covers and Grave-Slabs for marking the site of a grave or commemorating an individual. They vary in size, shape and decoration; some stood upright, others were laid flat.

GRIFFIN – A beast with the head and wings of an eagle and the body and hind quarters of a lion.

GROOVE – A design made by a channel cut into (usually) stone, wood or metal.

GROZE/GROZING – The process of trimming the edge of glass with a pair of pincers called "grozing irons".

HAMMER-HEAD – Hammer-shaped item with an unusually expanded head. Hammer-Head Cross-Heads have two additional horizontal arms integrated into and extending from each side of the top of the vertical arm of a free-arm cross-head.

HERRINGBONE (Opus Spicatum – literally "spike work") – Where stones, flints, tiles, or bricks, were laid on one of their short ends diagonally in rows of parallel lines. They may be placed in pairs of rows to provide an arrow shape imitating a herringbone, or, placed in rows where each row is angled in the opposite direction to the row above and below to provide a pattern in the shape of a zigzag. The row(s) are often incomplete with few individual stones, flints, tiles or bricks surviving. Herringbone pattern may also be used as a design on stonework – cross-shafts etc.

HOGBACK GRAVE-COVER – A recumbent grave-cover in the shape of an elongated house with a convex profile comprising a pitched roof above long side walls; often the roof has a top curved ridge. The overall effect is reminiscent in shape to a hog's back. Many have inward-facing bear-like beasts at each "gable" end gnawing at the roof and holding the long side walls and roof of the house with their paws.

HOLLOW-CHAMFER OR HOLLOW-MOULDING – A chamfer or moulding comprising an inverted, top quarter, of a circle – part of a concave shape. Sometimes used in the description of imposts and the arched heads of archways and doorways.

HOOD-MOULDING – A length of moulded stonework integral to, or protruding from, the face of a wall concentric to, or abutting, the heads of individual archways, doorways, or windows (rarely), or belfry-openings forming part of the "frame" around these architectural features. See also **PILASTER-STRIPS** and **STRIP-WORK**.

IMPOST(S) – A horizontal section of stonework which supports on each side the bottom of an arched or triangular (gable)-head spanning an archway, doorway, window or belfry-opening. Imposts have four sides, three when through-stones/two when half-through-stones, exposed to view – the fourth or third and fourth sides is/are internal to the stonework of the walling and consequently hidden from view. Imposts may be flush with, or protrude from, some or all of the faces/sides of the adjoining walling. Imposts may be chamfered, concave, angled, stepped, bulbous, conical, tapered or moulded. They may have a modelled surface sometimes with a shaped pattern in relief, or sculptured with a variety of abstract, geometrical, plant and architectural designs which may or may not be in relief.

INCISED – Lines or a design cut into, or engraved in, stonework.

INTERLACE DESIGN – A design developed from plait-work design (see **PLAIT-WORK DESIGN**) which consists of a pattern of ribbon-like strands intricately entwined and woven together constantly passing over and under each other. It may include internal strands (see **STRANDS**) which turn and proceed in a different direction rather than continuing downwards towards the bottom of the design.

IRREGULAR ANGLO-SAXON WALLING – Where the walling comprises irregularly-shaped roughly-faced rubble, which is randomly sized and placed, and not in recognisable courses.

JAMB(S) – The straight vertical side of an archway, doorway, window or belfry-opening. Jambs have four sides, three when through-stones/two when half-through-stones, exposed to view – the fourth or third and fourth sides is/are internal to the stonework of the walling and consequently hidden from view. Jambs may be constructed of a single, vertical, megalithic through-stone, alternatively, and more commonly, they may be constructed with roughly-dressed half-through-stones, three-quarter-through-stones, or through-stones (see **THROUGH-STONES**) through the full thickness of the walling laid in a similar fashion to Escomb jambs (see **ESCOMB JAMBS**) or side alternate quoining (see **SIDE ALTERNATE QUOINING**) – some examples may include megalithic stonework. There are no "standard" number of stones forming the jambs and the stonework in one jamb may not be the mirror image of the stones forming the opposite jamb. Many jambs were constructed with large "facing stones" (see **FACING-STONES**), but some were constructed of, and faced with, coursed or random rubble stonework, including flints and the reuse of Roman stonework including tile-like bricks, displaying few differences to the stonework forming the adjoining walling. Jambs may have recesses in which there are angle-shafts (see **ANGLE-SHAFTS**) and may have in the centre of the opposing faces of the jambs soffit-shafts (see **SOFFIT-SHAFTS**). Whatever their construction details Anglo-Saxon jambs were cut straight through the depth of the walling without recesses or rebates – a characteristic of Anglo-Saxon origin - unless, in the case of doorways, there were internal rebates for the specific provision of a door.

JELLINGE DESIGN – A design distinguished by ribbon-like reptilian S-shaped creatures who are fettered. In use in the 10th century. Named after the creature which decorates a small silver cup found at the royal burial ground in Jellinge in Jutland in Denmark.

JOISTS – Horizontal timbers carrying a floor or ceiling.

KEY-HOLE WINDOW – Mostly found in Lincolnshire. A window whose head is shaped into more than half a circle resulting in the overall shape resembling a key-hole.

KEY-PATTERN DESIGN – See **MEANDER-PATTERN DESIGN**.

KEY-STONE – The single, central, stone in an arch.

KNOT-WORK DESIGN – A variation of interlace design where the ribbon-like strands change direction in an angular way and were loosely knotted with adjoining strands of similar appearance.

LABEL-STOPS – Protruding, often, three-dimensional, stonework in the shape of a beast or creature or human head at both terminals of stonework defining the shape of an archway, doorway or window, and also both terminals of hood-moulding where this occurs.

LANCET – Tall and narrow archways and windows terminating in a pointed head. Characteristic of the Early English Gothic period circa 1180 to 1275.

LEWIS (LEWISSON) – An iron lifting-aid used to assist in the movement and raising of heavy blocks of stonework; often used by the Romans. See adjacent illustration: continuous solid lines indicate exposed stonework or metalwork; dashed lines indicate hidden stonework or metalwork. A wedge-shaped mortise was cut into the centre of a large block of stonework. Three separate pieces of metalwork, with a hole cut at right-angles through their heads, were placed on edge in line into the mortise. Each was greater in height than the depth of the mortise and were wedge-shaped. The third, smaller, central, rectangular piece was inserted last of all. A shackle was placed around the top ends of the metalwork enabling a moveable bar or pin to be placed through both the shackle and the tops of the three pieces of metalwork; the pin would be secured at both ends. Once fully assembled the lewis resembled the shape of a dovetail and acted like a tight-fitting lever with the weight of the stonework ensuring stability. A lifting hook would then be placed around the shackle for moving the block of stonework.

LEWIS-HOLE – A wedge-shaped mortise cut into the centre of a large block of stonework. A distinctive characteristic of some Roman stonework and often identifiable in Roman reused in Anglo-Saxon churches. See adjacent illustration which provides a cross-section of a lewis-hole: continuous solid lines indicate exposed stonework, dashed lines indicate hidden stonework, and hatched lines indicate where stonework has been cut in two to show lewis-hole. See **LEWIS (LEWISSON)**.

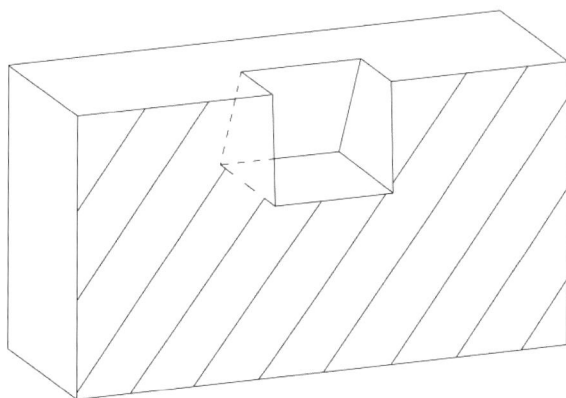

LIGHT – A vertical division of a window or opening in a wall which admits light. Plural "lights" can also refer to encased sections of glass forming part of a larger window particularly when referring to the tracery in Gothic windows.

LINEAR DESIGN – A design involving the use of a line or series of lines.

LIMESTONE – A sedimentary rock which forms mostly on the sea floor. It contains the skeletal remains of marine organisms. When available, commonly used in the construction of Anglo-Saxon churches.

LINTEL – A horizontal beam bridging an archway, doorway, window or belfry-opening – it may be wooden or stone, usually stone in churches. It may comprise a single through-stone stone or two half-through-stones – one on each face of the wall. Through-stone lintels have four sides, three of which are exposed to view when they are through-stones – one on each face of the wall and most of the side opposite the floor/ground which has the arch of the doorway, window or belfry-opening cut out of its underside – the fourth side is internal to the stonework of the walling and consequently hidden from view. Where lintels are not though-stones only two sides are exposed to view – one on one face of the wall and most of the side opposite the floor/ground which has the arch of the doorway, window or belfry-opening cut out of its underside – the third and fourth sides are internal to the stonework of the walling and consequently hidden from view.

LITURGY – The service of the Holy Eucharist - the Communion; a form of public worship in a Christian church.

LONG AND SHORT QUOINING – Where quoins are laid alternately so that on one wall one quoin displays horizontally one long or short side with another quoin above displaying one long face or side vertically, whilst on the adjoining walling the same quoins display a horizontal long or short side with a vertical long face or side above.

LONG AND SHORT QUOINING - "SUSSEX" VARIATION – A variation found in some churches, predominantly in Sussex but also in other counties - its use is not uniform. It is where more than one horizontal quoin forms the "short" between the vertical "long" narrow-sided quoins in long and short quoining. Quoins are laid alternately so that on one wall two or more quoins display horizontally one long or short side with another quoin above displaying one long face or side vertically, whilst on the adjoining walling the same quoins display a horizontal long or short side with a vertical long face or side above. The short quoins are laid so that on each wall a long horizontal side alternates with a short horizontal side above. The number of horizontal "short" quoins between the vertical "long" quoins can vary within the same angle of walling.

MASS - A service to celebrate the Lord's Supper or Sacrament of the Body and Blood of Christ, the Eucharist - Holy Communion.

MASS DIAL - See **SUNDIALS**.

MEANDER-PATTERN DESIGN OR KEY-PATTERN DESIGN - A design involving a regular pattern, in an alternating row, representing exaggerated meanders in a winding river with their long sides facing in opposite directions. Alternatively, a design resembling the letter "T" or key-shapes in an alternating row.

MEGALITHIC - A description used to identify distinctive larger than average sized stones which are not uniform in size or shape. Used in the construction of walling, quoining, and the jambs of archways and doorways. They may be used collectively to form a row of walling, the jambs of archways and doorways, or they may be used individually.

MILLEFIORI (Glass) - A process involving fusion of fine strands of coloured glass which are then cut across to provide the required detail for decorative purposes. Millefiori glass inserted into metalwork was used to decorate the covers of illuminated manuscripts and books.

MINSTER - A church from which a community of clergy served a wide area.

MISERICORD - A bracket placed under a hinged seat to provide support to the occupant when standing. Under this hinge there can be elaborate carvings.

MONASTERY - A place of residence and prayer for a community of monks and secular clergy.

MONOLITH/MONOLITHIC - A single large block of stonework which on occasions, may, for example include both a cross-head and its supporting cross-shaft.

MORTAR - A mixture of cement or lime, sand and water used to make the joints between stones and bricks and seal them together.

MORTISE - A shaped void, usually centrally placed, within one piece of stonework or woodwork, into which some other piece of stonework or woodwork specifically made to fill the void is inserted. The result joins the two pieces securely together - see **TENON**.

MOULDED - Describes the shaping of the surface of a piece of metalwork, woodwork or stonework by the use of an implement. Used to describe architectures features, such as capitals and bases of cylindrical shafts, imposts, corbels, pilaster-strips and string-courses where they have a modelled surface which may be described as "chamfered", "concave", "angled", "stepped", "bulbous", "conical", "tapering and expanding", "tapering with concentric grooves indicating an increasing or reducing circumference", or simply "square", "cylindrical", "rounded", or "sculptured".

MOULDING - A length of metalwork, woodwork or stonework with defined parallel borders. Moulding is often used as decoration on artefacts and architectural features; it can be in a single band, a pair of adjacent bands, or two bands separated by a groove, or a series of alternating grooves and bands. (See **BAND**.) The edges of the moulding may be flat, square or rounded.

NAME-STONES - A small stone denoting a grave usually with a cross and inscribed with the name of the individual in letters, sometimes in runes. Similar but larger than Pillow Stones.

NARTHEX - A covered western porch with adjacent north and south porticus or annexes bonded with, or built up against, the west face of the west wall of the nave. See **PORTICUS** and **ANNEXES**.

NAVE - The main body of the church from west to east intended for the congregation.

NEWEL - The central pillar from which the steps of a winding stairway radiate. Also the post at the head or foot of a stairway supporting a hand-rail.

NICHE - A vertical arched recess usually intended to house a statue.

NORMAN OR ROMANESQUE STYLE OF ARCHITECTURE - This term is applied to churches built around 1066 to 1170. Typically the construction of the church involved the widespread use of ashlar in both the walling and to provide the facing stonework on the quoining, archways, doorways, windows and belfry-openings. The heads of archways, doorways and windows were generally semi-circular in shape. Typically, the building style emulated the Roman style; known as "Romanesque" in mainland Europe.

OGEE – S-shaped moulding consisting of a continuous double curve, convex above and concave below.

OPUS SIGNINUM – A red flooring material made by mixing and pounding together very hard waterproof cement with crushed tile and brick. In Britain this type of flooring was first used by the Romans.

ORATORY – A small room or chapel intended for private prayer.

ORDER – An architectural term used when classifying stonework leading up to and surrounding an opening, doorway or window in terms of classical architecture. Classical architecture evolved in terms of differences in height, lightness of weight bearing elements, and decoration, from Tuscan, Doric, Ionic, and Corinthian through to Composite.

ORNAMENTED – Something embellished with decoration.

PALMETTE DESIGN – A design consisting of individual, or rows of, vertically placed, narrow-stemmed leaf shapes.

PANEL – A self-contained area having a defined border or frame within a larger construct or design. It can be in relief or recessed within the overall design and may encompass a wide range of decoration, sometimes including an inscription.

PARAPET – A low wall to provide protection where there is an abrupt drop.

PARCLOSE SCREEN – A screen which separates a chapel from the rest of the church.

PARVISE CHAMBER – A room over the porch.

PELLET(S) - A moulding or design which incorporates rounded, sometimes elongated, shapes in relief. They may be of similar or varying sizes, placed individually, in rows, or in groups. They may form part of a larger design. Pellets may also be used singularly or collectively to infill otherwise vacant spaces in decorative designs.

PELTA DESIGN – An elliptical or crescent-shaped design reminiscent of interlocking shells. A design occurring in some Roman mosaics and rarely in Anglo-Saxon stone friezes.

PERPENDICULAR GOTHIC PERIOD OF ARCHITECTURE – See "**GOTHIC PERIOD**" **STYLE OF ARCHITECTURE**.

PEW – A wooden or stone bench with a long back and square-ends.

PIER – A large section of stonework which supports an arch or other vertical pressure.

PILASTER-BUTTRESS – Small buttress-like Pilaster-Strips which are usually affixed on or near the corners of walling; demonstrably wider than Pilaster-Strips. Found mostly in Kent, but also in Essex, often where Roman bricks or tiles have been reused in the building fabric.

PILASTER-STRIP(S) – A vertical strip or length of moulded stonework integral to, or protruding from, the face of a wall intended to assist in the bonding of the stonework, the application of plaster, and for decorative purposes. Lengths of pilaster-strips may also be used and placed parallel to, or abutting, the jambs of individual archways, doorways, or belfry-openings forming part of the "frame" around these architectural features. See also **HOOD-MOULDING** and **STRIP-WORK**.

PILLAR – A distinctive vertical section of stonework usually slender in proportion to its height which often supports architectural structures but may also be found standing alone as a memorial.

PILLAR-STONE – A stand alone, irregularly-shaped, stone memorial to an individual slender in proportion to its height and incised with lettering on one face only. Some examples may have a Chi-Rho (see **CHI-RHO**) monogram depicted in different combinations. Pillar-Stones usually date from the fifth to the eighth centuries. Note: from the eleventh century "Stone Pillars" appear similar in physical characteristics, and with abstract and figurative designs poorly depicted, sometimes on more than one side.

PILLOW-STONE - A small stone denoting a grave incised with a cross and inscribed with the name of the individual concerned in letters, sometimes in runes. Despite its name it did not support the head of the deceased. Often found in conjunction with recumbent slabs covering the body with a similar small stone at the foot of the deceased. Pillow-Stones were similar but smaller than Name-Stones.
PISCINA - A basin, with a drainage hole, incorporated into the fabric of a wall, used for washing Communion vessels.
PITCH - The shape or angle of a roof.
PLAINSONG - An early form of vocal music in the Christian church. A simple melody or theme sung in unison.
PLAIT-WORK DESIGN - A design involving a pattern of ribbon-like strands intricately entwined and woven together constantly passing over and under each other making a continual progression downwards. The individual stands (see **STRANDS**) included an incised groove in the centre running parallel to its long borders.
PLANT DESIGNS - involve an individual or collective representation of plants, bushes and trees without being part of the more common "Plant-Scroll Design". See **PLANT-SCROLL DESIGN**.
PLANT-SCROLL DESIGN - A variation of scroll design comprising a circuitous design representing plants, shrubs, vines and trees which are usually described as "Bush-Scroll", "Vine-Scroll" or "Tree-Scroll".
PLASTER - A composition of lime, sand and other material, used for covering walls and ceilings.
PLATE OR PLATE-RING CROSS-HEADS - Where the ring of a Ring-Head Cross-Head comprises solid stonework from the spaces between the junctures of the arms to near or at the top of the ring.
PLINTH - The part of a wall immediately above the ground which may project from the face of the wall. Also stonework at ground level whose specific purpose is to support a cross-shaft or font.
POINTING - The mortar jointing between blocks of stonework or bricks.
PORCH - The structure surrounding and enclosing an entrance. Used for both secular and religious purposes. Sometimes there is an upper chamber.
PORTHOLE OPENINGS - See **SOUND-HOLE**.
PORTICUS - A structure up to two storeys high adjacent and attached to the north and south walls of the main body of a church; sometimes overlapping both nave and chancel. They could be a single structure or a series of attached structures similar in effect to an aisle. Porticus were usually entered through a narrow doorway or archway in an inward-facing wall but there were exceptions where it was possible to go directly into one porticus to another. On occasions describes as "annexe" or "annexes" see **ANNEXES**.
PORTRAIT - A representation of a figure, including Christ, angels, saints, humans and gods, beasts or creatures or some hybrid, as seen from the front in full face.
PRIEST - A minister of religious worship.
PRIESTS - When priests or monks were depicted on stonework, they are shown with either a Celtic or Roman tonsure and usually hold a book, often the Bible, or sometimes a cross. Additionally those following the Celtic form of Christianity were often carved with a reliquary or book satchel hanging from their neck and with both feet pointing the same way sideways.
PROFILE - A representation of a face or figure, including Christ, angels, saints, humans and gods, beasts or creatures or some hybrid, as seen from the side.
PROKROSSOS - A corbel-like feature projecting from a wall decorated with the head, and usually the neck, of an enigmatic beast.
PULPIT - A raised, and sometimes enclosed structure used for the preaching of sermons.
QUARRY WINDOWS/QUARRIES - Pieces of window glass trimmed to a shape for placement

in a design for a window.
QUOIN(S) – Collectively "quoining" are dressed sections of stonework which support the corners of a church or building. Individually, one side of a quoin forms the last stone in one wall and another side of the same quoin forms the last stone in the wall adjoining. Usually quoins are distinctly larger than other individual stones in the rest of the walling and are not always uniform in shape and size. Facing stonework in the jambs to archways, doorways, windows and belfry-openings may be constructed in a similar fashion to quoining.
RANDOM QUOINING - Where quoining may include fabric similar to the adjoining walling but with individual large stones added but not in any recognisable pattern such as side alternate, face alternate, or long and short quoining.
REBATE – A small section of stonework cut out of a jamb of an archway, doorway, window or opening to enable the insertion and retention of a door, shutter or window.
RECESS – A niche or alcove.
REGULAR ANGLO-SAXON WALLING – Where the walling comprises shaped, unevenly-faced and differently-sized stonework or rubble placed in discernible regular courses.
RELIEF – A design protruding from a flat or level surface of the stonework to provide a distinctive, solid, appearance. The elevation of relief can vary between "low" and "high" relief.
RELIQUARY – A small box or casket, often elaborately decorated, which contains/contained some carefully preserved and venerated part of the body or personal item connected with a departed saint or other holy person.
RENDERED – A process resulting in the shape of a section of stonework being altered and smoothed to fit in a particular place. For example, the side of a cross-shaft rendered so that it can fit into a particular section of walling, or to provide a lintel or sill for an archway, doorway, window or belfry-opening. This often results in any decoration being damaged or completely removed.
RENDERING – Where a coat of plasterwork or whitewash has been applied to stone surfaces, usually for protective purposes. Often covering a wall to provide a uniform surface.
REREDOS – A stone or wooden ornamental screen covering the wall behind an altar.
RESPOND – A half-column supporting a single arch or pier at the end of an arcade.
RHENISH-HELM – A square stone tower having four triangular gables on to which a pyramidal roof is affixed, thus giving the impression of a hood or helm. This is achieved by constructing the roof of four diamond shapes conjoined to form a pyramid-shape with the open triangular-shape at their base built directly on to the four matching gables of the tower walls.
RIBBON-SHAPED BEAST – A beast whose body and features are long and narrow; usually depicted in profile. Their bodies may be doubled outlined with bands of incised lines. They may be fettered by body extensions or by stand-alone strap-bands.
RING-TWIST DESIGN OR RING-CHAIN DESIGN – A variant of interlace design consisting of ribbon-like strands woven together and passing over and under each other which formed a pattern containing a series of "rings" in a row. The rings were connected by long, curving or diagonal strands. The patterns often comprised a series of rings each containing a pair of concentric circles. On occasions a single "ring", or a pair of connected rings, referred to as "free-rings" may have been incorporated into a design.
RING-HEAD CROSS-HEAD – A cross-head where the four arms of a free-arm cross-head are linked to each other by curved sections of metalwork, woodwork or stonework – known as quadrants - to give the overall appearance of a ring; they are often also referred to as "wheel-head" Cross-Heads. There are voids between the junctures of the arms of the cross-head and the underside of the quadrants forming the ring.
RING-CRYPT – A crypt with an ambulatory forming an outer curve around an apsidal chancel. The ambulatory allowed pilgrims to view relics and reliquaries in recesses in the walling, and, in addition, or instead, view a shrine in the central chamber of the crypt.

RING-KNOT DESIGN – A variant of ring-twist or ring-chain design (see **RING-TWIST DESIGN OR RING-CHAIN DESIGN**). It comprised ribbon-like strands woven together and passing over and under each other which formed a pattern containing a series of "rings" in a row. The rings were connected by long, curving or diagonal strands (see **STRANDS**). The strands at the ends of the pattern were loosely knotted to provide angular terminals. Often the rings and their accompanying strands were repeated within the length and width of the same design and formed a figure-of-eight pattern.

RINGERIKE DESIGN – A design distinguished by a large quadruped or bird with extensions from its body erupting in fans and taking on a foliate appearance. In use in the late-10th and 11th centuries. Named after a group of beast and plant motifs on ornamental slabs in the Ringerike district in Norway.

ROLL-MOULDING – A band (length) of moulding comprising a three-quarter circle in its cross section.

ROMAN BRICKS - Where available Roman bricks are often used in walling and in architectural features, sometimes collectively, sometimes individually. Physically they appear long and thin whichever side they display and whether laid horizontally or at an angle; they seldom, if ever, are used with one of their wide faces showing. They seem more like tiles hence the phrase "Roman Tile-Like Bricks" is often, but not always, used. See: **ROMAN TILE-LIKE BRICKS**.

ROMAN TILE-LIKE BRICKS – A description which better fits what many Roman bricks look like when used in Anglo-Saxon walling and architectural features. See: **ROMAN BRICKS**.

ROMAN TOOLING - Found on re-used Roman stonework. Such a description usually refers to the actions of craftsmen who have applied their skills to produce incised, angled or feathered striations on the surface(s) of the stonework. Diamond-hatched patterns, sometimes described as "broached", are characteristic of Roman workmanship intended to assist in the adhesion of plaster. Roman stonework is usually regularly shaped and sized. Some Roman stonework includes distinctive "Cramp-Holes" (see **CRAMP-HOLE**) and "Lewis-Holes" (see **LEWIS-HOLE**).

ROOD OR HOLY ROOD – Usually a sculptural representation of Christ on the Cross, sometimes including other figures such as The Virgin Mary, St John the Evangelist, the spear-bearer Longinus and the sponge-bearer Stephaton. It can be in wood, in stonework, or painted onto walling. Sometimes used to decorate cross-heads or cross-shafts.

ROOD LOFT – A gallery built above the rood screen. Sometimes used by singers during a service, also used to maintain the rood screen.

ROOD SCREEN – A wooden, stone, or wrought iron screen separating the nave from the chancel supporting a sculptural representation of Christ on the Cross, sometimes with other figures such as The Virgin Mary and St John the Evangelist. Many would have elaborate carved or applied designs.

ROPE-WORK DESIGN – See **CABLE-PATTERN DESIGN**.

ROSETTE – A decorative ornamental design resembling a rose with a distinctive centre with flower-like petals radiating from it.

RUBBLE – Rough and ready building material comprising irregularly-shaped, roughly-faced, and randomly-sized stone or flint, or reused broken or unbroken Roman bricks and tiles – on occasions some or all of these components may be mixed together.

RUDE – A description used when the stonework or design is simple, or where poor quality workmanship is exhibited.

RUNES OR RUNIC OR FUTHORC ALPHABET – A form of early writing incised on wood or stone. Futhorc denotes the first six letters of the alphabet f, u, "th" being a thorn, i.e. "þ" or "d" (hence one letter), and o, r, and c. The Anglo-Saxon runic alphabet contained thirty-one characters. See top of Page 25.

SACRISTY - For storing sacred vessels and vestments. Now more commonly known as the vestry.
SANDSTONE - A sedimentary rock consisting of sheets of sand and mineral particles formed as a result of rivers transporting the accumulation and sediment which is deposited in river estuaries or out to sea where the water is calmer. These sediments become compressed as they are buried deeper turning into rocks such as sandstone. When available commonly used in the construction of Anglo-Saxon churches.
SANCTUARY - The area immediately around the main altar of a church.
SCABBARD - A sheath which protects the blade of a sword, seax, or knife.
SCRAMASAX - A term sometimes used to describe a single-edged knife, a "seax" which was used as a weapon rather than for hunting or domestic use. No Old English source material uses this term; it may come from a single description in the "History of the Franks" by Gregory, Bishop of Tours, AD 539-594.
SCRATCH DIAL - See **SUNDIALS**.
SCROLL DESIGN AND SPIRAL-SCROLL DESIGN - A series of interconnecting circular, coiling, ribbon-like strands which extended in a vertical, horizontal or angled way. Those designs described as "spiral-scroll" coiled in a cylindrical, conical or helical way. These designs included examples of Plant Design and Plant-Scroll Design (see **PLANT DESIGN** and **PLANT-SCROLL DESIGN**). They also included examples where they formed an idiosyncratic design within a panel containing other designs.
SCULPTURED - Architectural features and stonework on which there are a variety of abstract and architectural designs in relief.
SEAX (SÆX/SAEX) - A single-edged knife, large dagger or short sword used for hunting or domestic purposes. This weapon gave its name to the people known as the "Sæx" - the Saxons.
SEDILIA - A seat for officiating priests usually on the south side of the chancel.
SERPENTS - See **ANIMALS**.
SET-BACK - Usually where the face of one wall is recessed from the face of the wall below as in each of the stages of a tower.
SHAFT - A slender vertical half-round or three-quarter round column usually with a capital and base. Used in the jambs of archways, doorways and windows. Also used as in the mid-wall to separate the two lights in double belfry-openings and double-windows.
SIDE ALTERNATE QUOINING - Where the quoins are laid alternately so that on one wall one quoin displays horizontally one long face with above another quoin displaying one short side vertically, whilst on the adjoining walling the same quoins display a vertical short side with above a horizontal long face. The quoins stand on their sides hence the name "Side

Alternate".
SILL – The horizontal section of stonework or woodwork at the bottom of an archway, doorway, window or belfry-opening.
SINGLE BELFRY-OPENINGS – These openings are found in the chamber of a tower housing the church bells. The openings comprise either a single light (opening) on its own or two separate lights (openings) forming a "pair". Both varieties are cut straight through the wall without being recessed from the face of the walling. With pairs of single belfry-openings the two lights are separated from each other by a central solid block of walling which runs through the entire thickness of the wall.
SINGLE-SPLAYED WINDOWS – These have their narrowest aperture at the external face of the wall. The opening widens inwards to the internal face of the wall.
SLAB – A flat and broad section of stonework.
SOFFIT - The underside of a lintel, vault or arch.
SOFFIT-FACE – The underside of a soffit-roll – facing the floor, or the internal vertical face of a soffit-shaft – facing the opposite jamb.
SOFFIT-ROLL - A distinctive band of roll-moulding on the underside, but integral to, an arch of an archway or doorway, and rarely, a belfry-opening. Often in the centre of the underside of the arch it may be set-back or separated from the arch by a distinctive groove which can be of some width (height) and depth.
SOFFIT-SHAFT – A continuation of a soffit-roll on the jambs of an archway or doorway, albeit interrupted by the imposts of the arch, which extends vertically in the centre of the face of the jamb opposite the face of the other jamb across the central void. In shape they are usually half or three-quarter-round. They often have distinctive moulded or sculptured shaped capitals and bases.
SOUND-HOLE – A recognisable "hole" in the stonework in the belfry stage of a tower intended to assist in the amplification of the sound of the bells, and/or to allow light into the belfry if the main belfry-openings were shuttered. Often, but not always, in pairs they are usually circular, but they can be other shapes. On occasions referred to as "portholes".
SPANDREL – The triangular space between adjacent archways in a wall or between the arms of a cross.
SPLAY(ED) – An angled jamb of a window used to increase the amount of light coming into a building. Usually found on the internal face of a single-splayed window or on both the internal and external faces of a double-splayed window.
SPRING(ING) – The point where an arch rises from its supports.
STOPPED PLAIT-WORK DESIGN – This is where strands in a pattern stop short of crossing over and under each other; they are described as "stopped".
SQUINT (HAGIOSCOPE) – A hole in a wall to allow sight of an altar from a position in the church otherwise blocked by stonework.
ST ANDREW'S CROSS – A design in the shape of a diagonal cross – the symbol of St Andrew. St Andrew was said to have been crucified on a diagonal-shaped cross at his own request since he didn't consider himself worthy enough to be crucified on the same type of cross as Jesus.
STAGE – A storey or floor of a building.
STELE – An upright, often cylindrical, section of stonework sometimes decorated with sculptured designs or inscriptions.
STEPPED-PATTERN DESIGN – A design depicting a row of distinctive steps placed together in a regular pattern whose central feature is noticeably thicker than its attached extensions.
STONEWORK – Masonry comprising stones sometimes without mortar.
STOREY – A stage of a building at one level.
STOUP – A recess or niche to hold holy water.
STRANDS – Ribbon-like threads with defined parallel borders used in the patterns of

decorative designs.
STRAP-WORK DESIGN – A plain design resembling a flat band mostly used in decorative patterns to depict the fettered or restrained bodies of ribbon-shaped or coiled beasts or creatures or humans.
STRING-COURSE – A distinctive line of horizontal stonework which protrudes from the face of a wall. Intended to assist in the bonding of stonework, to divert rainwater from running down the face of a wall, or for decorative purposes. It often separates the various stages of a tower. Usually found on the external faces of walling but occasionally found on internal faces of walling. Sometimes string-courses formerly on the exterior face of a wall may now be identified inside the church following the addition of aisles and towers in later centuries.
STRIP-WORK – A vertical strip or length of moulded stonework integral to, or protruding from, the face of a wall parallel to, or abutting, the jambs of individual archways, doorways, or belfry-openings forming part of the "frame" around these architectural features. See also **HOOD-MOULDING** and **PILASTER-STRIPS**.
SUNDIALS – A stone slab incorporated into the fabric of the church used for measuring the passing of the time of the day to indicate the time for the liturgy (service or mass). The vertical face was incised with a semi-circle with radiating lines extending from its horizontal line to indicate the time for the liturgy (service or mass). At the central intersection of these lines a wooden or metal peg or stele – the "gnomon" – would cast a shadow and indicate the time. Some examples comprised a full circle with lines radiating both above and below the central horizontal line. Sundials can be accompanied by wording, plants, serpents, and human figures.
SUPPEDANEUM - a short, wedge-shaped, horizontal, support for a crucified person which projects from the base of the lower vertical arm of the cross.
SWAGS – A distinctive pendulous decorative feature with a lower semi-circular centre linked to two higher "ends". These are found on some cross-shafts, particularly near the juncture of those with a circular lower half and an angular upper half.
SYNOD – An assembly of the clergy, sometimes including representatives of the laity, held for the purposes of discussing and deciding ecclesiastical affairs.
TEGULATED – A design comprising, or arranged like, a series of overlapping tiles similar in effect to roofing tiles and plate-armour.
TENON – A projection from one piece of stonework or woodwork for the purposes of inserting into another piece of stonework or woodwork which contains a mortise (a shaped void) specifically made to receive it. The result joins the two pieces securely together – see **MORTISE**.
TERRACOTTA – Moulded and fired unglazed clay.
"THE FOUR EVANGELISTS" – Some decorative designs include the depiction of the symbols of the Four Evangelists: Matthew represented by a winged man or angel symbolising the Incarnate Christ; Mark represented by a winged lion symbolising the triumphant resurrected Christ; Luke represented by a winged ox or bull or calf symbolising the atonement made by Christ's sacrifice on the Cross; and John represented by an eagle symbolising the ascended Christ of the Second Coming.
THROUGH-STONE – A single stone which may extend right through the depth of the wall, a quarter of the way through the wall –"quarter-through-stones", halfway through the wall – "half-through-stones" – or three-quarters of the way through the wall – "three-quarter-through-stones". Quarter, half or three-quarter through-stones require additional stonework to form the remaining depth of the wall.
TILES – Thin flat slabs of burnt clay (unglazed) or stone or slate covering the roof or floor of a building.
TOMB-CHEST – A large stone coffin often decorated - similar in size to a chest of furniture.
TONSURE – The heads of ecclesiastical figures depicted on stonework had either: the Celtic

tonsure where the head is shaved at the front, across the forehead, from ear to ear – the hair covers the rest of the top and the back and sides; or the Roman Tonsure where the head is shaved on the crown in a circular fashion so that the surrounding hair might symbolise the Crown of Thorns.
TOOLED – Where the surface and/or shape of a piece of stonework, woodwork, leatherwork or metalwork, have been worked with an implement.
TORUS – A roll-moulding design used on a column base.
TOWER – A structure taller in height than its width, mostly square in plan but also circular. It may be built on top of and incorporate in its lower stages an earlier porch. Towers are placed often attached to the west end of the nave but may also be more centrally placed, especially in a cruciform church, above a central chamber or crossing separating the nave from the chancel. The tower usually houses the church bells.
TOWER-ARCHWAY – Mostly in the east wall of the tower at the west end of the nave providing ground floor access between the tower and nave; they are often tall and narrow. Also found in the central crossing in a cruciform church providing ground floor access between the central crossing and the nave, south and north transepts, and chancel. In addition, on a few occasions, at the east end of the nave providing ground floor access to a central chamber from which access is gained to the chancel – there are no transepts.
TRACERY – Intricate ornamental stonework separating the lights (encased windows) in the upper part of Gothic (circa 1180 to 1520) windows. The stonework to support glass within a large window aperture.
TRANSEPT – The transverse sections (arms) of a cruciform church.
TRANSENNAE – A screen with open fretwork with geometrical decorative patterns occasionally used in belfry-openings but more widely used to surround a shrine or tomb.
TRANSITIONAL STYLE OF ARCHITECTURE – This dated from around 1170 to 1200. As the name implies this was when the style of architecture changed from Norman/Romanesque to Early English Gothic displaying characteristics of both building styles.
TRANSOM – The horizontal bar across the openings of a window.
TREE-SCROLL DESIGN – See **PLANT-SCROLL DESIGN**.
TRIFORIUM – An arcaded wall passage below the clerestory.
TRILOBED – Three similar rounded, projecting or hanging, lobes narrowly separated. A description mostly used in various forms of plant designs but also for the plant-like tops of ecclesiastical rods – particularly those held by angels.
TRISKELE – A design resembling three legs radiating from a common centre.
TRIQUETRA – A distinct variation of knot-work design. A knot-work design is described as "Triquetra(s)" where it comprises entwined triangular-shaped knots, representing God the Father, Son and Holy Spirit.
TUDOR, ELIZABETHAN, STUART, JACOBEAN STYLES OF ARCHITECTURE – These terms are individually applied to churches built between 1520 and 1714. Few churches were built during this period. However, many monuments and brasses do survive. Elizabeth 1, who reigned 1558-1603, decreed that the congregation should no longer have to stand in church but be provided with seating.
TUFA – A very light and porous variety of limestone filled with small holes used for building purposes when available in the construction of Anglo-Saxon churches.
TYMPANUM – A distinctive semi-circular border of a solid piece, or collection, of stonework directly above the lintel(s) of a doorway or double belfry-opening. With doorways their effect can be to change what ostensibly would have been a round-headed doorway into a flat-headed doorway. Also with doorways, they may be placed in the central depth of the opening resulting in semi-circular recesses in the faces of the doorways on both faces of the wall. Some tympanums accompanying doorways may be decorated with geometrical, plant or figurative designs, or a combination of these.

URNES DESIGN – A design distinguished by elongated stylised beasts and creatures entwined with spiral and scroll strands. In use during the second half of the 11th century and the first half of the 12th century. Named after the wood carvings on Urnes Church in Norway.

VAULT/VAULTING – An arched or semi-cylindrical ceiling with stones or bricks placed to support each other, sometimes within a ribbed framework.

VESTRY – A room primarily now used as a robing room by the clergy and choir. Formerly, it also stored the church plate and church records.

VICTORIAN PERIOD STYLE OF ARCHITECTURE – This term is applied to churches built between 1837 and 1901. Many churches were restored or rebuilt during this period, often in a style imitating work of an earlier period particularly medieval Gothic circa 1180 to 1520. – see **"GOTHIC PERIOD" STYLE OF ARCHITECTURE**.

VINE-SCROLL DESIGN – see **PLANT-SCROLL DESIGN**.

VOLUTE – A spiral scroll-like curve used to decorate architectural features, particularly capitals, but also used in descriptions of geometrical and plant designs on stone sculpture.

VOUSSOIR – Each of the wedge-shaped, tapered, stones laid in a row forming a half-round-headed arch – they may not be all of the same size or shape. Some, but not all, may be through-stones or half-through-stones. Voussoirs have four sides, three when through-stones/two when half-through-stones, exposed to view – the fourth or third and fourth sides is/are internal to the stonework of the walling and consequently hidden from view. Usually, but not always, voussoirs are flush with all of the faces/sides of the adjoining walling. Voussoirs may comprise a number of concentric adjoining bands and may be moulded to form, for example, a half-roll shape, part of the lower half of a "U"-shaped curve or a half-square flat shape. Collectively voussoirs had no obvious single central key-stone – a characteristic of Anglo-Saxon origin. Alternatively, some stonework described as "voussoirs" may comprise a mixture of stonework with rubble, flints and reused Roman stonework including brick-like tiles, placed radially to form a discernible half-round arched head – they are not wedge-shaped or through-stones.

WEATHERED OR WEATHERING – An artefact, or section of stonework, seasoned by the weather rather than deliberately damaged.

WHEEL-HEAD CROSS-HEAD – See **RING-HEAD CROSS-HEAD**.

WHITEWASH – A liquid composition of lime and water to provide a lighter colouration to built surfaces.

ZIGZAG DESIGN – A design comprising a row of short, joined, ribbon-like stands which were angled at right-angles to the ribbon-like strands adjacent.

ZOOMORPHIC DESIGN – A design representing or imitating beasts or creatures.

WHO WERE THE ANGLO-SAXONS?

The Anglo-Saxon period is defined as the years from 400 up to 1100 AD.

The predecessors to the Anglo-Saxons in Britain were the Romans with the native British; how much these peoples could be accurately described as "Romano-Britons" and how much the native British retained their separate identity is a matter of conjecture.

Around 428 AD Vortigern, a British ruler, invited the Angles and Saxons in to the country to help fight the Picts who at that time dominated modern day Scotland. Traditionally these Angles and Saxons were led by Hengist and Horsa. In return for their services Vortigern offered them land. On seeing how rich and sparsely populated the country was, the Angles and the Saxons rebelled around 441 AD and took land on their own behalf. Growing populations in the Anglo-Saxon homelands, the need for farmers to seek better land for their crops, and for some, the fear of their land being flooded by the rising North Sea, prompted migration of the Anglo-Saxons to Britain.

Initially the Anglo-Saxons crossed the North Sea in relatively small groups in the late-fourth and early-fifth centuries, but subsequently their numbers increased so that during the later fifth and sixth centuries they began to dominate the population. As well as warriors the settlers were predominantly arable farmers wanting better and more land for their crops and families. As the number of Anglo-Saxon settlers increased, the language of the native Romano-Britons/British population was replaced by English, reflecting the domination of the newcomers. In lowland Britain this was exemplified by the use of English to describe names for topographical features, settlements and groups of settlers. In response, some Romano-Britons/British intermingled with the newcomers whilst others moved westwards into Cornwall, Wales and Brittany either as a result of warfare or their own volition.

THE ANGLES came from the Danish peninsula, some of the islands in the Danish archipelago and southern Norway. They settled north of the River Thames and established the kingdoms of Bernicia (Northumberland, County Durham, parts of Cumbria and parts of southern Scotland), and Deira (Yorkshire). After 600 AD Bernicia and Deira were united to become the kingdom of the "people north of the River Humber", "Northanhymbre" - Northumbria, which extended from the River Humber in the south to the Firth of Forth in the north; including Edinburgh - "Edwin's burgh", named after King Edwin of Northumbria, who reigned 616-633.

The Angles also established the kingdoms of Lindsey (Lincolnshire), Mercia (Cheshire, Derbyshire, Nottinghamshire, Leicestershire, Staffordshire, Shropshire, Herefordshire, Worcestershire, Warwickshire, Northamptonshire, Bedfordshire, Hertfordshire, Greater London, Middlesex, Buckinghamshire, Oxfordshire and Gloucestershire), and East Anglia (Norfolk, Suffolk and Cambridgeshire).

THE SAXONS came from North Germany; they lived to the southwest of the Angles on the North Sea coastal plain around and up to the River Weser. They settled south of the River Thames and established the kingdoms of Wessex (Devonshire, Somerset, Dorset, Wiltshire, Berkshire and Hampshire), Essex (including parts of Greater London, Hertfordshire and possibly parts of Surrey), and Sussex (extending into parts of Hampshire and Surrey).

THE JUTES came from Jutland in Denmark and settled in Kent, the Isle of Wight and the coastal lands in Hampshire opposite the Isle of Wight.

THE FRISIANS were from the north of Holland; their numbers were increased by Angles and Saxons who used Frisia as a staging point in their migration. The Frisians settled mostly in Kent. Franks from the German Rhineland also settled in Kent.

WHO WERE THE VIKINGS?

The Viking period is defined as the years from 793 to 1100 AD.

The Vikings were people from modern day Denmark, Norway and Sweden. The "Age of the Vikings" was prompted by:

1. Economic factors. The populations were expanding; there was not enough land and wealth for everyone in the homelands.

2. The climate. The northern hemisphere was experiencing a periodic improvement in climate, making formerly inhospitable land desirable. In contrast, some areas experienced a rise in water levels making the land less hospitable.

3. Political factors. Warfare, consolidation and enlargement of kingdoms resulted in numbers of people becoming displaced.

4. Technological factors. The improvement of their ships in terms of construction, speed and manoeuvrability, and their ability to navigate.

Among the first recorded attack of the Vikings on England is the one on Lindisfarne off the Northumberland coast in 793. Initially, a few ships crewed by both Danish and Norwegian Vikings, undertook small-scale raids on undefended coastal sites ideally avoiding, if possible, any contact with local military forces. These raiders were intent on acquiring portable wealth for either trade or use at home. As their successes became known the numbers of raiders increased with raiding fleets of between thirty and forty ships. These raiders targeted rich trading centres and systematic pattern of raiding evolved as a result. Raids by these larger groups then developed into attempts at conquest by armies involving hundreds of ships.

Viking conquest of England began in 865 with "The Great Army" led by two sons of Ragnar Lothbrok, Ivar "the Boneless" and Halfdan. They landed in East Anglia and in the succeeding years the army moved back and forth between York, Mercia, East Anglia (where they killed King (Saint) Edmund the Martyr of East Anglia in 869), Wessex, London and Northumbria. In 874 the Great Army divided into two. One part, under the leadership of Halfdan went to the area around the mouth of the River Tyne in Northumbria. This resulted in 876 with the settlement of many of his soldiers in lands in modern day Yorkshire. The second part of the Great Army under the leadership of Guthrum, Oscytel and Anund moved to the Cambridge area. In 876, this part of the army attacked Wessex, moving between Wessex and Mercia in succeeding years. King Alfred's Treaty of Wedmore with Guthrum in 886 divided much of England between Saxon Wessex and Anglian south and west Mercia, with Viking "Danelaw" covering much of England north and east of a line from London to the Mersey. Part of northern Northumbria, with its capital at Bamburgh, Northumberland, remained English (Anglian) rather than Viking. Over the next eighty years the English gradually re-imposed their authority over the areas settled by the Great Army and their descendants.

During 900-925 Norwegian settlements extending from west of the Pennines to York were augmented by displaced Vikings from Ireland.

In 1014 the Vikings conquered all of England under Sweyn Forkbeard, King of Denmark and Norway. Shortly after his success Sweyn died and was succeeded by Canute who initially battled with King Edmund II "Ironside" for control of the country. With Edmund's death in 1016, Canute reigned as the unopposed King of England until 1035. He was succeeded as King of England by Harold I (1035-1040). Harold I was in turn succeeded by Hardecanute (1040-1042). On Hardecanute's death in 1042 Viking rule of England ceased. Hardecanute was succeeded by Edward the Confessor (1042-1066) who was one of the sons of King Æthelred II (the Unræd – The Unready) of England and Emma of Normandy.

The next Viking attempt at conquering England occurred in 1066. A Norwegian led army under Harald III "Hardrada" of Norway landed in Yorkshire. After initial success at the battle of Fulford Harald Hardrada and his army were defeated by King Harold II of England at the battle of Stamford Bridge.

In 1069 King Sweyn Estrithson of Denmark sent a composite fleet of Danes and Norwegians to join the English in their attempts to overthrow William I. After testing defences in Dover, Sandwich, Ipswich and Norwich the fleet went to safe anchorages in the River Humber. In 1070 King Sweyn himself led another Viking fleet to join the fleet he had sent in 1069. These Vikings were involved in the events orchestrated by Hereward leader of the English in the Isle of Ely. In the summer of 1070 Sweyn and William made a peace treaty involving William paying money to Sweyn to leave the country. There were no further attempts by the Vikings to affect a conquest of England.

Vikings who settled in England, whilst retaining their language, laws and customs, gradually adopted Christianity and adapted their life-style and culture to that prevailing in Anglo-Saxon England. This resulted in their becoming "Anglo-Scandinavian" similar, but not the same, as their relations in the Scandinavian homelands. Thus in this book the term "Anglo-Scandinavian" is used rather than "Viking". This indicates stonework has been commissioned by, has subject matter or stylistic influences, of the Scandinavians who settled in England.

THE HIBERNO-NORSE

Hiberno-Norse is a term often used to describe the similarities and influences between the culture of the Norse and other Scandinavian settlers living in Ireland with the Isle of Man, the Western Isles (Hebrides), Western and South-Western Scotland, Cumbria and parts of Lancashire and Cheshire, with each other and with the indigenous Celts, Irish, British, and Anglo-Saxon peoples. The amalgam of these cultures began in the mid-tenth century and continued into the twelfth century.

THE CELTIC AND ROMAN CHURCH PRACTICES, AND THE SYNOD OF WHITBY

In 664 King Oswy of Northumbria called a Synod at Whitby to resolve differences creating tension between the followers of the Celtic or Irish and the Roman practices of Christianity. Both were derived from the same Latinised Western European conversion sponsored by the Popes in Rome. But the very different circumstances of land-holding and political power in Ireland had given rise to different practices and patterns of development.

Celtic or Irish Christian communities were sponsored by local political dynasties. As there was no single regional or national central authority these communities were indifferent to conformity and did not adhere to a particular "Rule". Local variations of liturgy and ritual and a system of penitential discipline developed. Many individuals within these communities preferred isolation from the "world", an ascetic lifestyle, living in poverty, ideally preferring a hermit-like existence where they could concentrate on contemplation and prayer. Other individuals within the community were involved in missionary work often travelling alone long distances and spending weeks away from their communities to evangelise local populations and provide pastoral care.

Bishops in the Celtic or Irish communities were chosen for their perceived spiritual qualities rather than their abilities as an administrator. They avoided special treatment and lived simply like the rest of their community undertaking a ministerial role. Within a monastery, administrative authority remained with the abbot who answered only to their patron, not to a bishop.

In contrast, Roman Christianity was propagated by missions from Rome whose members were trained in the traditions of the Benedictine Rule (written advice by Saint Benedict of Nursia in Italy, 480-547, on the precepts for monks living in a community headed by an abbot). Roman Christianity was organised on a centralised, hierarchical structure, aiming at universality rather than insularity and parochialism. It was imposed on a "top-down" basis stemming from the conversion of regional kings. Its promotion was dependent on bishops who exercised spiritual, administrative and judicial roles within their dioceses. Bishops established local churches and enabled local landowners to do the same. Bishops also established monasteries which followed the "Benedictine Rule" to provide stability and conformity for the monks who, as well as undertaking contemplative study, maintained the "Daily Offices of Prayer"; some monks were also involved in the production of books and manuscripts. See Pages 37 to 38 "Anglo-Saxon Churches".

Irish missionaries had contributed to the process of conversion to Christianity of the Anglo-Saxons especially in the north of England. When Colman (of the Celtic or Irish tradition) was appointed Bishop of Northumbria in 660, disputes came to a head. The principal arguments related to the calculation of the date of Easter; details of church liturgy and canon law; the style of the monastic tonsure; the Celtic or Irish practice of following the example of the "Desert Fathers" who lived as hermits, ascetics and monks in the Egyptian desert (Saint Anthony the Great who died in 356 became known as the father and founder of desert monasticism); and also baptismal and fasting practices.

King Oswy's synod took place at Whitby (Streanaeshalch) where the monastery was ruled by Abbess Hild (later Saint Hilda). The principal advocate of the "Roman" party was Wilfrid, Abbot of Ripon monastery (later Saint), and the principal advocate of the "Irish" party was

Colman, Bishop and Abbot of Lindisfarne and its monastery. Regarding the method of calculating the timing of Easter, Colman based his arguments on the authority of Saint John the Apostle, the teachings of the church in Iona and the tradition of Saint Columba. Wilfrid based his arguments on the authority of Saint Peter the keeper of the "Keys of Heaven" whose authority had been inherited by his church in Rome; the folly of only the two "outer" islands of Christianity each using a different method of calculating Easter; and the advantages of conformity across the Christian world. The Synod determined that the "Roman" rather than the "Celtic or Irish" form of Christianity would be adhered to in England. Most accepted the decision but Colman, many of his Irish clergy, and some English monks, left for Iona.

SUGGESTED READING

Anglo-Saxon England: Sir Frank Stenton. Oxford University Press. First Published 1943.

The Anglo-Saxons: James Campbell. Phaidon Press Limited. First Published 1982.

Anglo-Saxon Architecture: H M Taylor and Joan Taylor. (Three Volumes.) Cambridge University Press. First Published 1965.

Anglo-Saxon Architecture: Mary and Nigel Kerr. Shire Publications Ltd. First Published 1983.

The Corpus of Anglo-Saxon Stone Sculpture Series published by Oxford University Press:
Grammar of Anglo-Saxon Ornament: A General Introduction to the Corpus of Anglo-Saxon Stone Sculpture: Rosemary Cramp. 1991.
Volume I: County Durham and Northumberland: Rosemary Cramp. 1984.
Volume II: Cumberland, Westmorland and Lancashire North-of-the-Sands: Richard N. Bailey & Rosemary Cramp. 1988.
Volume III: York and Eastern Yorkshire: James Lang. 1991.
Volume IV: South-East England: Dominic Tweedle, Martin Biddle & Birthe Kjølbye-Biddle. 1995.
Volume V: Lincolnshire: Paul Everson & David Stocker. 1999.
Volume VI: Northern Yorkshire: James Lang. 2001.
Volume VII: South-West England: Rosemary Cramp. 2006.
Volume VIII: Western Yorkshire: Elizabeth Coatsworth. 2008.
Volume IX: Cheshire and Lancashire: Richard N. Bailey. 2010.
Volume X: The Western Midlands: Richard Bryant. 2012.
Volume XI: Early Cornish Sculpture: Ann Preston-Jones and Elizabeth Okasha. 2013.
Volume XII: Nottinghamshire: Paul Everson and David Stocker. 2015.
Volume XIII: Derbyshire and Staffordshire: Jane Hawkes & Philip Sidebottom. 2018.

Northumbrian Crosses of the Pre-Norman Age: W G Collingwood. London: Faber & Gwyer. First Published 1927. Reprinted by Llanerch Enterprises. 1989.

Anglo-Saxon Cambridgeshire: Alison Taylor. The Oleander Press. First Published 1978.

Anglo-Saxon Sculpture: James Lang. Shire Publications Ltd. First Published 1988.

The Arts in Early England: G Baldwin Brown. John Murray Ltd. First Published 1903, 1915 and 1921.

PART 2

ANGLO-SAXON CHURCHES

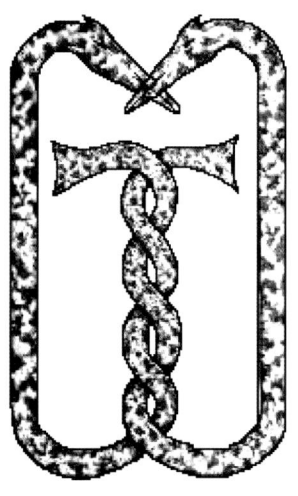

ANGLO-SAXON CHURCHES

Monastic Minster or Mother Churches were those from which a community of clergy served a wide area. Built as part of an organised clerical settlement whose members may or may not have followed a disciplined "Rule" of the Church.

The minsters varied in nature, some containing a community of monks in a monastery whose primary purpose was contemplative study, the production of books and manuscripts, and the maintenance of the "Daily Offices of Prayer". Note: Monks were not necessarily ordained as priests, secular clergy usually were. Others contained mainly secular clergy who undertook missionary work among the local inhabitants and returned to the minster church when their missions were completed. They covered a wide area where they often preached at standing crosses of wood or stone which acted as a focal point for worship. See Part 3, "Crosses", Page 250. As local churches established and serviced by these secular clergy became permanent the priests involved were given jurisdiction and eventually severed their links with the minster church. When this happened on a numerically significant scale reducing the numbers of secular clergy in the minster church it could re-establish itself as a collegiate or monastic establishment.

Those established as a monastic community were usually founded by kings, nobles and important landowners with the abbot of the monastery usually related to the founder's family. These monasteries were endowed with grants of land with rights and entitlements in a defined territory, some exempt from certain obligations – often military. Some held lands "royally and freely" (Anglo-Saxon Chronicle) with the monastery answerable only to Rome, not the king. Within the limits of their jurisdiction, abbots' had the judicial rights of a lord to hold a court for criminal and civil matters and were able to retain the fines imposed. The monastery also retained exclusively the taxes and rents levied on the people within their landholdings.

The network of local churches was expanded in a number of different ways. One of the duties of a bishop was considered to be the foundation of churches within his diocese to bring teaching and baptism to the inhabitants of the surrounding countryside; it was their responsibility to provide the priest(s) and ensure funding.

In addition, out of piety, some local landowners' established churches (usually with graveyards) and chapels (without graveyards) endowing them with land and income and appointing a priest to service them. Although often initially for the benefit of the families of the founder the churches and chapels often evolved to include the wider local community. The number of churches also expanded as a result of ceorls[1] wishing to obtain the status of a thegn[2]. Those who had accumulated wealth in their own right and were able to own, in addition to five hides[3] of land, a fortified gate or tower, and a chapel and bell tower, i.e. a church. In such circumstances the ownership of a church included the provision of the maintenance of the living for a priest.

Churches established by the laity – those not in holy orders - were often regarded as the hereditary property of the founder who provided church income through land endowment

---

[1] A ceorl was the lowest class of freemen.
[2] A thegn was the middle class of freeman; an earl/eorl was the upper class of freemen.
[3] A hide was an area of land deemed sufficient to support a family of household. A measure of the value of land rather than a measurement of area; the size of a hide could vary from one area to another.

and appointed the priest. A church was somewhere oaths could be sworn and contracts witnessed, they lent an air of probity to the proceedings, the undertakings agreed, and the decisions determined. Churches could take on many of the attributes of a court of law and for the services provided the founder and their heirs could charge and derive an income.

The Anglo-Saxons built churches from the seventh century and up to the 1060s. Whilst some churches were built in stone from their seventh century origin the majority were built in wood. An extensive building and rebuilding of churches in stone took place in the late-tenth and early-eleventh centuries. However, throughout the Anglo-Saxon period many more churches were built in wood. With the coming of the Danes in the ninth century and the Norse in the tenth century many churches were abandoned or destroyed in whole or in part. With the conversion of the Danes and Norse to Christianity, churches were built in the Anglo-Saxon architectural style; crosses were also raised.

A religious revival, led by King Edgar (959-975), and the coming of the first millennium and its aftermath, encouraged the building of more churches in both wood and stone. Some existing wooden churches were replaced by new ones built in stone, some existing stone churches were rebuilt, altered or extended, and new, additional, stone churches were constructed. Further encouragement to build churches to display landowners Christianity was provided as a result of the activities of the Danes under King Sweyn of Norway and Denmark who became King in England in 1013. King Sweyn was not averse to converting his subjects to Christianity - forcibly if necessary - and the building of a church could persuade him from taking such drastic action. During what is sometimes referred to as the "Saxo-Norman period", from 1066 to 1100, characteristic Anglo-Saxon building features can sometimes be identified in new works built under the direction of the Normans.

Typical Anglo-Saxon churches were rectangular in plan with thin and tall walls; the nave in particular being high in relation to its length and width. Some churches had a western porch or a square or round tower and some an eastern chancel or apse. Other churches were cruciform in shape with a tower rising above the central crossing. Anglo-Saxon churches often have distinctive features such as walling with irregularly shaped and sized stonework, megalithic quoining, double-splayed windows, pilaster-strips and strip-work parallel to the jambs of archways, doorways and openings - see the following pages.

The Anglo-Saxons also raised crosses to denote preaching places, places of prayer and contemplation within a monastic community, and memorials to the dead. They also commemorated places connected with the life or funeral route of a saint. They indicated a route-way for pilgrims, boundaries of an estate or other significant sub-division of land, and the site of wells - see Part 3. Pages 215 to 312, "Anglo-Saxon & Anglo-Scandinavian Stone Sculpture".

Anglo-Saxon Church Architecture & Stone Sculpture

PLANS OF ANGLO-SAXON CHURCHES

Churches were often built on a plan similar to that of a basilica (see Glossary). The following four examples illustrate the common variations in plan of Anglo-Saxon churches; a key is provided.

Most of the Anglo-Saxon features indicated – those in red – are likely to have had later, not Anglo-Saxon, additions and restorations. They may have been drastically altered in later centuries in line with the building styles and fashions of the time with few, if any, Anglo-Saxon walling or architectural features surviving. Later additions of towers, north and south aisles, new or extended chancels, may by now have altered the plan of the church so that it bears little resemblance to its original, Anglo-Saxon, footprint. However, there are examples of later archways cutting into part of Anglo-Saxon windows which are now blocked and are still readily identifiable. Often Anglo-Saxon stonework will survive in the lower courses of church walling, above and between later inserted archways and windows, and less frequently, surrounding doorways.

Note: Later, not Anglo-Saxon, windows, doorways and most archways, are not shown.

For Walling see Pages 47 to 51.
For Archways see Pages 57 to 89.
For Doorways see Pages 89 to 108.
For Windows see Pages 108 to 136 and in particular: Single-Splayed Windows Pages 110 to 111 and Double-Splayed Windows Page 111.

TWO-CELL CHURCH

The illustration adjacent gives an indication of the plan of the church and some of the likely architectural features to be encountered: a single-storey building comprising a rectangular nave with a smaller rectangular chancel attached – often termed "two-cell".

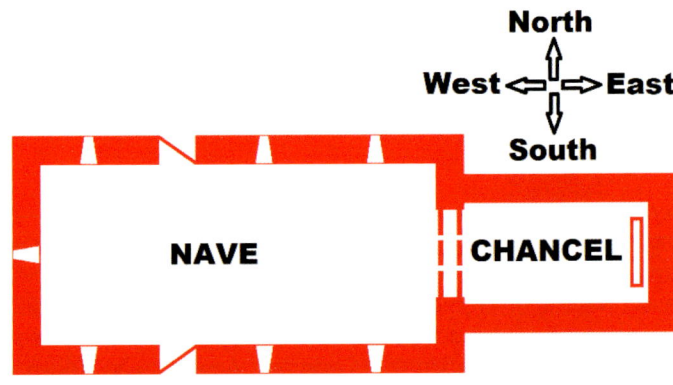

Entry to the church is by a ground floor doorway in either the north or south wall of the nave; the doorways open internally and are opposite each other (this was not always the case). At the east end of the nave, the "chancel" archway, provides ground floor access into the chancel area. The archway is supported by walling with its arched head having a void below and solid walling above. The nave is lit by single-splayed windows in the upper levels of the ground floor in the north, west and south walls. Often, but not always, there were no windows in the chancel. The only altar is at the east end of the chancel.

Escomb Church, County Durham, provides an example of a two-cell church constructed with coursed stone walling. It includes a flat-headed doorway and flat-headed single-splayed windows in the north wall with round-headed single-splayed windows in the south and west walls. See adjacent: PHOTO 1. Escomb 1.

PHOTO 1. Escomb 1.

CHURCH WITH TOWER

The illustration adjacent gives an indication of the plan of the church and some of the likely architectural features to be encountered: a western three-storey tower, a single-storey rectangular nave with a single-storey smaller rectangular chancel attached. The "main" entry to the church is through a ground floor doorway in the west wall of the tower and then through a ground floor "tower" archway

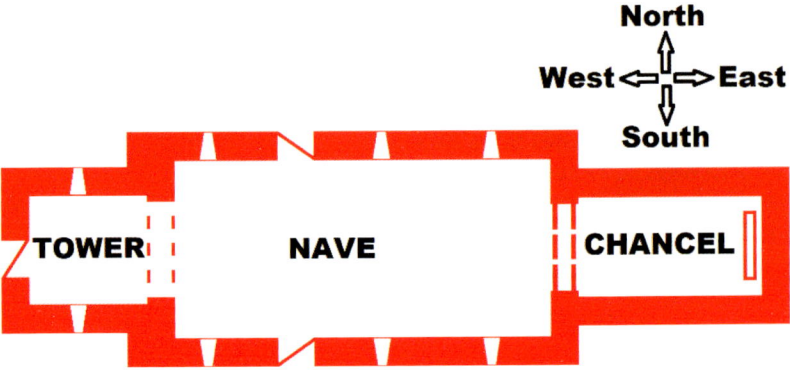

into the nave. At the east end of the nave, the "chancel" archway, provides ground floor access into the chancel area. The archway is supported by walling with its arched head having a void below and solid walling above. The tower and nave are lit by single-splayed windows. In the tower these windows are at first floor level and above in the north, west (above the doorway and not indicated in the illustration) and south walls. In the nave the windows are in the upper levels of the ground floor in the north and south walls. Often, but not always, there were no windows in the chancel. In addition there are ground floor doorways in the north and south walls of the nave; the doorways open internally and are opposite each other (this was not always the case). The only altar is at the east end of the chancel.

St John the Baptist Church, Kirk Hammerton, North Yorkshire, provides an example of a church with a square west tower, nave and chancel constructed with coursed stone walling. It includes megalithic side alternate quoining, a round-headed western doorway, flat-headed single-splayed windows, square string-course, round-headed double-belfry-openings with cylindrical mid-wall shafts, and a restored south doorway with hood-moulding and strip-work. See adjacent: PHOTO 2. Kirk Hammerton 1.

PHOTO 2. Kirk Hammerton 1.

CRUCIFORM CHURCH

The illustration on Page 42 gives an indication of the likely architectural features encountered: a single or two-or-more storied building a long rectangular nave leading into a central crossing usually comprising four walls constructed to form a square into which four archways have been inserted to provide ground-floor access to, and between, the nave, south and north transepts or porticus extending at right angles, and, to the east a sizable rectangular chancel. Above the central crossing is a tower.

The widths of the sides of the rectangle formed by the walling of the central crossing were wider than the width of any of the four buildings joined on to it. This resulted in the quoining – see Pages 52 to 57 - jutting out from the lines of the walling forming the nave, north and south transepts, and the chancel – a distinct characteristic of Anglo-Saxon Cruciform Churches.

Entry to the exemplar church illustrated on Page 42 is at ground floor level and is provided by a single doorway which opens internally into the west end of the nave. The north and south walls of the nave include ground floor arcades comprising interlocking archways supported by square pillars each of whose arched heads have a void below and solid walling above; these arcades provided ground floor access into to the Anglo-Saxon north and south aisles and still provide access into the current north and south aisles which were altered at a later date - not Anglo-Saxon. In the east walls of both the north and south aisles there are ground floor archways supported by walling with their arched heads having voids below and solid walling. These archways provided direct ground floor access from the north and south aisles into the north and south transepts or porticus. (In this illustration, later, not Anglo-Saxon walling, has been indicated to show how the church might have been extended resulting in the removal of the Anglo-Saxon north and south walls of the north and south aisles.)

At the east end of the nave a ground floor archway supported by walling with its arched head having a void below and solid walling above provides ground floor access to the central crossing. In the central crossing similar ground floor archways, supported by walling with their arched head having a void below and solid walling above, provide access to the north and south transepts or porticus, and to the chancel. In the central crossing, the jambs of the archways, and the walling above, may support a central tower.

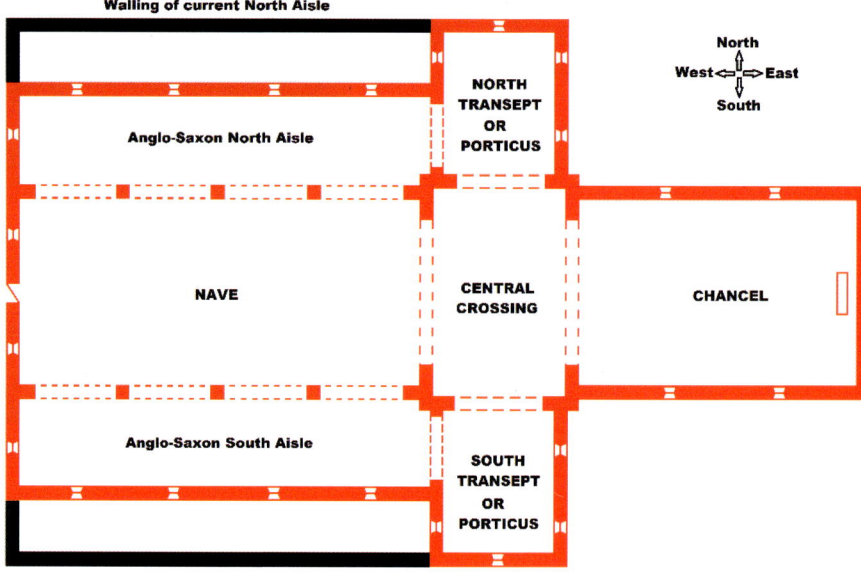

The church is lit by double-splayed windows. In the north and south walls of the nave windows are placed at first floor level between the archways. The windows in the west wall of the nave, and those in the west walls of the north and south aisles, are placed in the upper level of the ground floor. (Note: the illustration omits the windows, not Anglo-Saxon, in the current north and south aisles.) The windows in the north or south, west and east, walls of the north and south transepts, and in the north and south walls of the chancel, are placed in the upper level of the ground floor. The only altar is at the east end of the chancel.

St Mary's Church, Stow-in-Lindsey, Lincolnshire, provides an example of a cruciform church with transepts constructed with coursed rubble walling. It includes side alternate quoining jutting out from the lower part of the tower, see adjacent: PHOTO 3. Stow-in-Lindsey 1, red arrow indicates relevant quoining (ignore the ashlar stonework to its immediate left in the walling of the current nave).

PHOTO 3. Stow-in-Lindsey 1.

There are indications of stonework from Anglo-Saxon aisles surviving in Hexham Abbey, Northumberland, see Part 4, Pages 371 to 373, Number 85; and All Saints Church, Wing, Buckinghamshire, see Part 4, Pages 426 to 427, Number 175. Most Anglo-Saxon aisles appear to have been demolished and replaced by larger aisles built in later centuries.

MONASTIC CHURCH

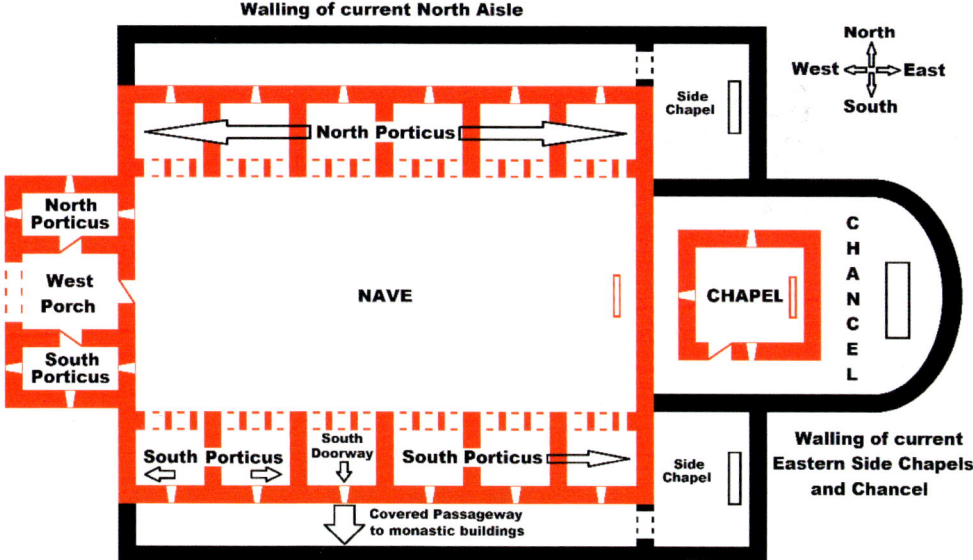

The illustration above gives an indication of the plan of the church and some of the likely architectural features to be encountered: a western two-storey porch with a single-storey north and south porticus attached – collectively these three buildings form the "narthex;" a two-storey rectangular nave; a row of single-storey porticus adjoining the north and south walls of the nave. Separately, to the east of the main monastic church, is a small, single-storey, square chapel. A separate chapel to the east of the main monastic church is often a characteristic of Anglo-Saxon monastery complexes.

The west porch contains an archway in its west wall which provides ground floor entry to the church; the archway is supported by walling with its arched head having a void below and solid walling above. The west porch also provides separate access through ground floor doorways into porticus adjoining the north and south walls.

From the west porch a ground floor doorway in the west wall of the nave provides access into the nave itself. The north and south walls of the nave include ground floor arcades comprising interlocking archways supported by square pillars with arched heads with a void below and solid walling above; these arcades provide ground floor access into porticus adjoining the north and south walls of the nave. Note: access from the nave into the porticus may be through archways but, alternatively, access may be through doorways inserted into the solid walling of the north and south walls of the nave. (In this illustration, later, not Anglo-Saxon walling, has been indicated to show how the church might have been extended resulting in the removal of the Anglo-Saxon east wall of the nave and the removal of the walls of the Anglo-Saxon porticus adjoining the north and south walls of the nave.)

At first floor level (not indicated in the illustration), the west porch has a single-splayed window in its west wall above the archway in the ground floor. The north and south porticus entered from the porch are lit by single-splayed windows in the upper levels of the ground floor in their external facing west and north or south walls. In the porticus adjoining the north and south walls of the nave the windows are in the upper levels of the ground floor in their external facing north or south walls.

The nave is lit by single-splayed windows. These windows are placed at first floor level and at a sufficient height so that they look above the roofs of, and not into, the porticus flanking the north and south walls of the porch and the porticus flanking the north and south walls of the nave. The windows in the north and south walls of the nave are placed between the archways below - these windows are not indicated in the illustration. The only altar in the church is at the east end of the nave.

The separate small chapel to the east of the main monastic church is entered at ground floor level through a doorway opening inwards in the south wall. The chapel has a single-splayed window in the upper level of the ground floor in three of its four walls. There is an altar adjacent to the east wall.

All Saints Church, Brixworth, Northamptonshire, provides an example of a former monastic church constructed with rubble walling. The square tower incorporates an earlier porch with round-headed doorways into the former north and south porticus adjoining. The nave includes round-headed interlocking archways, now blocked, and formerly providing access into porticus (now demolished) adjoining the north and south walls of the nave. At first floor level there are round-headed single-splayed windows. A later Anglo-Saxon stair turret providing access into the tower was added. See adjacent: PHOTO 4. Brixworth 1.

PHOTO 4. Brixworth 1.

CONSTRUCTION OF ANGLO-SAXON CHURCHES

Typical Anglo-Saxon churches consisted of a western rectangular nave with a smaller eastern square chancel or semi-circular apse attached. Entrance was through a ground floor doorway in the west wall of the nave sometimes instead of, or in addition to, doorways in the north and south walls. See Page 94: PHOTO 118. Escomb 3 (doorway in north wall of nave); and Page 104: PHOTO 147. Earls Barton 2 (doorway in west wall of the tower-nave).

In some churches the north and south walls of the nave were pierced by arcades of interlocking round-headed archways providing access into north and south aisles - see Page 76: PHOTO 83. Wing 1, and PHOTO 84. Wing 2; or, into a row of north and south porticus - see Page 76: PHOTO 85. Brixworth 3, and PHOTO 86. Brixworth 4.

Walls were thin and tall, the nave in particular was high in relation to its length and width. Archways, doorways, and windows were often narrow in comparison with their height and were usually cut straight through the depth of the wall without recesses or rebates.

Some churches had a western porch (with external access) or a western porticus (without external access). Others had a square tower (some at one time may have had north and south porticus attached) which might incorporate an earlier porch.

St Peter's Church, Monkwearmouth, Sunderland, County Durham, has a square tower incorporating an earlier porch both constructed with coursed rubble walling. The western archway in the porch/tower (on the left-hand side of the photograph) provided the main entrance to the church and a southern doorway (on the right-hand side of the photograph) provided access to an adjoining south porticus - now demolished. See adjacent left: PHOTO 5. Monkwearmouth 1, showing the roofline of the former porch arrowed red.

Some churches had round towers. St Peter's Church, Forncett St Peter, Norfolk, has a round tower constructed with coursed rubble walling with flints. See adjacent right: PHOTO 6. Forncett St Peter 1.

PHOTO 5.
Monkwearmouth 1.

PHOTO 6.
Forncett St Peter 1.

The tower usually housed the church bells. Other rooms in the tower may have been used as chapels, to house reliquaries and relics, or for the storage of books and manuscripts. They may also have provided accommodation for a priest, acted as a schoolroom, and used as a secure refuge in times of danger.

Doorways in the east wall of a tower, at first floor and higher levels, may indicate a western gallery or balcony extending into the nave, or an upper room in the nave itself. These doorways are now mainly blocked and often appear as opening into space – particularly those external facing. Reliquaries and relics kept in the tower may have been displayed from a balcony accessed through these doorways to the congregation below assembled outside the church, or inside the nave, at church festivals or on other special occasions.

Sometimes western galleries or upper rooms in the nave may have been accessed by wooden stairway(s): in the nave itself, or, from within attached north and south porticus or aisle(s) or, attached to the north and south walls of the nave externally. What these western galleries or upper rooms were used for is open to question, some, in a monastic church for example, could have been used as a scriptorium or a library.

St Peter's Church, Monkwearmouth, Sunderland, County Durham, has a nave with a likely interior first floor wooden gallery which at one time extended eastwards from the west wall. What is now a first-floor doorway was formerly an Anglo-Saxon round-headed single-splayed window. See below left: PHOTO 7. Monkwearmouth 2, with the position of the likely gallery indicated by the rectangular red box.

St Mary's Church, Deerhurst, Gloucestershire, has a nave with a likely interior first floor wooden gallery extending eastwards from the west wall. It has separate moulded corbels surviving which probably supported the gallery. At first floor level there is a blocked, round-headed, doorway which provided access to the gallery from the porch/tower. See adjacent right: PHOTO 8. Deerhurst 1, showing the corbels arrowed red, and the blocked doorway arrowed black.

 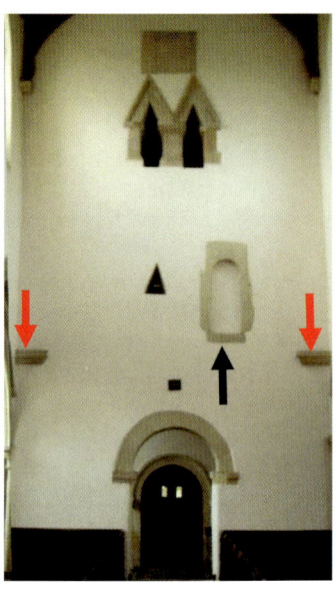

PHOTO 7. Monkwearmouth 2.   PHOTO 8. Deerhurst 1.

Some churches were cruciform in shape with a western nave extending to a central crossing with a tower rising above, with porticus or transepts extending north and south, and a chancel to the east. See Page 210: PHOTO 429. Breamore 5. Cruciform churches may have had accompanying aisles accessed through an arcade of round-headed archways in the north and south walls of the nave with separate eastern archways piercing the west walls of the north and south porticus or transepts.

Some cruciform churches, or those churches with a central area but without porticus or transepts, had upper rooms with doorways at first floor or higher levels enabling communication between the upper room(s) in the central crossing and the nave, porticus or transepts, and chancel - see Page 102. PHOTO 140. Langford 10.

Examples survive of churches with a crypt - see Pages 195 to 208: "15. Crypts". A few churches had a "Tower-Nave" comprising a nave within the lowest stage(s) of the tower with a chancel extending directly from the east wall: see Pages 73 to 75: "Tower-Naves and their Archways".

Whilst many Anglo-Saxon churches would originally have been constructed in wood, some were constructed in stone from the outset, often utilising stonework from nearby Roman buildings. There are no known wooden Anglo-Saxon churches surviving apart from the one at Greensted Church in Essex. At Greensted, the nave walls include original Anglo-Saxon vertical split trunks of oak trees, which now rest on a Victorian wooden sill supported by Victorian bricks. Often Anglo-Saxon stone churches, and some of their distinctive characteristic architectural features, survive to a greater or lesser extent incorporated in whole or in part into extensive later, not Anglo-Saxon, church rebuilding and restoration programmes.

Limestone and sandstone were common building materials used in the construction of Anglo-Saxon churches; knapped flints were also used. Where available, Roman stonework including tile-like bricks, were used. Anglo-Saxon mortar was of good quality, it hardened with age, and was similar in mixture and average particle size to that used today. The quality of the Anglo-Saxon mortar is one of the reasons why some fabric survives in its original form and one of the reasons why Anglo-Saxon walling can carry weight for which it was not originally intended. This is exemplified by the retention of original Anglo-Saxon walling in the nave walls above "new" arcades of interlocking round-headed archways inserted in later centuries; also the lower stages of original Anglo-Saxon porches and towers can support "new" stages of towers built on top of them in later centuries. See Page 45: PHOTO 5. Monkwearmouth 1. The quality of the mortar also enables identification of courses of Anglo-Saxon stonework among those built by Norman and later builders where although their mortar was finer in composition and neater in presentation it had less inherent strength.

The floors of many churches would have comprised pressed soil identical to the soil on which the church stood sometimes covered by straw. Others might have floors covered with cobbles or flints where these were available, some might have had the floor covered with flagstones or with mortar. The floors of monastic or minster churches, or where the patron was wealthy, might be covered with opus signinum a white or grey coloured mortar often with large pieces of pink or red crushed tiles or bricks throughout the composition; sometimes the tiles and bricks were only on the surface in more fragmentary form.

Windows in most churches would be open with wooden or fabric shutters; some might have plain glass and sometimes in addition coloured glass.

Roofs were supported by a wooden framework and covered with mainly thatch or turf, or triangular wooden shingle or stone tiles. Monastic buildings would more likely be tiled; some might have lead roofing, or stone tiles with lead flashing along the edges.

Often Anglo-Saxon churches were plastered white externally and plastered and painted internally. Red seems to have been a popular colour internally and narrow bands or stripes may have been used to indicate architectural details in the fabric such as pilaster-strips and the outline of doorways and to indicate the horizontal courses in the walling. To assist in the binding of the plaster the Anglo-Saxons used cow hairs in its composition whereas Norman and later builders usually used horse hairs in their plaster composition. Some indications and some vestiges of plaster survive.

1. WALLING
The walls of the naves in most Anglo-Saxon churches were less than 36 inches/91 centimetres thick/deep - similarly the walls of porticus or transepts, and chancels where these survive. The relative lack of depth is a characteristic of Anglo-Saxon workmanship; inevitably there are exceptions where the depth of the walling was greater. Although churches may have

extant Anglo-Saxon material in their porches and towers, many have been drastically altered by Norman and later builders, and consequently no similar assumption can be made regarding the thickness/depth of the walling in these structures or in the walling supporting the central towers in cruciform churches.

Anglo-Saxon walling may comprise shaped or irregularly-shaped, roughly-faced, and differently-sized stones, flints or rubble. It may include through-stones extending right through the depth of the wall, or half or three-quarter-through-stones. The absence of neatly shaped and regularly-sized dressed stones is an indication of stonework of Anglo-Saxon origin.

PHOTO 9.
Appleton-le-Street 1.

PHOTO 10. Little Bardfield 1.

PHOTO 11. Oxford 1.

Sometimes the stonework was laid in discernible regular courses and termed "Coursed Stone" or "Coursed Rubble". The stonework used in "Coursed Stone" was generally of rectangular shape of approximately similar size. Individual stones were seldom carefully dressed, and surfaces were "rough" – rarely smoothed. Although laid in fairly uniform courses, individual courses may show a change in the nature and shape and size of the stonework used. This can result in the shape and size of the stonework used in the courses below and above being altered to compensate for this change. All Saints Church, Appleton-le-Street, North Yorkshire provides an example of a church constructed with coursed stonework where there is a noticeable variation in some of the sizes of the individual stones used. See above left: PHOTO 9. Appleton-le-Street 1.

The stonework used in "Coursed Rubble" was generally of irregular shape and size, its only requirement was that its height more or less fitted in with the stones adjacent in the same individual course of the wall. "Rubble" may also include flints or reused Roman tiles or tile-like bricks and stonework. St Katherine's Church, Little Bardfield, Essex, provides an example of a church constructed with coursed rubble stonework including flints, and is a rare example of a square tower built without quoining constructed with roughly-dressed stonework. See above middle: PHOTO 10. Little Bardfield 1.

Alternatively, Anglo-Saxon stonework may comprise irregularly-shaped, roughly-faced and randomly-sized rubble comprising any mixture of small pieces of stone, flint, or reused Roman tiles or tile-like bricks, not laid in discernible courses and termed "Random Rubble Walling". St Michael's Church, Oxford, Oxfordshire, provides an example of a church constructed with random rubble stonework. See Page 48 above right: PHOTO 11. Oxford 1.

Large "megalithic" stones may be randomly placed in both coursed and un-coursed stonework and rubble – their use is characteristic of Anglo-Saxon workmanship.

St Andrew's Church, Wroxeter, Shropshire, is constructed with coursed stonework including megalithic work from reused Roman stonework. See adjacent: PHOTO 12. Wroxeter 1.

PHOTO 12. Wroxeter 1.

On other occasions stonework may be laid in a herringbone pattern.

St James Church, Selham, West Sussex is constructed with random rubble stonework including herringbone stonework. See adjacent: PHOTO 13. Selham 1.

Some churches include two types of stonework indicating two likely different building periods.

PHOTO 13. Selham 1.

St Helen's Church, Skipwith, North Yorkshire, provides an example of where it is possible to identify two different types of stonework indicating two different construction periods. The lower part of the tower is constructed with coursed stonework (larger stones) including megalithic side alternate quoining up to the tops of the lowest windows in the north and south walls. Above, the remaining Anglo-Saxon part of the tower, was constructed with coursed rubble stonework (smaller stones). See adjacent: PHOTO 14. Skipwith 1, showing the coursed stonework arrowed red, coursed rubble stonework arrowed black.

St Mary's Church, Broughton, Lincolnshire, provides another example of where it is possible to identify two different types of stonework indicating two different construction periods. The stair turret is mostly constructed with large roughly-dressed "ashlar-like" stonework with some coursed rubble stonework below whilst the tower, formerly a "Tower-Nave", is constructed with both random and coursed rubble including stonework laid in herringbone fashion.

PHOTO 14. Skipwith 1.

See adjacent: PHOTO 15. Broughton 1, showing the ashlar-like stonework arrowed red, the rubble stonework arrowed black, and the herringbone arrowed blue.

Other churches may have one type of stonework internally and another type of stonework externally, whether this indicates two construction periods is open to debate. St Mary's Church, Seaham, County Durham, provides just such an example. Internally it is constructed with coursed stonework whilst externally it is constructed with coursed rubble stonework including herringbone stonework. See below left: PHOTO 16. Seaham 1 – internally, and below right: PHOTO: 17. Seaham 2 – externally.

PHOTO 15. Broughton 1.

PHOTO 16. Seaham 1.

Where it was readily available existing tooled stonework or tiles and bricks from nearby Roman remains were reused collectively or individually to construct the walling itself or to decorate features such as archways, doorways and windows.

Roman stonework is usually regularly shaped and sized. Some Roman stonework includes distinctive "cramp-holes" – an identifiable hole in a piece of Roman stonework to receive a locking-pin or clamping bolt (see Glossary). Other Roman stonework may

PHOTO 17. Seaham 2.

include a "Lewis-Hole" - a rectangular, usually centrally placed, groove in the centre of large blocks of stone to assist their movement and requiring the use of a "Lewis" (see Glossary). Where cramp-holes and lewis-holes can be identified among Anglo-Saxon stonework they are unlikely to have been reused in the same way as they were originally intended by the Romans.

What is often described as "Roman tooling" appears as incised, angled or feathered striations on the surface(s) of the stonework often resulting in diamond-hatched patterns (also referred to as "brocading") which are characteristic of Roman decoration.

Where Roman bricks were used, they often appear long and thin whichever side they display and whether laid horizontally or at an angle; they were seldom used with one of their wide faces showing. Some are clearly tiles rather than bricks but for the avoidance of doubt the phrase "Roman Tiles or Tile-Like Bricks" is used in this book.

Holy Trinity Church, Colchester, Essex, provides an example of a tower constructed with random rubble stonework including the reuse of Roman bricks and tiles. See adjacent: PHOTO 18. Colchester 1.

For reused Roman stonework rather than tiles or tile-like bricks see Page 49: PHOTO 12. Wroxeter 1.

Rarely did the Anglo-Saxons use smoothly-dressed stones of a uniform shape and size – often described as "ashlar" stonework favoured in Norman and later periods.'

PHOTO 18. Colchester 1.

St Laurence Church, Bradford-on-Avon, Wiltshire, provides an example of an Anglo-Saxon church constructed with ashlar stonework: See adjacent: PHOTO 19. Bradford-on-Avon 1, showing the roofline of the former south porticus arrowed red.

For ashlar-like stonework also see Page 50: PHOTO 15. Broughton 1.

2. PLINTHS - EXTERNAL WALLING

Externally stone or rubble plinths projecting from the bottom of walling may be Anglo-Saxon in origin where they accompany stonework which has no alterations, additions or removals which are not Anglo-Saxon. Confirmation may be provided when, for example, the stonework includes an Anglo-Saxon Doorway, or, internally, by its support of the base of an Anglo-Saxon Archway. See Pages 67 to 68, "Plinths of Archways".

PHOTO 19. Bradford-on-Avon 1.

Whilst many examples of plinths will comprise a single, flat or square-shaped, course of stonework, some churches have plinths comprising two or three "steps" which may be square or chamfered, or a combination of both with the square step always being the lowest step.

St Andrew's Church, Brigstock, Northamptonshire, provides an example of a single square stone plinth at the base of its stair turret. See adjacent: PHOTO 20. Brigstock 1, showing the square plinth arrowed red.

PHOTO 20. Brigstock 1.

St Katherine's Church, Little Bardfield, Essex, provides an example of a square, single, plinth at the base of the tower constructed with rubble and flints – gravel and vegetation now obscures much of its length. See adjacent: PHOTO 21. Little Bardfield 2.

St Helen's Church, Skipwith, North Yorkshire, provides an example of a square and chamfered double stone plinth at the base of the tower – gravel now obscures much of the square base. See below left: PHOTO 22. Skipwith 2, showing the square plinth arrowed red, and the chamfered plinth arrowed black.

PHOTO 21. Little Bardfield 2.

PHOTO 22. Skipwith 2.

PHOTO 23. Diddlebury 1.

St Peter's Church, Diddlebury, Shropshire, provides an example of a square, three-stepped, stone plinth. See above right: PHOTO 23. Diddlebury 1, showing each step arrowed red.

Note: Not all Anglo-Saxon walling had a plinth(s), but more may be discovered if, and when, the adjoining ground is lowered for some reason or adjacent, not Anglo-Saxon, paving stones or gravel abutting the walls, are removed.

3. QUOINING

Quoins, collectively "quoining", are sections of stonework which support the corners of a building to assist and stabilise the construction; they also ameliorate the effects of damage, weathering and decay. Quoins are usually roughly "dressed" – see Glossary. Individually, one side of a quoin forms the last stone in one wall and another side of the same quoin forms the last stone in the wall adjoining. Most sides of the quoins are hidden from view by the interior fabric of the walling.

Individual quoins are usually distinctly larger than other individual stones used in the adjoining walling. The height of an individual quoin may equate to two or three courses of the stonework used in the adjoining walling. Quoins are not usually uniform in shape and size and may include the use of distinctly large "megalithic" stones - a characteristic of Anglo-Saxon workmanship. In some church towers the size of the quoining may reduce in size as the walls increase in height.

Some churches may have variations in types of quoining reflecting a change of masons undertaking the work, or different periods of building work. The tower and nave may have different types of quoining.

St Peter's-At-Gowts, Lincoln, Lincolnshire, provides an example of two types of quoining. The tower has side alternate quoining and the nave long and short quoining. See adjacent left: PHOTO 24. Lincoln 1, showing the side alternate arrowed red, and the long and short arrowed black.

St Bartholomew's Church, Whittingham, Northumberland, also provides an example of two types of quoining. The tower has side alternate quoining and the nave long and short quoining. See adjacent right: PHOTO 25. Whittingham 1, showing the side alternate arrowed red, and the long and short arrowed black.

PHOTO 24. Lincoln 1.

PHOTO 25. Whittingham 1.

Quoins may be made up of stone, rubble and flint; reused complete or broken Roman tiles or tile-like bricks may also be used where these are available. Where this occurs it is often described as "Rubble Quoining".

St Katherine's Church, Little Bardfield, Essex, provides an example of where the quoining of both the tower and nave are constructed of rubble stonework with flints – there are no facing stones. See adjacent: PHOTO 26. Little Bardfield 3, showing the quoining of tower arrowed red, and the quoining of nave arrowed black.

All Saints Church, Brixworth, Northamptonshire, provides an example of where the quoining is constructed with rubble stonework. See Page 44. PHOTO 4. Brixworth 1.

Holy Trinity Church, Colchester, Essex, provides an example of where the quoining is constructed with rubble stonework with reused Roman tiles or tile-like bricks. See Page 51. PHOTO 18. Colchester 1.

There are some examples of "cut-back" quoining where part of the surface of the quoining has been removed on both sides of the same quoin – said to assist the plastering of the faces of the walling

PHOTO 26. Little Bardfield 3.

but also the cut-back part of the quoining provided a decorative band similar to a pilaster-strip (see Pages 172 to 179: "10. Pilaster-Strips, Pilaster-Buttresses, Hood-Moulding and Strip-Work"). This results in a distinctive vertical divide between the part of the quoin "cut-back" and the remaining part of the quoin which stands in relief.

St Mary's Church, Stow-in-Lindsey, Lincolnshire, provides an example of "Cut-Back Side

Alternate Quoining" - see below right: PHOTO 28. Stow-in-Lindsey 2. All Saints Church, Wittering, Cambridgeshire, provides an example of "Cut-Back Long and Short Quoining" - see also Page 55: PHOTO 32. Wittering 1.

Facing stones on the exposed surfaces of jambs of internal and external archways, doorways, windows and belfry-openings are often constructed in a similar way to quoining including the use of megalithic stonework. When used to form through-stone jambs in archways, doorways, windows, or belfry-openings each quoin-like stone displays three sides, but when they are not through-stones each quoin-like stone displays only two sides.

Most quoining is laid either in "side-alternate", "face-alternate", or "long and short" fashion. However, some quoining does not conform to these descriptions and is more appropriately described as "random quoining". This is where quoining may include stonework laid in similar fashion to the adjoining walling which may or may not be coursed. Random quoining may also include individual large stones placed in no recognisable pattern.

SIDE ALTERNATE QUOINING
Side Alternate Quoining is where the quoins are laid alternately so that on one wall one quoin displays horizontally one long face with above another quoin displaying one short side vertically, whilst on the adjoining walling the same quoins display a vertical short side with above a horizontal long face. The quoins stand on their sides, hence the name "Side Alternate". Where appropriate Side Alternate Quoining may include examples prefixed with the terms "Megalithic" or "Cut-Back".

See adjacent illustration: black lines denote exposed stonework, hatched black lines denote hidden stonework.

St Andrew's Church, Bywell, Northumberland, provides an example of where the tower has side alternate quoining. See adjacent middle: PHOTO 27. Bywell 1.

St Mary's Church, Stow-in-Lindsey, Lincolnshire, provides an example of where the north transept has cut-back side alternate quoining. See adjacent right: PHOTO 28. Stow-in-Lindsey 2, showing the vertical groove indicating cut-back arrowed red.

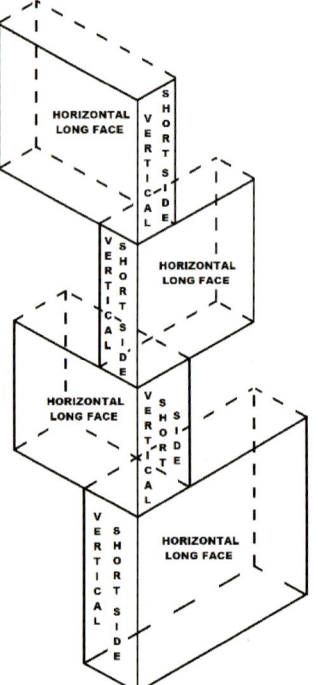

PHOTO 27. Bywell 1.

PHOTO 28. Stow-in-Lindsey 2.

FACE ALTERNATE QUOINING
Face Alternate Quoining is where the quoins are laid alternately so that on one wall one quoin displays horizontally one long side with above another quoin displaying one short side

horizontally, whilst on the adjoining walling the same quoins display a horizontal short side with above a horizontal long side. The quoins are laid horizontally flat on their faces, hence the name "Face Alternate". Given its nature it is the variant of quoining least easy to confidently identify. See the illustration below: black lines denote exposed stonework, hatched black lines denote hidden stonework.

St Matthew's Church, Langford, Oxfordshire, provides an example of where the tower has face alternate quoining. See adjacent middle: PHOTO 29. Langford 1.

St John the Baptist Church, Barnack, Cambridgeshire, also provides an example of where the tower has face alternate quoining but above there is long and short quoining (see next entry). See adjacent right: PHOTO 30. Barnack 1, showing the face alternate quoining arrowed red.

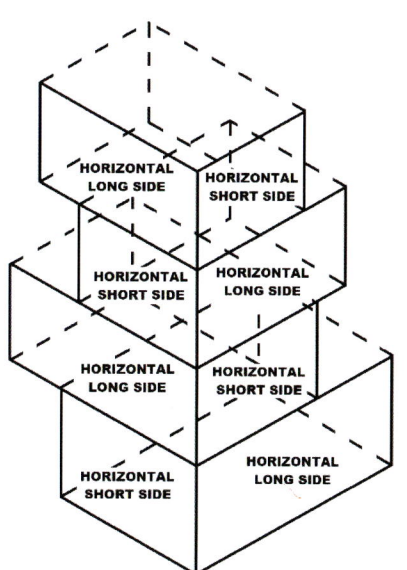 

PHOTO 29. Langford 1.   PHOTO 30. Barnack 1.

LONG AND SHORT QUOINING

Long and Short Quoining is where the quoins are laid alternately so that on one wall one quoin displays horizontally one long or short side with another quoin above displaying one long face or side vertically, whilst on the adjoining walling the same quoins display a horizontal long or short side with a vertical long face or side above.

The narrow vertical quoins are the "Long" and the wider horizontal quoins are the "Short". The "Longs" may sometimes be described as "narrow pillar-like column(s)", particularly where the difference between the width of the long face and the adjacent long side is not easily apparent. "Long" and "Short" quoins are

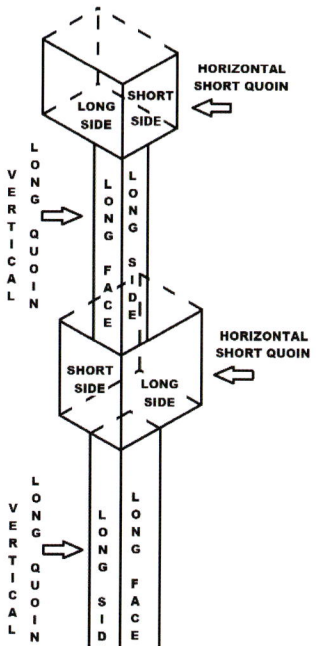  

PHOTO 31. Wilsford.   PHOTO 32 Wittering 1.

characteristic of Anglo-Saxon workmanship – their use is not uniformly spread over the country. Where appropriate Long and Short Quoining may include examples prefixed with the terms "Megalithic" or "Cut-Back". See the illustration at the bottom of Page 55: black lines denote exposed stonework, hatched black lines denote hidden stonework.

St Mary's Church, Wilsford, Lincolnshire, provides an example of where the nave has megalithic long and short quoining. See Page 55 bottom left: PHOTO 31. Wilsford.

All Saints Church, Wittering, Cambridgeshire, provides an example of where the chancel has cut-back side long and short quoining. See Page 55 bottom right: PHOTO 32. Wittering 1, showing the vertical groove indicating cut-back arrowed red.

It has been suggested that in Lincolnshire where the churches sometimes display two types of quoining, the fact that the nave has long and short quoining and the tower has side alternate quoining, indicates an earlier preference for long and short rather than side alternate.

LONG AND SHORT QUOINING – SUSSEX VARIATION
The variation known as "Sussex" is where more than one horizontal quoin forms the "short" between the vertical "long" narrow-sided quoins. Mostly found in Sussex – its use is not uniform; there are a few examples elsewhere.

Quoins are laid alternately so that on one wall two or more quoins display horizontally one long or short side with another quoin above displaying one long face or side vertically, whilst on the adjoining walling the same quoins display a horizontal long or short side with a vertical long face or side above.

The narrow vertical quoins are the "long" and the wider horizontal quoins are the "short". The number of horizontal "short" quoins between the vertical "long" quoins can vary within the same angle of walling and are laid so that on each wall a long horizontal side alternates with a short horizontal side above.

The adjacent illustration shows three quoins in the lower "short" and two quoins in the upper "short". Black lines denote exposed stonework, hatched black lines denote hidden stonework.

Holy Trinity Church, Bosham, West Sussex, provides an example of

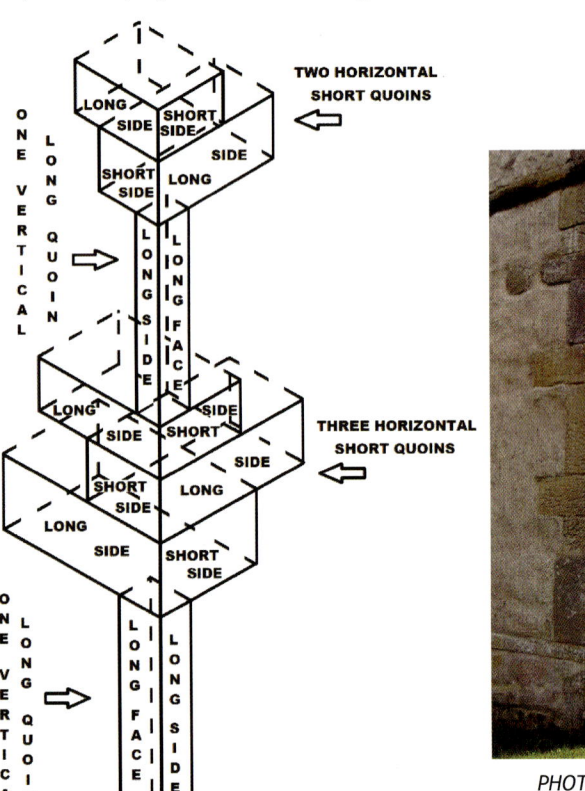

PHOTO 33.
Bosham 1.

Anglo-Saxon Church Architecture & Stone Sculpture   57

where the tower has long and short quoining with the "Sussex" variation. See Page 56 bottom right: PHOTO 33. Bosham 1.

4. ARCHWAYS

- From top to bottom most archways comprise: a half-rounded arched head; square or rectangular imposts*; jambs*; and often, but not always, a plinth* which supports the whole structure, including, on occasions, the adjoining walling. See the illustration below and on the following page.

- Many archways were constructed with large facing stones*, individually of a self-evident difference in terms of size and finish to the stonework used in the adjoining walling. Facing stones varied in size and shape and were roughly-dressed* but not to the uniformity of size, shape and careful dressing as ashlar* favoured by Norman and later builders although there are some examples where the Anglo-Saxon builders used ashlar.

- Alternatively, the heads, imposts, jambs and sills of some archways were constructed of, and faced with, rubble* stonework displaying few differences to the stonework forming the adjoining walling whether laid in courses* or randomly. Such archways could include the use of a mixture of rubble and flints and the reuse of Roman stonework, including Roman tiles or tile-like bricks, where these were available.

- Archways were mostly cut straight through the full depth of the walls without rebates or recesses unless they were accompanied by angle-shafts* or soffit-shafts* - see Page 58 text and illustration. All examples were open with no rebate around the head, imposts or jambs to accommodate the provision of a door.

- Some archways were accompanied by *hood-moulding*, strip-work* and pilaster-strips*. Examples may also have label-stops* at the bottom of the hood-moulding.

*See Glossary and for other such terms in the following pages.

The illustrations below provide examples of "typical" archways and indicate the differences between the more common types, those enabling access between the tower and the nave - "tower archways" - and those enabling access between the nave and the chancel – "chancel archways".

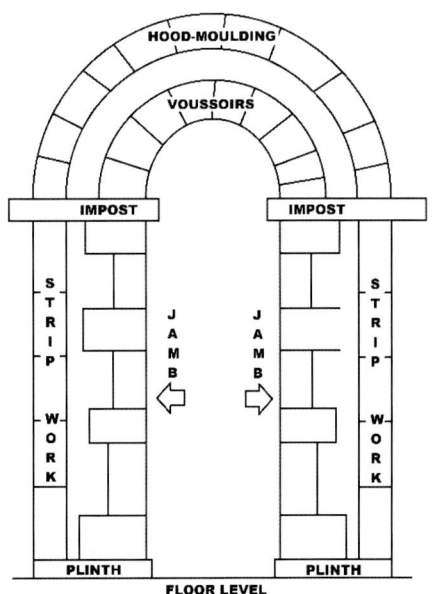

The adjacent illustration is intended to give an indication of a typical round-headed tower archway facing the nave.

Its arched head is constructed with voussoirs, supported by rectangular imposts which extend into the void between the jambs and below, and, between and beyond the accompanying strip-work and hood-moulding.

Below the imposts are the jambs whose three exposed sides are faced with roughly-dressed facing stones of varying shapes and sizes and laid in a similar fashion to side alternate quoining; some of the stonework may be described as "megalithic". The archway is accompanied by strip-work parallel to the jambs and hood-moulding concentric with the voussoirs; stonework from the walling separates the hood-moulding from the voussoirs and the strip-work from the jambs. The whole archway, including the accompanying strip-work, stands on a single rectangular plinth protruding from the faces of the walls. For an example with features indicated see Page 72: PHOTO 77. Barnack 4 - St John the Baptist Church, Barnack, Cambridgeshire (it has pilaster-strips rather than strip-work).

Some archways, particularly in Lincolnshire and Norfolk, may be noticeably taller and narrower than indicated in the illustration on Page 57 and may not have pilaster-strips or strip-work and hood-moulding.

The adjacent illustration is intended to give an indication of a typical round-headed chancel archway facing the nave.

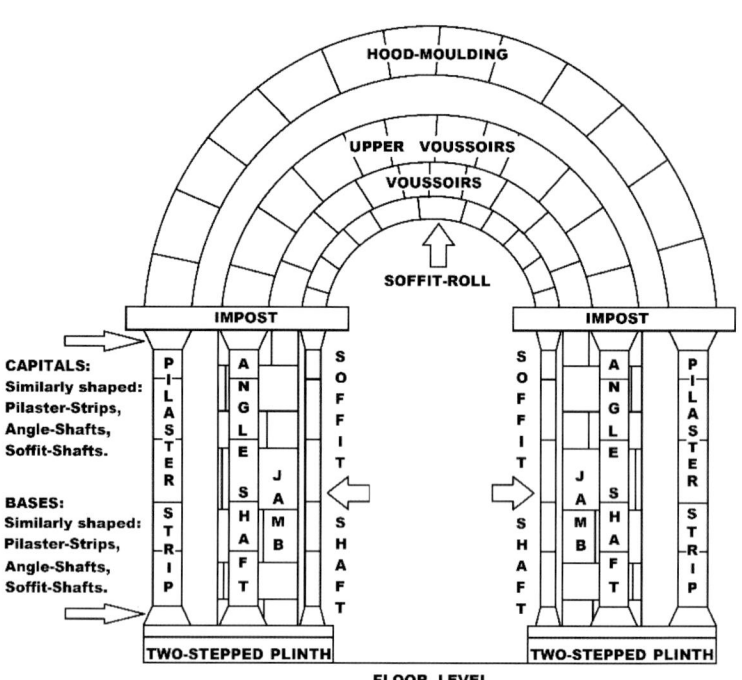

Its arched head is constructed with two adjacent rows of voussoirs, one on top of the other. Below the lower row of voussoirs is a soffit-roll placed centrally on the underside of the arch and viewed from the west or east sides set-back from the lower row of voussoirs. The arched head is supported by rectangular imposts which extend into the void between the jambs and below, and, between and beyond the accompanying pilaster-strips and hood-moulding.

Below the imposts are the jambs whose three exposed sides are faced with roughly-dressed facing stones of varying shapes and sizes and laid in a similar fashion to side alternate quoining; some of the stonework may be described as "megalithic". In addition, the jambs are recessed on both the west and east sides. In the angle of the jambs formed by the recesses are "angle-shafts". In addition, in line with the soffit-roll above, and in the centre of the opposing faces of the jambs of the archway are "soffit-shafts". Both angle-shafts and soffit-shafts are cylindrical in size and shape and usually have similar shaped capital and bases – often the accompanying pilaster-strips will also have similar capitals and bases – as indicated in this illustration. Where the jambs including angle-shafts and soffit-shafts most of the facing stones of the jambs are hidden from view but where they can be identified the exposed sides are faced with roughly-dressed facing stones of varying shapes and sizes and often laid in a similar fashion to side alternate quoining.

The archway is accompanied by pilaster-strips parallel to the jambs and hood-moulding concentric with the voussoirs; stonework forming the walling separates the pilaster-strips/hood-moulding from the voussoirs and the pilaster-strips from the jambs. Note: See Pages 172 to 179, "10. Pilaster-Strips, Pilaster-Buttresses, Hood-Moulding and Strip-Work".

The whole archway, including the accompanying pilaster-strips, stands on a two-stepped rectangular plinth protruding from the faces of the walls. For an example with features indicated see Page 87: PHOTO 107. Wittering 5 - All Saints Church, Wittering, Cambridgeshire. Other examples encountered may not have angle-shafts, soffit-shafts and soffit-rolls. Others may not have pilaster-strips or hood-moulding. Not all archways have plinths. The following pages set out the component parts of archways and their various locations within churches – photographic examples are provided.

ARCHED HEADS OF ARCHWAYS
Arched heads were usually constructed with a semi-circular row of tapering, wedge-shaped voussoirs which were often roughly-dressed half-through-stones, three-quarter-through-stones, or through-stones through the full depth of the walling. Not all examples have identifiable, single, vertically placed, central key-stones. Some may have an off-set central single key-stone – see below PHOTO 34. Wootton Wawen 1, others may not have an identifiable single, vertically placed, central key-stone – see Page 60. PHOTO 36. Brigstock 2.

St Peter's Church, Wootton Wawen, Warwickshire, provides an example of an arched head of an archway constructed with a semi-circular row of tapering, wedge-shaped, voussoirs, with, in the centre, an off-set stone shaped in the form of a free-arm cross with short arms – its left-hand (southern) arm is missing. It is the "chancel" archway in the central crossing. See adjacent: PHOTO 34. Wootton Wawen 1.

Some arched heads of archways were constructed with more than one row of voussoirs.

PHOTO 34. Wootton Wawen 1.

St John the Baptist Church, Kirk Hammerton, North Yorkshire provides an example of the arched head of a chancel archway constructed with three concentric semi-circular rows of voussoirs – the lowest "inner" row is recessed. See adjacent: PHOTO 35. Kirk Hammerton 2.

Other examples had a row of voussoirs accompanied by concentric hood-moulding. (See Page 172 to 179, "10. Pilaster-Strips, Pilaster-Buttresses, Hood-Moulding and Strip-Work"). Hood-moulding may be placed immediately on top of, not separate, from the voussoirs – there is no intervening stonework. Examples often have pilaster-strips or strip-work and hood-moulding only on one face of the archway, but sometimes it may be on both.

PHOTO 35. Kirk Hammerton 2.

St Andrew's Church, Brigstock, Northamptonshire, provides an example of the arched head of a tower archway constructed with through-stone voussoirs with no identifiable, single, vertically placed, central key-stone, and with hood-moulding placed directly on top of the voussoirs. See Page 60 top left: PHOTO 36. Brigstock 2, showing the hood-moulding arrowed red.

PHOTO 36. Brigstock 2.

PHOTO 37. Wittering 2.

Alternatively, hood-moulding may be separated from the voussoirs by stonework similar to that in the adjoining walling – see above right PHOTO 37. Wittering 2. The arched heads of some archways may have voussoirs shaped in the form of protruding bands of roll-moulding. Some examples may have a half-round soffit-roll on the underside of the arch.

All Saints Church, Wittering, Cambridgeshire, also provides an example of the arched head of a chancel archway constructed with three concentric rows of stonework - also see above right: PHOTO 37. Wittering 2. These rows comprise: an outer band of voussoirs similar in shape to a band of roll-moulding – arrowed red; a narrow middle band of voussoirs similar in shape to a half-square with an integral inner curve on its lower side – arrowed black; and an inner half-round soffit-roll – arrowed blue. Above the upper row of stonework is stonework similar to that in the adjoining walling (now plaster-covered) which separates the head of the archway from the hood-moulding above – arrowed green.

A few arched heads of what were considered the more important archways and doorways had label-stops at the bottom of the hood-moulding (above). They depicted the complete figure of a creature in profile, or the head only of a beast in portrait. Internally they are found on the side of archways facing the congregation, or externally on doorways.

The east face of the tower archway in St Bene't's Church Cambridge, Cambridgeshire, provides an example of label-stops in the shape of crouching beasts in opposite profile with tilted heads. See adjacent: PHOTO 38. Cambridge 1, showing the label-stops arrowed red, the outer half-square band of hood-moulding arrowed black, and the inner half-round band of hood-moulding arrowed blue. Also see adjacent close-ups of label-stops: PHOTO 39. Cambridge 2, showing the left label-stop, and PHOTO 40. Cambridge 3, showing the right label-stop.

PHOTO 38. Cambridge 1.

PHOTO 39. Cambridge 2.

PHOTO 40. Cambridge 3.

St Mary's Church, Deerhurst, Gloucestershire has examples of three-dimensional beasts' heads with paint, and indications of paint, surviving. Two are at the base of the hood-moulding on the west face of the blocked chancel archway. See adjacent: PHOTO 41. Deerhurst 2, showing the label-stops arrowed red. Also see below close-ups of the label-stops: PHOTO 42. Deerhurst 3, showing the left label-stop, and PHOTO 43. Deerhurst 4, showing the right label-stop – the detail of this beast is not clear.

PHOTO 41. Deerhurst 2.

St Mary's Church, Deerhurst, Gloucestershire has other beast-head label-stops with the hood-moulding on doorways – see Page 98, PHOTO 125. Deerhurst 5 and PHOTO 126. Deerhurst 6.

Where there is intervening stonework between the voussoirs on each face of the archway, i.e. where the voussoirs are not through-stones, the stonework will be similar to that used in the adjacent walling.

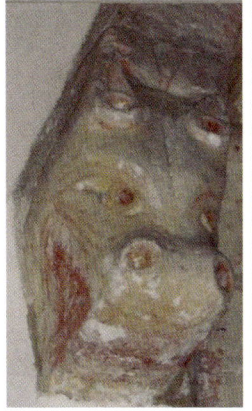

PHOTO 42. Deerhurst 3.

PHOTO 43. Deerhurst 4.

St Mary's Church, Norton, County Durham, provides an example of the arched head of the south transept archway constructed with voussoirs which are not through-stones. On each face of the archway there are distinctive voussoirs separated from each other by intervening stonework. See adjacent: PHOTO 44. Norton 1.

Instead of voussoirs the arched head may be constructed with a mixture of stonework comprising irregularly-shaped and sized rubble, flints and reused Roman stonework, similar to the fabric of the adjoining walling with no indication of wedge-shaped voussoirs.

To construct a half-round arched head, individual stones were shaped, if required, and placed radially with a square or rectangular

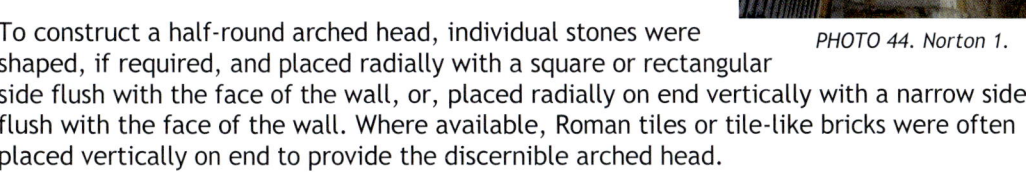

PHOTO 44. Norton 1.

side flush with the face of the wall, or, placed radially on end vertically with a narrow side flush with the face of the wall. Where available, Roman tiles or tile-like bricks were often placed vertically on end to provide the discernible arched head.

Holy Trinity Church, Colchester, Essex, provides an example of an arched head of a tower archway constructed with reused Roman tiles or tile-like bricks with hood-moulding, also with reused Roman tile-like bricks, placed directly on top. See Page 62: PHOTO 45. Colchester 2.

The placement of moulded and sculptured "decoration" on and around the archway, the numbers of rows of voussoirs, the provision of cylindrical-shaped angle-shafts, the nature of the plinths supporting the jambs, can indicate the importance of the area which it faced. Thus tower archways were often decorated only on the east face of the wall – towards the congregation - whilst chancel archways were often decorated only on the west face of the wall - again towards the congregation. See Page 172 to 179. "10. Pilaster-Strips, Pilaster-Buttresses, and Hood-Moulding and Strip-Work".

Note: Whatever the nature of the individual stones used to construct the arched head they are often still described as "voussoirs" despite not being wedge-shaped.

PHOTO 45. Colchester 2.

IMPOSTS OF ARCHWAYS
Imposts are usually square in section and profile and may be flush with, or protrude from, some or all of the faces of the walls of which they form a part. Imposts may also protrude into the central void below the head and between the opposing jambs. Imposts may be half-through-stones, three-quarter-through-stones, or through-stones through the full depth of the walling.

Some imposts may be chamfered, concave, angled, stepped, bulbous, conical, or tapered or moulded with a modelled surface sometimes with a shaped pattern in relief, or decorated with a variety of abstract, plant and architectural designs in relief.

PHOTO 47. Wittering 3.

PHOTO 48. Langford 2.

PHOTO 46. Barnack 2.

St John the Baptist Church, Barnack, Cambridgeshire provides an example of a round-headed tower archway with moulded imposts divided into three horizontal bands each with a horizontal central groove - central band recessed but other two bands protrude. See above left: PHOTO 46. Barnack 2.

All Saints Church, Wittering, Cambridgeshire, provides an example of a round-headed chancel archway with unusually large, inverted trapezoid-shaped, moulded imposts divided into two by a central horizontal groove. See above middle: PHOTO 47. Wittering 3.

Other examples may have extended imposts which separated the pilaster-strips or strip-work from the hood-moulding.

St Matthew's Church, Langford, Oxfordshire, provides an example of a round-headed archway with chamfered, moulded, extended, imposts which separate, the strip-work below from the hood-moulding above - these are on the west face only. See above right: PHOTO 48. Langford 2.

St Mary the Virgin Church, Strethall, Essex, provides an example of a round-headed chancel archway with chamfered, moulded, imposts which are also decorated with horizontal bands comprising, from top to bottom: a band of flat-moulding, a deep groove, a band of cable-moulding, a deep groove, a band of flat-moulding divided into two by a horizontal shallow groove, a deep groove, a band of flat-moulding, and a band of moulding angled inwards decorated in relief with a row of diamond-shaped lozenges with vertically bevelled centres. The extended imposts separate, the pilaster-strips/strip-work below from the hood-moulding above. See adjacent: PHOTO 49. Strethall 1.

PHOTO 49. Strethall 1.

Some imposts may also extend across the full face of the wall providing a string-course.

St Mary Magdalene Church, Rothwell, Lincolnshire, provides an example of a round-headed tower archway which has imposts which extend across the full width of the west wall of the nave. The imposts provide a string-course-like feature. See adjacent: PHOTO 50. Rothwell 1.

PHOTO 50. Rothwell 1.

JAMBS OF ARCHWAYS

Archways had individual stones which collectively formed two sets of jambs on opposite sides of the central void. Jambs were usually square in section and profile. They may be constructed with a single, vertical, megalithic through-stone. Alternatively, they may be constructed with roughly-dressed half-through-stones, three-quarter-through-stones, or through-stones through the full depth of the walling laid in a similar fashion to Escomb jambs or side alternate quoining. They may also be constructed of similar stonework to the adjoining walling and coursed in a similar fashion – some examples may include megalithic stonework. There are no "standard" number of stones forming the jambs and the stonework in one jamb may not be the mirror image of the stones forming the opposite jamb.

Corhampton Church, Hampshire, provides an example of a round-headed chancel archway which has through-stone Escomb jambs with accompanying pilaster-strips. (See Page 68 "Escomb Jambs") See adjacent left: PHOTO 51. Corhampton 1, showing the pilaster-strip arrowed red.

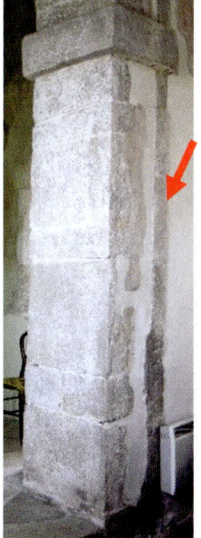 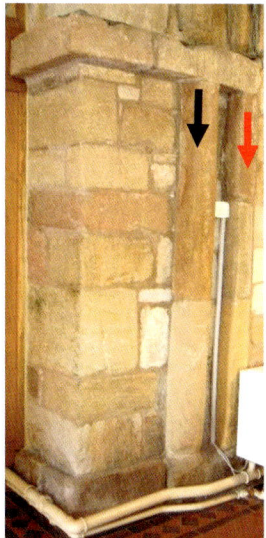

PHOTO 51. Corhampton 1.   PHOTO 52. Skipwith 3.

St Helen's Church, Skipwith, North Yorkshire, provides an example of a round-headed tower archway which has jambs laid in side alternate fashion, including megalithic stonework. The jambs are accompanied by two variations of pilaster-strips. See Page 63 bottom right: PHOTO 52. Skipwith 3, showing the outer half-square pilaster-strip arrowed red, and the inner half-round pilaster-strip arrowed black.

Alternatively, jambs may comprise rubble stonework displaying few differences to the stonework forming the adjoining walling whether laid in courses or randomly. Such jambs could be constructed with a mixture of rubble and flints similar to the stonework of the adjoining walling including the reuse of Roman stonework and tile-like bricks where these were available. With such examples the jambs may be covered with plaster so that the detail of the walling is hidden. See Page 76: PHOTO 85. Brixworth 3, and Page 86: PHOTO 106. Strethall 2.

JAMBS OF ARCHWAYS WITH SHAFTS
Each jamb may have a recess on one or two sides of the archway (not on the face fronting the central void) to accommodate a cylindrical-shaped "angle-shaft" - in the angle of the jambs. The jambs may also have a "soffit-shaft" moulded onto the face fronting the central void; it will mirror the position of the "soffit-roll" on the underside of the arched head above.

The angle or soffit-shafts may be constructed with one section of stonework or a series of sections of stonework placed one on top of another. They may be half-round, three-quarter round, or completely round (circular). Where provided they may have similarly shaped moulded or sculptured capitals and bases which may not all be of a similar size.

St Matthew's Church, Langford, Oxfordshire, provides an example of a round-headed chancel archway with half-round cylindrical "angle-shafts" and centrally-placed half-round cylindrical "soffit-shafts"; between them on the west face only, is a narrow band of stonework with a square edge. All have: moulded, half-round capitals with a vertical top third, a tapering lower two-thirds, a horizontal band of roll-moulding below; and, half-round, two-stepped bases tapering apart from vertical bottom one-fifth. The archway stands on a large, protruding, square plinth. See adjacent left: PHOTO 53. Langford 3, showing the angle-shaft arrowed red, the soffit-shaft arrowed black, and the band of square edged stonework arrowed blue.

All Saints Church, Wittering, Cambridgeshire, provides an example of a round-headed chancel archway with half-round cylindrical "angle-shafts" and centrally-placed half-round cylindrical "soffit-shafts". Both types of shaft have expanding bases which taper downwards and stand on the same square plinth as the jamb. Both also have expanding capitals tapering upwards towards the imposts. See above right: PHOTO 54. Wittering 4, showing the angle-shaft arrowed red, and the soffit-shaft arrowed black.

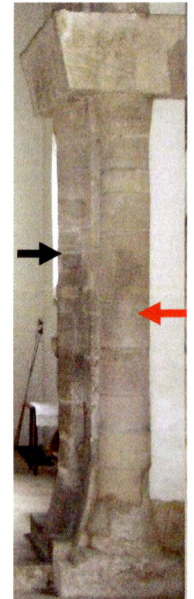

PHOTO 53. Langford 3.   PHOTO 54. Wittering 4.

Where the jambs include angle or soffit-shafts most of the facing stones of the jambs are hidden from view but where they can be identified the exposed sides are faced with roughly-dressed facing stones of varying shapes and sizes which may be laid in a similar way to side alternate quoining, or the stonework in the adjoining walling.

Other jambs may have moulded onto the face fronting the central void a series of adjacent vertical half-round shafts rather than a single soffit-shaft. They may be of alternating radii – large half-round shafts alternating with smaller half-round shafts.

Holy Trinity Church, Great Paxton, Cambridgeshire, provides an example of a round-headed archway into the former north transept with jambs incorporating a series of adjacent vertical half-round shafts of alternating radii with bulbous and tubular-shaped capitals. See adjacent: PHOTO 55. Great Paxton 1. Also see below: PHOTO 56. Great Paxton 2, showing a close-up of the capitals.

JAMBS OF ARCHWAYS WITH SHAFTS - CAPITALS
Capitals take various forms, and they may be square, rectangular, round, conical, or trapezoid in shape, some may be described as a "cushion-capital" – see Glossary. Capitals may be decorated with a variety of abstract and architectural designs in relief. They may be moulded with a modelled surface which may be described as "chamfered", "concave", "angled", "stepped", "bulbous", "conical", "tapering and expanding", "tapering with concentric grooves indicating an increasing or reducing circumference", or simply "square", "cylindrical", "rounded", or "sculptured".

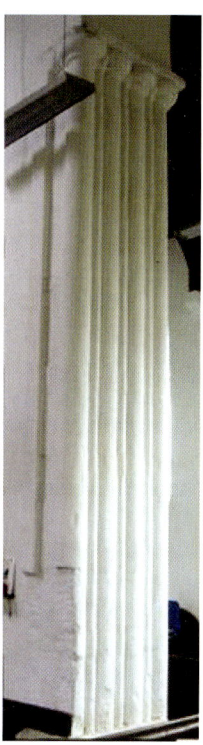

PHOTO 55. Great Paxton 1.

Holy Trinity Church, Great Paxton, Cambridgeshire, provides an example of a round-headed archway into the former north transept with jambs incorporating a series of adjacent vertical half-round shafts of alternating radii with bulbous and tubular-shaped capitals. See adjacent: PHOTO 56. Great Paxton 2.

PHOTO 56. Great Paxton 2.

St Mary's Church, Broughton, Lincolnshire, provides an example of a round-headed archway former chancel now tower archway with the capitals of the cylindrical soffit-shafts shaped square at top, with below chamfered, pendant, triangles, and below a horizontal band of roll-moulding. See adjacent left: PHOTO 57. Broughton 2.

St Gregory's Minster, Kirkdale, North Yorkshire, provides an example

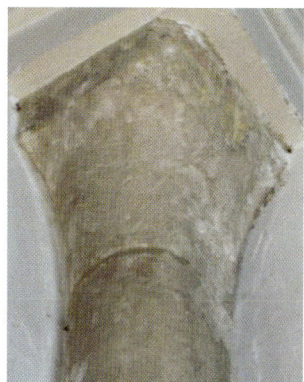

PHOTO 57. Broughton 2.   PHOTO 58. Kirkdale 1.

of where Anglo-Saxon jambs and cylindrical angle-shafts survive incorporated into a chancel archway with a 13th century arched head and imposts. The capitals on the angle-shafts have square tops with the lower part rounded, and tapering from top to bottom, to fit into the top of the cylindrical angle-shafts. See Page 65 bottom right: PHOTO 58. Kirkdale 1.

Holy Trinity Church, Great Paxton, Cambridgeshire, provides examples of round-headed archways in an arcade in the nave. These archways have cylindrical shafts with capitals each comprising an integral lower moulded horizontal band which expands into a larger bulbous shape above. See adjacent left: PHOTO 59. Great Paxton 3. (For the base to these capitals see below: PHOTO 61. Great Paxton 4.)

PHOTO 59. Great Paxton 3.

PHOTO 60. Langford 4.

St Matthews Church, Langford, Oxfordshire, provides an example of a round-headed chancel archway with accompanying angle-shafts and soffit-shafts. Both shafts have moulded, tapering, half-round capitals with a horizontal band of roll-moulding below. See above right: PHOTO 60. Langford 4, showing the angle-shaft arrowed red and the soffit-shaft arrowed black.

JAMBS OF ARCHWAYS WITH SHAFTS - BASES
Bases of shafts also take various forms, and they may be square, rectangular, round, conical or trapezoid in shape. Bases may be moulded with a modelled surface which may be described as "chamfered", "concave", "angled", "stepped", "bulbous", "conical", "tapering and expanding", "tapering with concentric grooves indicating an increasing or reducing circumference", or simply "square", "cylindrical", "rounded", or "sculptured". Bases of shafts are usually supported by plinths – see Page 67 "Plinths of Archways".

Holy Trinity Church, Great Paxton, Cambridgeshire, provides examples of round-headed archways in an arcade in the nave. These archways have cylindrical shafts with bases each comprising four concentric rings increasing in size towards their base and separated from each other by a square block of protruding stonework which forms part of the supporting square, single, plinth. See above right: PHOTO 61. Great Paxton 4.

PHOTO 61. Great Paxton 4.

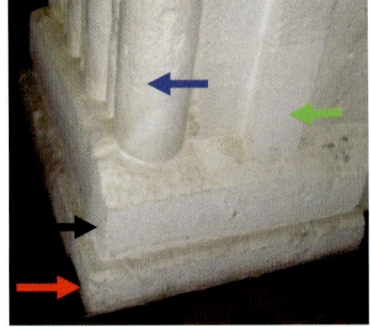

Holy Trinity Church, Great Paxton, Cambridgeshire, also provides an example of a round-headed archway into the former north transept with a single square plinth supporting the base of each jamb which also provides the bases of the cylindrical shafts and pilaster-strips. See adjacent: PHOTO 62.

PHOTO 62. Great Paxton 5.

Great Paxton 5, showing the plinth arrowed red, the base of jamb arrowed black, the cylindrical shafts arrowed blue, and the pilaster-strip arrowed green.

St Gregory's Minster, Kirkdale, North Yorkshire, provides an example of where Anglo-Saxon jambs and cylindrical angle-shafts survive incorporated into a chancel archway with a 13th century arched head and imposts. The bases on the angle-shafts have a lower part divided into four horizontal bands by three horizontal grooves, and an upper part with two bell-like collars, tapering from bottom to top, to fit into the bottom of the cylindrical angle-shafts – the two collars are separated by a horizontal ridge. The bases are supported by a single square plinth which projects from the wall. See below left: PHOTO: 63. Kirkdale 2.

St Matthews Church, Langford, Oxfordshire, provides an example of a round-headed chancel archway with accompanying angle-shafts and soffit-shafts. Both shafts have two moulded, bell-like collars, tapering from bottom to top, to fit into the bottom of the cylindrical angle-shafts and soffit-shafts – the two collars are separated by a horizontal step. The collars are supported at the bottom by a vertical band of stonework slightly angled inwards. The bases are supported by a single square plinth which projects from the wall. See above right: PHOTO 64. Langford 5, showing the angle-shaft arrowed red and the soffit-shaft arrowed black.

PHOTO: 63. Kirkdale 2.

PHOTO 64. Langford 5.

PLINTHS OF ARCHWAYS
The archway, including some of its associated adjacent walling, may all be supported by a distinctive plinth which projects from the bottom of the bases of the jambs and shafts and sits directly on top of the floor or ground below. Plinths may comprise a single or a number of stepped sections of stonework some of which may be square or chamfered, or a combination of both. They may also protrude from one, two or all three faces of the walling of each jamb. In addition to the examples below see the examples included in Pages 66 and 67 "Jambs of Archways with Shafts – Bases".

St John the Baptist Church, Barnack, Cambridgeshire, provides an example of a round-headed tower archway with the base and jambs supported by a square, two-stepped, plinth. Alterations in the 13th century resulted in the plinth now appearing as a single plinth along its west faces and its west ends opposite the central void. See adjacent left: PHOTO 65. Barnack 3, showing the two stepped, original, plinth arrowed red.

PHOTO 65. Barnack 3.

PHOTO 66. Langford 6.

St Matthew's Church, Langford, Oxfordshire, provides an example of a round-headed archway with the base and jambs supported by a chamfered single plinth; the archway provides access into a square, central, area. See above right: PHOTO 66. Langford 6, with the plinth arrowed red.

St Mary's Church, Stow-in-Lindsey, Lincolnshire, provides an example of a round-headed chancel archway with the jambs supported by a square and chamfered five-stepped plinth. The north side of the archway now provides the better example with the lowest step on the west (on the right-hand side of Photo 67. Stow-in-Lindsey 3) hidden by later flooring not Anglo-Saxon. See adjacent: PHOTO 67. Stow-in-Lindsey 3, showing the north side of the plinth arrowed red.

PHOTO 67. Stow-in-Lindsey 3.

ESCOMB JAMBS
This is a description applied to the roughly-dressed stonework forming the jambs of an archway, doorway, window or belfry-opening where the construction technique is similar to that employed in the jambs supporting the chancel arch in the Anglo-Saxon church at Escomb, County Durham. Escomb jambs are constructed with roughly-dressed through-stones, which are often, but not always, "megalithic" in nature.

The illustration adjacent shows jambs laid in Escomb fashion: black lines denote exposed stonework, hatched black lines denote hidden stonework. The stonework comprises through-stones laid alternately vertically and horizontally. On each side of the central void the opposing "faces" of the two jambs, demonstrably large vertical "upright" stones, display one of their tall wide "faces" which alternate with horizontal "flat" stones displaying one of their narrow long "sides". On each of the two other sides of the jambs visible the vertical stones display one of their long sides vertically and the horizontal stones display one of their short sides horizontally.

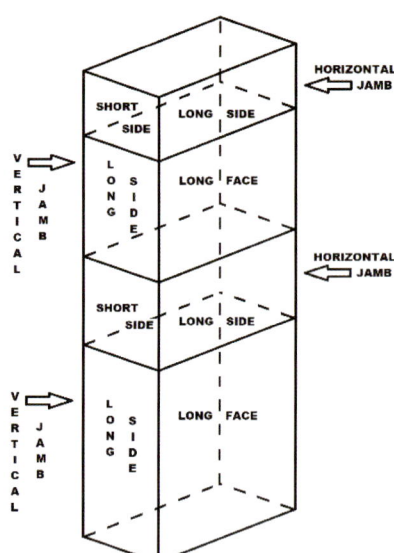

Ostensibly similar to long and short quoining the critical difference is that the "longs" display a tall, wide, face, they are not a narrow pillar-like column encountered with typical long and short quoining. See adjacent left: PHOTO 68. Escomb 2, and adjacent right: PHOTO: 69. Cambridge 4.

ARCHWAYS IN PORCHES
Anglo-Saxon porches were usually attached to the main, western, entrance to a church. The porch had an external western entrance comprising an "open" round-headed archway or a round-headed doorway. Once inside the porch the entrance into the main church was either through a round-headed doorway or a round-headed archway in the east wall. If the external entrance to the porch was under a round-headed archway, then the

PHOTO 68. Escomb 2.   PHOTO 69. Cambridge 4.

entrance into the main church would be a round-headed doorway, if the external entrance to the porch was a round-headed doorway then the entrance into the main church would be under a round-headed archway. Porches were usually one or two storeys high with a gabled roof above.

Some porches also provided internal ground floor access through round-headed doorways to flanking north and south porticus which did not have their own access to the church interior or the exterior space outside the church – see Page 45: PHOTO 5. Monkwearmouth 1.

St Peter's Church, Monkwearmouth, Sunderland, County Durham, has a west porch which originally provided access to the main entrance into the church - see below left: PHOTO. 70. Monkwearmouth 3. The porch was entered from the outside, at ground floor level, through a round-headed archway in its west wall. Inside the porch there were round-headed doorways in the north, south and east walls – these all still survive. Those in the north and south walls provided access into porticus (now demolished), and the doorway in the east wall provided the main entrance into the church. The porch was later incorporated into a late-10th/early-11th century tower.

The west wall contains a round-headed archway with an arched head constructed with through-stone voussoirs divided into two-thirds/one-third by a central concentric groove. The archway has through-stone half-chamfered imposts which are flush with two faces of the walls and overhang the central void between the opposing jambs. The jambs comprise stonework laid in Escomb fashion decorated with two entwined serpents with pairs of balusters above. See adjacent right: PHOTO 71. Monkwearmouth 4, showing the serpents' arrowed red and the pair of baluster-shafts above.

PHOTO 70. Monkwearmouth 3.

PHOTO 71. Monkwearmouth 4.

All Saints Church Brixworth, Northamptonshire, had a west porch which originally provided access to the main entrance into the church. The porch was entered from the outside, at ground floor level, through a round-headed archway in its west wall. Inside the porch there were round-headed doorways in the north, south and east walls – these all still survive. Those in the north and south walls provided access into porticus (now demolished), and the doorway in the east wall provided the main entrance into the church. The porch was later incorporated into a 10th century tower.

The round-headed archway formerly providing the external entrance into the porch can be viewed within the ground floor of the tower. It can now only be identified on the east face of the west wall of the tower. It has been blocked and a round-headed doorway inserted to provide access to the 10th century stair turret; this doorway, similarly, constructed to the archway, shares its southern jamb with part of the southern jamb of the archway.

The large round-headed western archway had its arched head constructed with reused Roman tiles or tile-like bricks placed on end and formed into a discernible arch. The imposts were also constructed with reused Roman tiles or tile-like bricks but laid horizontally, one on top of another. Whilst the imposts do not protrude from the face of the wall, they were probably stepped to provide the identifiable angle to slightly overhang the central void between the jambs. The jambs were constructed of rubble similar to the stonework of the adjacent walling. The archway is rather hidden from view by modern clutter on the east face and completely hidden by the walling of the stair turret on the west face. See adjacent: PHOTO 72. Brixworth 2.

PHOTO 72. Brixworth 2.

St Peter's Church, Titchfield, Hampshire, had a west porch which originally provided access to the main entrance into the church. The porch was entered from the outside, at ground floor level, through a round-headed archway in its west wall. Inside the porch, in its east wall, a round-headed doorway provided the main entrance into the church. The porch was later incorporated into a 12th/13th century tower. The round-headed archway has subsequently been converted into a doorway at a later, not Anglo-Saxon, date.

At ground floor level the west wall contains a round-headed archway with an arched head constructed with through-stone voussoirs which end, at the bottom of the arch, placed at an angle rather than horizontally as would be expected. The archway has no imposts. It has through-stone, including half-through-stone, square jambs which are not laid in any particular way. See adjacent: PHOTO 73. Titchfield.

PHOTO 73. Titchfield.

TOWER ARCHWAYS - see illustration on Page 57
In the east wall of the tower at the west end of the nave providing ground floor access between the tower and nave. Tower archways provide probably the most numerous examples of Anglo-Saxon archways but many were replaced by Norman and later tower archways. Sometimes Anglo-Saxon features survive incorporated into the "new" archways; see Page 73: PHOTO 80. Whittingham 2.

St Peter's Church, Forncett St Peter, Norfolk, has an example of a tall and narrow round-headed tower archway which provides ground floor access between the round tower and the adjoining rectangular nave. The archway has been built into coursed rubble walling with flints similar to that of the adjoining walling; plaster now obscures most of the construction details. It has chamfered imposts which are flush with two faces of the walls and overhang the central void between the opposing jambs. It has square jambs whose construction details are covered with plaster. It represents the basic form of a tower archway with few architectural embellishments. See Page 71 top left: PHOTO 74. Forncett St Peter 2.

Holy Trinity and St Mary the Virgin Church, Old Clee, Lincolnshire, has a tall and narrow round-headed tower archway in a Saxo-Norman tower. It provides ground floor access between the square tower and the adjoining rectangular nave. The archway has been built into coursed rubble walling flush with the faces of the wall. The arched head is constructed with two concentric rows of voussoirs. The voussoirs are supported by rectangular, chamfered, imposts which are flush with two faces of the walls and overhang the central void between the opposing jambs. The jambs are laid in a side alternate fashion and are not through-stones despite their almost "Escomb-like" appearance. The whole archway stands and is supported by a chamfered, three-stepped, plinth. See above right: PHOTO 75. Old Clee 1. There are a number of other similar examples of such tower archways in Lincolnshire.

PHOTO 74. Forncett St Peter 2.

PHOTO 75. Old Clee.1.

St Andrew's Church, Brigstock, Northamptonshire, has a round-headed tower archway providing ground floor access between the square tower and the adjoining rectangular nave. The archway has been built into coursed rubble walling. The arched head is constructed with a single row of large through-stone voussoirs supported by rectangular imposts which protrude from all three faces of the walls including overhanging the central void between the opposing jambs. In addition, the imposts extend across the full width of the west wall of the nave providing a string-course-like feature. The jambs below are constructed with roughly-dressed through-stones laid in a similar fashion to Escomb jambs. The whole archway is supported by a plinth which protrudes from the faces of the walls. In addition on the east face (facing the nave) the archway is accompanied by strip-work which is parallel but separated from the jambs with intervening coursed rubble stonework, and hood-moulding which sits on top of the voussoirs. Note: parts of the strip-work have been rendered flat. See adjacent: PHOTO 76. Brigstock 3.

PHOTO 76. Brigstock 3.

St John the Baptist Church, Barnack, Cambridgeshire, has a round-headed tower archway providing ground floor access between the square tower and the adjoining rectangular nave. The archway has been built into coursed rubble walling. The arched head is constructed with a single row of large through-stone voussoirs supported by moulded imposts which are divided into three distinct horizontal bands. The central band is recessed whilst the other two bands protrude from all three faces of the walls including overhanging the central void between the opposing jambs. The imposts also extend across the west wall of the nave providing a string-course-like feature. The archway has megalithic, including through-stone, square jambs laid in a similar way to Escomb jambs. The whole archway is supported by a two-stepped plinth. In addition on the east face (facing the nave) the archway is accompanied by pilaster-strips laid in long and short fashion, and parallel to, and abutting, the jambs, and hood-moulding which sits on top of the voussoirs. See adjacent: PHOTO 77. Barnack 4.

St Bene't's Church, Cambridge, Cambridgeshire, has a round-headed tower archway providing ground floor access between the square tower and the adjoining rectangular nave. The archway has been built into random rubble walling. The arched head is constructed with a single row of large through-stone voussoirs supported by moulded imposts. These imposts are divided into three distinct horizontal bands – the upper and lower bands with rectangular faces and the central band with a half-round face – with each band interrupted to replicate the position of the vertical bands of half-round and half-square pilaster-strips below. The imposts

PHOTO 77. Barnack 4.

protrude from all three faces of the walls including overhanging, and angled downwards, the central void between the opposing jambs. Additionally the imposts extend across the full width of the west wall of the nave providing a string-course-like feature. The jambs are constructed with roughly-dressed through-stones laid in a similar fashion to Escomb jambs. The whole archway is supported by a two-stepped plinth.

In addition, both west and east faces of the archway are accompanied by separate outer half-square and inner half-round bands of pilaster-strips and bands of hood-moulding. The pilaster-strips are separated from each other by what seems a flat groove but it is just part of the stonework forming the face of the walling. The pilaster-strips are parallel, but mostly separated from the jambs, by intervening rubble stonework. The hood-moulding is concentric with, and sits on top of the voussoirs, with the two bands separated by a deep groove. Additionally, on the east face of the walling, at the bottom of the hood-moulding, there are label-stops decorated with crouching beasts in opposite profile - see Page 60: PHOTO 38. Cambridge 1, PHOTO 39. Cambridge 2, and PHOTO 40. Cambridge 3. See adjacent: PHOTO 78. Cambridge 5.

PHOTO 78. Cambridge 5.

St Helen's Church, Skipwith, North Yorkshire, has a round-headed, former porticus now tower, archway providing ground floor access between the square tower and the adjoining rectangular nave. The archway has been built into coursed stone walling. The arched head is constructed with a single row of large through-stone voussoirs supported by rectangular imposts which protrude from all three faces of the walls including overhanging the central void between the opposing jambs. The rectangular-shaped stonework forming the jambs includes through-stones and megalithic stones. The whole archway is supported by a protruding single square plinth.

In addition, both west and east faces of the archway are accompanied by hood-moulding and pilaster-strips. Both the hood-moulding and the pilaster-strips comprise separate half-square outer bands, and half-round inner bands. The hood-moulding is concentric with, but separated from, the arched head by intervening coursed stonework. The pilaster-strips are parallel to the jambs but mostly separated by intervening coursed stonework. See adjacent: PHOTO 79. Skipwith 4.

St Bartholomew's Church, Whittingham, Northumberland, is an example of where much of the original Anglo-Saxon tower archway survives despite most of its arched head being replaced in 1840. The tower archway provides ground floor access between the square tower and the adjoining rectangular nave.

PHOTO 79. Skipwith 4.

The archway has been built into coursed rubble walling. The arched head is constructed with a single row of voussoirs with original voussoirs surviving above the imposts. On the south side of the archway these comprise two voussoirs on the east face and four voussoirs on the west face, and, on the north side of the archway, these comprise four voussoirs on both the east and west faces. There is some damage to the voussoirs on both the south and north sides. There is some original stonework separating the voussoirs on the west and east faces. The damaged through-stone chamfered imposts are decorated horizontally in the centre with a row of horizontal pellets in a groove. The jambs are constructed with roughly-dressed through-stones laid in a similar fashion to Escomb jambs. The whole archway is supported by a protruding, chamfered, single square plinth. See adjacent: PHOTO 80. Whittingham 2.

PHOTO 80. Whittingham 2.

TOWER-NAVES AND THEIR ARCHWAYS
In a few churches there were "Tower-Naves" where the tower provided the nave and a small chancel was added immediately to the east. In such cases what is now the tower archway was the former chancel archway and confirmation of this can be identified by:

- North-east and south-east quoining of the tower extending from roof to floor height with the archway midway between.

- Decoration in the form of pilaster-strips or strip-work, hood-moulding, or angle-shafts in the recessed jambs, on the west face of the east wall of the tower – not the east face.

- Indications of the foundations of a small rectangular or apsidal chancel below the existing floor between the north-east and south-east quoining of the tower, to the east of the former chancel archway and to the east wall of the tower.

- Indications of former chancel walling on the walling of the east face of the east wall of the tower.

St Peter's Church, Barton-Upon-Humber, Lincolnshire, is distinctive from the other churches with former tower-naves' insofar as the nave (the tower) had, additionally, access to a western baptistery through a western archway. Like other examples the tower-nave provided access to an eastern chancel through an eastern archway. The archways were built into random rubble walling.

The eastern, former chancel, archway has through-stone voussoirs, through-stone double-stepped imposts which are flush with two faces of the walls and overhang the central void the opposing jambs; it has through-stone Escomb jambs. The west face of the archway is accompanied by pilaster-strips parallel to, but separated from, the jambs by intervening random rubble stonework, and hood-moulding which is concentric with, but separated from, the voussoirs by intervening random rubble stonework. Above the west face of this archway is a representation of the head of Christ.

The western tower archway has through-stone voussoirs, through-stone imposts which are flush with two faces of the walls and overhang the central void between the opposing jambs; it has through-stone Escomb jambs. The east face of the archway is accompanied by pilaster-strips which are parallel but separated from the jambs by intervening random rubble stonework, and hood-moulding which sits on top of the voussoirs. See above right: PHOTO 81. Barton-upon-Humber 1, showing the eastern faces of the two archways with the eastern archway arrowed red and the western archway arrowed black.

PHOTO 81. Barton-upon-Humber 1.

St Mary's Church, Broughton, Lincolnshire, had an eastern archway providing access from the tower-nave into the chancel. The archway was built into random rubble walling. See adjacent: PHOTO 82. Broughton 3.

The round-headed tower, formerly chancel, archway has through-stone voussoirs (some restoration) supported by rectangular imposts. The imposts are flush with the east faces of the walling and extend into, and provide the shaped capitals, of the soffit-shafts forming part of the jambs – see next paragraph. The east faces of the imposts, flush with the faces of the east wall, has determined the off-centre position of the soffit-shafts – usually in a central position.

PHOTO 82. Broughton 3.

The three exposed sides of the through-stone jambs have roughly-dressed facing stones of varying shapes and sizes and laid in a similar fashion to side alternate quoining. The cylindrical soffit-shafts have capitals within the extended imposts – as indicated above.

The top half of the capitals are square-shaped with below a tapering triangular shape on each of their three sides; there is a horizontal band of roll-moulding separating each of the capitals from the cylindrical shafts below. (There is some damage to the west faces of the capitals obscuring the detail.) The bases of the soffit-shafts have a cylindrical, tapering and expanding top half with a square bottom half. (Unusually these soffit-shafts do not support voussoirs or a soffit-roll above and noticeably reduce the width of the archway.)

On the west side of the archway the jambs are recessed with the imposts above protruding from both the west faces of the walling of the tower and extending into the central void between the opposing jambs. The imposts have a top rectangular half with an inwardly angled and chamfered lower half.

In the angle of the jambs formed by the recesses are cylindrical angle-shafts - there is some damage. The top third of the capitals are rectangular-shaped with below a tapering triangular shape on each of their three sides; there is a horizontal band of roll-moulding separating each of the capitals from the cylindrical shafts below. The bases of the angle-shafts have a cylindrical, tapering and expanding top half with a square bottom half. The jambs of the archway, including the soffit-shafts and angle-shafts, stand on a slightly protruding single square plinth.

ARCADES OF INTERLOCKING ARCHWAYS IN THE NORTH AND SOUTH WALLS OF THE NAVE
There are a few surviving examples of Anglo-Saxon arcades of interlocking round-headed archways in the north and south walls of the nave providing access into adjacent north and south aisles or porticus. Often both arcades of archways and aisles or porticus have been replaced with later archways not Anglo-Saxon. However, on occasions Anglo-Saxon walling and indications, or parts, of round-headed archways may survive adjacent and above later inserted arcades or individual "new" archways.

Where Anglo-Saxon arcades do survive the archways are round-headed with imposts and often have large rectangular pillars - but some are square. Internally the arcades of archways may be plastered with their construction details hidden, but for an exception see Page 76: PHOTO 85. Brixworth 3, where the arched heads are not hidden; and also externally, Page 76: PHOTO 86. Brixworth 4 where none of the construction details are hidden.

All Saints Church, Wing, Buckinghamshire, has plaster obscuring most of the construction details of the arcades of interlocking round-headed archways in the north and south walls of the nave. These archways formerly provided access into the adjacent Anglo-Saxon north and south aisles.

The wide round-headed arched heads are supported by two-stepped (north wall)/three-stepped (south wall) imposts which are flush with two faces of the walls and overhang the central void between the opposing jamb. The imposts and arched heads are supported by large rectangular pillars with square jambs. See Page 76 top left: PHOTO 83. Wing 1, showing the south face of the north wall, and Page 76 top right: PHOTO 84. Wing 2, showing the north face of the south wall.

76 *Anglo-Saxon Church Architecture & Stone Sculpture*

PHOTO 83. Wing 1.

PHOTO 84. Wing 2.

All Saints, Church, Brixworth, Northamptonshire, has arcades of interlocking round-headed archways in the north and south walls in the nave which formerly provided access into the adjacent Anglo-Saxon north and south porticus. The round-headed arched heads are constructed with two roughly concentric rows of reused Roman tiles or tile-like bricks displaying one of their thin sides – the placement of the tiles is somewhat haphazard on occasions. The three-stepped imposts are constructed with reused Roman tiles or tile-like bricks laid horizontally which protrude from all three faces of the walls, including, overhanging the central void between the opposing jambs. Internally the construction details of the large rectangular pillars with square jambs are hidden by plaster. Externally, the pillars can be seen as constructed with rubble, including reused Roman tiles or tile-like bricks, similar to the stonework in the adjacent walling.

Additionally, in the north and south walls of the nave, there are vestiges of the outer arched heads of an arcade – north to south - of interlocking round-headed archways separating the nave from the from the "Monks' Choir" and the eastern part of the church. The remains of the archways, and by known excavation, indicate by their curvature that there were three interlinking archways bridging the intervening space. See below left: PHOTO 85. Brixworth 3, showing internally: the arcades arrowed red, the fragmentary remains of triple arcade north/left to south/right arrowed black, and the clerestory windows arrowed blue. See below right: PHOTO 86. Brixworth 4, showing externally: the north face of the north arcade with the clerestory windows above.

PHOTO 85. Brixworth 3.

PHOTO 86. Brixworth 4.

In the 10th century the church was restored for use as a parish rather than a monastic church and the archways were blocked; in the 19th century the current round-headed windows were inserted into the blocked, former, archways.

Holy Trinity Church, Great Paxton, Cambridgeshire, is another church with arcades of interlocking round-headed archways in the north and south walls of the nave formerly providing access into the adjacent Anglo-Saxon north and south aisles. It is thought that each of these arcades originally consisted of four archways. The westernmost archways in both walls are now missing, probably destroyed when the tower was built in the 15th century. What is now the westernmost archway in the north wall consists of the blocked remains of the eastern arm of the arched head, the imposts and the pillars. What is now the westernmost archway in the south wall retains its Anglo-Saxon characteristics in the eastern pillar including its shafts, and the impost above, the rest of the archway is a 15th century rebuild resulting in a narrow archway with an off-centre pointed arched head.

The arched heads comprise an outer arch whose faces are level with those of the adjoining walls and an additional inner (set-back) arch. Each arch is supported by two-stepped imposts which protrude from the faces of the walls including overhanging the central void between the opposing pillars.

The rectangular pillars include four large half-round cylindrical shafts separated from each other by centrally-placed smaller half-round cylindrical and triangular-shaped shafts. The cylindrical shafts have bulbous capitals each comprising an integral lower moulded horizontal band which expands above into a larger bulbous shape. The bases of the cylindrical shafts each have four concentric rings increasing in size towards their base and separated from each other by a square block of protruding stonework. The archways are all supported by a large square plinth. Additionally, the eastern arms of the eastern archways have no cylindrical shafts but instead have jambs constructed with roughly-dressed through-stones jambs laid in a similar way to Escomb jambs; the jambs do not stand on a plinth. See Page 66: PHOTO 59. Great Paxton 3, showing the capitals in these arcades, and Page 66: PHOTO 61. Great Paxton 4, showing the bases in these arcades. See adjacent: PHOTO 87. Great Paxton 6, showing the north arcade with above the chamfered string-course arrowed red.

PHOTO 87. Great Paxton 6.

ARCHWAYS IN A CENTRAL CROSSING IN A CRUCIFORM CHURCH
The central "crossing" in a cruciform church comprises four interlocking walls formed into a square into which four round-headed archways have been inserted to provide ground floor access to, and between, the nave, south and north transepts or porticus, and the chancel. The walling extending above these archways usually support a central tower.

Whilst the size of all four archways may be the same, some examples may have only the opposing pairs of similar size, with the west and east archways being larger than the north and south archways. Differences between the surviving examples can vary greatly, in terms of the number of rows of voussoirs in the arched heads and whether there are any accompanying pilaster-strips/strip-work and hood-moulding, whether the jambs are ornamented with quarter or half-round shafts with distinctive capitals and bases, and the nature of the plinths supporting the archways.

St Peter's Church, Wootton Wawen, Warwickshire, is an example of a former Anglo-Saxon cruciform church but both its north and south transepts or porticus no longer survive. Despite plaster covering much of the construction details the four megalithic round-headed archways in the central crossing can still be identified.

The north and south archways are similar in size to each other but smaller in size than the west (nave) and east (chancel) archways. The arched heads are constructed with voussoirs which project from the face of the wall and vary in shape and size towards the centre. The west and east archways voussoirs comprise one band of voussoirs, whereas the north and south archways comprise two bands of voussoirs, the lower band is thinner than the upper band with plaster obscuring some of the details. Off-set, in the centre of the east face of the east (chancel) archway, is a stone shaped in the form of a Free-Arm Cross with short arms – the south arm is missing. The archways have through-stone megalithic square imposts which protrude from all three faces of the walls including overhanging the central void between the opposing jambs.

The through-stones jambs are laid in a similar way to Escomb jambs. There is hood-moulding on the west face of the east (chancel) archway which is laid on top of the voussoirs. The northern archway is blocked and a later window inserted, not Anglo-Saxon. See adjacent left: PHOTO 88. Wootton Wawen 2, showing the east face of chancel archway, and adjacent right: PHOTO 89. Wootton Wawen 3, showing the south face of south transept archway with the exposed stone walling arrowed red.

PHOTO 88. Wootton Wawen 2.

PHOTO 89. Wootton Wawen 3.

St Mary's Church, Norton, County Durham, is also a former Anglo-Saxon cruciform church but only two of the original four Anglo-Saxon archways survive. (The western and eastern archways were replaced in the twelfth century.) It is likely that each of the four original archways were of a similar size given the Anglo-Saxon stonework surviving, and the gable rooflines of the transepts or porticus, nave and chancel indicated externally on the tower.

The round-headed archways provided access between the central crossing and the north and south transepts or porticus. Rather than voussoirs the arched heads appear to be faced with large, shaped curving stones with intervening stonework in the depth between them. They are supported by two-stepped imposts which protrude from all three faces of the walls including overhanging the central void between the opposing jambs. The jambs are constructed with coursed stone similar to the stonework in the adjoining walling. (It has been suggested than when the "new" western nave archway and the eastern chancel archway replaced their Anglo-Saxon predecessors in the twelfth century, rather than replace the existing north and south archways they were altered so that all four archways had the same wider width. This involved the removal of their voussoirs, and the alteration and removal of some of the stonework forming their imposts and jambs.) See adjacent: PHOTO 90. Norton 2.

PHOTO 90. Norton 2.

St Nicholas Church, Worth, West Sussex, a restored cruciform church, has three round-headed archways; there is no fourth western nave archway surviving or indicated.

The archways into the north and (restored) south transepts each have an arched head constructed with through-stones voussoirs supported by large through-stone two-stepped imposts which protrude from all three faces of the walls including overhanging the central void between the opposing jambs. The through-stone jambs include megalithic stonework and are otherwise constructed with coursed rubble similar to the stonework in the adjoining walling.

The archways have pilaster-strips and where the facing stones of the jambs are of insufficient size to abut the pilaster-strips additional stonework is in evidence. The pilaster-strips are unusually placed aligned with the outer edges of the facing stonework of the jambs rather than vertically in line with the base of the hood-moulding above the imposts as would usually be expected. The hood-moulding has been placed on top of the voussoirs. See above right: PHOTO 91. Worth 1, showing the south face of the north transept archway.

PHOTO 91. Worth 1.

The round-headed chancel archway has an arched head constructed with through-stone voussoirs. It is supported by through-stone two-stepped imposts comprising two square slabs separated by a quarter-round band of roll-moulding – the lower slab has a rounded profile towards its base. The imposts protrude from all three faces of the walls including overhanging the central void between the opposing jambs. The jambs are constructed with coursed stone similar to the stonework in the adjoining walling and each has a large half-round cylindrical soffit-shaft which extends almost the full west/east thickness of the walling. See adjacent: PHOTO 92. Worth 2, showing the west face of the chancel archway.

PHOTO 92. Worth 2.

Both faces of the archway have pilaster-strips and, like the archways into the transepts, they are aligned with the outer edges of the facing stonework of the jambs. However, this archway has some evidence on the west face above the northern impost that it may have had two bands of hood-moulding, one on top of the other. If this was the case then the pilaster-strips would be vertically in line with the base of the outer band of the hood-moulding above the imposts. The surviving band of hood-moulding has been placed on top of the voussoirs.

Holy Trinity Church, Great Paxton, Cambridgeshire, is a former Anglo-Saxon cruciform church with a central crossing with three archways; there is no fourth western nave archway surviving. Some of the construction details are now obscured by plaster including those of the only original arched head surviving – that of the northern archway.

It has megalithic, tall, round-headed archways providing access into the former north and south transepts. The details of the construction of the arched heads are now hidden by plaster. The archways have rectangular imposts which protrude from all three faces of the walls including overhanging the central void between the opposing jambs. The jambs are constructed of through-stones laid in Escomb fashion and incorporate on their soffit-faces, vertical half-round shafts of alternating radii; four large half-round shafts alternating with three smaller half-round shafts. The larger half-round shafts have bulbous capitals and the smaller half-round shafts have capitals which are triangular-topped, tubular-shaped, and set-back to take account of their intervening position. Incomplete half-square pilaster-strips extend from the top of a two-stepped base to the level of the adjoining imposts supporting the arched heads. The base of each jamb also provide the base of the cylindrical shafts and the pilaster-strips. The whole of each archway stands on a single rectangular plinth protruding from the faces of the walls.

PHOTO: 93. Great Paxton 7.

The northern archway is nearly complete and retains most of its original features. All the archways have damage. The southern archway has had its arched head replaced in the 13th century and its jambs reduced in height to facilitate the replacement. Only the jambs of the chancel archway can confidently be described as Anglo-Saxon. See above right: PHOTO: 93. Great Paxton 7, showing the south face of the archway into the former north transept.

Holy Trinity Church also has a megalithic round-headed chancel archway with a 13th century arched head and with imposts difficult to date. The head and imposts are supported by Anglo-Saxon through-stone jambs. These jambs incorporate on their soffit-faces vertical quarter-round cylindrical shafts alternating with smaller triangular-shaped shafts; these stand on three-stepped rounded bases increasing in size towards the bottom. The whole of the archway stands on a single rectangular plinth protruding from the faces of the walls. See above right: PHOTO 94. Great Paxton 8.

PHOTO 94. Great Paxton 8.

St Mary's Church, Stow-in-Lindsey, Lincolnshire, is a former Anglo-Saxon cruciform church with four surviving megalithic round-headed archways - all four of the archways are of similar size and are the largest Anglo-Saxon archways surviving. (Ignore the late-15th century pointed "Perpendicular" arches.) See adjacent: PHOTO 95. Stow-in-Lindsey 4, looking east to west with the east face of chancel archway arrowed red, and the east face of nave archway arrowed black.

PHOTO 95. Stow-in-Lindsey 4.

Each of the arched heads are constructed with two bands of voussoirs adjacent and concentric with each other which have been similarly subdivided into three distinctive moulded shapes. The lower band of voussoirs is constructed with: an inner (the lowest) moulded shape comprising a half-roll; above, a middle moulded shape comprising part of the lower half of a "U"-shaped curve; and, above, an outer, moulded half-square flat shape. The upper band of voussoirs repeats this sequence. The accompanying hood-moulding is on top of these two bands of voussoirs. The hood-moulding is similarly divided into three distinctive moulded shapes: an inner (the lowest) moulded shape almost wholly sculptured to provide part of the lower half of a "U"-shaped curve; above, a middle moulded shape comprising part of another "U"-shaped curve; and, above, an outer, moulded half-square flat shape along the top edge. See adjacent: PHOTO 96. Stow-in-Lindsey 5, showing the west face of the west nave archway with each half-roll shape arrowed red, and with the hood-moulding with palmette design arrowed black.

PHOTO 96. Stow-in-Lindsey 5.

The imposts supporting the arched heads are horizontally divided into two, the upper half is rectangular and the lower half is chamfered. The imposts protrude from all three faces of the walls including overhanging the central void between the opposing jambs. The imposts extend across the whole width of the walling in which the archways have been placed: separating the bottom of the voussoirs, including the accompanying hood-moulding, above, from the tops of the outer half-square and inner pilaster-strips, and the jambs, below.

The archways have square jambs are constructed with coursed rubble similar to the stonework in the adjoining walling not resembling in construction any recognisable pattern of quoining; the jambs include megalithic facing stones. In addition, the "outer" west, south, east, and north faces of the jambs have two separate bands of pilaster-strips.

The pilaster-strips nearer to the jambs are "half-round", and the outer ones are "half-square". (The "inner" faces of the jambs probably had similar pilaster-strips but the 15th century construction of the polygonal pillars to support the current tower removed any trace.) The tops of the pilaster-strips directly abut the imposts. The pilaster-strips terminate below with inner "half-round" and the outer "half-square" protruding bulbous corbels immediately above the top of the five-stepped plinth - one flat course is now integral with floor, with four chamfered courses above. The five-stepped plinths support the jambs of the archways and all the accompanying stonework. (Page 68, PHOTO 67. Stow-in-Lindsey 3, showing the north-west corner of the north jamb of the chancel archway with all five steps of the plinth.)

St Wystan's Church, Repton, Derbyshire, has little surviving of what was once the central crossing of a cruciform church apart from some of the walling, above the 19th century archways in the north and south walls of what is now the eastern part of the nave, and the two columns and their bases, which once formed part of the supports for the eastern arms of the archways into the north and south transepts.

Whilst the bases, now supporting a single "drum" of the columns, can still be seen in their original positions, the rest of the columns and their capitals, have been removed and now stand separately in the south porch.

Both of the columns in the south porch comprise nine "drums" each horizontally bordered by a distinctive groove; their capitals rest directly on the top drum. The capitals are similar in design to those supporting the columns and pilaster-strips in the crypt, i.e., rectangular-shaped capitals with the top half divided into three equal parts by two horizontal grooves supported by a tapering lower half with a horizontal band of roll-moulding below. The bottom drums of these columns and their supporting rectangular bases can be seem, along with vestiges of the accompanying flooring, adjacent to the stairways leading down to the crypt. See adjacent left: PHOTO 97. Repton 1, showing the rectangular base and one "drum", and adjacent right: PHOTO 97: PHOTO 98. Repton 2, showing most of one of the columns with its capital.

PHOTO 97. Repton 1.

PHOTO 98. Repton 2.

NAVE AND CHANCEL ARCHWAYS PROVIDING ACCESS INTO A SEPARATE CENTRAL AREA
There are a few examples of an eastern archway in the nave providing access at ground floor level to a central area which also provides access at ground floor level through a separate eastern, chancel, archway into the chancel. Ostensibly the layout is similar to a central crossing in a cruciform church but in these examples there are no north and south transepts or porticus although above there is a central tower.

St Matthew's Church, Langford, Oxfordshire, has a round-headed "nave" archway in the east wall of the nave, providing access at ground floor level into to a square central area between, and separating, the nave from the chancel. The nave archway is constructed of large, smoothly-dressed, stonework. It has an arched head constructed with voussoirs which are not dissimilar to half-through stones but nearly all require additional random stone rubble in-filling. The nave archway has through-stone chamfered square imposts which, on the west face only, extend beyond the accompanying hood-moulding. Below, the megalithic through-stone square jambs are constructed of large rectangular stonework of different sizes placed standing horizontally on one of their long sides (not their faces). The jambs have protruding rectangular bases. The whole nave archway stands on a large, chamfered plinth protruding from the faces of the walls.

Additionally, on the west face only, there is strip-work abutting the edges of the jambs (little survives adjacent to the south jamb). There is also hood-moulding concentric with, and placed on top of, the voussoirs. Both the strip-work and hood-moulding protrude sufficiently from the face of the walling so that the arched head and jambs appear "set-back". See adjacent left: PHOTO 99. Langford 7, showing the west view of nave archway arrowed red, the central area arrowed black, and the chancel archway arrowed blue. See adjacent right: PHOTO: 100. Langford 8, showing the east view of chancel archway arrowed blue, the central area arrowed black, and the nave archway arrowed red.

PHOTO: 99. Langford 7.   PHOTO: 100. Langford 8.

Internally, in the east wall of the square central area, a round-headed chancel archway provides access at ground floor level into the chancel. The archway has an arched head constructed with through-stone voussoirs which, on its west face, have been moulded to form a three-quarter-round roll-shape, whilst on its east face takes the more standard square-shaped and flat form; the voussoirs are accompanied by a half-round soffit-roll. The arched head is supported by moulded, rectangular, imposts which are divided horizontally into three with the top and bottom bands separated by a central groove. See adjacent: PHOTO 101. Langford 9, showing the west face of chancel archway.

Below, on the west face only, the through-stone square jambs have half-round cylindrical shafts (similar in position to angle-shafts but without their required recesses). On the faces of the jambs fronting the central void, there are centrally-placed half-round cylindrical soffit-shafts mirroring the placement of the half-round soffit-roll above. Both pairs of shafts have moulded, half-round capitals which comprise: at the top, two protruding horizontal bands of flat-moulding, each chamfered in opposite vertical directions, and separated by a distinctive groove; with below a cylindrical band on top of a conical band; the bottom of the capital has a horizontal band of roll-moulding separating it from the cylindrical shaft below. Both pairs of shafts also have half-round, conical, two-stepped bases most of which expand outwards apart from the vertical bottom one-fifth.

PHOTO: 101. Langford 9.

Additionally, on the west face only, a narrow band of stonework with a square-edge, is evident between the voussoirs and the soffit-roll, and between the half-round cylindrical shafts and the soffit-shafts; this narrow band of stonework has similar capitals and bases to both the half-round cylindrical shafts and the soffit-shafts. The whole chancel archway, including the half-round cylindrical shafts, the narrow band of square-edged stonework and soffit-shafts, stands on a large square plinth, protruding from the faces of the walls.

Holy Trinity Church, Great Dunham, Norfolk, has a round-headed "nave" archway in the east wall of the nave, providing access at ground floor level into to a square central area between, and separating, the nave from the chancel.

Most of the construction details of the round-headed nave archway are hidden by plaster but apparently the arched head was constructed with reused Roman tiles or tile-like bricks and rubble including flints similar to those that can be seen externally in the construction of some of the windows and belfry-openings. The jambs were constructed of rubble similar to the fabric in the adjoining walling – see externally the random rubble walling including flints and reused Roman tiles or tile-like bricks.

The imposts are one of only two features that can now be identified. These are chamfered rectangular imposts decorated with a horizontal band of diagonal crosses each contained within a rectangle. The east face of the impost survives on north side of the archway only. The imposts protrude from two/three faces of the walls including overhanging the central void between the opposing jambs. Hood-moulding is the other feature that can still be identified with its incomplete arched head surviving only on the west (nave) face of the archway.

Internally, in the east wall of the square central area, a round-headed chancel archway provides access at ground floor level into the chancel. Like the western nave archway most of the construction details are now hidden by plaster but apparently the arched head was constructed with reused Roman tiles or tile-like bricks and rubble including flints similar to those that can be seen externally in the construction of some of the windows and belfry-openings. The jambs were constructed of rubble similar to the fabric in the adjoining walling – see externally the random rubble walling including flints and reused Roman tiles or tile-like bricks.

See adjacent left: PHOTO 102. Great Dunham 1, showing the west view of nave archway arrowed red, the central area arrowed green, and the chancel archway arrowed blue. See also adjacent right: PHOTO 103. Great Dunham 2, showing the east view of chancel archway arrowed blue, the central area arrowed green, and the nave archway arrowed red.

PHOTO 102. Great Dunham 1.   PHOTO 103. Great Dunham 2.

The imposts are one of the only two features that can now be identified. These are decorated with a horizontal band of cable-pattern moulding with two stepped narrow bands of horizontal flat moulding below. The imposts protrude from the west faces of the walls including overhanging the central void between the jambs; there is no evidence of the imposts surviving on the east face of the walling even allowing for the plaster. Two, incomplete, and separate, bands of hood-moulding can be identified on the west (central area) face of the archway only. The outer band of hood-moulding is supported by small impost-like features, with, below, vestiges of half-round pilaster-strips. The inner band of hood-moulding is supported by the tops of the imposts of the archway itself; these imposts are decorated with cable-moulding – there is no indication of pilaster-strips below.

CHANCEL ARCHWAYS – see illustration on Page 58
Mostly in the east wall of the nave a single round-headed archway provided ground floor access to the west end of the chancel. They are often more extensively and elaborately moulded and sculptured than tower archways. Many were replaced by Norman and later chancel archways. Sometimes Anglo-Saxon features survive incorporated into the "new" archways.

The church of St Peter-on-the-Wall at Bradwell-on-Sea in Essex may provide an example of an arcade of interlocking round-headed archways rather than a single archway separating the nave from the chancel. In what is now the east wall of the nave, parts of the arched heads, imposts and jambs of these archways can be identified; they are now blocked and incorporated into the stonework.

The arched heads are constructed with the reused Roman brick-like tiles placed to form a discernible arch – little survives of the southern arched head. Only the reused Roman brick-like tiles placed horizontally, one on top of another, of the impost of the

PHOTO 104. Bradwell-on-Sea 1.

southern archway seem clearly identifiable. This impost protrudes slightly into what originally would have been the adjacent void, and has a curving, almost quarter-circle profile, placed vertically. The impost of the northern archway is difficult to confidently identify. Below the arched heads and imposts of both archways, the jambs are mostly constructed with reused Roman brick-like tiles placed horizontally, one on top of another. In addition, there is a distinctive square through-stone, of a similar size, and placed at a similar height, into each of the jambs of both archways.

The vestiges of the arched heads indicate by their curvature that there may have been three narrow archways rather than a single arch to bridge the intervening space. See above: PHOTO 104. Bradwell-on-Sea 1, showing the fragmentary arched heads arrowed red, the difficult to identify imposts arrowed black, the jambs arrowed blue, and the square through-stones arrowed green.

Corhampton Church, Hampshire (No Dedication), has a round-headed chancel archway providing ground floor access between the east end of the nave and the adjoining chancel. It has been built into flint walling and its construction details can easily be identified despite much of the walling now being incompletely covered with plaster. See below right 86: PHOTO 105. Corhampton 2.

The arched head is constructed with a single row of large through-stone voussoirs supported by rectangular through-stone imposts which protrude from all three faces of the walls including overhanging the central void between the opposing jambs. The jambs are constructed with roughly-dressed through-stones laid in a similar fashion to Escomb jambs; some of the narrower jambs may be half-through-stones. The whole archway is supported by a single square plinth.

In addition the west face of the archway is accompanied by pilaster-strips parallel to the jambs; much of the former stonework of the pilaster-strips protruding from the walls the walls has been removed. Hood-Moulding rests on top of the voussoirs and protrudes sufficiently from the face of the walling so that the arched head and jambs appear "set-back".

PHOTO 105. Corhampton 2.

Unusually, the hood-moulding has a single central key-stone which rises in height above the adjacent stonework, protrudes to a greater extent from the face of the wall, and extends into the voussoirs below.

St Mary the Virgin Church, Strethall, Essex, has a round-headed chancel archway providing ground floor access between the east end of the nave and the adjoining chancel. It has been built into random rubble walling with flints and its construction details can mostly be identified despite the adjacent walling being covered with plaster. See below: PHOTO 106. Strethall 2.

The arched head is constructed with a single row of voussoirs (now plaster covered) supported by rectangular imposts which extend beyond the accompanying hood-moulding and pilaster-strips. The imposts are decorated with horizontal bands of moulding, from top to bottom: flat-moulding with below a horizontal groove; cable-moulding with below a horizontal groove; roll-moulding with below a shallow horizontal groove separating it from a similar band of roll-moulding; below a horizontal groove; a narrow band of flat-moulding with an angled (inwards) lower two-thirds decorated with diamond-shaped lozenges with vertically bevelled centres. The imposts protrude from the west face of the walls and overhang the central void between the opposing jambs; there is no evidence of imposts on the east faces of the walls.

PHOTO 106. Strethall 2.

The archway has jambs constructed of through-stone Escomb jambs (now plaster covered). In addition the archway has hood-moulding and pilaster-strips which protrude sufficiently from the face of the walling so that the arched head, imposts and jambs appear "set-back". Both the hood-moulding and pilaster-strips are divided into three bands; half-square

- the inner band nearest the archway; wide half-round – the middle band; and a narrow band angled and raised on its outer edges but rounded on its inner edges – the outer band. The extended imposts provide the capitals for the pilaster-strips. The cubical bases for the pilaster-strips protrude from the west wall. Note: The east face of chancel archway is not decorated. The whole archway, including the accompanying pilaster-strips, stand on a square plinths projecting from the face of the north, south and west, not the east, faces of the walling.

All Saints Church, Wittering, Cambridgeshire, has a round-headed chancel archway providing ground floor access between the east end of the nave and the adjoining chancel. It has been built into coursed rubble walling. See below: PHOTO 107. Wittering 5.

The arched head is constructed with voussoirs subdivided into three distinctive moulded shapes: an outer (top), largest shape, comprising a wide, half-roll; below in the middle, a narrow moulded half-square, flat, shape; and below at the bottom, a narrow moulded shape comprising part of the lower half of a "U"-shaped curve. Below, and abutting the voussoirs, is a soffit-roll.

The archway has large, inverted trapezoid-shaped, imposts which extend beyond the hood-moulding on the west face of the wall; each impost is divided into two by a central horizontal groove. The imposts protrude from all three faces of the walls including overhanging the central void between the opposing jambs.

PHOTO 107. Wittering 5.

The through-stone square jambs are constructed of large rectangular stonework of different sizes placed standing horizontally on one of their long sides (not their faces); they do not resemble in construction any recognisable pattern of quoining. The jambs are complemented on three sides by "half-round" cylindrical shafts – those on the west and east faces of the archway "angle-shafts" and those on the faces of the jambs fronting the central void and in line with the soffit-roll above, "soffit-shafts". Between the angle-shafts and soffit shafts the jambs display a vertical square edge. Both angle-shafts and soffit-shafts have expanding capitals which taper upwards to the imposts and expanding bases which taper downwards.

The archway has accompanying half-square pilaster-strips and hood-moulding. The pilaster-strips have square bases and stand on the same square plinth protruding from the faces of the walls as the bases of the angle-shafts, soffit-shafts and jambs.

Holy Trinity Church, Bosham, West Sussex, has a Saxo-Norman round-headed chancel archway providing ground floor access between the east end of the nave and the adjoining chancel. The chancel archway has been built into coursed rubble walling. See Page 88: PHOTO 108. Bosham 2.

On both the west and east faces of the archway the arched head is faced with two bands of voussoirs. Below, and abutting the lower band of voussoirs, is a soffit-roll. The lower band of voussoirs is subdivided into three distinctive moulded shapes: above the soffit-roll, a moulded shape comprising part of the lower half of a "U"-shaped curve; above, a moulded half-square, flat, shape; above moulded half-roll shape. The upper band of voussoirs is also subdivided into three distinctive moulded shapes: above the half-roll at the top of the lower band of voussoirs, a moulded shape comprising part of the lower half of a "U"-shaped curve; above, a moulded, wide, upward curving shape; above, a moulded half-square, flat, shape forming the top edge of the voussoirs.

The archway has two-stepped imposts cut from a single stone, the lower step is circular and the upper step is rectangular and larger. The imposts protrude from all three faces of the walls including overhanging the central void between the opposing jambs.

The jambs have large facing stones not resembling in construction any recognisable pattern of quoining. In addition, moulded onto, and forming an integral part of the

PHOTO 108. Bosham 2.

jambs, are three-quarter round cylindrical angle-shafts – on both the west and east faces of the walling - and soffit-shafts. The soffit-shafts are larger than the angle-shafts and they are separated from each other by the intervening facing stones of the jambs.

Both the angle-shafts and the soffit-shafts, as well as the intervening facing stones of the jambs, have similarly shaped bell-shaped capitals and two-stepped bases – the lower step larger than the upper. The two-stepped bases of the soffit-shafts are distinctly more round and larger than those of the angle-shafts which are more rectangular in shape. The bases of both angle-shafts and soffit-shafts all stand on a large three-quarter-round base. These and the whole archway are supported by a large square single plinth protruding from the faces of the walls. See adjacent: PHOTO 109. Bosham 3, showing bases of soffit-shafts and angle-shafts.

PHOTO 109. Bosham 3.

St James Church, Selham, West Sussex, has a round-headed chancel archway providing ground floor access between the east end of the nave and the adjoining chancel. It has been built into coursed rubble walling. See Page 89: PHOTO 110. Selham 2.

The arched head is constructed with voussoirs which on the west face only have been subdivided into three distinctive, differently sized, moulded half-roll shapes by two distinctive grooves. The inner, lowest, half-roll shape is the largest, the middle half-roll shape the smallest. The archway has chamfered rectangular imposts which protrude from all three faces of the walls including overhanging the central void between the opposing jambs.

The south impost is decorated on its north face with a horizontal scroll design with two adjacent horizontal bands of roll-moulding above. On its west side it is decorated with a serpent in profile to the left with a distinctive head, including an eye and open jaws (towards the top left-hand corner), and with a scroll-like body. Below the impost is a tapering abacus decorated with a horizontal band of roll-moulding at the bottom and top providing a border for decoration involving a plant design with vertical leaves, forming, and encompassing, a scroll design. See below left: PHOTO 111. Selham 3, showing the south impost, abacus and soffit-shaft capital.

The north impost is decorated on its south face with a horizontal band of roll-moulding at the bottom, with a wide band of flat-moulding above, and with a further two adjacent horizontal bands of roll-moulding at the top. On its west side it is decorated with a scroll design involving vertical leaves – possibly part of a reused Roman string-course with the scroll design added at a later date, not Roman. Below the impost is a tapering abacus decorated with a horizontal band of roll-moulding at the bottom and top providing a border for a horizontal band of interlace design.

PHOTO 110. Selham 2.

Both jambs, now plaster-covered, are recessed and include three-quarter round soffit-shafts with decorated capitals and moulded, circular, bell-like bases. The capital on the soffit-shaft on the south side of the archway is decorated with a mixture of interlace and scroll designs with the entwined bodies of two creatures on the face opposite the north side of the archway. In north-west corner is a creature in profile to the right, with its head in portrait but slightly turned; it has distinctive ears, eyes and snout – it appears to be biting its tail. In the top left-hand corner is a small head of another creature in profile to the left, it emerges from one of the strands in the scroll design; its neck, eye, snout and drooping lower jaw can be identified. The capital on the north side of the archway is decorated with a vertical scroll design. See adjacent right: PHOTO 112. Selham 4, showing the north impost, abacus and soffit-shaft capital. The whole archway, including the accompanying soffit-shafts, stand on a two-stepped square plinth protruding from the faces of the opposing jambs with their soffit-shafts only.

PHOTO 111. Selham 3.

PHOTO 112. Selham 4.

Note: the date of the decoration on the imposts, abaci and the capitals of the shafts is a matter of debate. The nature of the decoration is suggestive of some Anglo-Saxon designs but a 12th century date for the decoration has also been suggested. Clearly the decoration was not completed by one individual - the designs are too inconsistent.

5. DOORWAYS
- From top to bottom most doorways comprise: a half-rounded arched head, or flat-headed lintel*, or triangular (gable) – head; square or rectangular imposts*; jambs*; and a sill*. See text and illustrations provided in the following pages.

- Many doorways were constructed with large facing stones*, individually of a self-evident difference in terms of size and finish to the stonework used in the adjoining walling. Facing stones varied in size and shape and were roughly-dressed* but not to the uniformity of size, shape and careful dressing as ashlar* favoured by Norman and later builders although there are some examples where the Anglo-Saxon builders used ashlar.

- Alternatively, the heads, imposts, jambs and sills of some doorways were constructed of, and faced with, rubble* stonework displaying few differences to the stonework forming the adjoining walling whether laid in courses* or randomly. Such doorways could include the use of a mixture of rubble and flints and the reuse of Roman stonework including Roman tiles or tile-like bricks, where these were available.

- Doorways were mostly cut straight through the full depth of the walls without rebates or recesses unless a rebate was required because the door hung below the head of the doorway and within the central void between the jambs. The rebates were cut into the stonework of the head, of whatever shape, imposts (they would probably not have extended into the central void between the jambs), and jambs to allow doors to open internally into a defined space. Where no such rebates were provided the door would have been hung against, and fitted flush, with the inner face of the walling adjacent to the doorway allowing the door to open internally.

- Some round-headed doorways and triangular-headed doorways were accompanied by strip-work* and hood-moulding* - a very few with label-stops* at the bottom of the hood-moulding*. Round-headed doorways may have angle-shafts* – see Pages 91 to 93 "Round-Headed Doorways with Arched Heads constructed with Voussoirs: also with Angle-Shafts, Strip-Work and Hood-Moulding".

- Doorways in upper rooms in a church were reached by permanent wooden stairways or ladders, and sometimes by stone stairways. See Pages 179 to 185, "11. Stairways".

*See Glossary and for other such terms in the following pages.

The following pages set out the component parts and types of doorways and their various locations within churches – photographic examples are provided.

ROUND-HEADED DOORWAYS
Round-Headed Doorways have half-rounded arched heads which may be constructed with wedge-shaped voussoirs or cut out of the centre of the lower horizontal face of a monolithic lintel. They may also be shaped from a single stone. They may comprise a horizontal row of stones shaped individually to form a discernible arch, or individual stones placed on end to form a discernible arch.

However the arched head is constructed the stonework used may or may not comprise half-through-stones, three-quarter-through-stones or through-stones through the full thickness of the walling. Whilst in many examples of round-headed doorways the inner and the outer sides of the arched head are identical, there are examples where the inner face has an arched head constructed with voussoirs and the outer face has the arched head cut out of a half-through-stone monolithic lintel.

There are also some examples of what ostensibly are round-headed doorways which are in fact flat-headed doorways because of the inclusion of a tympanum directly underneath the arched head. Whilst the tympanum is usually aligned with the outer faces of the walling of the doorway it may occasionally be placed in the central depth of the wall.

ROUND-HEADED DOORWAYS WITH ARCHED HEADS CONSTRUCTED WITH VOUSSOIRS

The illustration adjacent provides an example of a round-headed doorway whose arched head is constructed with voussoirs. The voussoirs are supported by rectangular imposts which do not protrude from the faces of the walls and do not overhang the central void. Below, the jambs are constructed with roughly-dressed through-stones laid in a similar fashion to Escomb jambs. Between the jambs is a sill comprising a monolithic stone lying flat on one of its faces. The inner face of the bottom vertical jambs are notched into the sill. There are no rebates indicated for the door. Both internally and externally the view of the doorway is similar.

St Peter's Church, Monkwearmouth, Sunderland County Durham, has a round-headed doorway which seems to have preserved most, if not all, of its original construction details. It is in the south wall of the late-seventh century west porch supporting above a late-tenth/early-eleventh century Anglo-Saxon tower. The doorway at one time provided access at ground floor level from the west porch into a south porticus – now demolished.

The arched head is constructed with through-stone voussoirs supported by through-stone imposts flush with all three faces of the walls of which they form a part; the imposts do not overhang the central void between the jambs. The jambs each comprise a single megalithic vertical through-stone; the bottom of the jambs are notched into the sill. The sill comprises a monolithic stone lying flat on one of its faces. See above left: PHOTO 113. Monkwearmouth 5, showing the north face of the doorway. See above right: PHOTO 114. Monkwearmouth 6, showing the south face of the doorway with the rebate for the inward opening door arrowed red. (Ignore the late-19th/early-20th century base with iron railings.)

PHOTO 113. Monkwearmouth 5.   PHOTO 114. Monkwearmouth 6.

ROUND-HEADED DOORWAYS WITH ARCHED HEADS CONSTRUCTED WITH VOUSSOIRS: ALSO WITH ANGLE-SHAFTS, STRIP-WORK AND HOOD-MOULDING.

The illustration on Page 92 provides an example of the outward or external face of a round-headed doorway with an arched head constructed with voussoirs. The voussoirs are supported by rectangular imposts protruding from the faces of the walls and overhanging the central void and extending below and beyond the accompanying hood-moulding.

Below the imposts are the jambs which are recessed on the outer or external side. In these recesses are "angle-shafts" – in the angle of the jambs - cylindrical in size and shape and with similar shaped capitals and bases. Most of the facing stones of the jambs are hidden from view by the angle-shafts but where they can be identified the exposed sides are faced with roughly-dressed stones of varying shapes and sizes and laid in a similar fashion to side alternate quoining. Between the jambs is a sill comprising a monolithic stone lying flat on one of its faces. There are no rebates indicated for the door. The doorway is accompanied by strip-work parallel to the jambs with intervening stonework similar to that in the adjoining walling. It also has hood-moulding which is concentric with, and sits directly on top of, the voussoirs.

St Botolph's Church, Hadstock, Essex provides not only an example of a restored round-headed doorway but also a rare surviving Anglo-Saxon door dendrochronologically dated to 1034-1042. The door is hung against, and fitted flush, with the inner face of the adjacent walling. The restored doorway is in the north wall of the nave at ground floor level.

The arched head of the doorway is constructed with through-stone voussoirs decorated around the bottom edge externally with a recessed band of roll-moulding. The arched head has accompanying hood-moulding which is concentric with, and sits directly on top of, the voussoirs; the hood-moulding is decorated with a design similar to palmette design. See adjacent: PHOTO 115. Hadstock 1, showing the north face of the doorway, with the hood-moulding arrowed black.

PHOTO 115. Hadstock 1.

The three-quarter through-stone imposts protrude from only the north face of the wall and overhang the central void between the jambs. The south wall is heavily plastered with no indication of the imposts on the south face of the doorway. The upper two-thirds of the three-quarter through-stone imposts are decorated horizontally with a honeysuckle design not dissimilar to palmette design. The lower third of the imposts comprise a protruding band of roll-moulding.

The through-stone jambs do not resemble in construction any recognisable pattern of quoining; they appear to include some megalithic stonework - plaster obscures some of their details. Externally, the jambs are recessed and contain free-standing cylindrical angle-shafts with capitals decorated with a design resembling palmette design; the bases of the shafts are sloping, rounded, and not decorated. Between the jambs the sill comprises a monolithic stone lying flat on one of its faces. Note: There are no rebates for the door.

St John the Baptist Church, Barnack, Cambridgeshire, provides an example of a round-headed doorway decorated with accompanying strip-work and hood-moulding. The doorway is in the south wall of the tower at ground floor level.

The arched head of the doorway is constructed with through-stone voussoirs supported by rectangular through-stone imposts protruding from all three faces of the walls including overhanging the central void between the opposing jambs. The imposts of the doorway extend horizontally across most, but not all, of the top of the strip-work below. Below, the jambs are constructed with roughly-dressed through-stones laid in a similar fashion to Escomb jambs. The jambs stand on square bases protruding from the face of the wall. These bases form the ends of a plinth running along the bottom of the rest of the wall of the tower. The plinth supports the bases of the strip-work. Between the jambs is a sill comprising a monolithic stone lying flat on one of its faces.

The doorway has accompanying strip-work which abut, and are not separated, from the jambs; the strip-work is on square bases protruding from the face of the wall. The hood-moulding is concentric with, and sits directly on top of, the voussoirs and has square corbels at its base which protrude further from the face of the wall than the imposts immediately below. Note: There are no rebates for the door. See adjacent: PHOTO 116. Barnack 5, showing the south face of the doorway with the strip-work arrowed red and the hood-moulding arrowed black.

PHOTO 116. Barnack 5.

ROUND-HEADED DOORWAYS WITH ARCHED HEADS CUT OUT OF A MONOLITHIC LINTEL

The illustration adjacent shows a doorway with the arched head cut out of a through-stone monolithic lintel supported by through-stone rectangular imposts which do not protrude from the faces of the walls or overhang the central void. Below, the jambs are constructed with roughly-dressed through-stones laid in a similar fashion to Escomb jambs.

Between the jambs is a sill comprising a monolithic stone lying flat on one of its faces. The inner face of the bottom vertical jambs are notched into the sill. There are no rebates indicated for the door. The view from the inner or internal or the outer or external sides is similar.

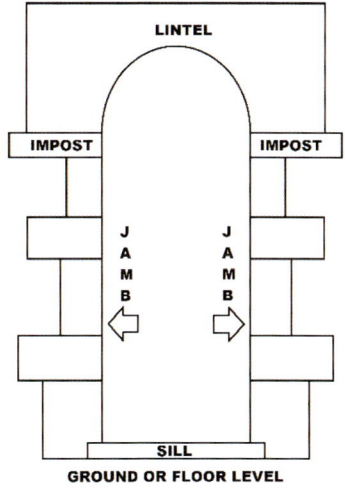

St Cuthbert's Church, Billingham, County Durham, provides an example of a round-headed doorway with its arched head cut out from the centre of the lower horizontal face of a through-stone monolithic lintel. It is supported by through-stone rectangular imposts which protrude from all three faces of the walls including overhanging the central void between the opposing jambs. The imposts extend to provide the tops of the strip-work below and support the corbel-like bases of the hood-moulding above. Below, the jambs are constructed with roughly-dressed through-stones laid in a similar fashion to Escomb jambs. The jambs stand on protruding bases which extend to, and also provide support for, the bases of the accompanying strip-work. Between the opposing jambs, but below the bottom of the bases of the jambs, is a monolithic stone forming the sill protruding from the face of the wall – its position indicates a step down from the bases of the jambs. Note: There are no rebates for the door.

A protruding, semi-circular, band of hood-moulding extends above the lintel with the intervening stonework similar to the adjacent walling and creating a tympanum. In addition strip-work abut the stonework forming the jambs.

This doorway is at second floor level in the south wall of the tower. It opened outwards into space probably providing access to an external balcony for the displaying of relics to the congregation below. See adjacent: PHOTO 117. Billingham 1, showing the south face of the doorway, with the strip-work arrowed red and the hood-moulding arrowed black.

PHOTO 117. Billingham 1.

FLAT-HEADED DOORWAYS
The illustration adjacent provides an example of a flat-headed doorway. The head comprises a through-stone monolithic lintel; there are no supporting imposts. Below, the jambs are constructed with roughly-dressed megalithic through-stones laid in a similar fashion to Escomb jambs. Between the jambs is a sill comprising a single, monolithic, stone lying flat on one of its faces. The inner faces of the bottom vertical jambs are notched into the sill. Between the jambs is a sill comprising a monolithic stone lying flat on one of its faces. There are no rebates indicated for the door. The view from the inner or internal or the outer or external sides is similar.

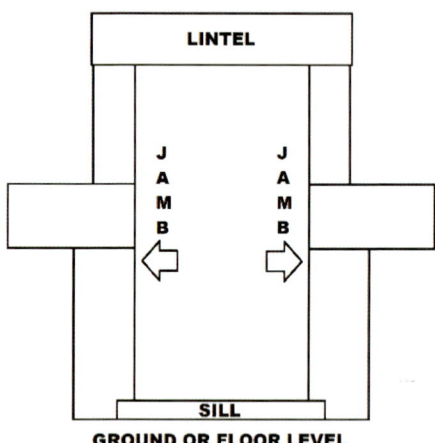

Escomb Church, County Durham, provides an example of a flat-headed doorway with its head comprising a through-stone monolithic lintel. It has no imposts but the tops of each of the large vertical stones forming part of the jambs and supporting the lintel are notched into the lintel – resembling mortise and tenon jointing. The large, megalithic, jambs are constructed with roughly-dressed through-stones laid in Escomb fashion. The jambs are rebated for the hanging of a door in the central depth of the walling. The sill is a single, large, stone lying flat on one of its faces. The doorway is at ground floor level in the north wall of the nave. See adjacent: PHOTO 118. Escomb 3, showing the north face of the doorway.

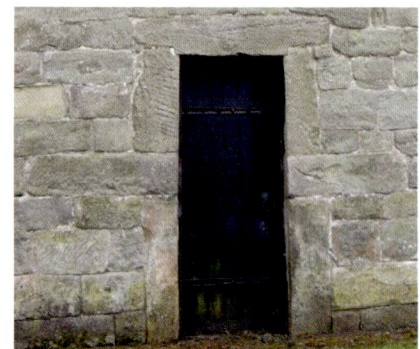

PHOTO 118. Escomb 3.

TRIANGULAR (GABLE)-HEADED DOORWAYS
The illustration on Page 95 provides an example of a triangular (gable)-headed doorway. The head comprises two through-stones – each a trapezium - placed together at one of their ends to form a triangular shape; their other ends are placed on top of the supporting imposts. The head is supported by through-stone rectangular imposts which do not protrude from the faces of the walls or overhang the central void. Below, the jambs are constructed with roughly-dressed through-stones laid in a similar fashion to Escomb jambs. Between the jambs is a sill comprising a monolithic stone lying flat on one of its faces. There are no rebates indicated for the door.

The view from the inner or internal or the outer or external sides is similar.

St Andrew's Church, Brigstock, Northamptonshire, provides an example of a triangular-headed doorway. The head comprises two through-stones – each a trapezium – placed together at one of their ends to form a triangular shape; their other ends are placed on top of the supporting through-stone imposts. The through-stone imposts are flush with all three faces of the walls of which they form a part and do not overhang the central void between the jambs. Below, the jambs are constructed with roughly-dressed through-stones laid in a similar fashion to Escomb jambs. Between the jambs is a sill comprising two large stones which also provide the bottom support for the jambs – they are horizontally placed "L"-shaped. Placed on top of the stones forming the sill are two steps to assist access from the tower into the Anglo-Saxon stair turret when it was added at a later date. On the west side of the doorway it appears a rebate was added for a door to open westwards into the stair turret – presumably work undertaken at the same time the steps were added onto the sill. (When the west doorway provided the main entrance to the church, if the doorway then had a rebate, the door would have opened eastwards into the tower.)

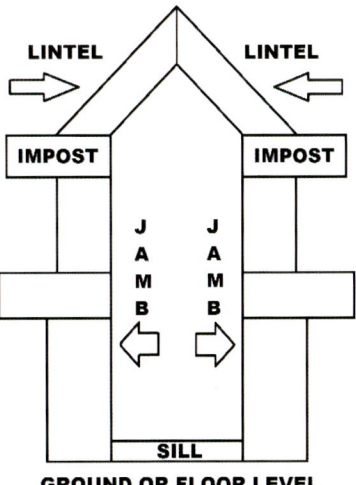

The doorway is at ground floor level in the west wall of the tower. It may have been the former western entrance to the church before the later, Anglo-Saxon, stair turret was added. See adjacent: PHOTO 119. Brigstock 4, showing the east face of the doorway.

PHOTO 119. Brigstock 4.

St Peter's Church, Barton-upon-Humber, Lincolnshire, provides an example of a triangular-headed doorway with strip-work and hood-moulding. It is at ground floor level in the north wall of the tower and was formerly one of the entrances to the "Tower-Nave" – it has now been blocked. See Page 96 top left: PHOTO 120. Barton-upon-Humber 2, showing the external north face of the doorway, with the strip-work arrowed red and the hood-moulding arrowed black, and Page 96 top right: PHOTO 121. Barton-upon-Humber 3, showing the internal south face of the doorway.

The head comprises two through-stones – each a trapezium – placed together at one of their ends to form a triangular shape. Externally the other ends are placed on top of the supporting imposts. Internally, the head appears to have been "restored" at some later, not Anglo-Saxon, date. The lower part of each trapezium has been replaced by two stones, one on top of the other, which now support the top of the triangular head. The upper stone with an angled interior face to compliment the trapezium above, and a lower stone extending into the void resulting in the imposts appearing two-stepped.

Externally, the through-stone imposts, which protrude from the faces of the walls and overhang the central void between the opposing faces of the jambs, are decorated with a horizontal band of flat-moulding along their bases. Internally the imposts are flush with the faces of the walls and do not protrude into the central void. Below, the jambs are constructed with roughly-dressed through-stones laid in a similar fashion to Escomb jambs; the jambs have protruding square bases. Externally, the sill of the doorway is now obscured by the stonework blocking the doorway, but internally, both jambs rest on a single, protruding, flat plinth. This plinth protrudes from the faces of the walls, including into the central void, and continues across the sill. Note: There are no rebates for the door.

PHOTO 120.
Barton-upon-Humber 2.

PHOTO 121.
Barton-upon-Humber 3.

Externally the doorway is accompanied by strip-work constructed in similar fashion to long and short quoining with protruding, square, corbel-like bases; the strip-work is parallel to, and slightly separate from, the jambs. The strip-work terminates with protruding, square, capitals decorated, like the abutting imposts, with a horizontal band of flat-moulding along their bases. The strip-work is identical in construction and size to the pilaster-strips decorating the wall and form part of the overall composition. Hood-moulding, in the form of two half-through-stones – each a trapezium – sits directly on top of the two through-stones forming the triangular head of the doorway. Additionally, the hood-moulding appears to have small, almost, corbel-like, bases sitting on top of part of the imposts and part of the square capitals of the strip-work below. Internally, the doorway is not accompanied by strip-work or hood-moulding.

Holy Trinity Church, Colchester, Essex, provides an example of a triangular-headed doorway constructed with random rubble fabric including flints and reused Roman tiles or tile-like bricks. It is also accompanied by pilaster-strips and hood-moulding. The doorway is in the west wall of the tower at ground floor level.

The whole of the doorway is faced with reused Roman tiles or tile-like bricks. The head is constructed with these bricks each placed at an angle on top of one another to form the two side arms of the triangle which converge in the centre to form the top of the head. A single brick has been placed on top to provide a "cap" for the head; below this cap are two small fragments of bricks mirroring the angle of the full-size bricks below and a single fragment of brick placed vertically in the centre between them. The head is supported by angled three-stepped imposts with each step constructed with two bricks placed horizontally on top of each other. The imposts are flush with two faces of the walls and overhang the central void between the opposing jambs. The jambs comprise bricks placed horizontally on top of one another. Between the jambs a protruding step, not of Roman or Anglo-Saxon origin, has been placed on top of the original sill of the doorway. Note: There are no rebates for the door.

Pilaster-strips, comprising bricks placed horizontally on top of one another, abut the jambs; the size of the bricks used to form the pilaster-strips appears to be smaller than the tiles used to form the jambs. Abutting the tops of the imposts the bases of the accompanying hood-moulding comprise bricks placed horizontally on top of one another with the top brick being the smallest but providing the base for the hood-moulding above. (There are five bricks providing the base abutting the top of the impost on the left-hand side but only four bricks providing the base abutting the top of the impost on the right-hand side.) The hood-moulding takes the form of bricks laid end to end in three rows placed on top of one another. These bricks have been placed on top of, and at right-angles to, the bricks forming the head of the doorway. Between the underneath of the apex of the hood-moulding, and above the apex of the head of the doorway, is a single stone of different dimensions to the bricks and the fragments of bricks used elsewhere in the construction of the doorway. See adjacent: PHOTO 122. Colchester 3, showing the west face of the doorway with the pilaster-strips arrowed red and the hood-moulding arrowed black.

HEADS OF DOORWAYS: ARCHED HEAD CONSTRUCTED WITH VOUSSOIRS
Arched heads were often constructed with a semi-circular row of tapering, wedge-shaped voussoirs which were often roughly-dressed half-through-stones, three-quarter-through-stones, or through-stones through the full thickness of the walling. Not all examples have identifiable single, vertically placed, central key-stones. See below PHOTO 123. Monkwearmouth 2, and Page 98. PHOTO 127. Breamore 1.

PHOTO 122. Colchester 3.

St Peter's Church, Monkwearmouth, Sunderland, County Durham, has in the south wall of the porch/tower at ground floor level an example of a round-headed doorway constructed with through-stone voussoirs with no identifiable single, vertically placed, central key-stone. See adjacent: PHOTO 123. Monkwearmouth 7, showing the north face.

PHOTO 123. Monkwearmouth 7.

The voussoirs providing the arched heads of some doorways may be accompanied by concentric hood-moulding. In contrast to archways, doorways are more likely to have hood-moulding placed on top of the voussoirs, rather than having intervening stonework separating it from the voussoirs.

St Botolph's Church, Hadstock, Essex, has in the north wall of the nave at ground floor level an example of a round-headed doorway whose arched head is accompanied by hood-moulding placed directly on top of the voussoirs. See adjacent: PHOTO 124. Hadstock 2, showing the north face with the hood-moulding arrowed red.

PHOTO 124. Hadstock 2.

Some doorways may have label-stops at the bottom of the accompanying hood-moulding. St Mary's Church, Deerhurst, Gloucestershire, provides examples with three dimensional beasts' heads with slight vestiges of red paint surviving. Two of these have been removed from their original position accompanying the hood-moulding on the external face of the west doorway providing access at ground floor level into the porch/tower. The label-stops have now been place on the interior face of the west doorway supporting the hood-moulding dating from the 1861 to 1862 restoration.

See adjacent left: PHOTO 125. Deerhurst 5, showing the label-stop on the south side, and above right: PHOTO 126. Deerhurst 6, showing the label-stop on the north side.

St Mary's Church, Breamore, Hampshire, has in the south wall of the nave at ground floor level a round-headed doorway into the former south porticus. The north face of the arched head of this doorway provides a rare example of where voussoirs have been decorated with an inscription. The inscription is in Old English and it precise interpretation is a matter of debate but it may be something like: "Here the agreement which ….reveals". The voussoirs have no identifiable single, vertically placed, central key-stone. See adjacent: PHOTO 127. Breamore 1.

PHOTO 125. Deerhurst 5.   PHOTO 126. Deerhurst 6.

HEADS OF DOORWAYS: ARCHED HEADS CONSTRUCTED WITH RUBBLE, FLINTS AND REUSED ROMAN STONEWORK
Instead of voussoirs the arched head may be constructed with a mixture of stonework comprising irregularly-shaped and sized rubble, flints and reused Roman stonework, similar to the stonework of the adjoining walling with no indication of wedge-shaped voussoirs.

PHOTO 127. Breamore 1.

To construct a half-round arched head, individual stones were shaped, if required, and placed radially with a square or rectangular side flush with the face of the wall, or, placed radially on end vertically with a narrow side flush with the face of the wall. Where available, Roman tiles or tile-like bricks were placed vertically on end.

All Saints Church, Brixworth, Northamptonshire, has in the south wall of the tower at ground floor level an example of a round-headed doorway whose arched head is constructed using Roman tiles and tile-like bricks. See above right: PHOTO 128. Brixworth 5, showing the south face.

PHOTO 128. Brixworth 5.

Note: Whatever the nature of the individual stones used to construct the arched head they are often still described as "voussoirs" despite not being wedge-shaped.

HEADS OF DOORWAYS: ARCHED HEADS CUT OUT OF A LINTEL
Alternatively the arched heads may be cut out of the centre of the lower horizontal face of a through-stone monolithic lintel or two half-through-stones lintels which abut each other in the central depth of the wall.

Anglo-Saxon Church Architecture & Stone Sculpture   99

St Cuthbert's Church, Billingham, County Durham, has at second floor level a round-headed doorway likely provided to gain access to an external balcony. It has a round-headed doorway with its arched head cut out of a through-stone monolithic lintel; it also has hood-moulding with corbel-like bases. See adjacent: PHOTO 129. Billingham 2, showing the south face with the hood-moulding arrowed red.

Some doorways, with an arched head cut out of a lintel may have a through-stone or half-through-stone tympanum. This can result in the doorway being flat-headed rather than round-headed.

PHOTO 129. Billingham 2.

St Cuthbert's Church, Billingham, County Durham, has at ground floor level in the west wall of the nave a round-headed doorway made flat-headed by the insertion of a mid-wall tympanum. See adjacent: PHOTO 130. Billingham 3, showing the west face.

HEADS OF DOORWAYS: FLAT-HEADED DOORWAYS
Flat-Headed doorways often have a through-stone monolithic lintel but some lintels may comprise two half-through-stones abutting each other in the central depth of the wall.

PHOTO 130. Billingham 3.

Escomb Church, County Durham, has in the north wall of the nave at ground floor level an example of a flat-headed doorway with its head constructed with a through-stone monolithic lintel with no supporting imposts; the top stones of the jambs have been notched into the lintel similar to mortise and tenon jointing. See adjacent: PHOTO 131. Escomb 4, showing the north face.

PHOTO 131. Escomb 4.

At All Saints Church, Hough-on-the-Hill, Lincolnshire, has two flat-headed doorways providing access between the tower and the stair-turret each lintel comprising two large half-through-stones abutting each other in the central depth of the wall. These half-through stones are stepped to allow for changes in height from one floor (the tower) to another (the stair turret).

At first floor level in the west wall of the tower there is a two stepped flat-headed doorway to allow for the change in height required for the three steps descending from the stair turret into the ringing room of

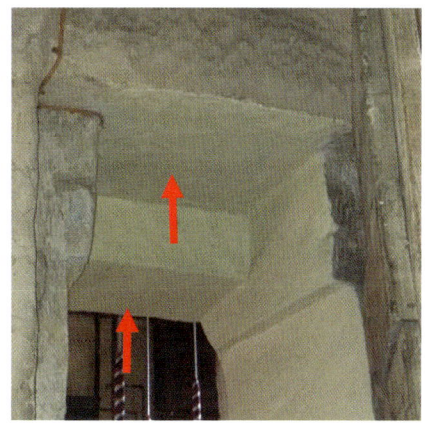

PHOTO 132. Hough-on-the-Hill 1.

the tower. See Page 99 bottom right: PHOTO 132 Hough-on-the-Hill 1, showing the west face with each step arrowed red. See also Page 105: PHOTO 149. Hough-on-the-Hill 2 and PHOTO 150. Hough-on-the-Hill 3.

HEADS OF DOORWAYS: TRIANGULAR (GABLE)-HEADED DOORWAYS
Some doorways were triangular (gable)-headed with the head constructed with two single through-stones, or two pairs of half-through-stones with each pair abutting each other in the central depth of the wall. Whether single or half-through-stones each stone is a trapezium which extends upwards from the imposts to meet centrally and form the triangle shape of the head of the doorway. Some examples may not have supporting imposts with the head extending directly from the tops of the jambs.

St Mary's Church, Deerhurst, Gloucestershire, has a ground floor triangular (gable)-headed doorway formerly providing access between the chancel and the choir porticus. It is constructed with two pairs of half-through-stones with each pair abutting each other in the central depth of the wall. Each half-through stone is a trapezium which extends upwards from the imposts to meet centrally and form the triangle shape of the head of the doorway. See adjacent: PHOTO 133. Deerhurst 7, showing the north face.

PHOTO 133. Deerhurst 7.

Holy Trinity Church, Colchester, Essex, has in the west wall of the tower at ground floor level an example of a triangular (gable)-headed doorway with its head constructed with reused Roman tiles or tile-like bricks. Each of these bricks has been placed at an angle on top of another to form the two side arms of the triangle which converge in the centre to form the top of the head. A single brick has been placed horizontally on top to provide a "cap" for the head; below are two small fragments of bricks mirroring the angle of the full-size bricks below and a single fragment of brick placed vertically in the centre between them. The head is supported by angled three-stepped imposts with each step formed of two bricks placed horizontally on top of each other. See adjacent: PHOTO 134. Colchester 4, showing the west face, with the hood-moulding arrowed red.

PHOTO 134. Colchester 4.

The accompanying hood-moulding takes the form of bricks laid end to end in three rows placed on top of one another. These bricks have been placed on top of, and at right-angles to, the bricks forming the head of the doorway. Between the underneath of the apex of the hood-moulding, and above the apex of the head of the doorway with its horizontal "cap" comprising a single brick, is a single stone of different dimensions to the bricks and the fragments of bricks used elsewhere in the construction of the doorway.

IMPOSTS OF DOORWAYS – applying to all shapes of head
Imposts are mostly found supporting the arched heads of doorways constructed with voussoirs and those doorways with triangular-shaped heads but even with these two varieties of head there may be no imposts.

Imposts were usually square in section and profile and may be flush with, and protrude from, some or all of the faces of the walls of which they form a part. Imposts may also protrude into the central void below the head and between the opposing jambs. Imposts could be half-through-stones, three-quarter-through-stones, or through-stones through the full depth of the walling. Some imposts were chamfered, concave, angled, stepped, bulbous or conical, or tapered or moulded with a modelled surface sometimes with a shaped pattern in relief, or decorated with a variety of geometrical and plant designs.

St Mary's Church, Stow-in-Lindsey, Lincolnshire, has in the west wall of the north transept at ground floor level a round-headed doorway with imposts chamfered along their lower edges. See below left: PHOTO 135. Stow-in-Lindsey 6.

PHOTO 135. Stow-in-Lindsey 6.

PHOTO 136. Hadstock 3.

St Botolph's Church, Hadstock, Essex, has in the north wall of the nave at ground floor level a round-headed doorway with imposts decorated with palmette design and, below, with a protruding horizontal band of roll-moulding. See above right: PHOTO 136. Hadstock 3, with the clearest example of palmette design arrowed red.

All Saints Church, Earls Barton, Northamptonshire, has a round-headed doorway in the west wall of the tower at ground floor level with imposts decorated with an arcade of blind, interlocking, round-headed archways. See adjacent: PHOTO 137. Earls Barton 1.

JAMBS OF DOORWAYS - applying to all shapes of head

PHOTO 137. Earls Barton 1.

Round, Flat and Triangular-Headed Doorways had individual stones which collectively formed two sets of jambs on opposite sides of the central void providing access to the door - whether the door was accompanied by rebates in the stonework or hung against, and fitted flush, with the inner face of the adjacent walling.

Jambs were usually square in section and profile. They may be constructed of a single, vertical, megalithic through-stone. Alternatively, they may be constructed with roughly-dressed half-through-stones, three-quarter-through-stones, or through-stones through the full depth of the walling laid in a similar fashion to Escomb jambs or side alternate quoining. They may also be constructed of similar stonework to the adjoining walling and coursed in a similar fashion – some examples may include megalithic stonework. There are no "standard" number of stones forming the jambs and the stonework in one jamb may not be the mirror image of the stones forming the opposite jamb. Sometimes the bottom stones forming the jambs of doorways were notched into the sill below.

St Peter's Church, Monkwearmouth, Sunderland, County Durham, has in the south wall of the porch/tower at ground floor level a round-headed doorway with jambs constructed with a single, vertical, megalithic through-stone notched into the sill below. See adjacent left: PHOTO 138. Monkwearmouth 8.

St Mary's Church, Stow-in-Lindsey, Lincolnshire, has in the west wall of the north transept at ground floor level a round-headed doorway with through-stone jambs constructed in Escomb fashion standing on a protruding base. See adjacent right: PHOTO 139. Stow-in-Lindsey 7.

PHOTO 138.
Monkwearmouth 8.

PHOTO 139.
Stow-in-Lindsey 7.

Alternatively, jambs may comprise rubble stonework displaying few differences to the stonework forming the adjoining walling whether laid in courses or randomly. Such jambs could be constructed with a mixture of rubble and flints similar to the stonework of the adjoining walling including the reuse of Roman stonework and tile-like bricks where these were available. With such examples internally, especially, the jambs may be covered with plaster so that the detail of the walling is hidden.

St Matthew's Church, Langford, Oxfordshire, has in the east wall of the central area at first floor level a blocked flat-headed doorway with jambs constructed with rubble similar to the stonework in the adjoining walling. See adjacent: PHOTO 140. Langford 10.

Each jamb of round-headed doorways only, may have a recess on the outer or external side to accommodate a cylindrical-shaped "angle-shaft" - in the angle of the jambs. Angle-shafts may be constructed with one section of stonework or a series of sections of stonework placed one on top of another. They may be half-round three-quarter round, or completely round (circular).

PHOTO 140. Langford 10.

Where provided they may have similarly shaped moulded or sculptured capitals and bases not necessarily of a similar size. Where the jambs include angle-shafts most of the facing stones of the jambs are hidden from view but where they can be identified the exposed sides are faced with roughly-dressed facing stones of varying shapes and sizes which may be laid in a similar way to side alternate quoining, or the stonework in the adjoining walling.

Both the jambs and the angle-shafts may stand on square bases which often project from the faces of the walling. These bases may themselves stand on a plinth which continues along the bottom of the adjoining walling. See Page 93: PHOTO 116. Barnack 5 (this doorway does not have angle-shafts).

SILLS OF DOORWAYS - applying to all shapes of head
Sills of doorways may comprise a "monolithic" stone lying horizontally between the base of the jambs or a row of two or three stones laid horizontally.

Holy Trinity Church, Bosham, West Sussex, has in the west wall of the nave at first floor level a triangular-headed doorway with a monolithic sill. See below left: PHOTO 141. Bosham 4, showing the east face.

PHOTO 141. Bosham 4.

St Mary's Church, Deerhurst, Gloucestershire, has in the west wall of the nave at first floor level a blocked round-headed doorway with a monolithic sill. See above right: PHOTO 142. Deerhurst 8, showing the east face.

PHOTO 142. Deerhurst 8.

On occasions where the sill comprises two or more stones laid horizontally in a row these stones may provide a base for the bottom stones forming the jambs above.

St Andrew's Church, Brigstock, Northamptonshire, has in the west wall of the tower at ground floor level an example of a round-headed doorway with a sill comprising two stones which extend in an "L" shape along the sill of the doorway and up each of the jambs to provide their bases. See adjacent: PHOTO 143. Brigstock 5, showing the east face with the internal "L" corners of the two stones arrowed red.

All Saints Church, Earls Barton, Northamptonshire, has in the south wall of the tower at first floor level an example of where the sill of the round-headed doorway is integral to the square string-course separating the first stage of the tower from the second stage. See Page 107: PHOTO 156. Earls Barton 3.

PHOTO 143. Brigstock 5.

DOORWAYS BELOW GROUND FLOOR LEVEL – examples providing access to a crypt and between their component areas. See Pages 195 to 208 "15. Crypts".

Hexham Abbey (St Andrew's Church), Northumberland, has a round-headed doorway providing an entrance into the main area of the crypt. The arched head is constructed with three, shaped, through-stones with the top stone being similar to a lintel. The doorway has no imposts and has through-stone jambs – there is now no door. See adjacent:

PHOTO 144. Hexham 1.

PHOTO 144. Hexham 1, showing the west face. (See Pages 198 to 202 for more text and photographs about Hexham Abbey crypt, including doorways.)

Ripon Cathedral, North Yorkshire, has a round-headed doorway providing the western entrance to the main area of the crypt. The arched head has been cut out of a through-stone. It has no imposts and the jambs are constructed with through-stones; paint obscures the details. See adjacent left: PHOTO 145. Ripon 1, showing the east face. (See Pages 202 to 205 for more text and photographs about Ripon Cathedral crypt, including doorways.)

PHOTO 145. Ripon 1.   PHOTO 146. Brixworth 6.

All Saints Church, Brixworth, Northamptonshire, has a round-headed doorway providing what was once the southern entrance to a ring-crypt with its arched head constructed with reused Roman tiles or tile-like bricks. The jambs have been restored in 1865 and are now similar to ashlar in their construction. See above right: PHOTO 146. Brixworth 6, showing the east face. (See Pages 207 to 208 for more text and photographs about Brixworth ring-crypt, including doorways.)

DOORWAYS AT GROUND FLOOR LEVEL - often provide:
- The main external entrance into the church comprising a single doorway in the west wall of the nave.

All Saints Church, Earls Barton, Northamptonshire, has a round-headed doorway which provided the western entrance to the former tower-nave at ground floor level. The arched head is cut out of two stones externally and a single large stone internally. The large, square, imposts which protrude from all three faces of the walls including overhanging the central void between the opposing jambs. On the faces overhanging the central void the imposts are decorated with an arcade of blind, interlocking, round-headed archways. The jambs are constructed in Escomb fashion supported by rectangular, protruding square bases.

PHOTO 147. Earls Barton 2.

The doorway is accompanied by hood-moulding and strip-work which have protruding square bases standing on the single square plinth at the bottom of the adjacent walling. See above right: PHOTO 147. Earls Barton 2, showing the west face with strip-work arrowed red and hood-moulding arrowed black.

All Saints Church, Brixworth, Northamptonshire, has a round-headed doorway which formerly provided the western main entrance to the nave at ground floor level. The arched head is constructed with reused Roman tiles or tile-like bricks with no supporting imposts. The jambs are mostly hidden by plaster but on the west face, where there is no plaster, they were constructed of random rubble walling similar to the stonework in the adjoining walling. See Page 105: PHOTO 148. Brixworth 7, showing the east face – note in the background an Anglo-Saxon round-headed doorway, arrowed red, which was inserted into walling when the western archway into the former porch was blocked.

- The main external entrance into the church where access to the church by single doorways in both the north and south walls of the nave, opposite each other, usually towards the west end of the nave. See Page 94: PHOTO 118. Escomb 3.

- Access into a porch or tower from the west end of the nave.

- Access from the western porch/tower into the adjacent north and south porticus.

PHOTO 148. Brixworth 7.

- Access from a western porch/tower where there is an adjoining stair turret.

All Saints Church, Hough-on-the-Hill, Lincolnshire, has a megalithic flat-headed doorway which provides access to the stair turret at ground floor level. The lintel is constructed with two half-through-stones which are stepped to allow for the rising of three steps which were added when Anglo-Saxon stair turret was built. See adjacent left: PHOTO 149. Hough-on the Hill 2, showing the stepped head of this doorway looking from the east: the west step, arrowed red, higher than the east step, arrowed black. See adjacent right: PHOTO 150. Hough-on-the-Hill 3, showing the eastern face. See also Page 99: PHOTO 132. Hough-on-the-Hill 1.

PHOTO 149.
Hough-on-the-Hill 2.

PHOTO 150.
Hough-on-the-Hill 3.

- Access from the nave and/or chancel into porticus running adjacent to their north and south walls, or, rarely, direct access between one porticus and another adjacent porticus.

St Mary's Church, Deerhurst, Gloucestershire, also has a ground floor triangular (gable) headed doorway formerly providing access between the chancel and the choir porticus. It is constructed with two pairs of half-through-stones with each pair abutting each other in the central depth of the wall. Each half-through stone is a trapezium which extends upwards from the imposts to meet centrally and form the triangle shape of the head of the doorway. The head is supported by square imposts. The jambs were constructed with random rubble similar to the stonework in the adjoining walling. See adjacent: PHOTO 151. Deerhurst 9, showing the north face.

PHOTO 151. Deerhurst 9.

St Mary's Church, Deerhurst, Gloucestershire, has a ground floor flat-headed doorway formerly providing access at ground floor level between the north choir porticus and the north-east apse porticus - both porticus have been demolished. The doorway has a single lintel forming its head - it is cracked. It has no imposts. The jambs are constructed with mostly large, vertical, stones standing on one of their narrow ends, and placed on top of each other - there is some rubble infilling. The sill is constructed with possibly a single stone internally but externally it appears there are now a row of three stones. See above left: PHOTO 152. Deerhurst 10, showing the internal west face, and above right: PHOTO 153. Deerhurst 11, showing the east face, now viewed externally.

PHOTO 152. Deerhurst 10.   PHOTO 153. Deerhurst 11.

- Access to stairways leading to crypts below ground; the position of these doorways, whether at the top, or towards the middle, of the stairway, may vary from one example to another. See Page 104, PHOTO 146. Brixworth 6.

DOORWAYS AT FIRST FLOOR LEVEL - often provide:
- Access from a western tower into a gallery or balcony or room extending eastwards from the west wall of the nave (east wall of tower).

Holy Trinity Church, Bosham, West Sussex, has a triangular-headed doorway at first floor level which formerly provided access from the western tower onto a gallery extending eastwards into the nave. The head is constructed with two single through-stones. Each stone is a trapezium which extends upwards from the tops of the jambs to meet centrally and form the triangle shape of the head of the doorway. It does not have imposts. The through-stone jambs are constructed in similar fashion to side alternate quoining. The doorway has a monolithic sill. See adjacent left: PHOTO 154. Bosham 5, showing the east face.

PHOTO 154. Bosham 5.

PHOTO 155. Deerhurst 12.

St Mary's Church, Deerhurst, Gloucestershire, has a blocked round-headed doorway at first floor level which formerly provided access from the western porch/tower onto a gallery extending eastwards into the nave. The doorway narrows from bottom to top. The arched head is cut out of a monolithic lintel, there are no supporting imposts, the jambs each comprise a single vertical through-stone, and there is a monolithic sill. See Page 106 bottom right: PHOTO 155. Deerhurst 12, showing the east face.

- Access from a western tower onto an external balcony used for the display of relics on special occasions, and/or, for the ringing of hand bells during funerals, and/or, for maintain a watch on the surrounding area.

All Saints Church, Earls Barton, Northamptonshire, has a round-headed doorway at first floor level on the south face of the tower; it is blocked internally. It may well have provided access to a former external balcony. The doorway narrows from bottom to top. The arched head is constructed with voussoirs horizontally-shaped and jointed rather than wedge-shaped and fitted together. The doorway has square imposts with pilaster-strips providing the external faces of the jambs. The sill is provided by the string-course separating the first and second stages of the tower. See adjacent: PHOTO 156. Earls Barton 3, showing the south face.

PHOTO 156. Earls Barton 3.

- Access in the internal facing walls of the north and south aisles or porticus into a gallery or balcony extending eastwards from the west wall of the nave (east wall of tower where appropriate). The doorways were accessed by interior stairways.

- Access in the external facing walls of the north and south walls of the nave into a gallery or balcony extending eastwards from the west wall of the nave (east wall of tower where appropriate). The doorways were accessed by exterior stairways.

- Access between the western tower and the attached stair turret.

- Access between the central crossing in a cruciform church and rooms above the nave, chancel and transepts or porticus.

- Access between a central area separating the nave from the chancel and rooms above the nave and chancel; the church has no transepts or porticus.

DOORWAYS AT SECOND FLOOR LEVEL - often provide:
- Access from a western porch or tower onto an external, probably timber, balcony used for the display of relics on special occasions, and/or, for the ringing of hand bells during funerals, and/or, for maintain a watch on the surrounding area.

St Andrew's Church, Bywell, Northumberland, has a round-headed doorway at second floor level on the south face of the tower and now used as a window. It may well have provided access to a former external balcony. The arched head is cut out of a monolithic lintel. Below extended imposts support the corbel-like bases of the hood-moulding above and

PHOTO 157. Bywell 2.

separate the hood-moulding from the strip-work below. The through-stone jambs are constructed in Escomb fashion each standing on a protruding rectangular base either side of a monolithic sill. A protruding, semi-circular, band of hood-moulding extends above the lintel with the intervening stonework similar to the adjacent walling and creating a tympanum. In addition strip-work abuts the stonework forming the jambs. See Page 107 bottom right: PHOTO 157. Bywell 2, showing the south face with the strip-work arrowed red and the hood-moulding arrowed black.

St Mary's Church, Deerhurst, Gloucestershire, has a doorway round-headed externally and flat-headed internally. It is at second floor level on the west face of the tower and now used as a window. It may well have provided access to a former external wooden walkway. Externally the arched head is cut out of a lintel which is cut away internally to form a flat head. It has no imposts. The jambs are constructed with large, vertical, through-stones standing on one of their narrow ends and placed on top of each other. The monolithic sill provides the base for the jambs. The accompanying hood-moulding sits on top of the lintel and is consequently of rectangular shape rather than being concentric with the arched head of the doorway. The hood-moulding has beast-head label-stops – there is no strip-work below. Above the hood-moulding is a prokrossos. See adjacent: PHOTO 158. Deerhurst 13, showing the west face with beast-head label stops arrowed red, the hood-moulding arrowed black, and the prokrossos arrowed blue.

PHOTO 158. Deerhurst 13.

- Access between the western tower and the attached stair turret.

All Saints Church, Hough-on-the Hill, Lincolnshire, has a triangular-headed doorway at second floor level which provides access from the stair turret into the tower. The head is constructed with two pairs of through-stones. Each stone is a trapezium which extends upwards from the tops of the jambs to meet centrally and form the triangle shape of the head of the doorway. It does not have imposts. The jambs are mostly through-stone mostly laid in similar fashion to Escomb jambs. The doorway has a monolithic sill with a shallow upper step. See adjacent: PHOTO 159. Hough-on-the-Hill 4, showing the west face.

PHOTO 159. Hough-on-the-Hill 4.

6. **WINDOWS**
- From top to bottom most windows comprise: a half-rounded arched head, or flat-headed lintel*, or triangular (gable) –head; jambs*; and a sill*. Most windows did not have imposts* but where they did they were square or rectangular in shape. St John the Baptist Church, Barnack, Cambridgeshire, provides rare examples of windows with imposts – see Pages 127 to 129. See text and illustrations provided in the following pages.

- Many windows were constructed with large facing stones*, individually of a self-evident difference in terms of size and finish to the stonework used in the adjoining walling. Facing stones varied in size and shape and were roughly-dressed* but not to the uniformity of size, shape and careful dressing as ashlar* favoured by Norman and later builders although there are some examples where the Anglo-Saxon builders used ashlar.

- Alternatively, the heads, jambs and sills of some windows were constructed of, and faced with, rubble stonework displaying few differences to the stonework forming the adjoining walling whether laid in courses* or randomly. Such windows could include the use of a mixture of rubble and flints, and the reuse of Roman stonework, including Roman tile-like bricks, where these were available. Often where some form of rubble was used the interiors of the windows are now plastered or painted obscuring the construction details.

- Some windows were circular and these were usually constructed of rubble* similar to the stonework in the adjoining walling. A template determined the shape. Often details of their construction are now hidden by plaster or paintwork.

- Windows were mostly cut straight through the full depth of the walls without rebates or recesses. Most windows comprised a single light*. In addition, there are a few examples of double-windows which have two adjacent lights separated by a mid-wall shaft which was often cylindrical in shape and sometimes comprised a baluster-shaft. The mid-wall shaft supported a through-stone slab, placed horizontally, which extended through the entire depth of the walling of the windows so that it sides overhung the mid-wall shaft. This through-stone slab supported above the junction of the heads of both windows.

- A few windows had an exterior face comprising a single slab which was pierced to form the shape of the aperture – internally their construction was similar to other single-splayed windows.

- Anglo-Saxon windows were seldom decorated. Some Lincolnshire churches may have windows decorated with palmette design*. See Page 113: PHOTO 164. Stow-in-Lindsey 8, and Page 114: PHOTO 169. Glentworth 1. Also see Page 129: PHOTO 236. Barnack 12, where the window has an exterior "frame" enclosing two confronting birds in relief. Decoration in the form of pilaster-strips*, strip-work* and hood-moulding* was rare.

- Windows were constructed in most parts of the church and at most levels. Some Anglo-Saxon windows may be incomplete because of their later replacement by larger windows, not Anglo-Saxon, or their partial destruction by the insertion of large new archways or arcades, not Anglo-Saxon, into the same walling nearby. See Pages 130 to 133. "Blocked and Incomplete Windows".

*See Glossary and for other such terms in the following pages.

- Most, but not all, Anglo-Saxon windows were splayed. They were either "single-splayed" or "double-splayed". In the depth of the interior of the church walling, the insertion and splaying of single or double-splayed windows often resulted in the exposure of stonework similar in shape, size and positioning to the coursed or randomly laid stonework in the adjoining main interior face of the church wall. On occasions the stonework facing the angles of the splaying and the main interior face of the church wall may be laid in a distinctly different way. Individual stones may be laid vertically rather than horizontally, or include megalithic stonework demonstrably of a different size, or be laid in similar fashion to side alternate or long and short quoining.

- A few churches had both single-splayed and double-splayed windows. Double-Splayed windows are indicative of Anglo-Saxon workmanship and are rarely found in churches built in Norman and later periods.

- Small single-splayed windows were common in both the Anglo-Saxon and Norman periods but those that have an arched head cut out of a half-through-stone or a through-stone, supported by rubble jambs similar to the stonework in the adjoining walling, or jambs including a single vertical stone, are more likely to be Anglo-Saxon rather than Norman in origin. Those of Norman or later origin, can often be identified by the facing stones comprising carefully-dressed ashlar blocks of a uniform shape and size.

SINGLE-SPLAYED WINDOWS

Most single-splayed widows were round-headed but a significant number were flat-headed. There are also a few examples of single-splayed windows circular in overall shape, triangular (gable) headed, and those with an external single slab pierced to form the shape of the aperture. Characteristics of Single-Splayed Windows:

- The narrowest aperture is at the outer (external) face of the wall of the church.

- The opening widens – "splays" - towards the interior of the church to let in the maximum amount of light.

- The splay of the sill, jambs and window head continues through the full thickness of the interior depth of the wall. The exception are the heads of flat-headed windows.

- The angle of the splay is not very acute and is similar for the head, jambs and sill.

- Internally, the splaying of the window resulted in the cutting into, and the removal, of parts of the stonework in the adjoining walling.

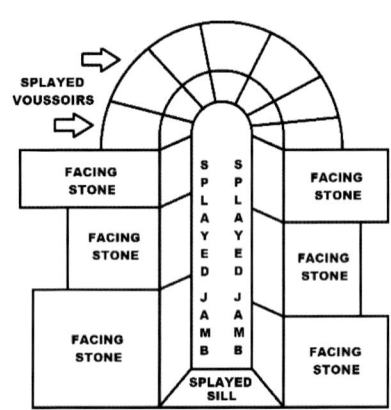

INTERIOR OF WINDOW

The illustration above right identifies the main features likely to be found in the internal view of a single-splayed window. It shows the sill, jambs and arched head of the window splayed inwards towards the interior facing wall of the church. The arched head is constructed with voussoirs; jambs with large, roughly-dressed facing stones, of different sizes, laid in a similar fashion to side alternate quoining; a single stone provides the sill.

The illustration adjacent identifies the main features likely to be found in the external view of a single-splayed window. It shows the sill, jambs and arched head of the window flush with the exterior facing wall of the church. The arched head has been cut out of the centre of the lower horizontal face of a single through-stone; jambs with large, roughly-dressed facing stones, of different sizes, laid in a similar

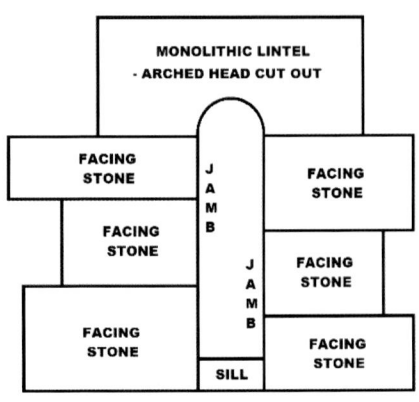

EXTERIOR OF WINDOW

fashion to side alternate quoining; sill comprise a single flat stone. See Page 120: PHOTO 198. Stow-in-Lindsey 11, showing the external view, and PHOTO 199. Stow-in-Lindsey 12, showing the internal view, of the same window.

DOUBLE-SPLAYED WINDOWS
Most double-splayed windows were round-headed but a significant number were circular in their overall shape; a few were flat-headed, none were triangular (gable)-headed. Characteristics of double-splayed windows:

- The narrowest aperture is close to the centre of the wall of the church.

- The opening widens – "splays" - inwards towards the interior facing wall of the church, and, similarly splays outwards towards the exterior facing wall of the church. Splaying was intended to maximise the amount of light received externally into the church and to maximise its spread internally.

- The outward and inner splays of the sill, jambs and window head continue through the full thickness of the interior depth of the wall. The exception are the heads of flat-headed windows.

- The angle of the splay is not very acute and is similar for the head, jambs and sill.

- Both externally and internally, the splaying of the window resulted in the cutting into, and the removal, of parts of the stonework in the adjoining walling.

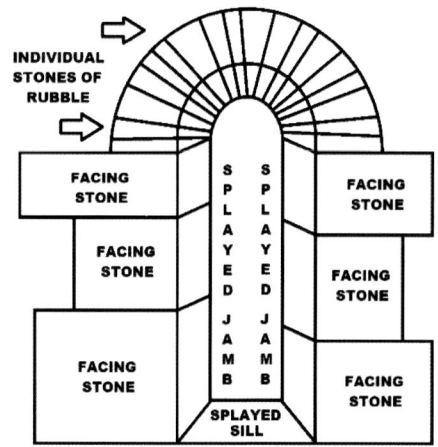

The illustration adjacent identifies the main features likely to be found in the internal and external faces of a double-splayed window - all features are splayed. The sill, jambs and arched head of the window are all splayed inwards towards the interior facing wall of the church and similarly splayed outwards towards the exterior facing wall of the church.

The arched head is constructed with individual stones placed radially on end vertically with a narrow side flush with the face of the wall. The jambs are constructed with large, roughly-dressed facing stones, of different sizes, laid in a similar fashion to side alternate quoining. A single stone provides the sill. See Page 122: PHOTO 210 (externally) and PHOTO 211 (internally) which are both of the same window in St Michael's Church, Oxford, Oxfordshire.

ARCHED HEADS CUT OUT OF A SQUARE LINTEL
The arched heads of many windows whether single and double-splayed were cut out of the centre of the lower horizontal face of a square lintel which may comprise a single through-stone or two half-through-stones or may comprise two smaller square lintels with rubble between them in the centre of the depth of the wall.

St Andrew's Church, Corbridge, Northumberland, has at ground floor level in the west wall of the porch/tower, a round-headed single-splayed window. It has an arched head cut from the centre of the lower horizontal face of two half-through-stones square lintels. The external lintel displays a cut-out indicating it is a reused piece of Roman stonework with a cramp-hole. The internal lintel includes a splayed head. See below views of the same window, left: PHOTO 160. Corbridge 1, showing the external view with the cramp-hole arrowed red, and right: PHOTO 161. Corbridge 2, showing the internal view.

PHOTO 160. Corbridge 1.

PHOTO 161. Corbridge 2.

St Mary the Virgin Church, Seaham, County Durham, has at ground floor level in the north wall of the nave, a round-headed single-splayed window. It has an arched head cut from the centre of the lower horizontal face of two half-through-stones square lintels. The internal lintel includes a splayed head. Externally and internally the face of each lintel is similarly decorated with two separate semi-circular grooves concentric with the arched head.

Additionally internally, the underside (soffit) of the lintel is decorated with cable-pattern, or "wheat-ear", design. See above showing views of the same window, left: PHOTO 162. Seaham 3, showing the external view, and right: PHOTO 163. Seaham 4, showing the internal view with the wheat-ear design arrowed red.

PHOTO 162. Seaham 3.

PHOTO 163. Seaham 4.

ARCHED HEADS CUT OUT OF A LINTEL EXTERNALLY AND CONSTRUCTED WITH VOUSSOIRS INTERNALLY
Many other round-headed single-splayed windows had their arched heads cut out of the lower horizontal face of a quarter-through-stone or half-through-stone lintel externally and constructed with wedge-shaped three-quarter through-stone or half through-stone voussoirs internally.

St Mary's Church, Stow-in-Lindsey, Lincolnshire, has at ground floor level in the south wall of the south transept, a round-headed single-splayed window. Externally, this window has its arched head cut out of the lower horizontal face of a half-through-stone lintel similar to well-dressed ashlar. Also externally, hood-moulding decorated with palmette design has been placed on top of the arched head; the hood-moulding is supported by protruding, narrow, imposts. Internally, this window has its arched head constructed with half-through-stone

Anglo-Saxon Church Architecture & Stone Sculpture   113

voussoirs separated by rubble walling from shaped facing stones. Internally the voussoirs are splayed. See below showing views of the same window, left: PHOTO 164. Stow-in-Lindsey 8, showing the external view with the palmette design arrowed red, and right: PHOTO 165. Stow-in-Lindsey 9, showing the internal view.

PHOTO 164. Stow-in-Lindsey 8.

PHOTO 165. Stow-in-Lindsey 9.

ARCHED HEADS CONSTRUCTED WITH VOUSSOIRS BOTH EXTERNALLY AND INTERNALLY

Some arched heads of windows were constructed with voussoirs both externally and internally. The voussoirs were constructed with a semi-circular row of tapering, wedge-shaped, stones which were often roughly-dressed half-through-stones or through-stones, through the depth of the walling. Not all examples have identifiable single, vertically placed, central key-stones.

All Hallows Church, Bardsey, West Yorkshire, has at ground floor level in the north wall of the porch/tower, a round-headed single-splayed window. It has an arched head constructed with half-through-stone voussoirs both externally and internally. Internally the voussoirs are splayed. See below showing views of the same window, left: PHOTO 166. Bardsey 1, showing the former external view now inside the north aisle, and right: PHOTO 167. Bardsey 2, showing the internal view now inside the porch/tower.

PHOTO 166. Bardsey 1.

PHOTO 167. Bardsey 2.

ARCHED HEADS SHAPED FROM A SINGLE STONE

Some round-headed single-splayed windows have their arched heads constructed with a single stone shaped to provide a curvature in both its upper and lower borders.

St Paul's Church, Jarrow, County Durham, has at ground floor level in the south wall of the chancel, three round-headed single-splayed windows. Both externally and internally, each of these three windows have an arched head constructed with a half-through-stone, shaped to provide a curvature in both their upper and lower borders - each

PHOTO 168. Jarrow 1.

window has a slightly differently shaped arched head. See Page 113 bottom right: PHOTO 168. Jarrow 1, showing the external view of the middle window.

St Michael's Church, Glentworth, Lincolnshire, has, at second floor level in the south wall of the tower, a round-headed, "key-hole", (see Pages 124 to 125) single-splayed window. Both externally and internally, its arched head has been constructed with a half-through-stone shaped to provide a curvature in both its upper and lower borders. Externally, in addition, this stone has been incised with angled divisions imitating the edges and jointing of individual voussoirs. Hood-Moulding (see Pages 173 to 179), decorated with palmette design has been placed on top of the arched head - a rare example of a window with hood-moulding. The hood-moulding is supported by protruding, narrow, impost-like features. See adjacent: PHOTO 169. Glentworth 1, showing the external view with the palmette design arrowed red.

PHOTO 169. Glentworth 1.

ARCHED HEADS CONSTRUCTED WITH RUBBLE, FLINTS AND REUSED ROMAN STONEWORK

Instead of voussoirs the arched head may be constructed with a mixture of stonework comprising irregularly-shaped and sized rubble, flints and reused Roman stonework, similar to the stonework of the adjoining walling with no indication of wedge-shaped voussoirs. Note: Whatever the nature of the individual stones used to construct the arched head they are often still described as "voussoirs" despite not being tapering, wedge-shaped, stones.

To construct a half-round arched head, individual stones were shaped, if required, and placed radially with a square or rectangular side flush with the face of the wall, or, placed radially on end vertically with a narrow side flush with the face of the wall. Where available, Roman tile-like bricks were placed vertically on end to provide the discernible arched head.

All Saints Church, Brixworth, Northamptonshire, has, at first floor level in the south wall of the tower, a round-headed single-splayed window. It has an arched head constructed with rubble and tile-like bricks. Internally the head of the window is splayed. See adjacent showing views of the same window, left: PHOTO 170. Brixworth 8, showing the external view, and right: PHOTO 171. Brixworth 9, showing the internal view.

PHOTO 170. Brixworth 8.

PHOTO 171. Brixworth 9.

HEADS OF FLAT-HEADED WINDOWS
Flat-Headed windows were often constructed with a rectangular lintel which may be a single-through-stone or two half-through-stones.

Escomb Church, County Durham, has at ground floor level in the north wall of the nave, a megalithic flat-headed single-splayed window. It has a head constructed with a monolithic through-stone lintel. Internally the head of the window is splayed. See below showing views of the same (north-west) window, below left: PHOTO 172. Escomb 4, showing external view, and adjacent right: PHOTO 173. Escomb 5, showing the internal view.

PHOTO 172. Escomb 4.

PHOTO 173. Escomb 5.

HEADS OF TRIANGULAR (GABLE)-HEADED WINDOWS

A few single-splayed windows were triangular (gable)-headed constructed with two through-stones or four half-through-stones – each a trapezium - which extended upwards from the imposts or jambs to meet centrally and form the triangle shape of the head of the window.

St John the Baptist Church, Barnack, Cambridgeshire, has at ground floor level in the west wall of the tower, a triangular-headed single-splayed window. Externally, its head is constructed with two half-through-stones, each a trapezium, which extend upwards from the imposts to meet centrally to form the triangular shape of the window. Additionally, and rarely, the whole external face of the window is set within a triangular-headed rectangular frame formed of stonework protruding from the face of the wall. Internally the head of the window is splayed.

See above showing views of the same window, left: PHOTO 174. Barnack 6, showing the internal view, and right: PHOTO 175. Barnack 7, showing the external view.

PHOTO 174. Barnack 6.

PHOTO 175. Barnack 7.

JAMBS OF WINDOWS – applying to all shapes of head

Round, Flat and Triangular-Headed Windows had individual stones which collectively formed two sets of jambs on opposite sides of the central void. Jambs were often angled vertically, narrowing towards the top. They may be constructed of a single, vertical, megalithic through-stone. Alternatively, they may be constructed with roughly-dressed half-through-stones, three-quarter-through-stones, or through-stones through the full depth of the walling laid in a similar fashion to Escomb jambs or side alternate quoining; or, constructed of similar stonework to the adjoining walling and coursed in a similar fashion – some examples may include megalithic stonework. There are no "standard" number of stones forming the jambs and the stonework in one jamb may not be the mirror image of the stones forming the opposite jamb.

Escomb Church County Durham has at ground floor level in the north wall of the nave, a megalithic flat-headed single-splayed window. Each of its jambs is constructed with a single vertical through-stone angled and narrowing slightly towards the top. See Page 116 top left:

PHOTO 176. Escomb 6, showing the exterior view of the north-west window and its western jamb.

St Paul's Church, Jarrow, County Durham, has at ground floor level in the south wall of the chancel, three round-headed single-splayed windows. Each of their jambs comprises one single, vertical, rectangular through-stone below a single horizontal through-stone. See adjacent right: PHOTO 177. Jarrow 2, showing the exterior view of the middle window and its eastern jamb.

St Andrew's Church, Bywell, Northumberland, has at ground floor level in the south wall of the tower, a round-headed single-splayed window. Each of its jambs comprise stonework similar to the coursed rubble stonework of the adjoining walling. See adjacent left: PHOTO 178. Bywell 3, showing the exterior view of its western jamb.

St Andrew's Church, Brigstock, Northamptonshire, has, at first floor level in the north wall of the tower, a round-headed double-splayed window. Each of its jambs comprise stonework similar to the coursed rubble stonework of the adjoining walling. See adjacent right: PHOTO 179. Brigstock 6, showing the exterior view of its eastern jamb.

All Saints Church, Brixworth, Northamptonshire, has at ground floor level in the south wall of the tower, a flat-headed single-splayed window. Each of its jambs comprise rubble stonework including stonework laid in herringbone fashion and re-used Roman tile-like bricks. See adjacent left: PHOTO 180. Brixworth 10, showing the exterior view of its western jamb.

Internally some windows may have the jambs comprising an inner and outer set of facing stones both laid in similar fashion to each other and separated by intervening coursed rubble walling.

St Mary's Church, Stow-in-Lindsey, Lincolnshire, has at ground floor level in the south wall of the south transept, a round-headed single-splayed window. Internally, this window has its jambs, and the facing stones on the angle of the splay and the main interior face of the church wall, laid in similar fashion to long and short quoining; between the two is coursed rubble stonework. See above right: PHOTO 181. Stow-in-Lindsey 10, showing the interior view of the eastern jamb.

PHOTO 176. Escomb 6.   PHOTO 177. Jarrow 2.

PHOTO 178. Bywell 3.   PHOTO 179. Brigstock 6.

PHOTO 180. Brixworth 10.

PHOTO 181. Stow-in-Lindsey 10.

Anglo-Saxon Church Architecture & Stone Sculpture   117

SILLS OF WINDOWS - applying to all shapes of head

The sills of windows may comprise a single "monolithic" stone lying horizontally between the base of the jambs or a row of two or three stones laid horizontally – these stones may also support the jambs. Where these stones are not through-stones, or stones of a size and shape different from those in the adjoining walling, windows will simply use as their sill the tops of the stonework directly below. Where this occurs, with many examples, the stonework below is unaffected in its composition and placement by the window above. However, with other examples, the splaying of the sill, particularly internally, may have resulted in the cutting into, and the removing, of part of the top of the stonework comprising the walling directly below.

All Hallows Church, Bardsey, West Yorkshire, has at ground floor level in the north wall of the porch/tower, a round-headed single-splayed window. The sill is provided by the coursed rubble stonework of the walling directly below with the internal splaying of the window resulting in the cutting into, and the removing, of part of the top of the stonework. See below showing views of the same window, left: PHOTO 182. Bardsey 3, showing the former external view now inside the north aisle, and adjacent right: PHOTO 183. Bardsey 4, showing the internal view obscured by a permanent wooden stairway.

PHOTO 182. Bardsey 3.

PHOTO 183. Bardsey 4.

St Peter's Church, Diddlebury, Shropshire, has at ground floor level in the north wall of the nave, a round-headed double-splayed window. The sill is provided by the coursed ashlar stonework externally, and the herringbone stonework internally, directly below with the splaying of the window both externally and internally resulting in the cutting into, and the removing, of parts of the tops of this stonework. See below showing views of the same window, left: PHOTO 184. Diddlebury 2, showing external view, and right: PHOTO 185. Diddlebury 3, showing the internal view.

PHOTO 184. Diddlebury 2.

PHOTO 185. Diddlebury 3.

TYPICAL WINDOWS

Escomb Church, County Durham, has at ground floor level in the north wall of the nave, two megalithic flat-headed single-splayed windows. Each has a head constructed with a monolithic through-stone lintel. Each of their jambs are constructed with a single vertical through-stone angled and narrowing slightly towards the top. The sills are constructed with rectangular through-stones. Internally, the heads, jambs and sills of the windows are splayed which resulted in the cutting into, and the removal, of parts of the stonework in the adjoining walling. See Page 118 showing views of the same (north-west) window, top left:

PHOTO 186. Escomb 7, showing the external view, and adjacent right: PHOTO 187. Escomb 8, showing the internal view, with the vertical grooves to hold a window shutter arrowed red.

Escomb Church, County Durham, has at ground floor level in the south wall of the nave, two megalithic round-headed single-splayed windows. Both externally and internally, each has an arched head cut out of the centre of the lower horizontal face of a half-through-stone lintel. Each of their jambs are constructed with a single vertical through-stone angled and narrowing slightly towards the top. The sills are provided by the tops of the coursed stonework directly below. Internally, the heads, jambs and sills of the windows are splayed which resulted in the cutting into, and the removal, of parts of the stonework in the adjoining walling. See adjacent showing views of the same (south-east) window, left: PHOTO 188. Escomb 9, showing the external view, and above right: PHOTO 189. Escomb 10, showing the internal view, with the vertical grooves to hold a window shutter arrowed red.

PHOTO 186. Escomb 7.

PHOTO 187. Escomb 8.

PHOTO 188. Escomb 9.

PHOTO 189. Escomb 10.

St Andrew's Church, Corbridge, Northumberland, has at ground floor level in the west wall of the porch/tower, a round-headed single-splayed window. It has an arched head cut out of the centre of the lower horizontal face of two half-through-stone lintels – the external lintel includes a Roman cramp-hole. The jambs are constructed with stonework all laid horizontally and include through-stones (supporting the lintels), and half-through-stones. The sill is provided by the top of the coursed rubble stonework directly below. Internally, the head, jambs and sill of the window are splayed which resulted in the cutting into, and the removal, of parts of the stonework in the adjoining walling. See below, showing views of the same window, left: PHOTO 190. Corbridge 3, showing the external view, with the Roman cramp-hole arrowed red, and right: PHOTO 191. Corbridge 4, showing the internal view.

PHOTO 190. Corbridge 3.

PHOTO 191. Corbridge 4.

St Mary's Church, Seaham, County Durham, has at ground floor level in the north wall of the nave, two round-headed single-splayed windows. Each has an arched head cut out of the centre of the lower horizontal face of two half-through-stone lintels. Internally and externally, the heads of both windows are incised with two separate semi-circular grooves concentric with their arched heads. In addition, the north-east window, internally, has the underside (soffit) of the lintel decorated with cable-pattern, or "wheat-ear", design. The jambs of both windows are constructed with roughly-dressed through-stones: each jamb has a single, large, vertical stone supporting a single, smaller, horizontal stone. Internally, vertical grooves have been cut into the middle depth of the jambs for the retention of window shutters. The sills are provided by the tops of the coursed stonework directly below.

Internally, the heads, jambs and sills of the windows are splayed which resulted in the cutting into, and the removal, of parts of the stonework in the adjoining walling. See adjacent, showing views of the same (north-east) window, left: PHOTO 192. Seaham 5, showing the external view, and right: PHOTO 193. Seaham 6, showing the internal view, with the vertical grooves to hold a window shutter arrowed red.

PHOTO 192. Seaham 5.   PHOTO 193. Seaham 6.

St Peter's Church, Diddlebury, Shropshire, has at ground floor level in the north wall of the nave, a round-headed double-splayed window. It has an arched head cut out of the centre of the lower horizontal face of two half-through-stone lintels. The jambs and sill are constructed with stonework similar to the coursed ashlar (externally) and herringbone (internally) stonework of the adjoining walling. Both externally and

PHOTO 194. Diddlebury 4.   PHOTO 195. Diddlebury 5.

internally, the head, jambs and sill of the window are splayed which resulted in the cutting into, and the removal, of parts of the stonework in the adjoining walling. The aperture of the window has been cut out of a single stone slab placed mid-wall. Externally there are two holes in this slab which may indicate provision for a window shutter. See above, showing views of the same window, left: PHOTO 194. Diddlebury 4, showing the external view with holes for the possible window shutter arrowed red, and right: PHOTO 195. Diddlebury 5, showing the internal view.

All Hallows Church, Bardsey, West Yorkshire, has at ground floor level in the north wall of the porch/tower, a round-headed single-splayed window. It has an arched head constructed with half-through-stone voussoirs. The jambs are constructed with coursed rubble stonework similar to that in the adjoining walling. The sill is provided by the top of the coursed rubble stonework of the walling directly below. Internally, the head, jambs and sill of the window are splayed which resulted in the cutting into, and the removal, of parts of the stonework in The adjoining walling. See Page 120, showing views of the same window, top left: PHOTO 196. Bardsey 5, showing the former external view now inside the north aisle, and top right:

PHOTO 197. Bardsey 6, showing the internal view obscured by a permanent wooden stairway.

St Mary's Church, Stow-in-Lindsey, Lincolnshire, has at ground floor level in the south wall of the south transept, a round-headed single-splayed window. Externally, this window has its arched head cut out of the lower horizontal face of a half-through-stone lintel similar to well-dressed ashlar. Also externally, hood-moulding, decorated with palmette design, has been placed on top of the arched head; the hood-moulding is supported by protruding, narrow, impost-like features. Internally, this window has its arched head constructed with half-through-stone voussoirs separated by rubble walling from similarly shaped facing stones on the angle of the splay and the main interior face of the

PHOTO 196. Bardsey 5.

PHOTO 197. Bardsey 6.

church wall. Externally, the jambs are laid in similar fashion to long and short quoining; some of the individual stones have dowel-holes for the addition of an external shutter(s). Internally, the jambs, and the facing stones on the angle of the splay and the main interior face of the church wall, are laid in similar fashion to long and short quoining; between the two is coursed rubble stonework. The sill is provided by the top of the coursed rubble stonework of the walling directly below. Internally, the heads, jambs and sill of the window are splayed which resulted in the cutting into, and the removal, of parts of the stonework in the adjoining walling. See adjacent, showing views of the same window, left: PHOTO 198. Stow-in-Lindsey 11, showing the external view with the surviving dowel-holes for shutters arrowed red – some may be doubtful, and right: PHOTO 199. Stow-in-Lindsey 12, showing the internal view.

PHOTO 198.
Stow-in-Lindsey 11.

PHOTO 199.
Stow-in-Lindsey 12.

St Andrew's Church, Brigstock, Northamptonshire, has, at first floor level in the north wall of the tower, a round-headed double-splayed window. Externally, it has an arched head constructed with irregularly-shaped and sized rubble similar to the stonework of the adjoining walling; the individual stones comprising the arched head have been placed on their ends and formed into a discernible arch. The jambs are constructed with coursed rubble stonework similar to that in the adjoining walling. The sill is provided by the top of the coursed rubble stonework of the walling directly below. Both externally and internally, the head, jambs and sill of the window are splayed which resulted in the cutting into, and the removal, of parts of the stonework in the adjoining walling – the splaying externally is not that distinctive. Internally the construction details are obscured by paint and plaster. See Page 121 showing views of the same window, top left: PHOTO 200. Brigstock 7, showing the external view, and adjacent right: PHOTO 201. Brigstock 8, showing the internal view.

St Peter's Church, Barton-upon-Humber, Lincolnshire, has at ground floor level in the south wall of the west porticus, a round-headed double-splayed window.

Externally its construction details are obscured by plaster. Internally it can be seen that it is constructed with rubble similar to the stonework in the adjoining walling. The arched head is constructed with individual stones placed on their ends and formed into a discernible arch. The individual stones comprising the jambs are of similar size to the rubble in the adjoining walling and are laid in a similar way. The sill is provided by the top of the rubble stonework directly below. Both externally and internally, the head, jambs and sill of the window are splayed which resulted in the cutting into, and the removal, of parts of the stonework in the adjoining walling. See above views of the same window, left: PHOTO 202. Barton-upon-Humber 4, showing the external view, and right: PHOTO 203. Barton-upon-Humber 5, showing the internal view.

PHOTO 200. Brigstock 7.   PHOTO 201. Brigstock 8.

PHOTO 202. Barton-upon-Humber 4.   PHOTO 203. Barton-upon-Humber 5.

Holy Trinity Church, Great Dunham, Norfolk, has at ground floor level in the north wall of the nave, a round-headed double-splayed window. It has an arched head constructed with reused Roman tile-like bricks placed on their ends and formed into a discernible arch – the present pointed nature of the glazed windows alters the shape of the original. Both the jambs and sill are constructed with a mixture of rubble and flints, including reused Roman tile-like bricks, similar to the stonework in the adjoining walling. Both externally and internally, the head, jambs and sill of the window are splayed which resulted in the cutting into, and the removal, of parts of the stonework in the adjoining walling. Plaster internally, and concrete rendering externally, obscures the construction details. See adjacent, views of the same window, left: PHOTO 204. Great Dunham 3, showing the external view, and right: PHOTO 205. Great Dunham 4, showing the internal view.

PHOTO 204. Great Dunham 3.   PHOTO 205. Great Dunham 4.

All Saints Church, Brixworth, Northamptonshire, has, at first floor level in the south wall of the tower, a round-headed single-splayed window. Its arched head, jambs and sill are constructed with a mixture of rubble and the reuse of Roman tile like bricks all similar to the stonework in the adjoining walling. Internally, the head, jambs and sill of the window are splayed which resulted in the cutting into, and the removal, of parts of the stonework in the adjoining walling. See adjacent, views of the same window, left: PHOTO 206. Brixworth 11, showing the external view, and right: PHOTO 207. Brixworth 12, showing the internal view.

PHOTO 206. Brixworth 11.

PHOTO 207. Brixworth 12.

Holy Trinity Church, Great Paxton, Cambridgeshire, has, at first floor level above the nave, round-headed double-splayed clerestory windows. They have their arched heads, jambs and sills constructed of rubble stonework similar to the adjoining walling. Externally, the arched heads are constructed with individual stones of similar size and shape placed radially – they are not wedge-shaped voussoirs. The jambs and sills display few differences to the stonework in the adjoining walling. Both externally and internally, the head, jambs and sill of the window are splayed which resulted in the cutting into, and the removal, of parts of the stonework in the adjoining walling. Internally the construction details of the window are hidden by plaster. (Note: Externally the horizontal string-course cutting across the jambs of the window is a later, not-Anglo-Saxon, addition to the stonework of the church.) See views of the same middle window in the south wall (the window to its left/west is incomplete and blocked), above left: PHOTO 208. Great Paxton 9, showing the internal view, and adjacent right: PHOTO 209. Great Paxton 10, showing external the view.

PHOTO 208. Great Paxton 9.

PHOTO 209. Great Paxton 10.

St Michael's Church, Oxford, Oxfordshire, has at ground floor level in the north wall of the tower, a round-headed double-splayed window. Its arched head, jambs and sill have been constructed with rubble similar to the stonework in the adjoining walling. Externally and internally, the head, jambs and sill of the window are splayed which resulted in the cutting into, and the removal, of parts of the stonework in the adjoining walling. See adjacent views of the same window, left: PHOTO 210. Oxford 2, showing the external view, and right: PHOTO 211. Oxford 3, showing the internal view.

PHOTO 210. Oxford 2.

PHOTO 211. Oxford 3.

CIRCULAR WINDOWS

Circular Windows are usually found in those churches constructed with a mixture of rubble and flints. They may include the reuse of Roman stonework, including Roman tile-like bricks, where these were available. During construction it is likely the stonework was laid around a template. Circular windows are nearly all double-splayed. They are mostly found in East Anglia with St Peter's Church, Barton-upon-Humber, Lincolnshire, providing one of the more notable exceptions.

In the western porticus of St Peter's Church, Barton-upon-Humber, Lincolnshire, there are at both ground and first floor level in the west wall, two circular double-splayed windows in vertical alignment with each other. Externally their construction details are obscured by plaster but internally it can be seen that they are constructed with rubble similar to the stonework in the adjoining walling. The circular nature of the windows was constructed by placing stones on end to form an irregular but discernible curvature at the top. The remaining curvature was constructed with horizontally-placed stones, similar in size and placement to those in the adjoining walling but reduced in size or removed to form the complete circular shape of the window. The lower window has a surviving wooden window frame, more easily identified externally. See adjacent, views of the same window, left: PHOTO 212. Barton-upon-Humber 6, showing the external view with the window frame arrowed red, and right: PHOTO 213. Barton-upon-Humber 7, showing the internal view.

PHOTO 212. Barton-upon-Humber 6.

PHOTO 213. Barton-upon-Humber 7.

St Matthias Church, Thorpe-next-Haddiscoe, Norfolk, has, at first floor level in the west wall of the nave, a circular double-splayed window. It is constructed with rubble and flints similar to the stonework in the adjoining walling. Both externally and internally, the splaying of the window resulted in the cutting into, and the removal, of parts of the stonework in the adjoining walling. Internally the construction details are now hidden by plaster. Its former external details were enclosed when the later Anglo-Saxon round tower was added. See adjacent: PHOTO 214. Thorpe-next-Haddiscoe 1, showing the internal view.

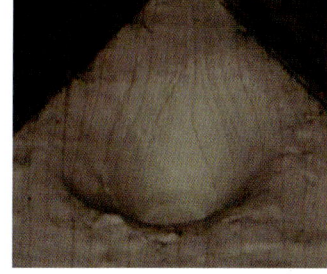

PHOTO 214. Thorpe-next-Haddiscoe 1.

St Mary's Church, Howe, Norfolk, has at ground floor level in the north and south walls of the tower, circular double-splayed windows. They are constructed with rubble and flints, including the reuse of some Roman tile-like bricks, similar to the stonework in the adjoining walling. Both externally and internally, the splaying of the windows resulted in the cutting into, and the removal, of parts of the stonework in the adjoining walling. Internally their construction details are now hidden by plaster. See adjacent: PHOTO 215. Howe 1, showing the external view of the window in the south wall.

PHOTO 215. Howe 1.

St Peter's Church, Forncett St Peter, Norfolk, has at second and top belfry floor levels in the tower, circular double-splayed windows. They are constructed with rubble and flints, similar to the stonework in the adjoining walling. Both externally and internally, the splaying of the windows resulted in the cutting into, and the removal, of parts of the stonework in the adjoining walling. Internally their construction details are now hidden by plaster. See adjacent: PHOTO 216. Forncett St Peter 2, showing the external view of the window in the south wall at second floor level.

PHOTO 216. Forncett St Peter 2.

KEY-HOLE WINDOWS

In Lincolnshire some single-splayed windows may be described as "key-hole windows" because the external appearance resembles the shape of a key-hole – hence the name. Key-Hole Windows were those where the shape of the arch of the window head was greater than a semi-circle; the arched head may have been cut out from the centre of the lower horizontal face of a lintel or constructed from a single shaped stone. The inner sides (those framing the glass) of the opposing jambs may be angled from bottom to top.

Holy Trinity Church, Old Clee, Lincolnshire, has, at first floor level in the west wall of the tower, a round-headed, key-hole, single-splayed window. It has an arched head cut out from the centre of the lower horizontal face of a through-stone lintel. The jambs each comprise a single, vertical, through-stone, angled along their inner edges, with small stones of rubble (not through-stones) below. The sill is provided by the top of the coursed rubble stonework of the walling directly below. Internally, the head, jambs and sill of the window are splayed which resulted in the cutting into, and the removal, of parts of the stonework in the adjoining walling. See adjacent: PHOTO 217. Old Clee 2, showing the external view.

PHOTO 217. Old Clee 2.

St Michael's Church, Glentworth, Lincolnshire, has, at second floor level in the south wall of the tower, a round-headed, key-hole, single-splayed window. It has an arched head shaped out of a single through-stone to provide a curvature in both its upper and lower borders greater than a semi-circle. The jambs each comprise a single, vertical, through-stone, with one small stone of rubble (not a through-stone) below. The sill is provided by the top of the coursed rubble stonework of the walling directly below. Externally, the shaped stone of the arched head has been incised with angled grooves to represent the jointing of individual voussoirs. Also externally, hood-moulding, decorated with palmette design has been placed on top of the arched head. The hood-moulding is supported by protruding, narrow, impost-like features. Internally, the head, jambs and sill of the window are splayed which resulted in the cutting into, and the removal, of parts of the stonework in the adjoining walling. See adjacent: PHOTO 218. Glentworth 2, showing the external view with the palmette design arrowed red.

PHOTO 218 Glentworth 2.

St Michael's Church, Glentworth, Lincolnshire, also has, at first floor level in the west wall of the tower, a round-headed, key-hole, single-splayed window – the key is not as distinctive as the one in the south wall. It has an arched head shaped out of a single through-stone to provide a curvature in both its upper and lower borders greater than a semi-circle. The southern jamb comprises a single, vertical, through-stone. The northern jamb comprises part of an early-11th century grave-cover decorated with cable-moulding enclosing a free-arm cross decorated with a chevron-pattern design – it is used as a through-stone; above is a single through-stone. The sill is provided by the top of the coursed rubble stonework of the walling directly below. Internally, the head, jambs and sill of the window are splayed which resulted in the cutting into, and the removal, of parts of the stonework in the adjoining walling. See adjacent: PHOTO 219. Glentworth 3, showing the external view with the grave-cover arrowed red.

PHOTO 219. Glentworth 3.

WINDOWS WITH A SINGLE STONE SLAB INSERTED WITHIN THE FRAME FORMED BY THE ARCHED HEAD, JAMBS AND SILL
St Paul's Church, Jarrow, County Durham, has at ground floor level in the south wall of the chancel, three round-headed single-splayed windows. The three windows each have an arched head constructed with a single through-stone shaped to provide a curvature in both its upper and lower borders – each is a slightly different shape. Each of their jambs comprises one single, vertical, rectangular through-stone below a single horizontal through-stone. Each of their sills comprises a single through-stone. Internally, the head, jambs and sill of the windows are splayed which resulted in the cutting into, and the removal, of parts of the stonework in the adjoining coursed stone walling.

The middle and eastern windows have an additional slab inserted within the "frame" provided by their heads, jambs and sills. The slabs are flush with the faces of the exterior wall. The middle window has a circular aperture cut out of the slab - it now contains reused Anglo-Saxon glass discovered on site during excavations in the 1960s and 1970s. The eastern window has an aperture cut out of the slab similar in shape to the window itself. See below showing views of the same (middle) window, left: PHOTO 220. Jarrow 3, showing the external view, and right: PHOTO 221. Jarrow 4, showing the internal view.

See also Page 126 showing views of the same (eastern) window, top left: PHOTO 222. Jarrow 5, showing the external view, and top right: PHOTO 223. Jarrow 6, showing the internal view.

PHOTO 220. Jarrow 3.

PHOTO 221. Jarrow 4.

WINDOWS WITH AN EXTERNAL FRAME

There are a few examples of where a single stone slab provided the head, jambs and sill framing the external faces of single-splayed windows. Some examples had various shapes of apertures which on occasions were ornamented with individual bands of roll-moulding or cable-moulding.

PHOTO 222. Jarrow 5.

PHOTO 223. Jarrow 6.

In addition some had a separate stone below providing a sill-like feature, whilst others had a separate stone above providing a lintel-like feature. Internally, the head, jambs and sill of the window are splayed in a similar way to other single-splayed windows.

The stair turret at All Saints Church, Hough-on-the-Hill, Lincolnshire, provides ten such examples of these single-splayed windows with an external frame provided by a single slab. Internally, the heads, jambs and sills of the windows are splayed which resulted in the cutting into, and the removal, of parts of the stonework in the adjoining coursed rubble walling.

In the south wall, at ground floor level, is a single-splayed window with, on its external face, a pentagonal-shaped aperture cut out of a through-stone slab providing the head, jambs and sill of the window – it is damaged. See above showing views of the same window, left: PHOTO 224. Hough-on-the-Hill 5, showing the external view, and right: PHOTO 225. Hough-on-the-Hill 6, showing the internal view.

PHOTO 224. Hough-on-the-Hill 5.

PHOTO 225. Hough-on-the-Hill 6.

In the west wall, at ground floor level, is a single-splayed window with, on its external face, a round-headed rectangular-shaped aperture cut out of a through-stone slab providing the head, jambs and sill of the window – there is some damage. See adjacent, showing views of the same window, left: PHOTO 226. Hough-on-the-Hill 7, showing the external view, and right: PHOTO 227. Hough-on-the Hill 8, showing the internal view with the wooden frame for glass arrowed red.

PHOTO 226. Hough-on-the-Hill 7.

PHOTO 227. Hough-on-the-Hill 8.

In the north wall, at ground floor level, is a single-splayed window with, on its external face, a round-headed aperture cut out of a through-stone slab – it is decorated with a concentric band of roll-moulding in relief. See adjacent, showing views of the same window, left: PHOTO 228. Hough-on-the-Hill 9, showing the external view, and right: PHOTO 229. Hough-on-the Hill 10, showing the internal view.

PHOTO 228. Hough-on-the-Hill 9.

PHOTO 229. Hough-on-the-Hill 10.

The stair turret at All Saints Church, Brixworth, Northamptonshire, has, at upper ground floor level in the south wall of the stair turret, another example of this variant of a single-splayed window. On its external face, a flat-headed rectangular-shaped aperture has been cut out of a single stone slab providing the head, jambs and sill of the window. In addition, separate, and above its head, is a single, protruding, horizontal lintel-like stone. Internally, the head, jambs and sill of the window are splayed which resulted in the cutting into, and the removal, of parts of the stonework in the adjoining rubble walling. See above, showing views of the same window, left: PHOTO 230. Brixworth 13, showing the internal view, and right: PHOTO 231. Brixworth 14, showing the external view.

PHOTO 230. Brixworth 13.

PHOTO 231. Brixworth 14.

WINDOWS WITH A PROTRUDING EXTERNAL FRAME
There are a few examples of single-splayed windows whose sills, jambs, imposts (a rare example of windows with imposts) and head all project from the face of the wall.

The west tower of St John the Baptist Church, Barnack, Cambridgeshire, provides three examples; all three windows are high up in the ground floor level of the tower.

In the north wall is a round-headed single-splayed window whose external face projects from the face of the wall. The frame comprises: a quarter-through-stone sill which extends beyond, and provides, the bases of the jambs; quarter-through-stone jambs laid in an Escomb fashion; through-stone imposts, the east/left-hand impost rectangular in shape, the west/right-hand impost square in shape; with the arched head cut out of the centre of the lower horizontal face of a quarter-through-stone lintel. The arched head also has hood-moulding placed directly on top which overhangs the window. Internally, the arched head is constructed with shaped and jointed stones with the remainder of the depth of the walling provided by a bespoke mixture of facing stones on the angle of the splay which extend onto the main interior face of the church wall. The head is supported by rectangular imposts which extend north to south in the internal splay of the window and onto the main interior face of the church wall. Its quarter-through-stone jambs, and the facing stones on the angle of the splay which extend onto the main interior face of the church wall, are laid in similar fashion to Escomb jambs; between the two is a narrow band of rubble stonework similar to the stonework in the adjoining walling. Internally, the head, imposts, jambs, and sill of the window are splayed which resulted in the cutting into, and the removal, of parts of the stonework in the adjoining coursed rubble walling. See adjacent, showing views of the same window, left: PHOTO 232.

PHOTO 232. Barnack 8.

PHOTO 233. Barnack 9.

Barnack 8, showing the external view, and right: PHOTO 233. Barnack 9, showing the internal view.

In the west wall is a triangular-headed single-splayed window whose external face projects from the face of the wall. The frame comprises: a quarter-through-stone sill which extends between, and provides, the bases of the jambs; quarter-through-stone jambs laid in an Escomb fashion, with one tall vertical stone supporting a short vertical stone above; through-stone square imposts, both rectangular in shape; and above two quarter-through-stones, each a trapezium, which extend upwards from the tops of the imposts to meet centrally and form the triangular shape of the head of the window. Internally, the head is constructed with quarter-through-stones - each a trapezium, with the remainder of the depth of the head provided by a bespoke mixture of facing stones on the angle of the splay which extend onto the main interior face of the church wall. The head is supported by rectangular imposts which extend west to east in the internal splay of the window and onto the main interior face of the church wall. Its quarter-through-stone jambs, and the facing stones on the angle of the splay which extend onto the main interior face of the church wall, are laid in similar fashion to Escomb jambs; between the two is a narrow band of rubble stonework similar to the stonework in the adjoining walling. Internally, the head, imposts, jambs, and sill of the window are splayed which resulted in the cutting into, and the removal, of parts of the stonework in the adjoining coursed rubble walling. See adjacent showing views of the same window, left: PHOTO 234. Barnack 10, showing the internal view, and right: PHOTO 235. Barnack 11, showing the external view.

PHOTO 234. Barnack 10.

PHOTO 235. Barnack 11.

In the south wall is a round-headed single-splayed window whose external face projects from the face of the wall. The frame comprises: a quarter-through-stone sill which extends between, and provides, the bases of the jambs; quarter-through-stone jambs laid in an Escomb fashion; through-stone imposts, the west/left-hand rectangular in shape, the east/right-hand square in shape; and the arched head which is cut out of the centre of the lower horizontal face of a quarter-through-stone lintel. Between the top of the lintel, and the arched head of the window below, most of the stonework has been hollowed out to enable the inclusion of two confronting birds in profile standing in relief. Internally, the arched head is constructed with shaped and jointed stones with the remainder of the depth of the walling provided by a bespoke mixture of facing stones on the angle of the splay which extend onto the main interior face of the church wall. The head is supported by rectangular imposts which extend south to north in the internal splay of the window and onto the main interior face of the church wall. Its quarter-through-stone jambs, and the facing stones on the angle of the splay which extend onto the main interior face of the church wall, are laid in similar fashion to Escomb jambs; between the two is a narrow band of rubble stonework similar to the stonework in the adjoining walling. Internally, the head, imposts, jambs, and sill of the window are splayed which resulted in the cutting into, and the removal, of parts of the stonework in the adjoining coursed rubble walling. See adjacent, showing views of the same window, left: PHOTO 236. Barnack 12, showing the external view with the birds arrowed red, and right: PHOTO 237.Barnack 13, showing the internal view.

PHOTO 236. Barnack 12.

PHOTO 237. Barnack 13.

EVIDENCE OF WINDOW SHUTTERS AND WINDOW FRAMES
Whilst windows were often open to the elements, some were shuttered with wood, animal horn or linen, or glazed - fragments of plain and coloured window glass survive. The intention was to keep out the rain, snow and wind, and, to keep out the birds.

Wooden frames were made of sufficient width to include in their construction dowel-holes, or, to enable flange-headed nails to be inserted. The dowel-holes, or nails, allowed string or laces to be threaded through the wooden frame and through the "shutter" comprising animal horn, linen or netting spread across the face of the window. Nails, whatever the shape of their head, might also be bent at right-angles to retain glass or a wooden shutter placed across the face of the window. Some of these wooden frames, usually made out of oak, were built into the stonework of the head, jambs and sill of the window. Other wooden frames were removable and to enable their insertion and removal vertical rebates were constructed in the stonework of both jambs of the window close to the inner face of the wall. Unusually, with some windows, it is possible to identify dowel-holes in the external stonework of the walling for the retention of externally placed window shutters.

St Mary and All Saints Church, Newton-by-Castle Acre, Norfolk, has at ground floor level in the external north wall of the chancel, an incomplete, blocked, round-headed single-splayed window. Only the east jamb and part of the arched head survives. Four dowel holes, and the part of the rebate for the window shutter cab be identified. It is unclear whether this is the external or internal face of the window as it is not thought to be in its original position. See adjacent: PHOTO 238. Newton-by-Castle Acre 1, showing the external view with the dowel holes arrowed red and the recess arrowed black.

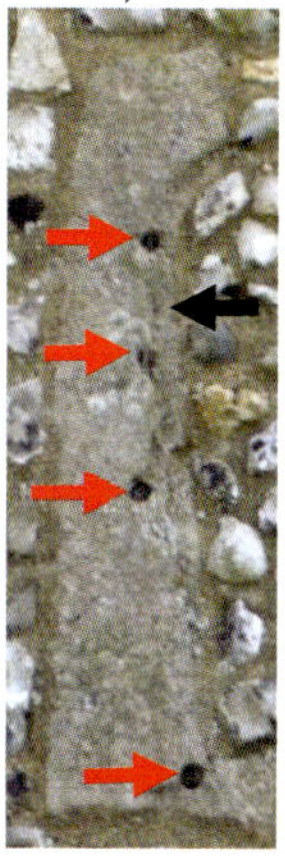

PHOTO 238. Newton-by-Castle Acre 1.

St Mary's Church, Stow-in-Lindsey, Lincolnshire, has at ground floor level in the north wall of the north transept, a single-splayed window which retains its characteristic Anglo-Saxon jambs laid in Escomb fashion despite a replacement flat-head with a rebate, not Anglo-Saxon, necessitated by the addition of a circular window, not Anglo-Saxon, above. Externally, four dowel holes on each jamb, and the rebate for the window shutter can be identified. See adjacent: PHOTO 239. Stow-in-Lindsey 13, showing the external view with the dowel holes arrowed red and the recess arrowed black.

There are some single-splayed windows where the rebates for the placement of the shutters survive – see Page 118. PHOTO 187. Escomb 8, and PHOTO 189. Escomb 10. See Page 119. PHOTO 193. Seaham 6. See Page 126, PHOTO 227. Hough-on-the-Hill 8, for indications of a wooden window frame in a single-splayed window. However, most wooden frames survive in the mid-wall of double-splayed windows see below and following.

PHOTO 239. Stow-in-Lindsey 13.

St Michael's Church, Thursley, Surrey, has at ground floor level in the north wall of the chancel, two round-headed double-splayed windows each with a mid-wall wooden window frame surviving. See adjacent, showing views of the same, eastern, window, left: PHOTO 240. Thursley 1, showing the external view with the mid-wall frame arrowed red, and right: PHOTO 241. Thursley 2, showing the internal view with the mid-wall frame arrowed red – in the splay there are also vestiges of a 13th century wall painting.

PHOTO 240. Thursley 1.   PHOTO 241. Thursley 2.

St Botolph's Church, Hadstock, Essex, has at ground floor level in nave four round-headed double-splayed windows each with a mid-wall wooden window frame surviving – two in the north wall and two in the south wall. See adjacent showing views of the same, eastern, Anglo-Saxon, window in the north wall, left: PHOTO 242. Hadstock 4, showing the external view with the mid-wall frame arrowed red, and right: PHOTO 243. Hadstock 5, showing the internal view with the mid-wall frame arrowed red.

BLOCKED AND INCOMPLETE WINDOWS
Many Anglo-Saxon windows survive only in part, with the glass removed and replaced with stonework – the window is now "blocked". How much survives can vary greatly from one example to another even in the same wall. The following examples give an indication of what can be found.

PHOTO 242. Hadstock 4.   PHOTO 243. Hadstock 5.

St Andrew's Church, Brigstock, Northamptonshire, has at ground floor level in the north wall of the nave, an incomplete, blocked, round-headed single-splayed window. On the internal face the arched head comprises through-stone, splayed, voussoirs, and below, vestiges of the coursed rubble stonework of the western jamb. Of the former external face, only the top arc of the through-stone voussoirs survive – they are not splayed. The building of a late-12th century archway - part of an arcade – has removed most of the jambs and sill of the window. See adjacent views of the same window, left: PHOTO 244. Brigstock 9, showing the internal view, and right: PHOTO 245. Brigstock 10, showing the former external view from inside the north transept – voussoirs arrowed red.

PHOTO 244. Brigstock 9.

PHOTO 245. Brigstock 10.

St Andrew's Church, Bolam, Northumberland, has at ground floor level in the west wall of the tower, an incomplete, blocked, round-headed single-splayed window – it is damaged. Below is a 12th century window whose construction removed its jambs and sill and contributed to its present damaged state. On the internal face the arched head comprises half-through-stone, splayed, voussoirs, supported by what were probably once through-stone square imposts – the southern impost now appears slightly out of position. Nothing can confidently be identified of the external face of this window. See adjacent showing the internal view of the window: PHOTO 246. Bolam 1.

PHOTO 246. Bolam 1.

St Mary Magdalene Church, Geddington, Northamptonshire, has at ground floor level in the north wall of the nave, an incomplete, blocked, round-headed single-splayed window. On the internal face the arched head is constructed with individual stones of rubble placed on end and formed into a discernible arch. What survives of the eastern jamb is constructed with half-through-stones laid in a similar way to long and short quoining; the western jamb and sill are missing. The coursed rubble stonework now blocking the window has removed almost all the indications of the internal splaying of the window. On the former external face the arched head has been cut out of the centre of the lower horizontal face of a rectangular half-through-stone lintel. The surviving eastern jamb comprises a single, vertical, megalithic, half-through-stone with parts of its eastern side

PHOTO 247. Geddington 1.

PHOTO 248. Geddington 2.

possibly changed by later alterations to the walling. The western jamb and sill are missing. See Page 131 showing views of the same window, bottom left: PHOTO 247. Geddington 1, showing the internal view, and bottom right: PHOTO 248. Geddington 2, showing the former external view from inside the north transept.

All Saints Church, Ledsham, West Yorkshire, has at ground floor level in the south wall of the nave, a nearly complete, blocked, round-headed single-splayed window.

Externally, its arched head has been cut from out of the centre of the lower horizontal face of a half-through-stone lintel with its jambs and sill comprising coursed stonework similar to the stonework in the adjoining walling. The eastern jamb has been partially destroyed by the insertion of a 14th century window to the east, and a 21st century "L"-shaped horizontal stone has been inserted at the base of the western jamb. Internally the arched head is constructed with half-through-stone voussoirs with its jambs and sill comprising coursed stonework similar to the stonework in the adjoining walling. The coursed stonework now blocking the window has removed the indications of the internal splaying of the window. See above, showing views of the same window, left: PHOTO 249. Ledsham 1, showing the external view, and right: PHOTO 250. Ledsham 2, showing the internal view.

PHOTO 249. Ledsham 1. *PHOTO 250. Ledsham 2.*

St Matthias Church, Thorpe-Next-Haddiscoe, Norfolk, has, at first floor level in the south wall of the tower, a complete, blocked, round-headed, apparently, single-splayed window. The arched head is cut from out of the centre of the lower horizontal face of a square through-stone lintel decorated. It is decorated with two separate, semi-circular grooves, concentric with the arched head. Each of the jambs comprise four square stones with the top stone being the narrowest. The sill is constructed of coursed rubble and flints similar to the adjoining walling directly below. Above the window is a prokrossos. See adjacent: PHOTO 251.Thorpe-next-Haddiscoe 2, showing the external view.

PHOTO 251. Thorpe-next-Haddiscoe 2.

St Katherine's Church, Little Bardfield, Essex, in the south wall of the nave at ground floor level has a complete round-headed double-splayed window which has been partly blocked externally by the gable roof of the later, not Anglo-Saxon, south porch.

Externally it is evident that the window was constructed and faced with stonework similar to the coursed rubble in the adjoining walling. The arched head has individual stones of rubble placed radially on end vertically to provide a discernible arch. The jambs and sill were constructed of, and faced with, rubble stonework displaying few differences to the stonework forming the adjoining walling. The sill was also probably constructed of similar coursed rubble but the roof of the south porch hides its details. As with many other windows constructed with rubble the interior is now plastered obscuring any construction details. See adjacent showing the views of the same window, left: PHOTO 252. Little Bardfield 4, showing the surviving external face, and right: PHOTO 253. Little Bardfield 5 showing the plastered internal face.

PHOTO 252. Little Bardfield 4. PHOTO 253. Little Bardfield 5.

DOUBLE WINDOWS

The former tower-nave of All Saints Church, Earls Barton, Northamptonshire, has, at first floor level in the south wall of the tower, possibly the only surviving example of a complete double-splayed double-window.

Externally, each window has similar, distinctive, facing stones on their heads and jambs. Each head comprises a single stone with a curvature similar to the top middle third of a semi-circle. These are decorated with two horizontal bands of roll-moulding, concentric with the curvature of the heads on the left-hand window apart from the centre of the top band which changes direction to provide a square frame enclosing a free-arm cross in relief. On the right-hand window the top band of roll-moulding continues its concentric course with the lower band apart from where it breaks to allow the lower vertical arm of the free-arm cross above to intervene. These heads are supported by three, square, corbel-like features which protrude from the face of the wall; the two outer corbels also support vertical pilaster-strips decorating the face of the wall. Below these corbels, the jambs, including the shared mid-wall jamb separating the two windows, are faced with baluster-shafts decorated with three, equally spaced, horizontal bands of protruding roll-moulding. Each of these baluster-shafts is supported by corbel-like features, which protrude from the face of the wall, and are similar in shape and size to the corbels supporting the facing stones on the curving heads above. The jambs of both windows, including the shared mid-wall jamb, interrupt the vertical pilaster-strips which protrude from the face of the walling.

Both externally and internally, both windows are flat-headed with plaster now obscuring the construction details of the heads, jambs and sills. Behind the facing stones, each of the splayed jambs comprises a single, vertical stone slab. In the central depth of each window, a single, blocking, stone slab, at right-angles to, and between, the jambs, has an aperture cut out in the shape of a free-arm cross. Each window has a sill provided by the coursed rubble stonework directly below. Both externally and internally, the head, jambs and sill of the window are splayed which resulted in the cutting into, and the removal, of parts of the stonework in the adjoining walling.

Internally, the only detail that can now be identified are the two protruding vertical and parallel half-round mouldings facing the mid-wall jamb shared by both windows. These half-round mouldings stand on a corbel-like feature comprising three stones placed one on top of the other which protrude from the face of the wall. There is a more conventional corbel comprising a single square stone above the top of the half-round mouldings. See Page 134: PHOTO 254. Earls Barton 4, showing the external view.

PHOTO 254. Earls Barton 4.

There is a similar double window in the west wall which is now incomplete and blocked. Externally, only the facing stones comprising the arched heads and the supporting square, outer corbels, survive. See below right: PHOTO 255. Earls Barton 5.

Each facing stone over the head comprises a single stone with a semi-circular shape. These are decorated with three incomplete bands of roll-moulding, concentric with the curvature of the heads apart from the centre of the middle band which changes direction to provide a square frame enclosing a free-arm cross in relief. These heads are supported by two outer corbels which also support vertical pilaster-strips decorating the face of the wall. These pilaster-strips do not appear to have been interrupted by the placement of the missing facing stones on the jambs – unlike the similar, complete window, in the south wall.

PHOTO 255. Earls Barton 5.

Both externally and internally, both windows are flat-headed with plaster now obscuring the construction details of the heads, jambs and sills. Internally, the only detail that can now be identified is a single protruding vertical baluster-shaft facing the mid-wall shaft shared by both windows. It has a square corbel at its base and a similar corbel above its top; both corbels protrude from the face of the wall.

St Nicholas Church, Worth, West Sussex, has, at first floor level in the north and south walls of the nave, three round-headed double-windows which are not splayed internally or externally. There were formerly four such windows, each one opposing another on the opposite wall but the east window in the south wall was destroyed when a large 15th century window was inserted in its place. Some of the stonework has been restored in the restoration of 1871 and at a later date.

See adjacent: PHOTO 256. Worth 3, showing the external view of the surviving double window in the south wall. See below right: PHOTO 257. Worth 4, showing the external view of both pairs of windows in the north wall, and near the bottom of this Page: PHOTO 258. Worth 5, showing the internal view of both pairs of windows in the north wall.

Each of the surviving double-windows have arched heads constructed with through-stone voussoirs. The supporting square imposts are also through-stones which protrude into the central void but are flush with the faces of the walls. The jambs are also through-stones with those in the north wall each comprising two, vertically placed, stones standing one on top of another.

PHOTO 256. Worth 3.

Those in the south wall comprise three stones with a single middle, horizontally placed, through-stone, separating a vertically placed through-stone below with a square through-stone above (south wall window). The jambs are supported by through-stone bases, similar in shape and size to the imposts, and likewise protruding into the central void but flush with the faces of the walls.

PHOTO 257. Worth 4.

Each of the single, cylindrical, mid-wall shafts increase slightly in diameter towards their centres. These mid-wall shafts support a rectangular through-stone slab, placed horizontally, and extending through the entire depth of the walling of the window so that its sides overhang the mid-wall shaft. This slab supports above the junction of the heads of both windows. The mid-wall shafts stand on through-stone square bases which also protrude into the central void opposite both jambs.

PHOTO 258. Worth 5.

The bases of the jambs, and the bases of the mid-wall shafts, all stand on the same sill provided by the chamfered horizontal string-course (see Pages 169 to 172 "9. String-Courses") which runs around the nave walls externally. Plaster obscures the construction details of the sills internally but it is likely that the sills are provided by the tops of the coursed rubble stonework of the walling directly below.

St Peter's Church, Barton-upon-Humber, Lincolnshire, has, at first floor level in the north and south walls of the tower-nave, two round-headed double-windows which are not splayed internally or externally.

The arched head of each window is constructed with a single through-stone shaped to provide a curvature in both its upper and lower borders. Externally, hood-moulding with label-stops (not decorated) has been placed directly on top the arched heads; the label-stops are above, and separate from, the imposts of the windows below. The arched heads are supported by horizontal through-stone imposts – internally their edges appear chamfered. The imposts protrude from the faces of the wall and into the central void between the jambs. The through-stone jambs are laid in Escomb fashion.

Each of the mid-wall shafts comprise a single baluster-shaft decorated with horizontal bands of roll-moulding: four separate bands in the centre, one band above the base, and one band below the capital. The mid-wall baluster-shaft supports a rectangular through-stone slab, placed horizontally, and extending through the entire depth of the window so that its sides overhang the mid-wall shaft. This slab supports above the junction of the heads of both windows. The bases of the jambs, and the bases of the mid-wall shafts, all stand on the same sill comprising three (south windows)/four (north windows with some restoration) stones laid horizontally in a row – the stone below the mid-wall shaft in both pairs of windows provides the top of the vertical pilaster-strip below. Internally, the construction details are now obscured by plaster but the mid-wall baluster-shafts are supported by square bases protruding from the splays of the windows. See adjacent: PHOTO 259. Barton-upon-Humber 8, showing the external face of the window in the south wall with the hood-moulding arrowed red.

PHOTO 259. Barton-upon-Humber 8.

ROUND-HEADED TRIPLE-OPENING
All Saints, Church, Brixworth, Northamptonshire, has, at first floor level in the east wall of the porch/tower a round-headed triple-opening with two "mid-wall" shafts; the opening is not splayed internally or externally. See below: PHOTO 260. Brixworth 15, showing the east face of the opening with part of the arched head of the first floor blocked doorway below.

The arched heads of each opening are constructed with reused Roman tile-like bricks placed on end and formed into a discernible arch. The three-stepped imposts are constructed with reused Roman tile-like bricks laid horizontally which slightly protrude from the faces of the walls but more noticeably protrude into the central void between the jambs. The jambs were constructed of rubble similar to the stonework in the adjoining walling but are now covered by 19th century facing stones on the west sides, and with plaster on the east sides and the faces of the jambs fronting the voids. The construction details of the sill are mostly hidden by plaster but it

PHOTO 260. Brixworth 15.

seems the bases of the jambs and mid-wall shafts all stand on the same sill now covered by a 19th century facing stone. On the east face it can be seen that this opening and its sill replaces the upper part of the arched head of a first floor, former doorway (now blocked) immediately below.

Both of the "mid-wall" shafts comprise a single baluster with square-shaped bases and capitals. Each baluster is decorated with three sets of horizontal bands of roll-moulding comprising a central band larger than the adjacent bands below and above; one set above its base, a middle set, and the third set below its capital. The mid-wall shafts support a rectangular through-stone slab, placed horizontally, and extending through the entire depth of the walling of the opening so that its sides overhang the mid-wall shaft. This slab supports above the junction of the heads of both openings. See above: PHOTO 261. Brixworth 16, showing the west face of the opening.

PHOTO 261. Brixworth 16.

TRIANGULAR-HEADED DOUBLE-OPENING
St Mary's Church, Deerhurst, Gloucestershire, has at second floor level in the east wall of the porch/tower a triangular-headed double-opening with a solid central pier supporting the junction of the heads of the opening instead of a mid-wall shaft and a through-stone slab that would usually feature in a double-opening. The openings are not splayed internally or externally.

The head of each opening is constructed with two angled rectangular, smoothly-dressed, through-stone slabs – each a trapezium - which extend upwards from the imposts to meet centrally and form a triangular shape. Hood-moulding has been placed on top of the trapezoid-shaped stones of the head and has a similar distinctive triangular shape boldly protruding from the faces of the walls. The opening is supported by five-stepped through-stone imposts (there is some damage) which protrude from the faces of the walls and into the central voids. The height of the top "step" of the imposts is distinctly larger than the four steps below which are all of a similar height. The imposts provide the capitals for the jambs and the central pier.

The jambs are constructed with single, rectangular, through-stones. The jambs, and the central pier, each originally had distinctive bases comprising a chamfered top half and vertical lower half. Additionally, below its lower vertical half, the base of the south jamb, on its west face, has stonework similar to the coursed rubble stonework in the adjoining walling. The northern opening now has stonework filling in the space of the original base and the space once occupied by the now blocked doorway. On the east face, the lower halves of the bases of the jambs are now covered with plaster – the base of the central pier is not plastered.

The east face of both jambs, and all four sides of the central pier, are decorated with bands of vertical reeded-fluting, also called cabled-fluting (a groove enclosing a straight-sided, round-ended, coped band of moulding with part its "roof" removed). A single "reed" is also evident at the east ends of the south and north faces of the respective jambs. Between the bases of each jamb and the central pier a single stone, not Anglo-Saxon, has been placed to provide the sills – presumably replacements for the original rubble sills.

See below left: PHOTO 262. Deerhurst 14, showing the east face of the opening. See below right: PHOTO 263. Deerhurst 15, showing the west face of the opening – Perspex has been placed in each opening.

PHOTO 262. Deerhurst 14.

PHOTO 263. Deerhurst 15.

TRIANGULAR OPENINGS

St Mary's Church, Deerhurst, Gloucestershire, contains three rare, if not unique, small triangular openings which have no separate component parts unlike other openings. Each of the three openings have been cut straight through the depth of the walls. These openings measure around 26 inches/66 centimetres high, and around 21 inches/53.3 centimetres wide at the base. See below right: PHOTO 264. Deerhurst 16, showing the east face of the opening in the east wall of the porch/tower/west wall of the nave – the blocked first floor doorway to the right gives an indication of its size and position.

These three openings are at first floor level in the east wall of the porch/tower/west wall of the nave, and the north and south walls of the nave. The two in the nave may indicate the centre of the first floor room of the north and south nave porticus thought to have been midway along the length of the nave. The opening in the west wall of the nave is not centrally placed, but the blocked doorway in the west wall, to the north of the opening, might have opened into a corridor leading to another doorway within the porch. The width of this speculative corridor could have reduced the width of the first floor room of the former porch resulting in the triangular opening placed in what may have been the centre of the room. Given their

PHOTO 264. Deerhurst 16.

size they were probably intended to assist the audio transmission of services rather than viewing services; they might also indicate the position of an altar adjacent in a chapel.

7. BELFRY-OPENINGS

- From top to bottom most belfry-openings comprise: a half-rounded arched head, or, sometimes, a triangular (gable) – head or, rarely, flat-headed lintel*; square or rectangular imposts*; jambs*; and a sill*. See text and illustrations provided in the following pages.

- The heads, imposts, jambs and sills of many belfry-openings were constructed of, and faced with, rubble stonework displaying few differences to the stonework forming the adjoining walling whether laid in courses* or randomly. Belfry-openings could include the use of a mixture of rubble and flints, and the reuse of Roman stonework, including Roman tile-like bricks, where these were available.

- Alternatively, some belfry-openings were constructed with large facing stones*, individually of a self-evident difference in terms of size and finish to the stonework used in the adjoining walling. Facing stones varied in size and shape and were roughly-dressed* but not to the uniformity of size, shape and careful dressing as ashlar* favoured by Norman and later builders although there are some examples where the Anglo-Saxon builders used ashlar.

- Belfry-openings were not splayed* like most Anglo-Saxon windows and they were left open, not glazed or shuttered, and thus not "windows" as they are often described but "openings".

- Belfry-openings were mostly cut straight through the full depth of the walls without rebates or recesses – a characteristic of Anglo-Saxon workmanship; Norman and later builders recessed the heads and jambs of the opening behind the faces of the walling.

- Some belfry-openings may have had circular-shaped Sound-Holes* – sometimes described as "circular double-splayed windows" or "portholes". These may have been placed singly, in pairs above or to the side of the belfry-openings. In view of their small size their purpose was probably more ornamental than sound amplification. See Page 164: PHOTO 333. Billingham 7, and Page 164: PHOTO 334. Cambridge 10.

- Belfry-openings were constructed in the upper stages of both square and round towers of churches. They usually comprised a set of four "openings", one set in the walling at each point of the compass (north, south, west and east). In the square west tower of a few churches the east opening may be missing because of the height of the former or current nave roofline and its supporting stonework made an east opening impracticable. Cruciform churches, and those with round towers, all appear to have had four sets of belfry-openings.

- Some Anglo-Saxon churches may have belfry-openings at more than one level or stage*. Where this occurs there may be a distinct difference in the nature of construction indicating different builders and likely different building periods. See Pages 165 to 166: PHOTO 336. Barton-upon-Humber 10, and: PHOTO 337. Barton-upon-Humber 11. See also Page 158: PHOTO 320. Appleton-le-Street 6. However, this assumption may not apply in all examples.

- Some Anglo-Saxon belfry-openings may now be incomplete because of their replacement or enlargement by later belfry-openings, not Anglo-Saxon. Others have been blocked up with walling because "new" belfry-openings, not Anglo-Saxon, have been built above in a higher stage in a heightened tower and the vestiges of the Anglo-Saxon belfry-openings may have only survived internally indicated by the "disturbed" nature of the walling.

*See Glossary and for other such terms in the following pages.

- Anglo-Saxon belfry-openings were either "single" or "double". The distinctive differences between the two are:

SINGLE BELFRY-OPENINGS
Single belfry-openings are those where a single opening only is provided. The illustration adjacent identifies the main features likely to be found in a single belfry-opening. This example has a triangular head constructed with two angled rectangular through-stone slabs. It has no imposts. The jambs are constructed with stonework of similar size, and laid in similar courses, to the adjoining walling. The sill is provided by the top of the coursed stonework directly below. See Page 152: PHOTO 307. Bolam 3 and PHOTO 308. Bolam 4.

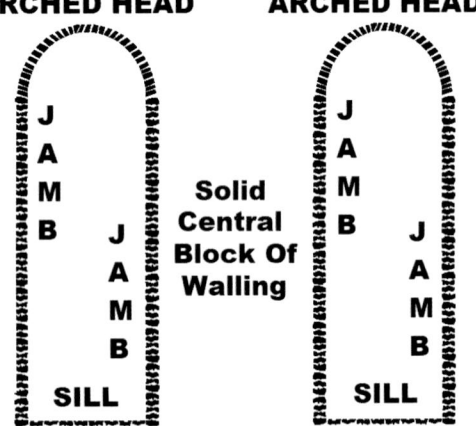

However, some single belfry-openings comprised a pair of similar openings separated from each other by a central solid block of stonework which extends through the entire depth of the wall. Single belfry-openings do not have imposts.

The illustration adjacent identifies the main features likely to be found in a pair of single-belfry-openings. The two openings are similar in construction and are separated by a central solid block of stonework which runs through the entire depth of the wall; this block is similar in construction to the adjoining walling. The arched heads of each opening are constructed with individual stones of rubble placed on end and formed into a discernible arch. The openings have no imposts. The jambs are constructed with rubble similar to the coursed rubble stonework in the adjoining walling. Each opening has a sill provided by the top of the coursed rubble stonework in the adjoining stonework directly below. See Page 154, PHOTO 313. Little Bardfield 6.

DOUBLE BELFRY-OPENINGS
Double belfry-Openings were those where the two openings were separated from each other by a narrow "mid-wall" shaft* in the centre of the depth of the wall, and in the centre of the void between the jambs. The mid-wall shaft could be cylindrical, polygonal, or bulbous in shape, in other examples, a baluster-shaft* may have been used. Sometimes

Anglo-Saxon Church Architecture & Stone Sculpture   141

they may be decorated with horizontal bands of roll-moulding. Some mid-wall shafts can have distinctively shaped capitals, such as "cushion-capitals", others may have capitals decorated with plant designs. See Page 160: PHOTO 325. Lincoln St Peter-at-Gowts 4.

The mid-wall shafts supported a rectangular through-stone slab, placed horizontally, which extended through the entire depth of the walling of the opening so that its sides overhung the mid-wall shaft. This through-stone slab supported above the junction of the heads of both openings, or, the centre of a megalithic lintel when both heads of the opening were cut out of the same single lintel. Note: there were no imposts above the mid-wall shaft. Some double belfry-openings were accompanied by hood-moulding and strip-work - see illustration below. Most belfry-openings were not decorated.

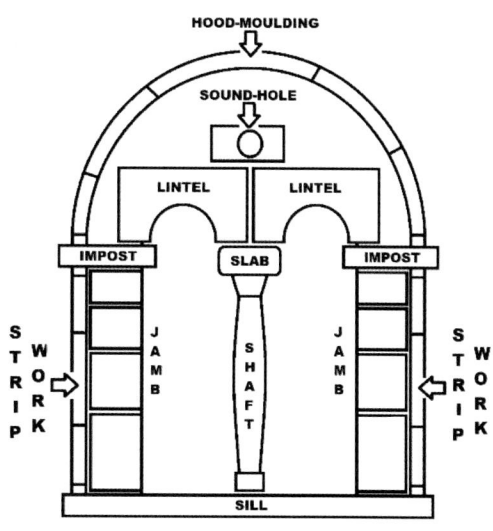

The adjacent illustration identifies the main features likely to be found in a double belfry-opening. This example has two openings separated from each other by a narrow, cylindrical, mid-wall shaft in the centre of the depth of the wall. The arched head of each opening is cut out of the centre of the lower horizontal face of a single lintel. The square imposts protrude from the faces of the wall and into the central void. The mid-wall shaft has an angled capital and square base. The mid-wall shaft supports a rectangular through-stone slab, placed horizontally, and extending through the entire depth of the walling of the opening so that its sides overhang the mid-wall shaft. This slab supports above the junction of the heads of both openings. Note: there is no impost above the mid-wall-shaft. The jambs are constructed with stonework of similar size, and laid in similar courses, to the stonework in the adjoining walling. The sill is a single, projecting, rectangular stone which supports the mid-wall shaft, the central voids, the jambs, and extends to support the strip-work parallel to the jambs. A band of protruding, semi-circular, hood-moulding extends above the lintels, separated by extended imposts, from a band of protruding, vertical, strip-work parallel to the jambs. Among the intervening stonework between the tops of the lintels heads and the hood-moulding, is a stone which has had a circular sound-hole cut out - see Page 162: PHOTO 331. Ovingham 3.

ARCHED HEADS CUT OUT OF A SQUARE LINTEL
The arched heads of many belfry-openings were cut out of the centre of the lower horizontal face of a square lintel which could comprise a single through-stone or two half-through-stones or comprise two smaller square lintels with rubble between them in the centre of the depth of the wall.

In both the lower and upper belfry stages of the east wall of the square tower of All Hallows Church, Bardsey, West Yorkshire, there are round-headed single belfry-openings. Each has an arched head cut out of the centre of the lower horizontal face of a

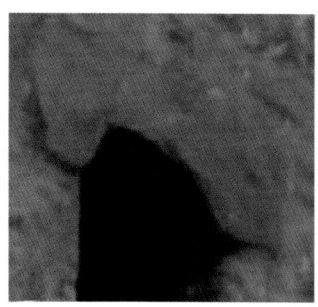

PHOTO 265. Bardsey 7.

single through-stone square lintel. See Page 141 bottom right: PHOTO 265. Bardsey 7, showing the single belfry-opening in the east wall in the upper belfry stage.

In the second stage of the square tower of All Saints Church, Appleton-le-Street, North Yorkshire, there are four round-headed double belfry-openings. Their arched heads are each cut out of the centre of the lower horizontal face of a half-through-stone lintel. See adjacent: PHOTO 266. Appleton-le-Street 2, showing the double belfry-opening in the south wall.

PHOTO 266. Appleton-le-Street 2.

Usually each arched head in a double belfry-openings had its own square lintel. Occasionally, instead of two separate lintels, the arched heads may have been cut out of the same single lintel.

In the fourth stage of the square tower of St Peter's Church, Monkwearmouth, Sunderland, County Durham, there are three round-headed double belfry-openings where the arched heads of each of opening have been cut out of the centre of the lower horizontal face of the same single lintel. See adjacent: PHOTO 267: Monkwearmouth 9, showing the double belfry-opening in the south wall.

PHOTO 267: Monkwearmouth 9.

In the third stage of the square tower of St Bene't's Church, Cambridge, Cambridgeshire, there are four round-headed double belfry-openings with the arched heads of three of the openings cut out of the centre of the lower horizontal face of the same single lintel. See adjacent: PHOTO 268. Cambridge 6, showing the double belfry-opening in the north wall.

PHOTO 268. Cambridge 6.

ARCHED HEADS CONSTRUCTED WITH VOUSSOIRS
Alternatively, the arched heads of some belfry-openings were constructed with a semi-circular row of tapering, wedge-shaped, voussoirs which were often roughly-dressed half-through-stones, three-quarter-through-stones, or through-stones through the full depth of the walling. Not all examples have identifiable single, vertically placed, central key-stones. See below: PHOTO 269. Glentworth 4, and Page 143: PHOTO 270. Bardsey 8.

In the upper stage of the square tower of St Michael's Church, Glentworth, Lincolnshire, there are four round-headed double belfry-openings. They have arched heads constructed with irregularly shaped voussoirs. See adjacent: PHOTO 269. Glentworth 4, showing the double-belfry-opening in the south wall.

PHOTO 269. Glentworth 4.

In the lower and upper belfry stages of the south wall of All Hallows Church, Bardsey, West Yorkshire, there are round-headed double belfry-openings. Each of their arched heads were constructed with voussoirs which are positioned set-back from both the square imposts and the through-stone jambs below. See adjacent: PHOTO 270. Bardsey 8, showing the lower double belfry-openings in the south wall.

PHOTO 270. Bardsey 8.

ARCHED HEADS CONSTRUCTED WITH RUBBLE, FLINTS AND REUSED ROMAN STONEWORK
The arched head may be constructed with a mixture of stonework comprising irregularly-shaped and sized rubble, flints and reused Roman stonework, similar to the stonework of the adjoining walling with no indication of wedge-shaped voussoirs.

To construct a half-round arched head, individual stones were shaped, if required, and placed radially with a square or rectangular side flush with the face of the wall, or, placed radially on end vertically with a narrow side flush with the face of the wall. Where available, Roman tile-like bricks were often placed vertically on end to provide the discernible arched head. Note: Whatever the nature of the individual stones used to construct the arched head they are often still described as "voussoirs" despite not being wedge-shaped.

In the lower and upper belfry levels of the square tower of St Michael's Church, Oxford, Oxfordshire, there are round-headed double belfry-openings with the arched heads each constructed with individual stones of rubble placed on end and formed into a discernible arch. See adjacent: PHOTO 271. Oxford 4, showing the arched head of the belfry-opening in west wall of the lower belfry stage.

PHOTO 271. Oxford 4.

In the upper belfry stage of the square tower of Holy Trinity Church, Colchester, Essex, there are four pairs of round-headed single belfry-openings. Each of the heads of the openings are constructed with reused Roman tile-like bricks placed on end and formed into a discernible arch - there is an occasional partial replacement with rubble. See adjacent: PHOTO 272. Colchester 5, showing the arched heads of the pair of single belfry-openings in the south wall.

PHOTO 272. Colchester 5.

HEADS OF FLAT-HEADED BELFRY-OPENINGS
In the east wall of the upper stage of the square tower of St Chad's Church, Harpswell, Lincolnshire, is a rare example of a flat-headed double belfry-opening. It has a head comprising a single rectangular lintel. See adjacent: PHOTO 273. Harpswell 1, showing the flat head of the belfry-opening in the east wall.

PHOTO 273. Harpswell 1.

144 Anglo-Saxon Church Architecture & Stone Sculpture

HEADS OF TRIANGULAR (GABLE)-HEADED BELFRY-OPENINGS
Some belfry-openings were triangular (gable)-headed constructed with two single through-stones, or two pairs of half-through-stones with each pair abutting each other in the central depth of the wall. Whether single or half-through-stones each stone is a trapezium which extends upwards from the imposts or jambs to meet centrally and form the triangular shape of the head of the belfry-opening.

In the second stage of the square tower of St Peter's Church, Barton-upon-Humber, Lincolnshire, there are four triangular-headed double belfry-openings – the west opening is now blocked. The heads of each opening are constructed with pairs of two angled rectangular through-stone slabs which extend upwards from the imposts to meet centrally and form the triangular shape of the head of each opening. Externally, parallel to, and on top of, these slabs, rectangular and trapezoid-shaped stones protrude from the face of the wall to provide hood-moulding. See adjacent: PHOTO 274. Barton-upon-Humber 9, showing the triangular heads of the belfry-opening in the north wall with the hood-moulding arrowed red.

PHOTO 274. Barton-upon-Humber 9.

Alternatively, the triangular head may be constructed with individual stones of rubble, flints or reused Roman tile-like bricks.

At third floor level in the round tower of St Peter's Church, Forncett St Peter, Norfolk, there are three triangular-headed double belfry-openings. Their heads were constructed with individual stones of rubble, flints and reused Roman tile-like bricks placed on end and formed into a discernible triangle. See adjacent: PHOTO 275. Forncett St Peter 3, showing the head of the belfry-opening in the south face of the tower.

PHOTO 275. Forncett St Peter 3.

HOOD-MOULDING ACCOMPANYING HEADS OF BELFRY-OPENINGS
Some heads of double belfry-openings may be accompanied by hood-moulding. Hood-Moulding may be placed on top of the stonework forming the arched or triangular head or, where the arched heads are cut out of monolithic lintels, separated from them by intervening stonework similar to that in the adjoining walling. See towards the of top this page: PHOTO 274. Barton-upon-Humber 9.

In the upper stage of the square tower of St Andrew's Church, Bywell, Northumberland, there are four round-headed double belfry-openings with hood-moulding, strip-work and sound-holes. Supported by the tops of the extended imposts a semi-circular band of hood-moulding with its own square bases (the east base appears mostly missing) projects from the face of the walling above the lintels. See adjacent: PHOTO 276. Bywell 4, showing the hood-moulding, arrowed red, above the belfry-opening in the south wall.

PHOTO 276. Bywell 4.

IMPOSTS OF DOUBLE BELFRY-OPENINGS

Single belfry-openings do not have imposts. Many, but not all, double belfry-openings do have imposts particularly those where the arched head is constructed with voussoirs and those with triangular-shaped heads. Imposts are usually square in section and profile and may be flush with, or protrude from, some or all of the faces of the walls of which they form a part. Imposts may also protrude into the central void below the head and between the opposing jambs. Imposts may be half-through-stones, three-quarter-through-stones, or through-stones through the full depth of the walling. They are not decorated but they may be chamfered or stepped.

In the second stage of the square tower of All Saints Church, Appleton-le-Street, North Yorkshire, there are four round-headed double belfry-openings. The arched heads are supported by through-stone square imposts which protrude from faces of walling and into central void. See adjacent left: PHOTO 277. Appleton-le-Street 3, showing the western impost of the belfry-opening in the south wall.

PHOTO 277.
Appleton-le-Street 3.

PHOTO 278.
Glentworth 5.

In the upper stage of its square tower of St Michael's Church, Glentworth, Lincolnshire, there are four round-headed double belfry-openings. They have square imposts which protrude from the faces of the walling and into the central void. See above right: PHOTO 278. Glentworth 5, showing the eastern impost of the belfry-opening in the south wall.

In the upper stage of the square tower of St Peter-At-Gowts Church, Lincoln, Lincolnshire, there are four round-headed double belfry-openings. They have square imposts flush with the faces of the walling but protruding into the central void where they are chamfered. See below left: PHOTO 279. Lincoln St Peter-At-Gowts 2, showing the western impost of the belfry-opening in the south wall.

At third floor level in the round tower of St Peter's Church, Forncett St Peter, Norfolk, there are three triangular-headed double belfry-openings. Their imposts were constructed with individual stones of rubble placed horizontally which protrude from the faces of the walling and into the central void. See adjacent right: PHOTO 280. Forncett St Peter 4, showing the western impost of the belfry-opening arrowed red in the south face of the tower.

PHOTO 279. Lincoln
St Peter-At-Gowts 2.

PHOTO 280.
Forncett St Peter 4.

Imposts may also extend to separate strip-work parallel to the jambs from hood-moulding around or on top of the arched or triangular heads.

In the upper stage of the square tower of St Cuthbert's Church, Billingham, County Durham, there are four round-headed double belfry-openings with hood-moulding, strip-work and sound-holes. The openings have square, through-stone, imposts protruding from the faces of the walling and into the central void, and also extending to separate the strip-work below from the hood-moulding above. See adjacent: PHOTO 281. Billingham 4, showing the eastern impost arrowed red separating strip-work below arrowed black, from hood-moulding above arrowed blue, in the belfry-opening in the north wall.

PHOTO 281. Billingham 4.

JAMBS OF SINGLE AND DOUBLE BELFRY-OPENINGS
Round, Flat and Triangular-Headed Single and Double Belfry-Openings had individual stones which collectively formed two sets of jambs on opposite sides of the central void.

Where a single belfry-opening was provided there were two sets of jambs opposite each other separated by the central void. Where single belfry-openings comprise a pair of openings separated from each other by a central solid block of stonework each opening has two sets of jambs opposite each other separated by the central void.

Double belfry-openings. The jambs were separated by a "mid-wall" shaft placed centrally in both the depth of the opening and in the void between the jambs - see Pages 148 to 149: "Mid-Wall Shafts of Double Belfry-Openings".

Jambs were usually square in section and profile. They may be with roughly-dressed half-through-stones, three-quarter-through-stones, or through-stones through the full depth of the walling laid in a similar fashion to Escomb jambs or side alternate quoining; or constructed of similar stonework to the adjoining walling and coursed in a similar fashion – some examples may include megalithic stonework. There are no "standard" number of stones forming the jambs and the stonework in one jamb may not be the mirror image of the stones forming the opposite jamb.

In the third stage of the square tower of St Bene't's Church, Cambridge, Cambridgeshire, there are four round-headed double belfry-openings with the jambs mostly laid in Escomb fashion. See adjacent left: PHOTO 282. Cambridge 7, showing the west jamb of the belfry-opening in the north wall.

In the upper stage of the square tower of St Peter-At-Gowts Church, Lincoln, Lincolnshire, there are four round-headed double belfry-openings. Their arched heads are each constructed with voussoirs with square imposts flush with the faces of the walling but protruding into the central void where they are chamfered. The jambs comprise through-stones laid in Escomb fashion. See adjacent right: PHOTO 283. Lincoln St Peter-At-Gowts 3, showing the west jamb of the belfry-opening in the south wall.

PHOTO 282. Cambridge 7.

PHOTO 283. Lincoln St Peter-At-Gowts 3.

Anglo-Saxon Church Architecture & Stone Sculpture   147

In the upper belfry stage of the square tower of St Andrew's Church, Bolam, Northumberland, there are three triangular-headed single belfry-openings, and one round-headed single-belfry-opening. The three triangular-headed openings jambs are constructed with stonework of a similar size, and laid in similar courses, to the stonework in the adjoining walling - the jambs include some megalithic stonework. See adjacent left: PHOTO 284. Bolam 2, showing the northern jamb of the triangular-headed single belfry-opening in the upper belfry stage in the east wall.

In the second stage of the tower of All Saints Church, Appleton-le-Street, North Yorkshire, there are four round-headed double belfry-openings. Their jambs were constructed of mostly larger stonework than the coursed stone in the adjoining walling and include some through-stones. See above right: PHOTO 285. Appleton-le-Street 4, showing the western jamb of the belfry-opening in the second stage of the south wall.

PHOTO 284. Bolam 2.   PHOTO 285. Appleton-le-Street 4.

Some jambs had accompanying parallel bands of strip-work.

In the upper stage of the square tower of St Cuthbert's Church, Billingham, County Durham, there are four round-headed double belfry-openings with hood-moulding, strip-work and sound-holes. They have bands of protruding, vertical, strip-work, with its own square bases, parallel to the jambs, below. See adjacent: PHOTO 286. Billingham 5, showing the eastern jamb of the belfry-opening in the north wall with the strip-work arrowed red.

Occasionally jambs may be constructed with smoothly-dressed, regularly shaped and sized, ashlar stonework - see Page 156: PHOTO 317. Langford 11.

PHOTO 286. Billingham 5.

Alternatively, jambs may comprise rubble stonework displaying few differences to the stonework forming the adjoining walling whether laid in courses or randomly. Such jambs could be constructed with a mixture of rubble and flints similar to the stonework of the adjoining walling including the reuse of Roman stonework and tile-like bricks where these were available.

At third floor level in the round tower of St Peter's Church, Forncett St Peter, Norfolk, there are three triangular-headed double belfry-openings. Their jambs were constructed with coursed rubble, flints and reused Roman tile-like bricks all laid horizontally similar to the stonework in the adjoining walling - the stones of the jambs are noticeably slightly larger than the adjoining stones. See adjacent: PHOTO 287. Forncett St Peter 5, showing the west jamb of the belfry-opening in the south face of the tower.

PHOTO 287. Forncett St Peter 5.

In the upper belfry stage of the square tower of Holy Trinity Church, Colchester, Essex, there are four pairs of round-headed single belfry-openings. Each of jambs of the openings are constructed with a mixture of rubble and facings provided by reused Roman tile-like bricks placed horizontally on top of one another. See adjacent: PHOTO 288. Colchester 6, showing the eastern jamb of the eastern opening of the pair of round-headed single belfry-openings in the south wall.

MID-WALL SHAFTS OF DOUBLE BELFRY-OPENINGS
Mid-Wall Shafts of double belfry-openings were centrally placed in both the depth of the wall, and in the void between the opposing jambs of a belfry-opening – they are not part of, or an extension of, another section of stonework. They supported a rectangular through-stone slab above – see Pages 149 to 150: "Through-Stone Slabs of Double Belfry-Openings".

Most mid-wall shafts were cylindrical in shape - some of which might be described as rectangular with rounded corners. They often stood directly on top of the sill of the opening, whether it was the top of the stonework below or a string-course, without any intervening bases. Whilst some mid-wall shafts had neither bases nor capitals others had both. Capitals and bases could be square, rectangular, round, conical, or trapezoid in shape, chamfered or moulded expanding in size towards the bottom or top; some capitals may be described as cushion-capitals. Capitals were more likely to be decorated.

PHOTO 288.
Colchester 6.

In the upper stage of the square tower of St Mary the Virgin Church, Ovingham, Northumberland, there are four round-headed double belfry-openings with hood-moulding, strip-work and sound-holes. The openings have cylindrical mid-wall shafts without bases or capitals. See adjacent left: PHOTO 289. Ovingham 1, showing the mid-wall shaft of the belfry-opening in the south wall.

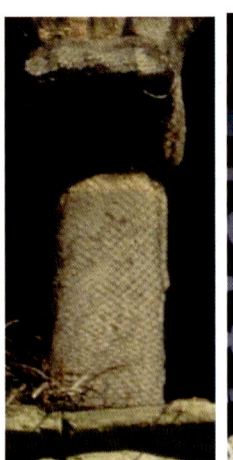

At third floor level in the round tower of St Peter's Church, Forncett St Peter, Norfolk, there are three triangular-headed double belfry-openings. The openings have cylindrical mid-wall shafts each with an expanding rounded base with a horizontal band of roll-moulding above, and a cushion-capital with a horizontal band of roll-moulding below. See above right: PHOTO 290. Forncett St Peter 6, showing the mid-wall shaft in the belfry-opening in the south face of the tower.

PHOTO 289.
Ovingham 1.

PHOTO 290.
Forncett St Peter 6.

In the upper stage of the square tower of St Michael's Church, Glentworth, Lincolnshire, there are round-headed double belfry-openings with both cylindrical and octagonal mid-wall shafts. These mid-wall shafts have square bases and capitals decorated mostly with volutes but the west wall mid-wall shaft appears to have heads of creatures rather than volutes. The mid-wall shaft in the south wall is decorated with a vertical band of cable- moulding in relief. See adjacent: PHOTO 291. Glentworth 6, showing the mid-wall shaft in the belfry-opening in the south wall.

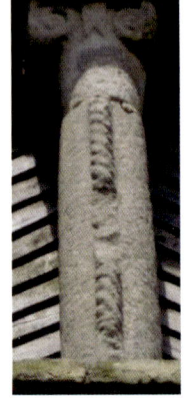

Some mid-wall shafts were baluster-shafts.

PHOTO 291.
Glentworth 6.

In the lower and upper belfry levels of the square tower of St Michael's Church, Oxford, Oxfordshire, there are round-headed double belfry-openings with mid-wall shafts provided by baluster-shafts. The baluster-shafts increase in circumference towards the centre where a single, narrow, central, horizontal, band of stonework is bordered, top and bottom, by the cutting away of the adjoining stonework to leave a distinctive horizontal, almost U-shaped, groove. The baluster-shafts do not have capitals but do have rounded, expanding, bases separated from the rest of the shaft, by a horizontal rounded band of stonework similar to roll-moulding. See adjacent: PHOTO 292. Oxford 5, showing the internal view of the mid-wall baluster-shaft in the lower belfry-opening in the west wall.

THROUGH-STONE SLABS OF DOUBLE BELFRY-OPENINGS

PHOTO 292. Oxford 5.

A rectangular through-stone slab was placed horizontally and extended through the entire depth of the walling of the opening, so that its sides overhung the mid-wall shaft below which provided its support. This rectangular through-stone slab supported above the junction of the heads of both openings, or the centre of a megalithic lintel when both heads of the opening were cut out of the same single lintel.

In the upper stage of the square tower of St Cuthbert's Church, Billingham, County Durham, there are four round-headed double belfry-openings with hood-moulding, strip-work and sound-holes. The mid-wall shafts support a rectangular through-stone slab, placed horizontally, and extending through the entire depth of the walling of the opening so that its sides overhang the mid-wall shaft. This slab supports above the junction of the heads of both openings. See above left: PHOTO 293. Billingham 6, showing the belfry-opening in the north wall.

PHOTO 293. Billingham 6. PHOTO 294. Appleton-le-Street 5.

In the second stage of the tower of All Saints Church, Appleton-le-Street, North Yorkshire, there are four round-headed double belfry-openings. Their mid-wall shafts support a rectangular through-stone slab, placed horizontally, and extending through the entire depth of the walling of the opening so that its sides overhang the mid-wall shaft. This slab supports above the junction of the heads of both openings. See above right: PHOTO 294. Appleton-le-Street 5, showing the belfry-opening in the south wall.

Alternatively, the through-stone slabs supported the centre of a megalithic lintel above - when both heads of the opening were cut out of the same single lintel.

In the third stage of the square tower of St Bene't's Church, Cambridge, Cambridgeshire there are four round-headed double belfry-openings with the arched heads of three of the openings cut out of the centre of the lower horizontal face of the same single lintel. Their mid-wall shafts of these belfry-openings support a rectangular through-stone slab, placed horizontally, and extending through the entire depth of the walling of the opening so that its sides overhang the mid-wall shaft. This slab supports above the centre of the single lintel above. See adjacent: PHOTO 295. Cambridge 8, showing the belfry-opening in the north wall with the northern end of the slab arrowed red.

At third floor level in the round tower of St Peter's Church, Forncett St Peter, Norfolk, there are three triangular-headed double belfry-openings. Their mid-wall shafts support a rectangular through-stone slab, placed horizontally, and extending through the entire depth of the walling of the opening so that its sides overhang the mid-wall shaft. This slab supports above the junction of the heads of both openings. See adjacent: PHOTO 296. Forncett St Peter 7, showing the through-stone slab in the belfry-opening in the south face of the tower.

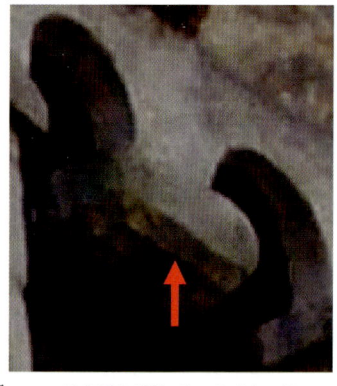

PHOTO 295. Cambridge 8.

PHOTO 296. Forncett St Peter 7.

SILLS OF BOTH SINGLE AND DOUBLE BELFRY-OPENINGS
Sills of both single and double belfry-openings were often provided by the top of the stonework below whether laid in courses or not; the stonework below is unaffected in its composition and placement by the opening above.

In both the lower and upper belfry stages in the south wall of the square tower of All Hallows Church, Bardsey, West Yorkshire, there are round-headed doubly-belfry-openings with their sills provided by the tops of the coursed rubble stonework below. See adjacent: PHOTO 297. Bardsey 9, showing the lower double belfry-opening in the south wall.

PHOTO 297. Bardsey 9.

In both the lower and upper belfry levels of the square tower of St Michael's Church, Oxford, Oxfordshire, there are seven round-headed double belfry-openings with their sills provided by the tops of the rubble stonework - not laid in courses - directly below. See below left: PHOTO 298. Oxford 6, showing the sill of the lower belfry-opening in the west wall.

PHOTO 298. Oxford 6.

PHOTO 299. Forncett St Peter 8.

At third floor level in the round tower of St Peter's Church, Forncett St Peter, Norfolk, there are three triangular-headed double belfry-openings with their sills provided by the tops of the coursed rubble stonework directly below. See above right: PHOTO 299. Forncett St Peter 8, showing the sill of the belfry-opening in the south face of the tower.

Sills were also provided by the top of the string-course below.

In the third stage of the square tower of St Bene't's Church, Cambridge, Cambridgeshire, there are four round-headed double belfry-openings with their sills provided by the tops of the string-course directly below. See adjacent: PHOTO 300. Cambridge 9, showing the sill of the belfry-opening in the north wall.

PHOTO 300. Cambridge 9.

In the upper stage of the square tower of St Michael's Church, Glentworth, Lincolnshire, there are four round-headed double belfry-openings with their sills provided by the tops of the square string-course directly below. See adjacent: PHOTO 301. Glentworth 7, showing the sill of the belfry-opening in the south wall.

PHOTO 301. Glentworth 7.

With some examples the sill may comprise a single horizontal row of protruding, narrow, stones which extend to support the square bases of the strip-work parallel to the jambs.

In the upper stage of the square tower of St Mary the Virgin Church, Ovingham, Northumberland, there are four round-headed double belfry-openings with hood-moulding, strip-work and sound-holes. The sills of the belfry-openings are provided by a single, projecting, rectangular stone which supports the mid-wall shaft, the central voids, the jambs, and extends to support the protruding, strip-work, parallel to the jambs – the strip-work also has distinctive, square, bases. The sill of the south opening appears to have been broken. See adjacent: PHOTO 302. Ovingham 2, showing the sill of the belfry-opening in the south wall.

PHOTO 302. Ovingham 2.

When available sills may also be constructed with reused Roman tile-like bricks placed horizontally in a row.

In the upper belfry stage of the square tower of Holy Trinity Church, Colchester, Essex, there are four pairs of round-headed single belfry-openings. Each of their sills are constructed with reused Roman tile-like bricks placed horizontally in a row. See adjacent: PHOTO 303. Colchester 7, showing the pair of round-headed single belfry-openings in the upper belfry stage of the south wall.

PHOTO 303. Colchester 7.

SOUND-HOLES
Some belfry-openings may have circular-shaped "sound-holes" – sometimes described as "circular double-splayed widows" or "portholes". These may be placed singly, in pairs above or to the side of the belfry-openings. A single stone which has had a circular sound-hole cut out may also be among the intervening stonework between the tops of the lintel heads and the hood-moulding – the semi-circular tympanum. In view of their small size the purpose of sound-holes was probably more ornamental than sound amplification; if the main belfry-openings were shuttered then they would also have provided some extra light.

In the upper stage of the square tower of St Andrew's Church, Bywell, Northumberland, there are four round-headed double belfry-openings with hood-moulding, strip-work and sound-holes. Among the intervening stonework between the tops of the lintel heads and the hood-moulding – the semi-circular tympanum - is a single stone which has had a circular sound-hole cut out. To the side of the opening, and roughly in line with the central sound-hole, are two further similar circular sound-holes cut out of a single stone, one on each side. See adjacent: PHOTO 304. Bywell 5, showing the sound-holes arrowed red accompanying the belfry-opening in the south wall.

PHOTO 304. Bywell 5.

In the fourth stage of the square tower of All Saints Church, Earls Barton, Northamptonshire, there are four pairs of round-headed quintuple-belfry-openings. The east wall belfry-opening only has circular openings similar to sound-holes above its two most northern openings. See adjacent: PHOTO 305. Earls Barton 6, showing the belfry-opening in the east wall with the two circular sound-holes arrowed red.

PHOTO 305. Earls Barton 6.

In the upper stage of its square tower of St Andrew's Church, Great Dunham, Norfolk, there are four round-headed double belfry-openings. Above the belfry-openings in the west and east walls there are pairs of double-splayed sound-holes constructed with rubble and flints similar to the stonework in the adjoining walling. See adjacent: PHOTO 306. Great Dunham 5, showing the double-splayed sound-holes above the belfry-opening in the west wall.

PHOTO 306. Great Dunham 5.

TYPICAL SINGLE BELFRY-OPENINGS
In the square tower of St Andrew's Church, Bolam, Northumberland, there are four single belfry-openings in the upper belfry stage - see below left: PHOTO 307. Bolam 3, showing the triangular-headed single belfry-opening in the upper belfry stage in the east wall. See below right: PHOTO 308. Bolam 4, showing the round-headed single-belfry-opening in the upper belfry stage in the south wall. See also the four double belfry-openings in the lower belfry stage – Page 157. PHOTO 319. Bolam 5.

It has three triangular-headed single belfry-openings, and one round-headed single-belfry-opening, in the upper belfry stage. The three triangular-headed openings have heads constructed with two, angled, through-stone slabs. The one round-headed opening

PHOTO 307. Bolam 3.   PHOTO 308. Bolam 4.

has an arched head constructed with a single stone shaped to provide a curvature in both its upper and lower borders – the curvature of the upper border is less regular than the lower border. None of the openings have imposts. All of their jambs were constructed with stonework of a similar size, and laid in similar courses, to the stonework in the adjoining walling – the jambs include some megalithic stonework. All of their sills are provided by the top of the coursed stonework directly below.

All Hallows Church, Bardsey, West Yorkshire, has, in its square tower, two round-headed single belfry-openings in both the lower and upper belfry stages of the east wall, and two round-headed double belfry-openings in the lower and upper belfry stages in the south wall. See Page 158: PHOTO 322. Bardsey 11, showing both single and double belfry-openings in the east and south walls, and Page 158: PHOTO 323. Bardsey 12, showing the lower double belfry-opening in the south wall.

The round-headed single belfry-openings each have an arched head cut out of the centre of the lower horizontal face of a single through-stone square lintel. They do not have imposts. The jambs are constructed of coursed rubble stonework similar to that in the adjoining walling and they include some megalithic stonework. The sills are provided by the top of the coursed rubble stonework directly below. See adjacent: PHOTO 309. Bardsey 10, showing the single belfry-opening in the upper stage of the east wall.

PHOTO 309. Bardsey 10.

In the upper level of the second stage of the square tower of St John the Baptist Church, Barnack, Cambridgeshire, there are four triangular-headed single belfry-openings; the belfry-opening in the west wall is a 1936 restoration. Their heads were constructed with two angled rectangular through-stone slabs. They do not have imposts. The jambs were constructed of coursed rubble stonework similar to that in the adjoining walling. The external sills are provided by a single large, splayed, stone in the west and east walls and by a similar stone, not splayed, in the north and south walls.

Set back in the depth of these openings, and extending across the width, each of the belfry-openings has stone fretwork in a surrounding frame - transennae. In the west and east walls the fretwork is in the form of a design with four long, vertical spaces, in two pairs, resembling vertical panels in a door. See adjacent: PHOTO 310. Barnack 14, showing the fretwork in the belfry-opening in the east wall. In the north and south walls the fretwork is in the form of a figure-of-eight ring-knot design. See adjacent right: PHOTO 311. Barnack 15, showing the fretwork in the belfry-opening in the south wall.

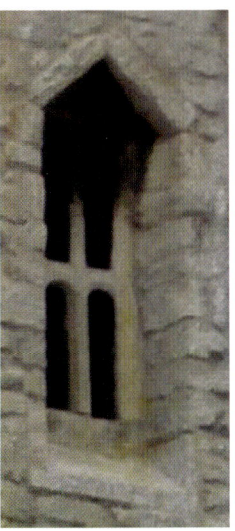

PHOTO 310. Barnack 14.

PHOTO 311. Barnack 15.

In the square tower of Holy Trinity Church, Colchester, Essex, there are four round-headed single belfry-openings in the lower belfry stage, and four pairs of round-headed single belfry-openings in the upper belfry stage. All are constructed with rubble and reused Roman tile-like bricks.

The round-headed single belfry-openings in the lower belfry stage have the heads of each opening constructed with reused Roman tile-like bricks placed on end and formed into a discernible arch – there is an occasional partial replacement with rubble. They do not have imposts. The jambs are constructed with a mixture of rubble and facings provided by reused Roman tile-like bricks placed horizontally on top of one another. The sills are provided by the top of the square string-course below.

In addition the whole opening is "framed" by protruding pilaster-strips which form part of an arcade extending along the whole width of the wall. The uprights of the pilaster-strips are constructed with reused Roman tile-like bricks placed horizontally on top of each other and extend way above the height of the jambs and the round-heads of the single belfry-openings. The arched heads of the pilaster-strips are constructed with reused Roman tile-like bricks placed on end and formed into a discernible arch – there is an occasional partial replacement with rubble. Like the single belfry-openings, the sills of the pilaster-strips, are provided by the top of the square string-course below. Note: The arcade of pilaster-strips can most easily be identified on the south wall.

PHOTO 312. Colchester 8.

See above right: PHOTO 312. Colchester 8, showing the round-headed single belfry-opening in the lower belfry stage of the south wall. Also see Page 155: PHOTO 315. Colchester 10, showing a pair of round-headed single belfry-openings in the upper belfry stage of the south wall.

SINGLE BELFRY-OPENINGS IN PAIRS
In the upper stages of the square tower of St Katherine's Church, Little Bardfield, Essex, there are pairs of single belfry-openings in three levels. String-courses, comprising rubble and flints rather than the usual dressed stone, separate the lower stage from the first belfry stage, the first belfry stage from the second belfry stage, and the second belfry stage from the third belfry stage. The construction of each of the belfry stages is set-back from the stage below. There are twenty-two openings in all, two pairs in all three levels in the north, west and south walls, and two pairs in the middle and

PHOTO 313. Little Bardfield 6.

Anglo-Saxon Church Architecture & Stone Sculpture   155

upper levels in the east wall. Those in the lowest level are the largest and separated by a considerable width of walling, those in the middle level are the narrowest and the closest together, and those in the upper level are of similar size to those in the middle level and separated by the widest width of walling.

Each of the openings were similarly constructed. Their heads were constructed with individual stones of rubble and flint placed on end and formed into a discernible arch. The openings do not have imposts. The jambs were constructed with coursed rubble and flints similar to the stonework in the adjoining walling. Each of the pairs of openings are separated by a block of walling, similarly, constructed to the jambs, which runs through the entire depth of the walls – as indicated above the width of their separation varies at each level. The sills are provided by the tops of the coursed rubble stonework directly below. See Page 154 bottom right: PHOTO 313. Little Bardfield 6, showing each of the three pairs of single-belfry-openings at different levels in the south wall.

In the square tower of Holy Trinity Church, Colchester, Essex, there are four round-headed single belfry-openings in the lower belfry stage, and four pairs of round-headed single belfry-openings in the upper belfry stage. All twelve belfry-openings were constructed with rubble and reused Roman tile-like bricks. See adjacent: PHOTO 314. Colchester 9, showing the south wall with the single belfry-opening in the lower belfry stage arrowed red, and the pair of single belfry-openings in the upper stage arrowed black.

PHOTO 314. Colchester 9.

The pairs of round-headed single belfry-openings in the upper belfry stage have the heads of each of the openings constructed with reused Roman tile-like bricks placed on end and formed into a discernible arch – there is an occasional partial replacement with rubble. The belfry-openings do not have imposts. Their jambs were constructed with a mixture of rubble and facings provided by reused Roman tile-like bricks placed horizontally on top of one another. Each pair of openings are separated by a thin block of walling, similarly, constructed to the jambs, which runs through the entire depth of the wall. The sills were constructed with reused Roman tile-like bricks placed horizontally in a row. See adjacent: PHOTO 315. Colchester 10, showing the pair of round-headed single belfry-openings in the upper belfry stage of the south wall.

PHOTO 315. Colchester 10.

In the belfry stage of the square tower of St Mary the Virgin Church, Sompting, West Sussex, there are pairs of triangular-headed single belfry-openings in the west and east walls.

Each of the heads of the openings in the west and east walls were constructed with two angled rectangular stones. The openings do not have imposts. The jambs were constructed with rubble and flints similar to that in the adjoining walling - the jambs of the openings in west wall also include reused Roman tile-like bricks. Each of the two openings are separated by a block of walling, similarly, constructed to the jambs, which runs through the entire depth of the walls; externally this walling has the addition of a centrally placed pilaster-strip. The sills are provided by the top of the rubble stonework directly below. See adjacent: PHOTO 316. Sompting 1, showing the pair of triangular-headed single belfry-openings in the west wall separated by a centrally placed pilaster-strip arrowed red. There are also pairs of round-headed double belfry-openings in the north and south walls - see Page 161: PHOTO 328. Sompting 2.

PHOTO 316. Sompting 1.

ATYPICAL EXAMPLE OF A PAIR OF SINGLE BELFRY-OPENINGS
In the third stage of the square central tower of St Matthew's Church, Langford, Oxfordshire, there are four pairs of round-headed single belfry-openings. All of the eight belfry-openings were constructed with through-stone ashlar stonework. Each of the single-belfry openings is constructed with similarly sized and faced wedge-shaped stones for the voussoirs and similarly sized and faced square stones for the jambs; there are no imposts. Each of the two openings are separated by a block of walling, similarly constructed to the jambs, which runs through the entire depth of the wall.

Externally, the addition of a half-round roll on the face of the arched heads and jambs on each of the openings, and the decoration of horizontal bands of roll-moulding between the arched heads and jambs where a capital might be expected, has the effect of transforming the appearance of each of the two separate belfry-openings into something similar to a double belfry-opening. Within the frame provided by the two horizontal bands of roll-moulding on both the half-round roll and the adjacent walling in effect set-back, there are vertical, plant-like, designs of different heights. Above the roll-moulding on the central vertical half-round roll is a single vertical leaf enclosed within its own bespoke border. The sills of each opening were constructed with a single stone, sloping outwards. See adjacent: PHOTO 317. Langford 11, showing the pair of single belfry-openings in the south wall.

PHOTO 317. Langford 11.

UNIQUE EXAMPLE OF QUINTUPLE BELFRY-OPENINGS
In the fourth stage of the square tower of All Saints Church, Earls Barton, Northamptonshire, there are four round-headed quintuple belfry-openings. See Page 157: PHOTO 318. Earls Barton 7, showing the belfry-opening in the south wall. Additionally, the east wall opening has circular openings similar to sound-holes above its two most northern openings – see Page 152: PHOTO 305. Earls Barton 6.

The five arched heads in each opening were cut out of the centre of the lower horizontal face of five, single, square through-stone lintels; each head was decorated with concentric, semi-circular, bands of "set-back" moulding. In the west wall the central lintel has a representation of a

PHOTO 318. Earls Barton 7.

free-arm cross in relief above the moulding similar to those on the facing stones of the arched heads of the round-headed double-splayed double-windows in the west wall (incomplete) and the south wall (complete) at first floor level. The openings have square imposts which support the arched heads above and overhang the tops of the baluster-shafts below.

The jambs comprise six vertical through-stone slabs which externally have been cut-back below their heads to allow baluster-shafts to be inserted. The baluster-shafts each stand on a square base. These baluster-shafts have three horizontal bands of protruding roll-moulding: one above its base, one in the centre, and one below its capital. (Note: The baluster-shafts are separate from the truncated external ends of the through-stone slabs apart from those in the belfry-opening in the east wall where, apparently, the baluster-shafts are integral to the through-stone slabs.) The sills are provided by the top of the string-course directly below.

TYPICAL DOUBLE BELFRY-OPENINGS
In the square tower of St Andrew's Church, Bolam, Northumberland, there are typical examples of both double belfry-openings in the lower belfry stage, and single belfry-openings in the upper belfry stage - see Page 152. PHOTO 307. Bolam 3, and PHOTO 308. Bolam 4.

It has four round-headed double belfry-openings in the lower belfry stage. Their heads were each cut out of the centre of the lower horizontal face of a single through-stone square lintel. The openings do not have imposts. The jambs were constructed with stonework of a similar size, and laid in similar courses, to the stonework in the adjoining walling - the jambs include some megalithic stonework. The openings have cylindrical mid-wall shafts with bulbous bases standing on a cuboid plinth - a distinctive horizontal groove separates the two shapes; the mid-wall shafts to not have capitals. The mid-wall shafts support a rectangular through-stone slab, placed horizontally, and extending through the entire depth of the walling of the opening so that its sides overhang the mid-wall shaft. This slab supports above the junction of the heads of both openings. The sills are provided by the top of the square string-

PHOTO 319. Bolam 5.

course directly below. See Page 157 bottom right: PHOTO 319. Bolam 5, showing the belfry-opening in the south wall.

In both the second and third stages of the square tower of All Saints Church, Appleton-le-Street, North Yorkshire, there are double belfry-openings. The round-headed double belfry-openings in the third stage are smaller and thought to be of a later date than those below. See adjacent: PHOTO 320. Appleton-le-Street 6, showing the double belfry-openings in the second and third stages in the south and east walls of the tower.

PHOTO 320. Appleton-le-Street 6.

In the second stage there are four round-headed double belfry-openings. Their arched heads are each cut out of the centre of the lower horizontal face of a half-through-stone lintel. The through-stone square imposts protrude from faces of walling and into central void. The jambs were constructed of mostly larger stonework than the coursed stone in the adjoining walling and include some through-stones. The openings have cylindrical mid-wall shafts with rounded, extending, bases interrupting the sills of the openings; the shafts do not have capitals. The mid-wall shafts support a rectangular through-stone slab, placed horizontally, and extending through the entire depth of the walling of the opening so that its sides overhang the mid-wall shaft. This slab supports above the junction of the heads of both openings. The sills are provided by the top of the coursed stonework below. See adjacent: PHOTO 321. Appleton-le-Street 7, showing the double belfry-opening in the second stage in the south wall.

PHOTO 321. Appleton-le-Street 7.

In the square tower of All Hallows Church, Bardsey, West Yorkshire, there are round-headed single belfry-openings in both the lower and upper belfry stages of the east wall, and round-headed double belfry-openings in both the lower and upper belfry stages of the south wall. See below left: PHOTO 322. Bardsey 11, showing the single belfry-openings in the east wall arrowed red, and the double belfry-openings in the south wall arrowed black – restoration of the upper opening has resulted in its arched heads appearing almost triangular in shape.

The round-headed double belfry-openings in the south wall each have an arched head constructed with voussoirs which are positioned set-back from both the square imposts and the through-stone jambs below. Both the imposts and jambs protrude into the central void, otherwise they are flush with the faces of the

PHOTO 322. Bardsey 11.

PHOTO 323. Bardsey 12.

walls. The jambs are mostly distinctly larger in size than the coursed rubble stonework in the adjoining walling.

The openings have cylindrical mid-wall shafts with large square bases; the shafts do not have capitals. The mid-wall shafts support a rectangular through-stone slab, placed horizontally, and extending through the entire depth of the walling of the opening so that its sides overhang the mid-wall shaft. This slab supports above the junction of the heads of both openings. The sills are provided by the top of the coursed rubble stonework below. See Page 158 bottom right: PHOTO 323. Bardsey 12, showing the double belfry-opening in the lower stage in the south wall. (See also Page 153: PHOTO 309. Bardsey 10, showing the single belfry-opening in the upper stage in the east wall.)

In the upper stage of the square tower of St Michael's Church, Glentworth, Lincolnshire, there are four round-headed double belfry-openings. Their arched heads are constructed with irregularly shaped voussoirs supported by square imposts protruding from the faces of the walling and into the central void. The jambs comprise facing stones of size and placed on top of each other but not in any distinctive design and are easily distinguished from the coursed rubble stonework in the adjoining walling. The openings have both cylindrical and octagonal mid-wall shafts with square bases and capitals decorated mostly with volutes but the west wall mid-wall shaft appears to have heads of creatures rather than volutes. The mid-wall shaft in the south wall is decorated with a vertical band of cable-moulding in relief.

PHOTO 324. Glentworth 8.

The mid-wall shafts support a rectangular through-stone slab, placed horizontally, and extending through the entire depth of the walling of the opening so that its sides overhang the mid-wall shaft. This slab supports above the junction of the heads of both openings. The sills are provided by the top of the square string-course directly below. The west belfry-opening may have had a bell hung between the mid-wall shaft and the left-hand (north) jamb - there are indications of a hole and concentric grooves - the larger where the bell cut into the stonework. See above right: PHOTO 324. Glentworth 8, showing the belfry-opening in the south wall.

In the upper stage of the square tower of St Peter-At-Gowts Church, Lincoln, Lincolnshire, there are four round-headed double belfry-openings. Their arched heads are each constructed with voussoirs with square imposts flush with the faces of the walling but protruding into the central void where they are chamfered. The through-stones jambs were laid in Escomb fashion. The openings have cylindrical mid-wall shafts with conical-cum-rectangular bases, and capitals, a rarity, with a conical lower half and a cylindrical upper half. The openings in the west and south walls have capitals decorated with a lower horizontal band of cable-moulding separating the capitals from the cylindrical mid-wall shaft below, and a centrally placed, narrow, band of roll-moulding, separating a lower palmette design from "wheat-ear" design above.

The mid-wall shafts support a rectangular through-stone slab, placed horizontally, and extending through the entire depth of the walling of the opening so that its sides overhang the mid-wall shaft. This slab supports above the junction of the heads of both openings. The sills are provided by the top of the string-course directly below. See adjacent: PHOTO 325. Lincoln St Peter-At-Gowts 4, showing the belfry-opening in the south wall, with the palmette design on the capital arrowed red, and above, the wheat-ear design on the capital arrowed blue.

At third floor level in the round tower of St Peter's Church, Forncett St Peter, Norfolk, there are three triangular-headed double belfry-openings. Their heads were constructed with individual stones of rubble, flints and reused Roman tile-like bricks placed on end and formed into a discernible triangle. The imposts were constructed with individual stones of rubble placed horizontally which protrude from the faces of the walling and into the central void. The jambs were constructed with coursed rubble, flints and reused Roman tile-like bricks all laid horizontally similar to the stonework in the adjoining walling – the stones of the jambs are noticeably slightly larger than the adjoining stones. The openings have cylindrical mid-wall shafts each with an expanding rounded base with a horizontal band of roll-moulding above, and a cushion-capital with a horizontal band of roll-moulding below. The mid-wall shafts support a rectangular through-stone slab, placed horizontally, and extending through the entire depth of the walling of the opening so that its sides overhang the mid-wall shaft. This slab supports above the junction of the heads of both openings. The sills are provided by the top of the coursed rubble stonework directly below. (Note: The one round-headed double belfry-opening in the west face of the tower is a 19th century restoration.) See above right: PHOTO 326. Forncett St Peter 9, showing the belfry-opening in the south face of the tower.

PHOTO 325. Lincoln St Peter-At-Gowts 4.

PHOTO 326. Forncett St Peter 9.

In the upper stage of the square tower of St Andrew's Church, Great Dunham, Norfolk, there are four round-headed double belfry-openings. Their heads were constructed with individual stones of rubble, flints and reused Roman tile-like bricks placed on end and formed into a discernible arch. The openings have stepped imposts constructed with individual stones of rubble and reused Roman tile-like bricks placed horizontally which protrude from the faces of the walling and into the central void. The jambs were constructed with coursed rubble, flints and reused Roman tile-like bricks all laid horizontally and similar to the stonework in the adjoining walling. The openings have cylindrical mid-wall shafts each with rectangular bases and cushion-capitals.

The mid-wall shafts support a rectangular through-stone slab, placed horizontally, and extending through the entire depth of the walling of the opening so that its sides overhang the mid-wall shaft. This slab supports above the junction of the heads of both openings. The sills are provided by the top of the rubble stonework directly below. Additionally, above the belfry-openings in the west and east walls, there are pairs of double-splayed sound-holes constructed with rubble and flints similar to the stonework in the adjoining walling. See adjacent: PHOTO 327. Great Dunham 6, showing the belfry-opening in the west wall with the sound-holes above.

The square tower of St Mary the Virgin Church, Sompting, West Sussex, has pairs of triangular-headed single belfry-openings in the belfry stage in the west and east walls (see Page 156: PHOTO 316. Sompting 1), and pairs of round-headed double belfry-openings in the north and south walls – see below right: PHOTO 328. Sompting 2, showing the pair of round-headed single belfry-openings in the south wall separated by a centrally placed pilaster-strip arrowed red.

Each of the arched heads of the pairs of round-headed belfry-openings in the south wall were constructed with a single stone shaped to provide a curvature in both its upper and lower borders. Each of the arched of the pairs of round-headed belfry-openings in the north wall appear to have been similarly constructed but with the single stone divided into three – the divisions do not result in traditional wedge-shaped voussoirs. The openings do not have imposts. The jambs were constructed with a mixture of horizontally placed, facing stones which are noticeably larger than most of the rubble stonework used in the adjoining walling, and rubble and flints which are similar to the adjoining walling. The openings have cylindrical mid-wall shafts with no bases but with cushion-like capitals. The openings in the north wall have capitals decorated in relief with vertically placed long, scroll-like, leaves above a horizontal band of roll-moulding.

PHOTO 327. Great Dunham 6.

PHOTO 328. Sompting 2.

To support the centre of the head of each of the double belfry-openings a rectangular through-stone slab has been placed horizontally on top of the mid-wall shaft. The slab extends through the entire depth of the walling of the opening so that its sides overhang the mid-wall shaft. The slab supports above the junction of the heads of both openings. The sills are provided by the rubble stonework directly below.

In both the lower and upper belfry levels of the square tower of St Michael's Church, Oxford, Oxfordshire, there are round-headed double belfry-openings. There are four round-headed double belfry-openings in the lower belfry level and three round-headed double belfry-openings in the upper belfry level – the belfry-opening in the east wall in the upper belfry level is not Anglo-Saxon. All seven surviving belfry-openings are of similar construction. See adjacent: PHOTO 329. Oxford 7, showing the belfry-openings in the lower and upper stages

PHOTO 329. Oxford 7.

of the west wall on the left-hand side and those in the south wall on the right-hand side. The arched heads are each constructed with individual stones of rubble placed on end and formed into a discernible arch. The openings have stepped, dressed, imposts protruding from the faces of the walling and into the central void. The jambs were constructed with some larger facing stones laid horizontally but they also include rubble little different to the random rubble stonework in the adjoining walling.

PHOTO 330. Oxford 8.

The openings have mid-wall shafts provided by baluster-shafts. The baluster-shafts increase in circumference towards the centre where a single, narrow, central, horizontal, band of stonework is bordered, top and bottom, by the cutting away of the adjoining stonework to leave a distinctive horizontal, almost U-shaped, groove. The baluster-shafts do not have capitals but do have rounded, expanding, conical-like bases separated from the rest of the shaft by a horizontal rounded band of stonework similar to roll-moulding.

The mid-wall shafts support a rectangular through-stone slab, placed horizontally, and extending through the entire depth of the walling of the opening so that its sides overhang the mid-wall shaft. This slab supports above the junction of the heads of both openings. The slab is similarly stepped like the imposts above the jambs of the opening. The sills are provided by the top of the rubble stonework directly below. See above right: PHOTO 330. Oxford 8, showing the lower belfry-opening in the west wall.

DOUBLE BELFRY-OPENINGS WITH HOOD-MOULDING, STRIP-WORK AND SOUND-HOLES
In the upper stage of the square tower of St Mary the Virgin Church, Ovingham, Northumberland, there are four round-headed double belfry-openings with hood-moulding, strip-work and sound-holes. Their heads were each cut out of the centre of the lower horizontal face of a single square lintel. The openings have square imposts protruding from the faces of the walling and into the central void, and also extending to separate the strip-work below from the hood-moulding above. The jambs were constructed with stonework of a similar size, and laid in similar courses, to the rubble stonework in the adjoining walling. The openings have cylindrical mid-wall shafts without bases or capitals.

The mid-wall shafts support a rectangular through-stone slab, placed horizontally, and extending through the entire depth of the walling of the opening so that its sides overhang the mid-wall shaft. This slab supports above the junction of the heads of both openings. The sills are provided by a single, projecting, rectangular stone which supports the mid-wall shaft, the central voids, the jambs, and extends to support the protruding, strip-work, parallel to the jambs – the strip-work also has distinctive, square, bases. The sill of the south opening appears to have been broken.

Supported by the tops of the extended imposts a semi-circular band of hood-moulding with its own square bases

PHOTO 331. Ovingham 3.

projects from the face of the walling above the lintels. Below the bottom of the extended imposts, and parallel to the jambs, are bands of protruding, vertical, strip-work with distinctive square bases. Among the intervening stonework between the tops of the lintel heads and the hood-moulding – the semi-circular tympanum - is a single stone which has had a circular sound-hole cut out. See Page 162 bottom right: PHOTO 331. Ovingham 3, showing the belfry-opening in the south wall.

St Andrew's Church, Bywell, Northumberland, has four round-headed double belfry-openings with hood-moulding, strip-work and sound-holes, in the upper stage of the square tower. Their heads were each cut out of the centre of the lower horizontal face of a single square lintel. The openings have square imposts protruding from the faces of the walling and into the central void, and also extending to separate the strip-work below from the hood-moulding above. The jambs were constructed with stonework of a similar size, and laid in similar courses, to the rubble stonework in the adjoining walling – the jambs include some larger stones. The openings have cylindrical mid-wall shafts without bases or capitals. See adjacent: PHOTO 332. Bywell 6, showing the belfry-opening in the south wall.

PHOTO 332. Bywell 6.

The mid-wall shafts support a rectangular through-stone slab, placed horizontally, and extending through the entire depth of the walling of the opening so that its sides overhang the mid-wall shaft. This slab supports above the junction of the heads of both openings. The sills are provided by a row of horizontal rectangular stones, originally projecting, which supported the mid-wall shaft, the central voids, the jambs, and extended to support the protruding, strip-work, parallel to the jambs – the strip-work has distinctive, square, bases. The stones of the sill supporting the mid-wall shaft and the two central voids are damaged and no longer project as much from the face of the wall as they once did.

Supported by the tops of the extended imposts a semi-circular band of hood-moulding with its own square bases (the east base appears to be mostly missing) projects from the face of the walling above the lintels. Below the bottom of the extended imposts, and parallel to the jambs, are bands of protruding, vertical, strip-work with distinctive square bases. Among the intervening stonework between the tops of the lintel heads and the hood-moulding – the semi-circular tympanum - is a single stone which has had a circular sound-hole cut out. To the side of the opening, and roughly in line with the central sound-hole, are two further similar circular sound-holes cut out of a single stone, one on each side.

In the upper stage of the square tower of St Cuthbert's Church, Billingham, County Durham, there are four round-headed double belfry-openings with hood-moulding, strip-work and sound-holes. Their arched heads are each cut out of the centre of the lower horizontal face of a half-through stone square lintels. The openings have square, through-stone, imposts protruding from the faces of the walling and into the central void, and also extending to separate the strip-work below from the hood-moulding above. The jambs were constructed with stonework of a similar size, and laid in similar courses, to the stonework in the adjoining walling – the jambs include some larger stones; none of the stones in the jambs are through-stones. The openings have roughly circular mid-wall shafts without bases or capitals.

The mid-wall shafts support a rectangular through-stone slab, placed horizontally, and extending through the entire depth of the walling of the opening so that its sides overhang the mid-wall shaft. This slab supports above the junction of the heads of both openings. The sills are provided by a single, projecting, rectangular through-stone. See adjacent: PHOTO 333. Billingham 7, showing the belfry-opening in the north wall – its sill appears to have had a partial replacement inserted – not Anglo-Saxon.

PHOTO 333. Billingham 7.

Supported by the tops of the extended imposts a semi-circular band of hood-moulding with its own square bases projects from the face of the walling above the lintels. Below the bottom of the extended imposts, and parallel to the jambs, are bands of protruding, vertical, strip-work with distinctive square bases. Among the intervening stonework between the tops of the lintel heads and the hood-moulding – the semi-circular tympanum - is a single stone which has had a sound-hole cut out. These sound-holes are octagonal star-shaped in the north and south walls, and circular-shaped in the west and east walls.

DOUBLE BELFRY-OPENINGS WITH ARCHED HEADS CUT OUT OF THE SAME SINGLE LINTEL
The third stage of the square tower of St Bene't's Church, Cambridge, Cambridgeshire, has four round-headed double belfry-openings with the arched heads of three of the openings cut out of the centre of the lower horizontal face of the same single lintel. The south opening is the exception with the arched head of each opening cut out of the centre of the lower horizontal face of its own square lintel. The openings have square imposts protruding from the faces of the walling and into the central void. The through-stone jambs were mostly laid in Escomb fashion. The openings have mid-wall baluster-shafts with several horizontal bands and grooves in the centre and above the bases and below the capitals.

The mid-wall shafts support a rectangular through-stone slab, placed horizontally, and extending through the entire depth of the walling of the opening so that its sides overhang the mid-wall shaft. This slab supports the centre of the single lintel above. The sills are provided by the top of the string-course directly below.

Each of the openings have two separate sound-holes at an angle above – one is now missing above the east opening. Externally, they have been constructed with a single facing stone through which a circular aperture has been cut. Internally, they have been constructed of rubble with stones placed to provide the circular aperture on the inner face. Note: each of the double belfry-openings are flanked by 16th century windows. See adjacent: PHOTO 334. Cambridge 10, showing the belfry-opening in the north wall.

PHOTO 334. Cambridge 10.

The fourth stage of the square tower of St Peter's Church, Monkwearmouth, Sunderland, County Durham, has three round-headed double belfry-openings with the arched heads of each of opening cut out of the centre of the lower horizontal face of the same single lintel. See Page 165: PHOTO 335. Monkwearmouth 10, showing the belfry-opening in the south wall. The openings have chamfered imposts protruding from the faces of the walling and into the central void, and also extending to separate the strip-work below from the hood-moulding above. The jambs were constructed with stonework of a similar size, and laid in similar courses, to the rubble stonework in the adjoining walling. The openings have cylindrical mid-wall shafts without bases or capitals.

The mid-wall shafts support a rectangular through-stone slab, placed horizontally, and extending through the entire depth of the walling of the opening so that its sides overhang the mid-wall shaft. This slab supports the centre of the single lintel above. The sills of the openings are provided by a row of horizontal rectangular stones, originally projecting from the faces of the walls, which supported the mid-wall shaft, the central voids, the jambs, and extended to support the protruding, strip-work, parallel to the jambs – the strip-work also has distinctive, square, bases. The stones of the sill supporting the mid-wall shaft and the two central voids are damaged and no longer project as much from the face of the wall as they once did.

PHOTO 335. Monkwearmouth 10.

Supported by the tops of the extended imposts a semi-circular band of hood-moulding with its own square bases projects from the face of the walling above the lintels. Below the bottom of the extended imposts, and parallel to the jambs, are bands of protruding, vertical, strip-work with distinctive square bases. High above the centre of each opening, above the hood-moulding, are two facing stones which have each had a semi-circle cut out to provide a circular sound-hole – these are now blocked and not in their original position which would have been closer to the top of hood-moulding.

DOUBLE BELFRY-OPENINGS CONSTRUCTED IN DIFFERENT STAGES OF THE TOWER INDICATING POSSIBLE DIFFERENT BUILDING PERIODS
In the square tower of St Peter's Church, Barton-Upon-Humber, Lincolnshire, there are four triangular-headed double belfry-openings in the second stage – the west opening is now blocked with its mid-wall shaft now hidden - and three round-headed Saxo-Norman double belfry-openings in the third stage – the west opening dates from the 14th century.

The triangular-headed double belfry-openings have the heads of each opening constructed with pairs of two angled rectangular through-stone slabs which extend upwards from the imposts to meet centrally and form the triangular shape of the head of each opening. Externally, parallel to, and on top of, these slabs, rectangular and trapezoid-shaped stones protrude from the face of the wall to provide hood-moulding. The east opening has label-stops each decorated with a human head – they are very weathered and worn and it is just about possible to discern the head on the south label-stop, the head on the north label-stop is almost unrecognisable. See adjacent: PHOTO 336. Barton-upon-Humber 10, showing the triangular-headed double belfry-opening in the north wall of the second stage with the strip-work arrowed red and the hood-moulding arrowed black.

PHOTO 336. Barton-upon-Humber 10.

The openings have through-stone imposts protruding from faces of walling and into central void and also extending beyond the accompanying strip-work below separating it from hood-moulding above. The through-stone jambs are laid in Escomb fashion. Externally, parallel to the jambs, bands of protruding, vertical, strip-work, with square bases, extend from the imposts to the top of the string-course below.

The openings have cylindrical mid-wall shafts each comprising a single baluster-shaft decorated with horizontal bands of roll-moulding: three separate bands in the centre, one band above the base, and one band below the capital. The mid-wall shafts support a rectangular through-stone slab, placed horizontally, and extending through the entire depth of the walling of the opening so that its sides overhang the mid-wall shaft. This slab supports above the junction of the heads of both openings. The sills of the belfry-openings are provided by the top of the string-course directly below externally, and by the top of the rubble stonework directly below internally.

The round-headed Saxo-Norman double belfry-openings have their arched heads constructed with voussoirs with accompanying concentric, protruding, hood-moulding placed directly on top of the voussoirs. The openings have chamfered imposts protruding from the faces of the walling and into the central void. The jambs were constructed with stonework of a similar size, and laid in similar courses, to the stonework in the adjoining walling. The openings have either cylindrical or square-shaped mid-wall shafts – the shaft of the north opening is decorated with two, separate, horizontal bands of cable-pattern moulding. Only the mid-wall shaft in the north belfry-opening has an identifiable square base. All three mid-wall shafts have cushion-capitals. The mid-wall shafts support a rectangular through-stone slab, placed horizontally, and extending through the entire depth of the walling of the opening so that its sides overhang the mid-wall shaft. This slab supports above the junction of the heads of both openings. The sills of the belfry-openings are provided by the top of the string-course directly below externally, and by the top of the coursed stonework directly below internally. See adjacent: PHOTO 337. Barton-upon-Humber 11, showing the round-headed double belfry-opening in the south wall in the third stage.

PHOTO 337. Barton-upon-Humber 11.

FLAT-HEADED DOUBLE BELFRY-OPENING
In the east wall of the upper stage of the square tower of St Chad's Church, Harpswell, Lincolnshire, is a rare example of a flat-headed double belfry-opening. It has a head comprising a single rectangular lintel. It does not have imposts. The jambs were constructed with a mixture of some larger facing stones laid roughly in a side alternate fashion, and stonework of a similar size, and laid in similar courses, little different to the rubble stonework in the adjoining walling.

It has a cylindrical mid-wall shaft without a base but with a horizontal band of roll-moulding below a conical capital whose shape is altered by the addition of a single, vertical, plant-like feature, on each of the corners. To support the centre of the

PHOTO 338. Harpswell 2.

head of the double-openings a rectangular through-stone slab has been placed horizontally on top of the mid-wall shaft so that its sides overhang the mid-wall shaft. The through-stone slab supports the centre of the flat lintel providing the head above. The sill is provided by the top of the string-course directly below. See Page 166 bottom right: PHOTO 338. Harpswell 2, showing the flat-headed double belfry-opening in the east wall.

The other double belfry-openings, including the now incomplete and blocked west opening, are round-headed. Apart from the head(s), the construction details of the east opening and the other openings are very similar. The round-headed double belfry-openings have each of the arched heads of the individual lights cut out of the centre of the lower horizontal face of a square lintel. See adjacent: PHOTO 339. Harpswell 3, showing the flat-headed double belfry-opening in the east wall on the left, and the round-headed double belfry-opening in the north wall on the right.

PHOTO 339. Harpswell 3.

8. BALUSTERS AND BALUSTER-SHAFTS

Baluster-Shafts were used to decorate each side of some archways, doorways and windows and to form balustrades around altars and shrines. They were also used as the mid-wall shafts in some double belfry-openings – see Page 149, PHOTO 292. Oxford 5, and, Page 162, PHOTO 330. Oxford 8. Some of the balusters and baluster-shafts were lathed turned with the holes at both ends for fitting onto a lathe for turning surviving - others were hand-carved with a chisel.

It is thought that the balusters in St Peter's Church, Monkwearmouth, Sunderland, County Durham, flanked archways or doorways, and provided support for balustrades enclosing altars. See Page 69: PHOTO 70. Monkwearmouth 3 and PHOTO 71. Monkwearmouth 4 showing the pairs of balusters forming part of the jambs flanking the western archway into the ground floor of the porch/tower. Although smaller in size than the balusters in St Paul's Church, Jarrow, County Durham (see Page 168), the balusters at St Peter's were more diverse in scale possibly indicating a variety of different uses.

Nearly all the surviving balusters in St Peter's Church are incomplete and most measure between around 3 inches/7.6 centimetres and 12 inches/30.4 centimetres in height, and between 6 inches/15.2 centimetres and 8 inches/20.2 centimetres in diameter. Two, now in the Monks Dormitory in Durham Cathedral, measure 22½ inches/57.1 centimetres high with an 8½ inch/21.5 centimetre diameter. The pairs of balusters forming part of the jambs of the western archway into the porch/tower in St Peter's Church have a height of 21 inches/53.3 centimetres with a 9¾ inch/24.7 centimetres diameter.

PHOTO 340. Monkwearmouth 11.

Around their circumference the balusters have sets of two, three or four horizontal grooves, in addition, some have rounded and chamfered mouldings. See Page 167 bottom right: PHOTO 340. Monkwearmouth 11, showing some of the baluster-shafts displayed in the church, one showing some of its distinctive original red paint.

Although most of the baluster-shafts at St Paul's Church, Jarrow, are incomplete, they are considered to have originally been of similar height of around 28¾ inches/73 centimetres with a similar diameter of around 12¼ inches/31.7 centimetres. Around their circumference the balusters have horizontal sets of three or four bands of moulding similar to roll-moulding; within each set the bands of moulding were separated from each other by horizontal grooves. Most had holes at both ends for fitting onto a lathe for turning; some of these holes can still be identified. See below: PHOTO 341. Jarrow 7, showing part of a former display of baluster-shafts at St Paul's Church, Jarrow, County Durham (some of these are still displayed) – arrowed red is a baluster showing a complete hole at the top to facilitate lathe-turning.

It is thought that some of the baluster-shafts may have been used to form a balustrade partitioning-off a particular section of the monastic church, for example, for a school for liturgical music. Such a use might be one of the reasons why the baluster-shafts in St Paul's Church. Jarrow, County Durham are generally larger than those in St Peter's Church, Monkwearmouth, Sunderland, County Durham.

PHOTO 341. Jarrow 7.

St John the Baptist Church, Greatham, County Durham, provides a rare example of a ground floor view of two baluster-shafts which at one time were used as mid-wall shafts for double belfry-openings. They each comprise a cylindrical baluster shape with square capitals and bases with chamfered corners. Below the capitals, and above the bases, are protruding horizontal collars of some size extending around the circumference. In addition the centre of the shaft has a similar horizontal collar which is contained within the shape of the baluster rather than protruding. It extends around the circumference and is bordered on each side by a horizontal groove. These baluster-shafts are now used to support the slab of altar in the chancel. See adjacent left: PHOTO 342. Greatham, showing the southern baluster-shaft.

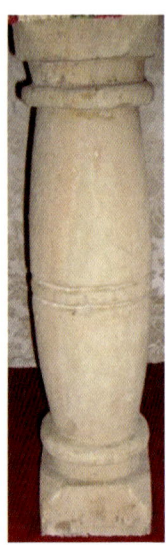

All Saints Church, Brixworth, Northamptonshire has a round-headed triple opening at first floor level in the east wall of the porch/tower. The opening has two baluster-shafts dividing it into three – see Page 136. PHOTO 260. Brixworth 15. See above right: PHOTO 343. Brixworth 17, showing part of the south-east view of the northern baluster-shafts with a round-headed single-splayed clerestory

PHOTO 342. Greatham.

PHOTO 343. Brixworth 17.

Anglo-Saxon Church Architecture & Stone Sculpture   **169**

window in the background. See also: Page 134, PHOTO 254. Earls Barton 4, where a double window externally has its jambs faced with baluster-shafts.

9. STRING-COURSES

String-courses were horizontal lengths of dressed stonework which protruded from the face of a wall up to 4 inches/10 centimetres and mostly measured between 6 inches/15 centimetres and 10 inches/25.3 centimetres in height. String-courses were mostly plain and square in section although some were chamfered and others were moulded. They assisted with the bonding of stonework, the application of plaster, and also, externally, diverted rainwater from running down the face of a wall.

Externally, string-courses often survive complete in length and height when used to help differentiate the external stages of a tower. They may also emphasise the different stages of a tower by the face of the upper stage being "set-back" by around 6 inches/15 centimetres from the face of the stage below. String-courses often provided the sills of belfry-openings, they sometimes provided the sills of windows – see Page 135. PHOTO 257. Worth 4, and also formed part of the external decorative panelling along with pilaster-strips – see Pages 172 to 179. "10. Pilaster-Strips, Pilaster-Buttresses, Hood-Moulding and Strip-Work".

Externally, St Bene't's Church, Cambridge, Cambridgeshire, has two separate square string-courses dividing the square tower into three stages. The upper string-course also provides the sills for each of the round-headed double-belfry-openings. See below left: PHOTO 344: Cambridge 11, showing the string-courses arrowed red on both the east (left-hand) and north (right-hand) sides.

Externally, St Michael's Church, Glentworth, Lincolnshire, has a square string-course which as well as indicating the separation of the square tower into two unequal stages also emphasises that the smaller upper stage is set-back from the larger lower stage. In addition the string-course provides the sill for each of the round-headed double-belfry-openings. See adjacent right: PHOTO 345: Glentworth 9, showing the string-course arrowed red on both the west (left-hand) and south (right-hand) sides.

PHOTO 344. Cambridge 11.

PHOTO 345. Glentworth 9.

Externally, the square tower of St John the Baptist Church, Barnack, Cambridgeshire, has two separate sets of moulded string-courses dividing the square tower into three stages – the top, belfry stage and spire date from the 13th century. What is now the middle stage (Anglo-Saxon) is set-back from the lowest stage (Anglo-Saxon), and what is now the top stage (13th century) is set-back from what is now the middle stage (Anglo-Saxon).

Both string-courses comprise three distinct horizontal bands of dressed stonework. The narrower upper and lower bands project from the face of the wall while the wide central band is set-back and level with the stonework of the face of the walling of the tower. See adjacent left: PHOTO 346. Barnack 16, showing a close-up of the south-west corner of the lower string-course. See adjacent right: PHOTO 347. Barnack 17, showing the string-courses arrowed red on both the west (left-hand) and south (right-hand) sides with rows of vertical pilaster-strips below and above the lower string-course.

PHOTO 346. Barnack 16.

More commonly used on the external facing of walling of square towers, they were seldom used on the external facing of round-towers, string-courses were also used on the external walling of some naves, porticus and chancels.

Externally, St Andrew's Church, Wroxeter, Shropshire, has an incomplete square string-course below the eaves of the north wall of the nave; a 15th century window has been inserted removing some of the string-course. See below right: PHOTO 348. Wroxeter 2, with the incomplete sections of string-course arrowed red.

PHOTO 347. Barnack 17.

Some former external walls of naves with string-courses may now be enclosed within the church because of the addition of later north and south aisles not Anglo-Saxon.

A few examples have string-courses on the internal faces of the walling in the nave. St Wystan's Church, Repton, Derbyshire, provides an exception with internal string-courses also in the crypt - see Page 197: PHOTO 405. Repton 5.

PHOTO 348. Wroxeter 2.

However, where string-courses survive internally on the walling of naves or aisles or chancels, they may not be complete because of the insertion of larger windows and doorways, or new archways or arcades, which are not Anglo-Saxon.

Now internally, St Andrew's Church, Bolam, Northumberland, has an incomplete square string-course below the former eaves of the south wall of the nave; it is now within the 12th century south aisle. See adjacent: PHOTO 349. Bolam 6, string-course arrowed red.

PHOTO 349. Bolam 6.

Internally, there are also some examples where the imposts of a tower archway extend across the whole width of the east face in similar fashion to a string-course.

Internally, St Mary Magdalen Church, Rothwell, Lincolnshire, has a round-headed tower archway with imposts which extend across the full width of the west wall of the nave in similar fashion to a string-course. Note: the imposts of the archway on the opposite sides of the central void are chamfered, the imposts extending along the west wall of the nave are square in section and not chamfered. See adjacent: PHOTO 350. Rothwell 2, with string-course-like imposts - those square in section arrowed red, those chamfered arrowed black.

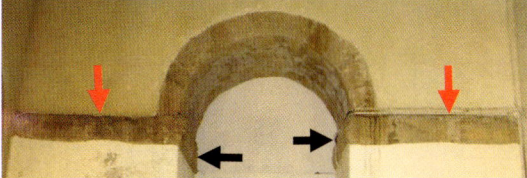

PHOTO 350. Rothwell 2.

Internally, St John the Baptist Church, Barnack, Cambridgeshire, has a round-headed tower archway with imposts which extend across the full width of the west wall of the nave and the east wall of the tower in similar fashion to a string-course. Similar to the string-courses on the external walling of the tower, these imposts comprise three distinct horizontal bands of dressed stonework. The narrow upper and lower bands project from the face of the wall while the wide central band is set-back and level with the stonework opposite the central void but noticeably less recessed along the west wall of the nave and the east wall of the tower. All three bands have a distinct horizontal groove in their centre. See adjacent: PHOTO 351. Barnack 18, showing the northern base, jamb, pilaster-strip and imposts of the archway with the string-course-like imposts arrowed red.

Internally, St Bene't's Church, Cambridge, Cambridgeshire, has a round-headed tower archway with imposts which extend across the full width of the west wall of the nave and the east wall of the tower in similar fashion to a string-course. These imposts are divided into differently sized half-round and half-square horizontal bands by grooves. See adjacent: PHOTO 352: Cambridge 12, showing the string-courses arrowed red.

PHOTO 351. Barnack 18.

PHOTO 352. Cambridge 12.

Internally, Holy Trinity Church, Great Paxton, Cambridgeshire, has a chamfered string-course above the arcades of round-headed archways on the north and south walls of the nave. The church has been extended westwards at a later, not Anglo-Saxon, date, so how far the string-courses extended westwards is now unclear, but the string-courses do extend from west to east to reach a point where it is thought was the position of the former western archway of then central crossing - just before the evident unevenness in the walling; all trace of this western archway has been removed. See adjacent left: PHOTO 353: Great Paxton 11, showing the string-course arrowed red along the south wall, and above right: PHOTO 354.

PHOTO 353. Great Paxton 11.

PHOTO 354. Great Paxton 12.

Great Paxton 12, showing the string-course arrowed red along the north wall.

Rather than dressed stonework the string-courses in the square tower at St Katherine's Church, Little Bardfield, Essex, were constructed with up to three rows of rubble, including flints, noticeably protruding from the faces of the walling unlike the similar stonework above and below. These string-courses help differentiate the set-back nature of the stages of the tower. See above left: PHOTO 355. Little Bardfield 7, showing the south wall with the string-courses arrowed red.

PHOTO 355. Little Bardfield 7.

PHOTO 356. Colchester 11.

In the square tower of Holy Trinity Church, Colchester, Essex, it has string-courses constructed with two horizontal rows of reused Roman tile-like bricks laid flat with their narrow edges projecting from the faces of the walls. See above right: PHOTO 356. Colchester 11, showing the south and west walls with the string-courses arrowed red.

10. PILASTER-STRIPS, PILASTER-BUTTRESSES, HOOD-MOULDING AND STRIP-WORK

Pilaster-strips, pilaster-buttresses, hood-moulding and strip-work were decorative architectural features on the faces of walling; along with string-courses (see Pages 169 to 172). They can be found both externally and internally across the faces of walling. They also provided the "frame" concentric or parallel to, or abutting, individual archways, doorways, windows (rarely) and belfry-openings with the pilaster-strips or strip-work extending vertically down from the hood-moulding sometimes separated from each other by extended imposts.

Some descriptions use the terms pilaster-strip and strip-work interchangeably when describing the decorative frame around an individual architectural feature. In the same sentence strip-work may be described as taking on the form of pilaster-strips or pilasters. Generally, the term pilaster-strip is used when describing the decorative frame internally of the more substantial archways, whereas the term strip-work is used when describing the decorative frame externally of smaller architectural features such as belfry-openings.

Externally, like string-courses, pilaster-strips, hood-moulding and strip-work could help to throw water clear of the wall and where they "framed" an architectural feature they also helped preserve the structural integrity of walling.

Pilaster-strips, hood-moulding and strip-work usually comprised, plain, variable, lengths of dressed stonework incorporated into, and protruding from the walling. Where the individual stones comprising this stonework were vertically-placed some were constructed in a similar fashion to long and short quoining, others, were horizontally-placed to mirror the coursing of the adjoining walling. Alternatively, where walling was constructed with rubble and flints, or reused Roman material, then pilaster-strips, hood-moulding and strip-work would be constructed with similar material.

Pilaster-Strips, hood-moulding and strip-work could extend between 4 inches/10.1 centimetres to 12 inches/30.4 centimetres wide and protrude between 1½ inches/3.7 centimetres to 6 inches/15.2 centimetres from the face of the wall. See also "Pilaster-Buttresses" following. Externally, weathering, the application of plaster at different dates, and restorations, can increase or decrease the width and how far pilaster-strips, hood-moulding and strip-work now protrude from the face of the wall. For an exception, and with distinctively large pilaster-strips internally, see Page 178: PHOTO 366. Stow-in-Lindsey 14.

Parts of three of the four sides of pilaster-strips, hood-moulding and strip-work were exposed to view, the full half-circumference or width of one face, parts of the depth of each of the two adjacent sides protruding from the face of the wall; the fourth side (face) of whatever shape was internal to the stonework of the walling and consequently hidden from view. Externally, some pilaster-strips and strip-work extended up the face of the walling from a corbel-like, base, and had corbel-like capitals supporting the arched or triangular heads of the hood-moulding above.

Pilaster-strips could be used externally across the face of the width of walling dividing it into panels, sometimes interrupted by doorways, windows and belfry-openings. They assisted in the vertical alignment of walling particularly where the walls were constructed of rubble or flint and could also assist with the application of plaster. They were too narrow and slight in projection from the face of the walling to add strength to a wall. On other occasions, both externally and internally, pilaster-strips formed a blind arcade with no voids between and with the individual bays having semi-circular or triangular heads.

In some internal examples an archway may be accompanied by two parallel bands of pilaster-strips, an inner half-round band and an outer half-square band both of which may continue in two similarly constructed and shaped bands of stonework forming the heads of the opening and described as "hood-moulding".

Hood-moulding was the term mostly used for the extension from the vertical pilaster-strips and strip-work of dressed and shaped stonework forming the heads of the bays of arcades, archways, doorways, belfry-openings and occasionally windows. Hood-moulding was concentric with, or placed directly on top of, the arched head, or, when the opening had a triangular head, the hood-moulding was similar in shape and size to the head itself and placed directly on top.

Hood-moulding could also be constructed with stonework similar to the rubble and flints in the adjoining walling, including, reused Roman material when this was available. Individual stones, flints and reused Roman tile-like bricks were placed on end to form a discernible arched or triangular head. With a few examples reused Roman bricks display one of their long sides and were carefully shaped and sized and placed horizontally on top of each other.

Internally, chancel and tower archways, and archways providing access into porticus or transepts, may be decorated with pilaster-strips, strip-work and hood-moulding only on the side facing the congregation, but some examples will have pilaster-strips, strip-work and hood-moulding on both sides.

In addition to hood-moulding a few examples of the most important archways and doorways had "label-stops" – see Page 60: PHOTO 38. Cambridge 1, PHOTO 39. Cambridge 2, and PHOTO 40. Cambridge 3; Page 61: PHOTO 41. Deerhurst 2, PHOTO 42. Deerhurst 3, and PHOTO 43. Deerhurst 4; Page 98: PHOTO 125. Deerhurst 5, and PHOTO 126. Deerhurst 6; Page 108: PHOTO 158. Deerhurst 13.

In Norman and later periods hood-moulding continued, but pilaster-strips and strip-work parallel to, or abutting, the jambs did not, perhaps because of the development of "orders" - shafts and columns accompanying the jambs. Openings with pilaster-strips and strip-work are indicative of Anglo-Saxon construction.

PILASTER-STRIPS AND HOOD-MOULDING EXTERNALLY
Both the north and south walls of the lower stage of the square tower at St Peter's Church, Barton-upon-Humber, Lincolnshire, are decorated with two arcades of pilaster-strips constructed with dressed stonework and laid in similar fashion to long and short quoining, and, with pilaster-strips forming the semi-circular and triangular heads.

The lower arcade is round-headed. At ground level the pilaster-strips extend upwards from distinctly large, square, corbel-like, bases to reach square, corbel-like, capitals supporting the round-headed arcading above. On top of the centre of each of the arched heads of the lower arcade, large, square, corbel-like bases support the pilaster-strips which extend upwards to reach square, corbel-like, capitals supporting the triangular-head arcading above. The triangular heads of the arcading support the horizontal, square, string-course separating the first stage from the second stage of the tower. In addition to the different nature of their heads, the positions of the heads of the two rows of pilaster-strip arcading provide an alternating pattern.

In both the north and south walls the positioning of the pilaster-strips varied to accommodate within the bays of the arcades ground-floor doorways which each necessitated a wider bay. At first floor level in both the north and south walls round-headed double-windows interrupt a vertical pilaster-strip. See adjacent: PHOTO 357. Barton-upon-Humber 12, showing the north wall of the tower with the arcade of round-headed of pilaster-strips arrowed red, and the arcade of triangular-headed pilaster-strips arrowed blue.

PHOTO 357.
Barton-upon-Humber 12.

The four stages of the square tower of All Saints Church, Earls Barton, Northamptonshire, were each decorated with an arcade of pilaster-strips constructed with dressed stonework and laid in similar fashion to long and short quoining, and, with pilaster-strips forming the semi-circular and triangular shapes on the second, third and fourth stages – those in the fourth, top, stage are incomplete. The pilaster-strips in the three lower stages extend vertically from square, corbel-like, bases up to each of the three horizontal string-courses without ending in a distinctive head; the square, corbel-like, bases were placed directly on top of the string-courses below separating the first from the second stage and the second from the third stage.

The top stage has angled pilaster-strips which meet centrally to form a triangular shape; they rise from the horizontal, square, string-course below. Above each of the triangular heads is a square, corbel-like, base from which a vertical pilaster-strip extends. The top stage is lacking most of its upper string-course and some sections of its vertical pilaster-strips.

Between the vertical pilaster-strips in the third stage there are additional pilaster-strips placed at angles to form an overall diamond shape comprising an upper triangle supported by a triangle below resting on the square string-course below. These diamond shapes extend from, and share with the vertical pilaster-strips, the square, corbel-like, bases which rest on the square string-course below. Above each of the heads of the diamond shapes is a square corbel-like base from which a vertical pilaster-strip extends.

Between the vertical pilaster-strips in the second stage there are pilaster-strips forming semi-circles. These extend from, and share with vertical pilaster-strips, the square, corbel-like, bases which rest on the chamfered string-course below.

In the south wall the pilaster-strips are interrupted in the first stage by a double-splayed double-window, in the second stage by a round-headed doorway, and in the third stage by a triangular-headed window. See above right: PHOTO 358. Earls Barton 8, showing the south wall of the tower with the rows of pilaster-strips arrowed red, and the string-courses arrowed black.

PHOTO 358. Earls Barton 8.

Whilst the other three walls have similar pilaster-strips there are gaps caused in the west wall by the ground-floor round-headed doorway and the round-headed window in the second stage. There are no gaps in the pilaster-strips on the north wall apart from the triangular-headed window in the third stage. The second stage of the east wall was originally beneath the nave roof and consequently was not decorated with pilaster-strips.

The walls of the two surviving Anglo-Saxon stages of the square tower of St John the Baptist Church, Barnack, Cambridgeshire, were each divided into four panels in each stage by vertical pilaster-strips constructed with dressed stonework and laid in similar fashion to long and short quoining. At the bottom of the walls in the first stage the pilaster-strips extend vertically from square, corbel like bases. The pilaster-strips have no capitals when they reach the lower part of the string-course above separating the first stage from the second stage. In the second stage the pilaster-strips extend from half-round, corbel like bases, placed on the upper part of the string-course separating the first stage from the second stage. The pilaster-strips have no capitals when they reach the lower part of the string-course separating the second Anglo-Saxon stage from the third 13th century stage above. The placement of the triangular-headed window in the west wall interrupts the central pilaster-strip. The position of the central pilaster-strip on the east wall indicates the position of the top of the ridge of the former Anglo-Saxon nave roofline. See Page 170. PHOTO 347. Barnack 17, showing the south and west walls of the tower.

St Peter's Church, Stanton Lacy, Shropshire, has a number of incomplete vertical pilaster-strips constructed with dressed stonework and laid in similar fashion to long and short quoining; some have square, corbel-like, bases. The pilaster-strips can be identified on the west and north walls of the nave, and the north and south walls of the north transept.

In the north wall of the nave there is a blocked, round-head doorway with vertical pilaster-strips with square, corbel-like, bases adjacent to its jambs and imposts. Dressed pilaster-strips, hood-moulding, extend from tops of the vertical pilaster-strips to form the semi-circular head of the doorway. See adjacent: PHOTO 359. Stanton Lacy 1, showing the north wall with the row of pilaster-strips arrowed red, and the blocked round-headed doorway arrowed black.

PHOTO 359. Stanton Lacy 1.

For further examples of pilaster-strips and hood-moulding and strip-work see also:
- Tower Archways: Pages 71 to 74, archways in a central crossing in a cruciform church on Pages 79 to 82, nave and chancel archways providing access into a separate central area on Pages 82 to 85, and chancel archways on Pages 85 to 87.
- Doorways: Pages 91 to 94, Pages 95 to 100, Page 104, and Pages 107 to 108.
- Windows: Page 120, Page 124, Pages 136 to 138.
- Double-Belfry-openings: Pages 162 to 166.

The round tower of St Mary's Church, Tasburgh, Norfolk, has two, blind arcades of pilaster-strips. Both arcades were constructed with a mixture of rubble and flints, and, with individual stones and flints placed on end to form the arched heads – the arched heads spring from the vertical pilaster-strips without any intervening corbel-like capitals or imposts.

The lower, first floor level, arcade is complete, whilst the arched heads of the upper, second floor level, arcade were probably removed when the upper part of the tower was rebuilt in 1385. For each of the arcades, the main rubble and flint stonework of the walling was recessed, or cut-back, to provide a "sunken" arcade. The positions of the two rows of arcading provide an alternating pattern with the arched head of each bay of the lower arcade below the solid walling between the jambs of the upper arcade. See adjacent left: PHOTO 360. Tasburgh, showing the south face of the tower with the lower complete row of arcading arrowed red, and the upper incomplete row of arcading arrowed black.

The round tower of St Matthias Church, Thorpe-Next-Haddiscoe, Norfolk, has an incomplete, probably round-headed, blind arcade of pilaster-strips constructed with a mixture of rubble and flints. The main rubble and flint stonework of the walling was recessed, or cut-back, to provide a "sunken" arcade. The likely round-heads of the

PHOTO 360. Tasburgh.   PHOTO 361. Thorpe-Next-Haddiscoe 3.

arcade were removed with the construction of the Norman belfry-openings above. See above right: PHOTO 361. Thorpe-Next-Haddiscoe 3, showing the south face of the tower with the row of arcading arrowed red.

In the lower belfry stage of the square tower of Holy Trinity Church, Colchester, Essex, there are arcades of round-headed pilaster-strips constructed with reused Roman bricks. All four walls have these arcades but only the arcade on the south wall is now easily identifiable.

PHOTO 362. Colchester 12.

The vertical pilaster-strips extend upwards from the square string-course of reused Roman tile-like bricks separating the second stage of the tower from the third stage. The reused Roman bricks display one of their long sides and have been carefully shaped and sized and placed horizontally on top of each other to form the arched heads. They have no supporting imposts.

Note: the vertical pilaster-strips of the western bay of the arcade in the south wall continue upwards past the sides of the arched head of the arcade up to the level of the upper belfry-stage. See above: PHOTO 362. Colchester 12, showing the south wall of the tower with the row of arcading arrowed red.

PILASTER-STRIPS AND HOOD-MOULDING INTERNALLY

Internally, St John the Baptist Church, Barnack, Cambridgeshire, has a round-headed tower archway with an east face (facing the nave) accompanied by pilaster-strips laid in long and short fashion, and parallel to, and abutting, the jambs, and hood-moulding which sits on top of the voussoirs. See adjacent left: PHOTO 363. Barnack 18, showing the east face

PHOTO 363. Barnack 18.   PHOTO 364. Wittering 6.

of the archway with the pilaster-strips arrowed red and the hood-moulding arrowed black.

Internally, All Saints Church, Wittering, Cambridgeshire, has a round-headed chancel archway with accompanying half-square pilaster-strips and hood-moulding. The pilaster-strips have stepped square bases standing on same square single plinth as the bases of the cylindrical shafts and square jambs of the archway. See above right: PHOTO 364. Wittering 6, showing the west face of the archway with the pilaster-strips arrowed red and the hood-moulding arrowed black.

Internally, the heads and jambs of archways may be complemented by double rows of adjacent but separate pilaster-strips – an inner half-round band and an outer half-square band. The top of such pilaster-strips may terminate in the imposts supporting the archways and the bases may terminate in bulbous corbels above a stepped plinth.

St Helen's Church, Skipwith, North Yorkshire, has an internal tower archway which on both sides has inner, half-round, and outer half-square, bands of pilaster-strips parallel to the jambs and hood-moulding concentric with the arched head. See adjacent left: PHOTO 365. Skipwith 5, showing east side of south jamb with inner, half-round, band of pilaster-strip arrowed red, and outer half-square, band of pilaster-strip arrowed black.

St Mary's Church, Stow-in-Lindsey, Lincolnshire has four megalithic round-headed archways with the jambs accompanied by two bands of parallel pilaster-strips. The pilaster-strips comprise an inner half-round band up to 15 inches/38.1 centimetres wide, which protrudes from the face of the wall up to 11 inches/27.9 centimetres, and an outer half-square band up to 11½ inches/29.1 centimetres wide, which protrudes from the face of the wall up to 11 inches/27.9 centimetres. The tops of the pilaster-strips terminate abutting the imposts supporting the arched heads above and the bases terminate in bulbous corbels above a stepped plinth. See above right: PHOTO 366. Stow-in-Lindsey 14, showing north-west face of north archway with inner, half-round, band of pilaster-strip arrowed red, and outer half-square, band of pilaster-strip arrowed black, impost arrowed blue, pilaster-strip bulbous corbel bases arrowed green.

PHOTO 365. Skipwith 5.

PHOTO 366. Stow-in-Lindsey 14.

Incomplete blind arcades of round-headed pilaster-strips decorate the interior faces of the north and south walls of the nave of St Andrew's Church, Great Dunham, Norfolk. The facing stonework of the walling has been recessed, or cut-back, to provide a "sunken" arcade. Within the arcade some of the bays have rectangular capitals in relief: one rectangular capital has two distinct stepped horizontal bands of roll-moulding below; another capital has a central band of raised and sunken vertical triangles; and one other capital has a central band comprising a series of diagonal crosses in a row, each contained within a rectangular box. All the round-headed pilaster-strips have stepped bases flush with the faces of the walls. See adjacent: PHOTO 367. Great Dunham 7, showing the arcade in the north wall arrowed red, with a round-headed double-splayed window above towards the west/left end arrowed black.

PHOTO 367. Great Dunham 7.

St Mary Magdalene Church, Geddington, Northamptonshire, has a triangular-headed arcade of pilaster-strips on the north face of the north wall of the nave; a later inserted Anglo-Saxon window has destroyed two of the bays of the arcading. The stones providing the vertical pilaster-strips, the imposts, and the triangular heads are all constructed with individual stones of requisite size and shape. To accommodate the arcade the facing stonework of the walling of the individual bays has been recessed but the vertical pilaster-strips, the imposts, and the triangular heads, are all flush with the face of the wall. See adjacent: PHOTO 368. Geddington 3, showing the row of triangular-headed arcading arrowed red.

PHOTO 368. Geddington 3.

PILASTER-BUTTRESSES

Despite the general lack of the use of buttresses during the Anglo-Saxon period, a few churches, mostly in Kent, but also in Essex, have what are described as "pilaster-buttresses" mostly used on the external angles of the walling. Pilaster-Buttresses were more than twice the width of pilaster-strips - up to around 24 inches/60.9 centimetres wide and protruded up to around 24 inches/60.9 centimetres from the face of the wall. They extended vertically from the base of the wall up to around mid-wall height in the wall. Usually placed near the corner of the building, one pilaster-buttress was placed on one wall and another was placed on the adjoining wall. Pilaster-Buttresses were also placed along the length of a wall. The material used in pilaster-buttresses was a mixture of rubble with reused Roman tile-like bricks where these were available. Most pilaster-buttresses surviving are incomplete and appear like rough vertical stubs of stonework protruding from the wall.

The nave of St Peter-on-the-Wall Church, Bradwell-on-Sea, Essex, has incomplete pilaster-buttresses: two on its south wall, two on its west wall, and three on its north wall. See adjacent: PHOTO 369. Bradwell-on-Sea 2, showing the pilaster-buttresses arrowed red on the south and west walls.

11. STAIRWAYS

Doorways at first floor level and above in porches, towers, naves, crossings and chancels were accessed by stairways or ladders but as these were mostly made of wood few traces of their existence survive – but see Pages 184 to 185, St Andrew's Church, Brigstock, Northamptonshire where there is a stone stair turret but without an internal spiral stone stairway. Stone stair turrets were also constructed with spiral stone stairways. Three stone stair turrets with spiral stone stairways survive, a fourth survives in a fragmentary and ruinous form. The methods used in the construction of these spiral stone stairways was distinctive and characteristically Anglo-Saxon rather than the methods used by Norman and later builders.

PHOTO 369. Bradwell-on-Sea 2.

Anglo-Saxon spiral stone stairways were constructed with a central pillar, the "newel", around which the steps radiated. The newel rose vertically from the ground floor of the stair turret to the top of where the stairway ended. In two of the surviving spiral stone stairways at St Mary's Church, Broughton, Lincolnshire, and All Saints Church, Hough-on-the-Hill, Lincolnshire, the newel consists of separate, jointed, vertical sections of cylindrical stonework with each section rising above several treads of the individual steps adjacent. See Pages 180 to 182. In the surviving spiral stone stairways at All Saints Church, Brixworth,

Northamptonshire, and the ruins of the Anglo-Saxon Cathedral and Bishops Palace at North Elmham, Norfolk, the newel consisted of a single, continuous, vertical column of rubble with no separate jointed vertical sections of cylindrical stonework. See Pages 182 to 184.

In all four examples of spiral stone stairways the treads of the individual steps were constructed separately from the newel with each tread notched into the newel on their inner side and notched into the inner face of the exterior wall of the stair turret on their outer side. In the examples of St Mary's Church, Broughton, Lincolnshire and All Saints Church, Brixworth, Northamptonshire, the individual steps and the stairway were supported by a roughly round vaulted rubble ceiling underneath. In the case of All Saints Church, Hough-on-the-Hill, Lincolnshire, the individual steps and the stairway have no supporting ceiling underneath. Given the fragmentary remains, it is not now possible to say what the support was underneath the stairway in the ruins of the Anglo-Saxon Cathedral and Bishops Palace at North Elmham, Norfolk.

The Anglo-Saxon method of construction of these spiral stone stairways contrasted with those methods used in Norman and later periods where both the central newel and individual treads of the steps were all formed of the same jointed sections of stonework – each tread an adjunct of the central newel. It is for this reason that St John the Baptist Church, Great Hale, Lincolnshire, has not been included in the group of churches identified in the following pages with stone stairways built in the Anglo-Saxon fashion.

St Mary's Church, Broughton, Lincolnshire, has a stair turret constructed with coursed rubble and ashlar-like stonework; it includes three flat-headed single-splayed windows. See adjacent: PHOTO 370. Broughton 4, showing the exterior view of the stair turret from the south.

Internally, the spiral stone stairway was built in "Anglo-Saxon fashion". The central newel consists of separate jointed vertical sections of cylindrical stonework which mostly measure between 31½ inches/80 centimetres and 42 inches/106.6 centimetres high; the base (ground) section of the newel is 14 inches/35.5 centimetres high, and the fourth section of the newel above this is 18 inches/45.6 centimetres high. The diameter of the newel is up to 13½ inches/34.2 centimetres.

PHOTO 370.
Broughton 4.

From the base of the turret there are twenty-seven complete steps up to a flat-headed doorway which provides access into the first floor of the adjacent square tower. Up from this doorway there are ten further complete steps and two incomplete steps. It is presumed the stairway continued upwards and led up to a doorway providing access into the second floor of the adjacent square tower. The steps comprise large, roughly dressed stones some with concrete, not Anglo-Saxon, to ensure a level tread. The individual steps measure on average up to 10½ inches/26.7 centimetres high, up to 28¼ inches/71.6 centimetres wide (between the newel and the inner wall of the stair turret), with a maximum depth of tread of up to 10½ inches/26 centimetres. The individual steps of the stairway were supported by a roughly round vaulted rubble ceiling underneath.

See adjacent: left: PHOTO 371. Broughton 5, showing part of the interior of the stair turret, with the newel arrowed red, the steps arrowed black, and the inner face of the exterior wall of the stair turret arrowed blue. See above right: PHOTO 372. Broughton 6, showing the top section of the newel where it has been cut away arrowed red.

PHOTO 371. Broughton 5.

PHOTO 372. Broughton 6.

All Saints Church, Hough-on-the-Hill, Lincolnshire, has a stair turret constructed with coursed rubble stonework. It includes ten windows where the external faces comprise a single stone slab through which differently-shaped apertures have been cut. See Pages 126 to 127: PHOTOS 224. Hough-on-the-Hill 5, to PHOTO 229. Hough-on-the Hill 10. See also:

- Page 99: PHOTO 132. Hough-on-the-Hill 1, showing the stepped head of the flat-headed doorway providing access at first floor level from the stair turret into the tower.

- Page 105: PHOTO 149. Hough-on-the-Hill 2, showing the stepped head of the flat-headed doorway providing ground floor access from the tower into the stair turret, and PHOTO 150. Hough-on-the-Hill 3, showing the east face of the flat-headed doorway providing ground floor access from the tower into the stair turret.

- Page 108: PHOTO 159. Hough-on-the-Hill 4, showing the west face of the triangular-headed doorway providing access at second floor level from the stair turret into the tower.

See adjacent: PHOTO 373. Hough-on-the-Hill 11, showing the exterior view of the stair turret from the north-west.

Internally, the spiral stone stairway was built in "Anglo-Saxon fashion". The central newel consists of separate jointed vertical sections of cylindrical stonework which mostly measure between 24½ inches/62.2 centimetres and 43½ inches/110.5 centimetres high. The diameter of the newel is 18 inches/45.6 centimetres and where it is replaced with a later, not Anglo-Saxon, newel it has an 8 inch/20.2 centimetre diameter – see Page 182 top right: PHOTO. 375. Hough-on-the-Hill 13, showing the top section of the newel with the Anglo-Saxon newel arrowed red, and the later, narrower newel, not Anglo-Saxon, arrowed black.

PHOTO 373. Hough-on-the-Hill 11.

From the base of the turret there are forty-five complete steps which reach up to five steps below the triangular-headed doorway providing access into the second floor of the adjacent square tower. At this point the newel has been replaced with a later, not Anglo-

Saxon, newel. The replacement newel is formed as part of the steps themselves which continue upwards – not an Anglo-Saxon method of construction. The Anglo-Saxon steps comprise large, roughly dressed stones some with concrete, not Anglo-Saxon, to ensure a level tread. The individual

PHOTO 374. Hough-on-the-Hill 12.

PHOTO 375. Hough-on-the-Hill 13.

steps measure between 3 inches/7.6 centimetres and 6 inches/15.2 centimetres high, up to 32 inches/81.2 centimetres wide (between the newel and the inner wall of the stair turret), with a maximum depth of tread of between 11 inches/27.9 centimetres and 18 inches/45.6 centimetres. The individual steps of the stairway have no supporting ceiling underneath. See above left: PHOTO. 374. Hough-on-the Hill 12, showing part of the interior of the stair turret, with the newel arrowed red, the steps arrowed black and the inner face of the exterior wall of the stair turret arrowed blue.

All Saints Church, Brixworth, Northamptonshire, has a stair turret constructed with random rubble stonework including herringbone masonry. It includes sixteen flat-headed single-splayed windows – some are now blocked. See adjacent: PHOTO 376. Brixworth 18, showing the exterior view of the stair turret from the south-west. See also Page 127: PHOTO 230. Brixworth 13, and Photo 231. Brixworth 14.

Internally, the spiral stone stairway was built in "Anglo-Saxon fashion". The central newel consists of a single cylindrical, continuous, column of rubble which rises vertically from the ground floor of the stair turret up to where it now terminates near second floor level – it does not consist of separate jointed vertical sections of cylindrical stonework. The diameter of the newel is 24½ inches/62.1 centimetres. The top of the newel has been damaged and cut away. See Page 183 top left: PHOTO 377. Brixworth 19, showing the top section of the newel where it has been cut away, arrowed red.

From the base of the turret almost to the top, fifty-seven steps survive. Just under half seem without additional stonework or concrete to restore their structure but some have been noticeably more restored than others at a later, not Anglo-Saxon, date to ensure a level tread. There are twenty-one steps up from the base of the

PHOTO 376. Brixworth 18.

stair turret to the round-headed doorway at first floor level. This round-headed doorway is an enlargement of a first floor round-headed window in the former porch onto which the tower, also Anglo-Saxon, was built. Two additional steps have been added at right-angles, cut into the twenty-second and twenty-third steps up from the base of the stair turret to enable access to what is now the round-headed doorway at first floor level providing entry into the room where the bells are rung in the adjacent square tower. Between the round-headed doorway at first floor level and the remaining part of the stairway, which nearly reaches the second floor round-headed doorway, there are thirty-four more steps.

Above what were the original Anglo-Saxon steps there is now a later medieval ladder not Anglo-Saxon; this wooden ladder now provides access to the second floor round-headed doorway providing entry to the "Clock Room". Above the top of the last surviving, complete, Anglo-Saxon step, scarring on the inner wall of the stair turret indicates where the Anglo-Saxon stairway continued to the top. The individual Anglo-Saxon steps comprise large, roughly dressed stones which measure on average up to 6¼ inches/15.8 centimetres high, up to 37 inches/93.9 centimetres wide (between the newel and the inner wall of the stair turret), with a maximum depth of tread of up to 20¾ inches/52.6 centimetres. The individual steps of the stairway are supported by a roughly round vaulted rubble ceiling underneath. See adjacent right: PHOTO 378. Brixworth 20,

PHOTO 377. Brixworth 19.

PHOTO 378. Brixworth 20.

showing part of the interior of the stair turret with the newel arrowed red, the steps arrowed black, and the inner face of the exterior wall of the stair turret arrowed blue.

The ruins of the Anglo-Saxon Cathedral and Bishops Palace at North Elmham, Norfolk, provide fragmentary remains of a round stair turret similar in construction to that at All Saints Church, Brixworth, Northamptonshire.

The stair turret was constructed of coursed rubble and built attached and integral to the south-east corner of the square west tower. The stonework surviving from the stair turret is up to 47 inches/119.3 centimetres high, by up to 74 inches/187.9 centimetres wide, by up to 101 inches/256.5 centimetres deep. See above right: PHOTO 379. North Elmham 1, showing the ruined stair turret from the south-east.

PHOTO 379. North Elmham 1.

It is not now possible to identify whether the treads, individual steps and stairway were supported by a roughly round vaulted rubble ceiling underneath - like the similar stairway at All Saints Church, Brixworth, Northamptonshire - see Pages 182 to 183.

See Page 184 top left: PHOTO 380. North Elmham 2, showing the internal view from above, and Page 184 top right; PHOTO 381. North Elmham 3, showing the internal view looking towards the south. On both photographs the position of the newel is arrowed red, the steps are arrowed black, and the inner wall of the stair turret is arrowed blue.

The spiral stone stairway was built in "Anglo-Saxon fashion". It is presumed the newel consisted of a single, formerly cylindrical, continuous, vertical column of rubble – it did not consist of separate jointed vertical sections of cylindrical stonework. The newel now only consists of part of the cylindrical rubble core – the surface is missing.

PHOTO 380. North Elmham 2.

PHOTO 381. North Elmham 3.

There are six steps surviving, from bottom to top:
1. Complete step up to 7 inches/17.7 centimetres high, by 34 inches/86.3 centimetres wide, by up to 18 inches/45.6 centimetres deep.
2. Complete step up to 6¾ inches/17.1 centimetres high, by 30¾ inches/78.1 centimetres wide, by up to 17 inches/43.1 centimetres deep.
3. More than half complete step up to 7 inches/17.7 centimetres high, by 22 inches/55.8 centimetres wide, by up to 15¾ inches/40 centimetres deep.
4. Complete but damaged step up to 7½ inches/19 centimetres high, by 30 inches/76.1 centimetres wide, by up to 15½ inches/39.3 centimetres deep.
5. Half complete and damaged step up to 8½ inches/21.5 centimetres high, by up to 19 inches/48.2 centimetres wide, by up to 13½ inches/34.2 centimetres deep.
6. Half complete step up to 10 inches/25.3 centimetres high, by up to 17½ inches/44.4 centimetres wide, by up to 11½ inches/29.1 centimetres deep.

St Andrew's Church, Brigstock, Northamptonshire, has a stair turret constructed with coursed rubble stonework with a single, square, external, plinth – see Page 51: PHOTO 20. Brigstock 1. The stair turret includes two flat-headed double-splayed windows. Access at ground floor level to the stair-turret is provided by a triangular-headed doorway which had steps added when the stair turret was built - see Page 95: PHOTO 119. Brigstock 4.

St Andrew's Church provides a rare example of where it is thought the stair turret had a wooden, not a stone, stairway. Inside the stair turret there is no indication of any stone stairway, nor is there any indication of damage to the interior walling had a stone stairway been removed at some later date; there is also no evidence of a central stone or rubble newel. See adjacent: PHOTO 382. Brigstock 11, showing the exterior view of the stair turret from the south-west.

PHOTO 382. Brigstock 11.

The interior walling of the stair turret has a series of square "holes" deliberately arranged and stepped to wind their way up the wall. They are presumed to be sized and positioned to secure the supports for a wooden stairway. At the base of the stair turret there are three wooden steps of uncertain date, but not Anglo-Saxon, providing access to the base of the modern step-ladder which leads up to the flat-headed doorway providing first floor access into the tower. See adjacent: PHOTO 383. Brigstock 12, showing some of the square "holes", arrowed red, which helped secure the wooden supports for the stairway. The original Anglo-Saxon wooden stairway has long since been destroyed and access is now by a step-ladder, not Anglo-Saxon.

PHOTO 383. Brigstock 12.

12. PORTICUS

Porticus were small buildings which were attached to the north and south walls of the nave and chancel; some may have overlapped the walling at the junction of the nave and chancel. They could be a single structure or a series of attached structures similar in effect to an aisle.

Each porticus was usually entered through its own archway or doorway in an inward-facing wall from the nave or chancel but occasionally it was possible to access one porticus directly into another. On occasions, and where practical, porticus may also have been accessed through an adjacent vestibule. Porticus were often single storied but on occasions they were two storeys high with possibly an internal stairway or a stairway rising from an adjacent vestibule providing the upper access.

Porticus could form a narthex which extended across the western end of the nave. Narthexes were often divided into three with a two storey central porticus providing at ground floor level the only direct access into the church. Porticus could also be an individual structure attached to the external west wall of the nave.

Porticus were often used as side chapels, those near the east end of the nave were sometimes used for important burials particularly senior ecclesiastics, those considered saints, and founders or benefactors of the abbey or church who had provided gifts or granted lands. Porticus were also used for the preparation of the Communion and the storage of sacred vessels, to house books, to act as a vestry, a baptistery, or an additional space for lay members of the congregation at important church festivals. In addition they could be used as schoolrooms, courtrooms and for accommodation for priests.

Who might have access to a porticus might be indicated by where in the church the porticus was entered. If entry was only possible from the chancel or apse this may indicate the porticus was intended for use only by the clergy so that they could gain access to sacramental vessels and church treasures. Where porticus were entered from the nave these were more likely to provide access to the congregation who would be able to venerate, and provide offerings, to those buried there and to any shrines the porticus contained.

Escomb Church, County Durham, formerly had two porticus. One extended across part north walls of both the chancel and nave and was entered directly from the chancel - the doorway, now blocked, survives. The flat-headed doorway can be identified both internally and externally and its position suggests it was for the exclusive use of the clergy. Internally, the east jamb of the doorway is decorated with faint vestiges of a "Tree of Life" design depicting a tree separating Adam and Eve.

The porticus may have measured around 146 inches/370.8 centimetres west to east and 119 inches/302.2 centimetres south to north; the walls were around 24 inches/60.9 centimetres deep. The position of the walls is now indicated externally by 20th century flagstones. See adjacent: PHOTO 383. Escomb 11, showing the position of the walls arrowed red; the head of the blocked doorway arrowed black, and the east end of the nave arrowed blue.

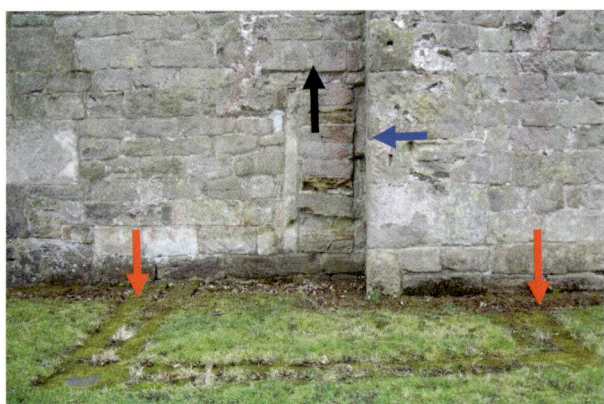

PHOTO 383. Escomb 11.

The second porticus extended from the west wall of the nave. Externally, scaring on the west wall of the nave indicates the position of the triangular head of the steeply pitched porticus roof. There appears to be no direct access from the porticus into the nave and from the position of the walls now indicated it may have had an external entrance in its north wall abutting the nave. The porticus may have measured around 155 inches/393.6 centimetres west to east and 178 inches/452.1 centimetres south to north; the walls were around 24 inches/60.9 centimetres deep. The position of the walls is now indicated externally by 20th century flagstones. The western porticus may have been used for the accommodation of priests who preached and undertook services for those in the wider community. Apparently the stones from this porticus were used to build the south porch in the 13th century. See adjacent: PHOTO 384. Escomb 12, showing the position of the walls are arrowed red and the former roofline arrowed blue.

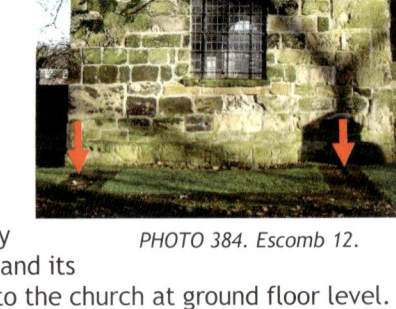

St Peter's Church, Monkwearmouth, Sunderland, County Durham, has a western narthex subdivided into three. Only the central porch with its external open western archway and its internal doorway provided external and internal access into the church at ground floor level.

PHOTO 384. Escomb 12.

Access into the north and south porticus was gained at ground floor level only through doorways in the north and south walls of the central porch. At first floor level in the surviving north wall of what is now the porch/tower there is a blocked, flat-headed doorway which provided access into the first floor of the central porch; presumably the north porticus contained either a wooden ladder or a wooden stairway. See Page 187: PHOTO 385. Monkwearmouth 12, showing the ground floor round-headed doorway – arrowed red – providing access from the central porch into the northern porticus; and the blocked first floor flat-headed doorway – arrowed black - providing access from the northern porticus into the central porch at first floor level.

At the eastern end of the nave of St Peter's Church, Britford, Wiltshire, both archways into the former north and south porticus survive - the adjacent porticus dating from the restoration of 1873 do not extend to the full dimensions of the former porticus.

The arched head of the round-headed archway of the northern porticus has individually shaped thin stones around the circumference of both faces in a similar position to voussoirs. These are separated on the soffit (underside) into three adjacent bands of square blocks of stone. The central soffit band has raised stones alternating with "sunken" stones of similar shape and size; the raised stones are separated from the adjoining stones in the two outer bands of stonework by reused Roman tile-like bricks placed on end. In the central soffit band, the lowest "voussoirs" on each side of the arch are separated by a vertical, corbel-like, stone which stands on top of the imposts and protrudes only into the central void. The arched head is supported by chamfered imposts which are flush with the faces of the walls of which they form a part but protrude into the central void below the arched head and between the opposing jambs. See adjacent left: PHOTO 386. Britford 1, showing the archway into the northern porticus,

PHOTO 385. Monkwearmouth 12.

PHOTO 386. Britford 1.

PHOTO 387. Britford 2.

Below the impost, on the west face of the eastern jamb, the central soffit band continues. On each side of the central soffit band, there is a single pilaster-strip, flush with the face of the jamb. These pilaster-strips are decorated with a plant-scroll design and framed by a band of flat-moulding. In the central soffit band, the three recessed squares are not decorated. The two squares flush with the face of the jamb have an upper square decorated with a floral plant-like design (see Pages 228 to 229) and a lower square decorated with a knot-work design (see Pages 224 to 226); each are framed with a band of flat-moulding (see Pages 217 to 218). See above right: PHOTO 387. Britford 2, showing the detail of the west face of the eastern jamb of the archway into the northern porticus.

On the east face of the western jamb, and on each side of the central soffit band, there is a single, undecorated, pilaster-strip, flush with the face of the jamb. In the central soffit band only, the lower square, flush with the face of the jamb, is decorated with a knot-work design (see Pages 224 to 226), and framed with a band of flat-moulding (see Pages 217 to 218).

On both jambs the archway has a restored chamfered plinth with a stone incorporating an almost corbel-like feature at the base of the central soffit band; the corbel-like feature protrudes only into the central void. There are apparently indications of accompanying hood-moulding and pilaster-strips but these are now obscured by plasterwork.

It is unclear as to what was the purpose of the corbels protruding from the arched head into the central void and the corbel-like features at the base of the central soffit band of the jambs. They seem to be incapable of supporting anything standing on top of them and may have only been decorative features. Also unclear is why only the western face of the eastern jamb is so elaborately decorated - it may indicate that the northern porticus housed relics or an important tomb.

The arched head of the round-headed archway of the southern porticus is constructed with three distinct bands of reused Roman tile-like bricks placed on end and formed into a discernible arch; in the centre of the soffit (underside) there are separated square-shaped stones reminiscent of those in the northern porticus. The arched head is supported by square imposts which are flush with the faces of the walls of which they form a part but protrude into the central void below the arched head and between the opposing jambs.

The west and east faces of the square jambs below each of the imposts have a central, recessed, soffit band with a single pilaster-strip, flush with the face of the jamb, on each side. At the bases of the central soffit bands there is a horizontal band of stonework which protrudes from the faces of the jambs and extends between the pilaster-strips. There is no decoration on either the west or east faces of the jambs. The archway has a restored square plinth. There are apparently indications of accompanying hood-moulding and pilaster-strips but these are now obscured by plasterwork. See adjacent: PHOTO 388. Britford 3, showing the archway into the southern porticus.

PHOTO 388. Britford 3.

The cruciform church of St Mary's, Breamore, Hampshire, retains much of its Anglo-Saxon south porticus, albeit altered, not too drastically, in later centuries. St Mary's also retains indications of its now demolished north porticus.

As well as the original flint rubble walling of the Anglo-Saxon south porticus it also retains in the external south-west and south-east corners long and short quoining which has been restored at some later, not Anglo-Saxon, date, but without the size and placement of the original. In addition, in the centre of the ground floor, the east wall retains a double-splayed Anglo-Saxon window which can be identified both internally and externally; a similar window existed in the south wall but now only the internal splay survives due to its replacement by a smaller 13th century window. See Page 189: PHOTO 389. Breamore 2, showing the external view of the south porticus – the walling arrowed red and the round-headed double-splayed window arrowed black.

Internally, the original Anglo-Saxon archway/doorway providing access into the south porticus survives. The arched head is constructed with six through-stone voussoirs; there is no single central keystone – a characteristic of Anglo-Saxon construction. On the north face of the voussoirs there is an inscription in Old English lettering which has been translated to mean "Here is made manifest the covenant to you" - the reference to the covenant is that given by God to Noah after the flood (Genesis, Chapter 9, verses 8 to 17). The text may have had some relevance to the function of the porticus as perhaps a chapel or a baptistery. See below right: PHOTO 390. Breamore 3.

(Given letters from other inscriptions, above the west face of the chancel arch, possibly the letters "DES", and in the external face of the west wall of the nave, possibly the letter "G", it is likely that there were a number of such inscriptions in the Anglo-Saxon church at Breamore.)

The arched head of the archway/doorway into the south porticus is supported by square imposts cut-back flush with the faces of the walls of which they form a part with the exception of the south face of the west impost. The square imposts protrude into the central void below the arched head and between the opposing jambs. The imposts are decorated with a band of cable-moulding (see Pages 219 to 220) along their upper and lower horizontal edges on the west face of the east impost, whilst the west impost has similar cable-moulding on the east face and the south face including, in addition, its vertical edges.

PHOTO 389. Breamore 2.

PHOTO 390. Breamore 3.

Note: The "doorway" into the south porticus as it is sometimes described may have been an archway. The south face of the western impost protrudes from the face of the wall and this would have prevented a door being placed flush with the inner face of the wall, inside the porticus, as would be expected. The south face of the eastern impost may also at one time have protruded from the face of the wall and have been cut back flush at a later date. There is no recess in the jambs of the "doorway" to facilitate the placement of a door so perhaps this is an archway.

The jambs, which may have been restored at a later, not Anglo-Saxon, date, are mostly half-through-stones and appear to be constructed in similar fashion to long and short quoining with inconsistencies in terms of size and placement of individual stones similar to the external examples of long and short quoining in the south porticus.

In the 15th century the north porticus was dismantled with a new window replacing the former archway/doorway providing access into the porticus - there are indications of the jambs of the former archway/doorway below this window - but see the "Note" above. In what is now the north wall of the central crossing much of the rest of the stonework of the walling appears undisturbed. The triangular (gable) shape of the roof of the former north porticus can clearly be identified. See adjacent: PHOTO 391. Breamore 4, showing the external view of north wall of the central crossing with the scaring on the wall indicating the position of the triangular head of the steeply pitched porticus roof – arrowed red; and the indications of the jambs of the former archway/doorway into the porticus arrowed black.

St Mary's Church, Deerhurst, Gloucestershire, formerly had a stand-alone two-storey porticus on both the north and south sides of the nave. Although interruptions to the string-course along the former exterior faces of the nave walls indicate their likely position, and the triangular-shaped openings they probably contained at first floor level greatly assist, little survives that can be confidently identified as belonging to the nave porticus. The exception is a section of the lower part of the south wall of the south nave porticus which is now part of the south wall of the south aisle – it is below the height of the triangular-shaped opening at first floor level in the south wall of the nave opposite.

PHOTO 391. Breamore 4.

See adjacent: PHOTO 392. Deerhurst 17, showing the interior of the current chancel with the north and south archways at first floor level in the former choir/chancel porticus arrowed red; the corbels supporting a second floor gallery arrowed black (see Pages 191 to 192, "13. Galleries"); and the blocked chancel arch arrowed blue with the beast head label-stops arrowed green.

Flanking the north and south sides of what is now the west end of the chancel, there were two rectangular single-storey vestibules. These vestibules were accessed through the surviving ground floor flat-headed doorways in the north and south walls of the chancel near their western ends - these doorways, opposite each other, are now blocked. It is thought that the vestibules provided both ground floor and first floor access to the adjoining two-storey choir/chancel porticus to the east which flanked the north and south sides of what is now the eastern part of the chancel. Access was probably through a flat-headed doorway at ground floor level, and a wooden stairway leading up to another flat-headed doorway at first floor level.

PHOTO 392. Deerhurst 17.

The round-headed archways surviving in the upper storeys of the choir/chancel porticus provided viewing of, or participation in, the liturgy in the choir/chancel below at ground floor level. The upper storeys could also have been used to seat high-status patrons when they attended services, church festivals and other special occasions, or for women when the community of the church included women and men, or for antiphonal singing. (It is thought that the two-storey choir/chancel porticus on the south side could have been used for the storage of liturgical vestments, books and vessels.) The sills of both the archways on the first floor have been lowered at later, not Anglo-Saxon, dates.

See below left: PHOTO 393. Deerhurst 18, showing the south face of the archway, arrowed red, at first floor level in the north choir/chancel porticus viewed from the archway at first floor level in the south choir/chancel porticus. See below right: PHOTO 394. Deerhurst 19, showing the north face of the archway at first floor level in the north choir/chancel porticus.

Two square single-storey apse porticus formerly flanked the north and south sides of the eastern part of the chancel and the western part of the apse. These were accessed through ground floor openings in the east walls of the adjacent two-storey choir/chancel porticus to the west. Now at the east end of the north aisle, there is a blocked flat-headed doorway formerly providing access between choir/chancel porticus and the north-east apse porticus – see Page 106: PHOTO 152. Deerhurst 10, and PHOTO 153. Deerhurst 11. A similar doorway may have existed at the east end of the south aisle now inside the vestry; the surviving blocked round-headed archway is a likely late-11th century replacement for the former doorway.

PHOTO 393. Deerhurst 18.   PHOTO 394. Deerhurst 19.

13. GALLERIES

Some churches have surviving corbels in the walling at first and occasionally second floor levels which may have provided support for former wooden galleries. Churches may have had rows of windows at first floor and second floor levels to provide light for these galleries. Precisely how far these galleries extended, and what they were used for, is a matter of conjecture.

Internally in St Mary's Church, Deerhurst, Gloucestershire, a pair of separate corbels in the east face of the west wall of the nave at first floor level provide indications of a gallery extending eastwards; the corbels would have supported its likely wooden floor. See Page 46: PHOTO 8. Deerhurst 1. Similarly, a pair of separate corbels in the west face of the east wall of the chancel provide indications of a gallery extending westwards; the corbels would have supported its likely wooden floor. See Page 190. PHOTO 392. Deerhurst 17. These corbels are at an equivalent height to the second floor of the west wall of the nave with its triangular-headed double-opening shown on Page 46: PHOTO 8. Deerhurst 1.

Access to these galleries would probably have been by wooden stairway(s) in the ground floor of the nave. It is not now possible to say confidently how far eastwards the gallery in the nave extended, or, whether it was "open" over the entire upper floor or sub-divided. Alternatively, there may have been separate, west to east, balconies, adjacent to the north and south walls of the nave, which overlooked a central void. The gallery extending westwards from the chancel must have had access through the former east wall of the nave above the apex of the former chancel archway. It is likely that this gallery extended westwards up to a point just east of the top of the current chancel steps where the former east wall of the nave was discovered during the restoration of 1861-1862. The gallery was probably not sub-divided.

St Peter's Church, Monkwearmouth, Sunderland, County Durham, also probably had a western gallery extending eastwards from the west wall of the nave at first floor level. It is thought that this western gallery may have accommodated the monastic scriptorium. For an indication of the position of this western gallery see Page 46: PHOTO 7. Monkwearmouth 2.

14. USE OF ROOMS IN TOWERS
Rooms in towers could be used for a variety of reasons similar to those for porticus, i.e., for the preparation of the Communion and the storage of sacred vessels, to house books, to act as a vestry, or a baptistery. They could also be used as schoolrooms, courtrooms and for the accommodation of priests. There is little specific evidence surviving to be confident about what individual rooms were used for, but there are some exceptions, as the churches mentioned below indicate.

Internally, in the ground floor of the tower, St John the Baptist Church, Barnack, Cambridgeshire, has a triangular-headed seat-like recess in the west wall and separate aumbries in the north and south walls. See adjacent: PHOTO 395. Barnack 19, showing the seat-like recess in the west wall. The aumbries provided storage for sacred vessels and also for books and documents. See below left: PHOTO 396. Barnack 20, showing the aumbry in the north wall, and below right: PHOTO 397. Barnack 21, showing the aumbry in the south wall.

It is thought this seat may have been used by a person presiding over matters of law, including the provision of legal proceedings, the swearing of oaths etc. One of the functions of Anglo-Saxon churches was a place where legal matters could be aired and determined. Alternatively, this seat may have been used by the person presiding over religious ceremonies. The seat is constructed with a head comprising two large stones – each a trapezium – placed together at one of their ends to form a triangular shape; their other ends are placed on top of the supporting through-stone rectangular imposts. The jambs are laid in long and short fashion just like the pilaster-strips accompanying the tower archway – see Page 177, PHOTO 363. Barnack 18. A single horizontal slab provides the seat. The head, imposts, jambs and seat all protrude from the

PHOTO 395. Barnack 19.

PHOTO 396. Barnack 20.

PHOTO 397. Barnack 21.

face of the wall. In the mid-19th century it was reported that there was some indication of wooden seating on each side of this stone seat.

St Mary's Church, Deerhurst, Gloucestershire, has flat-headed double-splayed windows in the north and south walls of the second floor room of the former porch/tower. The eastern jambs of both windows provide the western jambs of round-headed aumbries. Both aumbries have grooves concentric with the arched head and parallel to the jambs. The south aumbry has part of its west jamb and sill cut away and the window has been altered by the removal of its sill and the walling below to provide a doorway, not Anglo-Saxon, giving access into the room. These aumbries indicate the use of this room as a chapel. See below left: PHOTO 398. Deerhurst 20, showing the aumbry in the north wall arrowed red, and the flat-headed double-splayed window arrowed black. See below right: PHOTO 399. Deerhurst 21, showing the aumbry in the south wall arrowed red, and the flat-headed double-splayed window, now converted into a doorway, arrowed black.

PHOTO 398. Deerhurst 20.   PHOTO 399. Deerhurst 21.

Also in the second floor room of the former porch/tower, there is a round-headed (externally)/flat-headed (internally) doorway in the west wall – see Page 108: PHOTO 158. Deerhurst 13. It is thought that when this doorway was originally built it provided access from the porch onto an external, projecting, timber balcony or walkway which may have extended around the west, north and south walls of the porch as far as the west wall of the nave. The balcony or walkway may have had a wooden balustrade and it may have been roofed. This balcony or walkway was probably intended for the display of relics or reliquaries to the congregation assembled below on special occasions. However, such balconies or walkways may not have had a single purpose, they may have also assisted in liturgical practices such as the ringing of bells during a burial ceremony.

At St Michael's Church, Oxford, Oxfordshire, the second floor of the tower has in the north wall a round-headed doorway, now with a window, not Anglo-Saxon, inserted. This former doorway may have given access to a balcony from which relics could be displayed to the assembled congregation assembled at important church festivals and other special occasions. Alternatively, this doorway may have provided access onto a wall-walk leading off to the north forming part of the town's walled defences. At right-angles to the west wall of the tower there may have been a gate through the town wall. See adjacent: PHOTO 400. Oxford 9,

PHOTO 400. Oxford 9.

showing the former round-headed doorway in the north wall arrowed red.

The square tower of St Helen's Church, Skipwith, North Yorkshire, has a first floor room with three, linked, distinctive features – a recess in the east wall, a window in the south wall specifically placed to light the recess and, a doorway into the nave probably providing access to a balcony on the west wall of the nave.

On reaching the church one of the first things to notice is that in the tower at first floor level there are two round-headed double-splayed windows. The larger of the two is centrally placed and similar in size and position to the round-headed double-splayed window in the west wall – both windows in "standard" positions for Anglo-Saxon towers. Additionally, and unusually, in the south wall there is another, smaller, round-headed double-splayed window to the east of the central window and higher up the wall. Presumably the purpose of this additional window was to provide light to a particular part of the interior of the tower. See Page 49. PHOTO 14. Skipwith 1.

Inside the tower, at first floor level, there is a recess in the west face of the east wall provided with illumination by this additional window. See adjacent: PHOTO 401. Skipwith 6, showing the recess arrowed red and the interior of the additional double-splayed window arrowed black.

PHOTO 401. Skipwith 6.

The recess measures 30 inches/76.1 centimetres high with an internal width of 41½ inches/105.3 centimetres. It is 6 inches/15.2 centimetres deep with the protruding sill of the recess extending the depth by another 1 inch/2.5 centimetres. The recess has a stepped lintel comprising an upper horizontal, rectangular shaped, section of stonework protruding from the face of the wall, and below, a horizontal, rounded, section of stonework which does not protrude from the face of the wall. The recess has rectangular impost-like capitals which protrude from the face of the wall and also into the central void.

PHOTO 402. Skipwith 7.

The jambs comprise half-round cylindrical shafts with rounded bases with a tapering outwards angle-sided top complemented by a tapering inwards angle-sided bottom. The quarter-rounded sill sits inside the recess and comprises three stones laid horizontally in a row. The sill of the recess is 26 inches/66 centimetres up from the floor. See above right: PHOTO 402. Skipwith 7, showing the recess with its architectural features.

In the same room, in the east wall, to the north of the recess, is a round-headed doorway, now blocked. The west face of this doorway has a head constructed with differently sized voussoirs resulting in an arched head that is not that radial; there is no single central keystone – a characteristic of Anglo-Saxon construction. The imposts are flush with the face of the wall and protrude into the former central void between the opposing jambs where they are chamfered. The jambs are of similar shape and size, and laid in a similar way, to the coursed rubble stonework in the adjoining walling; the jambs stand on bases which, just like the imposts, protrude into the former central void where they are chamfered. Inside the nave what can be seen of the east face of this doorway - the imposts and head are obscured by the supports for the roof - appears similarly constructed to the west face. The stonework in the east wall blocking this doorway is recessed on both the west and east faces. This doorway may well have provided access to a first floor balcony on the east face of the west wall of the nave.

Construction of the recess, the additional window, and doorway opening into the nave, suggest the presence of something of significance. The recess itself may have housed reliquary(s), or perhaps a reredos, or provided some form of altar back decoration. There may have been an altar in front of the recess. Whatever this room contained it is likely that the relics housed in, or on an altar adjacent to, the recess, were displayed from a balcony on the east face of the west wall of the nave to the congregation assembled below at important church festivals and other special occasions.

Externally, above the head of the smaller round-headed double-splayed window illuminating the recess, there are indications of decorative panels which may have extended along the south, west and north walls of the tower. These panels may have protruded slightly from the face of the wall but weathering and some unsympathetic restoration have defaced their original appearance. These panels might have been decorated with scenes from the life of the individual whose relic(s) were kept in the first floor of the tower or had some other connection with whatever was within the tower. (One of these panels in the south wall has what looks like a boar in profile to the right. Another one of these panels, possibly depicting a chalice, has been repositioned out of context much lower down in the west wall.)

15. CRYPTS

Crypts were used for burials of members of the same, often extended, family over the generations. They were also used as mausoleums to particular individuals and to house a shrine or an altar dedicated to a saint. Often it was the skull and bones of the deceased which were placed in caskets of wood or iron in recesses within the thickness of the internal walls of the crypts whereas whole bodies were more likely to have been interred and placed in the centre of the crypt. When used to house a shrine or an altar dedicated to a saint caskets in the crypt may have contained some of their body parts or items owned by or directly associated with them. The caskets could be made of gold, silver or bronze with some richly ornamented and incorporating jewels.

Anglo-Saxon crypts were usually small, roofed, semi-underground, or underground, square-shaped areas with recesses around their internal walls. They were often located at or near the east end of the church, near, or directly below the main altar. Crypts were accessed by either a single stairway which entered the crypt from the west, or by a pair of separate stairways running west to east entering the crypt on or near their north-west and south-west corners. The number of stairways was probably determined by what the crypt contained, those where access was required infrequently with a single stairway and those where pilgrims required frequent access were more likely to have pairs of stairways. Archways or doorways may have been placed across the descending stairways or on the floor at the bottom of the stairways. Some churches may have had a small window in the floor near the main altar through which the priests when officiating at services could see the tomb(s) of the deceased or the shrines of saints or the casket(s) containing their reliquaries.

Where a shrine was involved, or where the main area was used as a chapel to venerate the deceased, crypts could require a more elaborate structure. This might have involved the building of additional stairways, passageways, ambulatories and roofs. All these structures would probably have been plastered and painted internally. To provide lighting the walls would have contained niches which included a centrally placed hollow in their sills to allow lighted wicks to float in oil, with, in the stonework above, centrally placed cone shaped cavities to help attract and dissipate the smoke. Some area(s) of the crypt may have had in their roof a ventilation shaft, now usually identified by its covering grate, extending upwards to the floor above.

Where there was provision, pilgrims were able to process around the shrine, venerate and worship beside the shrine, and leave offerings. Pilgrims may not always have been able to physically touch the shrine, their access may have been restricted to looking at the shrine through a gated archway inside the crypt, or, in some cases, looking from outside the crypt through window(s) in the external walling. In some examples pilgrims and clergy may have had separate entrances and exits, passageways and stairways.

At St Wystan's Church, Repton, Derbyshire, the structure we now see as a crypt may have originally been intended as a baptistery - it is half underground and built over a stream which was drained. Whatever was intended it was constructed at the behest of King Aethelbald of Mercia who reigned 716-757. Sometime after the initial construction it was converted into a royal mausoleum. It is believed that as well as the bones of King Aethelbald the crypt contained the bones of King Wiglaf of Mercia who reigned 827-839, and his grandson St Wystan who was murdered in 849.

The crypt is some 192 inches/487.6 centimetres square and 120 inches/304.7 centimetres high. The crypt is divided into nine vaulted, approximately square, bays in three rows. Recesses within the internal thickness of the north, east and south side walls probably contained bones and relics with perhaps King Wiglaf's bones or body occupying the centre of the crypt. Only the western recess is in something like its 9th century state; and in its west wall it has a small, curving, triangular-shaped, niche which might have been for a lamp.

Sometime early-9th century a first floor was added to the crypt and joined to the nave. It probably had a wooden floor and may have had triangular-headed windows in the north, east and south walls; the roof may also have been triangular-shaped. Before his death in 839 King Wiglaf made further changes to the crypt to create a suitable mausoleum for himself. This involved: the upward extension, and increasing the depth, of the north, east and south walls of the crypt to provide the supporting side walls for the chancel above; replacing the wooden floor of the upper room(s) of the crypt with a stone floor at a higher level for the chancel; the blocking of the triangular-headed windows in the former first floor of the crypt which would have been below the level of the new stone floor for the chancel; and the insertion of larger round-headed windows at a higher level in what had become the

PHOTO 403. Repton 3.   PHOTO 404. Repton 4.

heightened north, east and south walls of the chancel. Internally, he also had added the four centrally placed cylindrical columns and the eight, wide, vertical-sided, pilaster-strips in the side walls to support a new vaulted ceiling constructed with rubble stonework. Externally a chamfered string-course was added which also provided the sills for the new round-headed windows; pilaster-strips were also added to the new walls of the chancel.

Stairway passages descend down through the north-west and south-west corners of the crypt to provide access for pilgrims – only the north stairway is used by visitors today. See Page 196 bottom left: PHOTO 403. Repton 3, showing the south stairway and opening – the doorway is not Anglo-Saxon, it is a later addition, and see Page 196 bottom right: PHOTO 404. Repton 4, showing the north stairway and opening – the doorway is not Anglo-Saxon, it is a later addition.

Internally the crypt is mostly constructed with large blocks of ashlar stonework which almost extend through the whole depth of the wall – there is a thin band of rubble. All the stonework stands on a single plinth comprising large stones lying flat on one of their faces. The vaulting and ceiling was also constructed with rubble.

The walling includes a double-stepped string-course (incomplete) separated by more walling from an upper single string-course (incomplete). See adjacent: PHOTO 405. Repton 5, showing the double-stepped string-course arrowed red, and the single string course arrowed black.

PHOTO 405. Repton 5.

The nine bays of the crypt have a vaulted ceiling supported by round-headed interlinked arches which spring from two wide, vertical-sided, pilaster-strips on each of the four side walls and rest on the four free-standing columns in the centre; these four free-standing columns are also connected to each other by round-headed arches.

Vestiges of gesso and red paintwork can be identified on both the wide, vertical-sided, pilaster-strips and the central columns; particularly on the capitals. See adjacent: PHOTO 406. Repton 6, showing part of the vaulted ceiling and some of the supporting columns and pilaster-strips. One of the capitals of the pilaster-strips and one of the capitals of the columns show vestiges of red paint – both are arrowed black.

PHOTO 406. Repton 6.

On the side walls the eight wide, vertical-sided, pilaster-strips abut the walling - they are not integral to it. Some of the pilaster-strips are damaged and incomplete. They taper from bottom to top and appear not to have distinctive bases. Each of the three sides of the pilaster-strips visible display bands of flat-moulding along their two vertical edges which join together in an arched head just below the capital. Within these bands of flat-moulding there are two recessed panels separated in the centre by another band of vertical flat-moulding, almost ridge-like. The moulded capitals above have a lower half tapering upwards with a top half subdivided into three by two horizontal grooves. See adjacent left: PHOTO 407. Repton 7, showing one of the pilaster-strips with red paint surviving on its capital arrowed black.

Possibly sometime in the 16th century, the insertion of the current rectangular windows, in the east and south recesses, and the doorway in the north recess, led to most of the voussoirs forming the arched heads of the Anglo-Saxon round-headed windows being destroyed. However, vestiges of the original lower voussoirs of the arched heads do survive – particularly in the south recess.

In the centre of the crypt, the four free-standing columns have circular bases expanding as they taper downwards to become slightly more rectangular in shape. The columns were decorated sometime in the 9th century with a spiralling band of roll-moulding in relief which on each column spirals in an opposite direction to the spiralling on the adjacent column. The moulded capitals have a lower half tapering upwards with a top half subdivided into three by two horizontal grooves. See above right: PHOTO 408. Repton 8, showing one of the central columns.

PHOTO 407. Repton 7.   PHOTO 408. Repton 8.

Externally the crypt was constructed with coursed rubble stonework. The walling stands on a four-stepped plinth with the bottom step in particular including megalithic stonework. The south-east and north-east corners were constructed with large quoins placed in no regular pattern. There is a chamfered string-course from which pairs of pilaster-strips on each wall extend vertically up to short horizontal sections of stonework, above which are upwardly splayed capitals with narrow rectangular bands of stonework at their tops. The pilaster-strips on the east wall are incomplete. See adjacent: PHOTO 409. Repton 9, showing the external south and east walls of the crypt with, on the south wall, the pilaster-strips arrowed red, the string-course arrowed black, and the four-stepped plinth arrowed blue.

PHOTO 409. Repton 9.

The crypts at Hexham Abbey, Northumberland and Ripon Cathedral, North Yorkshire, were constructed as part of the monasteries established at the behest of Saint Wilfrid in the second half of the seventh century. Both a religious, and political figure, he was the chief spokesman for the advocacy of the Roman Church at the Synod of Whitby in 664 AD and his bishopric of York at one time extended over all the Kingdom of Northumbria.

The crypt at Hexham Abbey in Northumberland was constructed 674-678 AD to house the relics of saints. It was built beneath the High Altar of Wilfrid's church at the east end of the nave – it is now to the west of the centre of the central crossing. (The east end of the central crossing and the west end of the chancel overlie the incomplete foundations of a separate Anglo-Saxon chapel, possibly St Peter's Church. A large monastic church with a separate small chapel, centrally placed to the east, is typical of the layout of Anglo-Saxon monasteries.)

The crypt is constructed with ashlar stonework much of which came from the nearby Roman bridges at Corbridge and Chesters. The Roman origin of the stonework is clear from its shape, tooling and decoration, including architectural fragments with geometrical and plant designs thought to have been ornamentation taken from the mausoleum at Shorden Brae, west of Corbridge. The reuse of Roman decorated architectural fragments was not for their decorative appeal, but, for their ability to make the adhesion of plaster easier. The floors are mostly covered with 20th century concrete.

Access to the crypt is now provided, in the nave, by a single western stairway (only the top four steps are not original) which was formerly used for access by pilgrims and perhaps as well for ceremonial purposes at important church festivals. At the bottom of these steps is a western ante-chamber to the main chamber of the crypt.

Entrance into the western ante-chamber is provided by a round-headed doorway cut straight through the thickness of its west wall. The lintel forming its arched head is constructed with three through-stones, with an upper, central, stone providing a quarter-circle, supported on each side, by a stone shaped to provide the lower curvature of the arched head. The two lower stones are placed directly on top of the through-stone jambs below; there are no imposts. See adjacent: PHOTO 410. Hexham 2, showing the west face of the doorway into the western ante-chamber with individual stones forming the arched head each arrowed red.

PHOTO 410. Hexham 2.

The ante-chamber has a barrel-vaulted roof, orientated west to east. It was constructed with a wooden framework on top of which stone slabs were placed on end and shaped to the requisite curvature of the roof. These ribs provided the necessary structure to contain the mortar placed between their radii to cover the roof – a lighter coating of plaster enables the ribs to be identified. The roof contains a ventilation shaft, identified by its covering grate, extending upwards to the floor of the nave above. There is a niche in the south wall for a lamp. The niche includes a centrally placed hollow in its sill to allow a lighted wick to float in oil, with, in the stonework above, a centrally placed cone shaped cavity to attract and dissipate the smoke - see adjacent: PHOTO 411. Hexham 3.

PHOTO 411. Hexham 3.

The ante-chamber measures 57 inches/144.7 centimetres west to east, by 114 inches/289.5 centimetres north to south, with a height of 108 inches/274.3 centimetres. It provides access to the main chamber of the crypt to the east, and to the small north chamber to the north.

Entrance into the main chamber of the crypt is provided by a round-headed doorway cut through the thickness of its west wall. The lintel forming its arched head is constructed with three through-stones, with an upper, central, stone providing a quarter-circle, supported on each side, by a stone shaped to provide the lower curvature of the arched head. The two lower stones are placed directly on top of the through-stone jambs below; there are no imposts. The jambs are splayed on their western (ante-chamber) face possibly to enable pilgrims to have a better view; the south jamb was chamfered when the crypt was used for burials of members of the Andrewes and Clarke families in the 18th and 19th centuries. The doorway would probably have had a grill so that the pilgrims could see in, they would not have been allowed into the main chamber. See adjacent: PHOTO 412. Hexham 4, showing the west face of the doorway into the main chamber.

PHOTO 412. Hexham 4.

The main chamber has a barrel-vaulted roof, orientated north to south. It was constructed with a wooden framework on top of which stone slabs were placed on end and shaped to the requisite curvature of the roof. These ribs provided the necessary structure to contain the mortar placed between their radii to cover the roof. The walls of the main chamber stand on a single, flat, protruding plinth which can now only be confidently identified adjacent to the north wall.

PHOTO 413. Hexham 5.

Inside the main chamber relics of saints in gold, silver and bronze caskets would have been displayed – some possibly connected with St Andrew to whom the church was dedicated. Biblical scenes are likely to have been painted on its plastered walls and ceiling – the earliest surviving layers of plaster could date from the 7th century. In addition there may have been paintings hung on the walls. (The current altar dates from the 20th century). See above right: PHOTO 413. Hexham 5, showing the main chamber viewed from the west doorway with the north and south lamp niches arrowed red and the corbel replacing the lamp niche in the east wall arrowed black.

The main chamber would have been lit up by the lamps in the niches in the north, south and west walls, and the position of a fourth, in the east wall, is now indicated by a 13th century corbel. Each of these niches includes a centrally placed hollow in its sill to allow a lighted wick to float in oil, with, in the stonework above, a centrally placed cone shaped cavity to attract and dissipate the smoke. See adjacent: PHOTO 414. Hexham 6, showing the lamp niche in the west wall – ignore the 21st century candle.

The main chamber of the crypt measures 161 inches/408.9

PHOTO 414. Hexham 6.

centimetres west to east, by 94 inches/238.7 centimetres north to south, with a height of 108 inches/274.3 centimetres. A round-headed doorway in the south wall of the main chamber, near its west end, provides access to the south chamber.

Entrance into the small south chamber is provided by a round-headed doorway cut straight through the thickness of its north wall (the south wall of the main chamber). Its arched head has been cut out of the centre of the lower horizontal face of a through-stone monolithic lintel. The doorway has no imposts and its jambs were constructed with through-stones. The whole south wall of the main chamber of the crypt, including this doorway, is set-back (a distinctive feature) from the underside of the barrel-vaulted roof of the main chamber. See adjacent: PHOTO 415. Hexham 7, showing the north face of the doorway into the south chamber.

PHOTO 415. Hexham 7.

Inside the south chamber, pairs of stone slabs are placed on end to meet centrally to form a triangular roof, orientated north to south. The south chamber measures 66 inches/167.6 centimetres west to east, by 46 inches/116.8 centimetres north to south, with a height of 114 inches/289.5 centimetres.

The eastern entrance of the south chamber is indicated in the southern passageway extending eastwards by a round-headed arch cut out of the centre of the lower horizontal face of a through-stone monolithic lintel springing from the side walls. It is possible this arch might have been part of a round-headed doorway with no imposts and with the jambs provided by the side walls of the passageway. There is one floor step in the south chamber under the monolithic lintel of its eastern entrance, and then two more steps in the southern passageway. Reused Roman decorated architectural fragments, with geometrical and plant designs, can be identified incorporated into the south and east walls of the passageway.

The southern passageway is roofed with flat slabs resting on top of the adjacent walls; these slabs include a reused Roman stone with a lewis-hole. The southern passageway leads to the bottom of the south stairway, now blocked, where three steps and part of a fourth can be identified. This stairway originally led to a ground floor entrance/exit. This entrance/exit may have been housed in a small chamber attached to the main body of the church, or, just possibly, it may have opened directly outside the church into the open. The stairway was blocked in the 1907-1908 rebuilding of the Abbey church. (Note: Inside the south-east corner of the nave above, immediately to the west of the 13th century Parclose Screen, a glass floor panel reveals some of the stonework at the top of the southern stairway and some of the stonework of the eastern passageway, where it extended north to south, before reaching the former south entrance/exit. The glass floor panel is now covered by a carpet.) The south chamber, the southern passageway, stairway and entrance/exit may have been for the exclusive use of ecclesiastics.

Entrance from the western ante-chamber into the small north chamber is provided by a round-headed doorway cut straight through the thickness of its south wall (the north wall of the ante-chamber) – there is one floor step on its sill. The lintel forming its arched head is constructed with three through-stones, with an upper, central, stone providing a quarter-circle, supported on each side, by a stone shaped to provide the lower curvature of the arched head. The two lower stones are placed directly on top of the through-stone jambs;

there are no imposts. See adjacent: PHOTO 416. Hexham 8, showing the south face of the doorway into the north chamber.

Inside the north chamber, pairs of stone slabs are placed on end to meet centrally to form a triangular roof, orientated north to south. The small north chamber measures 71 inches/180.3 centimetres west to east, by 45 inches/114.2 centimetres north to south, with a height of 107 inches/271.7 centimetres.

The eastern entrance of the north chamber is indicated in the northern passageway extending eastwards by a round-headed arch cut out of part of a reused Roman altar shaped to match the triangular shape of the roof; the arched head springs from the side walls. It is possible this arch might have been part of a round-headed doorway with no imposts and with the jambs provided by the side walls of the passageway. The reused Roman altar was dedicated to the local god, Maponus Apollo, by P Aelius, centurion of the Vth Legion Victrix – the writing is on its western face.

PHOTO 416. Hexham 8.

There is one floor step in the north chamber and another step up to the northern passageway. The northern passageway is roofed with flat slabs resting on top of the adjacent walls; these include reused Roman stonework with cramp-holes. Reused Roman decorated architectural fragments, with geometrical and plant designs, can be identified incorporated into the north wall as can slight indications of vestiges of red paint. Near the current end of the passageway, and above a floor step, a roof slab reuses part of an inscription dedicating a granary at Corbridge Roman Fort during the time of Septimus Severus between 205 and 207 AD – it includes traces of an attempt to obliterate the name of the Emperor Geta. See

PHOTO 417. Hexham 9.

above right: PHOTO 417. Hexham 9, with the reused Roman altar, "Maponus Apollo stone", arrowed red, reused Roman decorated architectural fragments arrowed black, and part of the reused Roman inscription to Septimus Severus arrowed blue.

The northern passageway, now blocked at its current eastern end, originally made a right-angled turn which then led to the north stairway and the ground floor entrance/exit. Like its southern counterpart, this entrance/exit may have been housed in a small chamber attached to the main body of the church, or, just possibly, it may have opened directly outside the church into the open. During the 1907-1908 rebuilding of the Abbey church the stairway was blocked in by the construction of a wall to help stabilise the 13th century north-west pier of the central crossing above. The north chamber, passageway, stairway and entrance/exit was probably for the use of pilgrims and perhaps as well for ceremonial purposes at important church festivals.

The crypt at Ripon Cathedral in North Yorkshire was constructed as part of the monastery established at the behest of Saint Wilfrid - like the monastery and crypt at Hexham. It was probably constructed 669-678 AD to house the relics of saints. Although similar in layout and in many construction details to the crypt at Hexham there are differences - it has two, not three, passageways – and it has been subject to more alterations over the years. The crypt at Ripon was built beneath the High Altar of Wilfrid's church at the east end of the nave – it is now below the centre of the central crossing.

The crypt is constructed with ashlar stonework much of which came from the Roman site at Aldborough, near Boroughbridge. Plaster is in evidence obscuring some construction details particularly those in the main chamber and in the short passageways providing access to it. The floors are mostly covered with 20th century concrete.

Access to the crypt is now provided, in the nave, by a western stairway descending to a southern passageway which makes a right-angled turn where there is a lamp niche in the north wall. From this point eastwards the walling and the roof includes stonework constructed by the Anglo-Saxons. From the west wall of this southern passageway the second, third and fourth roof slabs east incorporate parts of three grave-covers. The fourth roof slab comprises part of an incomplete 8th or 9th century grave-marker or grave-cover - see Pages 276 to 279, "9. Grave-Markers" and Pages 279 to 289, "10. Grave-Covers and Grave-Slabs". It is decorated, in relief, with a band of roll-moulding (see Pages 218 to 219) forming a panel containing, in the centre, most of the lower vertical arm of a free-arm cross (see Glossary) which joins, by narrowing, inwardly curving, the lower parts of the two, incomplete, horizontal arms of the free-arm cross above. (An electrical fitting has been affixed to the exposed part of its east side.) The second and third roof slabs comprise parts of 13th century grave-covers.

The roof of what is now the southern passageway is constructed with flat slabs resting on top of the adjacent walls; these slabs include Roman stonework – one stone has a lewis-hole. At the end of the southern passageway, in the east wall, is a lamp niche which originally included a centrally placed hollow in its sill to allow a lighted wick to float in oil, with, in the stonework above, a centrally placed cone shaped cavity to attract and dissipate the smoke.

In the north wall of the southern passageway there is a floor step which leads down to a short passageway extending northwards towards the main chamber of the crypt. This short passageway is up to 41¼ inches/104.7 centimetres south to north, by 24 inches/60.9 centimetres west to east, by up to 78 inches/198.1 centimetres high. The arched head of the round-headed doorway providing the southern entrance into the main chamber can be identified 16 inches/40.6 centimetres along this passageway. There is another floor step in this passageway before the main chamber.

The round-headed doorway providing the southern entrance into the main chamber of the crypt has been cut straight through the thickness of the south wall of the main chamber. The lintel forming its arched head is constructed with three through-stones, with an upper, central, stone providing a quarter-circle, supported on each side, by a stone shaped to provide the lower curvature of the arched head. The two lower stones are placed directly on top of the through-stone jambs; there are no imposts. See adjacent: PHOTO 418. Ripon 2, showing the view looking along the short passageway leading to the main chamber. The set-back head of the doorway is arrowed red and the western lamp niche in

PHOTO 418. Ripon 2.

the north wall of the main chamber is arrowed black.

The main chamber of the crypt measures 135 inches/342.8 centimetres west to east, by 93 inches/236.2 centimetres north to south, with a height of 117 inches/297.1 centimetres. It has a barrel-vaulted roof, orientated north to south. It was constructed with a wooden framework on top of which stone slabs were placed on end and shaped to the requisite curvature of the roof. These ribs provided the necessary structure to contain the mortar placed between their radii to cover the roof. The walls were constructed with large blocks of ashlar stonework which stand on a single, flat, protruding plinth. Stonework of unknown date and purpose rises up from the floor and is similar in appearance to a flight of parts of three steps.

Inside the main chamber of the crypt there is a tall, shallow, recess at eye level in the east wall which was probably intended to house an important relic of a saint. Other relics in gold, silver and bronze caskets would also have been displayed in the main chamber. Biblical scenes are likely to have been painted on its plastered walls and ceiling – the earliest layers of plaster could date from the late-7th century. There may have been paintings hung on the walls. See adjacent: PHOTO 419. Ripon 3, showing the main chamber as viewed from the passageway from the western ante-chamber, with, in the east wall of the main chamber, the reliquary recess arrowed red and a lamp niche arrowed black.

PHOTO 419. Ripon 3.

The main chamber would have been lit up by the lamps in the niches in the north, south, west and east walls. Each of these niches originally included a centrally placed hollow in its sill to allow a lighted wick to float in oil, with, in the stonework above, a centrally placed cone shaped cavity to attract and dissipate the smoke. The north-west niche in the north wall seems in something like its original condition, as may be the niche in the west wall. See adjacent: PHOTO 420. Ripon 4, showing the east face of the west doorway looking from inside the main chamber, towards and through the short passageway which leads to the western ante-chamber. The lamp niche in the west wall of the main chamber is arrowed red and the western lamp niche in the north wall of the main chamber is arrowed black.

PHOTO 420. Ripon 4.

A round-headed doorway in the west wall of the main chamber has an arched head cut out of the centre of the lower horizontal face of a through-stone monolithic lintel. The doorway has no imposts and has through-stone jambs. It has been cut straight through the thickness of the wall. From this doorway there is a single step down to the main chamber of the crypt.

This doorway opened to a short passageway which measures up to 32 inches/81.2 centimetres west to east, by 25 inches/63.5 centimetres south to north, and 78 inches/198.1 centimetres high. This short passageway leads to the western ante-chamber which is orientated south/north.

The western ante-chamber has a quadrant-shaped, half-vaulted, roof, orientated west to east. It was constructed with a wooden framework on top of which stone slabs were placed on end and shaped to the requisite curvature of the roof. These ribs provided the necessary structure to contain the mortar placed between their radii to cover the roof - a lighter coating of plaster enables the ribs to be identified. Traces of pink plaster can be identified on the roof and the walls. The roof of the ante-chamber contains a ventilation shaft, identified by its covering grate, extending upwards to the floor of the nave above. In the north-west corner of the ante-chamber is a lamp niche. The ante-chamber measures 145 inches/368.2 centimetres north to south, by 50 inches/127 centimetres west to east, with a height of 109 inches/276.8 centimetres.

The western ante-chamber provides access in its north-east corner, under a round-headed arch, and up four floor steps, to a northern passageway which extends eastwards. The round-headed arch is cut out of the centre of the lower horizontal face of a through-stone monolithic lintel springing from the side walls. It is possible this arch might have been part of a round-headed doorway with no imposts and with the jambs provided by the side walls of the passageway. The northern passageway is roofed with flat slabs resting on top of the adjacent walls and its eastern end is now indicated by a lintel with a round-headed arch cut out - the lintel is not Anglo-Saxon.

The northern passageway leads to the current north stairway ending in a ground floor exit - the line of the original stairway is indicated in the north wall of the passageway. Originally, this entrance/exit may have been housed in a small chamber attached to the main body of the church, or, just possibly, it may have opened directly outside the church into the open.

At All Saints Church, Wing, Buckinghamshire, has an Anglo-Saxon crypt and chancel above. Both were built with coursed rubble walling including some reused Roman stonework. It is thought that originally the crypt was just one open chamber but when alterations later in the Anglo-Saxon period were made these included, in the crypt, the addition of the ambulatory, the barrel-vaulted roof, and, perhaps, the insertion of the lower windows to enable viewing of the central chamber. At the same time the chancel was provided with a new stone floor, its walls were extended vertically with additional round-headed windows inserted, and pilaster-strips added to the external faces of the walls. The round-headed double-window in the east wall of the nave was probably also inserted at the time of these alterations.

PHOTO 421. Wing 3.

The crypt comprises an outer, external, heptagonal shape enclosing an ambulatory around an octagonal-shaped central chamber - the two are separated by four large piers supporting the barrel-vaulted roof. Both the ambulatory archways and the more substantial archways in the central chamber were similarly constructed. Their arched heads have single stones of rubble laid on end to form a discernible arch, they have no imposts, and their jambs were constructed with individual, relatively large stones, laid in a roughly, sometimes inconsistent, fashion similar to side alternate quoining. See Page 205 bottom right: PHOTO 421. Wing 3, showing the interior of the crypt viewed externally through the round-headed window in the north wall, with part of the ambulatory arrowed red and part of the central chamber arrowed black.

The piers of the central chamber had their jambs angled to facilitate viewing through what are now the lower the round-headed windows in the centre of the north, east and south external walls of the crypt. These round-headed windows have arched heads constructed with individual stones of rubble placed on end and formed into a discernible arch, they have no imposts, and their jambs were constructed of similar stonework to the adjoining coursed rubble walling; the sills have been altered at a later, not Anglo-Saxon, date. The south window now has stone steps, not Anglo-Saxon, leading down from its sill into the crypt.

Access to the crypt was formerly gained by internal stairways at the east end of the nave, within the area now around and under the current chancel arch, one stairway on the north side and one on the south. These stairways led eastwards down to passages which made right-angled turns to continue eastwards to the crypt; they also enabled access when the ambulatory was built. The entrances to the stairways have been blocked below the ground and nothing is now visible within the church.

The relics, shrine or altar would have been located in the central chamber. Internally, at one time, a squint provided a view into the crypt from the east end of the nave – nothing now remains of this inside the nave but it is just possible that its position may be indicated inside the crypt on the east face of the west wall by the disturbed nature of the walling which might be infilling.

Externally the upper walls of the crypt and the chancel above were decorated with a blind arcade of round-headed pilaster-strips protruding from the faces of the walls – now incomplete because of the insertion of 14th century windows. The vertical pilaster-strips have shared rectangular imposts and are positioned on the corners of each section of the seven walls of the crypt. These vertical pilaster-strips continue above the interlocking round-headed archways and now disappear before they reach the current roof. Only the pilaster-strips on the north and south walls can now be confidently identified.

High above the centre of this round-headed blind arcade there is another blind arcade of pilaster-strips, this time triangular-headed, with the apex of their heads placed centrally similar to the round-headed blind arcade below. The pilaster-strips forming each angle of the triangular heads extend from the vertical pilaster-strips positioned on the corners of the walling. Only the pilaster-strips on the south wall can now be confidently identified. The individual stones forming the two blind arcades of pilaster-strips display externally a short, rather than a long, side giving the appearance similar to the ends of modern bricks.

In the north and south walls of the chancel, above the tops of the 14th century windows, and below the round-heads of the blind arcade, it is possible to identify individual rubble stones placed on end and formed into a discernible arch which were parts of the tops of the arched heads of Anglo-Saxon windows – possibly double-splayed given the estimate of their external radius.

In the south wall of the chancel, two round-headed single-splayed Anglo-Saxon windows, now blocked, can be identified in two of the bays of the upper arcade of pilaster-strips, below the apex of the triangular heads. The arched heads of these two windows were constructed with individual stones of rubble placed on end and formed into a discernible arch, they have no imposts, and their jambs and sills were constructed of similar stonework to the adjoining coursed rubble walling. It is possible that these windows may have been blind, intended for their decorative rather than lighting purposes. See adjacent: PHOTO 422. Wing 4, showing the external south-east view of the chancel with the blind arcade of round-headed pilaster-strips arrowed red, the blind arcade of triangular-headed pilaster-strips arrowed black, and one of the blocked round-headed windows arrowed blue.

All Saints Church, Brixworth, Northamptonshire, provides an example of a "ring-crypt" - a crypt with an ambulatory enclosing a central chamber containing a burial or a shrine or an altar dedicated to a saint. Additionally caskets containing bones and relics may have been placed in the recesses within the internal thickness of the side walls. The need to accommodate the height of this chamber may have necessitated the height of the floor of the current chancel and its predecessors being higher than the adjacent floor of the nave/monks' choir.

PHOTO 422. Wing 4.

Unfortunately, the Anglo-Saxon crypt at All Saints Church, was mostly destroyed by the 15th century replacement. The church was extensively restored in 1865 when the Anglo-Saxon foundations of the crypt were rediscovered. What survives of the crypt today is the ambulatory which would have been roofed, the blocked round-headed doorways leading onto the access stairways down to the floor of the ambulatory, and part of the external wall of the chancel with a restored round-headed window and incomplete pilaster-strips.

Internally, only the round-headed doorways in the east wall of the nave/monks' choir can be identified - these have been plastered so none of their construction details can be identified. However, only the top halves of the jambs upwards of these doorways are evident internally, they are cut in two by the current flooring. See adjacent: PHOTO 423. Brixworth 21, showing the blocked round-headed north doorway in the east wall of the nave/monks' choir internally.

PHOTO 423. Brixworth 21.

Externally, the round-headed doorways providing access from the church into the ambulatory can easily be identified in the east wall of the nave/monks' choir. The arched heads of these doorways were constructed with individual rubble stones placed on end to form a discernible arch, they have no imposts, and the jambs were similar to the random rubble stonework in the adjoining walling - displaying few differences; stonework, probably from the 1865 restoration, intrudes on the arched heads and jambs of these doorways. The doorways open onto a flight of steps leading down to the floor of the crypt and into the ambulatory, three steps survive below the northern doorway and part of one step below the southern doorway. When built the ambulatory would have been roofed. See Page 208: PHOTO 424. Brixworth 22, showing the showing the blocked round-headed north doorway in the east wall of the nave/monks' choir externally with the surviving steps arrowed red. For an exterior view of the south doorway see Page 104: PHOTO 146. Brixworth 6.

The surviving exterior walling of the ambulatory owes much to the restoration in 1865 but it is built on the foundations of its Anglo-Saxon predecessor. It may contain some original stonework at, and around, its base. There are two rectangular recesses in this walling, one on the north side and one on the south side, said to be for reliquaries or even tombs – they are probably not original features.

The present chancel was also restored in 1865 and although nothing Anglo-Saxon can be identified internally, externally Anglo-Saxon random rubble walling, a restored round-headed window, and incomplete pilaster-strips forming part of a round-headed blind arcade can be identified. The round-headed window has an arched head constructed of individual stones of rubble placed on end to form a discernible arch; its jambs and sill were constructed with stonework similar to the random rubble stonework in the adjoining walling. The pilaster-strips are incomplete and have been partly overlaid by buttressing and other "new" stonework from the 1865 restoration. They are on each side of the window in the north wall and abutting the window in the east wall of the nave/monks' choir. These pilaster strips probably formed part of a blind, round-headed arcade, and apparently some very slight vestiges of this arcading can just about be identified. See adjacent: PHOTO 425. Brixworth 23, showing the north wall of the chancel including the original random rubble walling arrowed red, the restored round-head window arrowed black, and the pilaster-strips arrowed blue. The stonework above the top of the arched head of the doorway shown in PHOTO 424. Brixworth 22 above right is arrowed green.

PHOTO 424. Brixworth 22.

PHOTO 425. Brixworth 23.

16. ROOFS

Whilst no Anglo-Saxon roofs now survive written records of the time do sometimes refer to the nature of church roofs. Bede, monk at the Wearmouth-Jarrow monastery in County Durham, refers to the church on Lindisfarne having a roof of oak and thatched with reeds which was later covered with sheets of lead. Eddius Stephanus, priest at the monastery of Ripon in North Yorkshire, refers to the roof at York having its roof ridges renewed and covered with lead. Alcuin of York, abbot at the monastery at Tours in Gaul (France), wrote to Archbishop Eanbald II of York donating one hundred pounds of tin for the belfry roof at York Cathedral. At the sites of the Wearmouth-Jarrow monastery archaeology has revealed nails, washers, and clips for sheets of lead, fragments of lead sheeting, lead flashing and stone roof flags/tiles from the roofs of the buildings.

Whilst some churches and monastic buildings had roofs with an oak frame covered with lead or stone tiles with lead flashing along the edges, most churches would probably not have gone to the expense that these roof coverings would have entailed. Churches usually had roofs with an oak frame, some were thatched with reeds or covered with turfs dependent on what material was available in the locality, and others might have triangular wooden shingles or stone tiles as represented by the tegulations on hogback grave-covers (see Pages 283 to 289 "Hogback Grave-Covers"), and in manuscript illustrations.

Church roofs were usually triangular (gable)-shaped, supported by an oak frame, some porticus and annexes may have had angled roofs up to the adjoining larger part of the church, a few roofs in porches, towers and crypts were barrel-vaulted.

Scaring in the walling surviving in the form of triangular (gable)-shaped "rooflines" on existing structures, often indicates the height of a former Anglo-Saxon nave abutting the walling of a tower, the height of a former porticus incorporated into a transept, and the height of a former porch incorporated into a tower. Sometimes the angle of an Anglo-Saxon roofline may survive in the current roofline, albeit reconstructed in later, not Anglo-Saxon, date, but perhaps with some vestiges of Anglo-Saxon stonework included.

St Mathew's Church, Langford in Oxfordshire, has the triangular (gable)-shaped roofline of its former chancel indicated internally, on the east face of the east wall of the Anglo-Saxon central room, above a blocked flat-headed Anglo-Saxon doorway. See adjacent: PHOTO 426. Langford 12, showing the roofline arrowed red and the flat-headed doorway arrowed black.

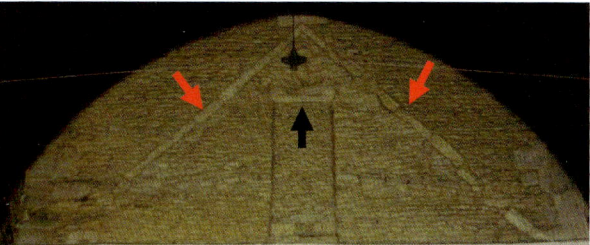

PHOTO 426. Langford 12.

St Peter's Church, Barton-upon-Humber, Lincolnshire, has the triangular (gable)-shaped rooflines of both its 10th and 11th century former chancels indicated internally on the east face of the tower. The upper, 11th century, former chancel roofline is easy to identify extending upwards at an angle from the long and short quoining on the south-east and north-east corners of the tower.

The lower, 10th century, former chancel roofline is more difficult to confidently identify with the angles of its roofline extending upwards from the tops of the scars in the walling indicating the position of the north and south side walls of the narrower 10th century chancel; the base of its roof was level with the sill of the 10th century round-headed doorway between the tower and the room in the chancel at first floor level. See adjacent: PHOTO 427. Barton-upon-Humber 13, showing the upper roofline arrowed red, the position of the lower roofline arrowed black with the approximate apex of the lower roofline arrowed green, and the scaring in the walls indicating the position of narrower 10th century chancel arrowed blue.

PHOTO 427. Barton-upon-Humber 13.

St Mary's Church, Deerhurst, Gloucestershire, has the triangular (gable)-shaped roofline of its former nave indicated externally, on the east face of the east wall of the tower above a lintel of a round-headed Anglo-Saxon doorway. See Page 210: PHOTO 428. Deerhurst 22, showing the roofline arrowed red and the top of the lintel of the round-headed doorway arrowed black.

St Mary's Church at Breamore in Hampshire has a central square tower with two receding pyramidal roofs separated by vertical walling. This is thought to represent a cut down version of the towers of major churches and cathedrals described in Anglo-Saxon literature and depicted in illustrations. (Ignore the later 12th century south porch towards the west end of the nave.) See below right: PHOTO 429. Breamore 5, showing the two receding pyramidal roofs arrowed red.

Some towers may have had what is described as a "Rhenish-Helm roof". This is where the roof has four triangular gables on to which a pyramidal roof is affixed, thus giving the impression of a hood or helm. This is achieved by constructing the roof of four diamond shapes conjoined to form a pyramid-shape with the open triangular-shape at their base built directly on to the four matching gables of the tower walls.

PHOTO 428. Deerhurst 22.

PHOTO 429. Breamore 5.

The "Rhenish-Helm" roof on the square tower of St Mary the Virgin Church at Sompting in Sussex is thought to replicate its Anglo-Saxon predecessor. See below left: PHOTO 430. Sompting 3, showing the west (left-hand) side and the south (right-hand) side of the tower.

The Anglo-Saxon square tower of St Bene't's Cambridge may have vestiges of stonework for a "Rhenish-Helm" roof. These comprise the remains of centrally placed pilaster-strips above the belfry-openings which would have extended upwards in the centre of the more traditionally shaped gables forming much of the roof. See adjacent right: PHOTO 431. Cambridge 13, showing the east (left-hand) side and the north (right-hand) side of the square tower with the pilaster-strips arrowed red.

PHOTO 430. Sompting 3.

PHOTO 431. Cambridge 13.

Scaring in the walling or the surviving triangular (gable)-shaped "rooflines" on existing structures is also indicated in other photographs already included in this book – see:
Page 45. PHOTO 5. Monkwearmouth 1. Roofline of former West Porch.
Page 51. PHOTO 19. Bradford-on-Avon 1. Roofline of former South Porticus.
Page 186. PHOTO 384. Escomb 12. Roofline of former Western Porticus.
Page 190. PHOTO 391. Breamore 4. Roofline of former North Porticus.

17. CHURCH SEATING AND OTHER FURNISHING
It seems from the surviving examples that permanent stone seating in churches was only provided for those ecclesiastics of importance with perhaps, wooden seating provided for some of their acolytes. (Note: seating for the congregation in churches was introduced at during the reign of Elizabeth I, 1558-1603.)

Hexham Abbey in Northumberland has what was probably the seat for the bishop in the diocese or the abbot of the monastery – it may have had connections with St Wilfrid – but it could also have been connected with the rite of sanctuary. It is known as the "frith stool".

The upper part of the seat was hollowed out of a single block of stone and decorated with linear, triquetra knots (see Page 224, PHOTO 459. Hexham 12) and ring-twist (see Pages 225 to 226) designs. The seat is incomplete with missing decoration and stonework on its top surfaces and its north and south sides- there is also damage on the back. It was broken in two in the 19th century and cemented back together; the lower half comprises a 19th/20th century concrete support. See adjacent: PHOTO 432. Hexham 10, showing the west view of the frith stool.

PHOTO 432. Hexham 10.

Beverley Minster in East Yorkshire has a similar, but more complete, chair than the one in Hexham Abbey. It too was hollowed out of a single block of stone with a chamfered seat, supported by a recessed vertical stone upright, and with a high, semi-circular, back. Like the chair at Hexham Abbey, it too is known as the "frith stool".

The chair was intended for the bishop but was also connected with the rite of sanctuary when it was granted by King Aethelstan in AD 938. The chair is not decorated and does have some repairs. On the back is a Latin inscription which has been translated to mean "The chair of peace was a full refuge and safety from the immediate infliction of punishment for any crime whatsoever". The inscription is not Anglo-Saxon, it was inscribed later in the Middle Ages. See above right: PHOTO 433. Beverley, showing the west view of the frith stool.

PHOTO 433. Beverley.

St John the Baptist Church, Barnack, Cambridgeshire, provides a different example of a stone seat. In the ground floor of the tower, in the interior face of the west wall, there is a triangular-headed seat-like recess. There are also separate aumbries in the interior faces of the north and south walls of the tower presumably for books and manuscripts. See Page 192: PHOTO. 395. Barnack 19, PHOTO 396. Barnack 20, and PHOTO 397. Barnack 21.

Examples of aumbries in a likely chapel are also to be seen in St Mary's Church, Deerhurst, Gloucestershire. These are in the north and south walls of the porch/tower at second floor level. See Page 193: PHOTO 398. Deerhurst 20, and PHOTO 399. Deerhurst 21.

In the Jarrow Hall Bede Museum in Jarrow, County Durham, there are parts from a monastic reading desk now displayed within a reconstruction. These parts were found on a floor, possibly in the monastic refectory, during archaeological excavations in 1965 associated with St Paul's Church, Jarrow. The reading desk comprises an octagonal shaft decorated with roll-moulding (see Pages 218 to 219) along its vertical edges enclosing plant designs (see Pages 228 to 229) and parts of what appears as extended ring-knot and ring-twist designs including figure-of-eight pattern (see Pages 225 to 226). Its base is not decorated but it does have large square sockets which may have been as a lifting aid during its construction and placement. See adjacent: PHOTO 434. Jarrow 8, showing three of the decorated sides.

PHOTO 434. Jarrow 8.

St James the Great Church, Melsonby, North Yorkshire, has a similar shaped piece of church furnishing to that in Jarrow. It is thought that this piece of furniture may have been used in the baptistry. It comprises most of a tapering, octagonal, shaft, split vertically in two, at some later, not Anglo-Saxon, date, and reused as part of a window sill.

Both pieces of the shaft have what survives of four incomplete vertical panels; those panels now forming the edges of these two pieces have been cut and reduced in size when the shaft was split in two. The surviving original sides of the panels are separated from each other by single bands of vertical roll-moulding along their adjoining edges.

The broad face of one piece, tapering from bottom to top, is decorated, at the top, with a large, incomplete, long-necked, long-legged, beast in profile to the left, but with its angled, and now defaced, head turned in portrait. Emerging from behind its neck and above its back, is a half-open wing. One of its forelegs is raised up to the level of its jaw and below part of the lower body of a coiled serpent which the beast holds horizontally in its mouth; the head of the coiled serpent touches what remains of the left ear of the beast. Below the beast, and between its hooves, there are the touching heads of two addorsed creatures in vertical profile with long, scrolling and entwining, tails with bulbous ends. Their tails are in being bitten by two incomplete, affronted, dog-like beasts below. See Page 213 top left: PHOTO 435. Melsonby 1, incomplete head of large beast arrowed red, head of serpent in mouth of large beast arrowed black, addorsed creatures arrowed blue, affronted dog-like beasts arrowed green. In what survives of the adjacent panel on the left is an extended knot-work design (see Page 224). In what survives of the adjacent panel on its immediate right is plant-scroll design (see Pages 228 to 229). To the right of this panel are four oval, vertically-placed, sub-panels three of which contain two human heads, which could possibly represent the

Apostles; some of the heads may be haloed, others are faint and incomplete. The fourth, top, sub-panel is badly damaged, and nothing can now be confidently identified. There are traces of gesso on the broad panel and the one to its right with plant-scroll design.

The broad face of the other piece, tapering from top to bottom – it is now upside down - is decorated with knot-work design including figure-of-eight ring-knot design (see Pages 224 to 226). In what survives of the adjacent panel on the left is plant-scroll design. In what survives of the adjacent panel on its immediate right is an extended knot-work design. To the right of this panel is another panel containing plant-scroll design. See adjacent right: PHOTO 436. Melsonby 2.

PHOTO 435. Melsonby 1.

PHOTO 436. Melsonby 2.

The left-arm from the abbot's chair, and the left-arm from a clergy bench, are displayed in St Peter's Church, Monkwearmouth, Sunderland, County Durham, both are damaged, but each is clearly decorated with a representation of a large four legged beast commonly described as a "lion". The display places the arm of the abbot's chair incorrectly as its right arm.

The arm of the abbot's chair comprises a "framed", crouching, beast within two vertical columns and attached to the top and bottom horizontal edges of a block of stonework of which it forms an integral part. The tail, body, legs and damaged claws can be identified forming part of the long side of the block of stonework.

The head of the beast is tucked under the front column and can be viewed from the front and what originally was the outer side of the arm. The head is turned horizontally to its left – the head has quite human characteristics. See adjacent: PHOTO 437. Monkwearmouth 13, showing the view of what was the outer face.

PHOTO 437. Monkwearmouth 13.

The arm of the clergy bench comprises a block of stonework decorated, on its inner side, with the beast, in relief, standing on a ledge. Its tail, body, legs and claws can clearly be identified with its head turned horizontally to its right and pressed up against the top of the block of stonework. See adjacent: PHOTO 438. Monkwearmouth 14, showing the view of what was its inner face.

The Yorkshire Museum in York displays two parts of

PHOTO 438. Monkwearmouth 14.

an Abbot's Chair with a modern intersection between. Top part comprises a three-dimensional head of a beast – the featured sides of the head are flat. It has It has distinctive eyes and open jaws – there is damage – a fang descends from the upper jaw in front of a more distinctive fang rising from the lower jaw. It has irregular linear designs on one of its cheeks and neck, and a leaf-like design on the top of its head. A separate lower part, not adjoining, is decorated with flat-moulding (see Pages 217 to 218), an extended version of interlace design (see Pages 222 to 226), an incomplete row of vertically placed leaf-like designs one above the other, and plant-scroll design (see Pages 228 to 229). See adjacent: PHOTO 439. York 1, showing part of the Abbot's Chair with the original pieces arrowed red and the "modern" intersection arrowed black.

Sunderland Museum displays from St Peter's Church, Monkwearmouth, Sunderland, a probable terminal from a stone chair or bench in the shape of a three-dimensional serpent's head. It has distinctive eyes, a slit-like mouth, grooves to indicate folded skin, a collar around its neck and roll-moulding on the back of its head. See below right: PHOTO 440. Sunderland.

PHOTO 439. York 1.

PHOTO 440. Sunderland. Photograph with permission of Sunderland Museum & Winter Gardens.

PART 3

ANGLO-SAXON & ANGLO-SCANDINAVIAN STONE SCULPTURE

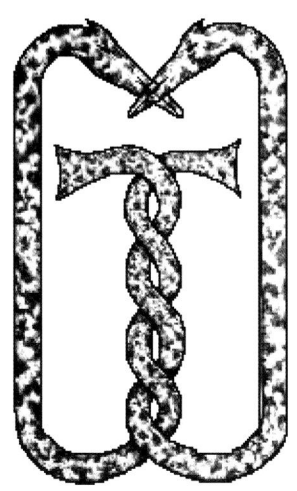

ANGLO-SAXON & ANGLO-SCANDINAVIAN DECORATION

The stonework comprising Anglo-Saxon cross-heads, cross-shafts, cross-bases, grave-markers, grave-covers, grave-slabs, memorials, sarcophagi, shrine-chests, wall-panels, wall-friezes were often, but not always, decorated with designs and patterns. These were "framed" or "enclosed" by moulding which often extended along the vertical and horizontal edges of the stonework.

The stonework was originally brightly painted in garish colours and was often coated with gesso and added pigment to give an appearance of more colours. Ornamentation on some examples included glass and metalwork.

The most common designs and patterns are set out in the following pages in numbered categories indicating their similarity or the subjects which they represent. It begins with moulding whose various manifestations may be encountered in whatever the pattern or design.

1. MOULDING

Moulding can be identified by its physical shape along the edges of vertical or horizontal stonework of whatever length and around the edges of the circumference where the stonework is circular or semi-circular. Additionally, moulding can provide a frame within which a variety of designs and patterns are enclosed within a panel. It was also used horizontally and vertically to separate one panel, or decorative design, from another. Moulding was also used to represent architectural features such as archways and arcades.

Moulding is a continuous section of stonework with defined parallel surface border edges. It may be integral to, in relief, or hollow below, the surface of the main stonework. Lengths of moulding are usually referred to as "bands". It can comprise a single narrow or wide band; a pair of adjacent narrow or wide bands, not necessarily of the same width or shape, and separated by a narrow groove; or a series of alternating bands and grooves with similar or different widths or shapes. The edges of the moulding may be flat, square or rounded. The most common forms of moulding are identified below.

FLAT-MOULDING is a band of moulding squared-off in cross-section. See adjacent illustration which is a cross-section of a band of flat-moulding: solid lines indicate exposed stonework and hatched lines indicate where the stonework has been cut in two.

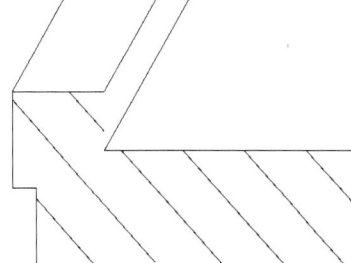

St John the Baptist Church, Low Dinsdale, County Durham, has an incomplete angular cross-shaft with one of its faces bordered along its vertical edges with a single band of flat-moulding. This moulding, with its horizontal extensions, provided the frames enclosing, and separating, three decorative panels. See Page 218, top left: PHOTO 441, Low Dinsdale 1, showing single bands of flat-moulding arrowed red.

St Andrew's Church, Middleton, North Yorkshire, has a billet-head cross-head (see Pages 257 to 258), which is bordered around the edges with a single band of flat-moulding. See below middle left: PHOTO 442, Middleton 1, showing single band of flat-moulding arrowed red.

PHOTO 441.
Low Dinsdale 1.

PHOTO 442.
Middleton 1.

PHOTO 443.
Low Dinsdale 2.

PHOTO 444. Low Dinsdale 3.

GROOVED-MOULDING is a band of narrow or wide flat-moulding separated from the adjacent stonework or design by an easily identifiable deep groove. It may also comprise a series of alternating deep grooves and bands of flat-moulding with similar or different widths. See adjacent illustration which is a cross-section of a band of grooved-moulding: solid lines indicated exposed stonework and hatched lines indicate where the stonework has been cut in two.

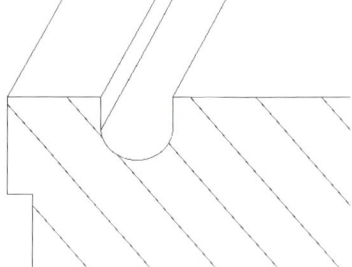

St John the Baptist Church, Low Dinsdale, County Durham, has an incomplete angular cross-shaft with one of its faces bordered along its vertical edges with bands of wide grooved-moulding; the moulding on the surviving horizontal edge at the bottom is unclear. See above, top middle right: PHOTO 443, Low Dinsdale 2, showing wide grooved-moulding arrowed red.

St John the Baptist Church, Low Dinsdale, County Durham, has another incomplete angular cross-shaft bordered along its vertical edges with two adjacent bands of grooved-moulding. This moulding, with its single horizontal band of grooved-moulding extensions, provided the frames enclosing, and separating, two, now incomplete, decorative panels. The lower panel contains interlace design and the upper panel contains the lower halves of the bodies, legs and feet, of two human figures facing each other in profile. See above, top right: PHOTO 444, Low Dinsdale 3, showing two bands of adjacent grooved-moulding arrowed red; single horizontal band of grooved-moulding arrowed black.

ROLL-MOULDING is a roll-shaped band of moulding comprising a three-quarter circle in its cross-section. See Page 219 top left illustration. It provides a cross-section of a band of roll-moulding: solid lines indicate exposed stonework and hatched lines indicate where the stonework has been cut in two.

Anglo-Saxon Church Architecture & Stone Sculpture   219

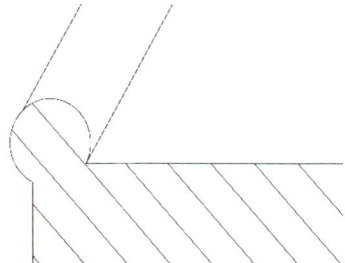

St Andrew's Church, Colyton, Devon has part of an angular cross-shaft with one of its narrow sides bordered along its vertical edges with two adjacent bands of roll-moulding – the outer bands are weathered and damaged. See above left: PHOTO 445. Colyton 1.

PHOTO 445. Colyton 1.

PHOTO 446. Newcastle 1.

At Newcastle Great North Museum: Hancock, the top vertical arm of a free-arm cross-head has its faces decorated with an outer band of flat-moulding with an adjacent inner band of roll-moulding. This cross-head is from Rothbury, Northumberland. See above right: PHOTO 446, Newcastle 1, showing outer band of flat-moulding arrowed red, adjacent inner band of roll-moulding arrowed black.

CABLE-MOULDING is a band of moulding depicting a series of distinctive thick lines in relief which take on a distended curved shape; often in a diagonal pattern. Sometimes cable-moulding is referred to as "rope-work". See adjacent left illustration which is a cross-section of a band of cable-moulding: solid lines indicate exposed stonework, thick black lines indicate the "cable" design of the moulding, and hatched lines indicate where the stonework has been cut in two. See adjacent right illustration showing an incomplete length of cable-moulding in plan indicating its diagonal pattern.

St Andrew's Church, Bishop Auckland, County Durham, has an incomplete angular cross-shaft with one of its faces bordered vertically by an outer band of cable-moulding and an adjacent inner band of roll-moulding. This moulding, with its horizontal extensions, provided the frames enclosing, and separating, what are now most of two panels. The inner band of roll-moulding provides an individual inner frame for each of the panels. See adjacent: PHOTO 447. Bishop Auckland 1, showing outer band of cable-moulding arrowed red, inner band of roll-moulding arrowed black.

PHOTO 447. Bishop Auckland 1.

Cable-Moulding may comprise two adjacent bands placed in opposite directions to provide a herringbone pattern. St Alkmund's Church, Blyborough, Lincolnshire, has part of a grave-cover with its top face decorated with two bands of adjacent cable-moulding along the vertical edges orientated to provide a herringbone pattern. See adjacent: PHOTO 448, Blyborough, showing cable-moulding forming a herringbone pattern arrowed red.

PHOTO 448. Blyborough.

BALUSTER-SHAFT MOULDING is a band of moulding comprising representations of individual baluster-shafts placed vertically, one on top of the other.

St Peter's Church, Codford St Peter, Wiltshire, has a face of part of an architectural feature or angular cross-shaft decorated along each of its vertical edges with a band of stonework comprising representations of baluster-shafts placed vertically one on top of the other. See adjacent: PHOTO 449, Codford St Peter 1, showing baluster-shaft moulding arrowed red.

BEADED-MOULDING is a band of moulding comprising vertical or horizontal rows of small circular-shaped flat beads. Unlike pellet-moulding – see below – they do not noticeably protrude from the surface of the stonework.

PHOTO 449. Codford St Peter 1.

St Luke's Church, Hickling, Nottinghamshire, has a coped hogback grave-cover decorated with geometrical designs and beasts. These include on the top face straight-sided bands of horizontal beaded-moulding, with single rows of small circular-shaped flat beads. See adjacent: PHOTO 450. Hickling 1, showing beaded-moulding arrowed red, flat-moulding arrowed black.

CHEVRON-MOULDING is a band of moulding comprising a series of "V" shapes, one under another, in an upright, curving or inverted sequence. Decoration may also be described as "chevron-pattern design."

St James Church, Burton-in-Kendal, Cumbria, has part of an angular cross-shaft decorated with incomplete bands of incised chevron-moulding which point in opposite directions along the vertical edges. See adjacent: PHOTO 451. Burton-in-Kendal 1, showing chevron moulding arrowed red.

PHOTO 450. Hickling 1.

PELLET-MOULDING is a band of moulding comprising vertical or horizontal rows of round-shaped pellets which protrude from the surface of the stonework. See also Pellet-Design, Page 227: PHOTO 468. Dearham 1, and PHOTO 469. Hickling 2.

PHOTO 451. Burton-in-Kendal 1.

St Andrew's Church, Hexham Abbey, Northumberland, has what may be part of the base of an archway decorated around all four sides with alternating horizontal bands of pellet-moulding, roll-moulding, cable-moulding. See adjacent: PHOTO 452, Hexham 11: pellet-moulding arrowed red, roll-moulding arrowed black and cable-moulding arrowed blue.

2. DESIGNS AND PATTERNS

Designs involving geometrical patterns were the most common ranging from simple lines and circles, to interlace and plant-scroll-designs, and to Scandinavian inspired designs such as "Jellinge", "Ringerike" and "Borre". The designs and patterns were

PHOTO 452. Hexham 11.

nearly always represented "in relief" – the height of the relief varied from one example to another. The complexity of designs and their patterns also varied from one example to another.

Within these designs and patterns, creatures, beasts, birds, serpents, and human or mythological figures, may be restrained by fetters or straps, surrounded and entwined with branching and tapering threads of interlace, spirals, scrolls or plants. Some may have had extensions to their tongues and tails, and plant-like extensions to their bodies. Those with similar characteristics might be linked or entwined together in a row.

Representations of Christ, human or mythological figures, including those from Norse mythology, beasts, creatures, birds and serpents were usually shown in portrait directly looking at the viewer, or in profile facing right or left, providing the viewer with a representation of one of their sides. Often examples may show a figure, beast, creature, bird or serpent in profile but with their head turned to face the viewer in portrait.

Creatures, beasts, birds, serpents, and human or mythological figures were often represented in their "full" size, but some examples represent them with only their head and shoulders, or show them complete in a representation of half their size (half-size) or three-quarter their size (three-quarter size).

Ribbon-like S-shaped creatures were sometimes depicted with serpent-like heads and characteristically long and narrow bodies – sometimes they were double-outlined with parallel grooves along the edges of their heads and bodies. Often in profile some serpents had their heads turned to appear in portrait. Sometimes the strands in a pattern provided the body of individual or pairs of serpents with the top of the strand(s) terminating in the head of the serpent(s).

Representations of animals on stonework was often not life-like and for this reason, this book uses the terms "beast" for the larger animals, "creature" for smaller animals, and "serpent" for snake-like creatures. Birds can sometimes be identified by species, but where this is not possible, they are described as "bird-like". Where such creatures, beasts, birds, serpents, and human or mythological figures, occur within a plant-scroll design it is often described as "inhabited" - see Pages 228 to 229.

As well as on stonework, these designs and patterns, also decorated jewellery, belt-fittings, metalwork and woodwork, and in some cases illuminated manuscripts.

PLAIT-WORK AND INTERLACE DESIGNS
Plait-Work Design was the basic design from which variations developed such as the often quoted "Interlace Design". Other variations included "Basket-Plait Design", "Knot-Work Design", "Ring-Twist Design" or "Ring-Chain Design", "Ring-Knot Design" and "Spiral-Scroll Design". These, and similar descriptions, either reflect the technical complexities of the construction of the design, or the physical resemblance of the design in total.

The formulation of these designs was aided by a grid, divided into equally sized squares by vertical and horizontal lines, and, in some examples, with the grid placed diagonally at a forty-five degree angle. The patterns of the design were placed on top of these grids. The designs consisted of a pattern of ribbon-like strands, each with defined parallel borders, which were set out at forty-five degree angles from the two opposite vertical sides of the grid. The strands were intricately entwined and woven together constantly passing over and under each other making a continual progression downwards. The strands adjacent to the top and bottom horizontal sides of the design, and those strands ending adjacent to the vertical sides of the grid, were broken and bent round to form a right-angle. Whilst many of these designs involved the pairing and duplication of "single" strands (see illustration left), some designs involved "double" strands where two separated strands of similar proportions, but of different sizes, follow the same direction - if they were circles they would be described as "concentric" (see illustration above right). The number of ribbon-like strands within a pattern can vary from one example to another. Several strands twisted together are often referred to as "cords".

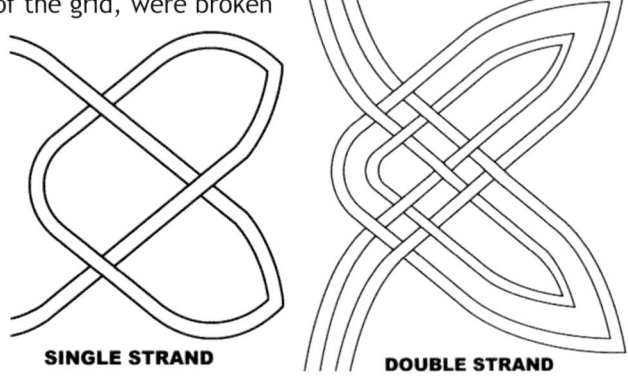

SINGLE STRAND   DOUBLE STRAND

Within the design the patterns used can be asymmetric or symmetric containing curved and pointed loops, U-bends, V-bends, single or concentric circles, and spirals. The same patterns may be repeated within the width and length of the same design sometimes mirroring each other. On other occasions the design may contain a number of different patterns. Some patterns may have identifiable ends – "terminals" – involving the joining of the ends of strands with a solid bar; see the adjacent illustration right with interlace design with bar terminals. Some identifiable patterns within a design may be "half-complete" comprising only one of the two sides of a pattern, rather than "fully-complete" with both sides of the pattern. The complexity of the pattern can vary from one example to another. Plait-

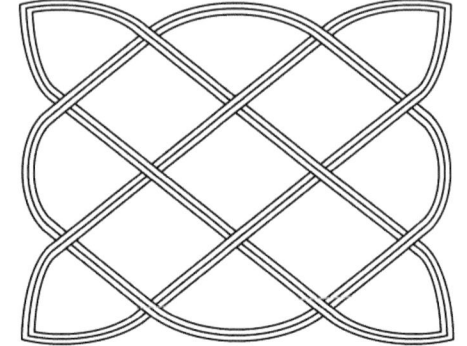

Work Design included strands with an incised groove in the centre running parallel to its long borders. See Page 222 illustration bottom left.

St John the Baptist Church, Low Dinsdale, County Durham, has part of an angular cross-shaft with one of its faces decorated with bands of flat-moulding surrounding the complete central panel and separating it from the incomplete panels on each side. Two panels contain plait-work design whilst the third panel has only the head of a beast in profile to the right. See adjacent left: PHOTO 453. Low Dinsdale 4, showing the head of a beast arrowed red. On one of the narrow sides of the same angular cross-shaft there are bands of flat-moulding along the vertical edges enclosing plait-work design. See adjacent right: PHOTO 454. Low Dinsdale 5.

PHOTO 453. Low Dinsdale 4.   *PHOTO 454. Low Dinsdale 5.*

Some designs included what are described as "Stopped Plait-Work". This is where the strands in the pattern stopped short of crossing over and under each other unlike most plait-work and interlace designs and their variants. See Page 278: PHOTO 568. Thornhill.

A variation of plait-work design can resemble the appearance of plaited wickerwork and this may be called "Basket-Plait Design". St John the Baptist Church, Kirkby Wharfe, North Yorkshire, has part of an angular cross-shaft with one of its faces decorated with a band of cable-moulding enclosing an incomplete panel containing basket-plait design. See adjacent left: PHOTO 455. Kirkby Wharfe 1.

Interlace design differed from plait-work design insofar the internal strands of the design may turn and proceed in a different direction rather than continuing downwards towards the bottom of the design. Additionally, interlace designs, may have diagonal, curving or angular strands, "outside" the main design linking similar patterns together; these additional strands may themselves form a diagonal pattern. However, a panel on a cross-shaft may be described as interlace design comprising a plait-work – see above right: PHOTO 456. Hope 1, showing part of a panel from an angular cross-shaft. Both plait-work and interlace designs involved strands which were intricately entwined and woven together constantly passing over and under each; the differences between the designs may not be obvious.

PHOTO 455. Kirkby Wharfe 1.   *PHOTO 456. Hope 1.*

KNOT-WORK DESIGN was a common variant of Interlace Design. It comprised ribbon-like strands which were intricately entwined and woven together constantly passing over and under each and changing direction in an angular way; the strands were loosely knotted with adjoining strands of similar appearance. They may form a single or a series of knots. See illustration below left; the illustration below in the middle has two similar images of knot-work design linked together by extended diagonal strands crossing over and under each other at the centre of the pattern.

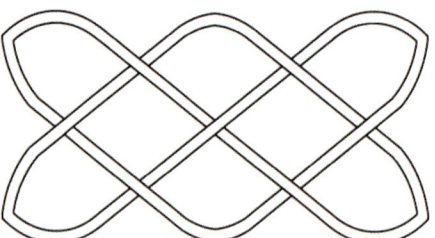

St John the Baptist Church, Colsterworth, Lincolnshire, has part of an angular cross-shaft with one of its faces decorated with a band of flat-moulding enclosing an incomplete panel containing knot-work design. See above right: PHOTO 457. Colsterworth.

PHOTO 457. Colsterworth.

A single "knot", formed by four single strands loosely crossing over and under each other, can often be identified decorating the arms of a cross-head. At times it appears almost "squashed in" by the surrounding moulding – see adjacent illustration.

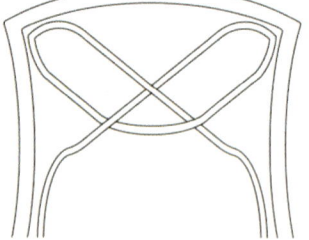

St Andrew's Church, Middleton, North Yorkshire, provides an example of a billet-head cross-head – see Pages 257 to 258 – with one of its faces decorated around the edges of each arm with a band of flat-moulding enclosing the ends of a single knot. See above right: PHOTO 458. Middleton 2.

PHOTO 458. Middleton 2.

Some examples display distinctly entwined triangular-shaped knots, often described as "triquetra(s)" – triquetra-knots, representing God the Father, Son and Holy Spirit. Triquetra-Knot Designs can decorate the faces of cross-heads. See adjacent illustration.

PHOTO 459. Hexham 12.

The "frith stool" (see Page 211: PHOTO 432. Hexham 10) at Hexham Abbey (St Andrew's Church), Northumberland, is decorated with two separate, but similar, triquetra-knot designs. See above right: PHOTO 459. Hexham 12, showing one example.

RING-TWIST DESIGN OR RING-CHAIN DESIGN was a common variant of Interlace Design. It comprised ribbon-like strands woven together and passing over and under each other which formed a pattern containing a series of "rings" in a row – also called "Ring-Chain Design. The rings were connected by long, curving or diagonal, strands. The patterns often comprised a series of rings each containing a pair of concentric circles.

See illustration adjacent left. On other examples, the inner or the outer circles may be divided into semi-circles by angular ribbon-like strands connecting them to other similar circles. See illustration adjacent right.

St Mary's Church, North Witham, Lincolnshire, has part of an angular cross-shaft with one of its narrow sides decorated with a band of cable-moulding enclosing an incomplete panel containing ring-twist design with a single knot-work design at the top. See above left: PHOTO 460. North Witham, showing ring-twist design arrowed red, single knot-work design arrowed black.

PHOTO 460. North Witham.

PHOTO 461. Nassington 1.

St Mary's and All Saints Church, Nassington, Northamptonshire, has part of an angular cross-shaft decorated on two sides with a band of flat-moulding enclosing an incomplete panel each containing ring-chain design. See above right: PHOTO 461. Nassington 1, showing the north face with ring-chain design arrowed red, and the east face with figure-of-eight knot-work design, a variation of ring-chain design, arrowed black.

On occasions a single "ring", or a pair of connected rings, referred to as "free-rings" forming a "free-ring design" may have been incorporated into a design. See adjacent left: PHOTO 462. Brigham 1, showing a free-ring, arrowed red, crossed by long diagonal strands linking it to an interlace design. On other occasions the individual rings in two parallel rows of a ring-twist design were linked together by "S"-shaped loops – sometimes referred to as "como-braid". See above right: PHOTO 463. Brompton 1.

PHOTO 462. Brigham 1.

PHOTO 463. Brompton 1.

RING-KNOT DESIGN was a common variant of Ring-Twist Design or Ring-Chain Design. See illustration adjacent. It comprised ribbon-like strands woven together and passing over and under each other which formed a pattern containing a series of "rings" in a row. The rings were connected by long, curving or diagonal, strands. The strands at the ends of the pattern were loosely knotted to provide angular terminals. Often the rings, and their accompanying strands, were repeated within the length and the width of the same design and formed a figure-of-eight pattern.

PHOTO 464.
Ramsbury 1.

PHOTO 465.
Colyton 2.

Holy Cross Church, Ramsbury, Wiltshire, has part of a reconstructed angular cross-shaft with one of its narrow sides decorated along its edges with a band of flat-moulding enclosing a panel containing figure-of-eight ring-knot design with the strands at the ends of the pattern loosely knotted to provide angular, knotted, terminals. See above left: PHOTO 464. Ramsbury 1.

St Andrew's Church, Colyton, Devon, has part of a reconstructed angular cross-shaft with one of its narrow sides decorated along its vertical edges with two, adjacent, bands of roll-moulding – there is some damage and much of the moulding along the left-hand (east) edge is missing. This moulding encloses a panel containing figure-of-eight ring-knot design – the knots reduce in size towards the top to cater for the tapering nature of the sides of the cross-shaft. Near the base of the cross-shaft diagonal strands extend from the figure-of-eight pattern to form part of the bar terminals completed by the inclusion of the horizontal band of roll-moulding which provides part of the frame containing the design. The upper horizontal border of the panel is now missing. See above right: PHOTO 465. Colyton 2.

OTHER DESIGNS
CHEQUER-BOARD DESIGN comprised squares flush with the surface of the stonework alternating with hollow squares below the surface - similar to a chequer or chess board in plan.

St Cuthbert's Church, Bewcastle, Cumbria, has an angular cross-shaft with one of its narrow sides decorated with two adjacent vertical bands of roll-moulding enclosing a panel bordered horizontally, top and bottom, by a single band of flat-moulding. Within the panel is a chequer-board design comprising rows of square chequers flush with the surface of the stonework alternating with hollow squares sunk below the surface. See adjacent: PHOTO 466. Bewcastle 1.

PHOTO 466. Bewcastle 1.

HERRINGBONE-DESIGN comprised parallel rows of individual stones placed on one of their short ends diagonally in rows of parallel lines. They may be placed in pairs of rows to provide an arrow shape imitating herringbones, or, placed in rows where each row is angled in the opposite direction to the row above and below to provide a pattern in the shape of a zigzag. See Page 49: PHOTO 13. Selham 1, and Page 50: PHOTO 15. Broughton 1. See also Cable-Moulding Pages 219 to 220: PHOTO 448. Blyborough.

MEANDER-PATTERN DESIGN is also known as KEY-PATTERN DESIGN. It comprised a design involving a regular pattern, in an alternating row, representing exaggerated meanders in a winding river with their long sides facing in alternating, opposite, directions. Alternatively the meanders may more resemble the letter "T" or the shape of keys. See illustration adjacent showing an incomplete length of meander or key-pattern design. On this example, but not all such designs, the main "T's" or keys are framed by an additional line of decoration.

PHOTO 467.
Kirkby Wharfe 2.

St John the Baptist Church, Kirkby Wharfe, North Yorkshire has part of an angular cross-shaft with one of its narrow sides decorated with a band of cable-moulding enclosing an incomplete panel containing a meander-pattern design. See above right: PHOTO: 467. Kirkby Wharfe 2. The church also has another, complete, angular cross-shaft with a band of flat-moulding enclosing an incomplete panel containing a meander-pattern design.

PELLET-DESIGN comprised a design which incorporates rounded, sometimes elongated, shapes in relief described as "pellets". They may be similar or varying in size, placed individually, in rows, or in groups. They may form part of a panel containing other designs. They were also used as space-fillers inserted singularly or collectively to fill otherwise vacant spaces in decorative designs – see below: PHOTO 469. Hickling 2. Also see Pellet-Moulding Pages 220 to 221: PHOTO 452. Hexham 11.

St Mungo's Church, Dearham, Cumbria has part of an angular cross-shaft with one of its faces decorated along the vertical edges by a band of flat-moulding enclosing three vertical lines of decoration. The central line contains spiral-scroll design with adjacent, on both sides, a ring-twist design with each ring enclosing a single pellet. See adjacent: PHOTO 468. Dearham 1.

PHOTO 468.
Dearham 1.

St Luke's Church, Hickling, Nottinghamshire, has a coped hogback grave-cover with two panels in its top face containing mostly knot-work designs, one with a beast, and both with pellets. See adjacent: PHOTO 469. Hickling 2, with a single pellet filler arrowed red in the left-hand panel, and a group of four pellets placed vertically in a zigzag line

PHOTO 469. Hickling 2.

providing a filler (see below "Decorative Fillers") arrowed black in the right-hand panel.

DECORATIVE FILLERS

On some designs and patterns the decoration within a panel may be augmented by what are referred to as "fillers" or "space-fillers" placed in spaces that otherwise would be empty. Often taking the form of a single or group of pellets – see Page 227 bottom right: PHOTO 469. Hickling 2. Alternatively they may be a triskele (see Glossary), or simply an elongated or round or ring-like shape perhaps reminiscent of an interlace design. They may also be bunches of berries or a single loose berry. Sometimes space-fillers may have no particular definition. Space-fillers are most commonly found in designs involving beasts, creatures and humans.

PLANT DESIGNS

PLANT DESIGNS involved an individual or collective representation of plants, bushes and trees without being part of the more common "Plant-Scroll Design" – see below Plant-Scroll Design.

PLANT-SCROLL DESIGN was a circuitous design which included the representation of plants, shrubs, vines and trees and is often described as "Bush-Scroll" or "Vine-Scroll" or "Tree-Scroll". It may even be described as in a vertical "scroll" or "spiral-scroll" format – see Pages 229 to 230, Scroll Design and Spiral-Scroll Design. Whatever their description the designs vary in shape, size and complexity. They include distinctive and variously styled stems, trunks, branches, buds, leaves, flowers with individual petals, fruits, and bunches of flowers, fruits, berries or grapes. The stems of plants and the trunks of the trees can be centrally placed with branches extending down from each side – see below: PHOTO 470. Rastrick 1, or, the stems can wind their way alternately between opposite edges of the design – see Page 229: PHOTO 471. Bishop Auckland 2.

The adjacent illustration provides an indication of what may be encountered when stonework is described as decorated with "vine-scroll-design" (the most common variant). The stem of the vine winds its way alternately between opposite edges of the design with sprouting buds and leaves, and bunches of grapes at the end of the stem in the centre circle. Each of the terminals of the main stem is provided by a sprouting leaf.

Examples include, within or adjacent to the scroll design, representations of both real and mythological creatures, beasts and birds sometimes reaching for or pecking at, or picking, the fruits, berries or grapes; humans may also be similarly depicted. Such examples may be described as "Inhabited Plant-Scroll", "Inhabited Bush-Scroll", "Inhabited Tree-Scroll", or "Inhabited Vine-Scroll".

St Matthew's Church, Rastrick, West Yorkshire, has a square cross-base with one side decorated with a band of roll-moulding providing a frame enclosing a single panel containing bush-scroll design. The design has a central vertical stem from which emerge, on each side, scrolling branches which end with flowers with large three-leaf petals. See adjacent: PHOTO 470. Rastrick 1.

PHOTO 470. Rastrick 1.

Anglo-Saxon Church Architecture & Stone Sculpture   229

St Andrew's Church, Bishop Auckland, County Durham, has an incomplete angular cross-shaft with one of its narrow sides decorated along the surviving vertical edges by an outer band of cable-moulding and an adjacent inner band of roll-moulding enclosing an inhabited plant-scroll design.

Within the plant-scroll design, at the bottom, is a three-quarter figure of an archer, most of whose body is rather compressed. The archer is in portrait and slightly turned to the right – upwards - and has been placed vertically rather than horizontally. The archer has a distinctive head with hair, eyebrows, eyes, nose, moustache, mouth and one ear. His right hand pulls the bow-string and his left hand is behind the bow so that its fingers can position the arrow. Above the archer, and placed one above the other, horizontally, and in the three separate plant-scrolls are: a beast in profile to the left with their neck and head turned back to the right, it has a distinctive ear, eye and open jaw, with its legs, feet and claws extending below the scroll and onto the stem of the plant; a bird-like creature in profile to the right but with its neck and head turned back to the left, it has a half open beak and an eye, with indications of body and tail feathers, with its legs, feet and claws extending below the scroll and onto the stem of the plant; a beast in profile to the left with their neck and head turned back to the right, it has a distinctive ear, eye and open jaw, with its legs, feet and claws extending below the scroll and onto the stem of the plant. See adjacent: PHOTO 471. Bishop Auckland 2.

*PHOTO 471.
Bishop Auckland 2.*

PALMETTE-DESIGN consisted of individual, or rows of, vertically placed, narrow-stemmed leaf shapes. Relatively common in Lincolnshire and occasionally in other counties. See Page 101: PHOTO 136. Hadstock 3; Page 113: PHOTO 164. Stow-in-Lindsey 8; and Page 124: PHOTO 218. Glentworth 2.

SCROLL DESIGN AND SPIRAL-SCROLL DESIGN comprised patterns with a series of interconnecting circular, coiling, ribbon-like strands which extended in a vertical, horizontal or angled way. Those designs described as "spiral-scroll" coiled in a cylindrical, conical or helical way. Scroll Design and Spiral-Scroll design included variations of plant designs and plant-scroll designs – see Pages 228 to 229, and also included examples where they formed an idiosyncratic design within a panel containing other designs. The scrolls may be rather more loosely connected than indicated in the illustration adjacent.

Some spiral-scroll designs could have been used to enhance what would otherwise be more standard features in a design. St Paul's Church, Irton,

PHOTO 472. Irton 1.

Cumbria, has an angular cross-shaft with one face decorated along its vertical edges with two separate bands of roll-moulding enclosing a single band of ring-twist design. This moulding frames five panels separated from each other by single, horizontal, bands of roll-moulding. Two separate panels enclose a free-arm cross with similar variations of spiral-scroll design filling each of the quadrants – the upper example interrupts the borders of its surrounding panel. See Page 229 bottom right: PHOTO 472. Ireton 1, showing each of the two relevant panels arrowed red.

STEPPED-PATTERN DESIGN comprised a row of distinctive steps placed together in a regular pattern whose central feature is noticeably thicker than its attached extensions. Some examples have the totality of the "steps" at a distinctive angle. See adjacent illustration.

St John the Baptist Church, Kirkby Wharfe, North Yorkshire, has an angular cross-shaft with one of its narrow sides decorated with a band of flat-moulding enclosing an incomplete panel containing a stepped-pattern design. See adjacent right: PHOTO 473. Kirkby Wharfe 3.

ZIGZAG-DESIGN comprised row of short, joined, ribbon-like strands which were angled at right-angles to the ribbon-like strands adjacent - at times they may be erratically executed. See illustration adjacent.

PHOTO 473.
Kirkby Wharfe 3.

St James Church, Burton-in-Kendal, Cumbria, has part of an angular cross-shaft with one of its faces and two of its sides decorated with a zigzag-design comprising rows of horizontally-placed zigzag lines. These lines are interrupted with vertical grooves which result in single bands of chevron-moulding along the vertical edges pointing in opposite directions to each other. See adjacent: PHOTO 474, Burton-in-Kendal 2, showing the zigzag-design arrowed red, the vertical, grooves arrowed black, and the chevron-moulding arrowed blue.

DESIGNS INCORPORATING CREATURES, BEASTS, BIRDS, SERPENTS AND HUMANS

Many designs incorporated individual, or groups of, creatures, beasts, birds, serpents and humans with geometrical and plant designs providing a subsidiary role. Designs on the same section of stonework did not necessarily involve one type of decoration or subject matter. Individual, or groups of, creatures, beasts, birds, serpents and humans may have been interposed between geometrical and plant designs. Inhabited plant-scroll design by its very nature contained creatures, beasts, birds and serpents, and sometimes humans.

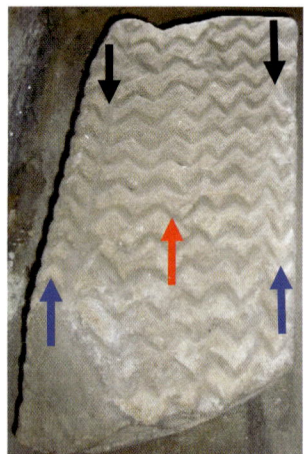

PHOTO 474.
Burton-in-Kendal 2.

St Andrew's Church, Middleton, North Yorkshire has a vertically-sided cross-shaft with one of its faces decorated with two adjacent bands of flat-moulding enclosing a panel containing a ribbon, "S"-shaped, beast. It has been placed vertically in portrait with its distinctive head, large eyes, and its extended, open, jaws linked together by a fetter. The body of the beast is double-outlined and fettered by body extensions and unconnected, stand-alone, moulded bands. See adjacent left: PHOTO 475. Middleton 3, showing head of beast arrowed red. (The other face of this cross-shaft has a seated warrior, see Page 248: PHOTO 512. Middleton 6.)

St Andrew's Church, Middleton, North Yorkshire has another vertically-sided cross-shaft with one of its faces decorated with two adjacent bands of flat-moulding enclosing a panel containing a ribbon, "S"-shaped, beast. It has been placed vertically in profile to the left and has a distinctive round eye with open jaws with a gag or possibly fangs. The body of the beast is double-outlined and fettered by body extensions and unconnected, stand-alone, moulded bands; within the panel there are pellets. See above right: PHOTO 476. Middleton 4, showing head of beast arrowed red. (The other face of this cross-shaft has a hunting scene, see Page 246: PHOTO 509. Middleton 5.)

PHOTO 475. Middleton 3.

PHOTO 476. Middleton 4.

Holy Cross Church, Ramsbury, Wiltshire, has part of a reconstructed angular cross-shaft with one of its narrow sides decorated with an incomplete band of flat-moulding enclosing a panel containing a coiled beast. The beast has been placed vertically with, in profile to the left, its head with a round extended eye, a row of teeth and a snubbed snout; it is in the process of biting its own body. Its body is incised with a chevron-pattern design along its length which becomes two adjacent rows, separated by a central incised line, as its body width increases. The beast is fettered by bands of interlace design with a central groove along their length. This interlace design expands within the spaces formed by the beasts coiled body, and in the spaces between its body and the flat-moulding enclosing the panel. In the top corners of the panel the interlace design has knot-work terminals. See adjacent: PHOTO 477. Ramsbury 2, showing head of beast arrowed red.

Conyers Chapel, All Saints Church, Sockburn, County Durham, has part of an angular cross-shaft with one of its faces decorated with a band of flat-moulding forming two complete and one incomplete panels. The lowest

PHOTO 477. Ramsbury 2.

complete panel contains a four-legged beast in profile to the right with its head turned back towards its tail which is curved forward. The complete middle panel above contains plait-work design. The top incomplete panel contains a different variant of plait-work design. See adjacent left: PHOTO 478. Sockburn 1.

Conyers Chapel, All Saints Church, Sockburn, County Durham, has part of an angular cross-shaft. See adjacent right: PHOTO 479. Sockburn 2. One of its faces is decorated along each of its vertical edges with a band of stonework comprising representations of baluster-shafts, arrowed red, placed vertically on end, one on top of another, which terminate, towards the bottom of the cross-shaft, with the heads of two serpents. The mouth of a larger headed serpent, arrowed black, points towards the top of the cross-shaft, whilst the mouth of a smaller serpent, arrowed blue, points towards the bottom of the cross-shaft – the head of the smaller serpent emerges from the back of the neck of the larger serpent. (Note. The two serpents' heads can be identified adjacent to both vertical edges of the cross-shaft.) The bodies of the two larger headed serpents converge at an acute angle to meet in the centre of the face of the cross-shaft and provide the neck of a fox-like creature in portrait with distinctive round eyes and pointed ears - arrowed green. Within the panel enclosed vertically by the baluster-shafts are a row of three beasts – the lowest beast arrowed yellow - restrained and interlocked, and in profile. These three beasts, shown vertically rather than horizontally, run towards the top of the cross-shaft. The two lower beasts have distinctive heads with open jaws and flowing ears; the head of the top beast is missing. The lower part of the cross-shaft is not decorated.

PHOTO 478. Sockburn 1.

PHOTO 479. Sockburn 2.

St Andrew's Church, Dacre, Cumbria, has part of an angular cross-shaft with one of its faces decorated with vestiges of an incomplete band of flat-moulding along the vertical edges enclosing an incomplete panel containing inhabited scroll-design involving a serpent, a lion-like beast, and two sets of legs and feet of humans.

See adjacent: PHOTO 480. Dacre. The lion-like beast is in profile to the right with its head, arrowed red, turned to appear in portrait but slightly angled; it has a human-like face with a mane, a drooping moustache, ears, eyes, nose and mouth. A flowing horizontal wing extends from the back of its neck and the top of its body, whilst the other wing extends vertically below its chin; a bunch of berries and their stem overlie part of the horizontal wing and a large serrated leaf overlies part of the vertical wing. Its legs are

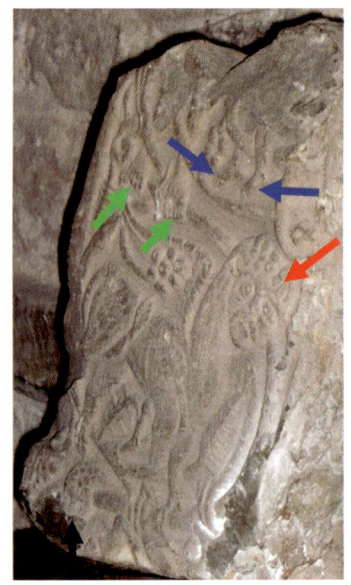

PHOTO 480. Dacre.

entwined in a plant scroll-design with leaves and their stems overlying parts of its body. Its tail curves around its rear and disappears and then re-emerges to curve ending in an almost leaf-like design. Below its rear legs is the head of a serpent, arrowed black, in profile to the right overlying a curving branch – its eyes and scaled head are distinctive. To the right of centre, and above the lion-like beast, two human legs and feet, arrowed blue, are in profile to the left emerging from and overlying the surrounding branches. To the left of centre, and above the lion-like beast, two human legs and feet, arrowed green, with distinctive individual toes, are angled downwards to the left but turned to appear in portrait.

All Saints Church, Ilkley, West Yorkshire, has an incomplete and damaged angular cross-shaft. One of its faces has a panel where the top and bottom borders are provided by a horizontal band of flat-moulding whilst the two vertical sides are decorated with a band of cable-moulding. The panel encloses two addorsed four-legged, winged, beasts in profile; their heads are turned back so that their snouts meet. Their features are distinctive and include oval pointed ears, round eyes, long jaws, legs, feet and tails. One foreleg of each beast is raised so that its foot bisects the upper corners of the panel whilst the other foreleg rests on top of their respective, curling, interlinked, tails. Their wings curve in front and behind their necks, cross over and behind their forelegs, and cross over their bodies to end in a distinctive tip opposite the wings of the other beast. Between their wings and below their chins are three round pellets. See above right: PHOTO 481. Ilkley.

PHOTO 481. Ilkley.

All Saints Church, Otley, West Yorkshire, has part of an angular cross-shaft with one of its faces decorated with most of an incomplete panel bordered by an outer wide band of roll-moulding with an adjacent inner, narrower, band of roll-moulding. The moulding encloses the standing, "S" - shaped figure, of a wyvern in profile to the left. Its features are particularly well-defined and include: a lip-like pointed ear, a sunken oval eye with eyebrow, an open beak, a mane at the back of its head and neck, a wing with details of its feathers, legs and claws, and a curling tail ending in a triangular, leaf-like shape, with distinctive veins. Below the tail is a single plant feature with a triangular leaf. See adjacent: PHOTO 482. Otley 1.

DESIGNS INVOLVING THE REPRESENTATION OF CHRIST, CRUCIFIXION SCENES AND THE VIRGIN MARY AND CHRIST-CHILD

The representation of the standing figure of Christ in portrait, with a dish-like halo, in "Majesty", or in the pose of giving a blessing, was often depicted on cross-shafts. The Crucifixion of Christ with various attendant figures and symbols was also depicted; on occasions the figure of Christ was omitted. The Virgin Mary, often sitting, was depicted holding the Christ-Child.

PHOTO 482. Otley 1.

Newcastle Great North Museum: Hancock, has part of an angular cross-shaft with one of its faces decorated with an outer band of flat-moulding adjacent to an inner band of roll-moulding enclosing an incomplete haloed figure of Christ in Majesty in portrait. Christ has a round-headed arch above his head emerging from the inner band of roll-moulding. On each side of his head there are detached flowers. This cross-shaft is from Rothbury, Northumberland. See adjacent left: PHOTO 483. Newcastle 2.

PHOTO 483. Newcastle 2.

The Minster Church of All Saints, Dewsbury, West Yorkshire, has a section of stonework cut out a circular lower part of a cross-shaft with an upper angular part. It has a face decorated with the representation of the seated figure of a haloed Christ in portrait. He gives giving a blessing with his raised right hand and holds a vertical scroll in his left hand. His hair and eyes are easily identified, his nose and mouth are damaged. Above his head is a protruding, frame-like band of flat-moulding with an inscription which is an abbreviation of the Latin form for "Jesus Christ". See above right: PHOTO 484. Dewsbury 1.

PHOTO 484. Dewsbury 1.

Two similar panels on different cross-shafts could have been based on the same "model". See below left: PHOTO 485. Ruthwell 1, (in good condition), and below right: PHOTO 486. Bewcastle 2, (in weathered condition).

Ruthwell and Mount Kedar Church, Ruthwell, Dumfriesshire, has most of an angular cross-shaft. Its north face is decorated with broad bands of vertical and horizontal flat-moulding providing the frame for a panel enclosing the standing, haloed, figure of Christ in Majesty in portrait. His right arm is raised as though in blessing but part of his hand is missing. In his left hand he holds a scroll, angled to the left; at first glance the scroll might be mistaken for his right hand. Christ stands on the heads of two four-legged creatures. On the flat-moulding providing the frame of the panel is a Latin inscription interpreted as "Jesus Christ", the judge of equity. Beasts and Dragons knew; in the desert, the Saviour of the World". See adjacent left: PHOTO 485. Ruthwell 1.

PHOTO 485. Ruthwell 1.

PHOTO 486. Bewcastle 2.

St Cuthbert's Church, Bewcastle, Cumbria, has most of an angular cross-shaft. The west face is decorated along its vertical edges with a band of roll-moulding with an adjacent inner, narrower, band of roll-moulding which provides the vertical part of the frame of a panel. The panel encloses the standing haloed figure of Christ in Majesty in portrait. His right arm is raised as though in blessing but part of his hand is missing. In his left hand he holds a scroll, angled to the left; at first glance the scroll might be mistaken for his right hand. Christ stands on the heads of two four-legged creatures. Above the head of Christ is the runic inscription "g[e]ssus kristtus" – Jesus Christ. See Page 234 bottom right: PHOTO 486. Bewcastle 2.

Crucifixion scenes are quite common, sometimes the Virgin Mary is depicted on the right-hand side of Christ and John the Evangelist on the left. Alternatively, the figures below, and on each side of Christ, may represent Stephaton the soldier who offered Christ a sponge soaked in vinegar, sometimes represented as a cup, and Longinus the soldier who pierced Christ's side with a spear. Christ may be depicted with one or more or all of the "Four Evangelists". They may be represented by different stylised figures: Mathew by a winged man or angel; Mark by a winged lion; Luke by a winged ox, bull or calf; and John by an eagle.

All Saints Church, Brixworth, Northamptonshire, has part of a panel decorated with an incomplete band of roll-moulding providing a "frame". The vertical bands of roll-moulding are half-curved, and on the right-hand side there is another, incomplete, adjacent band of roll-moulding. The frame encloses the figure of an eagle, the symbol of St John the Evangelist. It is shown in portrait but with its head turned in profile to the right. See adjacent: PHOTO 487. Brixworth 24.

PHOTO 487. Brixworth 24.

The Market Square in Sandbach, Cheshire has two, almost complete, reconstructed, angular cross-shafts and their supporting cross-bases; each has part of the lower vertical arm of their cross-head.

On the larger of the two angular cross-shafts the east face is decorated with a band of cable-moulding along each of its vertical edges with an adjacent, narrower, inner band of roll-moulding. This inner band of roll-moulding provides the vertical sides of an inner square frame for panels; the horizontal borders of this inner frame are now missing. This moulding encloses a panel containing a Crucifixion scene in relief. The facial and body features of Christ, the angel, humans and beasts, and the geometrical designs, can all be identified despite weathering and some damage. See Page 236: PHOTO 488. Sandbach 1.

The standing figure of the haloed Christ with outstretched arms and hands, is in portrait; his head is tilted slightly to the right. Christ is shown crucified on a free-arm cross with a long lower vertical arm supported by a stepped, hollow, cross-base. Above the head of Christ, at the top of, and within, the upper vertical arm of the cross, are two adjacent, rounded, boss-like features which represent the sun and the moon.

The symbols of the Four Evangelists, all holding books, are depicted as half-figures in the quadrants above and full figures in the quadrants below the horizontal arms of the cross: upper left, a haloed angel (Matthew), in profile to the right; upper right, a damaged lion (Mark), in profile to the left; lower left, a bull (Luke), in profile to the right, with a single pellet between its chest and the lower vertical arm of the cross; lower right, an eagle (John), in profile to the left. Both the bull (Luke) and the eagle (John) stand on a curving arch of flat-moulding linking the vertical sides of the inner frame of the panel and the vertical sides of the long lower vertical arm of the cross together.

Below, and flanking the bottom lower part of the long vertical arm of the cross, and the supporting stepped, hollow, cross-base, is, on the left, the standing, haloed, figure of John, in profile to the right but with his head turned in portrait, with a single pellet between his shoulder and the inner frame of the panel, he holds a scroll vertically. On the right, is the standing, haloed, figure of the Virgin Mary, in profile to the left, and leaning towards the feet of Christ, with her head turned in portrait; she has a single pellet between her shoulder and the inner frame of the panel, and another single pellet beneath her feet.

PHOTO 488. Sandbach 1

Between John and Mary, and framed by the stepped, hollow, cross-base, is a Nativity scene. Centrally placed, under the cross-base, is a haloed, half-figure, of an angel with its wings opened; it is in profile to the left but with its head turned in portrait. Below the right-wing of the angel, in profile to the right, is the head and neck of a large beast with part of its body and with one of its forelegs. Opposite the larger beast, and below the left-wing of the angel, in profile to the left, is a smaller beast; it is complete with head, neck, body, one foreleg and one hind leg. The heads of both beasts are lowered so that they appear to be looking down to a swaddled figure lying horizontally on a crib. The crib is represented at its head by a round vertical object with a mushroom top, and at its foot with a smaller vertical object. The swaddled figure, with its head on the left-hand side adjacent to the head of the crib, rests on an incomplete horizontal band of flat-moulding representing the bed of the crib joining its vertical head and foot together.

St Mary's and All Saints Church, Nassington, Northamptonshire, has part of an angular cross-shaft with one face decorated with a band of flat-moulding enclosing two incomplete panels separated by a horizontal band of flat-moulding. The larger, lower panel includes a weathered Crucifixion scene with the standing figure of Christ, in portrait, on the Cross; the head of Christ is damaged. The sun and moon are represented on each side of the head of Christ with a protruding (damaged) human face. Below the horizontal arms of the cross are two standing figures one on each side of the lower vertical arm of the cross. They are in opposite profile to each other and hold long pole-like objects reaching up towards Christ; the tops of these poles are damaged. These figures represent the Roman soldiers Stephaton, usually depicted on the left-hand side of Christ, who holds up a sponge soaked in vinegar, and Longinus,

PHOTO 489. Nassington 2.

usually depicted on the right-hand side of Christ, who pierces the body of Christ with a spear. The upper panel contains an incomplete figure with the lower half of their body and their legs in portrait and their feet turned in opposite directions in profile; it may represent an Ascension scene. See Page 236 bottom right: PHOTO 489. Nassington 2.

Although representing a Crucifixion scene Christ may not always be depicted. St John the Baptist Church, Kirkby Wharfe, North Yorkshire, provides just such an example. It has an angular cross-shaft with a face decorated with a band of flat-moulding enclosing a centrally placed long-stemmed free-arm cross with bush-like characteristics. The stem appears rounded and trunk-like and the top of each of the horizontal arms of the cross have a sprouting leaf design. Below each of the horizontal arms of the cross is a standing human figure in portrait who holds with one hand the stem/trunk of the cross which separates them. The figure on the right, turned towards the stem/trunk, represents the Virgin Mary and the figure on the left represents John. Both figures have what are slightly odd-shaped halos and incised facial features; each figure shows only one hand, their feet are missing. See adjacent: PHOTO 490. Kirkby Wharfe 4.

PHOTO 490.
Kirkby Wharfe 4.

St Peter and St Paul's Church, Shelford, Nottinghamshire, provides an example of the representation of the Virgin Mary and the Christ-Child. It has part of an angular cross-shaft which on one face is decorated along its incomplete vertical edges with a band of flat-moulding adjacent to an inner band of pellet-moulding. This moulding encloses a panel containing a round-headed archway with below a seated depiction of the Virgin Mary with the Christ-Child on her lap. See adjacent: PHOTO 491. Shelford 1.

The archway comprises three bands of adjacent moulding: an outer band of what was probably a band of pellet-moulding (now rather weathered and flat), a middle band of pellet-moulding which reduces in size just before it disappears above the imposts of the archway, and an inner band of flat-moulding. The imposts comprise two horizontal bands of roll-moulding, each with a hollow below, which extend to the vertical edges of the panel. The jambs comprise a vertical band of flat-moulding adjacent to a vertical band of pellet-moulding along with the bands of pellet-moulding and flat-moulding providing the vertical edges of the panel.

PHOTO 491.
Shelford 1.

The seated, haloed, Virgin Mary is in portrait with the Christ-Child sitting on her knee in profile to the right but with his head turned in portrait. In his right hand the Christ-Child holds a book vertically. Both the faces of the Virgin Mary and the Christ-Child were probably planed away in the 16th century removing all their facial features.

The other face of this cross-shaft is decorated along its incomplete vertical edges with a band of flat-moulding adjacent to an inner band of pellet-moulding. This moulding encloses a panel containing a round-headed archway with below the standing figure of a four-winged angel.

The archway comprises three bands of adjacent moulding forming its arched head: an outer band of what was probably a band of pellet-moulding (now rather weathered and flat), a middle band of single pellets in a row which reduce in size just before it disappears above the imposts of the archway, and an inner band of flat-moulding. The imposts comprise two horizontal bands of roll-moulding, each with a hollow below, which extend across to the vertical edges of the panel. The jambs comprise a vertical band of flat-moulding adjacent to a vertical band of pellet-moulding along with the bands of pellet-moulding and flat-moulding providing the vertical edges of the panel.

PHOTO 492. Shelford 2.

The four-winged angel has a long moustache and forked beard. In his right hand he holds horizontally a book or scroll. His left arm is raised with the hand above his head – his hand is damaged but he may be giving a blessing, or holding or supporting some object shining light. See above right: PHOTO 492. Shelford 2, with the mirror image arrowed red.

The Minster Church of All Saints, Dewsbury, West Yorkshire, also has part of an angular cross-shaft with one face decorated with the representation of the Virgin Mary with the Christ-Child. The haloed figure of the Mary is in portrait but her body is turned slightly to her left. She is seated with the haloed Christ-Child sitting on her left knee, the top of his haloed head is just below the top of her left shoulder. The Christ-Child is three-quarter turned to his right but his head is turned in portrait; he holds a vertically placed scroll. The facial and body details of both figures are very weathered. See adjacent: PHOTO 493. Dewsbury 2.

PHOTO 493. Dewsbury 2.

DESIGNS DEPICTING ANGELS AND SCENES FROM BIBLICAL STORIES
Angels are often depicted in portrait sometimes with both their bodies and heads slightly turned inwards towards a central figure of Christ or in pairs where both angels are turned inwards towards each other. They are usually, but not always, haloed and their wings may be closed, half-open or fully extended. They may be half, or three-quarter, or full size figures, some may be in profile and in a flying pose. Angels may be both male and female with the nature of their hairstyling and clothing indicating their sex. Archangels may also be depicted holding their individual distinguishing symbols. Representations of angels often appear associated with Crucifixion scenes.

The depiction of biblical stories is less common and it is not always clear what the scenes represent given that often only fragments survive. Those that do survive depict the representation of Christ, people, both individually and sometimes in "crowd" scenes, and beasts and creatures, sometimes all involved in, or accompanied by, plant designs.

St Andrew's Church, Bishop Auckland, County Durham, has part of an incomplete cross comprising a free-arm cross-head, angular cross-shaft, and a trapezoid-shaped cross-base –

all three components are incomplete. One face of the angular cross-shaft is bordered vertically by an outer band of cable-moulding and an adjacent inner band of roll-moulding which also separate two incomplete panels horizontally; the inner band of roll-moulding provides an individual frame for each of the panels.

In the centre of the lower, incomplete, panel, is a Crucifixion scene with the central figure probably depicting Christ bound on the Cross, or, possibly the martyrdom of St Andrew – the interpretation of the accompanying incomplete inscription leads to doubt about their identity. A haloed figure in portrait is bound to a free-arm cross; above the head, the top of the upper vertical arm of the cross is inscribed with the letters "PAS". Behind the surviving horizontal right arm of the cross, inscribed with the letters "AND", is a three-quarter length haloed figure in portrait; their haloed head is slightly higher than that of the central figure. Their right hand with extended fingers is placed upwards, diagonally, across their chest. Below the right arm of the cross, and towards the lower part of this figure, is the head and one hand of a smaller figure, who could represent Longinus the spear holder – what the figure is holding onto is unclear. On the left-hand side of the cross, slightly higher than the haloed head of the central figure, is part of the haloed head of another figure who is thought to be female given their hairstyle is similar to the female in the upper panel above on the right.

PHOTO 494.
Bishop Auckland 3.

In the upper complete panel there are two three-quarter length haloed figures who are probably angels. They are in portrait and slightly turned inwards towards each other; the figure on the right overlapping the figure on the left. The figure on the left is winged and their angled right arm and hand with three extended fingers reach the right shoulder of the figure on the right. The figure on the right appears to be female – given the nature of hairstyle. In her left hand she holds diagonally a trilobed-ended rod which ends level with her eyes; she may also be winged. See above right: PHOTO 494. Bishop Auckland 3.

All Saints Church, Bakewell Derbyshire, has what may be part of a square cross-base – it is weathered and damaged. One side is decorated along its vertical edges with a band of roll-moulding with an adjacent inner, narrower, band of roll-moulding providing both the vertical and horizontal borders of an inner "frame". Within the frame is the depiction of a three-quarter figure of a haloed, winged, angel in portrait. The facial feature, clothing and large wings on each side of the angel are distinctive. The damaged hands appear to hold a large trilobed-ended rod diagonally across the body with the top in the top right-hand corner of the panel. See adjacent: PHOTO 495. Bakewell 1.

The Minster Church of All Saints, Dewsbury, West Yorkshire, has part of an angular cross-shaft with its face decorated with biblical scenes. It has two separate horizontal bands of flat-moulding providing the top and bottom borders of an almost complete upper panel and

PHOTO 495. Bakewell 1.

separating it from an incomplete lower panel. The top band has an incomplete inscription interpreted as "(Jesus) made wine from water". It is thought that this inscription and the scene depicted below refers to the Miracle of Christ turning water into wine. The lower band has an incomplete inscription interpreted as "and two fishes [he divided] among them all". It is thought that this inscription and the scene depicted below refers to the Christ's Miracle of the Loaves and Fishes.

The almost complete upper panel contains the central, standing, haloed figure of Christ in portrait giving a blessing with his raised right hand and holding a vertical scroll in his left hand. On his right is the standing haloed figure of the Virgin Mary in portrait but turned to her left towards Christ. On the left of Christ is the standing haloed figure of St John holding in both hands a vertical scroll. The hair, eyes, noses and mouths of all three figures can be identified; their clothing is somewhat weathered and not that distinctive. In front of the lower bodies, legs and feet of Mary and Christ, in a horizontal row, are four vertical, bulbous-shaped, water jars with tops and bottoms indicated by horizontal grooves.

The incomplete lower panel contains, off-centre to the left, the top half of the haloed figure of Christ in portrait with his head turned to his right. It is thought he may be in the process of raising his right arm to give a blessing – only the horizontal part of the arm survives. Above what survives of his right arm are two incomplete rounded objects representing two of the five loaves. Below the left shoulder of Christ and above his stomach are two rounded objects, one diagonally above the other; these may represent the two fishes. The upper object seems to have two slanting eyes and an upturned snout which might represent a fish - it has a different shaped head and features to the human heads depicted. To the left side of Christ are two, possibly three, horizontal rows of human heads in portrait but turned to their right like the head of Christ – at least six heads representing the watching "crowd". The facial features of the head immediately on the left of Christ's head are the most distinctive of the "crowd". See adjacent: PHOTO 496. Dewsbury 3.

PHOTO 496. Dewsbury 3.

Newcastle, Great North Museum: Hancock, has an incomplete angular cross-shaft with one narrow side decorated with a flat-band of moulding enclosing part of a panel containing a "crowd scene" comprising eighteen human heads. These heads are arrayed in four horizontal rows with the details increasing in completeness as the rows descend. It is not clear as to whether these are heavenly – the scene is from the top of the cross-shaft - or earthly figures. This cross-shaft is from All Saints Church, Rothbury, Northumberland. See adjacent: PHOTO 497. Newcastle 3.

PHOTO 497. Newcastle 3.

Newcastle, Great North Museum: Hancock, has a free-arm cross-head which has on one of the faces of its horizontal arms a representation of a flying figure. The arm of the cross-head is decorated with an outer band of flat-moulding and an adjacent inner band of roll-moulding. This moulding encloses a figure, in profile to the left, holding a circlet in each hand - the folds in the drapery may indicate a flying figure. The cross-head is from Rothbury, Northumberland. See adjacent: PHOTO 498. Newcastle 4.

All Saints Church, Otley, West Yorkshire, has part of a weathered and damaged angular cross-shaft. One face is decorated with an incomplete band of roll-moulding along its vertical edges with an adjacent, narrower, inner band of roll-moulding which encloses and provides the frames for six panels. These comprise three narrow panels each originally containing a painted inscription, and three larger panels each containing the top half of the bodies and the heads of human figures - none are haloed. One narrow panel and one larger panel are incomplete.

PHOTO 498. Newcastle 4.

The figures are portrayed in portrait but with their heads turned in profile, alternating, from the bottom panel upwards, left, right, left. Each of the figures are shown recessed under arches supported by three-stepped imposts. In the two lower complete panels a form of plant design survives in the spandrels above the arch. All three figures hold a book although their hands are not depicted. The facial features and clothing of all three figures can be identified - the middle figure provides the best example. In the incomplete top panel, the top half of the head of the figure, and the arch and decoration above, are missing. The figures on this section of stonework, and another similar section more weathered and damaged in Otley, may depict the apostles. See adjacent: PHOTO: 499. Otley 2.

PHOTO 499. Otley 2.

DESIGNS DEPICTING PRIESTS AND MONKS
Designs depicting those monks and priests following the Celtic or Irish form of Christianity can usually be identified by a head with the Celtic tonsure where the head is shaved at the front, across the forehead, from ear to ear - the hair covers the rest of the top and the back and sides of the head. They often have a reliquary or book satchel hanging from the neck and they may have both feet pointing the same way sideways. Those following the Roman form of Christianity can usually be identified by a head with the Roman Tonsure where the head is shaved on the crown in a circular fashion so that the surrounding hair might symbolise the Crown of Thorns. They may be dressed in vestments and hold a chalice - see next paragraph.

St Mary and St Helen's Church, Neston, Cheshire, has part of an angular cross-shaft with one face decorated along each vertical edge with a band of cable-moulding - the top horizontal edge is broken and the lower horizontal edge appears to comprise a band of flat-moulding. The moulding encloses a panel containing the figure of a priest in portrait wearing his vestments whilst performing religious ceremonies. The vestments represented include: an alb - a tunic of white cloth reaching to the feet; a triangular shaped chasuble – a sleeveless outer garment worn over alb and stole; and a stole - a narrow strip of silk or linen worn over the shoulders and hanging down or crossed over the chest. The priest has his arms raised. He holds a chalice (a cup used in celebration of the Holy Eucharist – the Communion) in his right hand, and hanging from the wrist of his left hand is a maniple (another vestment item usually similar to a napkin) with two vertical strands each ending in a square shape. His facial features can all be identified but the top of his head is missing; his feet are placed at right-angles. See adjacent: PHOTO 500. Neston 1.

PHOTO 500. Neston 1.

Holy Trinity Church, Stonegrave, North Yorkshire, has an angular cross-shaft with one of its faces bordered with a band of flat-moulding enclosing a single panel containing plaitwork design within which is an incomplete standing human figure, a free-arm cross with a long lower vertical arm, and the figure of a priest following the Celtic form of Christianity. The priest stands in portrait, his head has the Celtic tonsure, he has a book-satchel hanging from his neck and his feet are both in profile to the right. See adjacent: PHOTO 501. Stonegrave 1.

DESIGNS DEPICTING SECULAR FIGURES
Designs depicting secular figures were not that common other than when they appeared in Christian scenes, scenes from Norse mythology, or where they are depicted as huntsmen (see Pages 246 to 247), or as warriors (see Pages 247 to 249). Some archers are depicted in inhabited plant-scroll designs – see Page 229: PHOTO 471. Bishop Auckland 2.

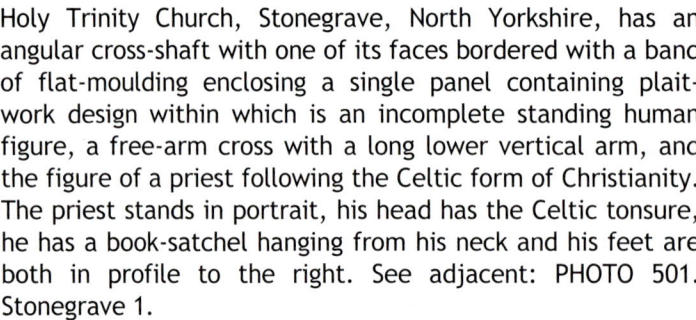

PHOTO 501. Stonegrave 1.

St Oswald's Church, Lythe, North Yorkshire, has a broken and incomplete angular cross-shaft known as the "Wrestlers Stone". The two parts show the same face of the cross-shaft.

The lower part of the cross-shaft is decorated with a broad horizontal band of flat-moulding providing a plinth-like feature. Set-back above, the stonework is decorated with the four legs of a beast whose head and body are depicted in the upper part of the cross-shaft; the legs are in profile to the right.

On the upper part of the cross-shaft an incomplete band of flat-moulding provides part of a frame within which is the body, neck and horned head of a large, "S" shaped, beast, in profile to the right – its legs are depicted on the lower part of stonework. Its neck and head are turned so that the end of its mouth is almost touching the top of its back. It has a horned head, a round eye, and its mouth is slightly open. Above the beast, two men are in profile, confronting each other,

PHOTO 502. Lythe 1.

and in the process of wrestling. Only their lower bodies, legs and feet, and one of their arms, survive. See Page 242 bottom right: PHOTO 502. Lythe 1.

St Peter's Church, Codford St Peter, Wiltshire has a decorated section of stonework tapering from bottom to top which may be part of an architectural feature or angular cross-shaft. The excellent condition of the detail of the decoration suggests that this stonework was an internal feature, possibly placed as part of a jamb to an opening, and never exposed to weathering as would be expected with a cross-shaft.

Its surviving face is decorated along each of its vertical edges with a band of stonework comprising representations of baluster-shafts placed vertically on end one on top of another. Single, horizontal, bands of roll-moulding divide the face into four panels.

At the base there is a narrow panel with a band of roll-moulding along its top border enclosing below a balustrade indicated by vertical grooves. Above this roll-moulding is the largest panel containing inhabited plant design with the half-turned standing figure of a man in profile to the left. His head is placed horizontally and he is looking upwards towards a bunch of berries on the plant above his head. His right arm is raised and his hand is grasping a stem of a plant. Above his waist his left arm holds vertically an object similar to a small pan or ladle. The position of his right leg and foot suggest he is stretching upwards with the foot almost off the ground; his left leg and foot are more solidly placed on the ground. His facial features, ornate hairstyle, and clothing are easily identified. Near to the top of the plant design are three-stepped imposts separated by two circular buds placed in a horizontal row. The plant design continues above these imposts until reaching a horizontal band of roll-moulding. The panel above contains stepped-pattern design with its top border provided by a horizontal band of roll-moulding. Above is a narrow section of stonework not decorated, with above, at the top of the cross-shaft, a horizontal band of roll-moulding. See above right: PHOTO 503. Codford St Peter 2.

PHOTO 503.
Codford St Peter 2.

DESIGNS DEPICTING FIGURES AND SCENES FROM NORSE MYTHOLOGY

Scenes depicted from Scandinavian mythology may refer to the main events in the Völuspá in the Edda, including figures such as Odin, Sigurd the Volsung, Fafnir and Weland the Smith.

St Mary's Church, Gosforth, Cumbria, has a cross decorated on the south side with a scene including the depiction of Odin the chief Norse god riding his horse Sleipnir. Each of the vertical sides enclosing Odin is decorated with a band of roll-moulding. Odin is depicted in profile to the right but with his upper body and head turned in portrait (his eyes and nose are distinctive). Sleipnir is depicted in motion and in

PHOTO 504. Gosforth 1.

profile to the right; Sleipnir has only four of his eight legs. Odin holds a spear in his outstretched right arm with the spear point towards the rump of Sleipnir whilst his left arm holds Sleipnir's bridle. See Page 243 bottom right: PHOTO 504. Gosforth 1.

Conyers Chapel, All Saints Church, Sockburn, County Durham, has part of an angular cross-shaft decorated on one face with a scene thought to represent Odin, the chief Norse god, with his horse Sleipnir (only four of his eight legs are depicted), and with one of his ravens "Thought" or "Memory"; there is also part of another scene. Both scenes are enclosed by an outer broad band of grooved-moulding with an adjacent inner, narrower, band of grooved-moulding - both bands are incomplete. See adjacent: PHOTO 505. Sockburn 3.

The lower, incomplete, scene contains on the left-hand side a female figure (her hair and the folds in her garments are indicative) in profile to the right with her head turned in portrait – her legs and feet are missing. She holds a drinking horn to the lips of the male figure opposite who is in profile to the left whose right arm supports the drinking horn – only part of his head and right arm survive. Between the two figures is a round shield probably being held by the missing left arm of the man.

The upper scene, which may be complete, has Odin riding his horse Sleipnir who is in motion; both are in profile to the right.

PHOTO 505. Sockburn 3.

In his extended left hand Odin holds up a large bird, Thought or Memory, with wings slightly extended. The bird is in portrait but with its head turned left so that it looks down on Odin. Odin holds Sleipnir's bridle in his right hand. Sleipnir's feet stand on the top of a horizontal band of ring-twist design which separates the lower scene from the upper scene. Above the top of the Sleipnir, Odin and the bird is an elongated serpent whose head, knotted body and tail provide an arch-like frame. Above the serpent is an incomplete band of plait-work design.

Kirkby Stephen Parish Church, Kirkby Stephen, Cumbria, has part of an angular cross-shaft decorated on one face with a figure which has resulted in it being referred to as the "Bound Devil" or the "Loki Stone" stone after the god Loki. There is some damage. See adjacent: PHOTO 506. Kirkby Stephen.

It is decorated with a band of flat-moulding enclosing an incomplete panel containing the figure of a large man in portrait, but, with lower part of his body, legs and feet in profile to the left. Large scrolls (inverted horns?) emerge from each side of his head where his ears should be; part of the top of his head is missing. He has distinctive eyes, nose and mouth, all of which by their representation and angle, are slightly odd-looking. His long arms, large hands and distinctive

PHOTO 506. Kirkby Stephen.

fingers hang down his sides – his fingertips reach to the level of his knees. Around, and hanging down from his waist, to his knees, is a broad circular strap-like band. It emerges from the circular bracelet-like features around his wrists to extend behind his legs to complete the "circle". Large bracelet-like features overlie both his legs and presumably fulfil a similar binding function as the smaller ones around his wrists. Between his feet, a band of moulding, initially shaped like an inverted "V", bifurcates to angle further towards the corners at the base of the cross-shaft. Single pellets are randomly scattered amongst the design.

St Mary's Church, Gosforth, Cumbria, has part of an angular cross-shaft known as the "Fishing Stone". Its surviving face is decorated with a scene depicting the story of the god Thor and the frost giant Hymir fishing for the Midgard World Serpent. The cross-shaft has two incomplete panels separated by a horizontal band of flat-moulding; no bands of moulding survive along the vertical edges. In the lower panel the fishing scene is depicted below a horizontal band of plait-work design.

PHOTO 507. Gosforth 2.

The scene comprises Thor and Hymir in a double-ended boat; they are separated by the central mast. Only their heads, upper bodies, arms and hands are shown in portrait. The figure of Thor, on the left, is better defined – his eyes are distinctive. In his outstretched right arm he holds in his right hand his hammer Mjolnir. In his left hand he hold a fishing line which extends below the boat and terminates in a bait comprising what is probably the head of an ox – its ears or horns can be identified. The figure of Hymir on the right holds in his outstretched right hand an axe (now very weathered), whilst his left hand holds the stern post of the boat. Below the boat, and on each side of the fishing line, one below the other, there are four fish, two in profile to the right and two to the left. In the bottom right-hand corner, between the tails of the fish in profile to the left, is a circular ring which could represent part of the body of the Midgard World Serpent. In the bottom left-hand corner there may be a representation, in profile to the right, of the head and part of the upper body of the Midgard World Serpent. See above right: PHOTO 507. Gosforth 2.

St Giles Church, Desborough, Northamptonshire, has part of an angular cross-shaft with one face which includes a panel decorated with an example of Ringerike design; whether it depicts a Christian or a pagan scene is a matter of debate. The complete panel is framed with vertical bands of cable-moulding and horizontal bands of flat-moulding.
The panel encloses two addorsed beasts who are in opposite profile. They have long necks ensnared with rather angular scroll-like ribbon-like strands. Between the legs of both beasts are round pellets – two beneath the body of the beast on the right and one beneath body of the beast on the left. In the centre of the panel is the head of a human-like figure portrait with, where the ears might be, lumps which have been interpreted as horns. The

head has a distinctive left eye (on the right), nose and mouth with possibly a moustache – the right eye (on the left) appears faintly. The top of the head brushes the top horizontal border of the panel. A pellet has been placed midway between the human head and the head of the beast on the right. See adjacent: PHOTO: 508. Desborough.

PHOTO 508. Desborough.

DESIGNS DEPICTING HUNTING SCENES
Designs depicting hunting scenes showed the huntsman and his hounds often with an antlered stag as their "kill". Sometimes only the depiction of the huntsman may survive. Scenes may depict other unidentified human figures, beasts and creatures – they may only survive as incomplete parts.

St Andrew's Church, Middleton, North Yorkshire has a complete cross with one face of its vertically-sided cross-shaft decorated with a panel depicting a hunting scene. The panel is enclosed by a band of flat-moulding with an adjacent inner band of flat-moulding providing an almost complete frame interrupted at the top right-hand side by the head of a standing figure – the huntsman – arrowed red.

At the bottom of the panel, and in profile to the right, is a stag with open jaws and large, branching, antlers – arrowed black. A large hound with head body, legs and tail, is in profile to the left vertically - its head, with open jaws, is upside-down and just above the rump of the stag. Placed above the curling tail of the larger hound, is the head of a smaller hound whose head, body and legs are also in profile to the left vertically. In the top right-hand quarter of the panel is the standing figure of the huntsman mostly in portrait but with his legs and feet in profile to the left – his facial features can be identified. In his right hand he holds a spear with a number of side lugs. He points the spear downwards vertically towards top of the antlers of the stag. In his left hand he is ready to draw his knife or seax from its sheath attached horizontally to the belt across his waist. See adjacent: PHOTO 509 Middleton 5. (The other face of this cross-shaft has a ribbon, "S"-shaped, beast placed vertically in profile to the left, see Page 231: PHOTO 476. Middleton 4.)

PHOTO 509. Middleton 5.

St Mary and St Helen's Church, Neston, Cheshire, has part of an angular cross-shaft with one face decorated with an incomplete panel containing a hunting scene. The panel is decorated along each vertical edge with a band of cable-moulding and has no lower horizontal band of moulding, nor any decoration below the hunting scene.

The hunting scene comprises humans and beasts depicted in profile. At the bottom of the scene there is a large stag standing in profile to the right; its pair of antlers, slightly raised head with a round eye and an open mouth, neck, body, legs, hooves, and tail, can all easily be identified. Standing on top of the back of the stag is a human – the huntsman - in profile to the right. He holds a spear which he is thrusting into and through the stag's back – the triangular-shaped, leaf-like, spear point can be identified below the body of the stag and behind its forelegs. A hound, in profile to the left, is biting the stag's throat, and grasping one of the stag's forelegs, with its forelegs.

In front of the head of the huntsman, to the right and above, are the lower parts of the bodies, arms, legs and feet, of a distinctly dressed woman and a man. They face each other in opposite profile given the positioning of their feet; the woman is placed slightly higher than the man. The woman on the left has behind her a vertical, knotted, pigtail which extends down towards the bottom of her skirt. She reaches across the body of the man with her left arm. Between the woman's pigtail, and the bordering band of cable-moulding, is a vertical band of plait-work design. See above right: PHOTO 510. Neston 2, showing the stag arrowed red and the huntsman arrowed black.

PHOTO 510. Neston 2.

DESIGNS DEPICTING WARRIORS

Some designs depicted individual warriors. A few surviving sections of stonework have two warriors in combat and some have groups of warriors. The manner in which they were depicted differs from one example to another, some may be seated on a chair, others may be riding a horse, and some may be standing upright. They may be depicted in portrait or in profile. Usually they were depicted with a sword or a spear but some were also depicted with a set of weapons. In addition to the examples shown in the following pages, see also, a group of warriors on the hogback grave-cover, "Warriors Tomb", in St Mary's Church, Gosforth, Cumbria, on Page 287, PHOTO 583. Gosforth 6.

Derby Museum displays part of a damaged and incomplete angular cross-shaft found at St Wystan's Church, Repton, Derbyshire, known as the "Repton Stone". One of its faces has part of a panel thought to depict King Aethelbald of Mercia who reigned from 716 to 757. See adjacent: PHOTO 511. Derby 1.

The panel is decorated along the surviving vertical edges with an incomplete band of roll-moulding enclosing a mostly complete warrior on a horse. The warrior's right hand, part of his right arm, and most of his left foot, are missing. The top of the horse's head, their feet and most of their forelegs are missing. The horse is in motion to the left. The warrior

PHOTO 511. Derby 1. Photograph Courtesy of Derby Museums.

and horse are in profile to the left. The upper body, arms and head of the warrior are turned in portrait. The warrior holds in his raised left hand a small round shield which has a plain band around the edge - the shield touches his head. In his missing, raised, right hand he probably held a sword whose surviving blade is angled above his head and shield. The warrior's facial features are indistinct but there are indications of his eyes, mouth and a moustache. Around his waist is a seax or short sword in a scabbard. The warrior sits on a saddle on the horse and has its reins looped around his upper right arm where they terminate in a ring - the reins are attached to the bit in the mouth of the horse by a large ring. The details of the horse's bridle can be identified and there is a large collar around its neck.

St Andrew's Church, Middleton, North Yorkshire, has an almost complete vertically-sided cross-shaft with one face decorated with a panel depicting a seated warrior - the base of the cross-shaft is missing. A band of flat-moulding along the vertical sides and the upper horizontal side provides the incomplete panel enclosing the seated warrior. The warrior is depicted in portrait with legs and feet turned in profile to his left; his facial features are easily identifiable. He wears a conical helmet and has a narrow belt across his waist from which hangs horizontally a knife or seax in a sheath.

Between his right side, and the vertical band of flat-moulding on the left, stands an upright spear. Between his left side, and the vertical band of flat-moulding on the right, are: an axe in profile to the right which stands level with his feet and extends up to his waist; a sword, slightly angled, and in portrait, has been placed level with his forehead extending down to his left hand; and a small circular shield, with a central boss, has been placed above his sword and level with his helmet. Above each of his shoulders is a single pellet with another pellet between the top pf his helmet and his shield. A triskele filler has been placed between his helmet and the spearhead on his right; there is also an irregular shaped filler between his legs. See above right: PHOTO 512. Middleton 6. (The other face of this cross-shaft has a ribbon, "S"-shaped, beast placed vertically in portrait, see Page 231: PHOTO 475. Middleton 3.)

PHOTO 512. Middleton 6.

St James Church, Nunburnholme, East Yorkshire, has part of an angular cross-shaft with one face decorated with a panel containing a seated warrior under an archway. In the top left and right-hand corners of the panel a diagonal arm emerges to enable hands to grasp the top of the semi-circular arch below. These arms and hands belong to angels whose heads are in the corners of the panel, they have small, rounded, ears, and pairs of differently sized wings which each end in a distinctive scroll. The heads of these angels are in portrait and disproportionately small compared to their angled arms.

Underneath the scroll-ended angel wings there are wide bands of flat-moulding which appear to include wider triangular-shaped and square-shaped features which represent capitals for the archway. The flat-moulding continues below to provide more of the archway providing a

PHOTO 513. Nunburnholme.

Anglo-Saxon Church Architecture & Stone Sculpture 249

frame enclosing the warrior. The warrior is in profile to the left and wears what is probably a hat rather than a helmet. He sits, unrealistically, on a small, angled, stool – one leg of which is on each side of the warrior's sword blade. The warrior holds in his left hand the hilt of a large, angled, sword. His right hand is shown in a rather unnatural position – protruding from below his chin. His knees, lower legs and feet are clearly identified. See Page 248 bottom right: PHOTO 513. Nunburnholme.

All Saints Church, Brailsford, Derbyshire, has an incomplete cross-shaft with a lower, complete, circular-shaped part and an upper, incomplete, angular-shaped part. The cross-shaft has a collar comprising two protruding, adjacent, horizontal, bands of cable-moulding which separate the lower, circular-shaped part from the upper angular-shaped part.

Just below the collar, on its south face, the cross-shaft is decorated with the figure of a warrior in portrait with somewhat angular facial features and body; his feet are shown in profile to the right. In his left hand he holds up, adjacent to the left side of his head, a circular shield with a small central circular boss. In his right hand he holds the hilt of his sword which appears to be in a scabbard angled across his waist. His body is covered in a plait-work design.

Above the hilt of his sword, adjacent to his right arm and the right side of his head, is plait-work design. The plait-work design is bordered to the left by an angled band of flat-moulding, parallel to his right arm, which extends below the hilt of his sword and then changes direction to extend horizontally to join the bottom of his mail coat or tunic. On the left side of the warrior, below his left arm and shield, there are pellets, and one of the ends of a band of spiral-scroll design which forms part of the decoration on the adjacent side of the circumference. See above right: PHOTO 514. Brailsford.

PHOTO 514. Brailsford.

St Peter's Church, Monkwearmouth, Sunderland, County Durham, has part of a frieze or wall panel with one face decorated with a scene depicting two figures in combat. Backed up against the left-hand vertical band of flat-moulding framing the scene, the figure on the left, in profile to the right, has raised what survives of his shield with his left arm. Below his extended right arm there is a broken sword which he may have dropped. The figure on the right, in profile to the left, is separate from the right-hand vertical band of flat-moulding framing the scene. He holds a spear at an angle which he appears to be thrusting under the shield of the figure on the left. The heads of both figures are missing and what survives of their arms, hands, bodies, legs and feet, clothing and weapons is mostly incomplete, weathered and damaged. See above right: PHOTO 515. Monkwearmouth 15.

PHOTO 515. Monkwearmouth 15.

3. CROSSES

Most crosses stood between 36 inches/91 centimetres and 240 inches/609 centimetres tall, varying in shape, size and in type of decoration. When complete they comprised a cross-head affixed or integral with a cross-shaft below; some were supported by a cross-base or plinth.

Where cross-head, cross-shaft and (where provided) cross-base, were carved out of separate pieces of stone they were often joined together by means of a stone carved tenon (a projection) and a mortise (a cavity or hole), or by lead-filled iron rods inserted into dowel-holes cut out of the adjoining pieces. The same method of jointing would be used to join sections of a cross-shaft when they were carved from separate pieces of stone.

Wooden and stone crosses were raised as a focal point for Christian worship and used as a preaching aid to assist the priest in explaining the Christian message to the congregation whether inside, or in close proximity to a church, or in the countryside where no church existed. Particularly in a monastic community they were also used as a central point for prayer and for contemplation. Churches and monasteries would use crosses and grave-memorials (see Pages 277 to 279) as memorials to the dead within a defined graveyard. Crosses would also have been used to indicate a route-way for pilgrims, and to commemorate places connected with the life of a saint or their funeral route. In addition crosses may have indicated boundaries of an estate, or other significant sub-divisions of land, and marked the position of wells and markets.

See adjacent illustration showing the constituent parts of a cross with the likely positions of moulding around their edges forming panels within which there was decoration as described in Pages 217 to 249 preceding.

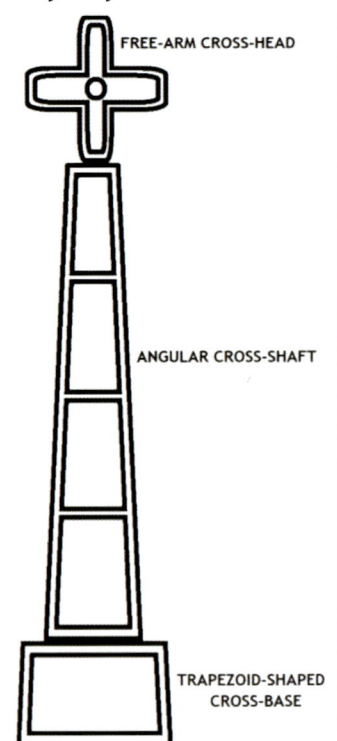

PHOTO 516. Ireton 2.

4. SURVIVING COMPLETE CROSSES

Few complete crosses survive: some examples are identified in the following pages.

St Paul's Church, Irton, Cumbria, provides an example of an almost complete cross with a free-arm cross-head, an angular cross-shaft below, supported by a square cross-base. See above right: PHOTO 516. Ireton 2, showing the west face.

There is no decoration on any of the sides of the cross-base. The cross-head and cross-shaft are decorated with designs and patterns including: cable-moulding, chequer-board design (raised diamonds and sunken St Andrew's crosses), interlace design, key-pattern design, pellets, plant-scroll design, ring-chain design, ring-knot design, ring-twist design, roll-moulding, spiral-scroll design, triquetra-knot design. There are faint traces of possible beasts and humans on the east face of the cross-head.

The west face of the cross-shaft is decorated along the vertical edges with two separate bands of roll-moulding enclosing a single band of interlace design. The top horizontal edge is similarly decorated but the interlace design is very weathered. There is no decoration on the bottom 8 inches/20.2 centimetres of the cross-shaft.

The moulding along the vertical edges frames four panels separated from each other by a single, horizontal, band of roll-moulding. The lower larger panel has a jumbled version of ring-chain design extending vertically, whilst the upper larger panel has a jumbled version of ring-knot design extending vertically. Separating these two larger panels is a single central panel which encloses three horizontal lines to assist the positioning of an inscription which is now illegible. The bottom border of the larger lower panel is provided by a separate narrow panel comprising a horizontal band of interlace design enclosed top and bottom by single bands of roll-moulding.

The west face of the cross-head is decorated along the edges with two adjacent bands of roll-moulding; the moulding is missing along the top horizontal edge. The moulding encloses a mixture of spiralling interlace and knot-work designs which vary in each arm. In all four arms within the spirals closest to the central boss there are three pellets. A circular band of cable-moulding surrounds the central boss which comprises five single pellets arranged in the shape of a free-arm cross - the central pellet is largest.

St Mary's Church, Gosforth, Cumbria, provides an example of an almost complete cross with a ring-head cross-head, with a cross-shaft comprising a lower circular shape and an upper angular shape (the junction of the lower circular shape and the upper angular shape is indicated by distinctive semi-circular, pendulous, downward facing, swags of roll-moulding). The cross-shaft is supported by a three-stepped cross-base which is not decorated on any side. The lower 48 inches/121.8 centimetres of the circular part of the cross-shaft is not decorated. See adjacent: PHOTO: 517. Gosforth 3.

The upper rectangular part of the cross-shaft is decorated along its vertical edges with bands of roll-moulding dividing each side into one large panel. These panels were mostly decorated with scenes from Norse mythology depicting the main events referred to in the Völuspá in the Prose Edda written by the Icelandic scholar Snorri Sturluson in about 1220 AD.

PHOTO: 517. Gosforth 3.

The scenes represent: 1. Chaos and creation; 2. The wars of the gods and giants; Ragnarök and the attack on the gods; 4. The new world with Vithar (one of Odin's sons) slaying Fenris the wolf, and the promise of rebirth of Baldr (another of Odin's sons), here identified with Christ. The panels also contain a Borre variation of ring-chain design and plait-work design; one panel contains a triquetra-knot design.

The ring-head cross-head is decorated with roll-moulding, cable-moulding, triquetra-knot design (on the west and south faces), and plait-work design.

St Mungo's Church, Dearham, Cumbria, provides an example of a complete cross comprising a ring-head cross-head supported by an angular cross-shaft. There is no decoration on the bottom up to 14½ inches/36.7 centimetres of the cross-shaft.

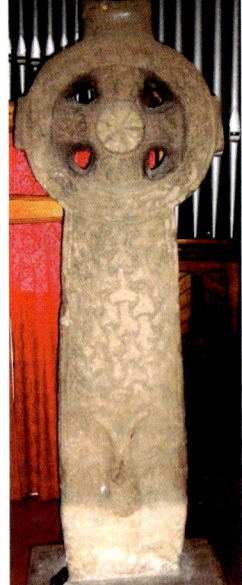

The south face of the cross-shaft is decorated with two adjacent, vertical, bands of roll-moulding which extend up to the band of roll-moulding around the outer "ring" of the cross-head above; there is no horizontal band of moulding at or near the bottom of the cross-shaft. Within the incomplete frame provided by the bands of roll-moulding there is a Borre variation of ring-chain design which in the centre, near its base, includes a bulb-like object. Adjacent to each side of this "bulb" is a flying bird in opposite profile with indications nearby of plait-work design and pellets. See adjacent: PHOTO 518. Dearham 2.

PHOTO 518. Dearham 2.

A description of the decoration on the south face of the ring-head cross-head is included in the example of a cross-head where the "ring" has been placed so that it appears on top of the face of the free-arm cross. See Page 260, PHOTO 535. Dearham 3.

"The Hewn Bar", Long Bar, Whitelyne Common, on the fells five miles to the north-east of Bewcastle, Cumbria, provides an example of a complete, but broken, cross still on the fell, left where it was quarried. It can be identified as a block of tapering stone shaped on three sides with its underside integral to an outcrop of rock. There is no decoration on any side.

It has similar dimensions to the cross surviving in the churchyard of St Cuthbert's Church, Bewcastle, Cumbria. It measures between 13 inches/33 centimetres and 27 inches/68.5 centimetres high – what would have been the depth of the cross, tapering 36 inches/91.4 centimetres from what would have been its base to 10 inches/25.3 centimetres which would have been its top, by 198 inches/502.8 centimetres long which would have been its height. The stone may have been split when it was being cut away from the surrounding rock. See above right: PHOTO 519. Bewcastle 3, showing the cross-shaft with the split at its presumed base arrowed red.

PHOTO 519. Bewcastle 3.

5. SURVIVING PARTS AND FRAGMENTS OF CROSSES

Whilst occasionally free-arm cross-heads are found almost intact, it is much more common to find that only an arm, or parts of arms and the centre has survived; the survival rate of ring or wheel-head crosses is better. Most cross-shafts have been broken up into pieces with perhaps only one or two fragments surviving. Some pieces may be reunited, but not always correctly reassembled, and some pieces may have "modern" inserts to assist reconstruction and maintain an upright position.

Parts, pieces and fragments from cross-heads, cross-shafts and cross-bases are sometimes incorporated both internally and externally into the fabric of the church anywhere from ground level to the top of the tower. They can be used as building material for the repair or infilling of walling or used as lintels or as part of jambs in archways, doorways and windows.

Internally, fragments may be found individually or in groups in wall niches and on window sills. Many may be placed on the floor and leaning against walling in the tower, the west end of the nave, or the north or south aisles; they may be beneath or behind pews. Some examples may be in the porch, integral to the walling, placed or cemented onto stone benches along its side walls, or placed on the floor. Some fragments may survive in their original position in the churchyard.

A display against the east wall of the south porch in All Saints Church, Bakewell, Derbyshire, includes: parts of angular cross-shafts; parts of cross-shafts with circular and angular parts; part of an angular cross-shaft with possibly part of a free-arm cross-head; and possibly part of a cross-base decorated with angels and possibly the Virgin Mary. The cross-shafts are decorated with designs and patterns including: cable-moulding, flat-moulding, interlace design, key-pattern design, knot-work design, pellets, plait-work design, plant-scroll design, ring-chain design, roll-moulding. Human figures, groups of human figures, and a bird. See adjacent: PHOTO 520. Bakewell 2.

PHOTO 520. Bakewell 2.

St Gregory's Church, Kirkdale, North Yorkshire, has most of a free-arm cross-head and its attached angular cross-shaft incorporated externally into the south wall of the nave; it has been placed horizontally rather than vertically. Some imagination will be required to recognise the rather weathered and damaged decoration which extends down from the cross-head into the top-half of the cross-shaft – mortar also obscures some of the detail.

The cross-head has an incomplete band of flat-moulding around its surviving edges which extends down the vertical sides of the cross-shaft. The cross-head and cross-shaft are decorated with a Crucifixion scene with a haloed Christ standing in portrait. He has outstretched arms with the palms of each hand passing behind an angled, vertical, bar.

Christ is bound at waist level by a distinctive strap. Enclosed within the flat-moulding around the edges of the cross-head are pellets and fillers in the right, now the upper vertical, arm. Below Christ's feet are two "s" shaped addorsed serpents in profile who can just about be identified. Beneath the serpents is a horizontal band of flat-moulding which terminates the panel enclosing the Crucifixion scene. Below, the remainder of the cross-shaft is not decorated, apart from a horizontal line. See adjacent: PHOTO 521. Kirkdale 3, showing the cross-head and cross-shaft turned vertically.

All Saints Church, Sinnington, North Yorkshire, has two incomplete free-arm cross-heads, both with their lower vertical arms missing, incorporated into the external face of the south wall of the nave. One cross-head has a flat, central, boss and is decorated with roll-moulding, knot-work design and pellets. The other cross-head depicts a Crucifixion scene with a centrally placed figure in portrait with outstretched arms and large hands with distinctive fingers all enclosed by a band of flat-moulding around the surviving edges. Rather than the usual halo around the head there is a horizontal ring-twist design. Below the right arm of the figure is a coiled, triangular-headed, serpent in profile to the right, and below the left arm of the figure is an abstract filler. See below left: PHOTO 522. Sinnington.

PHOTO 521. Kirkdale 3.

PHOTO 522. Sinnington.

St Giles Church, Acton Beauchamp, Herefordshire, has part of an angular cross-shaft reused as a lintel to the south doorway into the ground floor of the tower. It is decorated with adjacent bands of cable-moulding and flat-moulding enclosing a panel containing inhabited plant-scroll design with two incomplete dog-like creatures and a complete bird alternating in profile. See adjacent: PHOTO 523. Acton Beauchamp, showing the cross-shaft turned vertically.

PHOTO 523. Acton Beauchamp.

The Market Square in Sandbach, Cheshire has two, almost complete, reconstructed, angular cross-shafts and their supporting cross-bases; each has part of the lower vertical arm of their cross-head. Decoration on what survives of the cross-heads and the cross-shafts is extensive with the facial and body features of Christ, humans and beasts and geometrical designs mostly easy to identify apart from weathering and some damage.

Decoration on the cross-shafts include scenes depicting: Adoration of the Magi, Crucifixion Scene with the Evangelists' symbols, The Nativity, Transfiguration of Christ on Mount Tabor flanked by Moses and Elijah – a scene on both cross-shafts but with some differences, Christ committing the Keys of Heaven to Peter and the Book of the New Law to Paul, Christ's Road to Calvary, The Annunciation, Adoration of Mary holding the Christ-Child, and The Veneration of Christ. Other decorated scenes include incomplete and complete human figures some haloed and some seated, winged angels, beasts, and birds.

The cross-shafts are also decorated with designs including: cable-moulding, flat-moulding, interlace-design, knot-work design, pellets, plait-work design, ring-chain design, roll-moulding, inhabited plant-scroll design with human, beast and bird, figures. See adjacent: PHOTO 524. Sandbach 2.

6. CROSS-HEADS

Cross-Heads vary in shape, size and overall dimension. "Free-Arm" cross-heads and "ring-head" cross-heads (often referred to as a "wheel-head" cross-head) are the most common; there are also variants known as "plate-ring" and "disc-head" cross-heads.

PHOTO 524. Sandbach 2.

The shape, size and dimension of arms, rings and plates varies from one example to another, as does the shape and nature of the junctions of the arms, the ends of the arms, and the location and stepping of rings. Examples may have a distinctive central boss on each face of the cross-head – they may not necessarily be similar – with a protruding boss on one face and a flat boss on the other face.

Cross-Heads may be constructed from the same section of stonework as the supporting cross-shaft and be integral to it. Alternatively, they may be constructed from separate sections of stonework and joined to the supporting cross-shaft by mortise and tenon jointing, or by lead-filled iron rods inserted in dowel-holes.

The extent and nature of the decoration varies. Many will have some form of decoration on both faces, on both faces of the rings, and on the ends of each of arms where these exist; some may have decoration on both the top and under sides of the arms and the curves (quadrants) linking the arms together at their junctions. The decoration may be geometrical, plant or figurative, or any combination of these. The extent and nature of moulding around the edges also varies. Not all cross-heads had moulding and not all were decorated.

FREE-ARM CROSS-HEADS

Free-Arm Cross-Heads are those where the stonework comprises a representation of a standard Latin cross with a horizontal line placed across a vertical line. The horizontal arms are supported by centrally-placed vertical arms.

The illustration adjacent left has two vertical arms and two horizontal arms all of similar size. They emerge from the centre and the arms expand in size towards their curved ends. It has a central boss.

All Saints Church, Cawthorne, West Yorkshire, has an example of a large free-arm cross-head now incorporated into the external east wall of the Lady Chapel. The edges of the cross-head are decorated with two damaged, adjacent, bands of roll-moulding. This moulding encloses slight vestiges of decoration in the upper vertical arm and left-hand horizontal arm; the surviving indications of decoration on the other two arms cannot now be confidently identified. In the centre of the cross-head there may be indications of a central figure in portrait but if this existed it has been defaced beyond recognition. See above right: PHOTO 525. Cawthorne.

PHOTO 525. Cawthorne.

St Mary's Church. Ovingham, Northumberland, has a free-arm cross-head with wide, fan-shaped arms, rounded at the ends. It has a protruding central boss. It has no decoration on any side. See adjacent: PHOTO 526. Ovingham 4.

St Michael's Church, Cropthorne, Worcestershire, has a free-arm cross-head which is decorated round the edges on both faces with a band of cable-moulding, replaced by a row of horizontal single pellets along the lower vertical arm. Adjacent to this cable-moulding and this row of pellets is an inner band of flat-moulding. This moulding encloses inhabited plant-scroll-design with beasts and birds. On the ends and undersides of the arms, and in the junctions between the arms, it is decorated with a band of flat-moulding enclosing a rectangular meander-pattern design.

PHOTO 526. Ovingham 4.

On the south face, and filling most of the lower vertical arm, is a beast in profile to the left with head, body and legs. It has a round eye, open jaws, large clawed feet, and a vertical tail ending in a round ball. It appears to be biting an extended, entwined, plant stem. Around the centre of the cross-head is plant-scroll design enclosing a circular hole thought to have contained originally a raised boss. The plant-scroll design, has curling stems and single and clusters of fruits, with stems extending into the horizontal and upper vertical arms. Both horizontal arms have a bird in profile, one to the left and one to the right, with head, body, and a leg. Each has a round eye, a hooked beak, incised wing and tail feathers, and a large clawed foot. Each bird faces, and pecks at, a large single leaf ending in a curled tip. The upper vertical arm has a griffin in profile to the left with head, body and a leg. It has a round eye, a hooked beak, an enigmatic strand curves down from

Anglo-Saxon Church Architecture & Stone Sculpture   257

the back of its neck to end in a circular, hollow, ball. It has incised wing feathers, and a large clawed foot which rests on top of a large single leaf ending in a curled tip. See adjacent: PHOTO 527. Cropthorne, showing the south face on the right and west side on the left.

St Bridget's Church, Brigham, Cumbria has most of a free-arm cross-head which is missing its lower vertical arm and has some damage to the top vertical arm. One face is decorated with an incomplete band of roll-moulding around the edges of the arms enclosing the upper body of a human figure in portrait. The figure's head is mostly complete with distinctive eyes, nose and mouth, and a scroll-design suggesting curly hair. The figure has their arms extended, their left hand is displayed with the palm open, and their right hand grasps what maybe a serpent-like creature whose body surrounds the stomach of the figure. There is also some interlace design entangling the body of the serpent. See adjacent: PHOTO 528. Brigham 2.

PHOTO 527. Cropthorne.

St Lawrence's Church, Eyam, Derbyshire, has most of a decorated free-arm cross-head – the lower vertical arm is missing with the remaining vestiges cut away to form a level base enabling it to rest on the cross-shaft below. The cross-head has wide, square-ended arms, which curve inwards towards the encircled centre of the cross-head.

PHOTO 528. Brigham 2.

The west face is decorated around the edges with a band by a band of roll-moulding interrupted by a separate band of roll-moulding encircling the centre of the cross-head. Each of the three arms and the centre circle contain a weathered figure of an angel in portrait with facial features, bodies with a wing on each side, and clothing. Each angel holds with both hands a trilobed-ended rod placed diagonally across their body ending above their left shoulders. See adjacent: PHOTO 529. Eyam 1.

BILLET-HEAD CROSS-HEADS

PHOTO 529. Eyam 1. Photograph with permission of Eyam Parish Church.

In addition to the standard four-arm design, some free-arm cross-heads have in the juncture of their arms a small equal-size circular plate or roll of solid stonework which impinges on the angle between each arm and extends into the void between the arms. These plates or rolls are referred to as "billets". These billets extend right through the depth of the cross-head; they may be set-back from, or level with, the exterior faces of the stonework. The billets encroach into the vertical and horizontal arms of the cross-head.

The illustration adjacent left has a free-arm cross-head with distinctive round-shaped billets in the junctions between the arms. Both the vertical and horizontal arms are of similar size and are rounded at their ends. It has no central boss.

St Andrew's Church, Middleton, North Yorkshire, provides an example of a free-arm cross-head with billets between the junctions of the arms. Both faces are decorated with a band of flat-moulding around the edges of the arms which extend down the vertical sides of the supporting angular cross-shaft. The flat-moulding on the cross-head encloses knot-work design with a central protruding boss encircled by a design which it is difficult to identify with confidence. See above right: PHOTO 530. Middleton 7.

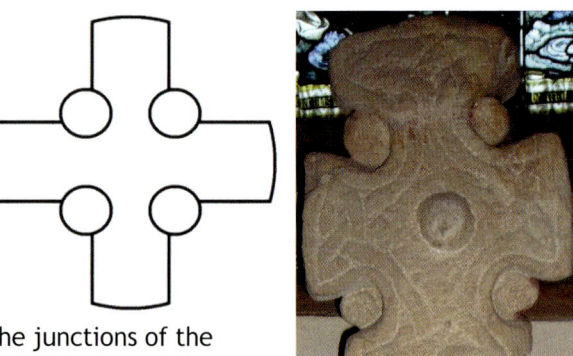

PHOTO 530. Middleton 7.

HAMMER-HEAD CROSS-HEADS

Other free-arm cross-heads may have two additional horizontal arms which are integrated into, and extend from each side of the top vertical arm giving the overall appearance of what is described as a "hammer-head"; the cross-head appears top heavy and shaped similarly to a hammer – hence its name. The top pair of horizontal arms of the cross-head can differ in height and width from the other arms, they can have similar, or much larger or much smaller, dimensions. Unlike most cross-heads, the top vertical arm does not extend above the top two horizontal arms; instead it acts as a link between the lower and upper pairs of horizontal arms.

The adjacent illustration has a free-arm cross-head with two additional horizontal arms extending from the top of what would otherwise be the top vertical arm; it has a lower and an upper pair of horizontal arms; the arms are rounded on their corners. Each pair of horizontal arms has a central boss.

St Chad's Church, Middlesmoor, North Yorkshire, provides an example of a hammer-head cross-head; it is weathered and damaged. On the west face both pairs of horizontal arms have a circular groove in the centre to indicate a central boss; the lower boss has the addition of an incised inner circle. Decoration on the lower horizontal arms consists of an incised scroll-design whilst decoration on the upper horizontal arms consists of incised lines adjacent to the vertical borders. The central vertical arm is incised with vestiges of curving lines. See above right: PHOTO 531. Middlesmoor.

PHOTO 531. Middlesmoor.

Carlisle Cathedral, reserve collection, has most of a hammer-head cross-head – part of its lower vertical arm is missing. One face is decorated with a protruding boss, off-centre on the lower horizontal arms, surrounded by a raised band of roll-moulding. From this roll-moulding similar, raised, angled, bands of roll-

PHOTO 532. Carlisle.

moulding emerge which extend into the ends of the lower horizontal arms - only vestiges survive in the lower right arm - and into the centre of the upper horizontal arms. The vertical band of moulding terminates in a circle enclosing a protruding boss in the upper horizontal arms. See Page 258 bottom right: PHOTO 532. Carlisle.

RING-HEAD CROSS-HEADS

A "ring-head" cross is where the four arms of a free-arm cross-head are linked to each other by curved sections of stonework which form "quadrants" to give the overall appearance of a ring; they may also be referred to as "wheel-head" cross-heads. There are voids between the junctures of the arms of the cross-head and the underside of the quadrants forming the ring.

The shapes of the arms of different cross-heads can vary greatly; they may be angular, rounded or fan-shaped with square or rounded ends which may or may not extend beyond the "ring". Some rings were placed so that they appear on top of the face of the free-arm cross uninterrupted by its arms.

The stonework forming parts of the ring linking the arms can vary in diameter (height) and depth, and placement from one cross-head to the next. Some rings may provide a "stepped" appearance comprising all one ring with what appears as smaller, narrower, outer rings on each side of a central larger ring.

The adjacent illustration has a free-arm cross-head where the arms emerge from the centre and the arms expand in size towards their curved ends. Midway along their length the arms are linked to each other by curved sections of stonework which form the "quadrants" of a ring. The cross-head has a central boss.

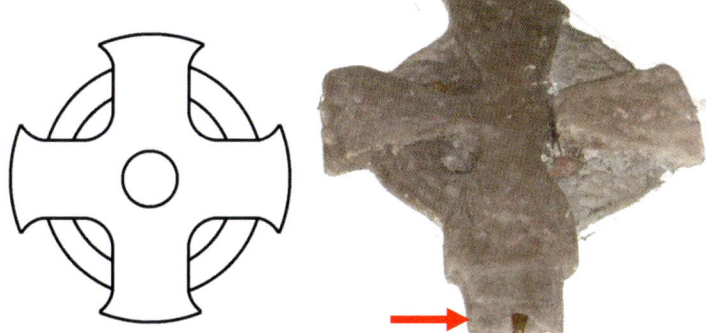

PHOTO 533. Gosforth 4.

St Mary's Church, Gosforth, Cumbria, provides an example of a ring-head cross-head formerly broken in two but now correctly restored as one. Additionally, and providing a rare example, it also has its surviving tenon extending from its lower vertical arm for attachment into the mortise in the supporting cross-shaft. See above right: PHOTO 533. Gosforth 4, with the tenon arrowed red.

The west face of the cross-head is decorated with a band of roll-moulding around the edges of the arms of the cross. This moulding encloses plait-work design in the upper and lower vertical arms, and ring-chain design in the two horizontal arms. The flat central boss is surrounded by a circular band of moulding now almost worn away. The lower left-hand quadrant of the "ring" is decorated with a band of roll-moulding around the edges enclosing two adjacent bands of cable-moulding; the decoration on the other three quadrants is almost all worn away and unidentifiable but was presume ably similar.

St Andrew's Church, Middleton, North Yorkshire, provides an example of where the quadrants forming the ring provide a "stepped" appearance. It has a ring-head cross-head comprising a free-arm cross – the lower vertical arm is noticeably more angular - with its arms linked by the four quadrants of a "ring". The larger, central ring, is bordered front and back, by stepped, smaller, narrower, outer rings. There are circular voids between the junctions of the arms.

Both faces of the cross-head are similarly decorated with a band of roll-moulding around the edges of the arms which enclose a knot-work design; there is also a pellet in the upper vertical arm and one face has an additional pellet in one of its horizontal arms. The quadrants of the ring now provide little evidence of decoration although, there may be slight vestiges of chevron-pattern design. See above right: PHOTO 534. Middleton 8.

PHOTO 534. Middleton 8.

The illustration adjacent left has a free-arm cross-head where the rectangular, square-ended, arms emerge from the centre. The ring has been placed so that it appears on top of the face of the free-arm cross uninterrupted by the arms of the free-arm cross. The cross-head has a central boss.

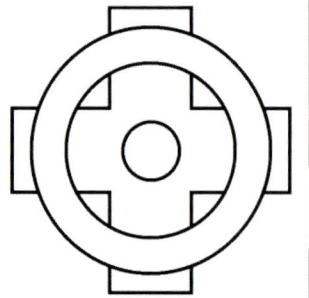

An example of where the ring appears on top of the free-arm cross is provided by in St Mungo's Church, Dearham, Cumbria. See above right: PHOTO 535. Dearham 3. It has a ring-head cross-head decorated on the south face of both the arms of the cross-head and the ring with a band of roll-moulding along their edges. This moulding encloses plait-work design on the ring, triquetra-knot design on the vertical arms, and figure-of-eight knot-work design on the horizontal arms and the part of the top upper vertical arm above the ring; no decoration survives on the horizontal arms protruding outside the ring. In the centre of the arms is a protruding boss whose surface is subdivided by grooves in imitation of the petals on a flower.

PHOTO 535. Dearham 3.

The illustration adjacent has a free-arm cross-head where the rectangular, round-ended, arms emerge from the centre. Attached to the ends of the arms are the "quadrants" which form the ring. The cross-head has a central boss.

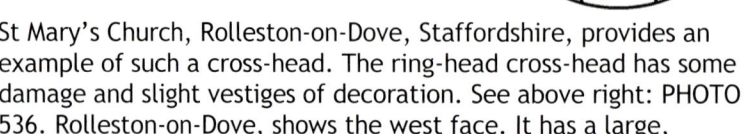

St Mary's Church, Rolleston-on-Dove, Staffordshire, provides an example of such a cross-head. The ring-head cross-head has some damage and slight vestiges of decoration. See above right: PHOTO 536. Rolleston-on-Dove, shows the west face. It has a large,

PHOTO 536. Rolleston-on-Dove.

protruding, central boss, surrounded by a circular band of roll-moulding. The right-hand horizontal arm, and the undersides of both lower north and south quadrants, have very slight indications of possible interlace design. The east face is now missing its central boss and accompanying roll-moulding; no other decoration survives. On each of the north and south sides of the supporting cross-shaft there are indications of a vertical band of roll or possibly cable-moulding providing the frame for a panel enclosing slight vestiges of a band of interlace design placed vertically. No decoration survives on the west and east faces of the cross-shaft. Both cross-head and cross-shaft were carved from a single piece of stonework.

St Bridget's Church, Brigham, Cumbria has most of a ring-head cross-head which has the quadrants of its ring attached to the ends of a free-arm cross. It is missing what was probably one of its horizontal arms and its accompanying quadrants; there is also damage to two of the surviving arms. One face of the cross-head is decorated around what survives of the edges with two adjacent bands of flat-moulding. In the centre there is a circular groove providing a flat, feature-less, boss. There is no decoration surviving on the quadrants of the ring. See adjacent: PHOTO 537. Brigham 3.

PHOTO 537. Brigham 3.

PLATE OR PLATE-RING CROSS-HEADS
On some examples the ring of a ring-head cross-head may comprise solid stonework out of which the arms of a free-arm cross have been cut - these may be termed "plate" or "plate-ring" cross-heads. The shape and extent of the spaces between the junctions, and the lengths, of the arms varies from one example to another. Some may have only a narrow gap between the whole length of the arm and the adjacent arms with the edges of the arms almost touching each other. Other examples may have circular eyelets at the junctions of the arms with a narrow gap between the remaining length of the arm and the adjacent arms. Other examples will have a more standard form of a free-arm cross. All can be identified as a solid plate quartered and overlaid by a free-arm cross in relief.

The illustration adjacent has a free-arm cross-head where the fan-shaped arms emerge from a central boss. The cross, blocked in black, is in relief cut out of a solid round "plate" of stonework.

St Giles Church, Chollerton, Northumberland, has two examples of plate-ring cross-heads with fan-shaped arms in relief overlaying a plate. One has its lower plate and supporting cross-shaft missing, the other is complete and has part of its supporting angular cross-shaft – both the cross-head and cross-shaft are carved out of the same piece of stonework. These have been incorporated in portrait into the external north wall of the chancel. See above right: PHOTO 538. Chollerton.

PHOTO 538. Chollerton.

St Peter's Church, Monkwearmouth, Sunderland, County Durham, has an almost complete consecration cross – one of a pair. It has been carved only on one face. It comprises a free-arm cross in relief with fan-shaped arms emerging from a central roundel. A short vertical narrow stem of stonework, also in relief, supports the centre of the lower vertical arm. Although similar to a plate-ring cross-head the stone out which it is carved is square rather than round. See adjacent: PHOTO 539. Monkwearmouth 16.

PHOTO 539. Monkwearmouth 16.

In Whithorn Museum, Wigtownshire, is a variation of a plate-ring cross-head with circular eyelets at the junctions of the arms and a narrow gap between the remaining length of the arm and the adjacent arms. One face has a distinctive band of grooved-moulding which extends around the edges of the circumference including around the edges of the eyelets separating the junctions of the arms. The overall effect of the moulding was to provide the outline of the shape of a free-arm cross with round-ended arms enclosing stopped plait-work design. See adjacent: PHOTO 540. Whithorn 1.

Although similar to disc-head cross-heads, this variation of plate or plate-ring cross-heads, were smaller in overall size, with a diameter that extended only slightly beyond the width of the supporting cross-shaft below, and the depth of the cross-head was noticeably larger, i.e. thicker, than disc-head cross-heads.

PHOTO 540. Whithorn 1.

DISC-HEAD CROSS-HEADS
Disc-Head Cross-Heads are usually identified by their large circumference and lack of depth. Although similar to plate or plate-ring cross-heads, disc-head cross-heads, were larger in overall size, their diameter extended well beyond the width of the supporting cross-shaft below, and the depth of the cross-head was noticeably less, i.e., thinner, than plate-ring-cross-heads.

Often a band of grooved-moulding extended around the edges of the circumference of the cross-head as well as extending around the edges of the "eyelets" between the junctions of the arms. The "eyelets" could surround voids, a sunken section of stonework, or a very large round pellet-like feature. The overall effect of the grooved-moulding provided the outline of the shape of a free-arm cross with round-ended arms. Some examples were only decorated on one face and few were decorated on the narrow side of their circumference.

The illustration on Page 263 top left has a free-arm cross-head where the fan-shaped arms emerge from a central boss. The circumference has a band of grooved-moulding around the edges as well as extending around the edges of the "eyelets" between the junctions of the arms.

Disc-Head Cross-Heads were concentrated in Wigtownshire and date from the 10th and 11th centuries. Whithorn Priory Museum, Wigtownshire, has a distinctive disc-head cross-head with part of the supporting angular cross-shaft below.

The face of the cross-head is decorated with a band of grooved-moulding around the edges which changes direction so that it also extends around the "eyelets" between the junctions of the arms. The eyelets surround sunken, solid stonework; there are no pellet-like features or voids in the eyelets. A central, circular, groove surrounds the centre providing a flat, boss-like, feature. The face of the supporting, vertically sided, incomplete, cross-shaft is decorated with a wide band of flat-moulding enclosing a single panel containing interlace-design. The decoration on both cross-head and cross-shaft is weathered. Only one face of both cross-head and cross-shaft is decorated. See above right: PHOTO 541. Whithorn 2.

PHOTO 541. Whithorn 2.

7. CROSS-SHAFTS

Cross-shafts supported the cross-head above and could themselves be supported by a cross-base. Cross-shafts may have been constructed from the same section of stonework as the cross-head and be integral to it, or, constructed from separate sections of stonework and joined to the cross-head by means of by mortise and tenon jointing, or, by lead-filled iron rods inserted in dowel-holes. The same method of jointing would also be used to join together sections of a cross-shaft when they were carved from separate pieces of stone.

Many cross-shafts were angular or vertically-sided in shape with four sides, others were circular, some were part circular and part angular, with the circular lower part supporting an upper angular part. There are examples where cross-shafts were circular from bottom to top and described as "columns" - whether they supported a cross-head or had some form of architectural capital is open to question. Whatever their shape many cross-shafts tapered from the ground/bottom to top; those with vertical sides from bottom to top provide examples of the more common exceptions.

Some examples of both angular cross-shafts, and those combining a circular-shaped lower part with an angular-shaped upper part, had distinctive horizontal collar(s) which protruded from the surface of the stonework. Collars could comprise bands of decorated moulding or contain panels enclosing a decorative design which may be in contrast to the decorative designs in the panels below and above on the body of the cross-shaft. Collars often indicated the junction between the lower circular part from the upper angular part of cross-shafts combining two shapes. They were also used to separate panels containing different decorative designs. Whether they were used to surround mortise and tenon jointing is open to debate.

Decoratively, moulding was common down the vertical edges of angular cross-shafts even when the sides were not sub-divided into panels. The subdivision of the sides, or the circumference, of cross-shafts was achieved by using bands of moulding mostly horizontally but also vertically in some cross-shafts which were circular or had a circular lower part. On some cross-shafts there may be no decoration on the lower parts of all four sides or the lower part of the circumference. This may indicate that the cross-shaft was intended to be embedded directly into the ground.

ANGULAR CROSS-SHAFTS
Angular cross-shafts usually taper from ground/bottom to top but there are examples that are vertical from ground/bottom to top. Some examples may have what are otherwise square vertical edges rounded on the corners with the adjacent face or side. The decoration can vary greatly from one example to another. Some may be decorated only with geometrical designs, some a mixture of geometrical designs, plant designs and figurative designs, and others may include inscriptions in Old English, Latin or runes. Angular cross-shafts usually had two opposite "faces" wider than the two other narrower sides. It is often on these faces that the decoration was more elaborate.

Angular cross-shafts may also have horizontal collar(s) which protrude from the surface of the stonework. These collars may comprise bands of horizontal moulding or moulding which may form panels enclosing similar or different designs, and these panels themselves may be sub-divided and enclose similar or different designs.

St Cuthbert's Church, Bewcastle, Cumbria, provides one of the best examples of an almost complete angular cross-shaft. It is decorated with geometrical, plant and figurative designs. See adjacent: PHOTO 542. Bewcastle 4, showing both the west face on the left and south side on the right of the cross-shaft.

The decoration on the west face includes: a vertical band of roll-moulding enclosing panels containing three standing figures separated from each other by horizontal bands of runic inscriptions. The lowest figure is that of St John the Evangelist in profile to the right but with his head in portrait - on his left fore-arm is a bird in portrait representing his symbol, an eagle. Above, a runic inscription interpreted "This token of victory Hwætred set up in memory of Icfri - the full name and most of the remaining runes are difficult to read but possibly include the words "to pray". (These runes may indicate that the cross was set up in memory of King Aldfrith of Northumbria who reigned 685 to 704.) Above, the standing figure in portrait of a haloed Christ in Majesty - his right arm is raised as though in blessing but part of his hand is missing, in his left hand he holds a scroll angled across his body, and he stands on the heads of two beasts. Above the head of Christ is the runic inscription "g[e]ssus kristtus" - Jesus Christ. Above, the weathered, standing figure in portrait is John the Baptist who holds a lamb with a halo around its head with its face turned in portrait. Above is a runic inscription which is now impossible to confidently interpret.

PHOTO 542.
Bewcastle 4.

The decoration on the south side includes: two adjacent vertical bands of roll-moulding - the outer band is broader than the inner band. These bands of moulding enclose five panels separated horizontally from each other by a band of flat-moulding. The lowest panel contains a variant of ring-knot design; above, there may be traces of a runic inscription - now indecipherable. Above a plant-scroll design including large bunches of berries; above, a different variant of ring-knot design; above, plant-scroll-design with a sundial divided below the horizontal into four which are then each subdivided into three -

its gnomon is missing (this is the only surviving example of a sundial on a cross-shaft); above, another variation of ring-knot design. Another possible runic inscription, now indecipherable, just below the broken top of the cross-shaft.

As well as having most of a decorated free-arm cross-head, see Page 257: PHOTO 529. Eyam 1, St Lawrence's Church, Eyam, Derbyshire, has an incomplete angular cross-shaft which now supports this cross-head. The cross-shaft is decorated with both geometrical and figurative designs. The truncated top has been cut away to provide a level base to support the incomplete cross-head above. The bottom has also been truncated and levelled flat and immersed in a cross-base, not Anglo-Saxon.

The west face is decorated along the surviving vertical edges with an outer, wide band of roll-moulding, with an adjacent, inner, narrower band of roll-moulding. The inner band of roll-moulding provides the bands linking the three rings of a ring-chain design placed vertically in the bottom part of the cross-shaft – the bottom ring is incomplete. Above the ring-chain design, this inner band of roll-moulding also provides the supports for the arching bands of roll-moulding below and above the complete figure. This figure above the ring-chain design is in portrait with distinctive facial features and clothing. Their right arm is angled downwards across their body with their right hand holding what may be a horn of some description. The "horn" is curving in shape with a narrowing curled end below the figure's right elbow, and a broader, almost upright end, level with their left shoulder, and supported by their left hand. It is thought this figure might represent a prophet. Above the prophet figure is another figure, thought to be the Virgin Mary. She is in portrait. All her features above her chin are missing having been cut away when the cross-shaft was truncated. Due to weathering her most distinctive features surviving are her clothing, and her right arm extending downwards across her body. In her right hand she holds the lower part of the Christ-Child whose legs and feet emerge below. The head of the Christ-Child is distinctive and directly below her chin – the hair, eyes, nose and mouth of the Christ-Child can be identified. Diagonally, across the chest of the Christ-Child is a rectangular panel which might represent a book. The Christ-Child is in portrait but slightly turned to his right. See adjacent: PHOTO 543, Eyam 2, showing the west face with the head of the Christ-Child arrowed red and the possible book across his chest arrowed black.

PHOTO 543. Eyam 2. Photograph with permission of Eyam Parish Church.

All Saints Church, Bakewell, Derbyshire, has an incomplete angular cross-shaft decorated along the vertical edges with a band of flat-moulding which is rounded on the corners providing a frame enclosing geometrical designs. See Page 266: PHOTO 544, Bakewell 3, with the south face on the left and east side on the right.

Within the vertical bands of flat-moulding the south face is divided into four panels of different sizes by further horizontal or arched bands of moulding. The bottom, incomplete, panel contains a horizontal band of plait-work design separated from the complete panel above by a horizontal band of flat-moulding. The complete second panel contains a vertical row of ring-chain design. The bottom and middle rings are similar in size and design apart from the addition of a single pellet in the vertical quadrants of the middle ring. The top ring is smaller and more compact in design than the lower two rings. It also has a single pellet in each of the four central quadrants, and, a single pellet on the "inside" of each of the curving strands linking it to the middle ring below. This panel is separated from the panel above by two adjacent arching bands of cable-moulding. The complete third panel contains a vertical row of ring-chain design with each of the individual rings similar in size and design to the top ring in the panel below. Whilst the bottom ring has a single pellet in each of the four central quadrants, just like the top ring in the panel below, the top ring in this panel does not include any pellets. Extending from both sides of the top of the outer concentric circle of the top ring, single strands join in an arched horizontal loop which encloses an arched row of three, single, pellets. Above the top of this loop is a circle surrounding a central boss-like feature. The circle is enclosed by each of the vertical bands of flat-moulding along the edges bifurcating: the lower halves joining to form the lower horizontal border, and, the upper halves each forming one of the vertical sides. Above the top of the left-hand side of this circle, is a pellet, with a similar pellet above the right-hand side. Above these pellets is a horizontal band of flat-moulding which may have formed part of the bottom vertical arm of a cross-head.

Within the vertical bands of flat-moulding the east side is divided into three complete panels of different sizes. The bottom of this side of the cross-shaft is not decorated, the stonework is plain up to the first panel. The bottom panel has no horizontal band of moulding at its base but it does contain knot-work design with its upper strands extending to form two distinctly shaped horizontal arches separating it from the panel above. The middle panel is decorated with a vertical band of plait-work design enclosed by a band of flat-moulding arched at the top and extending down both vertical sides to the top of the horizontal arches of the panel below. Above there are five thin, arched, bands of flat-moulding extending horizontally from the flat-moulding along the edges of the cross-shaft. There is a distinctive groove separating each of these bands; the fourth band has an incomplete circular feature at its centre. The top panel contains a triquetra-knot design with, below the lowest intersection of the strands, two separate single pellets placed at an angle outside the triquetra-knot design with a nondescript filler separate to their right. Above the triquetra-knot design is an irregular interlace design which seems to be divided into two parts by an angled strand and some plain, undecorated, stonework. Above this panel the cross-shaft is not decorated on this side - the stonework is plain. At the top is a horizontal band of flat-moulding which may have formed part of the bottom vertical arm of a cross-head.

An almost complete angular cross-shaft has been placed on a trapezoid-shaped base, not Anglo-Saxon, on an island in the middle of where the A377 bifurcates in the centre of Copplestone, Devon; the arm of the road to the left (west) leads to the A3072.

The cross-shaft is decorated with geometrical and figurative designs. On the most weathered north-east face there are faint indications of two standing figures in the middle panel and a horseman in profile to the left in the upper panel. See adjacent: PHOTO 545, Copplestone,

PHOTO 544. Bakewell 3.

PHOTO 545. Copplestone.

showing the north-west side of the cross-shaft. It is decorated along the vertical edges with a band of roll-moulding which weathering has now made virtually flat. The decoration is divided into three complete panels by single, horizontal, bands of roll-moulding. At the base there is an undecorated plain section of stonework. Above, the bottom panel is decorated with plait-work design, the middle panel with ring-knot design, and the upper panel with an irregular ring-twist design involving looping strands.

St Mary's Church, Newent, Gloucestershire, has an incomplete angular cross-shaft with one surviving horizontal collar around the edges of which are indications of a band of roll-moulding. On the east face of the cross-shaft the collar is decorated with the weathered remains of four figures who seem to be in pairs, facing each other in profile, each are under a round-headed archway forming part of the same arcade. On the right-hand end there is a human-like figure in profile to the left, and under the adjacent archway, to the left, in opposite profile, is what could be either a human-like figure or a bird. The other two figures in the arcade are too indistinct to identify with any confidence.

Below the collar, on each of the vertical edges of the cross-shaft, is an incomplete band of roll-moulding enclosing a representation of the standing figures of Adam and Eve. The two figures are separated by a central tree – the "Tree of Knowledge" – around which is curled a serpent. Eve, on the right, is striking the serpent with a long narrow rod she holds in her raised right hand. Adam, on the left, holds in his lowered left hand some form of a right-angled long-handled implement. Above Eve a small free-arm cross emerges from the top right-hand branch of the tree. By Adam's right foot is a stepped platform from which grows the trunk and branches of a small tree. See above right: PHOTO 546: Newent, showing the collar arrowed red with the head of the serpent arrowed black.

PHOTO 546. Newent.

The other sides of the collar include indications of figures, possibly including a winged figure with a spear. Below the collar the other sides of the cross-shaft are decorated with complete and incomplete human figures including a depiction of David and Goliath, inhabited interlace design with a beast, and inhabited plant-scroll design with birds.

St Mary's Church, Rockcliffe, Cumbria, has a ring-head cross-head supported by an angular cross-shaft with two, separate, horizontal collars. The cross-head, and the cross-shaft with its two collars are decorated with bands of roll-moulding along the edges enclosing mostly interlace design but some ring-chain design. Where decoration survives on the collars there are indications of fettered, ribbon-shaped, beasts in profile. The decoration on all sides of the cross-head and cross-shaft, including the two collars, is very weathered and often unidentifiable. The south-east face of the cross-head and cross-shaft are decorated with roll-moulding enclosing interlace design. Each of the two collars are decorated with slight vestiges of roll-moulding and a fettered, ribbon-

PHOTO 547. Rockcliffe.

shaped, beast with open jaws, in profile to the right. See Page 267 bottom right: PHOTO 547. Rockcliffe, showing south-east face with the collars arrowed red.

St Peter's Church, Creeton, Lincolnshire, also has an almost complete angular cross-shaft with a projecting collar. The sides of the collar are decorated with a band of flat-moulding enclosing complete panels containing plait-work design on the west face, knot-work design on the north and south sides, and a free-ring design on the east face. Below the collar it is decorated with a band of flat-moulding enclosing a complete panel containing on the west face a plant-scroll design with little indication of buds, flowers or berries, and a plait-work design on the north and south sides; the east face has no decoration within the panel. Above the collar it is decorated with a band of flat-moulding enclosing an incomplete panel containing plait-work design on the west face and south side, a knot-work design on the east face, and a key-pattern design on the north side. See adjacent: PHOTO 548. Creeton 1, showing the west face left and the south side right with the collar arrowed red.

St Andrew's Church, Wroxeter, Shropshire, has two separate panels thought to be from part of the collar of a cross-shaft now incorporated into the exterior south wall of the nave.

PHOTO 548.
Creeton 1.

Whether the cross-shaft was vertically-sided or angular is now uncertain. It is decorated with an outer band of flat-moulding with an adjacent inner band of cable-moulding. This moulding encloses and separates two complete panels. Below the lower panel (on the left in PHOTO 549. Wroxeter 3) is a plain, undecorated section of stonework thought to be the tenon which went into the socket of the collar below. The lower panel itself is decorated with inhabited design containing a standing figure, in profile to the left, of a long-necked, long-legged, beast whose tail extends upwards to form an evolving pattern reminiscent of a ring-twist design which extends above its head and fills the rest of the panel. Their body is outlined by incised lines enclosing contoured rows of hatching interrupted by a large spiral at shoulder level. Between the legs there are single, large, rounded, pellet-like features. The upper panel (on the right in PHOTO 549. Wroxeter 3) contains a plant-scroll design. See below: PHOTO 549. Wroxeter 3, showing the cross-shaft placed horizontally as it now. The bottom of the cross-shaft with its tenon is arrowed red, the eye on the front of the face of the long-legged beast is arrowed black.

PHOTO 549. Wroxeter 3.

The two panels thought to form part of the collar of the cross-shaft both depict dog-like creatures in profile with their bodies outlined by incised lines enclosing diagonal rows of overlapping, round-ended, scale-like, decoration to indicate their fur. Most of the details of their heads are missing apart from the closed jaw of the creature in profile to the left and the open jaw of the creature in profile to the right – an eye of this creature survives as a bulge on the front of the face. Around their necks is a collar with individual circular studs. They have short tails which curve

PHOTO 550. Wroxeter 4.

PHOTO 551. Wroxeter 5.

upwards. All four of their legs and large feet are depicted with the two legs furthest from the viewer in lower relief than those closest. See above left: PHOTO 550. Wroxeter 4, and above right: PHOTO 551. Wroxeter 5.

CROSS-SHAFTS COMBINING CIRCULAR AND ANGULAR SHAPES
Some cross-shafts may combine a circular-shaped lower part with an angular-shaped upper part – despite these differences they may be described as "circular". The junction between the two shapes is usually indicated by distinctive horizontal collar(s) which protrude from the surface of the stonework. Examples may have additional horizontal collars separating designs within both the circular-shaped and angular-shaped parts.

Collars may comprise bands of plain or decorated horizontal and/or vertical moulding around the angular shape of a cross-shaft, or around the circumference of a circular cross-shaft, or those having a combination of both shapes. Alternatively, rather than just forming plain or decorated bands, moulding may form panels enclosing similar or different designs. These panels themselves may be sub-divided into smaller panels enclosing similar or different designs.

In addition to a collar, or instead of a collar, the junction between the two shapes of the cross-shaft may be indicated by distinctive semi-circular, pendulous, downward facing, swags on the upper angular shape.

The illustration above left has a cross-shaft with a circular lower part, arrowed red, with an upper angular part, arrowed black. The junction between the two parts are separated by a horizontal collar arrowed blue. The pendulous swag in the upper angular part is arrowed green.

PHOTO 552. Stapleford.

St Helen's Church, Stapleford, Nottinghamshire, has most of a cross-shaft with a lower, incomplete, circular-shaped part, and an upper, incomplete, angular-shaped part; the cross-shaft has three "collars". Although weathered the decoration is easily identifiable. See above right: PHOTO 552, Stapleford showing the south face with the winged figure arrowed red.

The cross-shaft stands on a mostly mid-18th century base which conceivably might include some earlier material. All the decoration on the cross-shaft is weathered and the designs are not always that easy to confidently identify. (The horizontally placed capstone dates from 1830 and the concrete ball on top dates from the year 2000.)

The lower, circular-shaped, part of the cross-shaft is sub-divided into two by a protruding collar comprising two adjacent horizontal bands of roll-moulding. Below this collar there are slight vestiges of vertical bands of moulding which cannot now be confidently identified. The requirement for such vertical divisions is indicated by the different designs/patterns of decoration surviving below this lower collar; above this collar there is no indication of vertical divisions separating the decoration.

The designs both below and above the collar include variations of interlace design, knot-work design, free-ring design, ring-chain design, ring-knot design and possibly plant-scroll design. Whilst there are similarities between the different types of design identified some of the designs are more compacted than others. Some designs are enclosed in a loosely scroll-like pattern. The rows formed by these designs extend both vertically and horizontally.

A protruding middle collar comprising three adjacent horizontal bands of roll-moulding indicates the junction between the lower circular shape and the upper angular-shape of the cross-shaft. Above this collar, the angular shape is divided into two horizontally by a top collar comprising two protruding, horizontal, bands of roll-moulding forming a panel on each side enclosing an interlace design. This top collar separates one complete panel below, and one incomplete panel above, on each of the four sides. The bottom complete panels have vertical edges comprising a band of flat-moulding with an adjacent inner band of cable-moulding. As the band of cable-moulding extends along the vertical edges on each side towards the middle collar it evolves into a semi-circular, pendulous, downward facing, swag to reflect the lower circular shape of the cross-shaft. Within the borders provided by the swags each of the four panels contain a different design: knot-work design, plant-scroll design, ring-knot design, and a winged figure on the south face. It appears that the surface stonework on the winged figure has been removed with only their outline remaining. The figure is in portrait with strange looking eyes and a lop-sided mouth. It has triangular-shaped wings with possibly a serpent beneath each wing. Its legs are turned so that their feet point outwards in opposite directions. What the figure stands on is a matter of debate, it could either be a horizontal ledge, or, possibly, a creature of some sort in profile to the right. Above the top collar the cross-shaft is decorated on all four sides with plait-work design and free-ring design.

The Church of St Edward the Confessor, Leek, Staffordshire, has a complete cross-shaft comprising a lower circular-shaped part and an upper angular-shaped part. Only the lower part of the cross-head above survives comprising most of its lower vertical arm with parts of its junctions with the horizontal arms, and part of the central boss.

The cross-shaft has a protruding collar indicating the junction of the lower circular-shaped part with the upper angular-shaped part. It comprises a wide, central, horizontal band of interlace design, bordered, top and bottom, by a band of roll-moulding. Below the collar two of the "sides" are similarly decorated with bands of roll-moulding forming a triquetra-knot design enclosed within an inverted horseshoe-shape with a pair of volutes curving in opposite directions at the bottom. On another side the triquetra-knot design is replaced

Anglo-Saxon Church Architecture & Stone Sculpture   271

by a heart-shaped design ending with a pair of volutes curving in opposite directions; in the middle of the design is a single pellet. The fourth side has a weathered free-arm cross with fan-shaped arms. In the centre it has another small free-arm cross.

Above the collar the four panels are outlined by bands of flat-moulding which extend along the vertical edges on each side and evolve into semi-circular, pendulous, downward facing, swags to reflect the lower circular shape of the cross-shaft. Each panel within the swags contains a different design: plant-scroll, interlace, knot-work, and a meander-pattern.

See adjacent: PHOTO 553, Leek, showing the east side of the cross-shaft. The collar is decorated with interlace design which separates the lower circular shape with its triquetra-knot design from the upper angular shape with its interlace design.

St Bridget's Church, Beckermet, Cumbria, has a rectangular cross-base supporting a cross-shaft with a lower, complete, round-shaped part, separated by a collar, from an upper, incomplete, angular-shaped part. See below right: PHOTO 554. Beckermet, showing the west face.

The shape of the lower part of the cross-shaft is more of a square with round corners; it is not decorated on any side. It has an irregular fit into its supporting cross-base. At one time it was possible to see part of the tenon on the cross-shaft which fitted into the mortise in the cross-base.

PHOTO 553. Leek.

The junction of the lower part of the cross-shaft with the upper part is indicated by a collar comprising three adjacent horizontal bands of cable-moulding - the middle band is inset from the two outer bands. This junction is also indicated by distinctive semi-circular, pendulous, downward facing, swags on the upper angular shape. These swags emerge from the adjacent wide, outer, and narrow, inner, bands of grooved-moulding which extend along the vertical edges on each side down towards the collar.

Within the borders provided by the swags, three of the four panels contain a different design: plant-scroll, bush-scroll and tree-scroll in a vertical spiral-scroll format. On the west face, the fourth panel, contains an indecipherable inscription of five lines separated from each other by a horizontal groove. The inscription is probably in Latin but there is a debate about the identity of the language used.

St Peter's Church, Wolverhampton, Staffordshire, has a cross-shaft circular from bottom to top and usually described as a "column" – it may be Roman in origin. Given its height, and the indications of stonework at the top, it is likely that this "column" supported either a cross-head or some form of architectural capital.

PHOTO 554. Beckermet.

The column is very weathered and the exact nature of the decoration is often not clear. It appears that there are six, possibly seven, horizontal panels of different sizes extending around the circumference separated by horizontal bands of cable-moulding and roll-moulding. The lower part of the column is not decorated. See below: PHOTO 555. Wolverhampton. The surviving decoration appears to be:

1. The lowest decoration comprises interlinked triangular shapes of equal size extending downwards from a horizontal band of cable-moulding. Each triangle is bordered on its two downward extending sides by bands of flat-moulding. Within this moulding each triangle encloses a plant-scroll design or an inhabited plant-scroll design with a beast or a bird in profile.

2. Above is a horizontal panel containing inhabited plant-scroll design with a centrally placed row of pairs of affronted large beasts. These beasts are in profile and are enclosed within interlinked diamond-shaped narrow bands of flat-moulding with a centre foliate feature where these bands intersect between the bodies of the large beasts. Above and below these intersections are smaller bird-like creatures in profile to the left. Within the inhabited plant-scroll design, above the intersections, these bird-like creatures have their heads turned back in the opposite direction, but some, below the intersections, appear to be pecking at the foliage with their heads remaining in profile to the left, whilst others have their heads turned in the opposite direction.

3. Above this panel, is a narrow, horizontal, panel containing rows of interlinked, vertical, spreading and open, plants, bordered bottom and top by a horizontal, band of roll-moulding.

4. Above is a larger horizontal panel containing plant-scroll design separated from the horizontal panel above by a horizontal band of cable-moulding.

5. Above is a large horizontal panel containing inhabited plant-scroll design with alternating beasts and birds all in profile to the left with their heads turned to the right.

PHOTO 555.
Wolverhampton.

6. Above a band of unidentifiable moulding. Alternatively, it could possibly be a smaller, similar version of the vertical plants identified in "3" above.

7. Above a large horizontal panel containing plant-scroll design.

8. Above a horizontal band of roll-moulding.

The round, convex, cap-stone on the top of the column appears to be decorated around its base with a single horizontal band of roll-moulding. The centre of the cap-stone's circumference is decorated with two adjacent, horizontal, bands of roll-moulding separated by a deep groove. Above the centre there may be very slight indications of interlace design.

8. CROSS-BASES

Cross-Bases were usually provided for cross-shafts which were taller and physically more substantial examples. There were exceptions and not all large crosses were supported by cross-bases, some were directly embedded into the ground. Where cross-bases were provided the top surface had a trapezoid-shaped, square or circular socket, as a mortise, dependent on the shape of the base of the cross-shaft or its projecting tenon. Some cross-bases may have had lead-filled iron rods inserted in dowel-holes to join the cross-shaft to the cross-base but these examples are now difficult to identify. Other cross-bases may have had a "hole" straight through the cross-base so that the cross-shaft rested on the ground – smaller, pebble-like stones and earth would be used to pack-in the cross-shaft to ensure stability.

In shape, a cross-base could be a rectangular or tapering block. It could be low and flat or of some height and width. Particularly with the lower, flatter cross-bases which were multi-stepped, the distinction between the steps may not now be readily apparent due to weathering and damage. Additionally, the lower steps may be hidden by the surrounding undergrowth, soil accumulation, or ground subsidence. Cross-bases may now stand directly on the ground but others may be supported by separate, later, not Anglo-Saxon, plinths, some of which may be stepped.

Decoration on cross-bases with high sides is common usually involving bands of moulding along the vertical and horizontal edges of all four sides enclosing panels with geometrical, plant and figurative designs. Decoration on flat or stepped cross-bases is less likely.

The illustration adjacent identifies the main features likely to be found on a three-stepped flat cross-base with the socket ready to receive the base of a square-shaped cross-shaft above.

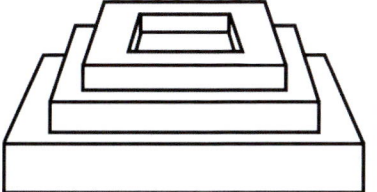

PHOTO 556. Gosforth 5.

St Mary's Church, Gosforth, Cumbria, has a three-stepped cross-base tapering from bottom to top. It is not decorated on any of its sides. The cross-base has a circular socket to receive and support a cross-shaft comprising a lower circular shape and an upper angular shape with a ring-head cross-head at the top. The cross-shaft and cross-head are decorated with designs and scenes mostly relating to Norse mythology. See above right: PHOTO 556. Gosforth 5.

St Wilfrid's Church, Halton, Lancashire, has a three-stepped cross-base tapering from bottom to top. It is not decorated on any of its sides. The cross-base is trapezoid-shaped. It has a socket to receive and support a reconstructed angular cross-shaft with a reconstructed free-arm cross-head above - these are decorated with geometrical, plant and figurative designs. See adjacent: PHOTO 557. Halton 1.

PHOTO 557. Halton 1.

274 Anglo-Saxon Church Architecture & Stone Sculpture

St Mary and St Cuthbert's Church (the Anchorage), Chester-le-Street, County Durham, has part of a vertically sided cross-base decorated with geometrical and incomplete figurative designs. The only side now complete has a panel edged at the top by a broad horizontal band of interlace design – there is some damage. Adjacent below is a narrower horizontal band of flat-moulding. These bands of moulding are supported by pillar-like features extending along both the vertical edges of the cross-base. The bottom of the panel is provided by a convex curve which links the two vertical pillar-like features together. Within the panel the stonework has been cut-back to provide a standing free-arm cross with a long lower vertical arm; in the centre of the cross-head is an incised circle to indicate a boss. The top of the cross-base is damaged but part of the square-shaped socket survives ready to receive the cross-shaft. See above right: PHOTO 558. Chester-le-Street, with position of socket arrowed red.

PHOTO 558. Chester-le-Street.

Walton Cross, Hartshead, West Yorkshire, has a complete weathered cross-base tapering from bottom to top and with both faces having a trapezoid appearance. In the centre of the top there is a rectangular socket to receive the cross-shaft. Some of the decoration is damaged.

The cross-base is decorated on each side, at its base, and at its top, with four, rounded, horizontal steps – ascending and descending; below the bottom step at the base there is also a horizontal band of flat stonework. The vertical edges on each side are rounded without any distinctive moulding. On three of the sides, adjacent to the top steps and the vertical rounded edges, there is an inner band of flat-moulding which provides three sides of a frame enclosing decoration – the fourth side of the frame is supplied by the top step at the bottom of the cross-base. The decoration within these frames includes interlace design, a variant of free-ring design, jumbled variants of figure-of-eight ring-knot design, inhabited plant-scroll design with two confronted winged beasts in profile, and inhabited bush-scroll design with birds.

The east face of the cross-base is differently decorated, see adjacent: PHOTO 559. Hartshead, with the socket arrowed red. At its base, and at its top, it has four, rounded, horizontal steps – ascending and descending; below the bottom step at the base there is also a horizontal band of flat stonework. The vertical edges are rounded without any distinctive moulding but they do have adjacent bands of vertical cable-moulding. This moulding provides three sides of a frame; the fourth side is supplied by the top rounded horizontal step at the bottom of the cross-base.

The frame formed results in four irregular trapezoid shaped bands comprising: interlace design; flat-moulding; a mixture of basket-plait, ring-twist and interlace designs; and a band of roll-moulding encloses a panel of inhabited bush-scroll design. The bush-scroll design has a central vertical stem from

PHOTO 559. Hartshead.

which emerge, on each side, scrolling branches which end with flowers or fruit. The design includes four birds in profile, two on each side of central stem, one above the other. The two lower birds are addorsed and the two upper birds face each other.

St Matthew's Church, Rastrick, West Yorkshire, has a complete cross-base tapering from bottom to top. In the centre of the top there is a rectangular socket to receive the cross-shaft. The cross-base is weathered with some of the decoration damaged.

A damaged horizontal band of flat stonework extends around the top and bottom of the cross-base on all four sides. Three of the sides have two adjacent horizontal bands of roll-moulding which also extend vertically to provide a frame. The outer band of roll-moulding is missing or damaged in places along the vertical sides and along the bottom of the cross-base. Within the frames provided there are variants of bush-scroll design on the south face and east side, and variants of interlace design and a free-ring design on the north face divided by a vertical band of roll-moulding. The east side has no indication of having been decorated other than a single band of roll-moulding providing a frame around the edges.

The south face of the cross-base has roll-moulding providing a frame enclosing bush-scroll design. The design includes a central vertical stem from which emerge, on each side, scrolling branches ending with flowers with large three-leaf petals. See adjacent: PHOTO 560. Rastrick 2, showing the south face with the socket arrowed red.

PHOTO 560. Rastrick 2.

St Andrew's Church, Bishop Auckland, County Durham, has part of a trapezoid-shaped cross-base comprising most of the east face (broken in two and placed together) and almost half of the north and south sides; no original stonework survives from the west face. There is some restoration and the use of modern concrete and stone. What survives is decorated along the edges, both vertically and horizontally, with a band of cable-moulding with an adjacent inner band of roll-moulding enclosing panels of haloed figures in portrait. Nothing survives to indicate the nature of the socket in the top.

See adjacent: PHOTO: 561. Bishop Auckland 4, showing the east face. It is decorated along the edges, both vertically and horizontally, with a band of cable-moulding with an adjacent inner band of roll-moulding – the moulding is incomplete. This moulding encloses a panel containing three haloed three-quarter length figures who are in portrait but with the two outer figures turned inwards towards the central figure who carries a jewel-covered book in their left hand. The

PHOTO: 561. Bishop Auckland 4.

figure on the left bends and angles their right arm across their chest so that the extended fingers of their right hand touch the top right arm of the figure in the centre. The figure in the centre bends their right arm so that it is angled across their chest and extends two fingers from their right hand. The figure on the right bends and angles their left arm across their chest so that the extended fingers of their left hand touch the top left arm of the figure in the centre. The figure on the right may be female as her hairstyle resembles the hairstyle of the figures identified as female on the cross-shaft above – see Page 239: PHOTO 494. Bishop Auckland 3.

9. GRAVE-MARKERS

Grave-Markers, including pillar-stones and name-stones, marked the grave of a deceased person and many stood vertically inserted directly into the ground whilst some were laid horizontally – they did not cover the body of the deceased. Grave-markers simply marked where the grave was or acted as a commemoration to the deceased. Grave-markers often comprised a short standing stone incised on one face with a simple free-arm cross with no inscription or any other markings or decoration on any of the sides.

St Andrew's Church, Haughton-le-Skerne, County Durham, has a square slab of stonework on which is incised a free-arm cross with square-ended arms extending to each of the edges of the slab. It could be a recumbent grave-marker or possibly a small head or foot stone accompanying a larger recumbent grave-cover. See adjacent left: PHOTO 562. Haughton-le-Skerne.

PHOTO 562. Haughton-le-Skerne.

PHOTO 563. Hackthorn.

St Michael and All Angels Church, Hackthorn, Lincolnshire, has a standing grave-marker which tapers slightly from top to bottom. Both faces are decorated along the edges with a band of cable-moulding enclosing a free-arm cross, double outlined with two incised parallel lines, and incised with a small, central, circle to indicate a boss. See above right: PHOTO 563. Hackthorn.

St Oswald's Church, Lythe, North Yorkshire, has a number of examples of long-stemmed grave-markers carved onto rectangular blocks of stonework. The cross-heads, carved on both faces, are in relief and comprise flat-headed crosses with triangular-shaped arms: the lower vertical arms merge with the long-stem below. Some examples have a central circular boss which may slightly protrude from the surface of the stonework. The cross-shaft may have chamfered edges along its vertical sides and it may also taper from top to bottom to provide a firm base to assist directly embedding them into the ground. See adjacent: PHOTO 564. Lythe 2, showing the cross-head without a central boss and with a damaged long-stem below.

PHOTO 564. Lythe 2.

PILLAR-STONES

Pillar-Stones were, stand alone, irregularly-shaped, stone memorials to an individual slender in proportion to their height and incised with lettering on one face only. Some may have a

Chi-Rho monogram depicted in different combinations. Pillar-Stones usually date from the fifth to the eighth centuries. Note: from the eleventh century "Stone Pillars" appear similar in physical characteristics, and with geometrical and figurative designs poorly depicted, sometimes on more than one side.

Whithorn Priory Museum, Wigtownshire, has a pillar-stone known as the "Peter Stone". The front face only has been incised with a free-arm cross-head supported by a small angular cross-shaft. The cross-head has fan-shaped arms surrounded by two concentric circles. The cross-shaft has vertical sides extending into a curving, flat-ended, base. Below is lettering interpreted as "The Place of Peter". There is no decoration on any other side. It is thought that this stone may have been brought to Whithorn by monks from St Peter's Monastery in Wearmouth (Sunderland), County Durham. See above right: PHOTO 565. Whithorn 3.

PHOTO 565. Whithorn 3.

NAME-STONES

Sometimes the grave-markers were more elaborate in their design with incised free-arm crosses, accompanied by the deceased name – a "name-stone", and all enclosed within a square frame of moulding around the horizontal and vertical edges of the grave-marker. Name-Stones were usually small, square, flat-headed or round-headed, with square bases. They were laid flat (recumbent) on the grave. Only the top face was decorated, usually with the lettering each side of the vertical arms of a free-arm cross which may have "expanded" (lengthened) arms. On occasions the lettering may be in runes. The centre of the cross and the ends of the arms may be angular, circular or stepped.

St Hilda's Church, Hartlepool, County Durham, provides an example of a recumbent, flat-headed, name-stone grave-marker. On its top face it is incised with a single line providing a border and forming a panel enclosing a free-arm cross with a square, box-like, centre, from which extend square-sided arms with box-like ends. The quadrants adjoining the arms of the cross have the symbol for "alpha" in the top left-hand quadrant, the symbol for "omega" in the top right-hand quadrant – the symbols for Christ as the beginning and the end. The bottom left-hand and right-hand quadrants have runes which together spell the feminine personal name "Hildithryth". See adjacent: PHOTO 566. Hartlepool.

PHOTO 566. Hartlepool.

GRAVE-MEMORIALS

Grave-Memorials commemorating an individual often took a more substantial physical form comprising a vertically standing cross with a cross-shaft supporting a cross-head. These were often decorated on all sides with geometrical designs. Some, but not all, had an inscription on one face indicating the name of the person who raised the cross and the name of the deceased. Usually only part(s) of the cross-shaft survive but this may include part, or all of, the inscription. Some grave-memorials took a different physical shape as exemplified by the memorial shown on Page 279: PHOTO 569. Whitchurch.

St Michael's Church, Great Urswick, Cumbria, has part of an angular cross-shaft used as a grave-memorial to a named individual. Known as the "Tunwini Cross" it was at one time was reused as a lintel for a window – hence it's curving shape. It is decorated along the surviving vertical edges with bands of flat-moulding enclosing knot-work design, ring-twist design, roll-moulding, human figures, inhabited plant-scroll design with humans and creatures, and runic inscriptions; the south side has been rendered and no decoration survives.

The east face shown adjacent in PHOTO 567. Great Urswick, has three panels. The lower incomplete panel contains a central long-stemmed free-arm cross. On each side of this cross stands a human figure – both sets of their legs are now missing. The figures are in portrait but with their heads turned in profile to face each other. The right arm of the figure on the left extends to the right shoulder of the figure on the right, the hand and raised thumb are clearly displayed; the arm overlies the long stem of the free-arm cross. The hair, eyes, ears and mouths of each figure are distinctive. On the chest of each figure is part of a runic inscription which has been interpreted as the maker's signature – Lyl made this.

PHOTO 567. Great Urswick.

The complete central panel has a square frame formed by a band of roll-moulding adjacent to the band of flat-moulding along the vertical edges. This frame encloses five lines of a runic inscription; the runes on the lowest line are smaller than those above. The runes have been interpreted to read "Tunwini put up (this) cross in memory of his lord Torhtred. Pray for the (his) soul". The incomplete top panel above is decorated with knot-work design.

St Michael and All Angels Church, Thornhill, West Yorkshire, provides another example of part of an angular cross-shaft used as a grave-memorial to a named individual. It is decorated along the surviving vertical edges with bands of flat-moulding enclosing "stopped" plait-work design; the south face includes an incomplete runic inscription.

The south face shown adjacent: PHOTO 568. Thornhill, is decorated with two incomplete panels separated by a horizontal band of flat-moulding. The lower panel contains an inner, incomplete, square frame outlined by incised lines which encloses an incomplete runic inscription comprising four lines.

Each complete line of runes is separated from the runes below by an additional horizontal incised line. The runes have been interpreted to read "Gilswiþ(th) raised up, in memory of Berhtswiþ(th), a beacon on a hill. Pray for her soul". This inscription provides an example of where the person commemorated, and the person who commissioned the stone, are female. The upper, incomplete, panel contains stopped plait-work design.

PHOTO 568. Thornhill.

All Hallows Church, Whitchurch, Hampshire, provides an example of a grave-memorial comprising a large section of stonework with a horizontal base, vertical sides, and a semi-circular head – there is some damage. The "front" face has a stepped recessed containing a half-figure of a haloed Christ in relief and in portrait. With his right arm he is giving a blessing and in his left arm he holds a book.

Around the vertical sides and the top of the grave-memorial is an incomplete band of flat-moulding within which are two lines of an inscription in Latin lettering including the Old English feminine name Friđburg, prefixed by an incised free-arm cross. There is some debate about whether the name is Friđburg or Frioburga as some of the lettering is unclear. The inscription has been interpreted to read as "Here rests the body of Frioburga buried into peace".

PHOTO 569. Whitchurch.

The flat, semi-circular head, of the back of the grave-marker is decorated with a semi-circular band of flat-moulding with a horizontal base enclosing a panel containing tree-scroll design. Adjacent to each side of the trilobed top of the central trunk, similar trilobed topped trunks or branches, extend downwards at an angle into a large scroll; there are smaller scrolls in the lower corners of the panel. See above right: PHOTO 569. Whitchurch.

10. GRAVE-COVERS AND GRAVE-SLABS

Grave-Covers including grave-slabs, were usually of considerable size, with a top which could be flat or coped in shape. They were laid flat over the grave – "recumbent" – usually covering what remained of the deceased body or their bones. Many were decorated around the edges of the top face with a band of moulding enclosing a centrally placed, large, long-stemmed, free-arm cross. On some examples bands of moulding extended along the vertical edges of the sides occasionally enclosing a geometrical design. It is rare that any indication of the name of the deceased survives on the top face. The most elaborate form of grave-covers were "hogback" grave-covers – see Page 283 to 289. Graves were sometimes covered by recumbent slabs with additional, smaller, vertical or flat, stones at the head and foot. These smaller stones at the head of the grave are sometimes referred to as "pillow-stones"– despite this name they were not used to support the head of the deceased.

At Hexham Abbey (St Andrew's Church), Northumberland, there is a round-headed grave-marker which could be either a foot-stone or a head-stone. It is decorated in relief with a long-stemmed free-arm cross. See adjacent: PHOTO 570. Hexham 13. (The design of the free-arm cross is reminiscent of the one on the grave-cover identified on Page 280 top left: PHOTO 571. Hexham 14.)

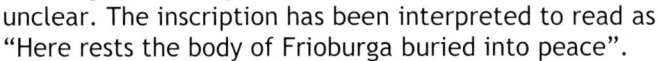

PHOTO 570. Hexham 13.

Hexham Abbey (St Andrew's Church), Northumberland, has most of a round-ended grave-cover which tapers towards the top and bottom ends; it is weathered and has some damage. The top face decorated in relief with a long-stemmed free-arm cross which expands and flattens towards its base. Separate, and above the top of the cross-head, is an incomplete band of roll-moulding in relief. There is no decoration on any other side. See adjacent left: PHOTO 571. Hexham 14.

Hexham Abbey (St Andrew's Church), Northumberland, also has a complete, rectangular-shaped, grave-cover with its top face decorated around the edges with a band of grooved-moulding enclosing a slightly raised panel within which is an incised long-stemmed free-arm cross emerging from a rectangular cross-base with rounded corners. See above right: PHOTO: 572. Hexham 15.

PHOTO 571. Hexham 14.   PHOTO: 572. Hexham 15.

St Mary and All Saints Church, Hawkesworth, Nottinghamshire, has most of a grave-cover which has now been placed vertically standing on one of its shorter ends; it tapers from top to bottom. Although weathered, it is clearly decorated on the north face and east side with a band of grooved-moulding around the edges enclosing one large central panel separated from two smaller outer panels by two, adjacent, horizontal bands of cable-moulding, placed in opposite directions to give a herringbone effect. The central panels contain on the east side a plait-work design reminiscent of ring-knot design including triquetra-knot design and a "bull's head" - see Pages 281 to 283, and on the north face a plait-work design enclosing a double-ended cross. The outer panels enclose a combination of a free-ring design and a knot-work design. The top and bottom ends of the grave-cover are not decorated. There is no decoration on the south face and only slight indications of grooved-moulding on the west side.

The north face shown in PHOTO 573. Hawkesworth, adjacent, has a central panel decorated with plait-work design sub-divided by a double-ended free-arm cross connected and sharing the same long, lower, vertical arm; the sub-divisions of plait-work design are linked by strands running across the ends of the arms of the free-arm crosses. The central panel is separated from two smaller outer panels by two, adjacent, horizontal bands of cable-moulding, placed in opposite directions to give a herringbone effect. The smaller panels contain a combination of a free-ring design and a ring-knot design.

PHOTO 573. Hawkesworth.

Holy Cross Church, Ramsbury, Wiltshire, has part of a recumbent coped grave-cover which is damaged and weathered. The grave-cover has a band of flat-moulding around the edges enclosing a panel which has a raised central ridge on the top which divides and terminates towards its surviving rounded end with the heads of two beasts whose tongues entwine into a distinctive knot; they are in profile and face each other. These two beasts each have a distinctive ear, eye, and open jaw from which their tongues emerge.

Below the central ridge on one side are three roundels of roll-moulding enclosing from top to bottom: a rosette of seven petals – the central petal is larger than the others; a bird-like beast in portrait but with its head turned in profile to the right to bite its curling tail – an eye and its beak can be identified; a dog-like beast in profile to the right with its head bent back to the left to bite its tail - an eye, its snout, and one leg can be identified.

Between the spandrels of the roundels there are rosettes with five petals. Below the central ridge on the other side are incomplete horizontal bands of figure-of-eight knot-work design. See above right: PHOTO 574. Ramsbury 3, showing beasts with entwining tongues arrowed red, the three roundels arrowed black, and the figure-of-eight knot-work design arrowed blue.

PHOTO 574. Ramsbury 3.

St Peter's Church, Monkwearmouth, County Durham, has most of a grave-cover now displayed vertically - there is some damage. See adjacent: PHOTO 575. Monkwearmouth 17.

Around the edges it has an incomplete band of flat-moulding with an adjacent inner incomplete band of roll-moulding. This moulding encloses an almost complete panel containing a large square-armed free-arm cross in relief with the remains of two wing-like features above the centre of the top vertical arm. Above and below the horizontal arms of the cross is a Latin inscription interpreted to read: "Here in the tomb rests Herebericht the priest in the body". The lowest two lines of the inscription, below the horizontal arms, are in smaller capitals than the rest of the inscription above. The letters "E" in particular are different: the "e's" above the horizontal arms are penannular, and the "e's" below the horizontal arm are vertical and horizontal. It is thought that the inscription was rewritten to commemorate a different individual than that originally intended. No decoration survives on any other side.

PHOTO 575. Monkwearmouth 17.

GRAVE-COVERS DECORATED WITH "BULL'S HEAD"
Mostly in Lincolnshire, but with occasional examples in other counties, the designs on some grave-covers may incorporate a representation in portrait of a bull's head. Usually a groove extends below the horns on its head to separate the bull from the rest of the design. The bull has a square jaw. A pair of incised lines outline a noseband, and further incised lines extend from opposite corners at the top of the noseband to form arcs which cross over the nose and extend into and along the centre of the horns. Holes represent the eyes of the bull, one each side of where the incised arching lines cross on the nose. The horns merge into the ribbon-

like strands which form the upper part of the patterns in the adjacent often plait-work designs. Note: some examples do not have the eyes or nosebands of the bull.

St Andrew's Church, Burton Pedwardine, has part of a grave-cover decorated with geometrical designs including a bull's head. An incomplete band of cable-moulding provides the top horizontal border of the grave-cover whilst the lower horizontal border appears to be a band of flat-moulding; the vertical borders have been cut away. Below the top border is an adjacent, horizontal, band of plait-work design, which, near what is now the left-hand end, incorporates the head of a bull in portrait.

A strand of the plait-work design provides the horns of the bull. The tops of these horns and the head of the bull are flat to accommodate the horizontal band of cable-moulding above. The bull has a square jaw with a pair of incised lines outlining a horizontal noseband. Further incised lines extend from opposite corners at the top of the noseband to form arcs which cross over the nose and extend into and along the centre of the horns. Holes represent the eyes of the bull, one each side of where the incised arching lines cross on the nose. Apart from its horns, the bull's head below its horns, is separated from the rest of the design on the grave-cover, by a distinctive, flat, groove which is at its narrowest below the bottom of the bull's jaw.

Below this groove is a horizontal band of cable-moulding which changes direction twice to accommodate the shape of the bull's head. Underneath the band of cable-moulding is a horizontal band of a ring-chain design which narrows and evolves into a plait-work design towards its left-hand end because of the intrusion of the band of cable-moulding above. See adjacent: PHOTO 576. Burton Pedwardine.

PHOTO 576. Burton Pedwardine.

All Saints Church, Hougham, Lincolnshire, has part of a grave-cover decorated with geometrical designs including a bull's head. It is divided vertically into three unequal parts. From left (east) to right (west) the decoration comprises: a "free-ring" design separated from the central panel by a rather jumbled looking, vertically placed, scroll-design.

The central panel contains a horizontal band of plait-work design with the head of a bull in portrait in the centre. A strand of the plait-work provides the horns of the bull. The bull has a square jaw with a horizontal noseband including a horizontal zigzag design. Below the noseband, the muzzle is decorated with a vertical design intended to give the impression of nostrils. Incised lines extend from opposite corners at the top of the noseband to form arcs which cross over the nose and extend into and along the centre of the horns. This bull does not have eyes.

To the right (west) of the central panel, the third panel is bordered vertically, to the left, by two vertical bands of different designs of cable-moulding connected top and bottom by a single strand. The panel contains knot-work design with its right-hand (western) border provided by two vertical bands of different designs of cable-moulding separated by a vertical groove. The right-hand band of cable-moulding is separated by a vertical groove from the west end of the grave-cover. See below: PHOTO 577. Hougham showing the bull arrowed red.

PHOTO 577. Hougham.

The Minster Church of All Saints, Dewsbury, West Yorkshire, has part of what probably is a grave-cover or a shrine – it has been referred to as a "hogback grave-cover". It is in the shape of a house resembling an upturned boat. The grave-cover has a central ridge on top of a curving roof with supporting "walls" and one complete gable end.

On the left-hand side of the grave-cover shown in PHOTO 578. Dewsbury 4, below, the roof is decorated with four incomplete, horizontal rows of tegulations which are separated from the gable end by five parallel bands of flat-moulding vertically placed. These bands abut a rectangular panel enclosing representations of baluster-shafts, one on top of the other, adjacent to the gable edge of the roof. The wall below is decorated with a band of flat-moulding forming an incomplete panel containing a horizontal plant-scroll design. The surviving edge of the wall has moulding in the form of a column with a base and capital – this design is not that different from the representations of baluster-shafts on the roof.

The right-hand side of the grave-cover is similarly decorated but with "L" shaped bands of flat-moulding rather than straight-sided vertical bands on the roof.

The surviving gable end is decorated with moulding in the form of a column with a base and capital on both vertical edges supporting a flat band of stonework which forms the end of the gable roof. These enclose a band of flat-moulding, outlining a shape like an upturned boat, including, off-centre, a free-arm cross standing on a raised section of the band of flat-moulding. See adjacent: PHOTO 578. Dewsbury 4.

PHOTO 578. Dewsbury 4.

HOGBACK GRAVE-COVERS

These are recumbent grave-covers in the shape of an elongated house with a convex profile comprising a pitched roof above long side walls; often the roof has a top curved central ridge. The overall effect is reminiscent in shape to a hog's back (the metaphor is emphasised by the nature of some of the decoration). Many examples, but not all, have inward-facing stylised bear-like beasts at each gable end gnawing at the top ridge and roof. They hold the sloping (pitched) roof and long side walls of the house with their paws. These bear-like beasts may have ears, eyes, be muzzled, and have one, two or three sets of paws.

The top curved central ridge may be decorated on its top (face) and adjacent sides. Below the top ridge, and along the pitched roof, the hogback may be decorated with curving horizontal rows of tegulations (there are various designs) or geometrical designs; the pitched roof often expands in volume at the centre. Below the pitched roof and along the side walls, and between the paws of the opposing beasts where these occur, there may be panels containing geometrical and figurative designs. In the centre of both of the long side walls some examples have an arched niche.

Moulding and decoration is usually, but not always, similar on both the sides of the top ridge, the pitched roof, the long side walls and, where they occur, both the backs of the bear-like beasts at each gable end.

See illustration below which shows one face of a hogback grave-cover. It has half of a muzzled bear-like beast at each end gripping the sloping roof with one of its paws. The top of their snouts are above the curving top ridge which has sides decorated with a stepped-pattern design. Their muzzled jaws are adjacent to the top row of three curving horizontal rows of tegulations along the roof. Their paws grip the curving horizontal rows of tegulations on the roof. Below, the upper parts of their bodies and arms extend over and onto the wall. The wall has a central semi-circular niche with, adjacent on both sides, two separate panels with bands of cable-moulding enclosing ring-knot and ring-twist designs placed vertically.

Other examples of hogback grave-covers do not have these bear-like beasts. Instead some may have representations of an inward facing serpent or beast head on the top face of the top ridge only; sometimes the sides of the face may be on the sides of the top ridge - see Page 288: PHOTO 584. Gosforth 7, and Page 289: PHOTO 586. Hickling 3. Alternatively, examples may have gabled, inwardly-sloping end panels which may be decorated with, for example, a Crucifixion Scene, beasts or a geometrical design - see Page 288: PHOTO 585. Gosforth 8.

St Oswald's Church, Lythe, North Yorkshire, has part of a weathered and damaged hogback grave-cover decorated on both faces with a mostly complete end bear-like beast, with open jaws, distinctive fang-like teeth, and incised circular eyes. See adjacent: PHOTO 579. Lythe 3, showing one face of the top ridge from which emerges from the upper part of the muzzle of the end bear-like beast. There is no decoration surviving along the top central ridge. The roof has three incomplete curving rows of tegulations extending from the lower jaw and neck of the bear-like beast to the missing likely bear-like beast opposite. There are indications of a horizontal band of flat-moulding separating the roof from the wall below.

PHOTO 579. Lythe 3.

One face of the wall, below the end-beast, retains part of a damaged panel containing a bird standing in profile to the right; it has distinctive tail feathers and an eye. To the right is a vertical band of flat-moulding. At the other end of what survives of this face of the wall there are slight vestiges of interlace design. See Page 284 bottom right: PHOTO 579. Lythe 3, showing the bird arrowed red, and the vestiges of interlace design arrowed black.

St Thomas's Church, Brompton-in-Allertonshire, North Yorkshire, displays a row of three hogback grave-covers with end bear-like beasts each with similar decoration on both their faces. See below the details of each one and below right: PHOTO 580. Brompton 2.

PHOTO 580. Brompton 2.

Hogback arrowed red on PHOTO 580. Brompton 2, adjacent. No decoration survives along the top ridge which emerges from the jaws of the end bear-like beasts. The roof has two rows of curving tegulations extending between the paws of the bear-like beasts and separated from the wall below by a horizontal band of flat-moulding. The walls have bands of flat-moulding forming a trapezoid panel extending between the paws and bodies of the bear-like beasts. Within this panel are a horizontal row of five, alternating, acute angle triangles, each enclosing a triquetra-knot design. The end-beasts are complete with muzzled jaws and fore-paws and have slight indications of individual toes, eyes and ears. The end-beasts are weathered and have no other distinctive characteristics.

Hogback arrowed black on PHOTO 580. Brompton 2, above. The top ridge emerges from the jaws of the end bear-like beasts with its top face decorated with bands of flat-moulding enclosing a ring-twist design. The roof has three rows of curving tegulations extending between the paws of the bear-like beasts and separated from the wall below by a horizontal band of cable-moulding. The walls have vertical bands of flat-moulding forming a row of four vertical panels separated from each other by a plain vertical band of stonework. Each of the four panels enclose plait-work design. These vertical panels are placed between the paws and bodies of the bear-like beasts. The end-beasts are complete with muzzled jaws, ears and fore-paws with individual toes. The end-beasts are weathered and have no other distinctive characteristics.

Hogback arrowed blue on PHOTO 580. Brompton 2, above. The top ridge emerges from the jaws of the end bear-like beasts with its top face decorated with bands of flat-moulding enclosing a stepped-pattern design. The roof does not have any rows of curving tegulations, instead, there is a large horizontal band of plait-work design extending between the paws of the bear-like beasts. There is no decorative separation of the roof and the walls below. No decoration survives on the walls other than a sizable semi-circular, recessed, niche. The end-beasts are complete and are reclined to show both sets of their front and back paws and as a consequence display more of their bodies. The end beasts are not muzzled, their jaws are slightly open, and their paws have individual toes. The end beasts have slight indications of eyes and ears. The end-beasts are weathered and have no other distinctive characteristics.

St Peters and St Patrick's Church, Heysham in Lancashire, has a complete hogback grave-cover with both faces depicting different scenes involving humans and beasts thought to derive from Scandinavian mythology, possibly involving Sigurd or Ragnarök, but a Christian interpretation, possibly, Adam naming the beasts, cannot be discounted.

PHOTO 581. Heysham 1.

See above: PHOTO 581. Heysham 1, showing the west face. The top ridge, with vestiges of cable-moulding, emerges from the ends of the snouts on the large heads of the end bear-like beasts who have small bodies. These beasts hold the roof and walls of the hogback with their upper and lower paws. The roof has a single curving row of tegulations extending between the snouts of the end-beasts. Below the left-hand side of the tegulations another curving band of tegulations begins but is interrupted by two incised, inverted, semi-circles with a central vertical band between the two semi-circles – these could possibly include the representation of the trunks of trees. The band of decoration continues to the right with a four-legged beast moving in profile to the left. Its head is turned to look over its rump; the beast has two distinct, round, hole-like, eyes. To the right of this beast is the figure of a human figure placed horizontally with its legs apart and its feet pointing in opposite directions. The human's arms form a semi-circle on each side of their body and the head has round, hole-like, eyes and an incised (vertical) slit for its mouth. To the right of the horizontal head of the human, the stonework is smooth but a series of incised lines gives the impression of square versions of the number "2". There is a curving row of five of these numbers with the left end number "2" incomplete. To the right of these numbers, at the right-hand end of this band of decoration, is an elongated ring-twist design.

The recessed wall below the roof is decorated with a rather jumbled scene. At the left-hand end of the wall are two standing human figures in portrait adjacent to each other. They hold their arms and hands level with their heads and have holes and horizontal slits representing their eyes and mouths. To the right of these figures, and moving in profile to the left, is a four-legged beast with a long "S" shaped tail. Above the tail of this beast, and in profile to the right, is a smaller, crouching, beast with open jaws. To the right of these two beasts, and moving in profile to the left, is a large four-legged beast; it has two distinctive antlers and a stubby tail. On the back of this beast, and in profile to the left, is a smaller four-legged beast with a curled tail. To the right of the stubby tail of the beast with antlers, and moving in profile to the right, is a four-legged beast with a long "S" shaped tail.

Above the tail of this beast, and moving along the eaves of the wall in profile to the left, is an upside down four-legged beast with its curling tail above the stubby tail of the antlered beast below. Adjacent to the right of these two beasts are two standing human figures in portrait adjacent to each other; they are similar to the humans depicted at the other end of the wall. They too hold their arms and hands level with their heads and have holes and horizontal slits representing their eyes and mouths. In addition, between them, and placed vertically rather than horizontally in profile, is a small four-legged beast with its curled tail intruding into the plain band of stonework representing the base of the wall.

Conyers Chapel, All Saints Church, Sockburn, County Durham, has an almost complete hogback grave-cover – it is broken in two but placed together; there is some stonework missing. Unlike many hogbacks it is not decorated with a bear-like beast at each end. The decoration on both faces is similar.

On the south face shown adjacent in PHOTO 582. Sockburn 4, at the undamaged end, an inward looking head of a small serpent – arrowed red – looks across the top ridge. The top ridge is decorated with a band of flat-moulding enclosing a ridge with a hollowed out centre. Below the top ridge there are three curving rows of tegulations on the "roof". There is no other decoration on the walls, or any other part, of the hogback.

PHOTO 582. Sockburn 4.

St Mary's Church, Gosforth, Cumbria, has a mostly complete, but damaged, hogback grave-cover known as the "Warrior's Tomb"; it has no end bear-like beasts. On one face it is decorated with tegulations on the roof, and a jumbled design involving interlace with a ribbon-beast, interlocking circles, and ring-knot design, on the wall. The other face is also decorated with tegulations on the roof but with two groups of standing warriors on the wall. Both gable ends slope inwards with one decorated with an incomplete human figure, and the other with a curled ribbon beast whose details are now difficult to identify confidently.

PHOTO 583. Gosforth 6.

See above right: PHOTO 583. Gosforth 6, showing the south face. There is no decoration on the top ridge. The roof is decorated with five curving horizontal, rows of tegulations which overhang the eaves. On the wall there are two groups of standing warriors. Each warrior stands behind the other, carries a spear over his shoulder, and holds a distinctive round-shaped shield which overlaps his neighbours; below some of the shields are indications of the warrior's legs. All stand on roughly the same axis and there is a central gap between the two groups. The fifteen warriors on the left stand in profile to the right and are led by a warrior whose lower left arm and hand extend at right-angles. The eleven warriors on the right stand in profile to the left and are led by a warrior who carries in front of him a staff with a triangular pendant in addition to the spear over his shoulder.

St Mary's Church, Gosforth Cumbria, has a damaged and mostly complete hogback grave-cover known as the "Saint's Tomb". The sides of the top ridge are decorated with plait-work design including the heads of two beasts confronting each other. The roof is decorated with a diamond-shaped pattern and the walls are decorated with inhabited plait-work design including humans and beasts. Both gable ends slope inwards and depict Crucifixion scenes.

On the top ridge the rectangular-shaped head of a large beast in profile to the right can be identified. Its head includes indications of a hollowed ear, round eye and upturned snout. Its open jaw has a single pointed tooth extending upwards, and a more distinctive, larger, pointed tooth extending downwards. The end of its snout

PHOTO 584. Gosforth 7.

replaces the top and bottom bands of cable-moulding extending along the top ridge. The end of its coiled tongue is in front of its front pointed tooth and between the jaws of a smaller beast it confronts. This smaller beast is in profile to the left. It has a round head with a rounded eye, hollowed ear and long open jaws – it emerges from the adjacent plait-work design. See above right showing the beasts on the south side: PHOTO 584. Gosforth 7.

The east gable end shown adjacent in: PHOTO 585. Gosforth 8, is decorated with an incomplete band of roll-moulding along the gable and vertical edges – the top of the gable is missing and the lower horizontal edge is damaged and mostly missing. This moulding encloses a Crucifixion scene showing a standing figure of Christ in portrait with his arms outstretched. His eyes, nose and mouth are distinctive. Above the band of moulding extending around the head of Christ, representing a halo, is a wide, curved, band of undecorated stonework with a narrower, curved, band of moulding above. There is not a cross depicted in this Crucifixion scene.

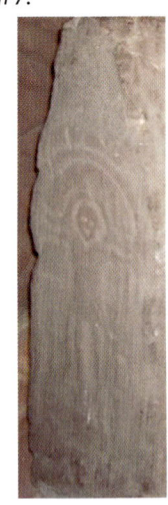

PHOTO 585. Gosforth 8.

St Luke's Church, Hickling, Nottinghamshire, has a combination of a hogback and coped grave-cover which is stylistically unique. The grave-cover tapers from one end to the other, has a top ridge with an angled roof on each side, all supported by a vertical wall on each side. The top face of the grave-cover is decorated with geometrical designs including beasts. The supporting long walls are decorated on the edges with bands of flat-moulding forming panels enclosing variants of ring-chain design with ring-knot design terminals – one wall has single pellets occasionally added to the design. No decoration survives on the gable ends.

PHOTO 586. Hickling 3.

The top of the grave-cover, see above: PHOTO 586. Hickling 3, is decorated at each end of the top ridge with an inward looking bear-like beast with a head – ears, nose and muzzled snout – shoulders and angled arms ending in claws. The beast's claws, at right-angles, hold a band of flat-moulding which extends along the bottom of both sides of the roof. From the mouth of each bear-like beast a band of flat-moulding emerges which extends along the top ridge into the mouth of the opposing bear-like beast.

Nearer to the head of one serpent than the other, the band of moulding along the top ridge abuts the centre of one of the triangular-shaped, vertical, arms of a free-arm cross. The cross is double-outlined and whilst it's vertical arms extend along the top ridge, its horizontal arms extend down the sides of the roof to the tops of the side walls. One of its horizontal arms has a serrated edge. Where the lower vertical arm of the free-arm cross ends, the band of flat-moulding continues along the top ridge. Where the top ridge reaches the mid-way point along the length of the grave-cover, it is joined by straight-sided bands of horizontal beaded-moulding, with single rows of small circular-shaped flat beads. This beaded-moulding extends up from the tops of the side walls, and up the sides of the roof, to join the top ridge. Together, at their junctions, the bands of moulding form another free-arm cross whose lower vertical arm continues along the top ridge.

Bands of flat-moulding, one on side, and two on the other, join the top ridge at right-angles to link it with the band of flat-moulding along the bottom of each side of the roof; these form sub-panels. The band of flat-moulding continues along the top ridge until it reaches the mouth of the other end bear-like beast.

Extending between the arms of the opposing end bear-like beasts, between the arms of the free-arm crosses, and in the sub-panels are: inhabited interlace and knot-work designs including some with triquetra-knot design, one with free-rings, some designs with loosely entangled beasts in profile whose heads and open jaws can be identified - two have a single eye; other interlace and knot-work designs with a single strand possibly ending in the head of a serpent or bird-like creature; affronted beasts; plait-work design with a strand possibly ending in the head of a serpent or bird-like creature; and one or more pellets.

11. SARCOPHAGI
Derby Museum has a rare, richly-decorated, Anglo-Saxon sarcophagus carved out of solid stone; only a fragment of its decorated lid survives. It is known as "St Alkmund's Sarcophagus" after the martyrdom around 800 of Alkmund, a son of Alhred, King of

Northumbria, who reigned 765 to 774. Whether or not the sarcophagus contained the remains of St Alkmund is open to question. It could be argued that given its decoration the sarcophagus was intended to be seen and therefore placed above ground rather than buried and that perhaps it was displayed as a shrine.

At the base there is a horizontal band of stonework which is not decorated, with above, an outer, wide, band of flat-moulding with an adjacent inner, narrower, band of roll-moulding which form panels on both the long and short sides of the sarcophagus. The panels contain variants of plait-work and interlace designs. On the long side shown in the adjacent: PHOTO 587. Derby 2, the panel contains ring-chain design laid horizontally in two separate, but linked, bands.

PHOTO 587. Derby 2. Photograph Courtesy of Derby Museums.

St Mary the Virgin Church, Wirksworth, Derbyshire, has part of a coped sarcophagus known as the "Wirksworth Stone" – there is some damage and some stonework missing. It may have been used to contain the body of the seventh century Northumbrian missionary "Betti" – it may even be his shrine. See Page 291: PHOTO 588. Wirksworth.

There are indications of a band of vertical moulding on the lower part of the vertical edge of the right-hand side; the rest of the right-hand edge and all of the left-hand edge are damaged with stonework missing. The top and bottom horizontal edges are slightly damaged with any indication of moulding removed. A horizontal band of roll-moulding separates the upper, surviving part, of the coped lid, from the lower, surviving, part of the side of the sarcophagus. Both parts are richly decorated in relief with figures depicting Biblical scenes, there are four surviving horizontal scenes in the upper row (the coped lid), and four surviving horizontal scenes in the lower row (the side/wall). The figures in the lower row are well defined with their facial features and clothing easily identifiable, the figures in the upper row are less well defined and are more weathered.

The scenes in the upper row, from left to right, depict:
1. Christ washing the feet of the feet of the disciples. There are three standing figures in portrait with the figure on the right standing in a large basin. The figure representing Christ bends in front of them in profile to the right but with his head turned in portrait. Both his hands grasp the right foot of the figure standing in the basin; around the waist of Christ are mouldings to indicate a cloth.

2. A Crucifixion scene. A large free arm cross with, in the centre, the representation of a lamb in profile to the left but with its head turned in portrait. In each quadrant of the cross there are the half-figures representing the different symbols of each Evangelist; they all hold a book.

3. The funeral procession of the Virgin Mary. Her body, on a semi-circular stretcher is being carried by two of the apostles in procession to the right. The stretcher-bearers are three-quarter turned to face the viewer. The swathed full-body of the Virgin Mary has, on the right, her head veiled but with her eyes turned to face the viewer. Above the body of the Virgin Mary is a semi-circular band of moulding representing a cloud.

Enclosed within the cloud is a top row of three heads and a bottom row of three and a half heads – all are in portrait and their facial features can mostly be identified; these heads represent singing angels. Below the stretcher with the Virgin Mary is a figure, the High Priest, lying on his back with his angled legs on the left and his head on the right and turned to face the viewer; he raises his hands to clasp the stretcher above. To the right of the front stretcher-bearer is a standing figure, representing St John, three-quarter turned to face the viewer, and holding in front with both his hands a vertically placed palm.

4. Presentation of Christ in the Temple. A standing figure representing Simeon is three-quarter turned to face the viewer. He holds diagonally across his body the Christ-Child whose head is three-quarter turned to face the viewer. The incomplete standing figure of the Virgin Mary is on the right – partly broken – her right arm reaches down towards the Christ-Child. The Hand of God, between the shoulders of Simeon and the Virgin Mary, points down from above. What this scene represents remains open to debate but see Page 292, "4. Mission".

PHOTO 588. Wirksworth.

The scenes in the lower row, from left to right depict:
1. The Descent into Hell. Two groups of figures, one above the other. The upper row has the head, right shoulder and right arm of Christ in profile to the right but with his head turned in portrait. He is in the process of releasing man, in the form of a babe in swaddling clothes, to re-birth. Below is a representation of a brazier with the heads of three figures in a row in portrait; these represent Cain, Herod and Judas Iscariot who are burning in the brazier.

2. The Ascension of Christ. Christ being conveyed into heaven by angels. An oval panel containing the standing figure of Christ in profile to the right but with his head turned in portrait. Christ holds with both hands, diagonally across his body and left shoulder,

a staff in the form of a long-stemmed free-arm cross. On each side, and clasping the sides of the oval panel are two winged angels, one above the other, placed horizontally in profile but with their heads turned in portrait; their wings, arms and hands are distinctive. The upper angels are in half-length whilst the angels below are in full length. Below, on each side of the oval panel, are the heads and shoulders of a pair of figures in portrait but with their heads three-quarter turned towards the panel, these figures comprise a veiled (female) figure who clasps the panel flanked by a winged angel. The angel on the left extends their left arm across their body to their right side and holds in their left hand an angled scroll.

3. The Annunciation. Virgin Mary seated on a wicker chair in profile to the left but with her head three-quarter turned in portrait. On the left is a half-figure of an angel in portrait with their right arm raised diagonally across their body with the hand giving a blessing-like gesture in the direction of Mary. In the angel's left hand is a vertically placed scroll signifying the word of God.

4. Mission. Three standing figures, three-quarter turned to the right, in a row – the first figure is male, the other two figures are female. The third figure represents the Virgin Mary who holds out the Christ-Child in her left arm. The Christ-Child holds a diagonally placed scroll in his right hand and his left arm and hand extend diagonally over the chest of the standing figure to his left. This standing figure, thought to represent St Peter, is three-quarter turned to the left towards the three figures and the Christ-Child. The figure of St Peter stands in a boat, signifying the church. This scene may be represent what is known as the "Presentation of Christ" involving Simeon meeting the Holy Family in a ceremony which took place outside the temple. Another similar ceremony which took place inside the temple may be depicted in the scene in "4. Presentation of Christ in the Temple" in the upper row – see Page 291.

12. SHRINE CHESTS
Shrine chest were usually rectangular-shaped with coped tops and box-like. They were often elaborately decorated with geometrical, plant and figurative designs.

The Cathedral Church of St Peter, St Paul and St Andrew, Peterborough, Cambridgeshire, has an example known as the "Hedda" or "Monks' Stone". It comprises a sloping, ridged roof with gable (triangular) ends supported by rectangular "walls". It was used as a grave-cover for Abbot Hedda and his monks killed by the Danes in 869.

The east and west walls are each decorated with a band of flat-moulding enclosing a single large panel - they are almost complete. Within each of these panels are arcades comprising six round-headed archways supported by capitals resting on pillars – the bases of the pillars are damaged. A plant design emerges from the tops of the capitals; the trunks of the plants bifurcate and sprout leaves. Under each of the archways is a haloed figure standing in portrait; these include Christ, the Virgin Mary, and the Apostles.

On the east face shown on Page 293: PHOTO 589. Peterborough, the figure arrowed red is Christ whose halo is divided by the ends of the arms of a free-arm cross behind his head. The right arm of Christ is angled across his body with his fingers extended to give a blessing. To the right of Christ, the figure arrowed black, is the Virgin Mary who carries a palm in her left hand. To the left of Christ, the figure arrowed blue, is St Peter who holds a key in his right hand.

On the west face: a beardless figure is said to depict the youthful figure of St John who is often shown as clean shaven, and a figure with spiked, flame-like hair, is said to depict St Andrew. Other figures represented are some of the apostles. No decoration survive on the north and south walls. The number 870 incised on the south wall is presumed a Victorian addition, if it were original, the lettering would be DCCCLXX.

PHOTO 589. Peterborough.

The east and west sloping roofs are each decorated with bands of roll-moulding (now rather flat) forming four complete panels enclosing ring-chain design and inhabited plant-scroll designs with possibly creatures and beasts. The north and south gable ends of the roofs are not decorated.

The Cathedral Church of St Peter, Lichfield, Staffordshire, has what is thought to be the left-hand part of an end panel from one side of a gabled box-like shrine chest. It has been broken into three and placed together. This chest may have contained the relics of St Chad (Bishop successively of York and Lichfield who died in 672). See adjacent: PHOTO 590. Lichfield.

The surviving face of the end panel is decorated around the edges with an incomplete band of flat-moulding. The figure enclosed by the moulding is thought to depict the Archangel Gabriel. The haloed, open-winged, figure stands in portrait with his head is turned to the right. His halo, his wings, his curled hair and facial features, his arms, hands, legs and feet, and his clothing, are all clearly defined. In front of his right wing his right arm and hand are raised giving a blessing. With his left hand he holds diagonally across his body a staff whose top ends in a foliate design above his right shoulder and reaches the upper border of the panel. His right foot is raised, as though in motion, and his left foot is firmly on the "ground" – the lower horizontal edge of the panel. There is also foliate design by his right foot extending half-way up what survives of the left-hand vertical edge of the panel. Paint clearly survives on much of the figure. Given the position of the figure it is thought he was communicating with another figure in the missing part of the panel.

PHOTO 590. Lichfield.

All Saints Church, Bakewell, Derbyshire, has a broken triangular-shaped section of stonework from part of a coped monument which could possibly be part of a shrine chest.

One face is decorated with a horizontal band of flat-moulding with above variants of ring-knot and plant-scroll designs. The other face is decorated with what are probably two different, incomplete, biblical scenes, separated by a horizontal band of flat-moulding. What exactly these scenes represent is now unclear. There is no decoration on any other side.

The east face shown adjacent: PHOTO 591, Bakewell 4, has an incomplete horizontal band of flat-moulding which divides the stonework into a smaller, incomplete, lower panel, and a larger, incomplete, upper panel.

The upper panel contains on the left an incomplete vertical, indistinct, object which rises to the full height of what survives of the panel. Adjacent on the right is a standing figure in profile to the left, their head and shoulders are missing. One of their arms is extended and from it hangs vertically what may be tapering drapery with distinctive horizontal folds. To the right is another incomplete standing figure in profile to the right but with their right leg and foot turned in portrait; their head and shoulders are missing. This figure appears to have been winged given the narrow, vertical,

PHOTO 591. Bakewell 4.

tapering, mouldings which can just about be identified on their back. To the right of the winged figure is the tail, most of the hind-legs, rump and part of the body of a horse or donkey in profile to the right – the front of the body, the fore-legs, neck and head are missing. It appears that the winged figure extends an arm, towards the back of the indistinct rider of the horse or donkey. The rider's lower body and a leg, and part of what they were sitting on, are not clear or easily identified – it is not now possible to say whether the rider sat astride or side-saddle.

The lower panel contains on the left-hand side part of a haloed head and vestiges of a left shoulder of a figure in portrait. To the right, and slightly lower down, is another figure who is more complete and in portrait. They have a haloed head, part of their right shoulder, and less of their left shoulder; their facial features are not distinctive. Adjacent to the left-hand side of the head of this second figure is part of the top of a crown-like object with three worn features with a central hollow below. In front of, and between, the shoulders of these two figures is a smaller haloed head in portrait.

St Kyneburgha's Church, Castor, Cambridgeshire, has what may be part of an eighth century shrine chest of St Kyneburgha who died sometime around 680 AD. The only face visible is decorated with a damaged horizontal band of roll-moulding at the top. Underneath are round-headed interlocking archways with shared capitals, shared central pillars and shared conical bases. From the surviving complete round capital a narrow vertical trunk emerges which bifurcates to end in leaves below the top band of roll-moulding. Under each arch are standing figures. The figure on the left is complete and is said to represent St Mark. He is haloed and stands in portrait but turned to his left with his head lowered; he is framed by an almost complete round-headed archway. The figure on the right and under the adjacent arch is incomplete but is also haloed and stands in portrait; most of their head and body are missing. See adjacent: PHOTO 592. Castor 1.

13. WALL FRIEIZES

Friezes which were incorporated into the stonework of walling were decorated with geometrical, plant and figurative designs. They were incorporated into walling, rather than protruding from walling (a characteristic of string-courses as they are sometimes described). Wall friezes were mostly incorporated into the internal faces of walling at, or around, first floor level. There are a few examples of wall friezes placed externally.

PHOTO 592. Castor 1.

St Peter's Church, Monkwearmouth, Sunderland, County Durham, provided an example of a wall frieze externally which extended horizontally across the width of the west face of the former porch at first floor level. It was decorated with cable-moulding enclosing a panel with running humans and beasts in profile. The frieze has now been removed and placed inside the church as it is both weathered and damaged; the decoration is now difficult to identify.

St Mary and St Hardulph Church, Breedon-on-the-Hill, Leicestershire, has a collection of wall friezes. For an example see below: PHOTO 593. Breedon 1, showing inhabited vine-scroll design with birds.

PHOTO 593. Breedon 1.

Many of the surviving friezes are framed by horizontal and vertical bands of flat-moulding to form panels containing mostly vine-scroll design, and inhabited vine-scroll design, with human-like figures, warriors, including horsemen, and variously styled birds and beasts, some are winged. Some are shown in profile and others with their heads turned in portrait. Also with ring-chain design, spiral-scroll design, and a pelta design which can occur in Roman mosaics.

St Margaret's Church, Fletton, Cambridgeshire, has seven sections of stonework from a wall frieze mostly bordered by flat-moulding forming panels. Some of the panels include inhabited scroll design with half-figures of haloed saints in portrait enclosed by an arcade of round-headed archways supported by capitals and pillars. Other panels include inhabited scroll design with half-figures of haloed, winged, angels in portrait or slightly turned with the accompanying scroll design containing what could be small human heads.

Some panels contain inhabited scroll designs with bird-like or duck-like creatures. One panel contains a central human figure between two strange looking bird-like or duck-like creatures in profile but with their heads turned in portrait. The human has their head at an angle and their arms are outstretched with his hands holding vertical pillar-like strands which form part of an inhabited scroll design; this human is sometimes interpreted as "Samson" – could the strands he hold be the extended tails of the bird-like creatures adjacent rather than pillars. See above: PHOTO 594. Fletton 1.

PHOTO 594. Fletton 1.

See below: PHOTO 595. Fletton 2, showing two panels of the frieze – the left-hand panel has inhabited scroll design with half-figures of haloed saints in portrait – the central figure may represent Christ - enclosed in an arcade of round-headed archways supported by capitals and pillars. The right-hand panel includes the figure of an angel in portrait, but slightly turned to their left, with open wings. The angel holds a staff in their right hand which extends up to the top of their right wing; the staff may possibly have a free-arm cross at the top. In the accompanying scroll design there may be small human heads.

PHOTO 595. Fletton 2.

Hexham Abbey (St Andrew's Church), Northumberland, has part of a wall frieze decorated with an angled band of flat-moulding with above most of the body of a running beast in profile to the right; there are slight vestiges of a white undercoat for painting. It is not decorated on any other side. See adjacent: PHOTO 596. Hexham 16.

Hexham Abbey (St Andrew's Church), Northumberland, also has what could be another part of the same wall

PHOTO 596. Hexham 16.

frieze shown in PHOTO 596. Hexham 16 on Page 296 bottom right. This second piece of stonework is decorated with a band of flat-moulding enclosing part of a panel with most of the body of a running beast in profile to the left; the stonework is covered with a white undercoat for painting. Unlike the frieze shown in PHOTO 596. Hexham 16, it is also decorated on a second narrow side with a band of flat-moulding around the edges enclosing a circle surrounding a double-diamond shape. Clearly both decorated sides were open to view, and, perhaps, the narrow side indicates that as well as terminating the frieze it also provided an impost where it reached an archway or doorway. It is not decorated on any other side. See above right: PHOTO 597. Hexham 17.

PHOTO 597. Hexham 17.

St Paul's Church, Jarrow, County Durham, has a part of a wall frieze decorated with an incomplete outer band of flat-moulding with an adjacent inner band of roll-moulding enclosing an inhabited plant-scroll-design. The design includes a standing human figure in profile to the left wearing a ribbed coat who is presumed to be a hunter - arrowed red. The hunter's raised left hand points towards a diagonal branch on which the snout, front two paws and parts of the front legs of a beast gnawing one of the branches can be identified – the snout of the beast arrowed black. The head of another human figure, placed horizontally and looking up towards the top of the frieze, can also be identified – it is arrowed blue. See above right: PHOTO 598. Jarrow 9.

PHOTO 598. Jarrow 9.

St Paul's Church, Jarrow, County Durham, has part of a wall frieze decorated with an incomplete band of flat-moulding enclosing what survives of a panel containing inhabited tree-scroll design including two birds. The central tree trunk separates the two birds. The figure of a bird on the left is complete and in profile to the right. The bird on the right is headless and in profile to the left but turned so that it is almost in portrait. See adjacent: PHOTO 599. Jarrow 10.

PHOTO 599. Jarrow 10.

St Paul's Church, Jarrow, County Durham, has parts of a wall frieze whose purpose and position in the monastery is uncertain. The upper section of stonework has been cut-back with below a wide flat border on which is an incised horizontal groove which forms the upper border of a horizontal band of roll-moulding which provides the upper frame for a

PHOTO 600. Jarrow 11.

representation of a horizontal row of vertical baluster-shafts. The baluster-shafts stand on a horizontal plinth. The baluster-shafts have a horizontal band of roll-moulding above their splayed bases and below their splayed capitals; they have a horizontal groove around their centres. See Page 297 bottom right: PHOTO 600. Jarrow 11.

Holy Trinity Church, Rothwell, West Yorkshire, has an incomplete wall frieze including part of an end panel perhaps indicating that it provided an impost where it reached an archway or doorway.

The frieze has a long face decorated with a band of flat-moulding along its horizontal sides. The top horizontal band of flat-moulding appears to be interrupted in places by short rows of equally spaced vertical grooves possibly representing baluster-shafts. It's one surviving vertical side has a band of moulding provided by representations of baluster-shafts placed one on top of the other. The bands of moulding form an incomplete panel enclosing inhabited plant-scroll design which is divided into four parts by three equally spaced, vertical, stubby, bushes whose foliage emerges on each of their sides near the top of each stem. Among the foliage long single curving branches connect it to the adjacent bush. The central bush appears to have foliage which pierces the horizontal border at the top of the panel rather than ending just below like the other two bushes.

On each side of these bushes are individual beasts in profile. From left to right: an incomplete winged bird-like beast in profile to the left; a dog-like, beast in profile to the left but with its head turned back over its body; a winged bird-like beast in profile to the left with a worm-like strand hanging from its jaws; a large, four-legged, winged beast in profile to the right. The heads, facial features, bodies, wings and legs of all four beasts can easily be identified. See below: PHOTO 601. Rothwell 1.

PHOTO 601. Rothwell 1.

At the right-hand end of this section of the frieze it continues at right-angles along another side. This side of the frieze includes a band of moulding provided by representations of baluster-shafts placed one on top of the other providing the left-hand vertical border and a band of moulding provided by representations of baluster-shafts one on top of the other but placed horizontally along the top horizontal border. The panel encloses the half-figure of a human, or possibly an angel, in profile to the left. The body of this figure is slightly angled to the left with its head tilted to the left. The figure clasps with their left hand a vertically placed book which the fingers of their right hand grip. Adjacent to the left side of the neck of this figure, and on top of, and

PHOTO 602. Rothwell 2.

around, their left shoulder and upper left arm, is a wing. The figure's hair, facial features, hand, fingers, and wing, and the book, are clearly defined. Whether the figure is an angel or the symbol of St Matthew – a winged man or angel – remains open to debate. See Page 298 bottom right: PHOTO 602. Rothwell 2.

14. WALL PANELS

Wall panels were usually of some size and often depicted a centrally placed figure within a frame provided by a band of flat-moulding. Sometimes within the frame an inner individual frame was provided by an archway, or, when a number of figures were involved an arcade. The figures were often standing, some were half-figures. Some were in portrait or in profile and half-turned to towards the viewer. The panels depicted Christ, the Virgin Mary, archangels, angles and saints. Some panels are described as "Holy Roods" signifying that they depicted representations of Christ crucified; sometimes with accompanying figures. Wall panels also included other figures and beasts, archways, plant designs and geometrical designs. Few panels are now in their original position but there are exceptions.

Bristol Cathedral, Somerset, has a wall panel with a band of flat-moulding along the surviving vertical edges with vestiges of a rounded archway along the top; no moulding survives along the bottom horizontal edge – it is damaged. The panel is decorated with a life-size standing figure of a haloed Christ in profile to the right, but half-turned towards the viewer, with his head inclined. His head and facial features, body, arms, legs and feet can all be identified. He holds up his right hand which has two fingers extended to give a blessing. In his left hand he holds a staff in the form of a long-stemmed free-arm cross; its base touches the top of a small standing figure in profile to the left reaching up towards him – the small figure is very weathered with few distinctive details. Above this small figure, below Christ's right hand and to the right of his staff, there appear to be three upstretched angled arms of human figures. Under the right foot of Christ is a writhing creature in profile to the left with a round head, open jaw, oval eye and a bound and fettered body – it represents Satan. Under the left foot of Christ is a creature in profile to the left with a round head, open jaw with a fang, oval eye and a large rounded body which fills the bottom right-hand corner of the panel. Christ's foot appears to be pressing down on the top of the head of this creature which represents the open mouth of Hell. The creature depicting Hell is larger than that depicting Satan. See above right: PHOTO 603. Bristol.

PHOTO 603. Bristol.

Romsey Abbey, Hampshire, has a wall panel, a Holy Rood, comprising three separate sections of stonework joined together. They are decorated in relief with a Crucifixion scene with the complete, large, standing, figure of a haloed Christ shown in portrait – his head is slightly turned to his right. He has, horizontal, outstretched arms and the palms of his hands are open. His vertical legs, slightly bend at the knees and then angle towards his feet. His angled feet are supported by a suppedaneum. Above his head, pointing vertically downwards toward the head of Christ, is the "Hand of God"; the open palm and fingers of a hand emerge from a sleeve with the stonework above decorated with a scroll design to represent a cloud. See Page 300 top left: PHOTO 604. Romsey 1.

Romsey Abbey, Hampshire, has another wall panel, also a Holy Rood, now built into a reredos. See adjacent right: Photo 605. Romsey 2.

The panel is decorated in relief with a Crucifixion scene with a centrally placed large free-arm cross with a stepped base. The haloed figure of Christ is shown in portrait affixed to the upper vertical arm, the two horizontal arms, and about half-way down the lower vertical arm of the cross. Christ's outstretched arms and the open palms of his hands are at right-angles to his body. His vertical legs, slightly bend at the knees and then angle towards his angled feet. Level with, and on each side of the head of Christ, are two haloed angels, one third in height, standing on the top edges of the horizontal arms of the cross. The angels are shown in portrait and have open wings. The angel on the left raises its left hand towards the head of Christ, and, in its right hand, holds an angled sceptre. The angel on the right is similar but damage has removed some of its facial features and the tip of its sceptre.

PHOTO 604. Romsey 1.

PHOTO 605. Romsey 2.

Below the horizontal arms of the cross, and on each side of the body of Christ, are two standing, haloed, figures. The figure on the left represents the Virgin Mary and the figure on the right represents St John. Both are shown in portrait but turned inwards looking up towards the body of Christ. Below the figure of the Virgin Mary is a standing figure, in profile to the right, looking up towards the head of Christ. His left leg is bent at the knee and he holds in his raised hands a long-stemmed spear with which he touches the chest of Christ; the figure represents Longinus. Below the figure of St John is a standing figure, in profile to the left, looking up towards the head of Christ. His knees are bent and he holds in his right hand a long-stemmed pole with a round sponge at its end with which he touches the cross level with the waist of Christ. In his left hand he holds a cloth; the figure represents the Stephaton. A plant design emerges, from both sides the cross, level with the waists of the figures of Longinus and Stephaton.

St Matthew's Church, Langford, Oxfordshire, has a wall panel, a Holy Rood, decorated in relief with a Crucifixion scene with three standing figures each on their own separate section of stonework. The larger, central, haloed figure of Christ is shown in portrait with his head angled to his right. His outstretched horizontal arms are turned to show the open palms of his hands, his knees bent with his legs angled to his right, and his feet angled. Below each of his hands is a smaller haloed figure also in portrait but turned outwards; the figure on the left represents St John and the figure on the right represents the Virgin Mary. When the panel was built into the 13th century porch it was incorrectly reassembled, the position of the figures of Mary and John were changed, originally they would have looked inwards towards Christ; in addition the arms of Christ would originally have sloped upwards with the hands hanging downwards. See Page 301 top left: PHOTO 606. Langford 13.

St Matthew's Church, Langford, Oxfordshire, has another wall panel, also a Holy Rood, comprising four separate sections of stonework joined together. They are decorated in relief with a Crucifixion scene with the incomplete, large, standing, figure of Christ shown in portrait - his head and accompanying halo are missing. His outstretched arms and the open palms of his hands are at right-angles to his body. His robe is tied at the waist with a central, knotted, belt. Below his robe his straight legs are placed vertically and his feet are damaged. It has been correctly reassembled and built into the 13th century porch. See above right: PHOTO 607. Langford 14.

PHOTO 606. Langford 13.

PHOTO 607. Langford 14.

The church of the Holy Rood, Daglingworth, Gloucestershire, has four separate wall panels two of which are Holy Roods.

One of the Holy Rood wall panels depicts a Crucifixion scene with a centrally placed, large, free-arm cross which tapers from top to bottom. All four ends of the cross have been roughly cut. The haloed figure of Christ is shown in portrait affixed to the upper vertical arm, the two horizontal arms, and what survives of the lower vertical arm of the cross. Christ's outstretched arms and the open palms of his hands are at right-angles to his body. His straight legs are placed vertically, and his angled feet are damaged and supported by a suppedaneum. The facial figures of Christ and the details of his clothing are easy to identify. See below left: PHOTO 608. Daglingworth 1.

The other Holy Rood wall panel depicting a Crucifixion scene has Christ flanked by two figures - see adjacent right: PHOTO 609. Daglingworth 2. The facial figures and details of the clothing of all three figures are easy to identify. The panel depicts a centrally placed, large, free-arm cross which tapers from top to bottom. The left-hand horizontal arm of the cross is incomplete. The bottom of the lower vertical arm of the cross has been cut damaging what remains of the feet of Christ. The haloed figure of Christ is shown in portrait affixed to the upper vertical arm, the two horizontal arms, and what survives of the lower vertical arm

PHOTO 608. Daglingworth 1.

PHOTO 609. Daglingworth 2.

of the cross. Christ's outstretched arms and the open palms of his hands are at right-angles to his body; the end of his right arm and his right hand are missing and his left hand is damaged. His straight legs are placed vertically, and his angled feet are damaged and supported by indications of a suppedaneum.

Below the horizontal arms of the cross, and on each side of the body of Christ, are two standing figures, both in portrait, and slightly angled away from the sides of the cross. The figure on the right of Christ represents Longinus – his face is damaged. He holds in his left hand a vertically placed spear with its head in line with the top of his head. His right arm is damaged but in his right hand he holds a scourge. His feet are missing. The figure on the left of Christ represents Stephaton who is in portrait. He holds in his raised right hand a cup or goblet and in his left hand a pot of wine. His feet are damaged.

The third panel, see adjacent left: PHOTO 610. Daglingworth 3, depicts Christ enthroned; his facial figures and details of his clothing are easy to identify. The haloed figure of Christ is in portrait sits on a centrally placed, rectangular bench-like, throne with raised armrests. Both his arms are raised and angled. With his right hand he gives a blessing and in his left hand he holds an incomplete long-stemmed shaft in the form of a free-arm cross. Christ has his legs in front of a rectangular footstool with his feet resting on its semi-circular front.

PHOTO 610. Daglingworth 3.   PHOTO 611. Daglingworth 4.

The fourth panel, see above right: PHOTO 611. Daglingworth 4, depicts a centrally placed standing figure of St Peter in portrait; his facial figures and details of his clothing are easy to identify. His right arm is angled and raised and in his right hand he holds a large key placed vertically. His left arm is angled in front of him and in his left hand he holds a book or scroll placed vertically at a slight angle. His feet are damaged. His stance is slightly angled to his right.

St Mary's Church, Deerhurst, Gloucestershire, has a panel which appears to be in its original position protruding from the face of a wall. It depicts, in relief, a representation of a haloed figure of the Virgin Mary standing in portrait. Mary holds up in her clasped hands a vertically placed, oval-shaped, shield on which the painted image of the Christ-Child was likely to have been depicted - it commemorated the child in the womb. See adjacent: PHOTO 612. Deerhurst 23.

The Virgin Mary stands under and within a semi-circular archway which in the centre of its arch has a slightly raised saucer-like object - a patera. The archway has stepped imposts and square

PHOTO 612. Deerhurst 23.

jambs all supported by a rectangular base on which is a horizontal row of four, recessed, stepped-sided, free-arm crosses; those in line with the inner sides of the jambs above are divided vertically into half-crosses. In each of the bottom corners of the panel is a single patera. Originally the panel would have been painted – some vestiges of paint survive.

St Mary and St Hardulph Church, Breedon-on-the-Hill, Leicestershire, has wall panels with round-headed interlocking archways providing frames for individual haloed standing figures who carry books and scrolls. The archways have stepped bases, pillars, and capitals. The pillars and the spandrels between the arched heads appear to be decorated with a plant design. The separate, central, panel with an archway framing a half-figure giving a blessing and holding a book may represent the Virgin Mary. See below: PHOTO 613. Breedon 2.

PHOTO 613. Breedon 2.

St Michael's Church, Winterbourne Steepleton, Dorset, has a carved block of stonework which may have formed a part of a much larger wall panel. It is decorated in high relief with the flying figure of a haloed, winged, angel in profile to the right. The head of the angel is half-turned in portrait and looks backwards over its horizontal body with upturned legs and feet; the halo and the wings are incomplete. The facial features and wing are clearly defined. See above right: PHOTO 614. Winterbourne Steepleton.

PHOTO 614. Winterbourne Steepleton.

St Margaret's Church, Fletton, Cambridgeshire, has two wall panels, one is thought to depict the Archangel Michael and the other may depict either the Archangel Gabriel or the Archangel Raphael.

One wall panel has a band of flat-moulding around the edges with an internal rounded head. Enclosed by the moulding is a standing figure, but with legs slightly bent, in portrait and turned to his left - the eyes and facial features can be identified. The figure has a halo and is carrying in his right hand a staff in the form of a long-stemmed free-arm cross which he holds diagonally across his body. It is thought this figure represents the Archangel Michael. See Page 304 top left: PHOTO 615. Fletton 3.

The other panel has a band of flat-moulding around the edges with an internal rounded head. Enclosed by the moulding is a standing figure, but with legs slightly bent, in portrait and turned to his right – the eyes and facial features can be identified. The figure has a halo and is carrying in his raised right hand, at an angle, what could be a scroll, or alternatively, and perhaps, less likely, a bottle or a flask. Could this figure represent the Archangel Raphael – there is doubt about who this figure is. See adjacent right: PHOTO 616. Fletton 4.

15. FONTS

It is difficult to confidently state that a font is Anglo-Saxon unless it is decorated with an attributable design (occasionally) or a script (rarely). However, plain, "tub" shaped, angled or vertically sided, font-bowls are sometimes identified as Anglo-Saxon and this may be correct. Sometimes the "old", possibly Anglo-Saxon, font is retained somewhere inside the church or abandoned in the churchyard in the vicinity of the south porch.

PHOTO 615. Fletton 3.   PHOTO 616. Fletton 4.

St Mary's Church, Potterne, Wiltshire, has an otherwise undecorated, cone-shaped, font with an inscription around the top, overhanging, rim. The inscription is bordered around its circumference, top and bottom, by a horizontal incised line. The inscription in Latin is taken from the "Roman" version of Psalm 41.2 with the addition of "Amen": "As the hart panteth after the fountains of water; so my soul panteth after thee, O God". Amen. 8 inches/20.2 centimetres above the base of the font there is a single, horizontal, incised line around the circumference. See adjacent: PHOTO 617. Potterne, with the inscription arrowed red.

PHOTO 617. Potterne.

St Lawrence's Church, Eyam, Derbyshire, has a font with a band of flat-moulding around the circumference at the bottom and a band of roll-moulding around the circumference at the top. This moulding encloses an arcade of interlocking round-headed archways with shared pillars, imposts and stepped bases, similar to those of an Anglo-Saxon chancel or tower archway or an arcade. A number of churches have similarly decorated fonts which may be Anglo-Saxon. See adjacent: PHOTO 618. Eyam 3.

St Mary's Church, Deerhurst, Gloucestershire, has a font and its supporting base decorated with geometrical, plant and figurative designs. Both taper from top to bottom.

PHOTO 618. Eyam 3. Photograph with permission of Eyam Parish Church.

The font-bowl is divided into three panels horizontally by two, separate, single bands of flat-moulding; the base of the font-bowl has a horizontal band of roll-moulding. The central panel, the largest of the three, is sub-divided by single, vertical, bands of flat-moulding into eight sub-panels. These sub-panels enclose three vertical and three horizontal bands of spiral-scroll design interlinked with each other and the enclosing bands of flat-moulding; there are nine scrolls in each sub-panel. The narrower horizontal panels, above and below the central panel, are each decorated with a single horizontal band of plant-scroll design.

PHOTO 619. Deerhurst. 24.

The font-base is divided into seven panels vertically by separate single bands of flat-moulding. The decoration in these panels alternates between inhabited interlace design – including ribbon-shaped creatures and beasts placed horizontally - and bands of spiral-scroll design all interlinked with each other and the enclosing bands of flat-moulding. The seventh panel does not seem to have been decorated. The decoration on the font-base is weathered, incomplete and damaged. The inhabited interlace design, and the ribbon-shaped creatures and beasts in particular, are difficult to identify with confidence. Below the decorated panels is a horizontal band of roll-moulding separating it from the tapering, undecorated, foot recesses below. The font-base stands on a stone plinth – not Anglo-Saxon. See above right: PHOTO 619. Deerhurst 24.

St Mary's Church, Melbury Bubb, Dorset, has part of a round cross-shaft reused as a font. It has been placed upside down and now tapers from top to bottom. The rectangular design along what is now the upper border may well be an addition when the lining to the font was added at a later, not Anglo-Saxon, date. What is now the lower border comprises a row of square-shaped billets.

Between these two borders there are two pairs of large beasts in profile who all stand on a horizontal band of flat-moulding. One pair comprises: a cat-like beast, probably a panther, with a plumed tail, an ear, an eye, a collar-like feature around its neck, open jaws, teeth and tongue, and clawed feet. It faces a beast with a horse-like head, probably a hyena, with a plumed tail, an ear, two eyes, two nostrils and clawed feet. The hyena bends its neck and head and turns them almost in portrait enabling it to hold in its jaws the neck of a smaller creature, in

PHOTO 620. Melbury Bubb 1.

PHOTO 621. Melbury Bubb 2.

profile vertically, and in mid-air between it and the panther. A loose ring-like interlace design ensnares the legs, bodies and tails of the panther and hyena and acts as a space filler. See Page 305 as the font would have been when part of a cross-shaft: bottom left: PHOTO 620. Melbury Bubb 1, showing the panther ensnared with a ring-like interlace design, and bottom right: PHOTO 621. Melbury Bubb 2, showing a close up of the heads of the facing the panther and hyena who holds the neck of a smaller creature between them.

The other pair comprises: a lion with a mane and plumed tail and clawed feet. It has an ear, an eye, open jaws with teeth, and its tongue licks a smaller creature in front of it which is in profile vertically and in mid-air. The lion faces a stag with a short tail, hoofed feet and branching antlers. It has an eye, an ear and open jaws holding a strand of interlace design. Its head is turned to look over its rump and towards another smaller creature in profile vertically, and in mid-air, who is touching its rump. The smaller creature is also holding a strand of interlace design in its open jaws and another strand of interlace design extends the length of its tail which ends in two flippers. A loose ring-like interlace design ensnares the legs, bodies and tails of the lion and stag – apart from tail of the stag – and acts as a space filler.

St Edmund King and Martyr's Church, Dolton, Devon, reuses two sections of stonework from an angular cross-shaft to provide the base and bowl for a font – parts of the decoration of the base has been subject to restoration. The base stands the right way round, tapering from bottom to top, whilst the bowl is upside down, tapering from top to bottom. See adjacent: PHOTO 622. Dolton 1, showing both the font-base and font-bowl as now configured.

The surviving vertical edges of both the font and base are decorated with a band of roll-moulding; none of the horizontal edges seem original. The font is decorated with inhabited interlace and knot-work designs including a human head, creatures with long curving ribbed bodies, and creatures with wings. The north side is decorated with ring-knot design only.

The base is mostly decorated with ring-knot designs including figure-of-eight ring-knot design. The east side is decorated with ring-knot design divided vertically into panels by bands of roll-moulding – there is an additional horizontal band of roll-moulding towards the bottom of the larger central panel. Within the central panel two of the end strands of the ring-knot design include the heads of serpents – these are very weathered. (The west side is a copy, not Anglo-Saxon, of the east side.)

PHOTO 622. Dolton 1.

The south face of the upper section of stonework, the font-bowl, has a band of roll-moulding along each of the vertical edges enclosing a centrally placed large human head with a narrow neck - all in portrait. The head has cropped hair, distinctive staring eyes, with a small mouth showing two teeth. From each nostril the curving ribbed body of a creature emerges in opposite, outward looking, profile; the upper body and the head of each creature is above the top of the human head. Their heads are upturned and each has an oval eye, two flowing ears and slightly opened jaws. These creatures give an impression of

PHOTO 623. Dolton 2.

an extended moustache-like feature on the face of the human. The panel also contains interlace design below and above the human head, and across the bodies of the creatures which develops into a knot-work design space-filler between the backs of their heads. See Page 306 bottom right: PHOTO 623. Dolton 2, showing the decoration on the south face of the font-bowl as it would have been when part of a cross-shaft.

16. SUNDIALS

Anglo-Saxon sundials and the more simple mass or scratch dials were used for measuring the passing of the time of the day to indicate the time for the liturgy (service or mass). They usually comprised a stone slab incised with horizontal, angled and vertical lines. Sundials were often either incorporated into, or protruding from, a south facing wall – occasionally a west facing wall; some may now be found inside a church where a south aisle has been added at a later date – not Anglo-Saxon.

The vertical face of the stone slab was incised with a semi-circle with its horizontal line having lines radiating below to indicate the time for the liturgy. At the centre of the horizontal line at the top a wooden or metal peg – the "gnomon" – would cast a shadow and indicate the time. Some sundials comprised a circle with lines radiating both above and below the central horizontal line. Others were accompanied by wording and designs including plants and human figures.

Most Anglo-Saxon sundials were divided into four day segments sometimes subdivided. Some had four additional night segments - eight in total for day and night. Other sundials were divided into twelve day segments and twelve night segments - twenty-four in total for day and night.

The adjacent illustration identifies the features likely to be found on most sundials. An incised semi-circle line extends below a horizontal line which together provide the "frame" of the sundial. Within the semi-circle incised lines, spaced equally apart from each other, radiate from a central hole in the horizontal groove at the top which indicates the position of the missing gnomon.
Near the ends of the three incised lines denoting the quartering of the semi-circle there is an addition of a short incised line at right-angles to create a free-arm cross.

PHOTO 624. Daglingworth 5.

Holy Cross Church, Daglingworth, Gloucestershire, has a sundial carved onto a square block of stone surrounded by a circular band of roll-moulding which also provides its lower semi-circular border. The roll-moulding encloses a centrally placed, incised, horizontal line from which four additional incised lines radiate from the central hole for the missing gnomon to divide the semi-circle below into five segments – three of which are similar in size with the upper left-hand segment divided into two smaller segments of equal size. Near the ends of the incised lines separating the three larger segments there is an addition of a short incised line at right-angles to create a free-arm cross. See Page 307 right: PHOTO 624. Daglingworth 5.

St Bartholomew's Church, Aldbrough, East Yorkshire, has a circular sundial which projects from a rectangular block of stonework. Around the edge of the circumference is a band of flat-moulding with adjacent concentric incised lines provide the upper and lower borders enclosing an inscription in Old English. The inscription has been interpreted to read "Ulf ordered the church to be built for himself and Gunwaru's soul"; it is prefixed by an incised free-arm cross. The sundial is divided into eight segments by diagonal, vertical and horizontal incised lines which extend from the centre to the border of the surrounding inscription; the hole for the missing gnomon is in the centre. See adjacent: PHOTO 625. Aldbrough.

PHOTO 625. Aldbrough.

St Andrew's Church, Bishopstone, East Sussex, has a sundial with an inscription on a semi-circular-headed, otherwise rectangular, block of stonework, whose vertical sides diverge towards its base; the apex of the roof of the south porch obscures the centre of its base. See below right: PHOTO 626. Bishopstone.

Around the edges of the block of stonework there are three (on the west side there are vestiges of four) parallel and concentric incised lines which result in three raised and narrow bands providing a "frame" enclosing the sundial. Two separate, but concentric, bands emerge from the vertical incised lines to provide the lower semi-circular part of the sundial itself. Adjacent to, and concentric with, the inner semi-circular incised line above the inscription, is a semi-circular band of stepped-pattern design.

The sundial is divided into twelve segments by incised lines radiating from the central hole for the missing gnomon – it has a modern replacement. Near the ends of the five incised lines denoting the quartering of the semi-circle there is an addition of a short incised line at right-angles to create a free-arm cross with the end of each arm "drilled" with a hole.

PHOTO 626. Bishopstone.

Incised into the stonework above the sundial, and below the semi-circular band of stepped-pattern design, is an inscription on two lines. The upper line, prefixed with an incised free-arm cross, has the letters "EAD"; the lower line has the letters "RIC". These have been interpreted as the name Eadric. Note: There is some indication that the inscription may have been recut at a later date, possibly during the 1848-49 restoration.

St Gregory's Minster, Kirkdale, North Yorkshire, has a sundial with flanking inscription panels on each side. All are on one block of stonework which has a band of flat-moulding providing an outer frame – additionally an adjacent inner band of flat-moulding extends across the top horizontal part of the frame only. Below, the flanking panels on each side, have an additional band of flat-moulding along the top horizontal edge and a pair of adjacent bands of flat-moulding for the vertical sides and the horizontal base; this results in both panels having similar frames enclosing an inscription.

The middle panel has a semi-circular sundial comprising at the top an incised horizontal line with in the centre a hole for the missing gnomon. From each end of this horizontal line two concentric incised lines extend to join and form a semi-circle below. This semi-circle is divided into eight segments by incised lines which radiate from the central hole for the missing gnomon. Near the ends of the three incised lines denoting the quartering of the semi-circle there is an addition of a short incised line at right-angles to create a free-arm cross. The incised line closest to the left-hand side of the top of the sundial, has two short incised lines at acute angles to create a diagonal cross.

An inscription in Old English can be identified above the horizontal incised line at the top of the sundial itself; this inscription continues within the two concentric semi-circular incised lines forming the lower part of the sundial. Both the start and end of the inscription are incised with a free-arm cross. This inscription has been interpreted to read "This is the day's sun-marker at every hour".

Below the sundial, and below a horizontal groove, is another inscription in Old English prefixed by an incised free-arm cross. The inscription has been interpreted to read "And Hawarth made me and Brand the priest" – the last word in this inscription continues above the horizontal groove.

The flanking panels on each side of the central panel contain an inscription in Old English; both the start and end of the inscription are inscribed with different versions of a free-arm cross. This inscription has been interpreted to read, left-hand panel: "Orm the son of Gamel bought St Gregory's minster when it was utterly ruined"; right-hand panel: "and collapsed and he had it rebuilt from the foundations (in honour of) Christ and St Gregory in the days of King Edward and in the days of Earl Tosti". See below: PHOTO 627. Kirkdale 4.

PHOTO 627. Kirkdale 4.

All Saints Church, Orpington, Kent has, an incomplete circular sundial with inscriptions, three are in Latin and one is in runes. The sundial stands in relief on an incomplete block of rectangular stonework. The sundial in the centre is surrounded by a frame comprising a band of cable-moulding, with an adjacent outer band of roll-moulding. These two bands provide the inner border for a recessed band of stonework on which there is an inscription in Old

English. The incomplete inscription provides two texts separated by an incised free-arm cross. These have been interpreted as "to (or "for") him who knows how to seek out how" and "to count (or "to tell") and to hold". The outer border of this inscription is provided by a band of roll-moulding with an adjacent outer band of cable-moulding. Note: the two bands of cable-moulding on this sundial are twisted in opposite directions.

What survives of the recessed circular sundial in the centre is divided into fourteen segments – two of which are incomplete - by thirteen, equally-spaced, incised lines radiating from the central hole for the missing gnomon. Each of these incised lines terminate at the inner band of cable-moulding on the sundial. Near the ends of alternate incised lines there is an addition of a short incised line at right-angles to create a free-arm cross.

PHOTO 628. Orpington.

Two complete and one incomplete letters survive in the segments adjacent to each side of the vertical damage at what is now the base of the sundial. Each segment contains a single letter or indications of a single letter – six letters altogether. Although there are missing letters those that can be identified read "OR[. .] VM". These letters are thought to have formed part of the Latin word "horologium" meaning clock but in this case referring to the sundial. Other segments have a runic letter – three letters in total. The runic inscription of which they formed a part is now incomprehensible. See above right: PHOTO 628. Orpington, with the runic letters arrowed red – they are upside down.

All Saints Church (the "new" church), Skelton-in-Cleveland, North Yorkshire, has an incomplete and damaged sundial with lettering– possibly Old Norse – and runes – also possibly Old Norse. Both lettering and runes are incomplete resulting in their meaning and translation being open to debate. Only part of the sundial survives, recessed and above, the accompanying wording and runes. See adjacent: PHOTO 629. Skelton-in-Cleveland, showing the sundial arrowed red, the lettering arrowed black, and the runes arrowed blue.

What survives of the sundial comprises part of a lower semi-circle divided into four segments by incomplete incised lines. Near the end of one of the incised lines there is an addition of a short incised line at right-angles to create a free-arm cross. It is thought that the sundial was divided into twelve segments. Note: these incised lines do not now extend to a central hole where the gnomon would have been.

PHOTO 629. Skelton-in-Cleveland.

Below the sundial are three, separate, and incomplete, horizontal incised lines. Above each of these incised lines, and below the bottom line, is an incomplete line of text. A vertical incised line joins the right-hand ends of the horizontal incised lines together. On the right-hand side of this vertical incised line is an incomplete line from a runic inscription. The runes have been placed horizontally one under the other. There are indications of another line of runes to the right of the one definite line.

St Cuthbert's Church, Bewcastle, Cumbria, has a rare, if not unique, surviving example of a sundial on a cross-shaft. It is on the south side of an angular cross-shaft. Two adjacent vertical bands of roll-moulding enclose a panel bordered horizontally by a band of flat-moulding. Within the panel is a plant-scroll design which includes a semi-circular sundial attached like a large leaf to the stem of the plant forming part of the scroll; above the sundial is a bunch of berries ready to sprout. The sundial is in relief like the rest of the decoration on the cross-shaft.

PHOTO 630. Bewcastle 5.

PHOTO 631. Bewcastle 6.

The sundial is divided into four main segments, each sub-divided into three, by incised lines radiating from the central hole for the missing gnomon at the top of the sundial. The incised lines indicating the four main segments extend up to the edge of the sundial whilst those indicating sub-divisions end in a circular depression before the edge of the sundial; these incised lines are faint and weathered. See adjacent left: PHOTO 630. Bewcastle 5, and adjacent right: PHOTO 631. Bewcastle 6, showing the sundial arrowed red incorporated into a plant-scroll design on the south side of the cross-shaft.

Corhampton Church, Hampshire, has a square block of stonework decorated in relief with a circular sundial. An incised circular line near the outer edge of the circular part of the sundial encloses some of the incised lines radiating from the hole for the missing central gnomon. These lines are difficult to identify – one, midway between "4 and 5 o'clock", appears to have an addition of a short incised line at right-angles to create a free-arm cross. However, extending from the circumference of the sundial are expanding bulbous shapes indicating the vertical and horizontal divisions, and stems ending with three narrow long leaves indicating the diagonal divisions. The bulbous shapes and stems with leaves divide the circumference into eight equal segments and help indicate where the radial divisions should be. The sundial is now faint in outline and weathered. See adjacent: PHOTO 632. Corhampton 3.

PHOTO 632. Corhampton 3.

Escomb Church, County Durham, has a semi-circular sundial in relief on a trapezoid-shaped slab of stonework. The sundial is framed along its top and vertical sides by the curving body of a serpent-like creature. The head of the serpent and its eye can be identified in profile to the left in the bottom left-hand corner. Its triangular ended fish-like tail is decorated with grooved-moulding and can be identified in the bottom right-hand corner.

Below the body of the serpent the sundial comprises a horizontal line with a hole in its centre indicating the position of the now missing gnomon. From this hole four rather faint lines radiate to meet a semi-circular groove separating the dial from a curving band of moulding decorated with ring-twist design.

PHOTO 633. Escomb 13.

Above the centre of the sundial, and possibly on the same slab of stonework, is what may be the head of a beast with protruding eyes on each side near the top. Near the bottom of the head of the beast is a horizontal band of ring-twist design. This beast lacks the associated supporting neck usually found on a prokrossos and it has been suggested it might even be a seated figure cut off above the waist. See above right: PHOTO 633. Escomb 13.

St Mathew's Church, Langford, Oxfordshire, has the faint semi-circular outline of a sundial on a protruding, trapezoid-shaped, block of stonework, widest along its top horizontal edge. No incised lines survive, but, at the top, the central hole for the missing gnomon can be identified. The block of stonework is decorated with two standing human figures in portrait. Their heads are turned in opposite profile and are tilted so they look upwards, and inwards, towards the raised semi-circular curve of the sundial above. They have raised, bent, arms which enable their hands to hold the lower part of the sundial. Their legs are angled to the right and their feet are in profile to the right; the figure on the left is missing a leg and foot. See adjacent: PHOTO 634. Langford 15.

PHOTO 634.
Langford 15.

PART 4

RECOMMENDED EXEMPLAR CHURCHES & MUSEUMS

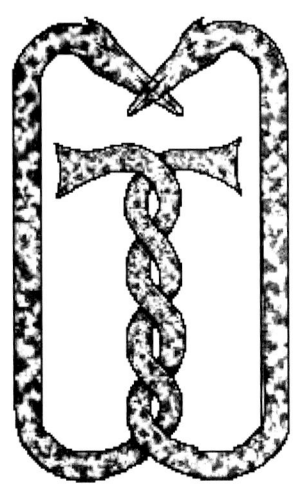

ACCESS TO CHURCHES

Access to churches can usually be obtained by using the contact details provided on www.achurchnearyou.com. Some churches may have their own websites but these will not always provide the information required. Alternatively, consult the current Crockford's Clerical Directory published by Church House Publishing, Great Smith Street, London SW1P 3NZ. This Directory includes details of Church of England clergy and identifies the church (es) for which they are responsible.

Opening times of the church, and the names and addresses of key holders, are sometimes included in notices on the internal walls of the porch, on the door into the church itself, or on freestanding notice boards outside. Often churches are open on Saturdays and Sundays and on these occasions special arrangements for access may not be necessary.

RECOMMENDED EXEMPLAR CHURCHES AND MUSEUMS

Each entry is alphabetically listed and consecutively numbered and identifies:

- Architectural features are prefixed by the red bullet point symbol indicated here.

- Anglo-Saxon church architectural features (internally then externally, and from west to east).

- Many of the architectural features identified can be see both internally and externally, although access to the features above ground floor level may not now be possible.

- Where the architectural features can only be seen internally they are prefixed with "Internally". Where Anglo-Saxon doorways are not at ground level their position is indicated.

- Later, not Anglo-Saxon, plaster may obscure the construction details of Anglo-Saxon architectural features.

- Where there is debate about the date of towers, archways, doorways, windows and belfry openings, they are described as "Saxo-Norman". All other entries without this prefix are of Anglo-Saxon, i.e., earlier vintage.

AND/OR,

- Sculptured stonework is prefixed by the blue bullet point symbol indicated here.

- Anglo-Saxon/Anglo-Scandinavian sculptured stonework and whether they are in the form of crosses, grave-markers, grave-covers and grave-slabs, sarcophagi, shrine chests, wall friezes, wall panels, fonts or sundials.

- The part of the church where they are located is indicated together whether they are to be found internally or externally or in the churchyard.

✠ The nature of decoration is identified where this is possible in geometrical designs and patterns, followed by where these are "inhabited" with beasts and creatures. Representation of Christian subjects, Norse mythological subjects, and human representations which cannot be confidently identified as falling within one of these subject groupings are given. Writing or runic inscriptions are then identified.

NOTE: The displays of stonework in churches and museums may be changed from time to time. Individual items may be loaned for temporary exhibitions elsewhere. Some items may be removed from display and put in store. A preliminary enquiry before a visit may identify such items but more than one visit with a reasonable intervening period may be required.

IDENTIFYING ANGLO-SAXON FABRIC AND FEATURES AMONG LATER BUILDING

Anglo-Saxon walling may survive both internally and externally:

- In the lower courses of stonework in the tower, above the tower and chancel archways, and below the roofline of the current nave.

- In the corners of the nave and the adjacent walling, and above and between later archways, not Anglo-Saxon, inserted into the north and south walls of the nave to provide access into the "new" north and south aisles.

- In the corners of the chancel, particularly, at the west end.

Anglo-Saxon archways, doorways and windows may now be blocked, or cut into, by later, not Anglo-Saxon, replacements resulting in Anglo-Saxon features surviving only in part e.g. part of a window-head or part of one of the jambs. Such surviving features may include both their former internal and external faces even though their external faces are now inside the church thanks to the addition of later aisles, not Anglo-Saxon.

Some Anglo-Saxon architectural pieces and sculptured stonework may be reused in a completely different context than their original intended use. They may be placed internally or externally upside down, vertically or horizontally, anywhere from ground level to the top of walling. Their reuse as lintels for doorways or windows, and sometimes quoining, is not uncommon.

Occasionally, the outline plan of an Anglo-Saxon church or its component parts may be indicated in stone or brickwork where a church has been demolished, or, where the present church overlays, or is adjacent to, or near to the site, of an Anglo-Saxon Church.

During 19th century restorations, parts and fragments of Anglo-Saxon and Anglo-Scandinavian stone sculpture was often re-discovered and incorporated into the fabric of the church or displayed internally. Often they can now be found internally, in bespoke displays, or on the floor or on window ledges, in the nave, south or north aisles or the tower, or in the porch now providing the usual entrance to the church.

1. ACTON BEAUCHAMP, Herefordshire – St Giles's Church.
TOWER EXTERNALLY:
- Part of Angular Cross-Shaft reused as lintel for doorway. Decorated with cable-moulding, flat-moulding and inhabited plant-scroll design with creatures and a bird.

2. ALDBROUGH, East Yorkshire – St Bartholomew's Church.
NAVE INTERNALLY:
- Sundial divided into eight segments by lines radiating above and below the horizontal line; central hole for missing gnomon. Inscription interpreted as "Ulf ordered the church to be built for himself and for Gunwaru's soul".

NORTH AISLE INTERNALLY:
- Incomplete Round-Headed Windows: arched heads each cut out of a monolithic lintel; decorated with a scroll design.

CHANCEL EXTERNALLY:
- Incomplete Round-Headed Window: arched head cut out of a monolithic lintel; decorated with inhabited plant design with two addorsed dragon-like beasts with long tails curled back over their bodies to below their jaws.

3. APPLETON-LE-STREET, North Yorkshire - All Saints Church.
SQUARE TOWER:
- Coursed Stone Walling – third (top) stage stonework smaller in size.
- Side Alternate Quoining.

FIRST STAGE:
- South Wall, Ground Floor. Blocked Flat-Headed Doorway; two large, square, stones forming lintel; no imposts; jambs laid in similar courses to the stonework in the adjoining walling.
- First Floor Level. Blocked Flat-Headed Doorways – north (only lintel survives), west and south walls: monolithic lintels; no imposts; each jamb, vertical stone, horizontal stone above and smaller horizontal stone up to lintel south wall/laid in similar courses to the stonework in the adjoining west wall; sills of both windows provided by the top of the coursed stonework of the walling directly below.
- Circular Window, not splayed, cut through a single through-stone – east wall, above current nave roof.
- Square String-Course separating first from second stage.

SECOND STAGE:
- Round-Headed Double-Belfry Openings: arched heads each cut out of single square lintel; through-stone imposts protruding from faces of walling and into central void; jambs, some through-stones, constructed with mostly larger stonework than the coursed stonework in the adjoining walling; cylindrical mid-wall shafts with rounded, extending, bases interrupting the sills of the openings – no capitals; above mid-wall shaft through-stone slab supporting junction of both arched heads; sills provided by the top of the coursed stonework of the walling directly below.

THIRD STAGE:
- Square String-Course separating second from third stage.
- Round-Headed Double-Belfry Openings: arched heads each cut out of single square lintel; through-stone imposts protruding from faces of walling and into central void; jambs are of similar size, and laid in similar courses, to the stonework in the adjoining walling; square mid-wall shafts curved and decorated externally with chevron and spiral patterns; above mid-wall shaft through-stone slab supporting central junction of both arched

heads; sills provided by the top of the string-course directly below.

NAVE:
- ❖ Coursed Stone Walling.
- ❖ Indications of Side Alternate Quoining on north-west and south-west corners – externally.

NORTH AISLE:
- ❖ North-West Quoining may include reused large Anglo-Saxon quoins.

4. AYCLIFFE, County Durham – St Andrew's Church.

NAVE INTERNALLY:
- ❖ Vestiges of Side Alternate Quoining above the first free-standing pillars east of the tower.

NORTH AISLE INTERNALLY:
- ✠ Incomplete Free-Arm Cross-Head and part of its Angular Cross-Shaft with designs and patterns including: flat-moulding, grooved-moulding, interlace design, plait-work design, roll-moulding; S-shaped creatures; long-necked birds. Crucifixion Scene with Christ, the sun and moon, and Stephaton and Longinus. Rows of three haloed figures in portrait whose haloes are joined – on one face each holds a book. Two, probably haloed, figures in portrait each holding a cross. Two haloed figures in portrait each holding a book and cross. Scene of St Peter being Crucified upside-down.

SOUTH AISLE INTERNALLY:
- ✠ Incomplete Free-Arm Cross-Head and part of its reconstructed Angular Cross-Shaft with designs and patterns including: concentric circles, flat-moulding, interlace design, knot-work design, open circles, pellets, stepped-pattern design; plait-work design with strands ending in the necks and heads of serpent-like creatures – on one face their bodies are double-outlined and their tails divide into strands; centaur-like beast with a horse-like head, body and legs but with human-like arms one holding a staff and the other its tail.
- ✠ Parts of Angular Cross-Shafts (one reused as a piscina) with designs and patterns including: flat-moulding, grooved-moulding, knot-work design, plait-work design, ring-twist design, roll-moulding; lower body, legs and feet of two figures in portrait; two out-turned human-like feet; two, possibly three, haloed figures in portrait each holding a book.
- ✠ Parts of Free-Arm Cross-Heads with designs and patterns including: flat-moulding, interlace design, plait-work design, roll-moulding. Two incomplete haloed figures in portrait each possibly holding a book. Bird in portrait standing on a perch with its head turned to the left and its wings partially outstretched; it may represent the eagle of St John.
- ✠ Part of a Grave-Cover with designs and patterns including: flat-moulding, free-arm cross, free-ring design, knot-work design, pellets.
- ✠ Part of a Round-Headed Grave-Marker with, on one face, most of a free-arm cross in relief decorated with interlace design and enclosed by flat-moulding and an adjacent inner band of grooved-moulding. On the other sides designs and patterns include flat-moulding and ring-twist design.

CHANCEL INTERNALLY:
- ✠ Part of Cross-Shaft with two incomplete panels with flat-moulding enclosing two haloed figures in portrait whose haloes are joined and two headless figures in portrait. See adjacent: PHOTO 635. Aycliffe.
- ✠ Fragment of Cross-Shaft with flat-moulding enclosing part of

PHOTO 635. Aycliffe.

two adjacent panels, one with the lower body, legs and feet of three figures in a row in portrait, the other the haloed heads of three figures in a row in portrait – their haloes are joined.
CHURCHYARD WALL:
✠ Part of a triangular panel with a band of flat-moulding enclosing a free-arm cross in relief with fan-shaped arms.

5. BAKEWELL, Derbyshire – All Saints Church.
SOUTH PORCH INTERNALLY:
✠ Parts and Fragments of Angular Cross-Shafts and Cross-Shafts with circular lower part and angular upper part. Decorated with designs and patterns including: cable-moulding, flat-moulding, interlace design, key-pattern design, pellets, plait-work design, plant-scroll design, ring-chain design, roll-moulding, spiral-scroll design; incomplete bird with part of a serpent; head and shoulders of veiled figure holding a short staff or rod; head, shoulders and upper body of a figure; upper part of a figure holding a staff in the form of a long-stemmed free-arm cross; lower parts of incomplete figures; scene comprising an incomplete group of figures possibly representing the Massacre of the Innocents – two apparently decapitated heads; remains of a group of three figures and separately two other figures on a ladder-like frame.
✠ Possible Cross-Base with panels with three-quarter figures of haloed, winged, angels on each side of a damaged panel probably depicting the Virgin Mary.
NORTH AISLE - INTERNALLY:
✠ Most of an arm from a Free-Arm Cross-Heads and Parts and Fragments of Angular Cross-Shafts with designs and patterns including: flat-moulding, interlace design, key-pattern design, knot-work design, plait-work design, spiral-scroll design; incomplete figure.
✠ Part of a Coped Grave-Cover which could have been part of a Shrine Chest with designs and patterns including: flat-moulding, plant-scroll design, ring-knot design; two Biblical Scenes with haloed heads, incomplete standing figures, one possibly winged, part of a horse or donkey with an indistinct rider.
✠ Three Fragments of stonework possibly from part of a shrine, frieze or panel with roll-moulding with pairs of human feet vertically placed in portrait.
EAST OF CHANCEL - EXTERNALLY:
✠ Part of lower vertical arm from a Free-Arm Cross-Head with an incomplete half-figure; inhabited plant-scroll design with an incomplete horseman – not confidently identified; knot-work design.
✠ Most of the Angular Cross-Shaft which supports the free-arm cross-head identified above. It has designs and patterns including: flat-moulding with the addition of an inner band of roll-moulding on one face, plant-scroll design; inhabited plant-scroll design with a beast, and separately, the bow and arrow, and extended arms, of an archer. Scenes including an incomplete Crucifixion Scene with below a panel with two standing figures facing each other with arms raised could possibly be the Visitation or figures in Adoration or Witnessing the Crucifixion. Other scenes involving a figure holding a large rod-like object, a larger figure with a smaller half-figure, an incomplete figure – none of these figures can confidently be identified. Some scenes have been suggested as reminiscent of Scandinavian mythology: See adjacent: PHOTO 636. Bakewell 5.

PHOTO 636. Bakewell 5.

SOUTH OF SOUTH PORCH EXTERNALLY:
- ✠ Part of Angular-Cross-Shaft with designs and patterns including: cable-moulding, flat-moulding but with rounded edges, interlace design, knot-work design, pellets, plait-work design, ring-chain design, spiral-scroll design, triquetra-knot design.

6. BARDNEY, Lincolnshire – St Lawrence's Church.
NAVE INTERNALLY:
- ✠ Most of a Cross-Base with projecting central extensions on two opposite sides giving the impression similar in shape to a squat free-arm cross; it is presumed that one of these projections has been removed to give the present shape. It has been placed standing vertically on its damaged side rather than correctly placed flat horizontally on the floor. The socket for the insertion of the cross-shaft measures 16 inches/40.6 centimetres, by 11 inches inches/27.9 centimetres, with a depth of 4 inches/10.1 centimetres. Within this socket there is a smaller central socket which measures 4½ inches/11.4 centimetres square with a depth of 1½ inches/3.7 centimetres. With incomplete band of roll-moulding and indications of Roman tooling. See adjacent: PHOTO 637: Bardney.

PHOTO 637. Bardney.

7. BARDSEY, West Yorkshire – All Hallows Church.
PORCH INCORPORATED INTO A LATER ANGLO-SAXON TOWER:
- ❖ Coursed Rubble Walling (west wall 15th century window).
- ❖ Megalithic Side Alternate Quoining.
- ❖ West Wall: former Gable Roofline of west porch – see adjacent: PHOTO 638. Bardsey 13, scarring indicating former roofline of porch arrowed red.
- ❖ North Wall Internally, Ground Floor: Round-Headed Doorway: arched head cut from two half-through-stone lintels; no imposts; mostly through-stone jambs.
- ❖ North Wall Internally, directly above ground floor doorway: Round-Headed Single-Splayed Window: half-through-stone voussoirs; coursed rubble jambs similar to stonework in adjoining walling; sill provided by coursed rubble stonework of the walling directly below.
- ❖ South Wall Internally, Ground Floor: Round-Headed Doorway (later restoration rather than Anglo-Saxon – not in alignment with north doorway or with window above in south wall): voussoirs, no imposts, and no through-stone jambs.

PHOTO 638. Bardsey 13.

- ❖ South Wall Internally, in the centre, opposite similar window in the north wall, Round-Headed Single-Splayed Window: half-through-stone voussoirs; coursed rubble jambs similar to stonework in adjoining walling; sill provided by coursed rubble stonework of the walling directly below.
- ❖ East Face of East Wall Internally: Incomplete Gable Roofline of earlier nave indicated by scaring on the walling – the lower of the two angular lines of scaring.

SQUARE TOWER:
- ❖ Coursed Rubble Walling.
- ❖ Side Alternate Quoining, not megalithic.

- Round-Headed Single-Belfry Openings - east wall, at second and third floor levels: individual arched heads cut out of a single square lintel; no imposts; coursed rubble jambs similar to stonework in the adjoining walling - some through-stones; sills provided by the coursed rubble stonework of the walling directly below.
- Round-Headed Double-Belfry Openings - south wall, at second and third floor levels: each of the arched heads constructed with voussoirs – positioned set-back from the square imposts and jambs below; both imposts and jambs protrude into central void, otherwise flush with the faces of the walls; jambs mostly larger in size than the coursed rubble stonework in the adjoining walling; cylindrical mid-wall shafts with square bases but no capitals; above mid-wall shaft through-stone slab supporting junction of both arched heads; sills provided by the coursed rubble stonework of the walling directly below.

NAVE:
- Coursed Rubble Walling.
- Megalithic Side Alternate Quoining.
- Internally: Indications of possible Anglo-Saxon blocked window in north wall, above the centre of the westernmost archway.
- Internally: Possibly part of an angle-shaft from an archway, with a separate, but integral, section of a baluster-like shaft incised with a groove.
- Internally. Possible Anglo-Saxon Grave-Marker incised with a long-stemmed free-arm cross.

8. BARNACK, Cambridgeshire – St John the Baptist Church.

SQUARE TOWER:
- Coursed Rubble Walling.
- Single, square, protruding, Plinth.
- Mostly Long and Short Quoining but with some Face Alternate Quoining in lower stage.
- Square String-Course comprising projecting lower and upper courses with middle course recessed.
- Pilaster-Strips laid in long and short fashion.

FIRST STAGE:
- Round-Headed Doorway: through-stone voussoirs with hood-moulding supported by corbels; protruding through-stone imposts; through-stone Escomb jambs with square bases protruding from the face of the wall and forming the ends of a plinth running along the bottom of the rest of the wall of the tower, the jambs have accompanying strip-work; sill.
- Round-Headed Single-Splayed Windows: arched head cut out of a single stone rectangular lintel (south window)/a single shaped stone (north window) externally/three-quarter through-stone voussoirs internally; imposts differently-shaped in each window externally/three-quarter through-stones internally; each jamb constructed with a single vertical stone externally/half-through stone jambs laid in Escomb fashion with additional coursed rubble internally; sills provided by a single narrow stone externally and by coursed rubble stonework of the walling directly below internally. Externally, heads, jambs and sills protrude from the face of the walls providing a distinctive "frame". South window with two birds in relief confronting each other in the hollowed out space between the arched head and the top of the window frame. North window has hood-moulding.
- Triangular (gable)-Headed Single-Splayed Window whose external face projects from the face of the wall, with: half-through-stone sill, quarter-through-stone jambs laid in Escomb fashion, through-stone imposts, head formed with two angled quarter-through-

stones. Internally, similar but with the adjoining coursed rubble walling adapted to provide the splaying and the stonework.
- Externally. Circular Stone incised with a sundial and leaf decoration above.
- Externally. Prokrossos.

SECOND STAGE:
- Externally. Decorated Panels: roll-moulding; plant-scroll design. South Wall Panel: plant-scroll surmounted by a farmyard cock in profile to the left. West Wall Panel: plant-scroll surmounted by a bird in profile to the left with its wings half-extended – its head is mostly missing but its beak is turned to the right. North Side Panel: bird feeding on the plants on which it stands and is integral to the plant-scroll design, rather than being placed on top like the other two panels.
- Round-Headed Single-Splayed Windows (one a 1936 copy): arched heads cut out of a monolithic lintels externally/voussoirs internally; one upright, one horizontal stone laid in Escomb fashion forming each jamb; single stone sills – some damaged. Externally, heads, jambs and sills protrude from the face of the walls providing a distinctive "frame" divided into two: the inner part of the frame set-back, and, the outer part of the frame splayed adjacent to the inner frame.
- Restored (1936) Opening now a Triangular-Headed Doorway.
- Flat-Headed Doorway (East Wall below the roofline of an earlier nave): monolithic lintel; through-stone Escomb jambs – top half visible externally, lower half internally.
- Gable Roofline of earlier nave indicated by scaring on exterior east wall.
- Triangular-Headed Single-Belfry Openings: heads constructed two angled rectangular through-stone slabs; no imposts; through-stone jambs constructed of coursed rubble stonework similar to that in adjoining walling; through-stone sills externally extend vertically to provide the bottom part of each jamb. Set back in the depth of these openings, and extending across the width, stone fretwork in a surrounding frame containing: a ring-chain design on the north and south sides; a design with four long, vertical spaces in two pairs resembling vertical panels in a door on the west and east sides. (Third stage of the tower and spire added in 13th century.)
- Internally. Round-Headed Tower Archway: through-stone voussoirs; moulded imposts divided into three distinct horizontal bands with the central band recessed – the imposts extend across the east wall providing a string-course; megalithic through-stone square jambs; all supported by two-stepped plinth. On east face of walling only: pilaster-strip laid in long and short fashion; also with hood-moulding.
- Internally. Triangular-Headed seat-like Recess (perhaps for an Abbot or for an individual presiding over legal matters): head with two angled, imposts, jambs laid in long and short fashion; single horizontal slab forms the seat.
- Internally. Small square-shaped Niches or Aumbries.

NAVE:
- Coursed Rubble Walling.
- Mostly Face Alternate Quoins but with Long and Short Quoins higher up.
- Internally, six stones forming part of an archway which may have provided access to a Northern Porticus; possible vestiges of Anglo-Saxon walling above.
- Internally. Possible Anglo-Saxon Panel: outlined with a band of flat-moulding containing a seated representation of Christ in Majesty in relief.
- Parts of Angular Cross-Shafts with flat-moulding, interlace design, ring-chain design, ring-knot design, roll-moulding.
- Part of a Saxo-Norman Grave-Cover with flat-moulding forming part of a panel containing a St Andrew's cross design.

9. BARTON-UPON-HUMBER, Lincolnshire – St Peter's Church. See below: PHOTO 639. Barton-upon-Humber 14.

WESTERN ANNEX/BAPTISTRY:
- Random Rubble Walling.
- Vestiges of Square Plinth.
- "Cut-Back" Long and Short Quoining.
- Indications of Blocked Round-Headed Doorway.
- Round-Headed Double-Splayed Windows: heads, jambs and sills constructed with rubble similar to the stonework in the adjoining walling.
- Circular Double-Splayed Windows: all constructed with rubble similar to the stonework in the adjoining walling; one with window frame.

SQUARE TOWER FORMERLY A "TOWER-NAVE":
- Random Rubble Walling.
- Coursed Stone Walling.
- Single Square Plinth.
- "Cut-Back" Long and Short Quoining.
- Side Alternate Quoining.
- Round-Headed and Triangular-Headed Pilaster-Strips laid in long and short fashion.
- Square String-Courses provide sills for triangular-headed double-belfry openings above in second stage, and round-headed double-belfry openings above in third stage.

PHOTO 639. Barton-upon-Humber 14.

FIRST STAGE:
- Round-Headed Doorway - Ground Floor: through-stones voussoirs with accompanying hood-moulding; protruding through-stone imposts; Escomb jambs with accompanying strip-work.
- Blocked Triangular-Headed Doorway - Ground Floor: head formed with two angled monolithic through-stones with accompanying hood-moulding; protruding through-stone imposts; Escomb jambs with accompanying strip-work.
- Round-Headed Double-Windows - Upper Ground Floor: arched heads constructed with a single shaped through-stone – externally hood-moulding with label-stops; protruding through-stone imposts; through-stone Escomb jambs; central, square, through-stone slabs supporting junction of both arched heads; central slabs supported by mid-wall baluster-shafts which internally are supported by square bases protruding from the splays of the windows; externally sills provided by five stones laid in a row.

SECOND STAGE:
- Triangular-Headed Double-Belfry Openings – west opening is blocked and mid-wall shaft now hidden. Heads of each opening constructed with pairs of two angled rectangular through-stone slabs which extend upwards from imposts to meet centrally and form the triangular shape of the head of each opening. Parallel to these slabs, rectangular and trapezoid-shaped stones protrude from the face of the wall to provide hood-moulding; through-stone imposts protruding from faces of walling and into central void and extending to the accompanying strip-work below separating it from hood-moulding above; rubble jambs similar in size, and laid in similar courses, to the rubble in the adjoining walling - plaster obscures. Parallel to the jambs, bands of protruding, vertical, strip-work with square bases, extend from the imposts to the top

of the string-course below. Mid-wall shafts comprising baluster-shafts; through-stone slab overhanging each of the mid-wall shafts; sills provided by top of string-course directly below externally and by rubble stonework directly below internally. East opening label-stops each decorated with a damaged human head.

THIRD STAGE:
- Coursed Stone Walling.
- Saxo-Norman Round-Headed Double-Belfry Openings: arched heads constructed with voussoirs with accompanying concentric, protruding, hood-moulding; chamfered imposts protruding from the faces of the wall and into the central void; jambs of similar size, and laid in similar courses, to adjoining stonework; cylindrical and square mid-wall shafts; only mid-wall shaft in north opening has a square base – the other openings are without bases; all three mid-wall shafts have cushion-capitals; above mid-wall shafts through-stone slab supporting junction of arched heads; sills provided by the top of the string-course directly below externally and by coursed stonework directly below internally.

INTERNALLY – FORMER NAVE, NOW TOWER:
- "Cut-Back" Long and Short Quoining - north-east and south-east quoining on east face of east wall of tower: extending from roof to floor height with the eastern, former chancel, archway, midway between.
- Indications of former chancel walling on east face of east wall of tower. Disturbed walling in tall vertical strips either side former chancel archway.
- Upper Gallery: providing access to the upper floor of the baptistry to the west and the room above the chancel (or a new, later, Anglo-Saxon nave - its roofline indicated by scaring on east face of wall).
- West Round-Headed Tower Archway: through-stone voussoirs; through-stone imposts flush with two faces of the walls and overhang the central void between the opposing jambs; through-stone Escomb jambs – on east face with pilaster-strips parallel, but separate from the jambs (random rubble stonework intervenes); on east face hood-moulding which sits on top of voussoirs; on east face hood-moulding and pilaster-strips separated by extended imposts.
- East Round-Headed Tower Archway (former Chancel Archway): through-stone voussoirs; through-stone double-stepped imposts flush with two faces of the walls and overhang the central void between the opposing jambs; through-stone Escomb jambs - on west face with pilaster-strips parallel, but separate from jambs (random rubble stonework intervenes); on west face hood-moulding concentric with voussoirs (random rubble stonework intervenes); on west face hood-moulding and pilaster-strips separated by extended imposts.
- Round-Headed Doorways: through-stone voussoirs; square imposts; through-stone Escomb jambs formerly providing access between the upper stages of the nave, chancel and western annex.
- Evidence of gables on walling indicating Rooflines of 10th and 11th century Chancels – east face of east wall.
- Slab with head of figure in portrait interpreted as Christ in Majesty or a Crucifixion Scene – above hood-moulding on west face of eastern, former chancel, archway.

CURRENT NAVE:
- Position of foundations of former Chancel walling and altar indicated on floor at west end of Nave.

10. BECKERMET, Cumbria - St Bridget's Church.
CHURCHYARD:
- Part of Cross-Shaft and its associated Cross-Base with socket. Cross-Shaft with "collar"

separating the circular lower part (square with rounded corners) with an angular upper part with swag with designs and patterns including: cable-moulding, flat-moulding, grooved-moulding, plant-scroll design including bush-scroll and tree-scroll in a vertical spiral-scroll format. Incomplete Inscription: subject of debate for centuries - mostly unintelligible and there is even uncertainty as to the language.
- Part of Cross-Shaft and its associated Cross-Base with Socket. Cross-Shaft with "collar" separating the circular lower part with an angular upper part with swag: with designs and patterns including: cable-moulding, pellets, roll-moulding, stopped plait-work design in a vertical spiral-scroll format.

11. BEVERLEY, East Yorkshire – Minster.
CHANCEL INTERNALLY:
- Bishop's Chair, also known as the "Frith Stool" – late-7th century. There is no decoration on any side but on the back is a later Latin inscription interpreted to read "The chair of peace was a full refuge and safety from immediate infliction of punishment for any crime whatsoever".

12. BEWCASTLE, Cumbria – St Cuthbert's Church.
CURCHYARD:
- Almost complete Angular Cross-Shaft with designs and patterns including: chequer-board design, flat-moulding, interlace design, knot-work design, plant-scroll design, ring-chain design, ring-knot design, roll-moulding; inhabited vine-scroll design with creatures, beasts and birds. Sundial. Runic inscriptions: two identifying Jesus Christ; another incomplete interpreted as "This token of victory Hwaetred…set up in memory"; and another interpreted as the feminine personal name "Cyneburh". Representations of Christ in Majesty, St John the Evangelist with his symbol the eagle, John the Baptist holding a lamb with a halo around its head. Cross-Base (no decoration survives).

CHURCHYARD OUTBUILDING "PAST & PRESENT EXHIBITION"
- Other stonework (not good examples): Part of a font (no decoration survives). Parts of Grave-Covers with incised crosses including cross-head, cross-shafts (one incomplete) and one with most of a stepped cross-base.

13. BILLINGHAM, County Durham – St Cuthbert's Church.
SQUARE TOWER:
- Coursed Stone Walling. South wall built up against the protruding west wall of nave; the east wall of the tower is built on top of the west wall of the nave.
- Megalithic Side Alternate Quoining.

FIRST STAGE:
- Megalithic Single-Splayed Window, First Floor in the west wall: externally, arched head cut out of a through-stone lintel which internally is flat-headed with no arch cut out; through-stone jambs similar to the coursed stonework in the adjoining walling; through-stone sill.
- Internally, north jamb of this west window, incorporates part of a cross-shaft decorated with interlace design and free-ring designs.
- Round-Headed Doorway, Second Floor, South Wall: arched head cut from through-stone monolithic lintel; protruding, rectangular, imposts; through-stone Escomb jambs supported by protruding plinths which extend to also provide support for the bases of the accompanying strip-work; projecting sill; strip-work with square bases standing on the plinth supporting the whole doorway; hood-moulding with "label-stops". This Doorway

opened outwards into space providing access to an external balcony.
- ❖ Square String-Course.
- ✠ Externally, Part of an Angular Cross-Shaft with designs and patterns including: roll-moulding, inhabited interlace design containing what may be interlinked birds – now placed horizontally.

NOTE STONE SCULPTURE:
- ✠ Both internally and externally, in the tower in particular, there are apparently other parts and fragments of cross-shafts decorated with interlace designs, plait-work designs and a figure who holds in each of their raised hands a bird. These are all difficult to identify confidently.

SECOND STAGE:
- ❖ Round-Headed Double-Belfry Openings: arched heads each cut out of single square lintel; through-stone imposts protruding from the faces of the walling and into the central void, and also extending to the accompanying strip-work separating it from the hood-moulding above; jambs are of similar size, and laid in similar courses, to stonework in the adjoining walling – some of the stones are larger; cylindrical mid-wall shafts without bases and capitals; mid-wall through-stone slab to support junction of both the arched heads above; sills provided by a single, projecting, rectangular stone which support the mid-wall shaft and central voids only. Band of protruding, semi-circular, hood-moulding extends above the lintels, separated by extended imposts, from the protruding, vertical, strip-work with square bases, parallel to the jambs below. Among intervening stonework between the tops of the lintel heads and the hood-moulding, a stone with a sound-hole cut out – octagonal and star-shaped in north and south walls, and circular shaped in west and east walls.

NAVE:
- ❖ Coursed Stone Walling.
- ❖ Side Alternate Quoining.
- ❖ Internally. Flat-Headed Megalithic Doorway – possibly former western entrance: arched head cut out of two monolithic lintels with a tympanum inserted in the centre rather than the outer/inner face of the wall; the placement of this tympanum results in the doorway becoming flat-headed. (Two later, not Anglo-Saxon, pieces of woodwork have been placed under the tympanum between and around the imposts.) Chamfered imposts; square jambs laid in similar courses to the stonework in the adjoining walling – rebated for door.

NORTH AISLE:
- ❖ Externally, large and megalithic Anglo-Saxon stonework, including monolithic head of a Round-Headed Window.

SOUTH AISLE INTERNALLY:
- ✠ Incomplete Grave-Marker decorated on one face with an incomplete free-arm with arms extending from a central circle and arms ending in a circle; the other face is decorated with a ring-head cross with its arms extending from an overlapping central circle.
- ✠ Incomplete Grave-Marker with one face decorated with an incomplete free-arm cross.

14. BILTON-IN-AINSTY, North Yorkshire – St Helen's Church.
SOUTH AISLE INTERNALLY:
- ✠ Damaged Ring-Head Cross-Head and part of its Cross-Shaft with designs and patterns including: cable-moulding, flat-moulding, interlace design, knot-work design, meander-

PHOTO 640. Bilton-in-Ainsty.

pattern design, ring-twist design, stepped-pattern design; creature; human figures. See Page 326 bottom right: PHOTO 640. Bilton-in-Ainsty.
- Parts of different Angular Cross-Shafts with designs and patterns including: basket-plait design, cable-moulding, flat-moulding, inhabited interlace design with probably a beast, linear designs, meander-pattern design, plait-work design, stepped-pattern design; two adjacent human figures possibly haloed, standing single human figure, lower half of human figure, three standing human figures in a row, two standing human figures – weathered.

15. BISHOP AUCKLAND, County Durham – St Andrew's Church.
NAVE INTERNALLY:
- Restored Cross – Free-Arm Cross-Head, Angular Cross-Shaft and Cross-Base with designs and patterns including: cable-moulding, flat-moulding, roll-moulding. Crucifixion Scene probably depicting Christ bound on the Cross but possibly depicting the martyrdom of St Andrew – the figure being bound on the cross, and the interpretation of the accompanying incomplete inscription, leads to doubt about the identity of the central figure. The central figure is flanked on each side by a haloed figure: left-hand figure has the head and one hand of another figure below; the right-hand figure has only part of their head surviving with the hair-dressing possibly indicating a female. Two haloed, winged, angels – one female given their hair-dressing. Part of a winged and haloed figure. Haloed figures – one may be female given their hair-dressing. Inhabited plant-scroll designs with an archer, creatures and beasts and birds.

NORTH AISLE INTERNALLY:
- Fragment of Cross-Shaft decorated with parts of human feet which may have formed part of the restored cross identified above in the previous bullet point.
- Part of Grave-Cover with grooved-moulding forming an incomplete panel containing roll-moulding outlining a standing free-arm cross with a central boss and an incomplete base. The panel also contains pellet and plait-work designs, with the cross also decorated with plait-work designs.
- Part of Grave-Marker with designs and patterns including: grooved-moulding, key-pattern design, stepped-pattern design, zigzag-design.

16. BISHOPSTONE, East Sussex – St Andrew's Church.
NAVE:
- Random Rubble Walling.
- Long and Short Quoining.
- Blocked, incomplete, Round-Headed Single-Splayed Windows; construction details now missing or hidden.

SOUTH PORCH (FORMER PORTICUS):
- Random Rubble Walling.
- Megalithic Long and Short Quoining – some restoration.
- Externally, Sundial divided into twelve segments with linear and stepped-pattern design and inscribed with the Old English name "Eadric" accompanied by a free-arm cross - the gnomon is not Anglo-Saxon.

17. BLYBOROUGH, Lincolnshire - -St Alkmund's Church.
NORTH AISLE INTERNALLY:
- Part of a Grave-Cover with cable-moulding placed in two bands to provide a herringbone pattern, figure-of-eight ring-knot design.

NAVE EXTERNALLY:
- ✠ Part of Grave-Cover built into base of south-west quoin with flat-moulding, interlace design including a free-ring design.
- ✠ Fragment with an indication of cable-moulding.

18. BOLAM, Northumberland – St Andrew's Church.
SQUARE TOWER:
- ❖ Coursed Stone Walling including some Herringbone Masonry.
- ❖ Side Alternate Quoining.
- ❖ Blocked incomplete Round-Headed Single-Splayed Windows, south and west walls – only indications of heads survive above later inserted windows: arched heads cut out of a monolithic half-through-stone lintels externally/half-through-stone voussoirs internally.
- ❖ Round-Headed Single-Splayed Windows: arched heads cut out of a monolithic lintels; jambs similar to coursed stonework in adjoining walling – central stone of each jamb comprises a large, horizontally-placed stone; sills provided by the top of the coursed stonework directly below.
- ❖ Square String-Course: provides sills for round-headed double-belfry openings above.
- ❖ Round-Headed Double-Belfry Openings: arched heads each cut out of a single square lintel; no imposts; jambs constructed of similar stonework, and coursed in a similar way, to the stonework in the adjoining walling, but with some megalithic stonework; cylindrical mid-wall shafts with bulbous bases – no capitals; above mid-wall shafts through-stone slabs supporting junction of both arched heads; sills provided by the top of the coursed stonework directly below.
- ❖ Triangular-Headed Single-Belfry Openings: heads constructed with two angled rectangular through-stone slabs – south is round-headed with its arched head cut out of a monolithic lintel; jambs laid in courses similar to adjoining stonework; sills provided by the top of the coursed stonework directly below.
- ✠ Grave-Cover incised with vertical and diagonal lines forming a herringbone pattern, St Andrew's cross designs, and incisions possibly indicating an additional design.
- ✠ Round-Headed Grave-Marker incised with linear design and free-arm crosses. See adjacent PHOTO 641. Bolam 7.

PHOTO 641. Bolam 7.

NAVE:
- ❖ Coursed Stone Walling.
- ❖ Square String-Course.
- ❖ Reused Anglo-Saxon columns for doorway.
- ❖ Side Alternate Quoining.

SOUTH PORCH:
- ❖ Parts of Imposts or Friezes with cable-moulding alternating with flat-moulding producing a herringbone pattern; rows of, and single, St Andrew's crosses.

19. BOSHAM, West Sussex – Holy Trinity Church.
SQUARE TOWER:
- ❖ Coursed Rubble Walling.
- ❖ Megalithic Long and Short Quoining including "Sussex" variation.
- ❖ Chamfered String-Courses.

THIRD STAGE:
- ❖ Incomplete, blocked, Round-Headed Double-Belfry Openings: arched heads with voussoirs; Escomb jambs.

FOURTH STAGE:
- Round-Headed Double-Belfry Opening: arched heads each constructed with voussoirs; square imposts; jambs and sill laid in courses similar to the rubble stonework in the adjoining walling – plaster obscures; cylindrical mid-wall shaft with inverted bell-shaped capital and rectangular base; above mid-wall shaft through-stone slab supporting junction of both heads.

INTERNALLY:
- Restored Round-Headed Tower Archway: voussoirs; chamfered imposts; megalithic, mostly, through-stone, Escomb jambs.
- Triangular-Headed Doorway - First Floor: head formed with two angled monolithic through-stones; no imposts; Escomb jambs; coursed stone jambs; monolithic sill. Doorway probably opened on to a balcony or gallery at the west end of the nave.
- Small Rectangular-Shaped Opening - First Floor: head, jambs and sill each cut out of a single stone.
- Round-Headed Doorway - Second Floor: head, jambs and sill formed of rubble similar to the fabric in the adjoining walling.

NAVE:
- Coursed Rubble Walling.
- Long and Short Quoining.
- Internally. Saxo-Norman Megalithic Round-Headed Chancel Archway: two bands of voussoirs; soffit-roll; two-stepped imposts; jambs with angle-shafts and soffit shafts with moulded capitals and bases; plinth.

CHANCEL:
- Coursed Rubble Walling with vestiges of Herringbone Masonry.
- Blocked Round-Headed Opening or Doorway above the Chancel Archway.
- Blocked Small Square-Shaped Opening.
- Part of blocked Round-Headed Single-Splayed Window: individual stones rather than voussoirs have been placed on end and formed into a discernible arch; east jamb survives in part, constructed with rubble similar to the stonework in the adjoining walling.
- Vestiges of blocked Round-Headed Doorway or Opening.
- Fragment from a decorated Frieze or Impost with a representation of a stepped capital and a foliate design.

20. BRACEBRIDGE, Lincolnshire – All Saints Church.
SQUARE TOWER – SAXO-NORMAN:
- Coursed Rubble Walling.
- Side Alternate Quoining – see Page 330: PHOTO. 642. Bracebridge.
- Round-Headed Doorway: voussoirs; rectangular imposts; jambs comprising horizontally placed stonework; accompanying hood-moulding.
- Round-Headed Single-Splayed Window: arched head constructed with a single shaped through-stone; jambs constructed with stonework similar to the coursed rubble in the adjoining walling; sills provided by the coursed stonework directly below.
- Square String-Course providing the sill for the round-headed double-belfry openings.
- Round-Headed Double-Belfry Openings: voussoirs; through-stone imposts protruding from the faces of the walling and into the central void; jambs mostly faced with slightly larger stones than those in the adjoining coursed rubble walling; cylindrical mid-wall shafts with angled bases and capitals decorated with triangular-shaped vertical leaves with a horizontal band of roll-moulding below; above mid-wall shafts

through-stone slab supporting the junction of both arched heads; sills provided by top of string-course directly below.
- Internally. Round-Headed Tower Archway: voussoirs; chamfered imposts; square jambs.

NAVE:
- Coursed Rubble Walling.
- Megalithic Long and Short Quoining. See adjacent: PHOTO. 642. Bracebridge, showing megalithic side alternate quoining of the nave arrowed red, side alternate quoining of the tower arrowed black.
- Internally. Round-Headed Chancel Archway: voussoirs; chamfered imposts; square jambs.

NORTH AISLE:
- Externally: blocked, rebuilt (with inaccuracies), Round-Headed Doorway: voussoirs; chamfered imposts; Escomb jambs.

SOUTH AISLE EXTERNALLY:
- Fragment of Cross-Shaft or Grave-Cover incised with two arms from a free-arm cross surrounded by interlace design - weathered.

PHOTO 642. Bracebridge.

21. BRADFORD-ON-AVON, Wiltshire - St Laurence's Church.

NAVE, CHANCEL AND PORTICUS:
- Ashlar Walling.
- Square Single Plinth.
- "Cut-Back" Megalithic Side Alternate Quoining.
- Round-Headed Doorways: through-stone voussoirs; protruding square imposts; jambs; accompanying strip-work and hood-moulding.
- Pilaster-Strips.
- Square String-Courses.
- Incomplete Round-Headed Sunken Blind-Arcading separated by pilaster-strips with trapezoid imposts/capitals and trapezoid bases; all between two square string-courses.
- Round-Headed Double-Splayed Windows: voussoirs; jambs and sills constructed of ashlar similar to the stonework in the adjoining walling.
- Evidence of gable on walling indicates Roofline of former South Porticus – now demolished.
- Round-Headed Chancel Archway: through-stone voussoirs; protruding square imposts; jambs; accompanying strip-work and hood-moulding.

CHANCEL INTERNALLY
- Two Panels with some damage depicting in high relief flying, haloed, winged, angels facing each other; their bodies extend horizontally and are in profile. See adjacent: PHOTO 643. Bradford-on-Avon 2, showing the angel on the south (right-hand) side.

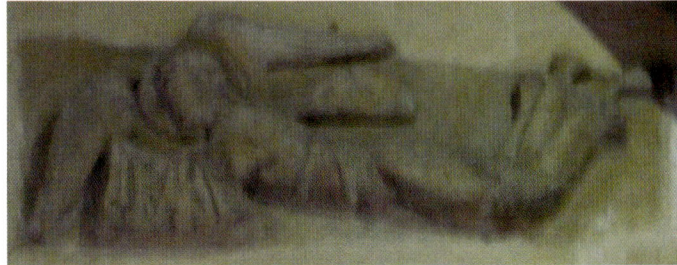

PHOTO 643. Bradford-on-Avon 2.

- Part of an Angular Cross-Shaft with flat-moulding and plait-work design with pelleted strands which could be the bodies of creatures.

✠ Three separate pieces from same panel now part of the altar frontal, with, flat-moulding, free-arm crosses enclosed within a serrated diamond-pattern design, and triangular knot-work design linked by angular twists.

22. BRADWELL-ON-SEA, Essex – St Peter-On-The-Wall Church.
RESTORED NAVE:
* Coursed Rubble Walling including re-used Roman Tile-like bricks.
* Rubble and occasional megalithic quoins, including reused Roman stones with lewis-holes and cramp-holes.
* Damaged and incomplete projecting, small, buttress-like pillars – sometimes referred to as "Pilaster-Buttresses" - rising up to a level in line with the sills of the windows.
* Restored Flat-Headed Single-Splayed Windows – one blocked and only vestiges surviving: wooden lintels; jambs similar to coursed rubble stonework in the adjoining walling but also include larger facing stones probably dating from the restoration in the 1920s; wooden sills.
* Restored Flat-Headed Doorway: wooden lintel; jambs similar to coursed rubble stonework in the adjoining walling.
* Restored Round-Headed Single-Splayed Window: arched head constructed with individual reused Roman tile-like bricks; jambs constructed with a mixture of reused Roman tile-like bricks and rubble; wooden sill.
* Archways East Wall: vestiges of the outer arched heads of archways; stepped imposts; jambs utilising Roman tile-like bricks. By their curvature these vestiges may indicate there may have been three narrow archways rather than a single archway to bridge the intervening space.

WESTERN PORCH:
* Slight indications of where the walling of the north and south walls of the attached porch abutted the west face of west wall of nave on each side of western doorway.

APSIDAL CHANCEL WITH NORTH PORTICUS:
* Externally, vestiges of Coursed Rubble Walling, including re-used Roman tile-like bricks for the archways separating the nave and former chancel, but mostly with the foundations outlined in cement.
* Externally, fragment of western jamb of possibly archway or doorway from chancel into the North Porticus. Scarring on the north wall of the nave indicating the position of the western wall of the North Porticus.

SOUTH PORTICUS:
* Internally, vestiges of blocked archway or doorway in south wall of nave opening into South Porticus; indications of possible eastern Escomb jambs.
* Externally, foundations outlined in cement with scarring on the south wall of the nave indicating the position of the western wall of the South Porticus. See adjacent: PHOTO 644. Bradwell-on-Sea 3, showing the nave from the south east with the foundations of the apsidal chancel outlined in cement arrowed red and

PHOTO 644. Bradwell-on-Sea 3.

the vestiges of the blocked archways arrowed black.

23. BRAILSFORD, Derbyshire – All Saints Church.
- ✠ Incomplete Cross-Shaft with circular lower part and angular upper part separated by bands of cable-moulding with designs and patterns including: floral design, interlace design, meander-pattern design, pellets, plait-work design, spiral-scroll design; figure of a warrior.

24. BREAMORE, Hampshire – St Mary's Church.
NAVE:
- ❖ Random Rubble Walling of Flints.
- ❖ Megalithic Long and Short Quoining.
- ❖ Pilaster-Strips laid in long and short fashion.
- ❖ Round-Headed Double-Splayed Windows – one blocked; insertion of 15th century windows, restoration, and plaster internally, obscure their construction details.
- ❖ Jambs of blocked megalithic doorway from nave to former north porticus.
- ❖ Evidence of a gable on the walling indicating Roofline of former north porticus; also indications of jambs of former archway/doorway into former north porticus.
- ❖ Indications of former western porticus.
- ✠ Internally, now within the south porch, a defaced rood with Crucifixion Scene with the Virgin and St John; with paint.
- ✠ One letter "G" from an Inscription on the external west wall of the nave.

SOUTH PORCH INTERNALLY:
- ✠ Painted Holy Rood Crucifixion Scene with Christ flanked by the Virgin Mary and St John – clarity of the detail and colouration affected by the removal of covering plaster on walls and possible repositioning of the Holy Rood.

CENTRAL SQUARE TOWER WITH TWO RECEDING PYRAMIDAL ROOFS SEPARATED BY VERTICAL WOODEN WALLING:
- ❖ Random Rubble Walling with Flints.
- ❖ Megalithic Long and Short Quoining.
- ❖ Vestiges of Round-Headed Double-Splayed Windows now replaced with flat-headed 15th century adaptations.
- ❖ Scaring on walling indicating Roofline of former Chancel.

SOUTH PORTICUS:
- ❖ Random Rubble Walling with Flints.
- ❖ Megalithic Long and Short Quoining.
- ❖ Round-Headed Double-Splayed Windows – one partly replaced by a 13th century window: restoration, and plaster internally, obscure their construction details.
- ❖ Internally. Round-Headed Megalithic Archway/Doorway from nave to south porticus with the arched head formed with through-stone voussoirs; imposts with cable-moulding. On the arched head is an Inscription in Old English lettering interpreted to read "Here is made manifest the covenant to you"; restored jambs retaining some Anglo-Saxon characteristics.

REBUILT CHANCEL:
- ❖ Random Rubble Walling of Flints.
- ✠ Internally. The letters "DE" and part of probably "S" from an incomplete inscription above chancel arch.

25. BREEDON-ON-THE-HILL, Leicestershire – St Mary and St Hardulph Church.
TOWER INTERNALLY:
- ✠ Friezes with designs and patterns including: flat-moulding, key-pattern design, ring-chain

design; inhabited vine-scroll design with beasts and birds.
- Frieze decorated with what is known as "The Breedon Angel" - a round-headed archway with plant design enclosing a standing, winged, figure giving a blessing with their right hand and holding in their left hand a shaft in the form of a long-stemmed free-arm cross.

NAVE INTERNALLY:
- Friezes with designs and patterns including: flat-moulding, pelta design, ring-chain design, spiral-scroll design, vine-scroll design; inhabited vine-scroll design, with human-like figures, warriors, including horsemen, birds and beasts - some winged.

SOUTH AISLE INTERNALLY:
- Friezes with designs and patterns including: round-headed interlocking archways with plant design and with a haloed saint framed within by each archway. Separate central panel with half-figure of possibly the Virgin Mary.
- Friezes with designs and patterns including: flat-moulding, key-pattern design; a lion-like beast; inhabited vine-scroll design with beasts and birds.

NORTH AISLE INTERNALLY:
- Parts of Angular Cross-Shafts with designs and patterns including: cable-pattern design, flat-moulding, interlace design, ring-chain design, ring-knot design, roll-moulding. Two *Scenes, one depicting Adam and Eve with the tree and serpent, the other depicting two figures - one with a drinking horn. "Jellinge-Style" beasts.
- Frieze decorated with inhabited vine-scroll design with birds.

26. BRIGHAM, Cumbria – St Bridget's Church.
SOUTH AISLE INTERNALLY:
- Parts of Free-Arm Cross-Heads (one may be part of a Hammer-Head Cross-Head), Ring-Head Cross-head, with designs and patterns including: flat-moulding, incised free-arm cross, interlace design, knot-work design, group of pellets, plait-work design, roll-moulding; human figure and human head; serpent-like creature.
- Parts of Angular Cross-Shafts with designs and patterns including: flat-moulding, incised lines preparatory to interlace design, interlace design, knot-work design, pellet, plait-work design, plant-scroll design, free-ring designs, ring-twist design, roll-moulding; part of fettered ribbon creature.
- Most of Cross-Base with its central socket. It has designs and patterns including: cable-moulding, interlace design, roll-moulding, spiral-scroll design; Creatures and beasts. See adjacent: PHOTO 645, Brigham 4, showing part of cross-base with a creatures head arrowed red and part of the socket rim arrowed yellow.
- Fragment of Hogback Grave-Cover with roll-moulding, spiral-scroll design, tegulations.

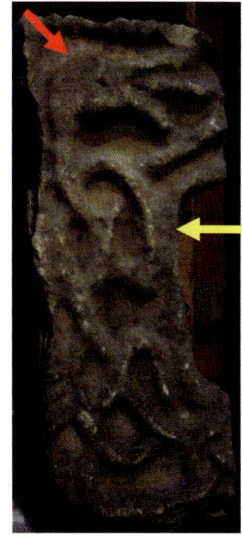

PHOTO 645. Brigham 4.

27. BRIGSTOCK, Northamptonshire – St Andrew's Church.
ROUND STAIR TURRET:
- Coursed Rubble Walling.
- Square Single Plinth projecting from the face of the wall.
- Flat-Headed Double-Splayed Windows: half-through-stone lintels which externally extend vertically to provide the top part of each jamb; single/two - upper north window only - vertical half-through-stone jambs; half-through-stone sills which externally extend

vertically to provide the bottom part of each jamb.

SQUARE TOWER INCORPORATING EARLIER PORCH:
- Coursed Rubble Walling.
- Square Single Plinth projecting from the face of the wall.
- Long and Short Quoining resting on projecting bases.
- Round-Headed Single-Splayed Windows: through-stone voussoirs; three-quarter through-stone jambs constructed with coursed rubble similar to the adjacent walling with two vertical facing-stones on the exterior faces forming the remainder of each of the jambs; single stone sills – south window sill appears to have been broken.
- First Floor North Wall: Round-Headed Double-Splayed Window: arched head constructed with individual stones placed on end and formed into a discernible arch; jambs constructed with rubble similar to the stonework in the adjoining walling; half-through-stone rectangular sill externally and half-through-stone sill internally. There was a similar window in the south wall, now blocked, and indications of its construction can only be identified internally.
- Internally. Round-Headed Tower Archway: through-stone voussoirs; rectangular imposts which extend across the full width of the east wall providing a string-course; megalithic, through-stone, Escomb jambs. East face only: strip-work (some now rendered flat), hood-moulding. All supported by a plinth which protrudes from the faces of the walls.
- Internally. Triangular-Headed Doorway (perhaps former western entrance to the church): head formed with two monolithic through-stones – each a trapezium; through-stone imposts; through-stone Escomb-like jambs; sill comprising two large stones which also provide the bottom support for the jambs – they are horizontally placed "L"-shaped. Placed on top of the stones forming the sill are two steps to assist access from the tower to the Anglo-Saxon stair turret when it was added at a later date; rebate for door also probably added at this time.
- Internally. First Floor West Wall: Flat-Headed Doorway: possible monolithic head; no imposts, jambs all similar to the adjoining walling – the head has being augmented by wooden planking and parts of the jambs have been whitewashed.
- Internally. First Floor East Wall: Blocked Flat-Headed Doorway into nave: lintel; jambs difficult to confidently identify; east face appears to be constructed in coursed rubble walling similar to that in the adjacent walling although a distinctive vertical stone from the south jamb can be identified.

NAVE:
- Coursed Rubble Walling.
- Square Single Plinth.
- Long and Short Quoining resting on projecting bases.
- Blocked Incomplete Megalithic Round-Headed Single-Splayed Window: through-stone voussoirs; coursed rubble jambs similar to the stonework in the adjoining walling.
- Square String-Course.

28. BRISTOL, Somerset – St Augustine's Cathedral.
SOUTH TRANSEPT INTERNALLY:
- Panel outlined with a band of flat-moulding (incomplete) containing a standing representation of Christ in relief known as "The Harrowing of Hell". As well as Christ there is a smaller human figure and the upstretched arms of other human figures. Under feet of Christ are creatures representing Satan and Hell.

29. BRITFORD, Wiltshire – St Peter's Church.
NAVE:
- Coursed Rubble Walling including Flints, reused Roman Bricks and Tiles.

Anglo-Saxon Church Architecture & Stone Sculpture 335

- Restored Round-Headed Doorway.

NORTHERN PORTICUS INTERNALLY:
- Round-Headed Archway: arched head has individually shaped thin stones around the circumference of both faces separated on the underside by three adjacent bands of square blocks of stone; the central, soffit-like band has recessed stones alternating with the face of the underside of the arch. Chamfered Imposts. Jambs with central Soffit Band have recessed stones alternating with the face of each jamb, with pilaster-strips of each side of the soffit band. East Jamb pilaster-strips and soffit band, decorated with knot-work, plant or plant-scroll designs; West Jamb pilaster-strips and soffit band not decorated apart from one square in the central soffit band. Restored Square Plinth. Corbel-like features above the imposts and at the bases of the jambs. Strip-Work and Hood-Moulding - now obscured by plaster.

SOUTHERN PORTICUS INTERNALLY:
- Round-Headed Archway: arched head formed by Roman tile-like bricks; square imposts; (inner) faces of the square jambs each have a central recessed soffit band with a single pilaster-strip flush with the faces of the jambs on each side; restored square plinth. Strip-Work and Hood-Moulding – now obscured by plaster.

30. BRIXWORTH, Northamptonshire – All Saints Church.

ROUND STONE STAIR TURRET:
- Random Rubble Walling including reused Roman tile-like bricks and stonework laid in herringbone fashion.
- Flat-Headed Single-Splayed Windows – four now blocked: most with heads, jambs and sills constructed with rubble similar to the stonework in the adjoining walling.
- South Wall, lowest two windows: external faces constructed from a single stone slab (the window frame) through which apertures have been cut; above each head a separate, protruding single horizontal lintel-like stone. Internally windows constructed of rubble stonework similar to the stonework in the adjoining walling.
- Stone Spiral Stairway: with fifty-seven roughly-dressed stone steps of Anglo-Saxon origin – some partially restored at a later, not Anglo-Saxon, date. The steps formed separately from the newel in the distinct Anglo-Saxon fashion. Newel comprising a thick continuous cylindrical column of rubble. Underside of the treads of the steps have vaulted supports in the form of a continuous rubble, round vault which also forms the ceiling of the stairway.

SQUARE TOWER incorporating earlier Two-Storey Porch formerly providing the main access to the church:
- Random Rubble Walling including reused Roman tile-like bricks and stonework laid in herringbone fashion.
- Square String-Course denotes upper limit of Saxon Walling.
- Fragments of west walls of former North and South Porticus.
- Ground Floor, Internally and externally. Blocked Round-Headed Archway, west wall, with Round-Headed Doorway inserted. Round-Headed Doorways east wall (access to nave), north wall (incomplete and blocked), and south wall. Archway and doorways have arched heads with reused Roman tile-like bricks; no imposts; jambs formed of rubble similar to the fabric of the adjacent walling.
- Ground Floor, South Wall. Flat-Headed Single-Splayed Window: head, jambs and sill constructed of rubble including reused Roman tile-like bricks and stonework laid in herringbone fashion – all similar to the stonework in the adjoining walling.
- First Floor, Internally. East Wall: Blocked Round-Headed Doorway formerly providing

access to balcony or gallery at the western end of the nave: arched head constructed with reused Roman tile-like bricks but top of head cut away by the triple opening above; no imposts; jambs formed of rubble similar to the fabric of the adjacent walling.
- First Floor, Internally. East Wall: Round-Headed Triple-Opening: arched heads constructed with reused Roman tile-like bricks; three-stepped imposts constructed with reused Roman tile-like bricks protruding into the central void; jambs constructed of rubble similar to the stonework in the adjoining walling despite the 19th century single, vertical, rectangular, facing stones on the west face and the plaster cover on the east face and elsewhere; decorated, bulbous-shaped, mid-wall shafts with bulbous, expanding, bases and capitals; mid-wall shafts each support a square through-stone slab beneath arched heads of openings above.
- First Floor, Internally. West Wall: Round-Headed Doorway: arched head constructed with reused Roman tile-like bricks; no imposts, and jambs constructed of rubble similar to the stonework in the adjoining walling. It was cut through a former window of western porch to provide access to the stair turret.
- First Floor, South Wall. Round-Headed Single-Splayed Window: arched head, jambs and sill constructed with a mixture of rubble and reused Roman tile-like bricks similar to the stonework in the adjoining walling.
- Note: Second Floor, West Wall: Round-Headed Doorway has been cut through to provide access to stair turret; its head and jambs formed of rubble similar to the fabric of the adjacent walling, no imposts. It is of uncertain date and given the medieval ladder now providing access it may have been constructed in later, not Anglo-Saxon, times.

NAVE:
- Random Rubble Walling including reused Roman tile-like bricks.
- Blocked Arcade of Round-Headed Archways formerly providing access to north and south porticus – now with 19th century round-headed windows inserted; the westernmost arch has been adapted to provide the current south door. Archways: arched heads - two roughly concentric rows of reused Roman tile-like bricks displaying one of their thin sides – the placement of the tiles is somewhat haphazard on occasions. Three-stepped imposts formed of reused Roman tile-like bricks laid horizontally. Internally, construction details of the large rectangular piers with square jambs are hidden by plaster. Externally, jambs formed of rubble, including reused Roman tile-like bricks, similar to the stonework in the adjacent walling.
- Above the top of the arcades a horizontal course of stonework provides a set-back in north and south walls identifying the support for the inner end of the shared roofs of the north and south porticus. This results in the Clerestory Stage set-back from the face of the nave walls below.
- Clerestory: Round-Headed Single-Splayed Windows – the restoration of the sills and the placement of the current window glass makes them appear almost double-splayed: arched heads constructed with reused Roman tile-like bricks; jambs and sills constructed with rubble similar to the stonework in the adjoining walling.
- Internally. In the north and south walls of the nave: vestiges of the outer arched heads of an arcade of interlocking round-headed archways separating the nave from the "Monks' Choir" and the eastern part of the church. The remains of the archways, and by known excavation, indicate by their curvature that there were three interlinking archways bridging the intervening space.
- Internally. A nearly complete decorated Panel framed by roll-moulding enclosing the figure of an eagle – the symbol of St John the Evangelist.
- Internally. "Brixworth Relic". A reliquary containing what was thought to be the throat bone of the West Saxon Saint Boniface who was the 8th century missionary to the Frankish Empire and Patron Saint of Germany.

- Externally. Part of an arm from a Free-Arm Cross-Head with what could be the centre of a triangle in the middle of the left-hand edge with curving angled sides extending vertically. With perhaps some groove and roll-moulding and even possibly an indication of a shape of a creature or beast – all rather indistinct.

NAVE/MONKS' CHOIR:
- Random Rubble Walling including reused Roman tile-like bricks.
- Internally. Tall Round-Headed Chancel Archway: arched head formed with reused Roman tile-like bricks; imposts; jambs now obscured by plaster.
- Nearly complete Round-Headed Single-Splayed Windows: arched heads constructed with Roman tile-like bricks; random rubble jambs similar to stonework in adjoining walling; through-stone sills.
- Incomplete Round-Headed Single-Splayed Window: arched head constructed with reused Roman tile-like bricks; parts of the jambs may survive but these are hidden by plaster.
- Blocked and partially obscured Round-Headed Doorways formerly providing access to the Ambulatory – they have been restored.
- Incomplete Blocked Round-Headed Doorway providing access to one of the North Porticus; externally arched head constructed with reused Roman tile-like bricks.
- Incomplete Blocked Round-Headed Window.
- Internally. Part of an Angular Cross-Shaft with flat-moulding, indications of cable-moulding; greyhound-like creature within an Urnes design. On top surface a hole or socket which if original may have been for the insertion of a rod to join it to another section of the cross-shaft or cross-head.

CHANCEL/APSE – replaced in 15th century and restored in 1865. On site of Anglo-Saxon Chancel.
- Random Rubble Walling.
- Round-Headed Window: arched head constructed with reused Roman tile-like bricks; jambs constructed with rubble similar to the stonework in the adjoining walling – restored 1865.
- Anglo-Saxon Pilaster-Strips.
- Externally, three Steps leading down from North Doorway, part of one Step leading down from South Doorway, to the Ambulatory from the blocked doorways identified in the Nave/Monks' Choir.

AMBULATORY: Originally roofed rather than open as at present. It formed part of a "Ring-Crypt" - now incomplete.

31. BROMPTON-IN-ALLERTONSHIRE, North Yorkshire – St Thomas's Church.
NAVE INTERNALLY:
- Three complete Hogback Grave-Covers with designs and patterns including: cable-moulding, flat-moulding, plait-work design, ring-twist design, stepped-pattern design, tegulations, triquetra-knot design; complete end bear-like beasts.
- Plate-Ring Cross-Head with part of its attached Angular Cross-Shaft with designs and patterns including: flat-moulding, incised rectangle enclosing a diagonal cross, knot-work design, pellets, plait-work design, shield-shaped design enclosing knot-work design.
- Part of Angular Cross-Shaft known as the "Cock Shaft" with designs and patterns including: cable-moulding, flat-moulding, plant-scroll design; birds; human figure with wing-like features; helmet and spearhead of a warrior, haloed ecclesiastic holding a book; head and shoulders of possibly another ecclesiastic.
- Incomplete Plate-Ring Cross-Head and Ring-Head Cross-Heads and incomplete Angular Cross-Shafts with designs and patterns including: flat-moulding, interlace design, knot-

work design, pellets, plait-work design, ring-knot design, scroll design.
NORTH AISLE INTERNALLY:
- ✠ Two incomplete Hogback Grave-Covers with designs and patterns including: cable-moulding, flat-moulding, pellets, plait-work design, ring-twist design, tegulations; complete and vestiges of end bear-like beasts.

CHANCEL INTERNALLY:
- ✠ Most of Plate-Ring Cross-Head with its attached Angular Cross-Shaft with designs and patterns including: flat-moulding, knot-work design, pellets, plait-work design, shield-shaped design enclosing triquetra-knot design.

CHANCEL EXTERNALLY:
- ✠ Fragments of Angular Cross-Shafts with designs and patterns including: flat-moulding, plait-work design, parallel rows of ring-twist design with the individual rings linked together by "S"-shaped loops forming a "como-braid".

32. BROUGHTON, Lincolnshire - St Mary's Church.
ROUND STAIR TURRET:
- ❖ Large roughly-dressed "ashlar-like" stonework and Coursed Rubble Walling.
- ❖ Flat-Headed Single-Splayed Windows: half-through-stone lintels; jambs narrow, vertical, half-through-stones externally/mostly similar to stonework in adjoining walling, but including some vertically placed stones internally; through-stone sills.
- ❖ Internally. Stone Spiral Stairway with thirty-nine roughly-dressed stone steps of Anglo-Saxon origin – some partially restored at a later, not Anglo-Saxon, date. Steps formed separately from the Newel in the distinct Anglo-Saxon fashion. Newel formed of separate, jointed, vertical sections of cylindrical stonework rising above several steps. Treads of individual steps supported by an underside comprising a roughly round vaulted ceiling.

SQUARE TOWER – formerly "Tower-Nave":
- ❖ Coursed Rubble Walling including stonework laid in herringbone fashion.
- ❖ Large Side Alternate Quoining; the north-east and south-east quoining, the west faces only, can be identified internally in the east wall of tower.
- ❖ Round-Headed Doorway: two concentric, adjacent, bands of voussoirs, the lower, roll-moulded band set-back from the face of the wall, and the upper band in the face of the wall divided into two by a central concentric groove. In addition, above, and concentric with these voussoirs is another row of voussoir-like stones in the face of the wall, similar in effect to hood-moulding, which may relate to some later, not Anglo-Saxon, alteration of the doorway. Restored, chamfered, imposts protruding into the void between jambs. Coursed three-quarter through-stone jambs with recessed cylindrical angle-shafts. Cylindrical angle-shafts with no bases but with capitals, square at the top, triangular below, with a horizontal band of roll-moulding at their base.
- ❖ Round-Headed Single-Splayed Windows: arched heads cut out rectangular half-through-stones; jambs one vertical half-through-stone on top of another externally/similar to stonework in adjoining walling internally; half-through-stone sills.
- ❖ Internally. Round-Headed Doorway providing internal access at ground floor level to stair turret: half-through-stone voussoirs set-back from the imposts and jambs below; half-through-stone imposts; three-quarter-through-stone jambs.
- ❖ Internally. Round-Headed Tower, formerly Chancel, Archway: through-stone voussoirs (some restoration); rectangular imposts flush with east faces of walling and extend into, and provide shaped capitals, of soffit-shafts forming part of jambs. Through-stone jambs laid in side alternate fashion. Cylindrical soffit-shafts: capitals top half square-shaped

with below a tapering triangular shape; horizontal band of roll-moulding below; bases with a cylindrical, tapering and expanding top half with a square bottom half. Cylindrical angle-shafts: top third of capitals rectangular-shaped with below a tapering triangular shape; horizontal band of roll-moulding below; bases with a cylindrical, tapering and expanding top half with a square bottom half. Note the soffit-shafts do not support voussoirs or a soffit-roll above.
- Internally. First Floor – access to Tower: Megalithic Flat-Headed Doorway: monolithic lintel; no imposts; megalithic square jambs.
- Internally. First Floor – access to a first floor gallery or balcony at the west end of the nave or providing access into first floor of former chancel: Megalithic Flat-Headed Doorway: monolithic lintel; no imposts; megalithic square jambs.

NAVE:
- Coursed Rubble Walling including Herringbone Masonry.
- Large Side Alternate Quoining.
- Internally. Foundations of Saxon Chancel extending eastwards 120 inches/304 centimetres from the current west wall of the nave and 100 inches/254 centimetres north to south (all measurements approximate, nothing can be seen at present).

NAVE INTERNALLY:
- Part of Grave-Cover with cable-moulding and figure-of-eight ring-knot design.

NORTH AISLE INTERNALLY:
- Part of Grave-Cover with cable-moulding and plait-work design,

33. BURGWALLIS, South Yorkshire – St Helen's Church.
NAVE:
- Coursed Rubble Walling including Herringbone Masonry.
- Square Single Plinth.
- Megalithic Side Alternate Quoining.

CHANCEL:
- Coursed Rubble Walling including Herringbone Masonry.
- Square Single Plinth.
- Megalithic Side Alternate Quoining.

34. BURTON-IN-KENDAL, Cumbria.
- Part of a Ring-Head Cross-Head with grooved-moulding.
- Part of an Angular Cross-Shaft and vestiges of the lower vertical arm of its Cross-Head with flat-moulding. Cross-Shaft with designs and patterns including: roll-moulding, scroll design, St Andrew's crosses one above the other; possibly a haloed figure under an archway.
- Part of an Angular Cross-Shaft and vestiges of the lower vertical arm of its Ring-Head Cross-Head with designs and patterns including: free-ring designs, interlace design, key-pattern design, ring-chain design, roll-moulding, stepped-pattern design, stopped plait-work design. Christ in Majesty standing on a serpent, other haloed figures.
- Part of an Angular Cross-Shaft with chevron-moulding, zigzag-design and interlocking curving lines.

35. BURTON PEDWARDINE, Lincolnshire – St Andrew's Church.
NAVE INTERNALLY:
- Fragment of Cross-Shaft with flat-moulding and plait-work design.
- Two sections of stonework probably from the same Grave-Cover with designs and

patterns including: cable-moulding, flat-moulding, interlace design, knot-work design, zigzag-design; plait-work design including "bull's head"; part of a free-arm cross – parts of its horizontal arms and its fourth arm are missing.
- ✠ Three sections of stonework probably from the same Grave-Cover with designs and patterns including: cable-moulding, free-ring design, interlace design, knot-work design, plait-work design.

36. BYWELL, Northumberland – St Andrew's Church.
SQUARE TOWER:
- ❖ Coursed Rubble Walling.
- ❖ Megalithic Side Alternate Quoining.
- ❖ Round-Headed Single-Splayed Window: externally arched head constructed from a single shaped stone/internally cut out of a half-through-stone lintel – some intervening stonework between. Coursed rubble jambs laid in similar courses to the stonework in the adjoining walling. Monolithic sill which internally has been extended by removal of two, courses of stonework.
- ❖ Square String-Courses – the lower course provides the sills for the Round-Headed Double-Belfry Openings above.
- ❖ Second Floor Level South Wall: Megalithic Round-Headed Doorway: arched head cut out of a monolithic lintel with separate hood-moulding above; imposts; Escomb jambs with accompanying strip-work and, protruding plinths; sill.
- ❖ Round-Headed Double-Belfry Openings: arched heads each cut out of single square lintel; imposts protruding from the faces of the walling and into the central void, and also extending to separate the strip-work below from the hood-moulding above; jambs are of similar size, and laid in similar courses, to the rubble stonework in the adjoining walling – some of the stones are larger; cylindrical mid-wall shafts without bases or capitals; above mid-wall shafts through-stone slabs supporting junction of both arched heads; stones of the sill supporting the mid-wall and the two central voids are damaged and no longer project from the face of the wall or align with the remaining parts of the original sill. A band of protruding, semi-circular, hood-moulding extends above the lintels. It is separated by the extended imposts, from the bands of protruding, vertical, strip-work parallel to the jambs below. Among the intervening stonework between the tops of the lintel heads and the hood-moulding, is a stone which has had a circular sound-hole cut out. Above the opening, and roughly in line with the central sound-hole, are two further circular sound-holes, one on each side of the opening.

NAVE:
- ❖ Coursed Rubble Walling.
- ❖ Megalithic Side Alternate Quoining.
- ❖ Impost with chequer-pattern design and grooved-moulding.

CHANCEL INTERNALLY:
- ✠ Part of an Angular Cross-Shaft with designs and patterns including: flat-moulding, key-pattern design, linear designs, pellets, ring-knot design, ring-chain design, a swag-like design on one face and a triangular-shaped design on the other face; part of a coiled creature.
- ✠ Supporting the angular cross-shaft identified in the previous bullet-point, an Impost with horizontal rows of grooved-moulding and cheque-board design.

37. CAMBRIDGE, Cambridgeshire – St Bene't's Church.
SQUARE TOWER:
- ❖ Random Rubble Walling.
  Square Single Plinth.

- ❖ "Cut-Back" Long and Short Quoining.
- ❖ Square String-Courses delineating each of the upper two stages of the tower: the Middle and Upper Stages are set-back from stage below. Upper Square String-Course forms the sill of the round-headed double-belfry openings above.
- ❖ Round-Headed Double-Belfry Openings: arched heads cut out of the same single lintel – apart from south opening where each of the arched heads has its own single square lintel; square imposts protruding from the faces of the walling and into the central void; jambs have facing stones laid in a similar fashion to Escomb jambs; mid-wall baluster-shafts; above mid-wall baluster-shafts through-stone slab supporting centre of the single square lintel above, and the junction of both arched heads above the south opening; sills provided by the string-course below. Each of the openings have two separate sound-holes at an angle above – one is now missing above the east opening. Externally, they have been constructed with a single facing stone through which a circular aperture has been cut. Internally, they have been constructed of rubble with stones placed to provide the circular aperture on the inner face.
- ❖ Above the Belfry Openings, a centrally placed Pilaster-Strip which possibly originally extended to a gable supporting a "Rhenish-Helm" Roof.
- ❖ Internally. Round-Headed Tower Archway: through-stone voussoirs; moulded imposts divided into three distinct horizontal bands – the upper and lower bands with rectangular faces and the central band with a half-round face – with each band interrupted by the bands of half-round and half square pilaster-strips – the imposts extend across the full width of the east wall providing a string-course; through-stone Escomb jambs; all supported by two-stepped plinth. Separate outer half-square and inner half-round pilaster-strips (parallel to the jambs) and hood-moulding (concentric with the arch) on both west and east faces of walling. Additionally on the east face of the walling, at the bottom of the hood-moulding, label-stops decorated with crouching beasts. See adjacent: PHOTO 646. Cambridge 14, showing the west face of the top of the archway with through-stone voussoirs and hood-moulding above, and moulded imposts.

PHOTO 646. Cambridge 14.

- ❖ Internally, First Floor. Round-Headed Doorway: through-stone oddly-shaped voussoirs; chamfered through-stone imposts; through-stone Escomb jambs with chamfered bases.

NAVE:
- ❖ Random Rubble Walling.
- ❖ Long and Short Quoining with indications of a Square Single Plinth.

38. CARLISLE, Cumbria – Carlisle Cathedral.
- ✠ Part of Hammer-Head Cross-Head with a protruding central boss. One face has roll-moulding enclosing the central boss and extends into the arms of the cross-head where the roll-moulding terminates in a circle surrounding a smaller boss.
- ✠ Part of a Free-Arm Cross-Head with designs and patterns including: flat-moulding, incised squares, knot-work design, a rosette. An inscription which continues on both faces interpreted as "Sig... set this up in memory of Suitberht".
- ✠ Parts of two arms from the same Free-Arm Cross-Head with designs and patterns

including: irregularly-shaped chevrons, flat-moulding, plant-scroll design, irregularly-shaped zigzag-design akin to a cat's cradle pattern. Possibly part of the hands from the outstretched arms of Christ.
- Part of an arm from a Free-Arm Cross-Head with flat-moulding, interlace design and an incomplete inscription including the letters "NIMA".

39. CASTOR, Cambridgeshire - St Kyneburgha's Church.
NAVE:
- Coursed stone walling.
- Some indication of side alternate quoining.

NORTH TRANSEPT:
- Jambs of a blocked Doorway with possibly Long and Short Quoins surviving.
- Internally. Part of a Roman Altar reused as an Anglo-Saxon Cross-Base. Designs and patterns including: roll-moulding, scroll design; inhabited tree-scroll design with birds, inhabited scroll design with a beast.
- Internally. Possibly part of shrine chest of St Kyneburgha (died circa 680 AD) with: a pair of interlocking round-headed archways – only one is complete - with shared capitals, pillars and conical bases; roll-moulding, tree design with leaves. Enclosed within each archway a tree design with leaves. One complete haloed figure, said to represent St Mark, and one incomplete haloed figure.

SOUTH PORCH EXTERNALLY:
- Panel with flat-moulding, interlace design, scroll-design. Half-figure of a haloed Christ in Majesty giving a blessing with his right hand and holding a book in his left hand - representations of sun and moon by the side of his head. See above right: PHOTO 647. Castor 2.

PHOTO 647. Castor 2.

40. CAWTHORNE, West Yorkshire. All Saints Church.
NORTH AISLE EXTERNALLY:
- Free-Arm Cross-Head with roll-moulding, possibly a central figure, indications of decoration in the arms which cannot now be confidently identified.

CHURCHYARD
- Free-Arm Cross-Head with linear designs in the shape of the letter "D" semi-circles, roll-moulding. It has been placed on top of the restored cross-shaft – see below.
- Restored Angular Cross-Shaft with part of an angular cross-shaft with linear designs in the shape of the letter "D" semi-circles and forming designs similar to straps involving vertical, horizontal and angular lines; roll-moulding; a bear-like figure missing its head. Also in this reconstruction a fragment of possibly the arm of a free-arm cross with roll-moulding.

41. CHESTER-LE-STREET, County Durham – Anker's House Museum – part of St Mary and St Cuthbert's Church.
FIRST FLOOR INTERNALLY:
- Complete and incomplete Cross-Bases with designs and patterns including: column-like features, flat-moulding, interlace design, knot-work design, ring-knot design, standing free-arm cross; human figures; creatures and beasts. Crucifixion Scene.
- Part of an arm from a Free-Arm Cross-Head and Parts of Angular Cross-Shafts decorated

with designs and patterns including: cable-moulding, flat-moulding, grooved-moulding, interlace design, key-pattern design, knot-work design, plait-work design, plant-scroll design, ring-knot design, spiral-scroll design, tree-scroll design; creatures and beasts. Warrior on horseback. Inscription – "Eadmund".

42. CHOLLERTON, Northumberland - St Giles Church.
CHANCEL EXTERNALLY:
✠ One complete Plate-Ring Cross-Head with part of its supporting Angular Cross-Shaft, one complete Plate-Ring Cross-Head missing its supporting cross-shaft, and one incomplete Ring-Head Cross-Head and part its angular Cross-Shaft.

43. CODFORD ST PETER, Wiltshire – St Peter's Church.
CHANCEL INTERNALLY:
✠ Part of an Architectural Feature or Angular Cross-Shaft with designs and patterns including: representations of baluster-shafts as moulding, plant-scroll design, roll-moulding, stepped-pattern design; inhabited plant-scroll design with human figure.

44. COLCHESTER, Essex – Holy Trinity Church.
SQUARE TOWER:
❖ Random Rubble Walling including reused Roman tile-like bricks.
❖ Re-used Roman tile-like brick Double Plinth – only the top course can now be seen.
❖ Quoining comprising re-used Roman tile-like bricks placed horizontally on top of each other.
❖ Triangular-Headed Doorway: head with accompanying hood-moulding, stepped imposts and jambs with accompanying pilaster-strips all constructed with reused Roman tile-like bricks.
❖ Round-Headed Double-Splayed Windows in north and south walls at ground floor level. Those in west wall at first floor are blocked. Arched heads, jambs and sills constructed with a mixture of mostly reused Roman tile-like bricks, but also rubble similar to the rubble stonework in the adjoining walling; externally sills of blocked first floor windows provided by lower square string-course.
❖ Square String-Course separating the first from the second stage. Constructed with two horizontal rows of reused Roman tile-like bricks laid flat with their narrow edges projecting from the faces of the walls.
❖ Round-Headed Doorway at First Floor Level in West Wall: arched head, jambs and sill constructed with a mixture of mostly reused Roman tile-like bricks, but also rubble and flints similar to the stonework in the adjoining walling. The String-Course separating the first from the second stage provides the imposts.
❖ String-Course separating the first from the second stage also provides the sills for the blocked Round-Headed Recesses in the north and south walls in the second stage above. These recesses similar to round-headed windows but not splayed. Arched heads, jambs and sills constructed with a mixture of mostly reused Roman tile-like bricks, but also rubble similar to the rubble stonework in the adjoining walling.
❖ Third Stage: String-Course separating the first from the second stage. Constructed with two horizontal rows of reused Roman tile-like bricks laid flat with their narrow edges projecting from the faces of the walls.
❖ Lower Round-Headed Single-Belfry Openings: arched heads constructed with reused Roman tile-like bricks placed on end and formed into a discernible arch – occasional replacement with a single stone of rubble; no imposts; jambs constructed with a mixture

of rubble and facings provided by reused Roman tile-like bricks placed horizontally on top of each other and some rubble similar to the rubble stonework in the adjoining walling; sills provided by the top of the square string-course below.
- ❖ Arcades of Round-Headed Pilaster-Strips on all four walls - only the arcade on the south wall can now easily be identified. The central arcade on each wall provides a "frame" around a lower single-belfry opening. Arched heads constructed with reused Roman tile-like bricks placed on end and formed into a discernible arch; jambs constructed with a mixture of rubble and facings provided by reused Roman tile-like bricks placed horizontally on top of each other; sills provided by the top of the square string-course below.
- ❖ Upper Round-Headed, Pairs of, Single-Belfry Openings: arched heads constructed with reused Roman tile-like bricks placed on end and formed into a discernible arch – occasional replacement with a single stone of rubble; no imposts; jambs constructed with a mixture of rubble and facings provided by reused Roman tile-like bricks placed horizontally on top of each other. The two openings are separated by a thin block of stonework, similarly constructed to the jambs, which runs through the entire depth of the wall. Sills are constructed with reused Roman tile-like bricks placed horizontally in a row.
- ❖ Internally. Round-Headed Tower Archway: arched head including hood-moulding, three-stepped imposts, jambs with accompanying pilaster-strips all resting on a three-stepped plinth. Pilaster-Strips and hood-moulding on both west and east faces of walling. All constructed with reused Roman tile-like bricks.

45. COLLINGHAM, West Yorkshire – St Oswald's Church.
SQUARE TOWER INTERNALLY:
- ✠ Parts of Angular Cross-Shafts with designs and patterns including: flat-moulding, interlace design, key-pattern design, line design, plait-work design, plant-scroll design, stepped-pattern design.
- ✠ Part of an Arm from a Free-Arm Cross-Head with designs and patterns including: flat-moulding, knot-work design, ring-knot design, roll-moulding.

NAVE:
- ❖ Coursed Rubble Walling.
- ❖ Megalithic Side Alternate Quoining.

NAVE INTERNALLY:
- ✠ Two parts of an Angular Cross-Shaft with some vertical lengths with chamfered or rounded edges. Known as the "Apostles' Cross" with designs and patterns including: cable-moulding, flat-moulding, plant design; weathered, three-quarter and full-length, haloed figures some of whom are standing, others are sitting, each framed by a round-headed archway. The figures include: possibly Christ, the Virgin Mary with the Christ-Child, most are thought to represent the Apostles. See adjacent left: PHOTO 648. Collingham 1, showing one almost complete figure and the head of another below.
- ✠ Two parts of an Angular Cross-Shaft joined together and known as the "Aerswith Cross" with designs and patterns including: flat-moulding, interlace design,

PHOTO 648. Collingham 1.   PHOTO 649. Collingham 2.

knot-work design, ring-twist design, plant-scroll design; single beasts including a headless beast, confronting beasts; incomplete runic inscription which some have interpreted as the feminine name "Aerswith". See Page 344 bottom right: PHOTO 649. Collingham 2, showing plant-scroll design on the narrow, left-hand side, and confronting beasts entangled with interlace design on the right-hand face. Part of a runic inscription can be identified on both sides – arrowed red.
- Parts of an Angular Cross-Shafts with designs and patterns including: flat-moulding, interlace design merging into knot-work design, linear designs, meander-pattern design, plait-work design, plant-scroll design, stepped-pattern design.
- Part of an arm from a Free-Arm Cross-Head with designs and patterns including: flat-moulding, knot-work design, lose ring design enclosed within interlace design which has some strands ending in curls, roll-moulding.

46. COLSTERWORTH, Lincolnshire. St John the Baptist Church.
NAVE INTERNALLY:
- Part of a Ring-Head Cross-Head with flat-moulding and knot-work design.
SOUTH AISLE INTERNALLY:
- Part of an Angular Cross-Shaft with flat-moulding, knot-work design, plait-work design and vine-scroll design.
NORTH AISLE INTERNALLY:
- Part of a Grave-Cover with cable-moulding, plait-work design and a scroll design interconnected with loops.
- Possibly part of a Consecration Cross comprising a round stone decorated on one face in relief with a free-arm cross with fan-shaped arms.

47. COLYTON, Devon – St Andrew's Church.
SOUTH AISLE INTERNALLY:
- Reconstructed Free-Arm Cross-Head, Angular Cross-Shaft and Cross-Base with designs and patterns including: basket-plait design, plant-scroll design, ring-knot design, figure-of-eight ring-knot design, roll-moulding; inhabited plant-scroll design with a beast and a bird; inhabited interlace design with creatures with a herringbone pattern on their bodies.

48. COPPLESTONE, Devon - Cross-Shaft.
ON ISLAND IN MIDDLE OF COPPLESTONE WHERE THE A377 BIFURCATES - the arm of the road to the left (west) leads to the A3072
- Almost complete Angular Cross-Shaft with designs and patterns including: interlace design, key-pattern design, knot-work design, plait-work design, ring-knot design, a ring-twist design involving loops, roll-moulding; faint indications of two standing figures in one panel and a horseman in another panel; possible panel for an inscription.

49. CORBRIDGE, Northumberland – St Andrew's Church.
"THE KING'S OVEN" – extending eastwards from churchyard wall towards porch/tower:
- Possible reuse of large Anglo-Saxon stonework in north-east and south-east corners.
EXTERNALLY EXTENDING WEST AND NORTH OF FORMER PORCH:
- Coursed Rubble Walling.
- Vestiges of Square and Chamfered Double Plinth.
PORCH - now incorporated into the Square Tower.
- Coursed Rubble Walling including reused Roman Stonework.

- Square Single Plinth.
- Megalithic Side Alternate Quoining.
- Blocked Round-Headed Doorway, providing the former entrance into Porch. An early-20th century window inserted into the original stonework forming the doorway may have necessitated reconstruction of what now seems to the arched head of the former doorway. This arched head comprises flat stones laid round the circumference rather than wedge-shaped voussoirs. The former doorway has no surviving imposts; but does have Escomb jambs rebated for a door. The original doorway may have been taller than currently indicated. The doorway would have had imposts, now missing, supporting a round-headed arch constructed with wedge-shaped voussoirs, now missing. It has been suggested that the current arch above the former doorway and below the sill of the separate round-headed window above may indicate the original doorway had hood-moulding with flat stones laid round the circumference - but there is little evidence of strip-work parallel to the jambs that would have supported this hood-moulding. See above right: PHOTO 650. Corbridge 5, showing the former west doorway with Escomb jambs arrowed red, and the side alternate quoining of the porch arrowed black.

PHOTO 650. Corbridge 5.

SQUARE TOWER INCORPORATING EARLIER PORCH:
- Coursed Rubble Walling mostly including reused Roman Stonework.
- Side Alternate Quoining smaller in size than the quoining of the Porch below.
- Megalithic Round-Headed Single-Splayed Window: arched head cut out of two half-through-stone lintels – with Roman Cramp-Hole externally. All stonework forming the jambs laid horizontally and includes through-stones (below the lintels), and half-through-stones, as well as rubble similar to the stonework in the adjoining walling. Sill provided by coursed stonework directly below.
- Round-Headed Single-Splayed Window in east wall formerly providing light into the nave and overlooking the top of the porch – its splay is now outside the tower above the current nave roof. Its external light was blocked when the Anglo-Saxon Tower was added in the late-10th/early-11th century, and when the Anglo-Saxon Nave was reduced to its current height in the 13th century its internal single-splay was exposed externally. Arched head constructed with through-stone voussoirs; most of each jamb comprises a single megalithic stone but with some rubble similar in size to the coursed rubble in the adjoining walling; sill constructed with rubble similar to the stonework in the adjoining walling. The alteration of this window at a later, not Anglo-Saxon, date, has compromised some of its original construction details – including a rudimentary splay on the face of the window now inside the tower.
- Externally. Scaring on east wall indicating former Nave Roofline partly obscured by clock face: above current nave roofline and above round-headed single-splayed window identified in previous bullet point.
- Externally. Position of stonework supporting base of the western gable of the former Nave indicated by the height of the buttresses on the south-east and north-east corners of the Tower; they may include some of the stonework from the gable.
- Externally. Square String-Course.

- Internally. Round-Headed Tower Archway – formed with reused Roman stones: through-stone voussoirs which are shorter than the depth of the wall; one of the imposts has indications of moulding; through-stone square jambs; all supported by a stone plinth.

NAVE:
- Coursed Rubble Walling including reused Roman stonework.
- Internally. North Wall: Incomplete blocked Round-Headed Single-Splayed Windows: only part of the arched heads cut out of a monolithic lintel can now be identified – the more easterly window includes part of a cramp-hole. The outer face of the western window can be identified from the North Aisle.
- Vestiges of foundations of north wall and associated flooring beside it – surrounding the two free-standing pillars under wooden blocks.

SOUTH TRANSEPT – Internally:
- ✠ Part of a Slab, possibly part of an altar. Incised with parts of two separate circles each containing a free-arm cross – one is incomplete.
- ✠ Part of a Slab with inscription interpreted as "here lies Eric".
- ✠ Possibly part of a Finial similar in shape to a free-arm cross with a supporting block of stone at its base. Incised with circles, St Andrew's crosses, linear designs.

50. CORHAMPTON, Hampshire – Church (No Dedication).
NAVE:
- Restored, lightly plastered, Flint Walling.
- Square Single Plinth.
- Long and Short Quoining.
- Pilaster-Strips, some with vestiges of plant design on the bases.
- Part of Square String-Course.
- Blocked Doorway (now window) – only partly surviving including: hood-moulding; projecting imposts divided by grooves horizontally into three, with a wide band of roll-moulding in the centre, framed above, and below, by a narrower rectangular band divided in the centre into two horizontally; strip-work separated from their projecting bulbous bases by a horizontal band of roll-moulding – their bases are supported by, and stand on, a wider stone protruding from the face of the wall.
- Restored Bell-Cote Double-Opening.
- ✠ Internally. Possible Saxo-Norman font.
- ✠ Externally. Sundial with foliate decoration and roll-moulding.

CHANCEL:
- Restored, lightly plastered, Flint Walling.
- Square Single Plinth.
- Pilaster-Strips, some with vestiges of plant design on the bases.
- Internally. Round-Headed Chancel Archway: through-stone voussoirs with accompanying hood-moulding resting on top; protruding through-stone imposts; through-stone Escomb jambs with accompanying, damaged, pilaster-strips; single square plinth.
- ✠ Internally. Possible Anglo-Saxon altar stone.

51. CREETON, Lincolnshire – St Peter's Church.
NAVE EXTERNALLY:
- ✠ Incorporated into the walling are five sections of stonework from Angular Cross-Shafts with flat-moulding, interlace design and plait-work design. Imagination will be required to give coherence to the vestigial markings as on some only a series of holes indicates that the surface was at one time decorated.

- ✠ Incorporated into the walling are six sections of stonework from Grave-Covers with flat-moulding, interlace design and knot-work design. Imagination will be required to give coherence to the vestigial markings as on some only a series of holes indicates that the surface was at one time decorated.

SOUTH TRANSEPT EXTERNALLY:
- ✠ Incorporated into the walling part of a Grave-Cover with flat-moulding and plait-work design.

CHURCHYARD:
- ✠ Part of an Angular, Collared, Cross-Shaft with designs and patterns including: flat-moulding, free-ring design, key-pattern design, knot-work design, plait-work design, plant-scroll design.
- ✠ Almost complete Grave-Cover redesigned and reused as a grave-cover in the 12th century, and subsequently reused as a lintel. The Anglo-Saxon decoration surviving has designs and patterns including: cable-moulding, diagonal crosses enclosed within a square in rows and filling concentrically large circular designs, interlace design, plait-work design, plant-scroll design, roll-moulding, zigzag-design; plait-work design including bull's heads. See above right: PHOTO 651. Creeton 2, showing the north-west side with the bull's head shown horizontally rather than its present vertical position.

PHOTO 651. Creeton 2.

52. CROPTHORNE, Worcestershire – St Michael's Church.
NORTH AISLE INTERNALLY:
- ✠ Free-Arm Cross-Head with designs and patterns including: cable-moulding, flat-moulding, rectangular maze-like pattern, pellets; inhabited plant-scroll design with beasts and birds.

53. DACRE, Cambria – St Andrew's Church.
CHANCEL INTERNALLY:
- ✠ Part of an Angular Cross-Shaft with designs and patterns including: flat-moulding, key-pattern design, pellets, plant-scroll design, spiral-scroll design. Inhabited plant-scroll design including a serpent, a winged lion-like beast, and two pairs of human legs and feet. Inhabited plant-scroll design with a large four-petalled flower with a central rosette, incomplete four-legged beast climbing up the branches.
- ✠ Part of an Angular Cross-Shaft with slight indications of Cross-Head: designs and patterns including: free-ring designs, pellets, plait-work-design, plant design, roll-moulding, tree-scroll design. Three horizontal scenes: a scene representing Adam and Eve, both in profile to the left, separated by the "Tree of Knowledge" with a coiled serpent; above, a flat curving band with above, a stag with a crouching hound-like creature on its back both in profile to the right; above, two human figures, in portrait, whose hands are joined over a rectangular object with pellet-like legs, with above, a large four-legged beast in profile to the right but with its head turned back over its body.

54. DAGLINGWORTH, Gloucestershire – Church of the Holy Rood.
NAVE:
- ❖ Random Rubble Walling.

- ❖ Chamfered Single Plinth.
- ❖ "Cut-Back" Long and Short Quoining.
- ❖ Chamfered String-Course.
- ❖ Round-Headed Doorway voussoirs externally/Flat-Headed with a monolithic lintel internally; imposts divided into a plain top-half and a bottom-half sub-divided by four horizontal grooves with two bands of herringbone design at the bottom with a plain band above; jambs include some through-stones – jambs rebated for a door.

NAVE INTERNALLY:
- ✠ Two Carved Holy Rood Panels with Crucifixion scenes; one with Christ only, the other with Christ with the figures of the cup/sponge-bearer Stephaton and the spear-bearer Longinus.

NORTH AISLE INTERNALLY:
- ✠ Holy Rood Panel with Christ Enthroned.
- ✠ Holy Rood Panel with St Peter holding the Key to Heaven.

SOUTH PORCH INTERNALLY:
- ❖ Re-Use of Anglo-Saxon material including Round-Headed Doorway which may have been part of the former western entrance to the church: voussoirs; chamfered imposts incised with a narrow groove; Escomb Jambs rebated for a door. See adjacent: PHOTO 652. Daglingworth 6, showing reused Anglo-Saxon Doorway in the south porch in the foreground and the south doorway into the nave with the Anglo-Saxon sundial above in the background – arrowed red.
- ✠ Sundial framed by a circular band of roll-moulding.

PHOTO 652. Daglingworth 6.

REBUILT CHANCEL:
- ❖ Random Rubble Walling.
- ❖ "Cut-Back" Long and Short Quoining.
- ❖ Internally. Rebuilt Round-Headed Chancel Archway: voussoirs; imposts with three horizontal bands – chamfered at the base, row of pellets in middle, square at top; jambs constructed in Escomb fashion but plaster now obscures their details.

55. DEARHAM, Cumbria – St Mungo's Church.
TOWER INTERNALLY:
- ✠ Part of Angular Cross-Shaft with designs and patterns including: flat-moulding, pellets, ring-twist design, spiral-scroll design, plait-work design, stopped plait-work design. Scene described as depicting legend of St Kenneth – horse and rider, human figure, baby and bird-like creature.

NAVE INTERNALLY:
- ❖ A Ring-Head Cross-Head supported by an Angular Cross-Shaft with designs and patterns including: Borre variation of ring-chain design, flat boss with a rosette in centre of cross-head, free-ring designs, key-pattern design, knot-work design, pellets, plait-work design, roll-moulding, triquetra-knot design; flying birds; plant design with a central bulb-like object said to represent Yggdrasil – the world tree of Norse mythology.

VESTRY INTERNALLY:
- ❖ Part of Hammer-Head Cross-Head with designs and patterns including: roll-moulding, spiral-scroll design, pellets.

56. DEERHURST, Gloucestershire – St Mary's Church.

SQUARE TOWER incorporating earlier Porch:
- Coursed Rubble Walling including Herringbone Masonry.
- Lower stages with Rubble Quoining and upper stages with Face Alternate Quoining indicating different construction dates.

GROUND FLOOR EXTERNALLY
- West Wall, above current west doorway, not Anglo-Saxon: parts of through-stone voussoirs providing the arched head of a former Anglo-Saxon Doorway; incomplete imposts – particularly the south side; incomplete hood-moulding concentric with, and siting directly on top of, the voussoirs. Above centre of hood-moulding incomplete Prokrossos.

GROUND FLOOR INTERNALLY
- Central Wall: Restored Round-Headed Doorway: mostly through-stone voussoirs; chamfered rectangular through-stone imposts; plaster obscures the jambs; hood-moulding with, on east face, original Anglo-Saxon beast head label-stops probably removed from one of the other doorways in the church.
- ✠ Central Wall: above ground floor doorway west face: Panel decorated with Virgin Mary holding up an oval-shaped shield on which the Christ-Child was probably depicted – it commemorated the child in the womb. The Virgin Mary stands under a round-headed archway with: a patera; stepped imposts; square jambs; rectangular base with horizontal row of recessed, stepped-sided, free-arm crosses; bottom corners of panel each with a single patera; vestiges of paint.

FIRST FLOOR LEVEL INTERNALLY - the floor has been removed:
- Central Wall: Blocked Flat-Headed Doorway monolithic sill with head and jambs constructed of coursed rubble similar to the stonework of the adjoining walling - the construction details of the east face are hidden by plaster.
- North and South Walls: Flat-Headed Single-Splayed Windows – their western jambs are not splayed: monolithic lintels, jambs and sills constructed of rubble similar to the coursed rubble of the adjoining walling.
- North and South Walls: Vestiges of doorways now blocked – their construction details appear to have been of coursed rubble stonework similar to the adjacent walling.
- South Wall: Fragment of Stepped String-Course with varied mouldings.

SECOND FLOOR LEVEL
- West Wall: Doorway (window inserted) wider at the base than the top: round-headed externally arched head cut out of a through-stone lintel which internally is cut away to provide a flat-head; no imposts; through-stone jambs; monolithic sill. Internally both the head and the jambs are rebated for the hanging of a door. Externally hood-moulding outlines the rectangular shape of the lintel rather than the arch of the doorway. Hood-Moulding has label-stops decorated with slab-sided beast heads in portrait; their features are not distinct. Above centre of hood-moulding incomplete Prokrossos.
- North and South Walls: Flat-Headed Double-Splayed Windows wider at the base than the top: monolithic lintels; jambs constructed of rubble similar to the coursed rubble of the adjoining walling; monolithic sill. Interior faces rebated for a shutter; east jambs shared with round-headed aumbries – see next bullet point. South window has been drastically altered with its sill and the walling below removed to form a doorway to provide access at second floor level.
- Internally. North and South Walls: Aumbries wider at the base than the top. Arched heads each cut out of a monolithic lintel divided into two; single large stone forming each of the jambs; monolithic sills; also interior faces rebated for a shutter.

THIRD FLOOR LEVEL – clock chamber

- East Wall: Doorway part above existing nave roofline, but below Anglo-Saxon roofline: round-headed on the west side with arched head cut out of a through-stone lintel which internally is cut away to provide a flat-head; no imposts; through-stone jambs; sill with two steps.
- Externally. Anglo-Saxon Nave Roofline: scaring on the east wall of the tower.

NAVE:
- Coursed Rubble Walling including Herringbone Masonry.

GROUND FLOOR LEVEL INTERNALLY WEST WALL:
- Restored Round-Headed Archway (former doorway): mostly through-stone voussoirs; chamfered rectangular through-stone imposts; plaster obscures the jambs; hood-moulding only on west side.

FIRST FLOOR LEVEL INTERNALLY WEST WALL:
- Parts of Moulded Corbels formerly supported floor of Western Gallery.
- Blocked Megalithic Doorway wider at the base than the top: round-headed, arched head cut out of a monolithic lintel east face/flat-headed, lintel west face (inside tower); no imposts; through-stone jambs; monolithic sill.
- Triangular-Shaped Opening – not splayed – it may indicate the placement of an altar adjacent in the first floor of the tower.

FIRST FLOOR LEVEL INTERNALLY NORTH AND SOUTH WALLS:
- Stepped String-Course with varied mouldings (view from aisles) – some lengths surviving, some cut-back.
- Single Triangular-Shaped Openings - not splayed – directly opposite each other. These may indicate the centre of the upper stories of the north and south two-storey nave porticus – see bullet point below: South Aisle Internally. Nave Porticus.

SECOND FLOOR LEVEL INTERNALLY WEST WALL:
- Double-Triangular-Headed Opening: individual lights each have two angled rectangular through-stones forming the heads with accompanying hood-moulding; protruding, stepped, through-stone imposts providing capitals for the jambs and central pier below; through-stone jambs with a central pier. East face of both jambs and central pier decorated with reed-fluting. Bases of jambs and central pillar with chamfered top half and vertical lower half – the northern light has vertical base to accommodate its one-time use as a doorway.
- Rectangular Panel above top of Double-Triangular-Headed Opening. Possibly decorated with a painted figure and an inscription.

NORTH AISLE WEST END INTERNALLY:
- Font-Bowl supported by separate Font-Base with designs and patterns including: flat-moulding, plant-scroll design, roll-moulding, spiral-scroll design; inhabited interlace design with ribbon-shaped creatures and beasts.

SOUTH AISLE INTERNALLY:
- Nave Porticus. Section of walling which formed part of the two-storey nave porticus is now part of the south wall of the South Aisle. It can be identified opposite the triangular-shaped opening at first floor level in the south wall of the nave. It extends from ground floor level up to 132 inches/335.2 centimetres in height.

PRESENT CHANCEL, THE "CHOIR" CENTRAL SPACE:
Formerly part of the central crossing separating nave from the chancel and providing access to porticus on both north and south sides. It may have supported a central tower.
- Coursed Rubble Walling with Herringbone Masonry.
- Double Chamfered Plinth.
- Blocked former Round-Headed Chancel Archway: through-stone voussoirs with

accompanying hood-moulding with beast-head label-stops; rectangular, chamfered, protruding, through-stone imposts with bands of horizontal and angled moulding resulting in a shape resembling the shape of the stern of a ship; cylindrical columns with no capitals and cylindrical bases. See adjacent: PHOTO 653. Deerhurst 25, showing the east face of the blocked former chancel archway.

FIRST FLOOR LEVEL INTERNALLY EAST WALL:
- Parts of moulded corbels supporting former eastern gallery.

SECOND FLOOR LEVEL INTERNALLY EAST WALL:
- Each side of the Perpendicular East Window: Triangular-Headed Panels with indications of paintings: north, left-hand, panel with a triangular-headed archway supported by pillars with stepped capitals, and bases; framed by the archway is a haloed standing figure who probably holds a book in their left hand. South, right-hand panel has slight indications of markings which cannot now be confidently interpreted.
- Externally. Large Stone providing indications of a sill of a Window or Doorway below the present East Window.

PHOTO 653. Deerhurst 25.

VIEWED FROM EAST ENDS OF CURRENT NORTH AND SOUTH AISLES INTERNALLY:
GROUND FLOOR:
- North Aisle: North Chancel/Choir Porticus. South wall with Triangular-Headed Doorway: head formed with two monolithic through-stones placed to form a triangle with moulded imposts providing their bases; jambs constructed of random rubble similar to the adjoining walling. The east arm of the head reuses part of a Grave-Cover with vestiges of interlace design.
- South Aisle: South Chancel/Choir Porticus. North wall with Flat-Headed Doorway could date from 12th century: monolithic lintel and jambs with large facing stones.
- South Aisle: South Chancel/Choir Porticus. South wall with Blocked Doorway now with window; wider at the base than the top, internally rebated for a door. Flat-Headed with a monolithic lintel internally/round-headed externally with voussoirs, accompanying hood-moulding with beast head label-stops. No imposts, jambs with dressed facing stones, possible monolithic sill. Above centre of hood-moulding incomplete Prokrossos.
- North and South Aisles: North and South Vestibules providing ground floor access to the adjoining two-storey Chancel/Choir porticus to the east: blocked Megalithic Flat-Headed Doorways with a monolithic lintel and jambs with large facing stones in the north and south walls of the chancel.

FIRST FLOOR LEVEL:
- North and South Aisles: Round-Headed Archways providing access to former North and South Chancel/Choir Porticus: through-stone voussoirs with hood-moulding – only vestiges survive on the north archway; moulded imposts protruding into the void between the opposing jambs and some indication they protruded from the faces of the other walls – particularly south archway; jambs constructed of random rubble similar to the adjoining walling; two stones in a row forming sills - sill of south archway lower than north archway.
- South Aisle: South Chancel/Choir Porticus. West wall with Round-Headed Window; arched head cut out of through-stone monolithic lintel; jambs and sill constructed of coursed rubble similar to the stonework of the adjoining walling. In the adjoining

walling to the north of this window are indications of a single jamb and the lintel from a Flat-Headed Doorway.

FLANKING THE EASTERN PART OF THE CHANCEL AND THE WESTERN PART OF THE APSE INTERNALLY:
- Coursed Rubble Walling including Herringbone Masonry of north and south apse porticus.
- North Aisle, East Wall: Blocked Megalithic Flat-Headed Doorway providing access to North-East Apse Porticus: monolithic lintel; no imposts; vertically placed stones forming jambs; sill of three horizontal stones in a row. It can also be identified externally.
- North Aisle, East Wall: Flat-Headed Aumbries of uncertain date.
- South Aisle, East Wall: Blocked Round-Headed Archway, replacing former doorway providing access to South-East Apse Porticus – it probably dates from late-11th century.

FLANKING THE EASTERN PART OF THE CHANCEL AND THE WESTERN PART OF THE APSE EXTERNALLY:
- Foundations of north and east walls of North-East Apse Porticus and part of east wall of South-East Apse Porticus.

RUINED HEPTAGONAL-SHAPED APSE EXTERNALLY:
- Some Coursed Stone Walling and foundations.
- Pilaster-Strips.
- Pilaster-Strips forming a Triangular-Headed Arch above Square String-Course.
- Below one surviving Triangular-Headed Arch formed by Pilaster-Strips is a panel on a rectangular stone decorated with: flat-moulding enclosing an incomplete haloed angel in portrait with distinct facial features and hair and vestiges of its left wing and slight indications of its right wing. See above right: PHOTO 654. Deerhurst 26.

PHOTO 654. Deerhurst 26.

57. DERBY, Derbyshire – Museum and Art Gallery.
- Part of an arm from a Free-Arm Cross-Head with flat-moulding, interlace design and roll-moulding.
- Part of Angular Cross-Shaft known as "St Alkmund's Cross" with designs and patterns including: flat-moulding, interlace design, pellets; incomplete and complete beasts and serpents; incomplete bird. See adjacent: PHOTO 655. Derby 3.
- Part of a damaged Angular Cross-Shaft with roll-moulding and incomplete and complete beasts.
- Part of a damaged Angular Cross-Shaft with flat-moulding, roll-moulding, plant design; arched panels enclosing a seated figure of a warrior and incomplete and damaged figures one with a raised sword or rod, part of a shield and possibly part of the legs of a horse.
- Part of Angular Cross-Shaft with flat-moulding, roll-moulding, strands from a design it is not now confident to identify; two standing, probably haloed, figures separated by a vertical band of flat-

PHOTO 655. Derby 3. Photograph Courtesy of Derby Museums.

moulding.
- St Alkmund's (martyred son of King Alhred of Northumbria) Sarcophagus with designs and patterns including: flat-moulding, interlace design, plait-work design, ring-chain design, roll-moulding.
- Coped Grave-Cover with roll-moulding and inhabited knot-work design with serpent-like creatures.
- Almost complete Grave-Cover with flat-moulding with a double-ended free-arm cross.
- Broken, but almost complete, Grave-Cover with a long-stemmed free-arm cross ending at its base in an arched shape with interlace design and triquetra-knot design – only vestiges of the upper arms of the cross.
- Part of a Hogback Grave-Cover with roll-moulding, interlace design; inhabited knot-work design with a serpent; weathered head of an end beast.
- Possibly part of a Hogback Grave-Cover with ring-chain design and roll-moulding.
- Part of Angular Cross-Shaft known as "The Repton Stone" with roll-moulding; a mounted warrior on horseback possibly depicting King Aethelbard of Mercia; a depiction of a monster with a human head devouring human figures – interpreted as "The Mouth of Hell"; an extended arm and hand on a horizontal arm of a cross-shaft – interpreted as that of Christ in a Crucifixion Scene.

58. DESBOROROUGH, Northamptonshire - St Giles's Church.
NAVE INTERNALLY:
- Part of an Angular Cross-Shaft with designs and patterns including: cable-moulding, flat-moulding, knot-work design, pellets, roll-moulding; Ringerike design including two addorsed beasts, a human-like head and pellets; inhabited scroll design with beasts.
- Possibly part of an Arm from a Free-Arm Cross-Head with ring-chain or ring-knot design and roll-moulding.
- Part of a Grave-Cover with what now appears as flat-moulding, a confused band of ring-chain or ring-knot design, roll-moulding.

59. DEWSBURY, West Yorkshire – The Minster Church of All Saints.
NAVE INTERNALLY:
- Internally. Coursed Stone Walling including a single quoin from the north-east corner of the nave.

PAULINUS PILGRIMAGE CHAPEL INTERNALLY:
- Part of a circular lower part of Cross-Shaft with an upper angular part: a seated figure of a haloed Christ giving a blessing with an inscription IHS XPVS - the abbreviated Latin name for Jesus Christ; indications of another haloed figure.

HERITAGE CENTRE INTERNALLY:
- Part of an arm from a Free-Arm Cross-Head with designs and patterns including: cable-moulding, flat-moulding, interlace design; part of a crouching beast or creature and possibly vestiges of another; part of a haloed, winged, angel with a human figure crouching at its feet.
- Two arms from a Free-Arm Cross-Head with cable-moulding, flat-moulding.
- Part of the centre of a Cross-Head with one face with a domed boss surrounded by interlace design; the other face could possibly be a human face, or a free-arm cross, surrounded be some form of moulding.
- Two parts from the circular lower part of a Cross-Shaft with an upper angular part – the same cross-shaft identified in the Paulinus Pilgrimage Chapel. One part comprising: an incomplete curving band of cable-moulding which may have formed part of the swag separating the lower circular part of the cross-shaft from the upper angular part; flat-moulding; two damaged and incomplete standing human figures. The other part

comprising: the lower halves of the bodies and feet of three standing human figures standing on the heads of two interlocking round-headed archways with a shared stepped capital; beneath each of the archways there are vestiges of the upper body of one and the heads of all four.
- Part of an Angular Cross-Shaft with designs and patterns including: part of an archway with a stepped base and stepped capital, cable-moulding, plant-scroll design. Seated figure of the Virgin and Child. Possibly the feet of two standing human figures.
- Part of an Angular Cross-Shaft with designs and patterns including: cable-moulding, flat-moulding. A haloed Christ giving a blessing flanked by the figures of the Virgin and St John with representations of water jar; an inscription interpreted as referring to the miracle of turning water into wine. A haloed Christ with representations of the loaves and fishes with a "crowd" represented by human heads; an inscription interpreted as referring to the miracle of the loaves and fishes.
- Part of an Angular Cross-Shaft with designs and patterns including: cable-moulding, flat-moulding, interlace design, plant-scroll design. Lower half of the figure of probably Christ Crucified; headless seated figure holding vertically a stick-like figure - possibly the Virgin and Christ-Child.
- Fragments of Angular Cross-Shafts with designs and patterns including: bush-scroll design, flat-moulding, plant-scroll design, roll-moulding; incomplete lower part of robed figure.
- Part of a Cross-Base with baluster-shaft moulding, plant-scroll design, roll-moulding.
- Part of a House-Shaped Grave-Cover or Shrine resembling an upturned boat with designs and patterns including: baluster-shaft moulding, flat-moulding, free-arm cross, linear design, moulding in the form of columns with capitals and bases, plant-scroll design, tegulations.

60. DIDDLEBURY, Shropshire – St Peter's Church.
NORTH WALL AND PART OF THE ADJOINING EAST WALL OF TOWER:
- Ashlar walling externally with herringbone walling internally.
- Square Three-Stepped Plinth.
- Round-Headed Double-Splayed Window: two half-through-stone lintels separated by a central slab; jambs and sill constructed with coursed ashlar laid in similar courses to the adjoining walling. Externally sill constructed with three stones in a horizontal row, internally, sill provided by coursed herringbone masonry of the adjoining walling.
- Blocked Round-Headed Doorway: through-stone voussoirs with accompanying hood-moulding; protruding, chamfered, through-stone imposts; through-stone jambs with square bases protruding from the face of the wall; sill provided by the lowest course of the three-stepped plinth; accompanying strip-work with similar imposts and bases to the doorway; the bases on the strip-work interrupt the top two courses of the three-stepped plinth.

NAVE INTERNALLY:
- Parts of Angular Cross-Shaft with inhabited tree-scroll design - two human figures climbing the tree; bird.
- Grave-Marker decorated with designs and patterns including: a honey-comb-like design; roll-moulding; free-arm cross entwined in a circle, standing on a narrow base.

61. DOLTON, Devon – Church of St Edmund King and Martyr.
NAVE INTERNALLY:
- Two Parts of Angular Cross-Shaft reused as a font, the upper part upside down and used as a font bowl, the lower part – the right way up – used as the base. On one side and part

of another the decoration is a reconstruction. Designs and patterns including: interlace design, knot-work design, figure-of-eight ring-knot design, roll-moulding. Inhabited knot-work design with human head with two reptile-like creatures extending from its nostrils; inhabited interlace design with two creatures forming a circle whose herringbone-patterned bodies cross at the neck; a pair of winged creatures with herringbone-patterned bodies and affronted heads; inhabited interlace design with two creatures whose bodies cross at the neck.

62. DOVER, Kent – St Mary-In-The-Castle Church – much restored in 1860-62.
NAVE:
- Coursed Rubble Walling with Flints and reused Roman tile-like bricks.
- Square Single Plinth.
- Side Alternate Quoining – a mixture of reused Roman tile-like bricks and some megalithic dressed stones.
- Blocked Round-Headed Doorway: Roman tile-like bricks forming arched head; chamfered imposts; mixture of stone, rubble and flint jambs.
- Large Round-Headed Double-Splayed Windows: arched heads constructed with reused Roman tile-like bricks placed on end and formed into a discernible arch; jambs mostly reused Roman tile-like bricks but also some individual pieces of rubble; sills mostly of rubble and flint similar to the stonework in the adjoining walling.
- Flat-Headed Double-Splayed Windows with a monolithic wooden lintel; jambs mostly reused Roman tile-like bricks but also some individual pieces of rubble; sills of rubble and flint similar to the stonework in the adjoining walling. See above: PHOTO 656. Dover 1, showing the south wall of the nave with the blocked round-headed doorway arrowed red, the round-headed double-splayed windows arrowed black, and the flat-headed double-splayed window arrowed blue.
- First Floor, West Wall: Round-Headed Doorway providing access to both the first floor gallery in the Nave and the Roman Lighthouse: mixture of, stone, rubble and flint forming arched head including voussoirs, stepped imposts and jambs.

PHOTO 656. Dover 1.

CENTRAL SQUARE TOWER – See Page 357: PHOTO 657. Dover 2, showing the central tower from the north-east:
- Coursed Rubble Walling with mixture of, stone, rubble, flint and reused Roman tile-like bricks.
- Square Single Plinth.
- Side Alternate Quoining – a mixture of reused Roman tiles and some dressed stones.
- Double-Splayed Circular Windows: mostly reused Roman tile-like bricks but also some individual pieces of rubble and flint similar to the stonework in the adjoining walling.
- Pairs of Round-Headed Single-Belfry Openings: arched heads constructed with reused Roman tile-like bricks placed on end and formed into a discernible arch; jambs mostly reused Roman tile-like bricks but also some individual pieces of rubble; sills mostly of rubble and flint similar to the stonework in the adjoining walling.
- Internally. East and West Walls: Round-Headed Archways: stepped, moulded, imposts; square jambs including reused Roman tile-like bricks; strip-work and hood-moulding on west faces only. Archways opening into the north and south transepts replaced in 12th century but there are indications they were smaller in size than the west (nave) and east

(chancel) archways.
- Internally. First Floor: Blocked Round-Headed Doorways formerly providing access between upper stages of nave, tower and chancel: Roman tile-like bricks forming arched heads; chamfered imposts; mixture of stone, rubble and flint jambs.

TRANSEPTS:
- Coursed Rubble Walling with Flints and some reused Roman Bricks and Tiles.
- Square Single Plinth.
- Side Alternate Quoining – a mixture of reused Roman tiles and some dressed stones.
- Flat-Headed Double-Splayed Window with a monolithic lintel.

CHANCEL:
- Coursed Rubble Walling with Flints and some reused Roman Bricks and Tiles.
- Square Single Plinth. Side Alternate Quoining – a mixture of reused Roman tiles and some dressed stones.
- Vestiges of Blocked Doorway.

PHOTO 657. Dover 2.

NAVE INTERNALLY:
- Rectangular, tapering, coped, Grave-Cover broken in three, with incomplete linear designs involving pairs of parallel lines providing a frame around the edges. Below, at its wider head, the parallel lines enclose a row of equally-spaced holes; possible plant design.
- Part of Baluster-Shaft with incomplete bands of roll-moulding and grooves.

63. DURHAM CATHEDRAL, County Durham – The Monk's Dormitory.
- Incomplete and parts of Free-Arm, Plate-Ring and Ring-Head Cross-Heads with designs and patterns including: flat-moulding, grooved-moulding, interlace design, knot-work design, pellets, plait-work design, plant design, ring-chain design, ring-knot design, roll-moulding, rosette design enclosed by roll-moulding, scroll design; creatures, beasts and birds. Crucifixion and baptismal scenes, the "Lamb of God", human figures – some haloed, winged, angels.
- Incomplete and parts of Angular Cross-Shafts with designs and patterns including: representations of baluster-shafts, cable-moulding, flat-moulding, grooved-moulding, interlace design, key-pattern design, knot-work design, linear designs, pellets, plait-work design, plant designs, plant-scroll design, roll-moulding, ring-chain design, ring-knot design, scroll design, berries used as space-fillers, spiral-scroll design, stepped-pattern design, triquetra-knots, vine-scroll design. Complete and incomplete creatures, beasts and birds. Complete and incomplete human figures – some haloed, haloed winged angels, horseman. Figures from Norse Mythology. Inscription interpreted to read "[Pray for Herebericht, priest. Alla raised this sign in memory of his brother.]".
- Part of a Cross-Base with flat-moulding, key-pattern design, plait-work design, roll-moulding.
- Incomplete Grave-Covers, including hogbacks, with designs and patterns including: cable-moulding, an incomplete cross-head and cross-shaft, incised cross, cable-moulding, flat-moulding, herringbone design, interlace design, key-pattern design,

knot-work design, pellets, plait-work design, plant design, ring-knot design, parallel rows of ring-twist design with the individual rings linked together by "S"-shaped loops – "como-braid", roll-moulding, scroll design, stepped-pattern design, tegulations, alternating triangular design. Creatures and beasts. Complete and incomplete end bear-like beasts. Human figures – some haloed, winged haloed angels. Inscription interpreted as "Alrihic set up".
✠ Complete Grave-Marker with incised lines forming a panel containing a free-arm cross and with an inscription - the female name "Beorhtgyd".
✠ Architectural Fragments including an impost, a possible support for a reading desk, some with patterns and decoration including: cable-moulding, chequer-pattern design, flat-moulding, grooved-moulding, interlace design, roll-moulding, scroll design.
✠ Fragments of Wall Panels with designs and patterns including: roll-moulding, scroll design, vine-scroll design. Inhabited plant-scroll design with an archer.
✠ Parts of Friezes with designs and patterns including: flat-moulding, representations of baluster-shafts placed vertically, horizontally and some in herringbone fashion – some with cable-moulding.
✠ Baluster-Shafts with sets of narrow and wide grooves alternating with plain bands of stonework.
✠ Casts of Ruthwell Cross, Dumfriesshire; Bewcastle Cross, Cumbria; "Acca's Cross", Hexham, Northumberland.

64. EARLS BARTON, Northamptonshire – All Saints Church.
SQUARE TOWER formerly "Tower-Nave" – See adjacent: PHOTO: 658. Earls Barton 9, showing the four stages of the west wall with the west doorway arrowed red, incomplete round-headed (externally)/flat-headed (internally) double-splayed double-windows arrowed black, megalithic triangular-headed doorway/window arrowed blue, round-headed quintuple-belfry openings arrowed green.

PHOTO 658. Earls Barton 9.

❖ Coursed Rubble Walling.
❖ Square Single Plinth.
❖ Long and Short Quoining. Internally, some of the horizontal "short" quoins, and even fewer of the vertical longs, protrude through the plastered wall – the north-east quoining provides more examples. Externally, uniquely, the entirety of each quoin protrudes from the surface of the walls – they are not "cut-back".
❖ Pilaster-Strips laid in long and short fashion.
❖ Chamfered (between first/ground and the second stage) and Square (between the second and third stages and between the third and fourth stages) String-Courses. These String-Courses delineate each of the upper three Anglo-Saxon stages of the Tower; each stage is set-back from the stage below. The String-Courses also provide the sills for: the Round-Headed Doorways above (second stage); Triangular-Headed Windows above (third stage); Round-Headed Quintuple-Belfry Openings above (fourth stage).
FIRST STAGE, GROUND FLOOR LEVEL. WEST WALL:
❖ Megalithic Round-Headed Doorway: arched head cut out of two large stones externally – accompanied by hood-moulding - and a single stone internally; protruding imposts decorated with a blind arcade of interlocking round-headed archways; Escomb jambs supported by square bases which also support the accompanying strip-work.
❖ Restored Round-Headed Single-Splayed Window with jambs of possible Anglo-Saxon

origin.

FIRST STAGE, GROUND FLOOR LEVEL. SOUTH WALL:
- Round-Headed (externally)/Flat-Headed (internally) Double-Splayed Double-Windows. Externally, heads provided by single-shaped facing-stones, curving similarly to the middle third of a semi-circle; these facing stones are decorated with bands of roll-moulding which provide a frame for the representation of a free-arm cross in relief. Externally, jambs, including the shared central jamb and the through-stone slab above, faced with decorated baluster-shafts with square-shaped bases and capitals; the jambs and their baluster-shaft facings interrupt the pilaster-strips decorating the tower overall. Each sill is faced with a single rectangular stone. Rubble walling evident behind the facing stones. In the middle depth of the walling each window has a single stone slab through which an aperture in the shape of a free-arm cross has been cut. Internally, most of the construction details are now hidden by plaster, with the exception of the mid-wall jamb faced with two protruding vertical and parallel half-round mouldings each with a base comprising two or three stones laid horizontally on top of each other, with the capital provided by the inner face of the through-stone slab beneath the arched heads of both windows.

  A similar decorated window existed in the west wall but all that now survives externally are the blocked facing stones of the semi-circular shape of the arched heads, and, the outer impost-like capitals of the jambs. Internally, both windows are flat-headed with most of the construction details hidden by plaster, with the exception of the mid-wall jamb faced with a single protruding baluster-shaft with a square-shaped base and capital.
- Circular Stone Slab with a free-arm cross in relief enclosed within a band of flat-moulding also in relief.

SECOND STAGE. SOUTH WALL:
- Megalithic Round-Headed Doorway: voussoirs horizontally-shaped and jointed rather than wedge-shaped and fitted together; square imposts. The outer face of the jambs are decorated with pilaster-strips and the sill is provided by the damaged string-course separating the first/ground and the second stages of the tower. West Wall has a similar doorway now blocked apart from its voussoirs and imposts which provide the arched head for a window. The East Wall also has a similar doorway, now restored, but without the pilaster-strips. It can be identified above the current nave roof; it was formerly beneath the roofline of the chancel (present nave).

SECOND STAGE. SOUTH AND WEST WALLS:
- Pilaster-Strips providing interlinked semi-circular arcading on top of the string-course separating the first/ground and the second stages of the tower.

THIRD STAGE:
- Megalithic Triangular-Headed Doorways (their construction seems more akin to doorways but they are also described as windows). Each head formed with two monolithic through-stones placed to form a triangle with square imposts providing their bases; each of the jambs are faced externally with a single vertical stone similar to the "longs" in the accompanying vertical pilaster-strips; sill provided by the string-course separating the second and third stages of the tower. East Wall Doorway, with a monolithic slab providing its sill, and with no pilaster-strips, is near the top of the stage below the string-course separating the third stage from the fourth stage.
- Pilaster-Strips providing an interlinked diamond-shaped row of arcading whose horizontal joints also have a protruding square base-like stone.

FOURTH STAGE:
- Megalithic Round-Headed Quintuple-Belfry Openings (rare, if not unique): arched heads

each cut out of a single square lintel and decorated with concentric bands of set-back moulding – west wall central lintel has a representation of a free-arm cross in relief above the moulding similar to those on the facing stones of the arched heads of the round-headed double-splayed double-windows in the west wall (incomplete) and the south wall (complete). No imposts. Jambs comprise six vertical slabs ornamented externally with baluster-shafts decorated with horizontal bands of roll mounding - despite their appearance the four intervening jambs are not mid-wall shafts. Above all six baluster-shafts, the tops of the through-stone slabs supporting the junctions of the arched heads can be identified. The sills are provided by the top of the string-course below. Additionally, east wall opening has circular openings similar to sound-holes above its two most northern openings.
- Pilaster-Strips similar, but less complete, than those in the third stage.

65. EDINBURGH, Lothian - National Museum of Scotland.
- Parts of Angular Cross-Shafts with designs and patterns including: cable-moulding, flat-moulding, interlace design, key-pattern design, knot-work design, pellets, ring-chain design, ring-twist design, roll-moulding, spiral-scroll design, stopped plait-work, plant-scroll design; creatures and beasts; inhabited interlace design with birds; inhabited plant-scroll design with creatures and birds; inhabited ring-chain design with a creature. Scenes depicting a building - on one face a gable-headed structure - with representations of round-headed archways/doorways with below haloed figures, human heads, the sun, the moon, round-headed window, panel for an inscription. Lower part of body, legs and feet of Christ with smaller human figures, pairs of human figures, the figure of David playing his harp. Lower part of body, legs and feet of Christ with human figures, hooded human figures.
- Parts of Free-Arm, Plate-Ring, and Disc-Head Cross-Heads with parts of their attached Angular Cross-Shafts with designs and patterns including: flat-moulding, interlace design, knot-work design, ring-knot design, roll-moulding, stopped plait-work design. Incised crosses with cross-heads and cross-shafts.
- Parts of Cross-Slabs with designs and patterns including: flat-moulding, free-arm crosses and their angular cross-shafts in relief, interlace design, key-pattern design, knot-work design, roll-moulding, scroll design, spiral-scroll design; creatures and beasts. Rider with drinking horn. Runic Inscription interpreted as "In memory of Þorgerðr Steinarsdóttir is the cross raised" - a feminine name.
- Section of Slate incised with part of a free-arm cross-head with an incomplete runic inscription.
- Triangular-Headed Stone known as the "Aberlemno Stone" ("Aberlemno 2"). One face is decorated with a billet free-arm cross-head and supporting cross-shaft with designs including: key-pattern design, knot-work design, scroll design. The other face is decorated with fighting mounted and unmounted warriors. It may represent the battle in AD 685 of Nechtansmere (near Aberlemno) where the forces of King Bridei of the Picts defeated the forces of King Ecgfrith of Northumbria – Ecgfrith was killed.

66. ESCOMB, County Durham – Church.
NAVE:
- Coursed Stone Walling.
- Megalithic Side Alternate Quoining.
- Flat-Headed Doorway: through-stone monolithic lintel head; no imposts but tops of each of the large vertical stones forming part of the jambs and supporting the lintel are notched into the lintel – resembling mortise and tenon jointing; Escomb jambs – rebated for door.

- ❖ Flat-Headed Single-Splayed Windows: monolithic through-stone lintel; jambs each formed with a single vertical through-stone slightly angled towards the top; single through-stone sill. Internally, each jamb with vertical groove enabling the placement of a window shutter - inside the present glazing.
- ❖ Round-Headed Single-Splayed Windows: arched heads cut out of two half-through-stone lintels; jambs each formed with a single vertical through-stone slightly angled towards the top; single through-stone sill. (The west window has two through-stones in each jamb and two narrow through-stones forming the sill.) Internally, each jamb with vertical groove enabling the placement of a window shutter - inside the present glazing.
- ✠ Internally: Consecration Cross.
- ✠ Internally: Font possibly Anglo-Saxon.
- ✠ Externally: Sundial with the body of a serpent – head on the left, fish-like tail on right - providing an upper, curving, frame, with the lower, semi-circular border of the sundial provided by a ring-twist design. Above prokrossos.

WESTERN PORTICUS EXTERNALLY:
- ❖ Evidence of gable roofline of former western porticus on west wall of nave.
- ❖ Foundations of porticus indicated by 20th century flagstones.

CHANCEL:
- ❖ Coursed Stone Walling.
- ❖ Megalithic Side Alternate Quoining.
- ❖ Round-Headed Chancel Archway: arched head formed of through-stone voussoirs, resting on through-stone chamfered imposts which do not project from the west and east faces of the walling but do project into the central void. Both Arch and Imposts are supported by Escomb jambs comprising through-stones laid alternately vertically and horizontally. On each side of the central void the opposing "faces" of the two jambs, demonstrably large vertical "upright" stones, display one of their tall wide "faces" which alternate with horizontal "flat" stones displaying one of their narrow long "sides". On each of the two other sides of the jambs visible the vertical stones display one of their long sides vertically and the horizontal stones display one of their short sides horizontally.
- ❖ Blocked Flat-Headed Doorway: through-stone monolithic lintel head; no imposts; single, vertical, megalithic stones forming each of the jambs – rebated for a door – east jamb decorated with faint vestiges of "Tree of Life" design apparently depicting a tree separating Adam and Eve.
- ✠ Internally: Grave-Marker with, in relief, a free-standing free-arm cross-head, angular cross-shaft and trapezoid-shaped cross-base, bordered along the vertical sides by flat-moulding. There are distinctive round bosses on either side of the cross-shaft and in the centre and on each of the surviving arms of the cross-head.

WESTERN PORTICUS EXTERNALLY:
- ❖ Foundations of porticus indicated by 20th century flagstones; stonework from this porticus may have been used to build 13th south porch.

SOUTH PORCH INTERNALLY:
- ❖ Part of the corner of possibly a shrine or altar with designs and patterns including: flat-moulding, ring-twist design, roll-moulding.
- ✠ Parts of Angular Cross-Shafts with designs and patterns including: cable-moulding, plant-scroll design, roll-moulding; inhabited plant-scroll design with creatures and a bird.

67. EYAM, Derbyshire – St Lawrence's Church.
CHURCHYARD:
- ✠ Most of Free-Arm Cross-Head and its associated Angular Cross-Shaft decorated with

designs and patterns including: knot-work design, plant-scroll design, ring-chain design, ring-knot design, roll-moulding, plant-scroll design. The Virgin Mary with Christ-Child – the top of Mary's head is missing; possibly the figure of a prophet; winged Angels. See adjacent: PHOTO 659. Eyam 4, showing west face of Cross-Head and Cross-Shaft.

NORTH AISLE INTERNALLY:
- Tub-shaped font tapering from bottom to top. Decorated in relief with an arcade of interlocking arches with shared columns, imposts and bases, similar to those of a chancel or tower archway in an Anglo-Saxon church; also with a broad band of flat-moulding around the bottom circumference and a band of roll-moulding around the top circumference.

68. FLETTON, Cambridgeshire – St Margaret's Church.
TOWER INTERNALLY:
- Part of an Angular Cross-Shaft with cable-moulding and inhabited plant-scroll design with creatures and birds.

PHOTO 659. Eyam 4. Photograph with permission of Eyam Parish Church.

NAVE INTERNALLY:
- Separate sections of stonework possibly from the Angular Cross-Shaft in the churchyard. Two sections appear to have vestiges of cable-moulding and indications of inhabited plant-scroll design with creatures and birds

CHANCEL INTERNALLY:
- Two Wall Panels framed with flat-moulding with an internal rounded head. In each panel is a single haloed figure. One is thought to represent the Archangel Michael (carrying a cross-shaped sword). The other is thought to represent the figure of the Archangel Gabriel holding his horn or trumpet in his right hand, or, the figure of the Archangel Raphael holding a bottle or flask in his right hand.
- Seven sections of stonework from a decorated Wall Frieze now placed together and mostly bordered by flat-moulding forming panels decorated with both designs and patterns including: plant-scroll design; inhabited scroll design with bird-like or duck-like creatures and a central human figure said to represent Samson – he has an angled head, arms outstretched, and with his hands holding vertical, pillar-like strands which form part of a scroll design; inhabited scroll design with half-figures of haloed saints, one may represent Christ, enclosed in an arcade of round-headed archways supported by capitals and pillars; inhabited scroll design with half-figures of winged angels and what could be small human heads. Inhabited scroll design with a shield-like feature, a bird-like or duck-like creature, and possibly human heads, creatures or fruit.

CHURCHYARD EXTRERNALLY:
- Later memorial incorporating part of an Angular, Collared, Cross-Shaft with the lower part of its Ring-Head Cross-Head attached, with cable-moulding and inhabited plant-scroll design with creatures and birds. Cross-Head enlarged and reshaped and crown on top added at later, not Anglo-Saxon, date(s).

69. FORNCETT ST PETER, Norfolk – St Peter's Church.
ROUND TOWER:
- Coursed Rubble Walling with Flints and some reused Roman tile-like bricks.
- Restored Round-Headed Doorway only interior contains original stonework with its arched head formed of rubble voussoirs supported by chamfered imposts; the jambs are formed of rubble and flint similar to the stonework in the adjoining walling.
- Round-Headed Single-Splayed Windows constructed with rubble, flints and reused Roman

tile-like bricks similar to the stonework in the adjoining walling.
- Three Circular Double-Splayed Windows constructed with rubble and flints similar to the stonework in the adjoining walling.
- Three Triangular and One (west wall) Round-Headed (restored) Double-Belfry Openings: heads constructed with individual stones of rubble, flints and reused Roman tile-like bricks placed on end and formed into a discernible triangle/arch; stepped imposts constructed with individual stones of rubble placed horizontally – the imposts protrude from the faces of the walling and into the central void; jambs constructed with rubble, flints and reused Roman tile-like bricks all laid horizontally similar to the coursed rubble stonework in the adjoining walling; cylindrical mid-wall shafts each with a expanding rounded base and cushion-capital; above mid-wall shafts through-stone slab placed horizontally – only overhangs the internal and external faces of the mid-wall-shaft – the slab supports junction of both triangular/arched heads above; sills provided by the top of the coursed rubble stonework below.
- Eight Circular Double-Splayed Windows: constructed with rubble and flints similar to the stonework in the adjoining walling.
- Internally. Round-Headed Tower Archway: constructed with rubble with flints similar to the stonework in the adjoining walling but now plastered over; chamfered imposts; square jambs.

NAVE:
- Coursed Rubble Walling with Flints and some reused Roman tile-like bricks.

CHANCEL:
- Coursed Rubble Walling with Flints and some reused Roman tile-like bricks.
- Slight vestiges of the arched head of a blocked Double-Splayed Window: individual stones, including a reused Roman brick-like tile, placed on end and formed into a discernible arch.

70. GEDDINGTON, Northamptonshire – St Mary Magdalene Church.
NAVE
- Coursed Rubble Walling.
- Incomplete Long and Short Quoining.
- Blocked, incomplete, Round-Headed Single-Splayed Window. South, former internal, face: individual stones placed on end and formed into a discernible arch; surviving eastern jamb constructed with through-stones laid in a similar way to long and short quoining. Western jamb and sill no longer survive. North, former external face: arched head cut out of rectangular half-through-stone lintel; eastern jamb constructed with a single, vertical, megalithic half-through-stone. Western jamb and sill no longer survive.
- Triangular-Headed Arcading constructed with pilaster-strips.

71. GLENTWORTH, Lincolnshire – St Michael's Church.
SQUARE TOWER:
- Coursed Rubble Walling.
- Side Alternate Quoining.
- Round-Headed "Key-Hole" Single-Splayed Windows: south window has an arched head shaped out of a single stone to provide a curvature in both its upper and lower borders greater than a semi-circle. Externally, the head is incised with grooves to represent the jointing of voussoirs. Also externally, hood-moulding, decorated with palmette design, has been placed on top of the head; the hood-moulding also has label-stops – not decorated. Jambs each comprise a single, vertical, through-stone with a small stone of

rubble below; sill provided by top of the coursed stonework below. West Window: externally arched head cut out of a monolithic lintel/internally flat-headed comprising two large stones. Monolithic through-stone jamb on its south side but on the north side jamb comprises two half-through-stones internally but externally there are two stones the lower one of which is part of an early-11th century grave-marker with cable-moulding enclosing a free-arm cross with chevron-pattern and herringbone pattern; sill provided by top of the coursed stonework below.

- ❖ Square String-Course forms the sill of the Round-Headed Double-Belfry Openings above and delineates the tall lower stage of the tower from the upper stage: the upper stage is set-back from the lower stage.
- ❖ Round-Headed Double-Belfry Openings: arched heads constructed with voussoirs; square imposts protruding from the faces of the walling and into the central void; jambs comprise facing stones of size and placed on top of each other but not in any distinctive design; cylindrical and octagonal mid-wall shafts with square bases and capitals decorated mostly with volutes but west opening appears to have creature or beast heads rather than volutes – additionally, mid-wall shaft in the south wall is decorated with a vertical band of cable-moulding in relief; above mid-wall shafts through-stone slab placed horizontally so that it sides overhang the mid-wall-shaft – the slab supports junction of both arched heads above; sill provided by the top of the string-course below. West belfry opening may have had a bell hung between the mid-wall shaft and the left-hand (north) jamb.
- ❖ Internally. Round-Headed Tower Archway: voussoirs: chamfered imposts; square jambs.
- ❖ Internally. First Floor: Blocked Megalithic Flat-Headed Doorway; lintel; no imposts; large stones forming jambs.

72. GOSFORTH, Cumbria - St Mary's Church.
NORTH AISLE INTERNALLY:
- ✠ Most of Hogback Grave-Cover known as the "Warrior's Tomb" with designs and patterns including: flat-moulding, free-ring designs, interlace design, interlocking circles, ring-knot design, tegulations; creatures and serpent-like creatures; human figure possibly carrying a book. Scene depicting two groups of standing warriors.
- ✠ Most of Hogback Grave-Cover known as the "Saints Tomb" with designs and patterns including: flat-moulding, cable-moulding, diamond-shaped pattern, knot-work design, plait-work design, roll-moulding; creatures, serpent-like creatures, and beasts; human figures, Crucifixion Scenes.
- ✠ Part of Ring-Head Cross-Head with designs and patterns including: cable-moulding, plait-work design, ring-chain design, roll-moulding.
- ✠ Almost complete Ring-Head Cross-Head with tenon (to fit into the mortise of a cross-shaft), and with designs and patterns including: cable-design, knot-work design, plait-work design, ring-chain design, roll-moulding.
- ✠ Part of Angular Cross-Shaft or Frieze with designs and patterns including: flat-moulding, plait-work design. Large four-legged beast fettered by the knotted body of a serpent. Known as the "Fishing Stone" it depicts from Norse Mythology Thor and the giant Hymir in a boat fishing for the Midgard World Serpent, their fishing line uses an ox's head as bait around which fish swim; below is a ring which may be part of (now indistinct) Midgard World Serpent.

CHOIR VESTRY INTERNALLY:
- ✠ Fragment of Angular Cross-Shaft with flat-moulding, plait-work design; serpent and another creature.

CHURCHYARD:
- ✠ Cross comprising: Ring-Head Cross-Head with designs and patterns including; cable-

moulding, triquetra-knot design, plait-work design, roll-moulding.
Lower Circular/Upper Angular Cross-Shaft with designs and patterns including: Borre variation of ring-chain design, cable-moulding, knot-work design, plait-work design, ring-chain design, roll-moulding. Various scenes are represented including: Christ Crucified with Longinus and Mary Magdalene. From Norse Mythology: Odin and his horse Sleipnir, the hart Eikthyrnir, Fenrir the wolf, Garm the wolf, Heimdall, Loki, Mímir, Sigyn, Surt, Vithar, as well as the heads of wolf-like creatures and beasts and serpents, and indistinct representations of the sun and moon. The scenes tell of the main events referred to in the Völuspá in the Prose Edda written by Snorri Sturluson in about 1220 AD. 1. Chaos and creation; 2. The wars of the gods and giants; 3. Ragnarök and the attack on the gods; the new world with Vithar (one on Odin's sons) slaying Fenrir the wolf and the promise of the rebirth of Baldr (another of Odin's sons), here identified with Christ. Lower part of cross-shaft not decorated.
- Three-Stepped Cross-Base – no decoration survives.
- Part of a Cross-Shaft reshaped and reused to support a sundial – not Anglo-Scandinavian (no decoration survives).

73. GREAT DUNHAM, Norfolk – St Andrew's Church.
NAVE:
- Random Rubble Walling with Flints including some reused Roman tile-like bricks.
- Long and Short Quoining.
- Blocked Triangular-Headed Doorway – construction details hidden by plaster - with strip-work and hood-moulding all decorated with distinctive sunken small squares.
- Complete Round-Headed Double-Splayed Window: arched head constructed with reused Roman tile-like bricks placed on end and formed into a discernible arch. The jambs and sill are constructed with a mixture of rubble, flints and reused Roman tile-like bricks similar to the stonework in the adjoining walling. Plaster and rendering obscures construction details.
- Vestiges of the heads of Round-Headed Double-Splayed Windows: reused Roman tile-like bricks aid identification.
- Internally. North and South Walls: Incomplete rows of Round-Headed Sunken Blind Arcading separated by Pilaster-Strips with stepped bases; some have decorated capitals Plaster now obscures much of the construction details. Note: later, not Anglo-Saxon, windows and doorways have been inserted into the arcading.

CENTRAL SQUARE TOWER (NOT CRUCIFORM):
- Random Rubble Walling with Flints including some reused Roman tile-like bricks.
- Long and Short Quoining. The south-west and north-west quoining extend from the level of the eaves of the nave up to the level of the added, not Anglo-Saxon, string-course below the battlements in the tower. Below the eaves of the nave there is no separation between the walling of the nave and the tower and consequently no quoining. On the east (chancel) side of the tower there is north-east and south-east quoining extending from ground level up to the level of the added, not Anglo-Saxon, string-course below the battlements in the tower.
- Round-Headed Double-Splayed Windows: arched heads, jambs and sills constructed with a mixture of rubble, flints and reused Roman tile-like bricks similar to the stonework in the adjoining walling. Plaster and rendering obscures some of construction details.
- Scaring on the east wall of the tower indicates the Roofline of the former Anglo-Saxon Chancel.
- Round-Headed Double-Belfry Openings: heads constructed with individual stones of

rubble, flints and reused Roman tile-like bricks placed on end and formed into a discernible arch; stepped imposts constructed with individual stones of rubble and reused Roman tile-like bricks placed horizontally - the imposts protrude from the faces of the walling and into the central void,; jambs, are constructed with rubble, flints and reused Roman tile-like bricks all laid horizontally; cylindrical mid-wall shafts each with rectangular bases and cushion-capitals; above mid-wall shafts through-stone slab placed horizontally so that it sides overhang the mid-wall-shaft – the slab supports junction of both arched heads above; sills provided by the top of the rubble stonework below.

- West and East Walls: Pairs of Circular Double-Splayed Sound Holes: constructed with rubble, flints and reused Roman tile-like bricks similar to the stonework in the adjoining walling.
- Internally. East Wall of Nave: Round-Headed Archway providing access to square central chamber - plaster now obscures many of the construction details: chamfered square imposts decorated with a horizontal band of diagonal crosses each contained within a rectangle. East face impost survives on north side only. Square jambs. West face only, incomplete hood-moulding.
- Internally, in the east wall of the square central chamber, is a round-headed chancel archway which provides access at ground floor level into the chancel – plaster now obscures many of the construction details: stepped imposts decorated with a horizontal band of cable-moulding; no evidence of the imposts survive on its east face. Below square jambs. West face only, two separate bands of hood-moulding – the outer band with small imposts and vestiges of half-round pilaster-strips below.
- Internally. First Floor, view from inside tower: Blocked Round-Headed Doorways providing access to nave and chancel. Voussoirs and jambs constructed of rubble walling with flints including some reused Roman brick and tile similar to the stonework in the adjoining walling.

74. GREAT PAXTON, Cambridgeshire – Holy Trinity Church.
NAVE:
- Random Rubble Walling.
- Internally. Arcade of Interlocking Megalithic Round-Headed Archways originally providing access into Anglo-Saxon north and south aisles – now demolished and replaced with existing aisles. Some construction details of the archways are now hidden by plaster: an "outer" arched head and an additional "inner" (set-back) arched head; two-stepped imposts; jambs comprising four large half-round cylindrical shafts separated from each other by centrally-placed smaller half-round cylindrical and triangular-shaped shafts; cylindrical shafts with capitals each comprising an integral lower moulded horizontal band which expands above into a larger bulbous shape; cylindrical shafts with bases each comprising four concentric rings increasing in size towards their base and separated from each other by a square block of protruding stonework; all supported by large square plinths.
- Additionally, the eastern arms of the eastern Archways have no shafts but instead have through-stone Escomb jambs.
- Above the Archways: Chamfered String-Course.

CLERESTORY - see Page 367: PHOTO 660. Great Paxton 13, showing the south wall of the clerestory with the incomplete round-headed double-splayed window arrowed red and the complete round-headed double-splayed windows arrowed black:
- Random Rubble Walling.
- Complete and Incomplete (Blocked) Round-Headed Double-Splayed Windows: arched heads constructed with stonework laid similarly to voussoirs; jambs and sill constructed with random rubble walling similar to the stonework in the adjoining walling.

- Part of Chamfered String-Course (not now visible from the ground).

CENTRAL CROSSING INTERNALLY:
- The former western archway has been removed and its position is now indicated by the uneven surface of the walling and the string-course ending just before the unevenness begins.
- Megalithic Round-Headed Archways providing access to the former North and South Transepts. The details of the construction of the arched heads are now hidden by plaster. The archways have rectangular imposts which protrude from all three faces of the walls including overhanging the central void between the opposing jambs. The jambs are constructed of through-stones laid in Escomb fashion and incorporate on their soffit-faces, vertical half-round shafts of alternating radii; four large half-round shafts alternating with three smaller half-round shafts. The larger half-round shafts have bulbous capitals and the smaller half-round shafts have capitals which are triangular-topped, tubular-shaped, and set-back to take account of their intervening position. Incomplete half-square pilaster-strips extend from the top of a two-stepped base to the level of the adjoining imposts supporting the arched heads. The base of each jamb also provide the base of the cylindrical shafts and the pilaster-strips. The whole of each archway stands on a single rectangular plinth protruding from the faces of the walls

PHOTO 660. Great Paxton 13.

Note: The Northern Archway is more complete and retains most of its original features. Both Archways have damage and the Southern Archway has had its arched head replaced in the 13th century and its jambs reduced in height to facilitate the replacement.
- Internally. Megalithic Round-Headed Chancel Archway with a 13th century arched head but with Anglo-Saxon through-stone jambs. These jambs incorporate piers which on their soffit-faces comprise vertical quarter-round cylindrical shafts alternating with smaller triangular-shaped shafts; these stand on three-stepped rounded bases increasing in size towards the bottom. The jambs, including their piers and soffit-shafts, are all supported by a single rectangular plinth. (There is some doubt about whether the imposts of the archway are Anglo-Saxon.)
- Former Roofline of north transept indicated by the current gable of the roof covering the eastern bay of the north aisle.

NORTH TRANSEPT:
- Random Rubble Walling.
- North Transept may occupy most of the footprint of the Anglo-Saxon North Transept.
- Externally in the north wall, between the middle and easternmost buttresses in what is now the north aisle, Anglo-Saxon random rubble walling may survive between 36 inches/91.4 centimetres and 38 inches/96.5 centimetres up from the ground, and protruding 3½ inches/8.2 centimetres from the face of the wall. These buttresses and the walling adjacent may also contain Anglo-Saxon walling up to 24 inches/60.9 centimetres up from the ground and protruding 3½ inches/8.2 centimetres from the face of the wall. (There are chamfered plinths extending along the ground and above the tops of the protruding stonework.)

75. GREAT URSWICK, Cumbria – St Michael's Church.
NAVE INTERNALLY:
- Part of Angular Cross-Shaft used as a grave-memorial to a named individual with designs and patterns including: flat-moulding, knot-work design, ring-twist design, roll-moulding; human figures; inhabited plant-scroll design with humans and creatures and possibly bird-like creatures. Runic inscriptions interpreted as "Tunwini put up this cross in memory of his lord Torhtred. Pray for his soul" and "Lyl made this".
- Fragment of Ring-Head Cross-Head and Angular Cross-Shaft with designs and patterns including: interlace design, free-ring design in a ring-knot design, roll-moulding, stepped-pattern design.

76. GREATHAM, County Durham – St John the Baptist Church.
CHANCEL INTERNALLY:
- Baluster-Shafts formerly the mid-wall shafts of double belfry-openings now reused to support altar.
- Fragment from another baluster-shaft.
- Part of an arm and part of the centre of a Cross-Head with roll-moulding.
- Part of an arm from a Ring-Head Cross-Head with roll-moulding and plait-work design.

77. HACKTHORN, Lincolnshire – St Michael's Church.
CHURCHYARD:
- Grave-Marker with cable-moulding providing a border for a free-arm cross.
- Two non-joining parts of a Grave-Cover with indications of cable-moulding on both parts enclosing parts of a panel. On one part there was an incomplete free-arm cross outlined with a band of cable-moulding. On the other part a distinctive fan-shaped, splayed, lower vertical arm from a free-arm cross outlined by a band of cable-moulding. Above, below, and adjacent to the sides of these arms of the cross were triquetra-knot designs, variations of interlace and square designs, and bird-like creatures. Both parts are very weathered and only limited indications of some of the designs can be identified.

78. HADSTOCK, Essex – St Botolph's Church. Cruciform Church.
NAVE:
- Coursed Rubble Walling with flints including flints, herringbone masonry, and reused Roman tile-like bricks.
- Single Square Plinth.
- Vestiges of Side Alternate Quoining.
- Round-Headed Double-Splayed Windows - one is blocked - arched heads, jambs and sills constructed with rubble similar to the stonework in the adjoining walling; they retain their mid-wall wooden frames. See adjacent: PHOTO 661. Hadstock 6, showing the interior of the blocked east window in the north wall.
- Restored Round-Headed (North) Doorway: through-stone voussoirs decorated with roll-moulding; three-quarter through-stone imposts decorated with palmette design, roll-moulding; through-stone jambs with angle-shafts with capitals decorated with palmette design and plain bases; sill; hood-moulding decorated with palmette design.

PHOTO 661. Hadstock 6.

SOUTH TRANSEPT:
- Coursed Rubble Walling.
- Restored Round-Headed Archway (original up to Imposts) with original Imposts divided

horizontally into two by an upper band decorated with a design similar to palmette design, and a lower band comprising a plain band of flat-moulding. Megalithic Jambs with the corners of each jamb comprising, additionally, recessed, free-standing cylindrical angle-shafts with capitals decorated with a design similar to palmette design; with plain, square, bases.

❖ Square-Stepped Double-Plinths which are separated from each other by a horizontal groove. Each is then divided into two halves by a further horizontal groove. Each of the upper halves subdivided by another horizontal groove above which the top quarter takes on a rounded shape. The double plinths are separated from the later, not Anglo-Saxon, plinths above by a horizontal groove, and separated from the adjacent stonework by a vertical groove. See adjacent: PHOTO 662. Hadstock 7, showing the double-plinth in the south transept with each of the grooves dividing each step into two arrowed red, and the grooves subdividing the upper halves into two arrowed black.

PHOTO 662. Hadstock 7.

NORTH TRANSEPT:
❖ Slight vestiges of Side Alternate Quoining.
❖ Later, not Anglo-Saxon, Archway has similar Square-Stepped Double-Plinths to those in the Archway in the South Transept with the lower two steps only of Anglo-Saxon origin.

79. HALTON, Lancashire – St Wilfrid's Church.
CHURCHYARD with reconstructed Cross-Head, Cross-Shaft and Cross-Base with original parts comprising:
✠ Upper vertical arm of Free-Arm Cross-Head with designs and patterns including: basket-plait design, cable-moulding, key-pattern design, knot-work design, pellets; design similar to a St Andrew's cross.
✠ Part of Angular Cross-Shaft. One part with square and arched headed, complete and incomplete, panels with designs and patterns including: cable-moulding, knot-work design, pellets, plant-scroll design, ring-twist design; incomplete single beast, entwined beasts upside down. The panels also contain: Christian scenes including on the west face: a scene with a seated angel with wings who holds a book – their legs are flanked by two squatting figures; a scene with a long-stemmed free-arm cross with a stepped base flanked on each side by a figure standing on a column with a cup-shaped capital. See adjacent left: PHOTO 663. Halton 2, showing the west face. See also adjacent right: PHOTO 664. Halton 3, showing left (west) face arrowed red, and right (south) side arrowed black.

PHOTO 663. Halton 2.   PHOTO 664. Halton 3.

The panels also contain scenes from Norse Mythology including: On the east face, Sigurd sucking his thumb after roasting the heart of the dragon Fafnir whose juices enabled him to understand the language of the birds in the tree above who told him the story of the cursed treasure and the intention of Reginn to kill Sigurd after Sigurd had killed the dragon Fafnir; Reginn the with his blacksmiths tools and raising a hammer working on a sword for Sigurd to kill the dragon Fafnir, also showing Reginn decapitated. On the north side, possibly a scene representing the horse Grani on which Sigurd carried away the treasure. See adjacent PHOTO 665 Smith. Halton 4, showing left (east) face arrowed red, and right (north) side arrowed black.

PHOTO 665. Halton 4.

- Another part of the same Angular Cross-Shaft identified above with incomplete panels with: cable-moulding, pellets, plant-scroll design; symbols of the Evangelists with haloed beast-headed, bird-headed and human half-figures probably each holding a book – some winged; incomplete, head and shoulders of other human figures.
- Fragment of the same Angular Cross-Shaft identified above with an incomplete panel with cable-moulding, pellets; part of probable half-figure.
- Three-Stepped Cross-Base, tapering bottom to top, with no surviving decoration.

TOWER INTERNALLY:
- Reconstructed parts of Angular Cross-Shafts with square and arched headed panels, complete and incomplete, with designs and patterns including: cable-moulding, bush-scroll design, pellets, interlace design, knot-work design, plant-scroll design, spiral-scroll design. Haloed, full and half figures, including Christ, probably seated, holding a book in his left hand and probably holding in his right hand a shaft in the form of a long-stemmed free-arm cross; a larger haloed figure, probably Christ, with a smaller figure in a tub; an angel holding an open book with a kneeling figure below; a group of three figures; incomplete heads and bodies of human figures; figure of an archer with a bird in a plant-scroll design above; a flock of probably sheep.
Note: how many of the parts and fragments identified above are from the same cross-shaft, and/or the reconstructed cross-shaft in the churchyard, is a matter of debate.

80. HARPSWELL, Lincolnshire – St Chad's Church.
SQUARE TOWER
- Coursed Rubble Walling.
- Face Alternate Quoining.
- Square String Course.
- First Stage. Flat-Headed Single-Splayed Window: head, jambs and sill constructed with rubble similar to the coursed stonework in the adjoining walling.
- Upper Stage. Three Round-Headed (one blocked) and one Flat-Headed Double-Belfry-Openings: arched heads cut out of a monolithic lintel/single rectangular monolith for flat-headed opening; no distinctive imposts; jambs constructed with a mixture of some larger facing stones laid roughly in side alternate fashion, and rubble, little different to the coursed rubble stonework in the adjoining walling; cylindrical mid-wall shafts without bases but with a horizontal band of roll-moulding below conical capitals whose shape is altered by the addition of a single, vertical, plant-like feature, on each of the corners; above each of the mid-wall shafts a through-stone slab placed horizontally so that it sides overhang the mid-wall-shaft – the slab supports the centre of the flat lintel in the flat-headed opening above and the junction of both arched heads in the round-headed openings above; sills provided by the top of the string-course below.

81. HARTLEPOOL, County Durham – St Hilda's Church.
   ST NICHOLAS CHAPEL INTERNALLY:
   - Recumbent, Flat-Headed, Name-Stone Grave-Marker: top face incised with a panel enclosing a free-arm cross with the symbols for "alpha" and "omega" and runes which together spell the feminine personal name "Hildithryth".

   BRUS CHAPEL INTERNALLY:
   - Grave-Markers in the form of plate-ring Cross-Heads.

82. HARTSHEAD, West Yorkshire – Walton Cross.
   - Cross-Base with a stepped base and socket for insertion of cross-shaft. Cross-Base with designs and patterns including: basket-plait design, cable-moulding, flat-moulding, free-ring design, interlace design, figure-of-eight ring-knot design, knot-work design, plait-work design, ring-twist design, roll-moulding. Inhabited bush-scroll design with birds. Inhabited scroll design with winged beasts.

83. HAUGHTON-LE-SKERNE, County Durham – St Andrew's Church.
   NAVE
   - Incomplete Angular Cross-Shafts with designs and patterns including: flat-moulding, grooved-moulding, knot-work design, pellet, plait-work design, ring-knot design. Rows of connected beasts.
   - Round-Headed Grave-Marker with flat-moulding enclosing a long-stemmed free-arm cross.
   - Possible fragment from Hogback Grave-Cover with stepped-pattern and plait-work designs.

   SOUTH PORCH
   - Part of a Cross-Head with an incoherent collection of strands.
   - Part of a Free-Arm Cross-Head.
   - Part of a Grave-Cover incised with the lower parts of the angled horizontal arms of a free-arm cross supported by part of its attached angular cross-shaft – it is displayed upside down. Part of a similar Grave-Cover with the lower parts of the (very) angled horizontal arms of a free-arm cross supported by part of its attached angular cross-shaft – it is displayed the correct way round.
   - Grave-Marker incised with free-arm cross.
   - Fragment of what may be from a Cross-Head or Cross-Shaft with grooved-mouldings enclosing what may be part of a linear design.

84. HAWKSWORTH, Nottinghamshire – St Mary and All Saints Church.
   TOWER INTERNALLY:
   - Most of a tapering Grave-Cover with designs and patterns including: bands of parallel cable-moulding placed to give a herringbone effect, grooved-moulding, combination of a free-ring design and a knot-work design, plait-work design enclosing a double-ended cross, plait-work design reminiscent of ring-knot design including triquetra-knot design and a "bull's head".

85. HEXHAM, Northumberland – Abbey (St Andrew's Church).
   NAVE INTERNALLY:
   - Damaged Impost with horizontal angled linear designs alternating with plain bands to create a herringbone pattern, representations of baluster-shafts placed vertically, horizontally – damaged.

- ❖ Impost with horizontal bands of flat-moulding providing the frame for bands of roll-moulding.
- ❖ Stonework at the top of the southern stairway and some of the stonework of an eastern passageway before reaching the south entrance/exit to the crypt - underneath a glass screen, now covered by carpet, south of the "Parclose Screen".
- ✠ Font Bowl – a reused base of a Roman pillar.
- ✠ Fragments forming an incomplete Holy Rood.
- ✠ Part of a Round-Headed Grave-Marker with a long-stemmed free-arm cross.
- ✠ Part of a Grave-Slab with an inscription including the letters "HIC".
- ✠ Eight fragments from a Panel representing a robed figure, possibly a Crucifixion Scene.

NAVE EXTERNALLY:
- ❖ West Wall - Vestiges of eight incomplete courses of coursed rubble stonework including reused Roman stonework.

NAVE AISLE INTERNALLY:
- ❖ Part of Impost or Frieze with representations of baluster-shafts placed vertically, and horizontally; flat-moulding.
- ❖ Part of a String-Course or Impost with flat-moulding framing an interlace design.
- ❖ Part of an Impost or Frieze with part of the body of a beast in movement; roll-moulding.
- ❖ Part of a String-Course or Impost with flat-moulding framing an interlace design.
- ✠ Fragment from a Frieze with a coiled serpent, flat-moulding.
- ✠ Fragment with incomplete horizontal and curving band of flat-moulding with three curling features.
- ✠ Part of probably a Free-Arm Cross-Head and part of a Vertical-Sided Cross-Shaft with designs and patterns including: flat-moulding, interlace design, roll-moulding, head of a creature.
- ✠ Part of a Grave-Marker with a free-arm cross with rosettes in each of the junctions of the arms.
- ✠ Grave-Cover reminiscent in shape of a hogback, but with no end bear-like beasts. Arcades in intersecting archways, circles, raised crosses, single pellets.
- ✠ Panel with a rosette surrounding an inner circle of tightly-packed petals; roll-moulding.
- ✠ Part of a Hogback Grave-Cover with plait-work design, roll-moulding; no end bear-like beasts survive.
- ❖ Architectural Fragment with horizontal bands of cable-moulding, chequer-board design, roll-moulding.

NAVE AISLE EXTERNALLY:
- ❖ Vestiges of between one and three incomplete courses of Coursed Rubble Stonework including reused Roman stonework; at and just above ground level.
- ❖ Fragments of a circular and a half-circular column.

CRYPT: INTERNALLY:
- ❖ Ashlar Walling including reused Roman stonework – some decorated, some with vestiges of plasterwork.
- ❖ Round-Headed Doorways: arched heads cut out of through-stone monolithic lintels or formed of three through-stones stones – an upper stone providing a quarter-circle supported on each side by a stone shaped to provide the lower curvature of the arched head; no imposts; through-stone jambs – west face of doorway in north passage has a Roman inscription to the god Maponus Apollo.
- ❖ Barrel-Vaulted Chambers.
- ❖ Triangular-Headed Chambers.
- ❖ Flat-Headed Passages.
- ❖ Lamp Niches.
- ❖ Ventilation Shaft.

- ❖ Stairs.

SOUTH TRANSEPT INTERNALLY:
- ✠ Reconstructed part of Free-Arm Cross-Head and part of its attached Angular Cross-Shaft known as "Acca's Cross" with designs and patterns including: pellets, plant-scroll, ring-knot design, roll-moulding, spiral-scroll design. Incomplete Inscriptions – letters difficult to identify.

CHANCEL INTERNALLY:
- ❖ Below Floor: St Peter's Church comprising: part of nave and apsidal chancel: Coursed Rubble Walling. Possible site of grave of St Acca.
- ❖ Bishop's Chair known as "Frith Stool" with linear, triquetra-knots and ring-twist designs.

NORTH AISLE INTERNALLY:
- ❖ Most of a Round-Headed Grave-Cover with a long-stemmed free-arm cross which expands and flattens towards its base; also with an incomplete band of roll-moulding.
- ❖ A complete Flat-Headed Grave-Cover incised with a free-arm cross-head, cross-shaft and cross-base.

VISITOR CENTRE INTERNALLY:
- ✠ Part of an Angular Cross-Shaft known as the "Spital Cross" with designs and patterns including: plant-scroll design, roll-moulding. Crucifixion Scene - the cup/sponge-bearer Stephaton and the spear-bearer Longinus. Possible Inscriptions. See adjacent: PHOTO 666. Hexham 18, showing plant-scroll design on one face and one side.
- ✠ Part of probably a Free-Arm Cross-Head and part of a Vertical-Sided Cross-Shaft with designs and patterns including: flat-moulding, plait-work design, roll-moulding, creatures.
- ✠ Part of an arm from probably a Free-Arm Cross-Head with only roll-moulding.
- ✠ Part of a Free-Arm Cross-Head and part of its supporting Vertical-Sided Cross-Shaft with designs and patterns including: flat-moulding, knot-work design, roll-moulding.
- ✠ Part of a Cross-Base with designs and patterns including: interlace design, plant-scroll design, roll-moulding.
- ✠ Part of a Round-Headed Grave-Marker with a free-arm cross with fan-shaped arms within an incised circle and an inscription spanning each of the arms thought to represent the name "Tondwine".
- ✠ Fragment from a Frieze with part of a fish-like creature.
- ✠ Fragment from a Panel with designs and patterns including: flat-moulding, roll-moulding, vine-scroll design, legs and an arm from two different human figures, bird, head of a goat.
- ✠ Part of a Frieze with an incomplete running beast below a horizontal band of flat-moulding.
- ❖ Part of Impost or Frieze with representations of vertically placed baluster-shafts; flat-moulding.
- ❖ Part of an Impost with an incomplete running beast within an incomplete frame of flat-moulding.
- ❖ Part of an Impost with flat-moulding, row of interlinked diamond-shaped loops, single similar loop.
- ❖ Part of the Base of possibly an archway with alternating horizontal bands of pellet-moulding, roll-moulding, cable-moulding.

PHOTO 666. Hexham 18.

86. HEYSHAM, Lancashire – St Peter's Church.

NAVE:
- Coursed Rubble Walling.
- Face Alternate Quoining.
- West Wall: Blocked Round-Headed Doorway: half-through-stone lintels fashioned to form a semi-circular shape (some damage); no imposts; large through-stone jambs. Doorway probably had a rebate for a door.
- Blocked, incomplete, Flat-Headed Doorway, possibly Anglo-Saxon. It may have led to first floor of former Annex or porticus.

CHANCEL INTERNALLY:
- Chancel Archway with possibly reused Anglo-Saxon imposts decorated with cable-moulding.

SOUTH AISLE INTERNALLY:
- Possible plinth with cable-moulding; its exact purpose is uncertain.
- Complete Hogback Grave-Cover with end bear-like beasts and designs and patterns including: cable-moulding, ring-twist design, tegulations, possible representations of tree trunks, a design reminiscent of a series of square versions of the number "2". Scenes with humans, beasts, birds, a snake's head or large fish most probably from Norse Mythology involving Sigurd or Ragnarök. Alternatively, the scenes could be Christian representing "Adam naming the beasts" or the "Tree of Life".

SOUTH PORCH EXTERNALLY
- Fragment from a cross-shaft with plant-scroll design running horizontally; reused as a quoin stone.

CHURCHYARD:
- Reconstructed (1864) Coursed Rubble Walling including Round-Headed Doorway: three parallel lintels each form about a third of the depth of the arched head; they have been fashioned to form semi-circular shapes both in their upper and lower borders. With through-stone imposts and through-stone Escomb jambs rebated for a door. See adjacent: PHOTO 667. Heysham 2, showing the north-east face.

PHOTO 667. Heysham 2.

- Part of Angular Cross-Shaft with designs and patterns including: cable-moulding, knot-work design, plait-work design, plant-scroll design, roll-moulding. On the south face, under a round-headed archway, a seated haloed figure, possibly Christ in Glory, giving a blessing with their right hand and holding a book in their left hand. On the north face a gabled structure - probably a mausoleum - with long-stemmed free-arm crosses extending from each side of the gable roof. In the body of the building below, a large central doorway or archway containing a half-figure – possibly in profile to the left - swathed in fabric, with above, three round-headed windows in which there is a human head with neck in portrait. On each side of the central doorway or archway are two, narrow, round-headed niches, one above the other, which contain standing human figures facing inwards – some imagination will be required. See adjacent PHOTO 668. Heysham 3, showing right-hand (north) face arrowed red, and left-hand (east) face arrowed black.
- Grave-Cover with a band of roll-moulding providing a frame enclosing a long-stemmed Hammer-Head Cross-Head with a

PHOTO 668. Heysham 3.

free-arm cross in the centre of its head.
- ✠ Damaged three-stepped Cross-Base with indications of socket for insertion of cross-shaft (no decoration survives).

87. HICKLING, Nottinghamshire – St Luke's Church.
NAVE INTERNALLY:
- ✠ A combination of a Hogback and Coped Grave-Cover; stylistically unique – it is almost complete. Designs and patterns including: beaded-moulding, flat-moulding, free-arm crosses, pellets; affronted beasts; inhabited interlace and knot-work designs including triquetra-knot design, free-rings, some designs with loosely entangled beasts and one design with a strand indicating head of a serpent or bird-like creature; plait-work design with one strand indicating head of a serpent or bird-like creature. At each end of the top ridge is an inward-looking head of a strange bear-like beast, with a head, shoulders and angled arms ending in claws.

88. HOLY ISLAND (LINDISFARNE), Northumberland – The Priory Museum (English Heritage).
- ✠ Fragments from arms of Free-Arm Cross-Heads with flat-moulding, interlace design and roll-moulding.
- ✠ Incomplete Angular and Vertically-Sided Cross-Shafts with designs and patterns including: flat-moulding, interlace design, linear design, plait-work design, ring-knot design, roll-moulding, creatures and beasts, birds, human figures. Seated Christ which could be a Crucifixion Scene or perhaps a Day of Judgement Scene with the attendant figures possibly blowing trumpets and holding books or scrolls.
- ✠ Most of Round-Headed Grave-Marker known as "The Viking Raiders Stone" – it may commemorate the attack on Lindisfarne in 793 AD or a similar attack at a later date. One face is decorated with a scene which may represent the Day of Judgement: a Free-Arm Cross around which are representations the sun and moon, two "human" hands, two human figures who may be praying. The other face is decorated with a scene said to represent a Viking raid: a procession of warriors carrying axes and swords above their heads. There is a band of flat-moulding around the edges of both faces.
- ✠ Parts of, and almost complete, Recumbent, Round-Headed, Name-Stone Grave-Markers: incised with panels enclosing a free-arm cross. Some examples have triquetra-knot design, one example has interlace design, plait-work design, ring-twist design in the enclosing border. Examples have inscriptions in Latin characters, Anglo-Saxon capitals, and runes. Some inscriptions are so incomplete it is not now possible to identify the personal name represented. Those that can be interpreted to read include the feminine personal name "Osgyth" and the masculine personal names: "Aedberecht"; possibly "Beanna"; possibly "Ethelhard".
- ✠ Part of a Grave-Cover with a Free-Arm Cross in relief with flat-moulding, free-ring designs and knot-work design.

89. HOPE, Derbyshire – St Peter's Church.
CHURCHYARD:
- ✠ Two parts of an Angular Cross-Shaft known now cemented together with designs and patterns including: flat-moulding which has been adapted to form protruding interlinking arches on each side of the cross-shaft (below the cemented join); interlace design, knot-work design, pellets, plait-work design, plant-scroll design, ring-chain design, roll-moulding. Indistinct and weathered: West Face: human figure – possibly a warrior; two

standing figures with a band of roll-moulding around their heads extending diagonally across their bodies and terminating in indistinct objects; East Face: two confronting, standing, human figures each grasping a central staff in the form of a long-stemmed free-arm cross. See adjacent: PHOTO 669. Hope 2, showing the west face arrowed red and the south side arrowed black.

PHOTO 669.
Hope 2.

90. HOUGH-ON-THE-HILL, Lincolnshire - All Saints Church.
STAIR TURRET:
- Coursed Rubble Walling.
- Flat-Headed, Single-Splayed Windows – four in south face, three in west face and three in north face: Externally, faces comprise a single stone slab (the window frame) through which the differently-shaped apertures have been cut; three round-headed, two circular, one pentangle, and one diamond-shaped. Some with Moulding reflecting the external shape of the aperture - cable-moulding, flat-moulding, roll-moulding. Some have an accompanying, but separate, single stone sill or single stone lintel. Internally windows are mostly flat-headed – the lowest window in the south wall, and the two lower windows in the west wall, are round-headed with the arched heads cut of a three-quarter-through-stone lintels. Jambs mostly three-quarter through-stones occasionally replaced with two stones. Sills are flat-three-quarter through-stones apart from the lowest window in the south wall with the face of the sill shaped so that the window has internally an overall circular appearance. The lowest window in the west wall has a wooden frame for glass.
- Stone Spiral Stairway with forty-five roughly-dressed stone steps of Anglo-Saxon origin – some have been partially restored at a later, not Anglo-Saxon, date. These steps are formed separately from the newel in the distinct Anglo-Saxon fashion. Newel comprising a thick continuous cylindrical column of rubble. Underside of the treads of the steps have no support underneath and simply rest on the step below.

SQUARE TOWER - built up against and on top of the west wall of the Nave:
- Coursed Rubble Walling.
- Vestiges of Square Double Plinth.
- Face Alternate and Side Alternate Quoining.
- Square String-Courses.
- First Floor. Round-Headed Single-Splayed Windows: arched heads constructed with a single, shaped through-stone. The lowest stone in each jamb is a square with a large vertical stone on top, above there are another three stones (where the absence of plaster enables their identification) similar in shape but reducing in size to accommodate the curvature of the single stone shaped to form the arched heads. The square string-courses provide the sills for these windows externally/faced with coursed rubble stonework internally. Lower window in north wall retains its Anglo-Saxon characteristics internally – a single shaped stone forms its arched head - but externally it has been altered at later, not Anglo-Saxon, date.
- Second Floor. Flat-Headed Single-Splayed Windows: Externally, the windows are faced with a monolithic lintel; each jamb comprises a square stone with a larger, rectangular, vertical, stone above – the jambs narrow towards the top; monolithic sills. Internally, two flat stones form the lintels; three-quarter-through-stones jambs; three-quarter-through-stone sills.
- Internally Ground Floor. Round-Headed Doorway into nave altered at a later, not Anglo-Saxon, date.

- Internally Ground Floor. Megalithic Flat-Headed Doorway into stair turret: two large half-through-stone lintels – the west higher than the east to allow for the rising of the three steps from the tower into the stair turret; through-stone imposts protruding into the void between the jambs only; through-stone jambs laid in discernible courses.
- Internally First Floor. Megalithic Flat-Headed Doorway plaster obscures construction details: two large half-through-stone lintels – the west higher than the east to allow for three steps descending from the stair turret into ringing chamber of tower; through-stone imposts protruding into the void between the jambs only; through-stone jambs similar to those laid in Escomb fashion; jambs only rebated for door.
- Internally Second Floor: Megalithic Triangular-Headed Doorway into tower: two pairs of angled rectangular stones forming the head; through-stone imposts; through-stone Escomb Jambs; single shallow-stepped sill of one large flat stone.
- Internally Second Floor: Blocked Triangular-Headed Doorway opening into the nave: two pairs of angled rectangular stones forming the head; imposts and jambs laid in similar courses to the adjoining walling; plaster obscures the construction details.
- Internally above Second Floor. Faint indications of scaring on east face of east wall indicates Roofline of former Nave - above the blocked Triangular-Headed Doorway, view from nave.

NAVE:
- Coursed Rubble Walling.
- Incomplete Long and Short Quoining.
- Slight vestiges of Square Double Plinth.

VESTRY:
- Internally, incomplete – four pieces now joined together - Architectural Frieze/String-Course with designs and patterns including: representations of baluster-shafts, cable-moulding, interlace design, roll-moulding; possibly part of the rear body, leg and tail of a beast.

NORTH AISLE:
- Externally: Grave-Cover incised with, small, free-arm cross.

91. HOUGHAM, Lincolnshire – All Saints Church.
SOUTH AISLE INTERNALLY:
- Part of a Grave-Cover reused as a lintel with designs and patterns including: cable-moulding, knot-work design, free-ring design, jumbled scroll design; plait-work design including bull's head with a noseband with zigzag-design.

92. HOVINGHAM, North Yorkshire – All Saints Church.
SQUARE TOWER:
- Coursed Stone Walling including Herringbone Masonry.
- Megalithic Side Alternate Quoining (including part or all of window or doorway heads reused as quoins not necessarily placed the correct way round – two in south-west quoining, one in north-west quoining and one in the fabric of the wall next to the north-west quoining).
- Megalithic Round-Headed Doorway. Arched head formed with four concentric bands of stonework: the lowest band is recessed, the band above comprises roll-moulding, the next band above is slightly inset and includes a distinct lower "hollow", and the top band is level with the face of the wall. Half-chamfered rectangular imposts which do not project from the faces of the walls but do project into the central void between the jambs. Through-stone jambs with external recesses to accommodate cylindrical angle-

shafts with narrow, angled, capitals, and with no bases.
- Square String-Courses separating each of the upper set-back two stages of the tower.
- Round-Headed Double-Splayed Window: arched head and jambs constructed mostly of rubble similar to stonework in the adjoining walling - with facing stones; a single narrow stone provides the sill.
- Flat-Headed Windows not splayed in north and west walls constructed of rubble similar to stonework in the adjoining walling - with facing stones. These narrow windows near the top of the second stage have their heads provided by the string-course separating the second stage from the third stage.
- Round-Headed Double-Belfry Openings: arched heads each constructed with differently sized stones and formed into a discernible arch – they are not voussoirs; chamfered through-stone imposts protruding from the faces of the walling and into the central void; half-through-stone jambs larger than the stones in the adjoining stonework but not constructed to a particular design; square mid-wall shafts which are curved externally; above mid-wall shafts through-stone slab placed horizontally so that it sides overhang the mid-wall-shaft – the slab supports junction of both arched heads above; sills provided by a narrow stone.
- Externally, Free-Arm Cross-Head protruding from the external face of the west wall.
- Externally, Plate-Ring Cross-Head and part of its Angular Cross-Shaft above the external face of the double belfry-opening in the south wall. Decorated with designs and patterns including: flat-moulding, interlace design, knot-work design, roll-moulding; birds; humans. See adjacent: PHOTO 670. Hovingham 1, with plate-ring cross-head and angular cross-shaft arrowed red.
- Internally. Megalithic Round-Headed Tower Archway: voussoirs; chamfered imposts; square jambs.
- Internally. First Floor: Megalithic Flat-Headed Doorway: single lintel; no imposts; Escomb jambs.

PHOTO 670. Hovingham 1.

NAVE:
- Coursed Stone Walling.
- Megalithic Side Alternate Quoining – only the west face of north-west quoining can now be identified.
- Internally: Shrine, reused as reredos, with architectural features including arcade of round-headed interlocking archways with shared capitals, columns and bases. Designs and patterns including: flat-moulding, inhabited plant-scroll design with birds and a beast. Weathered and damaged scenes depicting under an Arcade: The Annunciation, The Visitation, The Circumcision of St John the Baptist or the Presentation at the Temple, Part of a Nativity Scene including Joseph, haloed winged Angels (one facing inwards at each end). See adjacent: PHOTO 671. Hovingham 2.

PHOTO 671. Hovingham 2.

CHANCEL:

✠ Internally: Free-Arm Cross-Head and the top, angular part, of a Cross-Shaft with vestiges of a swag indicating a circular lower part below where the cross-shaft is now broken. Cross-Head and Cross-Shaft are decorated with designs and patterns including: flat-moulding, interlace design, knot-work design; creatures and beasts. See adjacent: PHOTO 672. Hovingham 3, showing the west face.

93. HOWE, Norfolk - St Mary's Church.
ROUND TOWER: See below right: PHOTO 673. Howe 2.
❖ Random Rubble Walling with Flints and occasionally reused Roman tile-like bricks.
❖ Round-Headed Double-Splayed Windows: arched heads, jambs and sills constructed with rubble, flints and reused Roman tile-like bricks similar to stonework in the adjoining walling.
❖ Circular Double-Splayed Windows: constructed with rubble, flints and reused Roman tile-like bricks similar to the stonework in the adjoining walling.
❖ Blocked Round-Headed Doorway formed of rubble similar to the stonework in the adjoining walling - now with modern window inserted.
❖ Internally. Round-Headed Tower Archway: construction details mostly hidden by plaster but with stepped imposts; square jambs.
❖ Internally. Blocked Flat-Headed Doorway formerly providing access to upper floor. Plaster obscures most of its construction details it does have moulded imposts.

NAVE:
❖ Random Rubble Walling with Flints.
❖ Rubble Quoining of Flints, Bricks and Stone.
❖ Double-Splayed Round-Headed Window: arched head, jambs and sill constructed with rubble, flints and reused Roman tile-like bricks similar to the stonework in the adjoining walling; slight indications of vestiges of other similar windows.

PHOTO 672. Hovingham 3.

PHOTO 673. Howe 2.

94. ILKLEY, West Yorkshire – All Saints Church.
TOWER INTERNALLY:
❖ Roman Altars re-used as Lintel Window-Heads.
✠ Two arms from a Free-Arm Cross-Head now reconstructed and placed on top of Angular Cross-Shaft identified in next bullet point. Decorated with flat-moulding, roll-moulding; inhabited plant-scroll design with birds; possible winged figure with halo representing the symbol of St Matthew the Evangelist.
✠ Almost complete, but weathered, Angular Cross-Shaft with designs and patterns including: possible baluster-shaft moulding, flat-moulding, plant-scroll design, roll-moulding, spiral-scroll design; beasts, inhabited scroll or interlace design with a beast, inhabited knot-work design with two confronted beasts. Haloed, seated, figure giving a blessing with his raised right hand is probably Christ in Majesty. Haloed half or three-quarter size figures of the Evangelists with their heads provided by their representative symbols: eagle - St John, bull – St Luke, lion - St Mark, a human-like head – St Matthew.
✠ Incomplete, weathered and damaged, Angular Cross-Shaft with designs and patterns

including: cable-moulding, flat-moulding, pellets, plant-scroll design; inhabited scroll or interlace design with a beast in one panel and an incomplete bird in another panel; inhabited bush-scroll design with birds facing each other; affronted beasts, two addorsed, winged, beasts; two figures facing each other – whether they are human or beasts is now uncertain.
- Incomplete, weathered, Angular Cross-Shaft with designs and patterns including: interlace design, pellets, mixture of inhabited interlace and knot-work designs including beasts; three-quarter size figure, possibly haloed.

95. IRTON, Cumbria – St Paul's Church.
- Cross comprising Free-Arm Cross-Head, Angular Cross-Shaft and Cross-Base: Free-Arm Cross-Head and Angular Cross-Shaft with designs and patterns including: cable-moulding, chequer-board design, interlace design, key-pattern design, pellets, plant-scroll design, ring-chain design, ring-knot design, ring-twist design, roll-moulding, spiral-scroll design, triquetra-knot design; inscription now illegible; faint traces of possible beasts and humans on cross-head. No decoration survives on Cross-Base.

96. JARROW, County Durham – Jarrow Hall, Bede Museum - internally.
- Possibly parts from the same Cross-Head with flat-moulding, roll-moulding, representations of baluster-shafts, zigzag-design.
- Part of Cross-Shaft with roll-moulding.
- Parts of Friezes with representations of vertical rows of baluster-shafts, flat-moulding, roll-moulding.
- Parts of an ornamental Panel with cable-moulding, roll-moulding, petals of a leaf and a pellet.
- Part of Grave-Marker with flat-moulding and incised with parts of free-arm crosses and a small free-arm cross enclosed within a circle. One an inscription "DIV" and separately the letter "R".
- Baluster-Shafts.
- Building stone with the inscription "Helmgyt", probably a personal name.
- Reconstruction of an eight-sided Reading Desk with some original sections of stonework. Decorated with roll-moulding, plant designs, extended figure-of-eight interlace and ring-twist designs – the base is not decorated but does have square sockets which may have been a lifting aid during its construction and placement.

97. JARROW, County Durham - St Paul's Church.
NAVE INTERNALLY:
- Foundations from north wall of former monastic church.
- Dedication Stone above what is described as the "chancel arch". Latin inscription interpreted as "The dedication of the basilica of St Paul on the 9th day before the Kalends of May in the 15th year of King Ecgfrith; and in the 4th (year) of abbot Ceolfrith, founder, by the guidance of God, of the same church."

NORTH AISLE INTERNALLY:
- Incomplete Angular Cross-Shafts decorated with designs and patterns including: flat-moulding, interlace design, plait-work design, plant-scroll design, roll-moulding. Inhabited plant-scroll design with creatures and beasts.
- Incomplete Grave-Cover known as the "Jarrow Cross". Now in two pieces and with cable-moulding, roll-moulding, and a Latin inscription interpreted as "In this unique sign life is returned to the world".
- Baluster-Shafts with sets of narrow and wide grooves alternating with plain bands of stonework.

- Incomplete Friezes decorated with both designs and patterns including: representations of baluster-shafts, flat-moulding, roll-moulding. Inhabited plant-scroll design with the figure of a hunter, the head of a woman, and an incomplete beast. Inhabited tree-scroll design with birds known as "The Tree of Life".
- Part of what may have been a Lamp with part of an incomplete Inscription.

CENTRAL OBLONG-SHAPED TOWER incorporating earlier Porch; linking former monastic church, replaced by current nave, to former separate chapel, current chancel.
- Coursed Stone Walling.
- Side Alternate Quoining.
- Ground Floor. Round-Headed Doorways blocked and restored: voussoirs; no imposts; restored jambs including some megalithic stonework.
- First Floor: Megalithic Round-Headed Double-Splayed Windows: voussoirs; large stones forming jambs. South wall window now a doorway. North wall window has hood-moulding and decoration suggesting Saxo-Norman work.
- First Floor: Blocked Round-Headed Doorway giving access between tower and western gallery in chancel: voussoirs; no imposts; megalithic jambs.
- Second Floor – Saxo-Norman Megalithic Triangular-Headed Doorway: head formed with two monolithic through-stones placed to form a triangle with square imposts providing their bases; jambs constructed of coursed stones similar to the stonework in the adjoining walling.
- Second Floor – Saxo-Norman Round-Headed Double-Belfry Openings: voussoirs some through-stones; square imposts protruding into the central void only; jambs, including megalithic stonework, laid in side alternate fashion; cylindrical mid-wall shafts with rounded bases and no capitals; above mid-wall shafts through-stone slab placed horizontally so that it sides overhang the mid-wall-shaft – the slab supports junction of both arched heads above; sills provided by rectangular stones laid in a horizontal row on the top of the coursed stonework below.
- Scaring on east wall indicates earlier Roofline of chancel.

CHANCEL – formerly a chapel separate from former monastic church:
- Coursed Stone Walling.
- Square Single Plinth.
- Megalithic Side Alternate Quoining.
- South Wall Ground Floor: Vestiges of Megalithic Doorway. Internally Round-Headed: single stone shaped to form part of the lower western arm of the arched head. Externally Flat-Headed: most of the western jamb laid in an irregular fashion.
- South Wall: Round-Headed Single-Splayed Windows: arched heads constructed with a single, shaped, through-stone; each jamb comprises one rectangular vertical through-stone supporting one rectangular horizontal through-stone above; sills comprise a single through-stone. Additionally, middle and east windows, single stone slab inserted into the frame provided by the external faces of the arched head, jambs and sill – slab in middle window has a circular opening, eastern window has an opening similar in shape to the head, jambs and sill of the window itself.
- South Wall First Floor: Blocked Round-Headed Doorway which may have given external access to western gallery in former chapel now chancel: Vestiges only surviving:
Internally: two voussoirs from the eastern arm of arched head; with below an impost and one large vertical stone from the jamb.
Externally: one weathered, angular, voussoir separated from one vertical stone from the jamb, by a stone not part of its original impost.
- North Wall Ground Floor. Blocked Megalithic Round-Headed Doorway: voussoirs with,

unusually, a distinct single key-stone which appears to include at the top part of a Roman lewis-hole or cramp-hole; differently sized imposts; a single, megalithic, vertical stone forming most of each jamb.
- Internally West Wall: East Face of Round-Headed Archway: voussoirs - long and roughly-faced in the centre – these may be Anglo-Saxon; other voussoirs below are of a regular size and dressed and of a later date.
- Internally West Wall of Chancel, East Face, First Floor: Blocked Round-Headed Doorway giving access between tower and possible western gallery in chancel: voussoirs only surviving. It can be identified directly below the centre of the horizontal wooden frame that supports the current roof.
- Internally north-west corner: tower construction may explain damaged face of stonework adjacent to current west wall which formerly provided part of the northern end of the west wall of the separate chapel (now the chancel).

MONASTERY BUILDINGS EXTERNALLY – possible Saxo-Norman workmanship surviving:
- Coursed Stone Walling.
- Flat-Headed Doorway with monolithic lintel, imposts and jambs constructed of coursed stones similar to the stonework in the adjoining walling. On the east face, above the flat-headed monolithic lintel, there is a round-head comprising two rows of voussoirs – the inner row set-back - supported by narrow rectangular imposts. Additionally, on the east face, the jambs contain recessed free-standing cylindrical angle-shafts each separated from their bases and capitals by a horizontal band of roll-moulding. Their capitals are square-shaped and angled to meet the imposts above, whilst their round expanding bases each stand on two horizontal stones which form part of the coursed stonework in the adjoining walling.
- Saxo-Norman Megalithic Triangular-Headed Doorway: head formed with two monolithic through-stones placed to form a triangle – the rest of the doorway appears of Norman construction with imposts and jambs constructed of coursed stones similar to the stonework in the adjoining walling.

98. JEDBURGH, Borders – Abbey, Visitor Centre.
- Parts of Free-Arm Cross-Heads and Angular Cross-Shafts with designs and patterns including: flat-moulding, interlace design including looping interlace design, key-pattern design, knot-work design, pellets, ring-knot design, roll-moulding.
- Parts of an Angular Cross-Shaft later reused as building stone with designs and patterns including: cable-moulding, flat-moulding, interlace design, roll-moulding; inhabited plant-scroll design with creatures. Two incomplete confronting human figures who may represent Adam and Eve; an incomplete similar human figure;
- Damaged Panel decorated in relief with a band of flat-moulding forming a panel containing Christ in Majesty. Above the top of the panel a horizontal row of human heads in portrait; also standing human figures one above the other.
- Part and two fragments of a Shrine possibly for St Boisil, Abbot of Melrose, who died AD 661. With designs and patterns including: flat-moulding, interlace design, knot-work design; inhabited plant-scroll design with creatures and

PHOTO 674. Jedburgh.

birds. See Page 382 bottom right: PHOTO 674. Jedburgh.

99. KIRKBY STEPHEN, Cumbria – St John's Church.

- Part of what may be a Reading Desk: with designs and patterns including: knot-work design, plait-work design, roll-moulding, spiral-scroll design including pellets or buds.
- Part of an Angular Cross-Shaft known as the "Bound Devil Stone" or "Loki Stone" with flat-moulding, plait-work design, ring-twist. Bound figure with large scrolls, inverted horns, emerging from the side of the head, also with large hands, circular strap-like band, bracelet-like features, and pellets.
- Parts of Free-Arm Cross-Head, Ring-Head Cross-Head, Plate-Ring Cross-Head with central bosses and with designs and patterns including: interlace design, parallel mouldings forming the shape of a free-arm cross with the moulding surrounding a pellet at the end of each arm; pellets, roll-moulding.
- Part of an Angular Cross-Shaft with vestiges of the lower arm of its attached Ring-Head Cross-Head with designs and patterns including: interlace design, plait-work design, roll-moulding, scroll design; beasts.
- Parts of Angular Cross-Shafts with designs and patterns including: free-ring designs, knot-work design, plant-scroll design including rosettes and pellets, stepped-pattern design.
- Part of Hogback Grave-Cover with roll-moulding, tegulations.

100. KIRKBY WHARFE, North Yorkshire – St John's Church.

- Possible Anglo-Saxon Font - no decoration.
- Part of a Free-Arm Cross-Head and part of its associated Angular Cross-Shaft with designs and patterns including: basket-plait design, flat-moulding, knot-work design, linear design, meander-pattern design, pellets, plait-work design, plant design, stepped-pattern design. One male, one female, haloed human figures – presumed to represent Mary and John at the Crucifixion – holding on to the long lower vertical arm of the free-arm cross with bush-like characteristics which separates them.
- Part of a Free-Arm Cross-Head with designs and patterns including: flat-moulding, knot-work design, pellets, plant-scroll design.
- Part of an Angular Cross-Shaft with designs and patterns including: basket-plait design, cable-moulding, meander-pattern design, pellets, plant-scroll design, possible stepped-pattern design.

101. KIRKDALE, North Yorkshire – St Gregory's Minster.
NAVE:
- Coursed Stone Walling.
- Megalithic Side Alternate Quoining.
- Restored Megalithic Round-Headed Doorway: voussoirs – west face has two rows, the inner set-back, east face one row; thin, square, through-stone imposts which do not protrude from the faces of the walls but do protrude into the central void between the jambs; jambs, some through-stone Escomb stonework, with additionally, on the west face, recesses containing cylindrical shaped angle-shafts. These angle-shafts have square, chamfered, capitals comprising a horizontal band of roll-moulding at the bottom with alternating triangular-shaped moulding above extending up to a square-shaped top, and, square, chamfered, bases with an upper conical half, tapering and expanding,

PHOTO 675. Kirkdale 5.

towards the lower, expanding, square half. The jambs and angle-shafts all stand on a protruding square plinth on the west face, but the plinth does not protrude from the east face. See Page 383 bottom right: PHOTO 675. Kirkdale 5, showing the east face.
- ❖ Chancel Archway: arched head and imposts 13th century. Anglo-Saxon square jambs: west face recesses containing cylindrical shaped angle-shafts with capitals square at top, with a larger, rounded, lower section tapering to fit on top of the cylindrical angle-shaft; and with bases with a tapering and expanding circular collar divided into two by a ridge with a tapering and expanding four-stepped square bottom below. Bases stand on two-stepped plinths whose lower halves protrude from the west face of the walls.

NAVE SOUTH WALL – NOW WITHIN SOUTH PORCH:
- ✠ Sundial with inscriptions divided into three panels by flat-moulding. Sundial divided into eight segments by lines radiating from the hole for the missing gnomon; alternate lines have an addition of a line to create a free-arm cross. Central panel contains sundial with above: inscription interpreted to read "This is the day's sun-marker at every hour", and below: inscription interpreted to read "And Hawarth made me and Brand the priest". The panels on each side of the sundial contain the main inscription interpreted to read: "Orm, the son of Gamel, bought St Gregory's church when it was utterly ruined and collapsed and he had it rebuilt from the foundations in honour of Christ and St Gregory in the days of King Edward the king and in the days of Earl Tosti". Incised free-arm crosses act as prefixes and suffixes to each inscription – apart from the inscription relating to Hawarth and Brand.

NAVE INTERNALLY - UNDER NORTH ARCADE:
- ✠ Grave-Cover with designs and patterns including: flat-moulding, long-stemmed free-arm cross with damaged cross-base, spiral scroll variation of plant-scroll design.
- ✠ Grave-Cover in two pieces with chevron-pattern moulding changing to a meander-pattern design, flat-moulding, mixture of interlace design including free-ring designs, pellets, ring-knot design.

NAVE SOUTH WALL EXTERNALLY:
- ✠ Incomplete Free-Arm and Angular Cross-Shaft with: fillers, flat-moulding, pellets, s-shaped addorsed serpents. Crucifixion Scene.
- ✠ Incomplete Hammer-Head Cross-Head and Angular Cross-Shaft with no decoration surviving.

NORTH AISLE INTERNALLY:
- ✠ Part of Cross-Head and Cross-Shaft with knot-work design.
- ✠ Part of Free-Arm Cross-Head with incised free-arm cross, spiral-scroll design; defaced human head and shoulder.
- ✠ Fragment of Cross-Shaft with flat-moulding, knot-work design, spiral-scroll design, stopped plait-work design; incomplete beast.

WEST WALL OF CHURCH EXTERNALLY:
- ✠ Part of Free-Arm Cross-Head and Angular Cross-Shaft with flat-moulding, spiral-scroll design, stopped plait-work design.

EAST WALL OF CHANCEL EXTERNALLY:
- ✠ Part a Hogback Grave-Cover with pellets, plait-work design and spiral-scroll design.

102.   KIRK HAMMERTON, North Yorkshire – St John the Baptist Church.
SQUARE TOWER:
- ❖ Coursed Stone Walling.
- ❖ Square Double Plinth.
- ❖ Megalithic Side Alternate Quoining.
- ❖ Round-Headed Doorway: two adjacent rows of through-stone voussoirs – inner row set-back; imposts – protruding west face; jambs including megalithic stonework –

additionally, on the west face, jambs recessed and contain free-standing cylindrical angle-shafts with differently-shaped capitals and no bases.
- Flat-Headed Megalithic Single-Splayed Windows – first and second floors; through-stone monolithic lintels, through-stone monolithic jambs, and through-stone monolithic sills.
- Square String-Course providing sill for Round-Headed Double-Belfry Openings above.
- Round-Headed through-stone Double-Belfry Openings: arched heads each cut out of a monolithic lintel; through-stone imposts protruding from the faces of the walling and into the central void; through-stone jambs laid in similar fashion to side alternate quoining; with cylindrical mid-wall shafts with splayed, rounded, bases and no capitals; above mid-wall shafts through-stone slab placed horizontally so that it sides overhang the mid-wall-shaft – the slab supports junction of both arched heads above; sill provided by the top of the string-course below.
- Internally. Megalithic Round-Headed Tower Archway: voussoirs; no imposts; through-stone square jambs.

NAVE:
- Coursed Stone Walling.
- Square Single Plinth.
- Megalithic Side Alternate Quoining.
- Restored Round-Headed Doorway: voussoirs; protruding imposts; jambs including megalithic stonework; strip-work and hood-moulding - not concentric with voussoirs and separated from voussoirs by other stonework.
- Blocked Round-Headed Doorway: voussoirs mostly missing; impost – internally only; megalithic jambs; vestiges of strip-work internally.

CHANCEL:
- Coursed Stone Walling.
- Square Single Plinth.
- Megalithic Side Alternate Quoining.
- Internally. Restored Round-Headed Chancel Archway: arched head formed with three adjacent concentric rows of voussoirs – the inner row is recessed; also with stepped-imposts. Some original Anglo-Saxon stonework survives in the right-hand (southern) arm of the arched head, the imposts and some of the upper part of the south jamb.
- Vestiges of Blocked Round-Headed Single-Splayed Window.

103.   LANGFORD, Oxfordshire – St Matthew's Church.
CENTRAL SQUARE TOWER (no indication of porticus or transepts):
- Random Rubble Walling.
- Square Single Plinth.
- "Cut-Back" Face Alternate Quoining.
- Square String-Courses.
- Incomplete Pilaster-Strips including one interrupted by a Sundial with two standing human figures reaching up to hold the semi-circular dial on which the divisions of time were incised – the hole for missing gnomon can be identified.
- Round-Headed Double-Splayed Windows: voussoirs; jambs and sills; plaster now obscures their construction details.
- Top (Belfry) Stage set-back from the stage below.
- Pairs of Round-Headed Single-Belfry Openings. Constructed with through-stone ashlar stonework with similarly sized and faced wedge-shaped stones for the voussoirs and similarly sized and faced square stones for the jambs; there are no imposts. Each of the two openings are separated by a block of walling, similarly constructed to the jambs,

which runs through the entire depth of the wall. Externally, the addition of a half-round roll on the face of the arched heads and jambs on each of the openings, and the decoration of horizontal bands of roll-moulding between the arched heads and jambs where a capital might be expected, has the effect of transforming the appearance of each of the two separate belfry-openings into something similar to a double belfry-opening. Decorated with vertical, plant-like, designs of different heights. Sills constructed with a single stone, sloping outwards.

NAVE INTERNALLY:
- East Wall. Round-Headed Archway providing access into square central chamber: voussoirs; through-stone chamfered square imposts extending beyond accompanying hood-moulding on west face only; megalithic through-stone square jambs; protruding square bases; all standing on protruding chamfered plinths overall providing a stepped appearance. Additionally, west face only, incomplete strip-work, and hood-moulding placed on top of voussoirs, protruding sufficiently so that the arched and jambs appear set-back.

SQUARE CENTRAL CHAMBER INTERNALLY:
- East wall. Round-Headed Chancel Archway providing access into chancel: through-stone voussoirs which on its west face takes the form of a half-round band of roll-moulding, whilst on its east face takes the more standard square-shaped and flat form; voussoirs accompanied by a half-round soffit-roll; moulded, rectangular, imposts divided horizontally into three with the top and bottom bands separated by a central groove; jambs with attached half-round cylindrical angle-shafts and attached centrally-placed half-round cylindrical soffit-shafts. Both pairs of shafts have moulded, half-round capitals comprising a vertical top third and a tapering lower two-thirds with a horizontal band of roll-moulding below. Both pairs of shafts also have half-round, cylindrical, two-stepped bases most of which taper apart from the vertical bottom one-fifth. The archway stands on large, protruding, square plinths. Additionally, on the west face only, a narrow band of stonework with a square edge, is evident between the voussoirs and the soffit-roll, and between the angle-shafts and the soffit-shafts; this narrow band of stonework has similar capitals and bases to both the angle and soffit-shafts.
- First Floor: Megalithic Flat-Headed Doorway facing nave: lintel comprising two larger stones separated by a narrower central stone; no imposts; Escomb Jambs with chamfered bases; monolithic sill.
- First Floor: Blocked Flat-Headed Doorway facing chancel: monolithic lintel; no imposts; jambs formed of rubble similar to the stonework in the adjoining walling.
- First Floor, above blocked flat-headed doorway facing chancel: Scaring in walling indicating gable of earlier Chancel Roofline.

SOUTH PORCH EXTERNALLY:
- ✠ Holy Rood with Crucifixion Scene – Christ with the Virgin Mary and St John. Incorrectly reassembled.
- ✠ Incomplete Holy Rood with Crucifixion Scene reassembled – Christ's head is missing.

104.   LAUGHTON-EN-LE-MORTHEN, South Yorkshire – All Saints Church.

NORTH AISLE (FORMER NORTH-WEST PORTICUS):
- Coursed Stone Walling.
- Square Triple Plinth.
- "Cut-Back" Megalithic Long and Short Quoining.

PHOTO 676. Laughton-en-le-Morthen.

- Incomplete Blocked Megalithic Round-Headed Doorway: through-stone voussoirs; damaged rectangular imposts; jambs now missing; strip-work, with protruding square bases above the triple plinth of the walling, and with hood-moulding also supported by protruding square bases. (The smaller doorway inserted below is not Anglo-Saxon.) See Page 386 bottom right: PHOTO 676. Laughton-en-le-Morthen, showing the external face of the doorway.

105.   LEDSHAM, West Yorkshire – All Saints Church.
SQUARE TOWER incorporating earlier Anglo-Saxon West Porch:
- Coursed Stone Walling.
- Megalithic Side Alternate Quoining.
- Megalithic Doorway with most of the decoration dating from 1871 restoration based on an interpretation of the original: Round-Headed externally - voussoirs/Flat-Headed internally - monolithic lintel; imposts with flat-moulding, roll-moulding, scroll design – decoration on inner faces may be original. Large stone jambs rebated for door. Strip-work decorated with roll-moulding, plant-scroll design – decoration on bottom stone on each side may be original.
- Round-Headed Single-Splayed Windows: externally, arched heads cut out of half-through-stones/internally, voussoirs; through-stone jambs and sills of similar coursed stonework to the adjoining walling. See adjacent: PHOTO 677. Ledsham 3, showing the megalithic doorway arrowed red, the round-headed single-splayed windows arrowed black, and the megalithic side alternate quoining in the south-west corner of the nave arrowed blue.

PHOTO 677. Ledsham 3.

- Internally, East Wall. Blocked, incomplete, Round-Headed Single-Splayed Window: east face (facing the Nave) arched head cut in two out of half-through stone/west face (facing the Porch/Tower) voussoirs; through-stone jambs and sills of similar coursed stonework to the adjoining walling.
- Internally, East Wall, West Face: Scaring indicates Roofline of former Western Porch.

NAVE:
- Coursed Stone Walling.
- Megalithic Side Alternate Quoining.
- Incomplete Blocked Megalithic Round-Headed Windows – one is almost complete: arched head cut out of a rectangular half-through-stone externally/voussoirs internally; jambs and sill constructed with stonework similar to the adjoining coursed stone walling externally/similar to Escomb jambs internally. Others more fragmentary: a rectangular half-through-stone lintel with stonework from one of the jambs; single stone of an arched head; voussoirs with stonework from one of the jambs; voussoirs with a large, single, vertical stone forming each of the jambs.
- Round-Headed Chancel Archway with through-stone voussoirs and megalithic jambs. Flower and pellet decoration on imposts mostly dates from 1871 restoration but with some original fragments.
- First Floor Nave, South Porticus: Incomplete Blocked, possible Round-Headed Doorway rather than Window: voussoirs with imposts below internally/monolithic lintel externally

(in south porch); large stone jambs with possible rebate for doorway; but it is not known whether, if a doorway, it extended up from the ground floor.

SOUTH PORCH incorporating the former South Porticus:
- Coursed Stone Walling.
- Side Alternate Quoining including stonework of considerable size.

NORTH AISLE INTERNALLY:
- Parts of Angular Cross-Shafts or Decorated Friezes with plant-scroll design, roll-moulding design; inhabited plant-scroll design with affronted birds.

106.   LEEK, Staffordshire – Church of St Edward the Confessor.
NORTH AISLE INTERNALLY:
- Part of a Ring-Head Cross-Head with a central protruding boss, flat-moulding and interlace design.
- Part of the lower vertical arm of a Cross-Head with part of its supporting Angular Cross-Shaft with designs and patterns including: most of a free-arm cross, interlace design, linear designs, pellets, concentric rings, roll-moulding.
- Part of a damaged Angular Cross-Shaft with little surviving decoration apart from indications of flat-moulding, some variation of a linear design, possibly a variation of interlace design.
- Part of an Angular Cross-Shaft with flat-moulding, interlace design, looping interlace ending in a spear-shape, pellet, plait-work design; inhabited knot-work design with a serpent; two incomplete figures with the more complete figure, possibly haloed, holding a long-stemmed free-arm cross.

CHURCHYARD:
- Part of Cross-Head support by a complete Cross-Shaft comprising a lower circular-shaped part separated by a collar from the upper angular part with designs and patterns including: flat-moulding, free-arm crosses, heart-shaped and horseshoe shaped designs with volutes, interlace design, knot-work design, meander-pattern design, pellet, plant-scroll design, roll-moulding, triquetra-knot design.
- Part of a reconstructed Angular Cross-Shaft with flat-moulding, knot-work design, interlace design; incomplete runic inscription which is difficult to interpret.

107.   LICHFIELD, Staffordshire – Cathedral Church of St Peter.
CHAPETER HOUSE INTERNALLY:
- Part of a reconstructed panel from a Shrine Chest, probably from the Shrine of St Cedd. Designs and patterns including: flat-moulding and plant design; the Archangel Gabriel with vestiges of paint.

108.   LINCOLN, Lincolnshire – St Peter-At-Gowts Church.
SQUARE TOWER:
- Coursed Rubble Walling.
- Chamfered Two-Stepped Plinth.
- Side Alternate Quoining.
- Restored Flat-Headed Doorway with tympanum and arched head above: vestiges of Anglo-Saxon stonework at most: chamfered imposts; large stone jambs.
- Round-Headed Single-Splayed Saxo-Norman Windows in west and south walls: arched heads cut out of a monolithic lintel externally/voussoirs internally; jambs with dressed stones externally and internally, mostly laid similar to long and short quoining, with some additional smaller stones towards the arched heads; single stone sill. Externally, the west window has damaged hood-moulding with label-stops, not decorated, placed on top, and concentric with, the arched head.

- Square String-Course forms sill of Round-Headed Double-Belfry Openings above and delineates the tall lower stage from the upper stage; the upper stage is set-back from the lower stage.
- Round-Headed Double-Belfry Openings: arched heads constructed with voussoirs; square imposts flush with the faces of the walling but protruding into the central void where they are chamfered; jambs comprise through-stones laid in Escomb fashion; cylindrical mid-wall shafts with conical-cum-rectangular bases, and conical capitals. The openings in the west and south walls decorated with horizontal bands of cable-pattern design, which separate the capitals from cylindrical mid-wall shaft below, and, separate the palmette design from "wheat-ear" design above; above mid-wall shafts through-stone slab placed horizontally so that it sides overhang the mid-wall-shaft – the slab supports junction of both arched heads above; sill provided by the top of the string-course below.
- Internally. Round-Headed Tower Archway – construction details now mostly covered with plaster: chamfered imposts; megalithic square jambs. See adjacent: PHOTO 678. Lincoln St Peter-at-Gowts 5.

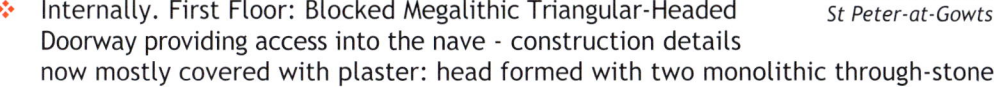

PHOTO 678. Lincoln St Peter-at-Gowts 5.

- Internally. First Floor: Blocked Megalithic Triangular-Headed Doorway providing access into the nave - construction details now mostly covered with plaster: head formed with two monolithic through-stones placed to form a triangle with square imposts providing their bases; megalithic square jambs laid similar to Escomb jambs – east face chamfered at a later, not Anglo-Saxon, date.

NAVE:
- Coursed Rubble Walling.
- Square Single Plinth.
- Long and Short Quoining.

NORTH AISLE - Internally:
- Possible Anglo-Saxon Font decorated with: roll-moulding and cylindrical columns supporting capitals, imposts and interlocking archways. See adjacent: PHOTO 679. Lincoln St Peter-at-Gowts 6.

PHOTO 679. Lincoln St Peter-at-Gowts 6.

109.   LITTLE BARDFIELD, Essex – St Katherine's Church.
SQUARE FLINT TOWER:
- Coursed Rubble Walling with Flints.
- Part of Square Single Plinth.
- Rubble Quoining with Flints.
- Square String-Courses dividing the tower into a tall lower stage, a narrow middle stage, and a tall upper stage which is sub-divided by the walling being set-back – unusually there is no accompanying string-course denoting the sub-division.
- Lower Stage West Wall: Possible indications of blocked doorway at ground floor level.
- Second Stage, Third Stage and Fourth Stage: Pairs of Round-Headed Single-Belfry

Openings. Each of the heads of the openings are constructed with individual stones of rubble and flint placed on end and formed into a discernible arch; no imposts; jambs and sills constructed with rubble and flints similar to the coursed rubble stonework in the adjoining walling. The amount of walling which runs through the entire depth of the wall and separates the pairs of openings differs between the three stages; this walling is constructed with rubble and flints similar to the stonework in the adjoining walling.

NAVE:
- Coursed Rubble Walling of Flints.
- Part of Square Single Plinth.
- Round-Headed Double-Splayed Windows: arched heads, jambs and sills constructed with rubble and flints similar to the stonework in the adjoining walling; north wall window blocked and incomplete its features can only now be identified externally.

110. LONDON - Victoria and Albert Museum.
- Reconstructed, but damaged, incomplete Cross from Easby, North Yorkshire: part of Free-Arm Cross-Head, and much of its supporting Angular Cross-Shaft, with designs and patterns including: cable-moulding, interlace design, plant-scroll design, roll-moulding, inhabited plant-scroll design with beasts and birds. Scenes including: upper body and head of Christ giving a blessing, also holding a book – part of his halo survives; seated, full figure of haloed Christ in Majesty giving a blessing with a haloed half-figure on each side; horizontal rows of haloed half-figures representing the Apostles – some holding books.
- Resin Casts of Crosses from: Bewcastle, Gosforth and Irton (Cumbria); Ruthwell (Dumfries & Galloway); Hexham (Northumberland); Wolverhampton (West Midlands). Cast of Shrine known as the "Hedda or Monks' Stone", Peterborough (Cambridgeshire). Doorway and Pillar from Norwegian Church of Urnes – "Urnes Design".

111. LOW DINSDALE, County Durham. St John the Baptist Church.
SOUTH PORCH INTERNALLY:
- Part of a Cross-Head with designs and patterns including: roll-moulding, interlace design, knot-work design.
- Parts of Angular Cross-Shafts with designs and patterns including: flat-moulding, grooved-moulding, interlace design, plait-work design, ring-twist design, ring-knot design. Parts of human figures. Part of a beast. Possibly parts of birds.
- Grave-Marker or Consecration Cross with free-arm cross.

SOUTH AISLE INTERNALLY:
- Hogback Grave-Cover with designs and patterns including: flat-moulding, knot-work design, stepped-pattern design. End bear-like beast and part of a claw of another.

CHURCHYARD:
- Part of an Angular Cross-Shaft with designs and patterns including: flat-moulding, free-ring designs, grooved-moulding, interlace design, plait-work design.
- Grave-Cover with a long-stemmed free-arm cross.

112. LOWTHER, Cumbria – St Michael's Church.
WEST PORCH INTERNALLY:
- Two almost complete and parts of one other Hogback Grave-Covers with designs and patterns including: long-stemmed free-arm cross, key-pattern design, loops, plant design, ring-twist design, stepped-pattern design, tegulations, roll-moulding; coiled, extended and undulating bodies of serpents, a fish, winged bird-like creature; on one hogback indications of bear-like beasts; boat containing warriors, warriors; human-like half-figures.
- Parts of Grave-Cover with designs and patterns including: cable-moulding, interlace

design, meander-pattern design, ring-knot design, roll-moulding; head of a beast.
NORTH TRANSEPT INTERNALLY:
- Part of Grave-Cover cable-moulding, interlace design, stepped-pattern design.
- Part of Free-Arm Cross-Head - no decoration survives.
- Fragment of Cross-Shaft with roll-moulding and plant-scroll design.

113. LYTHE, North Yorkshire – St Oswald's Church.
TOWER INTERNALLY:
- Part of what could be a Door Jamb from earlier Anglo-Saxon Church with knot-work design and roll-moulding.
- Part of Free-Arm Cross-Head with designs and patterns including: flat-moulding, interlace design, knot-work design; human head.
- Most of a Ring-Head Cross-Head without surviving decoration.
- Part of an Angular Cross-Shaft known as "The Wrestlers" with flat-moulding; a pair of incomplete, headless, human figures "wrestling"; incomplete S-shaped beast.
- Parts of Angular Cross-Shafts with designs and patterns including: cable-moulding, flat-moulding, interlace design, key-pattern design, plait-work design, meander-pattern design, stepped-pattern design.
- Almost complete and fragments of Grave-Markers in the form of long-stemmed free-arm crosses with deep grooves separating the arms. The upper vertical and horizontal arms of some examples are triangular-shaped, others are fan-shaped and some have central bosses at the intersection of these arms. None are decorated.
- Grave-Markers which could possibly be Anglo-Saxon decorated on one face with variants of a single free-arm cross.
- Incomplete and fragments of Hogback Grave-Covers with designs and patterns including: flat-moulding, interlace design, linear design, pellets, plait-work design, roll-moulding, ring-twist design, stepped-pattern design, tegulations; horned beast, birds, serpents; some with end bear-like beasts; parts of human figures. See above right: PHOTO 680. Lythe 4, showing north face of hogback grave-cover with a scene involving a human-like figure, creatures and beasts.

PHOTO 680. Lythe 4.

CRYPT:
- Incomplete and fragments of Grave-Covers including Hogback Grave-Covers with flat-moulding, grooved-moulding. None of these Hogback Grave-Covers have end bear-like beasts.

114. MARTON, Lincolnshire – St Margaret's Church.
SQUARE TOWER – Saxo-Norman:
- Coursed Rubble Walling with herringbone masonry.
- Side Alternate Quoining.
- West Wall: Round-Headed Single-Splayed Key-Hole Window: arched head shaped out of a single through-stone with hood-moulding with label-stops (not decorated) externally; jambs each comprise five half-through-stones with the only stone of any distinctive size, under the arched head, consisting of a rectangular, horizontal, stone; the sill is provided by a course of herringbone masonry externally. Internally, jambs

and sill were constructed similarly to the coursed rubble stonework in the adjoining walling.
- Flat Stone decorated with a human head in portrait in relief possibly Anglo-Saxon. A flat stone protrudes from the walling above the head - in the second course of herringbone masonry above the west window.
- Square String-Course forms sill of Round-Headed Double-Belfry Openings above and delineates the tall lower stage of the Tower from the upper stage: the upper stage is set-back from the lower stage.
- Round-Headed Double-Belfry Openings: arched heads each cut out of a single square lintel – the lower part of the arched head is slightly set-back from the rest of the arch above; chamfered imposts protruding from the faces of the walling and into the central void; jambs with dressed facing stones but not constructed to a particular design; cylindrical mid-wall shafts with capitals possibly decorated with volutes with a horizontal band of cable-moulding below; above mid-wall shafts through-stone slab placed horizontally so that it sides overhang the mid-wall-shaft – the slab supports junction of both arched heads above; sill provided by the top of the string-course below.
- First Floor – East Wall: Blocked Flat-Headed Doorway: monolithic lintel; no imposts; large stone jambs – most is now above the apex of the current Nave (view externally).
- First Floor – East Wall: Scaring on walling indicates former Roofline of the Anglo-Saxon nave - see nave below.
- Internally. Tower Archway: voussoirs; chamfered imposts; square jambs.

NAVE:
- Coursed Rubble Walling with Herringbone Masonry.
- Rubble Quoining.
- West wall extends buttress-like the north and south walls of the tower. The angled nature of the tops of these "buttresses" indicates part of the lower roofline of the Anglo-Saxon nave.
- Internally. Round-Headed Chancel Archway: voussoirs with a set-back band of roll-moulding below on the west face; with chamfered imposts. Additionally, on the west face, the jambs are recessed and contain free-standing cylindrical angle-shafts with chamfered plinths on square bases and with cushion-capitals; the capital on the north side of the arch is additionally decorated with odd-shaped upright leaves above a horizontal band of cable-moulding.

CHANCEL – Saxo-Norman:
- Coursed Rubble Walling with Herringbone Masonry.
- Internally: Panel incised with a Crucifixion Scene.

SOUTH AISLE EXTERNALLY:
- Part of a Ring-Head Cross-Head with chevron-moulding, flat-moulding, plait-work design.
- Part of a Cross-Base with roll-moulding and parts of the ends of rectangular panels – the larger enclosing the smaller.
- Parts of the same Grave-Cover with chevron-moulding some of which now appears more like roll-moulding, flat-moulding, figure-of-eight knot-work design.

115. MELBURY BUBB, Dorset - St Mary's Church.
NAVE:
- Part of a Round Cross-Shaft, now upside down, and reused as a font. The rectangular design along what is now the upper border may well be an addition when the lining to the font was added at a later, not Anglo-Saxon, date. What is now the lower border comprises a row of square-shaped billets. Between these two borders there are two pairs of large beasts in profile: a panther facing a hyena, and, a lion facing a stag. They all

stand on a horizontal band of flat-moulding. In addition there are three smaller creatures placed vertically in mid-air between these large beasts. A loose ring-like interlace design ensnares the legs, bodies and tails of the large beasts – apart from the short tail of the stag – and extends the tail of one of the smaller creatures which ends in flippers; this design acts as a space filler.

116. MELSONBY, North Yorkshire – St James the Great Church.
- Two parts of Octagonal Shaft, now split vertically into two. Possibly part of church furnishing and used in the baptistry. With designs and patterns including: extended knot-work design, knot-work design including figure-of-eight ring-knot design, plant-scroll design, roll-moulding; winged beast, serpent, addorsed creatures, affronted dog-like beasts; human heads. Traces of gesso.
- Two Fragments from different pieces of stonework one with an incomplete beast above a beast with antlers, and the other with a coiled serpent.

117. MIDDLESMOOR, North Yorkshire – St Chad's Church.
NAVE:
- Hammer-Head Cross-Head with part of its attached Angular Cross-Shaft with incised lines, scroll design.
- Possible Anglo-Saxon font bowl but with later, not Anglo-Saxon, decoration added.

118. MIDDLETON, North Yorkshire – St Andrew's Church.
SQUARE TOWER:
- Coursed Rubble Walling.
- Square Single Plinth.
- Megalithic Side Alternate Quoining.
- Blocked Incomplete Round-Headed Doorway West Wall (later, not Anglo-Saxon, window inserted): through-stone voussoirs; chamfered imposts; through-stone square jambs: accompanying pilaster-strips with projecting, chamfered, bases; hood-moulding.
- Megalithic Flat-Headed Single-Splayed Window South Wall in lower First Floor: monolithic lintel and sill; through-stone jambs laid in similar fashion to the coursed rubble stonework in the adjoining walling.
- Megalithic Flat-Headed Window South Wall in upper First Floor: monolithic lintel and sill; each of the jambs are constructed with a single vertical stone with two stones above, one on top of the other, laid in similar fashion to the coursed rubble stonework in the adjoining walling. The jambs are not through-stones, there is a square rebate in the depth of the wall; the window is not splayed.
- Square String-Course.

NAVE EXTERNALLY:
- Coursed Rubble Walling.
- Indication of extension of the west wall both north and south of Tower: South side Chamfered Double Plinth extending 59½ inches/151.1 centimetres. North side - plinth not Anglo-Saxon.
- Incomplete Megalithic Side Alternate Quoining 56 inches/142.2 centimetres south of tower, 52½ inches/133.3 centimetres north of tower. Parallel to this quoining, but extending only 10 inches/25.3 centimetres from the north and south walls of the tower: Quoining comprising mostly single vertical stones separated from each other by smaller stones suggestive of long and short quoining – Sussex variation. Whilst the megalithic side alternate quoining is similar to that in the tower the position of this

"inner" quoining may indicate the north-west and south-west corners of an earlier, narrower, nave.

NORTH AISLE INTERNALLY:
- Complete Ring-Head Cross-Head and its complete attached Vertically-Sided Cross-Shaft with designs and patterns including: flat-moulding, interlace design, knot-work design, pellets, roll-moulding; hunt scene with huntsman, stag and hounds; ribbon, S-shaped, beast.
- Most of Ring-Head Cross-Head and most of its attached Angular Cross-Shaft with designs and patterns including: flat-moulding, free-ring design, interlace design, knot-work design, lines incised in a triangular design, pellets, stepped-pattern design; ribbon beast; seated warrior with his weapons.
- Complete Billet-Head Cross-Head and its complete attached Angular Cross-Shaft with designs and patterns including: flat-moulding, interlace design and knot-work design possibly including creatures, plait-work design, stopped plait-work design, ring-knot design, spiral-scroll design.
- Fragment of Ring-Head Cross-Head and part of its attached Angular Cross-Shaft with designs and patterns including: flat-moulding, interlace design, ring-knot design; head and shoulders of a human figure. Cemented onto the stump of the cross-head is a fragment of an arm with flat-moulding, plait-work design and ring-twist design – it may have been part of the same ring-head cross-head.
- Part of an Angular Cross-Shaft with designs and patterns including: flat-moulding, pellets, plait-work design, roll-moulding; seated warrior with his weapons.

TOWER SOUTH WALL EXTERNALLY:
- Part of Arm from Cross-Head and part of its attached Angular Cross-Shaft with flat-moulding and spiral-scroll design.

TOWER WEST WALL EXTERNALLY:
- Free-Arm Cross in relief with flat-moulding, interlace design and a plant design.

NAVE NORTH WALL EXTERNALLY:
- Fragment with indications of a representation of a human face – some imagination required.

119.   NASSINGTON, Northamptonshire – St Mary's and All Saints Church.

NAVE:
- Coursed Rubble Walling.
- Slight vestiges of Square Single Plinth.
- Vestiges of "Cut-Back" Long and Short Quoining.
- Internally, First Floor Level, West Wall. Blocked Round-Headed Doorway or Window. Its origin and purpose is open to conjecture; plaster obscures construction details.
- Internally, Second Floor Level, West Wall. Blocked Triangular-Headed Doorway: head formed with two monolithic through-stones placed to form a triangle with square imposts providing their bases; jambs constructed of coursed rubble similar to the adjoining walling. Plaster obscures construction details. It may have provided access to a gallery or chamber.

NORTH AISLE INTERNALLY
- Part of an Angular Cross-Shaft with designs and patterns including: flat-moulding, plant-scroll design, ring-chain design, figure-of-eight ring-knot design. Crucifixion Scene with Christ with the sun and moon above, the cup/sponge-bearer Stephaton and the spear-bearer Longinus. Incomplete Figure possibly representing the Ascension.
- Incomplete, possible Saxo-Norman Coped Grave-Cover with a central ridge comprising a band of roll-moulding which provides the vertical arms of long-stemmed double-ended free-arm cross.

120. NESTON, Cheshire – St Mary and St Helen's Church.
SOUTH AISLE INTERNALLY:
- Fragments of Ring-Head Cross-Heads and parts of Angular Cross-Shafts with designs and patterns including: cable-moulding, flat-moulding, interlace design, knot-work design, plait-work design, ring-twist design, stepped-pattern design, triquetra-knot design; two moving beasts in profile. The figure of a priest, a haloed winged angel, individual human figures; two human figures fighting each other (possibly representing David slaying Goliath); two horsemen confronting each other with spears crossing above their horses heads. Hunting scene with beasts, one complete human figure, and two incomplete human figures, one a women given her dress and hairstyle.

121. NEWCASTLE-UPON-TYNE, Northumberland – Great North (Hancock) Museum.
- Most of a Free-Arm Cross-Head and part of a separate section of its Angular Cross-Shaft. The Free-Arm Cross-Head is decorated with designs and patterns including: flat-moulding, roll-moulding, interlace design, plant design; part of a human figure; three-quarter figure with a distinctive vertical coil below their hands. Incomplete Crucifixion Scene with part of the haloed head and arm of Christ with a winged angel; flying, winged angel holding a circlet in each hand. Angular Cross-Shaft decorated with designs and patterns including: flat-moulding, roll-moulding. Scene depicting Christ in Majesty under an archway with a plant design. Inhabited spiral-scroll design with an incomplete beast. Two miracles with Christ healing of a seated blind man and the healing of a woman whose body is mostly missing. Representation of eighteen people in galleried rows.
- End of an arm from a Free-Arm Cross-Head with roll-moulding and zigzag-design.
- Part of a damaged and incomplete Angular Cross-Shaft with designs and patterns including: flat-moulding, interlace design, key-pattern design, ring-knot design, interlace design, ring-twist design; and, an inscription interpreted to read "Myredah made me" and incomplete inscriptions which cannot now be interpreted. Incomplete Crucifixion Scene with Christ and representations of the sun and moon, incomplete human figures, also the cup-bearer Stephaton and the sponge-bearer Longinus.
- Part of a Two-Collared Angular Cross-Shaft with the lower collar now forming a plinth. Decorated with designs and patterns including: grooved-moulding; large, protruding, pellet-like studs; plant-scroll design; roll-moulding; spiral-scroll design; and inhabited plant-scroll design with paired birds and affronted beasts.
- Part of an Angular Cross-Shaft with designs and patterns including: interlace design, plant-scroll design, roll-moulding and inhabited plant-scroll design with a creature.
- Part of an Angular Cross-Shaft with flat-moulding and interlace design; also with indications of lower arm of its attached Free Arm Cross-Head.
- Part of a Cross-Shaft with cable-moulding, roll-moulding and an incomplete St Andrew's Cross – saltire – design.
- Part of an Architectural Feature with flat-moulding and inhabited knot-work design including two or three, entwined, double-outlined, ribbon, beasts.
- Incomplete house-shaped Casket Shrine with, flat-moulding which also forms a handle-like appearance on the top "roof", cable-moulding, plait-work design. Inscription both in letters and runes interpreted to read "in memory of Hroethberht, a monument of the uncle: pray for (his) soul".
- Grave-Marker with roll-moulding and an adjacent inscription too incomplete to interpret confidently; a horizontal representation of a row of baluster-shafts enclosed within frame provided by flat-moulding.
- Incomplete Round-Headed Grave-Marker with designs and patterns including: flat-

moulding, incomplete fee-arm cross, interlace design, knot-work design, ring-twist design, roll-moulding.
✠ Part of a Round-Headed Grave-Marker reused as a Grave-Cover. Originally a Roman or Anglo-Saxon millstone. Reshaped and decorated with a free-arm cross.
✠ Incomplete, Recumbent, Flat-Headed, Name-Stone Grave-Marker: top face incised with an incomplete panel enclosing a free-arm cross with a runic inscription spelling the feminine personal name "Hildigyth".
✠ Recumbent, Flat-Headed, Name-Stone Grave-Marker: top face with a slightly bevelled border providing a panel enclosing, in low relief, a free-arm cross with a Latin inscription in Anglo-Saxon capitals interpreted to read "Pray for Vermund (masculine personal name) – [and] Torhtsuid (feminine personal name)".

122. NEWENT, Gloucestershire – St Mary's Church.
SOUTH PORCH INTERNALLY:
✠ Part of Angular, Collared, Cross-Shaft with designs and patterns including: roll-moulding, tree-scroll design; inhabited interlace design including a beast, inhabited plant-scroll design including two birds. Scenes including: Adam and Eve with the Serpent and the Tree of Knowledge; David and Goliath; complete and incomplete human figures. Collar with indication of round-headed arcading with figures possibly representing the symbols of the Evangelists, also other figures including possibly a winged figure with a spear.
SOUTH AISLE INTERNALLY:
✠ Copy of Stone Tablet known as "The Newent Stone". It is decorated with: a Crucifixion Scene including a number of human figures and angels. A scene depicting a central human figure, probably a priest, surrounded by smaller human figures with the name "Edred" carved above a figure placed horizontally below the top left-hand side of the tablet. The four narrow-edges have inscriptions: "Matheus", "Marcus", "Lucas" and "Iohannes" – the names of the four Gospel writers - and the name "Edred" repeated.

123. NEWTON-BY-CASTLE ACRE, Norfolk – St Mary's and All Saints Church.
NAVE:
❖ Random Rubble Walling with Flints.
❖ Slight indications of Blocked Doorway.
CENTRAL SQUARE TOWER:
❖ Random Rubble Walling with Flints.
❖ Side Alternate Quoining.
❖ Round-Headed Double-Splayed Window: head constructed with individual stones of rubble, flints and reused Roman tile-like bricks placed on end and formed into a discernible arch; no imposts; jambs, constructed with rubble, flints and reused Roman tile-like bricks similar to the adjacent walling – some use of slightly larger facing stones; sill provided by the top of the rubble stonework below.
❖ Restored Triangular-Headed Double-Belfry Openings: heads constructed with individual stones of rubble, flints and reused Roman tile-like bricks placed on end and formed into a discernible triangle; no imposts; jambs, constructed with rubble, flints and reused Roman tile-like bricks similar to the adjacent walling – some use of larger facing stones; cylindrical mid-wall shafts – the nature of their bases and capitals is unclear; above mid-wall shafts through-stone slab placed horizontally so that it sides overhang the mid-wall-shaft – the slab supports junction of both triangular heads above; sills provided by the top of the rubble stonework below.
❖ Scaring on the west and east walls indicates earlier Rooflines of Nave and Chancel.
❖ Internally. Eastern Tower Round-Headed (Chancel) Archway: arched head is set-back from the faces of the chamfered square imposts and the square jambs which have

protruding, chamfered bases; plaster obscures most of the construction details. See adjacent: PHOTO 681. Newton-by-Castle-Acre 2.
* Internally: Blocked Triangular-Headed Doorways formerly providing access between upper stages of nave, tower and chancel; plaster obscures their construction details.

FORMER NORTH AND SOUTH TRANSEPTS EXTERNALLY:
* Uneven patchwork nature of the faces of the north and south walls probably indicates position of the archways into the central crossing and their associated walling.

CHANCEL:
* Random Rubble Walling with Flints.
* Incomplete, blocked, Round-Headed Single-Splayed Window: east Jamb and part of its arched head; rebate with four dowel-holes adjacent to secure a shutter.

PHOTO 681. Newton-by-Castle-Acre 2.

124. NORTH ELMHAM, Norfolk – Anglo-Saxon Cathedral.
* Ruins and foundations comprising: west tower with stair turret; nave with only the south wall standing, the north wall is destroyed; transepts apart from destroyed east wall; apsidal chancel only foundations and a small section of walling survive.
* Coursed Rubble Walling.
* Square Plinth constructed with flint and rubble.
* Bases of Tower Archway survive.
* One jamb of north doorway of north transept.
* West Tower Quoining.

125. NORTH WITHAM, Lincolnshire – St Mary's Church.
SOUTH PORCH INTERNALLY:
✠ Part of Angular Cross-Shaft with cable-moulding, knot-work design, plait-work design, ring-twist design.

126. NORTON, County Durham – St Mary's Church. Cruciform Church.
CENTRAL CROSSING WITH SQUARE TOWER ABOVE:
* Walling of the Central Crossing and the Tower above is wider than the width of any of the original four buildings (nave, chancel, south and north transepts) joined to it - a distinct Anglo-Saxon characteristic. As a result quoining juts out from the lines of the adjacent walling – see externally north-west and south-west quoining; and internally, south-west and north-west quoining which extends down to the floor; only some of this internal quoining is now visible because of the later inserted, not Anglo-Saxon, archways.
* Coursed Stone Walling.
* Megalithic Side Alternate Quoining.

GROUND FLOOR INTERNALLY.
* Round-Headed Archways into North and South Transepts: arched heads faced with large shaped curving stones; two-stepped imposts; square jambs. The structure of these archways may have been altered in the 12th century.

FIRST FLOOR:
* Flat-Headed Doorway for access to upper gallery – view from south transept and central crossing: monolithic lintel; no imposts; jambs laid in similar courses to stonework in

adjoining walling.

SECOND FLOOR: See adjacent: PHOTO 682. Norton 3, showing the view from the north-west with, on the north wall, the triangular-headed window arrowed red, the round-headed windows arrowed black, and the scaring on the walling indicating former roofline arrowed blue.

- ❖ Megalithic Triangular-Headed Windows – formerly doorways providing first floor access to nave, chancel and transepts – later restorations have comprised their original construction details: heads formed with two monolithic through-stones placed to form a triangle; through-stone imposts which project from the faces of the walling but not on the external faces; jambs mostly through-stones laid in courses similar the adjoining walling.
- ❖ Round-Headed Single-Splayed Windows: arched heads cut out of monolithic lintels; vertical and horizontal megalithic jambs – some restoration; monolithic sills – some restoration.
- ❖ Externally. Scaring on walling indicates earlier Rooflines of nave, chancel and transepts – modern restoration obscures, particularly towards and at the apexes.

PHOTO 682. Norton 3.

TRANSEPTS:
- ❖ Coursed Walling.

NAVE INTERNALLY:
- ❖ Vestiges of Coursed Walling above arches in the north and south walls.

CHANCEL INTERNALLY:
- ❖ Jagged vestiges of the north and south walls protrude from the east wall of the tower. See adjacent: PHOTO 683. Norton 4, showing the vestiges of the former walling in the west wall of the chancel arrowed red.

CENTRAL CROSSING INTERNALLY:

PHOTO 683. Norton 4.

- ✠ Part of Angular Cross-Shaft with flat-moulding and ring-knot design.

SOUTH PORCH INTERNALLY:
- ✠ Part of Angular Cross-Shaft decorated with diamond-shaped interlace design and roll-moulding.

127.   NUNBURNHOLME, East Yorkshire - St James Church.
TOWER INTERNALLY:
Incorrectly reconstructed incomplete Angular Cross-Shaft with nearly complete panels containing various scenes and designs; each panel contains a different "scene". The top of the cross-shaft has a mortise.
- ✠ Top-Half including: flat-moulding, pellets. Heads, wings, and arms of angels with hands grasping the top of an archway on three sides under which scenes depicting: a seated warrior; a hooded monk or nun; a saint separated from the angels by an additional arch held by the hands of the angels enclosing an S-shaped beast. On one face instead of angels at the top there are confronting wyverns (part eagle, part snake) above the archway with the Virgin and Christ-Child below.
- ✠ Bottom-Half including: flat-moulding with scenes depicting: incomplete seated human figure with a centaur and an adjacent human head; a ring-chain design entwining two

beasts; incomplete Crucifixion Scene with a headless Christ with a headless bird (angel) on each shoulder and with Christ's hands clasping below the heads of two smaller human figures; representation of a mass with a priest (part of his head is missing) with a chalice and host, and below, a feast with two sitting confronting figures from Norse Mythology - Sigurd and the beast-headed Reginn the smith.

128. OLD CLEE, Lincolnshire - Holy Trinity and St Mary the Virgin Church.
SQUARE TOWER - Saxo-Norman: See below right: PHOTO 684. Old Clee 3, from the north-west, with round-headed doorway arrowed red, round-headed single-splayed key-hole window arrowed black, possible roofline of northern porticus arrowed blue, string-course arrowed green and round-headed double-belfry openings arrowed yellow.

PHOTO 684. Old Clee 3.

- Coursed Rubble Walling.
- Square Single Plinth.
- Side Alternate Quoining.
- Round-Headed Doorway: two concentric rows of voussoirs – the inner row set-back – with accompanying hood-moulding; projecting rectangular imposts; jambs rest on plinth running around base of tower; sill.
- Round-Headed Single-Splayed Windows -"Key-Hole" Window in west wall: arched heads cut out of monolithic through-stone lintels; jambs each comprise a single vertical through-stone, angled on its inner edge, with small stones of rubble below; sill provided by top of the coursed stonework below.
- Incomplete Roofline of possible Northern Porticus to the Tower.
- Square String-Course forms the sill of the Round-Headed Double-Belfry Openings above and delineates the tall lower stage of the tower from the upper stage: the upper stage is set-back from the lower stage.
- Round-Headed Double-Belfry Openings: arched heads shaped out of a single stone to provide a curvature in both its upper and lower borders; chamfered imposts protruding from the faces of the walling and into the central void; rubble jambs laid in courses similar to the adjoining walling; cylindrical mid-wall shafts with bulbous bases and cushion-capitals; above mid-wall shafts through-stone slab placed horizontally so that it sides overhang the mid-wall-shaft – the slab supports junction of both arched heads above; sills provided by the top of the string-course below.
- Weathered and nondescript "Prokrossi".
- Internally: Round-Headed Tower Archway: two concentric rows of voussoirs; square, protruding, chamfered, imposts; jambs rest on chamfered, three-stepped, plinth.
✠ Stonework includes Free-Arm Cross internally and stone with a human face externally which may be Anglo-Saxon.

NAVE:
Coursed Stone Walling.
- Side Alternate Quoining in north-west angle.

129. ORPINGTON, Kent – All Saints Church.
SOUTH WALL OF "OLD CHURCH" INTERNALLY:
✠ Incomplete Sundial with central hole for missing gnomon, and divided into fourteen

surviving segments; with cable-moulding, roll-moulding; four inscriptions. Three inscriptions are in Latin lettering and the fourth is in runes: two inscriptions have been taken together and interpreted to read "to (or for) him who knows how to seek, how" and "to count (or to tell) and to hold"; the third "OR....VM" has been interpreted as referring to the sundial rather than the "clock"; the fourth inscription is in Runes and provides no obvious textural reading.

130.   OTLEY, West Yorkshire – All Saints Church.
SOUTH AISLE INTERNALLY:
- ✠ Sections of stonework from the same incomplete Angular Cross-Shaft known as the "Evangelist Cross" - it may have representations of some of the Evangelists and Angels. Decorated with designs and patterns including: plant design, plant-scroll design, roll-moulding; inhabited plant-scroll design with creatures and birds; panels originally each containing a painted inscription; beneath round-headed archways complete and incomplete human half-figures, complete and incomplete human heads - some damaged including two figures with vestiges of wings.
- ✠ Incomplete Angular Cross-Shaft and part of its attached Free-Arm Cross-Head known as the "Dragon Cross" with designs and patterns including: flat-moulding, roll-moulding; inhabited interlace design with beasts; two panels each with inhabited plant design with a dragon or wyvern (part eagle, part snake); beneath round-headed archway incomplete haloed human half-figure – including vestiges of plant design; inhabited plant-scroll design with haloed half-figure; vestiges of incomplete human figures.
- ✠ Parts of Angular Cross-Shafts with designs and patterns including: with flat-moulding, interlace design, plait-work design, plant-scroll design, mixture of knot-work design and ring-knot design; inhabited interlace design with beasts.
- ✠ Grave-Cover incised with lines ending in a spiral-scroll design.
- ✠ Incomplete Grave-Marker incised linear designs and a design suggestive of Ringerike Design.
- ✠ Fragments of stonework with interlace design.

CHURCHYARD:
- ✠ Half-Barrel-Shaped Cross-Base with Socket for insertion of Cross-Shaft; incised with panels within which are long-stemmed free-arm crosses.

131.   OVINGHAM, Northumberland – St Mary the Virgin Church.
SQUARE TOWER:
- ❖ Coursed Rubble Walling.
- ❖ Megalithic Side Alternate Quoining.

LOWER STAGE (BELOW STRING-COURSE). GROUND AND FIRST FLOORS:
- ❖ Round-Headed Single-Splayed Windows: arched heads each cut out of a monolithic lintel; jambs each including a single megalithic stone supporting the head with below a stone similar to those in the adjoining coursed rubble walling – south window/jambs each with a single vertical stone with a horizontal stone above – west window; sills provided by the top face of the coursed stonework below.

SECOND FLOOR SOUTH WALL:
- ❖ Megalithic Round-Headed Doorway: arched head constructed from a single stone to form a semi-circular shape both in its upper and lower borders; no imposts; megalithic jambs; sill. This Doorway opened outwards into space providing access to an external balcony for the displaying of relics to

PHOTO 685. Ovingham 5.

the congregation below. See Page 400 bottom right: PHOTO: 685. Ovingham 5.

UPPER STAGE (STRING-COURSE AND ABOVE):
- Square String Course.
- Round-Headed Double-Belfry Openings: arched heads each cut out of a single square lintel; square imposts protruding from the faces of the walling and into the central void, and also extending to the accompanying strip-work below separating it from hood-moulding above; jambs are of a similar size, and laid in similar courses, to the rubble stonework in the adjoining walling; cylindrical mid-wall shafts without bases or capitals; placed horizontally on top of mid-wall shafts, rectangular through-stone slabs whose sides overhang the mid-wall shafts – the slabs support the junction of both of the arched heads above; sills provided by a single, projecting, rectangular stone which supports the mid-wall shaft, the central voids, the jambs, and extends to support the protruding, strip-work parallel to the jambs – the strip-work also has distinctive, square, bases, The sill of the south opening appears to have been broken into three. A band of protruding, semi-circular, hood-moulding extends above the lintels. It is separated by the extended imposts, from the bands of protruding, vertical, strip-work parallel to the jambs below. Among the intervening stonework between the tops of the lintel heads and the hood-moulding, is a stone which has a circular sound-hole cut out. See adjacent: PHOTO: 686. Ovingham 6, showing west wall on left and south wall on right.

PHOTO 686. Ovingham 6.

- Internally. Round-Headed Tower Archway. Nothing can now be seen of any definite construction details of this archway.
- Internally. First Floor. Round-Headed Doorway providing access to a western gallery in the nave; arched head cut out of half-through-stone lintels; jambs similar to the coursed rubble stonework in the adjoining walling. Nothing can now be seen of any definite identifiable details of construction of this doorway.

NAVE:
- Coursed Rubble Walling.
- Vestiges of Side Alternate Quoins in south-west quoining only.
- Internally. Part of Angular Cross-Shaft with designs and patterns including: cable-moulding, flat-moulding, interlace design, knot-work design, pellets, roll-moulding, stepped-pattern design. Under an archway an incomplete human figure in portrait holding a book against their chest, with possibly a bird on their right shoulder. Possibly a hunting scene with incomplete human figures: on the left a standing figure with their body three-quarter turned and their head in profile to the right; this figure appears to be holding a four-legged creature placed vertically tail to head whose feet touch the body of the figure on the right; on the right a human figure in portrait who holds a large club or horn-like object in their right hand – between the heads of these two human figures is a round object. Alternatively this scene could come from Norse Mythology – Ragnarök - with Loki on the left, the wolf Fenris in the middle, and Heimdall with his horn on the right.

SOUTH PORCH INTERNALLY:
- Part of Angular Cross-Shaft with roll-moulding and interlace design.

EXTERNALLY - Formerly in part of the churchyard but now separate from it:
- ✠ "The Goose Fair Cross": Free-Arm Cross-Head on a reconstructed Cross-Shaft and Cross-Base – both not Anglo-Saxon.

132.   OXFORD, Oxfordshire – St Michael's Church.
SQUARE TOWER:
- ❖ Random Rubble Walling.
- ❖ Long and Short (both northern angles) and Rubble (both southern angles) Quoining; also modern ashlar insertions.
- ❖ Blocked Round-Headed West Doorway: arched head constructed with individual stones placed on end and formed into a discernible arch; jambs include megalithic through-stones but also rubble similar to the stonework in the adjoining walling.
- ❖ Round-Headed Double-Splayed Windows: arched heads constructed with individual stones placed on end and formed into a discernible arch; jambs and sills constructed with rubble and flints similar to the stonework in the adjoining walling – west window at first floor level enlarged to form a doorway.

SECOND FLOOR:
- ❖ Blocked Round-Headed Doorway which opened outwards into space – it may once have provided access to the adjacent Town Walls: arched head constructed with individual stones placed on end and formed into a discernible arch; jambs and sill constructed with rubble and flints similar to the stonework in the adjoining walling.
- ❖ Lower Round-Headed Double-Belfry Openings: arched head constructed with individual stones placed on end and formed into a discernible arch; jambs and sill constructed with rubble and flints similar to the stonework in the adjoining walling; mid-wall baluster shafts which increase in circumference towards the centre where a single, narrow, central, horizontal, band of stonework is bordered, top and bottom, by the cutting away of the adjoining stonework to leave a distinctive horizontal, almost U-shaped, groove. The baluster-shafts do not have capitals but do have rounded, expanding, bases separated from the rest of the shaft, by a horizontal rounded band of stonework similar to roll-moulding. To support the centre of the head of each double-opening a rectangular through-stone slab has been placed horizontally on top of the mid-wall baluster-shaft so that its sides overhang the mid-wall baluster-shaft. The through-stone slabs support the junction of both of the arched heads above. The sills are provided by the top of the rubble stonework below.
- ❖ Upper Round-Headed Double-Belfry Openings: arched head constructed with individual stones placed on end and formed into a discernible arch; jambs and sill constructed with rubble and flints similar to the stonework in the adjoining walling; mid-wall baluster shafts which increase in circumference towards the centre where a single, narrow, central, horizontal, band of stonework is bordered, top and bottom, by the cutting away of the adjoining stonework to leave a distinctive horizontal, almost U-shaped, groove. The baluster-shafts do not have capitals but do have rounded, expanding, bases separated from the rest of the shaft, by a horizontal rounded band of stonework similar to roll-moulding. To support the centre of the head of each double-opening a rectangular through-stone slab has been placed horizontally on top of the mid-wall baluster-shaft so that its sides overhang the mid-wall baluster-shaft. The through-stone slabs support the junction of both of the arched heads above. The sills are provided by the top of the rubble stonework below. East Opening is of a later date, not Anglo-Saxon.

133.   PETERBOROUGH, Cambridgeshire – Cathedral Church of St Peter, St Paul and St Andrew.
IN VAULTS BELOW THE FLOOR OF THE PRESENT NAVE AND SOUTH TRANSEPT INTERNALLY:

- Coursed Rubble Walling: comprising several courses of stonework forming much of the former North and South Transepts and some of the western parts of the joining north and south walls of the Chancel.

"NEW BUILDING" INTERNALLY:
- "Hedda" or "Monks' Stone". A coped, box-shaped Shrine with inhabited plant design with arcades of round-headed archways with capitals and piers – their bases are damaged. These archways each enclose a single, standing, haloed figures in portrait representing Jesus and Mary and the Apostles. Also with flat-moulding, ring-chain design, roll-moulding, now rather flat, and scroll designs with possibly creatures and beasts.

SOUTH TRANSEPT INTERNALLY:
- Wall Panel. A band of roll-moulding forming an almost complete panel containing two standing figures separated by a central column which they both clasp with one hand – their legs nearer to the central column are angled and bend towards it. The figures are sometimes referred to as the "Bishop and King" but with their pointed headgear seem more typical of Anglo-Saxon military figures.

NORTH TRANSEPT INTERNALLY:
- Parts of Grave-Markers decorated with Free-Arm Crosses.

134. POTTERNE, Wiltshire – St Mary's Church.
- Font with, around its top circumference, incised lines bordering a Latin Inscription from Psalm 41.2: "As the hart panteth after the fountains of water; so my soul panteth after thee, O God. (added) Amen"; above the base of the font additional incised line around the circumference.
- Grave-Marker with a Free-Arm Cross with a base all in relief.

135. RAMSBURY, Wiltshire – Holy Cross Church.

NORTH AISLE INTERNALLY:
- A reconstructed column incorporates three sections of stonework from two, possibly three, different Angular Cross-Shafts:
  Part of an Angular Cross-Shaft with flat-moulding, figure-of-eight knot-work design, ring-chain design; inhabited plant-scroll design with beasts, rosettes and pellets; top with dowel-holes to connect it to the now missing section of cross-shaft above.
  Part of an Angular Cross-Shaft with inhabited interlace design with creatures with bodies decorated with chevron design.
  Part of an Angular Cross-Shaft with flat-moulding, knot-work design; inhabited interlace design with coiled beasts with bodies decorated with chevron design.
- Part of recumbent round-ended and coped Grave-Cover with figure-of-eight knot-work design, roundels of roll-moulding enclosing a rosette, a bird-like beast, a dog-like beast; rosettes; heads of beasts whose tongues entwine in a knot.
- Part of recumbent round-ended and coped Grave-Cover with flat-moulding and plant-scroll design. See adjacent: PHOTO 687. Ramsbury 4.
- Part of a damaged Grave-Cover with a free-arm cross in relief including an "Agnus Dei" (haloed Lamb of God) in the centre, below is a panel of interlace design, with below a figure either with upstretched arms or wings; flanking the cross a winged creature, an incomplete beast, a serpent.

PHOTO 687.
Ramsbury 4.

- ✠ Fragment of damaged cross-shaft with inhabited interlace design with parts of two creatures with on one side bodies decorated with herringbone pattern and on another side with one body decorated with a row of pellets – the other body has only a central incised line.
- ✠ Fragment with flat-moulding and knot-work design.
- ✠ Fragment with roll-moulding and indications of drapery.
- ❖ Foundations of possible Anglo-Saxon Cathedral underlying and overlapping present chancel; its precise extent is a matter of conjecture – nothing is now visible.

136. RASTRICK, West Yorkshire – St Matthew's Church.
CHURCHYARD:
- ✠ Complete Cross-Base with socket. Tapering from bottom to top with designs and patterns including: bush-scroll design, interlace design, loosely connected rings, roll-moulding.

137. REED, Hertfordshire – St Mary's Church.
NAVE:
- ❖ Random Rubble Walling.
- ❖ Long and Short Quoining most of whose "longs" alternate to provide a wider width on one wall with the next "long" with its wider width on the adjoining wall. Additionally, on the west face of the wall, the lowest long quoin in the north-west and south-west angles have a chamfered "short" above and this accommodates a set-back in the west wall which continues around the Tower; the north-east and south-east quoining having a similar, but not as distinctive, adaptation. It seems that when the 15th century Tower was built the quoining was adapted to reflect the design on the Tower.
- ❖ Blocked Flat-Headed Doorway: half-round tympanum whose horizontal base provides the flat-head of the doorway. Above the tympanum is a semi-circular band of roll-moulding with a narrow, flat, set-back, strip of stonework above and below. Concentric with the roll-moulding, the remaining part of the arched head of the doorway, comprises two bands of stonework, the upper band wider, and flat on the face of the walling, with the lower, narrower, band set-back but not as far as the flat strip of stonework above the roll-moulding below. Chamfered imposts; square jambs with cylindrical angle-shafts with conical bases and tapering capitals both decorated with a scroll design. In line with the base of the overall arched head of the doorway, below the imposts, a band of roughly faced walling extends parallel to both jambs; a narrow band of random rubble walling separates this stonework from the jambs. A plinth projects from the wall supporting the doorway. Internally, the opening appears as an arched head formed with voussoirs with imposts and square jambs below – much of the detail of construction is hidden by plaster. See above right: PHOTO 688. Reed, showing the exterior north face of the doorway.

PHOTO 688. Reed.

138. REPTON, Derbyshire – St Wystan's Church.
NAVE - incorporating parts of the former Anglo-Saxon Central Crossing and Transepts.
  Internally. Coursed Rubble Walling: above the two, easternmost archways (not Anglo-Saxon), in both the north and south walls which, on both walls, include lengths of a Moulded String-Course.

- Internally: Fragments of Coursed Rubble Walling including Flooring: in both the north-east and south-east angles of the former Central Crossing adjacent to the stairways leading down to the Crypt.
- Internally: Flooring includes the rectangular bases and stumps comprising a single "drum" of the columns which supported the eastern arms of the archways separating the former Central Crossing from the North and South Transepts. (See South Porch below.)
- Internally, First Floor Level. Blocked Flat-Headed Doorway: through-stone Escomb jambs – a "modern" wooden door has been inserted in the walling adjacent to the internal face of the southern jamb. The two jambs are separated by stonework up to fourteen courses high and between three and eight horizontal stones wide; within these courses is the modern wooden door. The position of these jambs may indicate that there were interlocking arches perhaps springing from baluster shafts.
- Externally, east wall: incomplete Chamfered String-Course. It continues around the Chancel level with the bottom quarter of the 13th century window in the north wall and its 20th century window (a copy of the window in the north wall) in the south wall, and the bottom third of the 14th century window in the east wall.
- Externally, east wall, high above the Chamfered String-Course identified in the previous bullet point, either side of the chancel, just below the top of the Coursed Rubble Stonework surviving: two short sections of a Double String-Course comprising a lower half-round course and an upper square course. (Ignore other string-courses, not Anglo-Saxon, above in the ashlar stonework on top of this string-course.)

FORMER NORTH TRANSEPT - now part of north aisle:
- Coursed Rubble Walling – east wall and lower courses of the eastern part of north wall.

CENTRAL CROSSING - east wall, parts of north-east and south-east corners:
- Coursed Rubble Walling: see externally extending north and south of the walls of the crypt.

CHANCEL/CRYPT - Internally:
- Chancel with Coursed Rubble Walling.
- Stairway passages descending down through the north-west and south-west corners of the crypt.

CRYPT/CHANCEL - Internally:
- Megalithic Ashlar Walling.
- Plinth formed of large, flat, stones.
- Incomplete Double-Stepped String-Course and above, separated by walling, a Single Square String-Course.
- Vaulted ceiling supported by: round arches springing from eight wide, vertical-sided, pilaster-strips, abutting but not integral to the side walls. Pilaster-strips taper from bottom to top and appear not to have distinctive bases. Each of the three sides of the pilaster-strips visible display bands of flat-moulding along their two vertical edges which join together in an arched head just below the capital. Within these bands of flat-moulding there are two recessed panels separated in the centre by another band of vertical flat-moulding, almost ridge-like. The moulded capitals above have a lower half tapering upwards with a top half subdivided into three by two horizontal grooves.
(Note: some of the pilaster-strips are damaged and incomplete. Their capitals are similar to those of the central columns.)
- Vaulted ceiling supported in the centre of the crypt by: round arches spring from four free-standing columns with circular bases expanding as they taper downwards to become slightly more rectangular in shape. The columns were decorated sometime in the 9th century with a spiralling band of roll-moulding in relief which on each column spirals in

an opposite direction to the spiralling on the adjacent column. The moulded capitals have a lower half tapering upwards with a top half subdivided into three by two horizontal grooves. Vestiges of gesso and red paintwork on both the pilaster-strips and central columns; particularly on the capitals.
- Recesses within the thickness of each of the four walls for housing burials, relics and shrines; only the western recess is in something like its original state.

CHANCEL/CRYPT - Externally:
- Coursed Rubble Walling.
- Ashlar Square-Stepped Triple Plinth including megalithic stonework.
- Face and Side Alternate Quoining.
- Chamfered String-Course from which pairs of Pilaster-Strips on each wall extend vertically up to short overlapping horizontal sections of stonework, above which are upwardly splayed capitals with a narrow rectangular band of stonework at their tops. The pilaster-strips on east wall incomplete.

SOUTH PORCH INTERNALLY:
- Most of the two eastern columns – each comprising nine "drums" horizontally bordered by a distinctive shallow groove; their capitals rest directly on the top drum. These columns once supported the eastern arches separating the former Central Crossing from the North and South Transepts (their bases with stumps of the piers remain in situ – see Nave above).
- Part of an Angular Cross-Shaft reused as a monolithic lintel head of a window with a set-back inner arch; indications of a possible interlace design and roll-moulding on the face forming what was the top of the window.
- Part of an Angular Cross-Shaft from Ingleby. Decorated with designs and patterns including: cable-moulding, herringbone design, plant-designs with tree-like features, roll-moulding. Standing human figure in profile to the right holding an implement with a shaft with a curving blade.
- Part of an Angular Cross-Shaft from Ingleby with interlace design and plant design.

CHURCHYARD:
- Arched heads cut out of a monolithic lintel with upwardly tapering vertical sides; both may be from Round-Headed Windows.

139. RIPON, North Yorkshire - Cathedral.
CRYPT INTERNALLY:
- Ashlar Walling including reused Roman stonework with layers of plasterwork.
- Northern and Southern Passageways running west to east roofed with flat slabs resting on top of the adjacent walls.
- Northern Passageway: lintel with a round-headed arch cut out at both its western and eastern entrances; to the east, in the north wall, is an indication of the line of one of the original stairways.
- Southern Passageway roof: reused 8th or 9th century Grave-Cover with incomplete free-arm cross in relief with long lower vertical arm joining two incomplete horizontal arms.
- Southern Passageway: lamp niches.
- Southern Passageway with a short passageway leading off north to provide access to the south doorway into the main chamber.
- Round-Headed Doorways into main chamber: south doorway with arched head formed of three shaped through-stones – an upper stone providing a quarter-circle supported on each side by a stone shaped to provide the lower curvature of the arched head; no imposts; through-stone jambs. West doorway with arched head cut out of monolithic through-stone lintel; no imposts; through-stone jambs.
- Main Chamber: barrel-vaulted roof; walls comprising large blocks of ashlar stonework;

single, flat, protruding plinth; reliquary recess; lamp niches. Stonework of unknown date and purpose rises up from the floor and is similar in appearance to a flight of parts of three steps.
- Western Ante Chamber: half-vaulted roof; ventilation shaft; lamp niche.
- Western Ante Chamber with a short passageway leading off east to provide access to the west doorway into the main chamber.

Note: the stairways providing access are not Anglo-Saxon.

NORTH TRANSEPT EXTERNALLY:
- Lengths of Imposts with designs and patterns including: flat-moulding, interlace design, ring-chain design, spiral-scroll design.

CATHEDRAL TREASURY:
- Incomplete Free-Arm Cross-Head with one central protruding boss surviving with designs and patterns including: flat-moulding, ring-twist design, two confronting birds.
- Parts of two joined arms from a Free-Arm Cross-Head with designs and patterns including: flat-moulding, knot-work design. From Norse Mythology, part of a scene in which the figure of Sigurd (sucking his thumb) roasts and eats the heart of the dragon Fafnir.
- Part of what may be the corner of an architectural feature or a piece of furniture with vertical "posts" and horizontal "rails" with designs and patterns including: possible baluster-shaft moulding, cable-moulding, plant design, ring-twist design, roll-moulding, zigzag design.

CHAPEL OF RESURRECTION INTERNALLY:
- Reused likely Roman capital from a pillar now supporting altar.

140.   ROCKCLIFFE, Cumbria – St Mary's Church.
CHURCHYARD:
- Almost complete Cross with Ring-Head Cross-Head, Angular Cross-Shaft with two "collars", and Cross-Base. Ring-Head Cross-Head and Angular Cross-Shaft with designs and patterns including: roll-moulding, interlace design, ring-chain design; fettered, ribbon-shaped, beasts.

141.   ROLLESTON-ON-DOVE, Staffordshire – St Mary's Church.
- Ring-Head Cross-Head with supporting Square-Sided Cross-Shaft with possibly cable-moulding, indications of possible interlace design, roll-moulding.

142.   ROMSEY, Hampshire - Abbey.
- Rood with Crucified Haloed Christ and the Hand of God.
- Rood Panel with Crucifixion Scene – Haloed Christ; haloed angels with wings each holding a sceptre (one is incomplete); haloed figures of the Virgin Mary and St John; the spear-bearer Longinus and the cup/sponge-bearer Stephaton; an extended plant design.

143.   ROTHWELL, Lincolnshire - St Mary Magdalene Church.
SQUARE TOWER – Saxo-Norman: See Page 408: PHOTO 689. Rothwell 3, showing west wall on left and south wall on right, and, on the south wall, an incomplete section of a square string-course which might indicate a flanking porticus below - arrowed red.
- Coursed Rubble Walling.
- Two-Stepped Chamfered Plinth.
- Side Alternate Quoining.
- Megalithic Flat-Headed Doorway: base of half-round tympanum provides the flat-head

and is set-back from the arched row of voussoirs directly on top; above voussoirs a concentric band of protruding hood-moulding placed on top; protruding (not on internal east wall) imposts; Escomb-like jambs supported by chamfered two-stepped plinth which runs around the base of tower. Internally, the tympanum extends only across the depth of the door itself, a round-headed arch, set-back from the jambs, has been cut through the remaining internal depth of the head of the doorway.
- Round-Headed externally/Flat-Headed internally Single-Splayed Windows: arched heads cut out of a half-through-stone lintel externally/uncut, flat, half-through-stone internally. Externally, each jamb of upper windows constructed with one (west window)/two (north and south windows) large, horizontal, half-through-stones – the lower south window has jambs each constructed with a single vertical stone. Internally, jambs constructed with rubble similar to the coursed rubble in the adjoining walling. Sills provided by the coursed rubble stonework directly below.

PHOTO 689. Rothwell 3.

- Incomplete sections of Square String-Courses which might indicate a flanking porticus below. String-Course can be identified level with the sill of the upper window in the south wall and just above the level of the sill of the only window in the north wall.
- Near the top of the Lower Stage: Scaring on the east wall indicates earlier Roofline of Nave.
- Square String-Course forms the sill of the Round-Headed Double-Belfry Openings above and delineates the tall lower stage of the tower from the upper stage: the upper stage is set-back from the lower stage.
- Round-Headed Double-Belfry Openings: arched heads each cut out of a single square lintel; square imposts protruding from the faces of the walling and into the central void; jambs are of similar size, and laid in similar courses, to the adjoining walling but including some individual megalithic stones; cylindrical mid-wall shafts with conical bases and cushion-capitals; placed horizontally on top of mid-wall shafts rectangular through-stone slabs whose sides overhang the mid-wall shafts – the slabs support the junction of both arched heads of the openings above; sill provided by the top of the string-course below.
- Internally: Round-Headed Tower Archway – plaster obscures much of the construction details: voussoirs; square imposts which extend across the full width of the east wall providing a string-course; square jambs; all supported by a double chamfered plinth.

NAVE:
- Coursed Rubble Walling.

Megalithic Long and Short Quoining can easily be identified in the buttress-like feature in the corner of the south wall of the Tower and the west wall of the south aisle.

144. ROTHWELL, West Yorkshire - Holy Trinity Church.
- Two parts of a decorated Frieze with designs and patterns including: round-headed interlocking arches with shared capitals, shared central columns and shared conical and vertical bases; baluster-shaft moulding, flat-moulding, interlace design, knot-work design, plant design, roll-moulding, ring-twist design; inhabited plant-scroll design with winged bird-like beasts, a dog-like beast, and a winged beast; beast ensnared in knot-work design; half-figure winged human or angel.

145.   RUTHWELL, Dumfries & Galloway – Ruthwell and Mount Kedar Church.
Almost complete Cross comprising Cross-Head, Cross-Shaft and Cross-Base – some 19th century stonework reconstruction. See adjacent: PHOTO 690. Ruthwell 2, showing the south face.
- ✠ Free-Arm Cross-Head with flat-moulding. St John the Evangelist with his symbol the eagle. An Archer. A large dove or eagle. Two figures possibly representing two of the Evangelists.
- ✠ Angular Cross-Shaft with flat-moulding; inhabited vine-scroll design with creatures and birds. Scenes depicting: The Visitation of Mary, Christ with Mary Magdalene washing His feet, Christ healing the man born blind, The Annunciation, John the Baptist with the Lamb of God, Christ in Majesty, the meeting in the desert of the hermit Saints Paul and Anthony, the Flight into Egypt. Inscriptions in Latin and Runes including the opening words of the Fourth Gospel, and "Dream of the Rood" by Caedmon of Whitby, North Yorkshire.
- ✠ Cross-Base designs and patterns including: vine-scroll design and a Crucifixion Scene.

PHOTO 690.
Ruthwell 2.

146.   SANDBACH, Cheshire – Market Square.
Two Reconstructed Crosses comprising parts of lower vertical arms of Free-Arm Cross-Heads, most of Angular Cross-Shafts, and most of Cross-Bases (no decoration survives on the cross-bases).
- ✠ Cross-Heads and Cross-Shafts with scenes including: Adoration of the Magi, Crucifixion Scene with Christ with the Evangelists' symbols, The Nativity, Transfiguration of Christ on Mount Tabor flanked by Moses and Elijah, Christ committing the Keys of Heaven to Peter and the Book of the New Law to Paul, Christ's Road to Calvary; The Annunciation, Adoration of Mary holding the Christ-Child, The Veneration of Christ. Other decorated scenes include incomplete and complete human figures some haloed and some seated, haloed winged angels, beasts and birds. Designs and patterns include: cable-moulding, flat-moulding, interlace design, knot-work design, pellets, plait-work design, ring-chain design, roll-moulding, inhabited plant-scroll design with human, beast and bird figures.
- ✠ [In the churchyard of St Mary's Church nearby there are three other very weathered sections of stonework from Cross-Shafts with vestiges of incomplete and complete human figures including possibly winged figures. Whether these formed part of the Crosses in the Market Square is unlikely but remain a matter of debate. Also two, now separate, parts of probably the same Coped Grave-Cover with cable-moulding, interlace design, parallel lines, a pellet, roll-moulding; a beast; a bird-like creature; a human figure, two seated human figures facing each other.]

147.   SEAHAM, County Durham – St Mary's Church.
NAVE:
- ❖ Coursed Stone Walling internally.
- ❖ Coursed Rubble with Herringbone Masonry externally.
- ❖ Chamfered Single Plinth.
- ❖ Megalithic Side Alternate Quoining.
- ❖ Megalithic Round-Headed Single-Splayed Windows – three complete, one blocked and incomplete – some later, not Anglo-Saxon restoration: arched heads cut of half-through-stone lintels each decorated with concentric, semi-circular, grooves. Internally, the

underside of the lintel of the eastern window in north wall, is decorated with two adjacent bands of cable-moulding or "wheat-ear" design. Jambs comprise one vertical, one horizontal half-through stone externally and internally including half-through stones and other smaller stonework similar to the coursed stonework in the adjoining walling; internally, vertical grooves cut into the middle depth of the jambs for shutters. Sills provided by the tops of the coursed stonework directly below.
- Foundations of an Anglo-Saxon Chancel (under the western part of the current Chancel); these foundations cannot now be viewed.
- Foundations of a western Annex or Porch under and out with the current Tower; these foundations cannot now be viewed.

148. SELHAM, West Sussex – St James Church.
NAVE:
- Random Rubble Walling including Herringbone Masonry.
- Side Alternate, including some Megalithic, Quoining.
- Megalithic Round-Headed Doorway: voussoirs; chamfered imposts.
- Internally: Round-Headed Chancel Archway: voussoirs which on the west face only comprise three concentric, but differently sized, bands of roll-moulding; chamfered rectangular imposts with roll-moulding, scroll design and creatures and beasts; tapering abacus with interlace design, plant design, roll-moulding, scroll design; jambs with soffit-shafts with moulded bases and capitals decorated with interlace design, scroll design, creatures and beasts; two-stepped plinth.

CHANCEL:
- Random Rubble Walling including herringbone masonry.
- Side Alternate, including some Megalithic, Quoining.

149. SHELFORD, Nottinghamshire – St Peter and St Paul's Church.
SOUTH AISLE INTERNALLY:
- Part of Angular Cross-Shaft with designs and patterns including: flat-moulding, interlace design, pellet-moulding, possible plant-scroll design; round-headed archway with seated, haloed, Virgin Mary and Christ-Child; four-winged angel.

150. SINNINGTON, North Yorkshire. All Saints Church.
NAVE INTERNALLY:
- Parts of Angular Cross-Shafts with designs and patterns including: cable-moulding, flat-moulding, interlace design, pellets, plait-work design, scroll design; ribbon beasts.
- Part of Coped Grave-Cover with cable-moulding and ring-knot design

NAVE EXTERNALLY:
- Parts of Free-Arm Cross-Heads with designs and patterns including: flat-moulding, knot-work design, pellets, ring-twist design, roll-moulding; serpent. Crucifixion scene.
- Parts and Fragments of Angular Cross-Shafts with designs and patterns including: cable-moulding, flat-moulding, interlace design, knot-work design, pellets, plait-work design, roll-moulding, scroll design; ribbon beast; incomplete human figures.
- Fragment of Hogback Grave-Cover with flat-moulding, meander-pattern design and an end bear-like beast.
- Part of Coped Grave-Cover with no decoration surviving.

CHANCEL INTERNALLY:
- Part of Angular Cross-Shaft with designs and patterns including: flat-moulding, interlace design, free-ring designs, ring-twist design, roll-moulding.

151. SKELTON-in-CLEVELAND, North Yorkshire. All Saints Church (the "new" church).
SOUTH PORCH INTERNALLY:
- ✠ Incomplete and damaged sundial with incomplete lettering and runes.

152. SKIPWITH, North Yorkshire – St Helen's Church.
SQUARE TOWER - incorporating earlier single storey western annex:
- ❖ Coursed Stone Walling (lower level)/Coursed Rubble Walling (upper level).
- ❖ Square and Chamfered Double Plinth.
- ❖ Megalithic Side Alternate Quoining up to just above the tops of the lowest/lower original windows in the south and north walls and at a similar level on the west wall.
- ❖ Round-Headed Double-Splayed Windows, Ground Floor Level: arched heads half-through-stone voussoirs internally/cut out of a rectangular half-through-stone externally; half-through-stone jambs similar to the coursed stonework in the adjoining walling; sills provided by the top of the coursed stonework directly below.
- ❖ Coursed Rubble Walling and some smaller sized quoining extending above the coursed stonework and megalithic side alternate quoining up to the upper Anglo-Saxon Chamfered String-Course.
- ❖ Round-Headed Double-Splayed Windows, First Floor Level: half-through-stone voussoirs; jambs similar to the stonework in the adjoining coursed rubble walling; sills provided by the top of the coursed rubble stonework directly below.
- ❖ Round-Headed Double-Splayed Window, First Floor Level, South Wall, off-centre to the east: half-through-stone voussoirs internally/cut out of a rectangular half-through-stone externally; jambs similar to the stonework in the adjoining coursed rubble walling; sill provided by the top of the coursed rubble stonework directly below.
- ❖ Prokrossos in the west wall just below the Square (lower) String-Course – it can no longer be confidently identified.
- ❖ Square String-Course separating the tall lower Anglo-Saxon stage from the shorter upper Anglo-Saxon Stage.
- ❖ Chamfered String-Course separating the Anglo-Saxon stonework from the 14th century belfry stage above.
- ❖ Internally: Round-Headed Tower Archway: through-stone voussoirs with concentric bands of hood-moulding; rectangular imposts supporting both arched head and hood-moulding; jambs including through-stones and megalithic stones with parallel pilaster-strips; both the hood-moulding and pilaster-strips comprise separate half-square outer bands and half-round inner bands; all supported by protruding single square plinth.
- ❖ Internally First Floor: Blocked Round-Headed Doorway providing access to a first floor gallery or balcony at the west end of the nave: voussoirs; chamfered imposts; jambs and sill similar to the coursed stonework in the adjoining walling.
- ❖ Internally First Floor: In the west face of the east wall: Rectangular Recess probably indicating the presence of an altar and/or a reliquary (box).
- ✠ Internally. Stone Slab: graffiti probably depicting a scene from Norse Mythology, destruction of the gods at Ragnarök – Thor fighting the world serpent, Odin eaten by Fenrir the wolf.
- ✠ Externally. Possible Decorative Panels in the lower first stage of the tower. One panel depicts in profile to the right a boar – it has a rather square body, a neck, angled head, a closed snout, a half-round eye, and an ear. It can be identified in the south wall adjacent to the tenth quoin up from the plinth in the south-west corner of the tower. Another panel, decorated with a chalice, may also survive but it is very difficult to see – it is in the west wall, on the stone to the right at the top of the

bottom window. Other panels may survive elsewhere not necessarily in their original position but these are difficult to confidently identify.

NAVE:
- Coursed Rubble Walling above later inserted arches accessing the north and south aisles.

153. SOCKBURN, County Durham – All Saint's Church and Conyers Chapel.

NAVE:
- Vestiges of Coursed Rubble Walling.
- Side Alternate Quoining.

CONYERS CHAPEL INTERNALLY:
- Nearly complete and incomplete parts of Free-Arm and Ring-Head Cross-Heads with designs and patterns including: flat-moulding, grooved-moulding, plait-work design, plant-scroll design, ring-chain design. Parts of human bodies.
- Incomplete Angular Cross-Shafts with designs and patterns including: baluster-shaft moulding, cable-moulding, flat-moulding, grooved-moulding, interlace design, key-pattern design, knot-work design, pellets, plait-work design, ring-chain design, ring-knot design, ring-twist design, roll-moulding, spiral design, triquetra-knot design. Figures of warriors, horseman holding a bird, male and female human figures. Creatures and beasts, serpents, and a bird. Scenes with figures from Norse Mythology.
- Nearly complete and incomplete Hogback Grave-Covers with designs and patterns including: incised cross, diamond-pattern, flat-moulding, grooved-moulding, interlace design, key-pattern design, linear pattern design, pellets, plait-work design, ring-chain design, roll-moulding, spiral design, tegulations, zigzag-design. Human figures, including female (incomplete), horsemen. Creatures and beasts including serpent-headed creatures and beasts, end bear-like beasts and a bird. Scenes with humans and beasts.

154. SOMPTING, West Sussex – St Mary the Virgin Church.

WEST SQUARE TOWER:
- Random Rubble Walling with Flints, Roman tile-like bricks.
- "Cut-Back" Long and Short Quoining, although much of the south-east quoining appears to be a "Pilaster-Buttress"; the north-east quoining has slight indications of vestiges of what may have been a similar Pilaster-Buttress.
- "Rhenish Helm" Roof.
- Square String-Course, mostly complete, separating the shorter lower stage from the taller upper stage. It is decorated with a horizontal design involving protruding, vertically angle-sided, interconnected squares which alternate above and below the mid-way height of the string-course; the stonework above or below these squares appears to have been removed.
- Pilaster-Strips laid in long and short fashion – mostly incomplete. Where they survive below the string-course the square-shaped pilaster-strips have semi-circular bases comprising a chamfered stone on top of a square stone. In the south wall the pilaster-strip is demonstrably out of alignment with the central pilaster-strip above the string-course. Above the string-course, in the centre of each wall, half-round pilaster-strips have corbel-like capitals. In addition, on each wall below the level of the belfry openings, the pilaster-strips include an inverted, half-round, bell-like shaped capital decorated top and bottom with a horizontal band of roll-moulding in relief. Between the bands of roll-moulding the capital on the north wall is decorated in relief with three tapering rows of vertical, leaf-like features, whilst the capital on the west wall is decorated in relief with vertically-placed long, scroll-like, leaves; the decoration on the south and east walls has indications of a plant design but both are heavily weathered.

- The base of the pilaster-strip in the east wall terminates with a square horizontal stone just above the apex of the current roof of the nave.
- North Wall, Ground Floor: Round-Headed Double-Splayed Window: arched heads, jambs and sill - facing stones but mostly constructed with rubble and flints similar to the adjoining walling.
- South Wall, First Floor: Triangular-Headed Window – not splayed: two angled rectangular half-through stones forming the head; each jamb one vertical and one horizontal half-through-stones; half-through-stone sill.
- North Wall, First Floor. Pair of Triangular-Headed Windows – not splayed: two angled rectangular half-through stones forming each of their heads; externally jambs faced with half-round moulded stonework with a pilaster-strip overlying their shared central jamb, but jambs and sills mostly constructed with rubble and flints similar to the adjoining walling. Internally, mid-wall jamb decorated with a human head in portrait.
- North Wall, Second Floor. Pair of Round-Headed Windows – not splayed: voussoirs (the eastern window with its half-round moulded head may have been restored at a later, not Anglo-Saxon, date); externally jambs faced with half-round moulded stonework with a pilaster-strip overlying their shared central jamb, but jambs and sills mostly constructed with rubble and flints similar to the adjoining walling; sills with protruding facing stones.
- North and South Walls, Belfry Stage: Round-Headed Double-Splayed Belfry Openings: each of arched heads constructed with a single stone shaped to provide a curvature in both its upper and lower borders; no imposts; jambs a mixture of larger, horizontally placed, facing stones, with rubble and flints similar to the adjoining walling; cylindrical mid-wall shafts with no bases and cushion-like capitals – north wall capitals decorated in relief with vertically placed long, scroll-like, leaves above a horizontal band of roll-moulding. Above mid-wall shafts rectangular through-stone slab placed horizontally so that its sides overhang the mid-wall shaft – the slab supports junction of both arched heads above; sill provided by the top of rubble stonework below.
- East and West Walls, Belfry Stage: Triangular-Headed Single-Belfry Openings: two angled rectangular stones forming each head; jambs and sills constructed with rubble and flints similar to the adjoining walling – jambs of opening in west wall also include reused Roman tile-like bricks. The two openings are separated by a block of walling, similarly constructed to the jambs, which runs through the entire depth of the wall; externally this walling has the addition of the centrally placed pilaster-strip.
- Internally. Tower Archway: voussoirs with half-round soffit-roll; recessed imposts. Square jambs whose opposing faces have protruding, integral, central half-round moulded cylindrical soffit-shafts with an inverted, half-round, bell-like, shaped capital decorated in relief with three horizontal rows of vertically placed leaves with club-like ends; all the decoration is above a narrow band of horizontal roll-moulding. The bases of the soffit-shafts are half-round. Between the bottom of the imposts and a narrow band of horizontal roll-moulding, the capitals on the faces of the jambs are decorated with a vertical scroll design surrounding a bunch of berries. All the stonework forming the jambs and shafts stand on a rectangular, extending, plinth. The Archway is placed off-centre in the wall and this may have been to accommodate an altar which was at one time to the north of the archway and inside the tower.

NAVE INTERNALLY:
- Random Rubble Walling with Flints.
- Most of arched head of a blocked Round-Headed Double-Splayed Window: voussoirs.

CHANCEL INTERNALLY:
- Reused parts of String-Course decorated with plant designs.

NAVE INTERNALLY:
- ✠ Parts of Frieze decorated with roll-moulding, plant-scroll design and inhabited plant-scroll design with a creature. A fragment is in the chancel, another is in the chapel on the north side of the tower.
- ✠ Panel with haloed figure below an arch – it was altered in the 12th century and the identity of the figure is a matter of debate.
- ✠ Fragment with flat-moulding and plant-scroll design.

155. SPROXTON, Leicestershire – St Bartholomew's Church.
CHURCHYARD:
- ✠ Cross: tapering rectangular cross-base, angular cross-shaft, ring-head cross-head with designs and patterns including: flat-moulding, interlace design, plait-work design, ring-chain design, inhabited vine-scroll design including a beast. See adjacent: PHOTO 691. Sproxton, showing the west face on the right and the north side on the left.

156. STANTON LACY, Shropshire – St Peter's Church.
NAVE:
- ❖ Coursed Rubble Walling.
- ❖ Megalithic Side Alternate Quoining.
- ❖ Pilaster-Strips constructed in long and short fashion.
- ❖ Blocked Round-Headed Doorway: through-stone voussoirs with accompanying hood-moulding placed on top of the voussoirs. The hood-moulding comprises mostly a band of roll-moulding which is chamfered on its upper part. Above the adjacent stonework has been arranged to reflect the curvature of the hood-moulding with a square stone placed in its centre. This central single stone has been incised with a free-arm cross in relief with a central pilaster-strip above with a rectangular base with four pellets below. The doorway has through-stone chamfered imposts; through-stone square jambs with protruding chamfered bases. Pilaster-Strips parallel and adjacent to the jambs with square bases above ground and above the bases of the jambs. See adjacent: PHOTO 692. Stanton Lacy 2, showing the exterior north face.

PHOTO 691. Sproxton.

PHOTO 692. Stanton Lacy 2.

NORTH TRANSEPT:
- ❖ Coursed Rubble Walling.
- ❖ Megalithic Side Alternate Quoining.
- ❖ Pilaster-Strips, constructed in long and short fashion, with short horizontal cross pieces.
- ❖ Blocked, incomplete round-headed doorway which has lost its dressed facings.
- ❖ Megalithic Round-Headed Single-Splayed Window: arched head cut out of half-through-stone lintel; two megalithic stones forming each of the jambs, single stone forms the sill. Date of window uncertain.

157. STAPLEFORD, Nottinghamshire - St Helen's Church.

- Most of a Cross-Shaft with a lower circular-shaped part and an upper angular-shaped part with three collars; with designs and patterns including: cable-moulding, flat-moulding, bands of now unidentifiable moulding, interlace design, knot-work design, plant-scroll design, ring-chain design including free-rings, ring-knot design, roll-moulding, scroll design; winged figure.

158.   STONEGRAVE, North Yorkshire – Minster (Holy Trinity Church).
TOWER:
- Possible Saxo-Norman Round-Headed Doorway – now with a 13th century window inserted in its head.
- Possible Saxo-Norman Round-Headed Single-Splayed Window: arched head is cut out of a monolithic lintel; jambs each comprise two stones.

NAVE INTERNALLY:
- Incomplete Ring-Head Cross-Head with most of its Angular Cross-Shaft with designs and patterns including: flat-moulding, interlace design, knot-work design, plait-work design; standing human figure; long-stemmed free-arm cross; probably a Celtic priest. See adjacent: PHOTO 693. Stonegrave 2, showing the west face on the left and the south side on the right.
- Parts of Angular Cross-Shafts with designs and patterns including: flat-moulding, incised lines, interlace design, free-ring designs, knot-work design, pellets, plait-work design, incomplete human figure and part of head of another.
- Parts of a Cross-Base with designs and patterns including: cable-moulding, flat-moulding, plait-work design; beast with bird on its back; another beast.
- Part of weathered Grave-Cover with roll-moulding, plait-work design; faint hunting scene with standing archer and stag. Possible fragment from this Grave-Cover with cable-moulding and plait-work design.

PHOTO 693. Stonegrave 2.

159.   STOW-IN-LINDSEY, Lincolnshire – St Mary's Church. Cruciform Church.
NAVE INTERNALLY:
- Part of Grave-Cover with cable-moulding and figure-of-eight knot-work design.

NAVE EXTERNALLY:
- Part of Grave-Marker with cable-moulding.

STAIR TURRET, - not Anglo-Saxon, possible reuse of Anglo-Saxon Windows:
- Round-Headed Single-Splayed Windows: external arched heads cut out of half-through-stone lintels; jambs each comprise a single megalithic half-through-stone; tops of coursed rubble stonework below provide sills.
- Circular Single-Splayed Windows: external faces constructed with a single stone slab (the window frame) through which circular apertures cut – one with concentric circular grooves around the aperture.

CENTRAL CROSSING AND BASE OF THE TOWER:
- The church displays a distinct characteristic of Anglo-Saxon cruciform churches with the walling of the lower Anglo-Saxon part of the current tower wider than the width of any of the original four buildings (nave, chancel, south and north transepts) joined to it. See externally, quoining and some of its adjacent walling can be identified in all four corners of the tower jutting out from the lines of the present walls of the nave, chancel and

transepts.

CENTRAL CROSSING:
- Coursed Rubble Walling.
- Three-Stepped Plinth with a square base with two upper chamfered courses.
- Megalithic Side Alternate Quoining – some restoration at a later, not Anglo-Saxon, date. In the south-east and north-east corners some of the lower quoins have been "Cut-Back" and some of the upper quoins appear to have been laid in Face Alternate fashion.
- Internally: Megalithic Round-Headed Archways – all four of the archways are of similar size and are the largest Anglo-Saxon archways surviving. (Ignore the later 15th century pointed "Perpendicular" arches.) Arched heads - two bands of voussoirs, adjacent and concentric, both have been similarly subdivided into three distinctive moulded shapes a protruding band of roll-moulding, above a sunken lower half of a "U"-shaped curve, above a band of half-square flat-moulding in line with the faces of the walls. With accompanying hood-moulding divided into an outer half-square band and an inner band sculptured to provide the lower half of a "U"-shaped curve. Additionally, west face of western arch has the hood-moulding decorated with "palmette design". Imposts horizontally divided into an upper rectangular half and a lower chamfered half; they extend across the full width of the walls. Square jambs with two separate bands of half-round and half-square pilaster-strips whose bases terminate in bulbous corbels immediately above the top of the five-stepped plinth supporting all the stonework above forming the archways.
- ✠ Internally: Incised on stonework on the right-hand side of Chancel Archway is a representations of a Viking longship - believed to be the earliest such representation in England. Apparently there is another on the right-hand/east side of the South Transept Archway, behind the War Memorial.

TRANSEPTS:
- Coursed Rubble Walling noticeably more neatly coursed and squared stonework higher up the walls, adjacent to where the quoining is not damaged and in good condition. This change in construction detail indicates two separate building periods.
- Megalithic Side Alternate Quoining with some of the lower quoins in the north-east corner of the North Transept "Cut-Back".
- North Transept North Wall. Megalithic Flat-Headed Single-Splayed Window: Escomb jambs with an exterior rebate with nine surviving dowel-holes all for a shutter; top of coursed rubble stonework below provides sill. Window head is a later replacement, not Anglo-Saxon. Internally, much of the stonework has been altered at a later, not Anglo-Saxon, date.
- North Transept West Wall. Blocked, incomplete, Flat-Headed Window: four stones, three laid in Escomb fashion forming part of the south jamb, and one stone probably forming part of its head above. (Nothing can be seen internally.)
- North Transept West Wall Internally. Round-Headed Doorway: through-stone voussoirs; chamfered imposts; Escomb jambs standing on a protruding base. Adjacent coursed rubble stonework of walling. See adjacent: PHOTO 694. Stow-in-Lindsey 15, showing the east face of the doorway.
- South Transept South Wall. Round-Headed Single-Splayed Window: externally arched head constructed from well-dressed ashlar lintel with hood-moulding decorated with palmette design with label-stops – not decorated, internally three-quarter-through-stone voussoirs. Internally, jambs

PHOTO 694. Stow-in-Lindsey 15.

comprise an inner and an outer set of facing stones laid similarly to long and short quoining with intervening coursed rubble stonework. Externally, facing stones laid similarly to long and short quoining – some stones with dowel-holes for shutter(s). Through-stone sill.

160. STRETHALL, Essex – St Mary the Virgin Church.
NAVE:
- Random Rubble Walling with Flints.
- Long and Short Quoining. See adjacent right: PHOTO 696. Strethall 4.
- Round-Headed Double-Splayed Window: constructed with rubble with flints similar to the stonework in the adjoining walling – internally plastered and its external face now enclosed by the tower.
- Circular Double-Splayed Window constructed with rubble with flints similar to the stonework in the adjoining walling - internally plastered and its external face now enclosed by the tower. See adjacent left: PHOTO 695. Strethall 3, showing the round-headed double-splayed window arrowed red, and the circular double-splayed window arrowed black.
- Internally. Megalithic Round-Headed Chancel Archway – plaster obscures some of the construction details; apparently with voussoirs; imposts extending beyond hood-moulding and pilaster-strips. Imposts decorated with horizontal bands of flat-moulding and roll-moulding alternating with horizontal grooves. The lower band of flat-moulding includes an angled (inwards) band of diamond-shaped lozenges with vertically bevelled centres. The Archway has apparently through-stone Escomb jambs standing on square plinths projecting from the face of the north, south and west walls but not the east walls. In addition the Archway has hood-moulding and pilaster-strips which are divided into three bands; half-square – the inner band nearest the archway; wide half-round – the middle band; and a narrow band angled and raised on its outer edges but rounded on its inner edges – the outer band. The extended imposts provide the capitals for the pilaster-strips. The cubical bases for the pilaster-strips protrude from the west wall. Note: east face of chancel archway is not decorated.

PHOTO 695. Strethall 3.

PHOTO 696. Strethall 4.

161. SUNDERLAND – Museum.
All items identified from St Peter's Church, Monkwearmouth, Sunderland.
- Four Fragments from what appears as half of an Ionic Capital probably originally set against a wall rather than free-standing. One face decorated with part of a spiral shape.
- Architectural Fragment with roll-moulding, ring-chain design.
- Two almost complete Baluster-Shafts decorated around their circumference with horizontal sets of grooves.
- Probable Terminal from a stone chair or bench in the shape of a three-dimensional serpent's head with distinctive eyes, a slit-like mouth, grooves to indicate folded skin, a collar around its neck and roll-moulding on the back of its head.
- Fragment of the end of an arm of a Free-Arm Cross with roll-moulding.

- Fragment of the end of an arm from a Free-Arm Cross-Head decorated on one face with flat-moulding and petals from a flower.
- Fragment of probably a cross-shaft with cable-moulding, meander-pattern design, roll-moulding.
- What could be part of a cross-shaft or a piece of furniture. On one face is part of a panel outlined by flat-moulding containing interlace design with pellets, with on the top, part of a panel outlined by flat-moulding containing a zigzag design including pellets.
- Incomplete Grave-Marker with parallel grooved-moulding forming part a panel containing the left-hand, horizontal, arm of a square ended, free-arm cross, part of its square centre, and part of its lower vertical arm. All of the cross is outlined by parallel grooves apart from the horizontal arm which has an additional central groove – the lower vertical arm may be similar but its width is incomplete. Above the horizontal arm are the letters "EO" in runes and below are the letters in capitals "AID" thought to be parts of the name of the individual before and after entering the monastery.
- Incomplete Grave-Marker broken horizontally in two and placed together with flat-moulding, parallel grooves. One face is decorated with two standing human figures, in opposite profile, facing each other. Both figures hold the opposite sides of a rectangular box above a free-arm cross. Above the break in stonework is a runic inscription spelling the masculine name "Tidfirth". (Possibly commemorating the last Bishop of Hexham, Tidfirth, who was on his way to Rome and died at St Peter's Church, Monkwearmouth, Sunderland in 821.) Above the runes an incomplete design involving uprights with a loop in between. The other face has a standing human figure in movement indicated by the bend in their right leg. The figure is in portrait, but with their head turned to their left; it has distinctively long arms.
- Fragment of stonework whose purpose cannot now be confidently identified decorated with flat-moulding providing part of a panel containing a mixture of ring-chain and ring-knot designs.
- Fragment of stonework whose purpose cannot now be confidently identified decorated with ring-chain design and roll-moulding.

162.   SUNDERLAND – MONKWEARMOUTH, County Durham – St Peter's Church.
WEST PORCH - now incorporated into Square Tower.
- Coursed Rubble Walling.
- Megalithic Side Alternate Quoining (much restored).
- Round-Headed Archway: through-stone voussoirs divided into two-thirds/one-third by a central concentric groove; through-stone half-chamfered imposts; through-stone Escomb jambs, each with a pair of baluster-shafts and below a unique decoration of entwined serpents.
- Round-Headed Doorways into porticus – rebated for doors: through-stone voussoirs; through-stone imposts; jambs each comprise a single megalithic vertical through-stone whose bases are notched into monolithic sill.
- Frieze decorated with humans and creatures and beasts in motion framed by bands of cable-moulding; now faint. Replaced in 19th century with original now on floor at west end of nave.
- Barrel-Vaulted Roof added when tower was built.
- First Floor, North Wall: Blocked Flat-Headed Megalithic Doorway: monolithic lintel; jambs mostly comprising large vertical stones; monolithic sill.
- First Floor, West Wall: Restored Megalithic Round-Headed Single-Splayed Window: half-through-stones externally/arched head cut out of a half-through-stone lintel divided into two internally; externally, jambs mostly faced with stones from 1866 restoration/internally, jambs appear original, each jamb comprises two half-through-

stones. Internally, vestiges of red paint and indications of cable-moulding on arched head in particular. Single stone sill externally dates from 1866 restoration/faced with coursed rubble stonework internally.
- First Floor, South Wall: Blocked Megalithic Flat-Headed Single-Splayed Window - jambs now their most distinctive feature.
- First Floor, West Wall: Base of Gabled Roof indicated by the chamfered string-course identifiable on each of the three walls; vestiges of a statue; scaring indicating gable roof of former porch.

SQUARE TOWER - built on top of former Porch.
- East wall of the tower built on top of the gable roofline of west wall of nave.
- Tower narrows slightly towards the top but with no set-backs.
- Coursed Rubble Walling - more carefully dressed and built using larger stones above the base of the gable roofline of the former porch.
- Side Alternate Quoining no longer megalithic above the porch.
- Chamfered and Square String-Courses - lower two string-courses on north wall incomplete.
- West Wall, Third Stage: Round-Headed Window: externally the aperture has been cut out of a single slab, internally arched head cut out of three-quarter-through-stone lintel; jambs and sill constructed of rubble similar to the stonework in the adjoining walling.
- West, North and South Walls, Fourth (top) Stage: Round-Headed Double-Belfry Openings: arched heads each cut out of the same single lintel; chamfered imposts protruding from the faces of the walling and into the central void, extending to separate the strip-work below from the hood-moulding above; rubble jambs of similar size, and laid in similar courses to the rubble stonework in the adjoining walling; cylindrical mid-wall shafts without bases or capitals. The mid-wall shafts support a rectangular through-stone slab placed horizontally and extending through the entire depth of the walling so that its sides overhang the mid-wall shaft. The through-stone slabs support the centre of the single lintel above. The sills are provided by a row of horizontal rectangular stones, originally projecting from the faces of the walls, which supported the mid-wall shaft, the central voids, the jambs, and extended to support the protruding, strip-work, parallel to the jambs - the strip-work also has distinctive, square, bases. The stones of sill supporting the mid-wall shaft and the two central voids are damaged and no longer project as much from the face of the wall as they once did. A band of protruding, semi-circular, hood-moulding with its own square bases extends above the single lintels. It is separated by the extended imposts, from the bands of protruding, vertical, strip-work with its own square bases parallel to the jambs below. High above the centre of each opening, above the hood-moulding, are two facing stones which have each had a semi-circle cut out to provide a circular sound-hole - these are now blocked.

NAVE:
- Coursed Rubble Walling including vestiges of Herringbone Masonry (internally).
- Megalithic Side Alternate Quoining: North-West original but with evidence of reconstruction towards the top - probably dating from the 1866 restoration. South-West is mostly an 1866 reconstruction.
- Internally, West Wall. Restored Round-Headed Doorway - rebated for door: through-stone voussoirs (splaying is 19th century); through-stone imposts; jambs each comprise a single megalithic vertical through-stone whose base is notched into monolithic sill.
- First Floor Internally: Round-Headed Window: half-through-stone voussoirs internally (inside nave), arched head cut out of half-through-stone lintel externally (inside tower); circa 1866 jambs lengthened vertically for a doorway to provide access into the Tower.

- Second Floor Internally. Round-Headed Single-Splayed Windows: arched heads cut out of quarter-through-stone lintels externally/three-quarter through-stone voussoirs internally; through-stone imposts; through-stone jambs; through-stone sills - internally, extended in 1866 to accommodate the inclusion of Anglo-Saxon baluster-shafts in the splays of each jamb.
- Second Floor Internally: Chamfered String-Course; surviving now inside the Tower but with a section surviving externally in the south-west corner of the Nave.

NORTH PORTICUS - now internally in North Aisle and below glass panel in the Exhibition Centre:
- Part of the foundations of the easternmost Porticus on the north side of the Nave.

CHURCHYARD - west of porch/tower along south edge of driveway.
- Stonework of various dates and purposes which may include stonework from the Anglo-Saxon church and its associated monastic buildings.

EXHIBITION CENTRE - Internally:
- Part of "Abbot's Seat" and Clergy Bench – each with representation of a lion.
- Consecration Crosses (one still in the tower, one in Exhibition Centre): Each is similar and comprises a free-arm cross with fan-shaped arms in relief.
- Almost complete Grave-Cover with incomplete wing-like features, flat-moulding, large square-armed free-arm cross in relief. Latin inscription interpreted as "Here in the tomb rests Herebericht the priest in the body", known as "Herebericht Stone".
- What may have been part of a Shrine with decoration reminiscent of the carpet pages in the Lindisfarne Gospels and the Book of Durrow. Decorated with flat-moulding, interlace design, ring-chain design, roll-moulding, ribbon-shaped creature. See adjacent: PHOTO 697. Monkwearmouth 18, showing part of the creature with its angled beak arrowed red, and tapering body arrowed black.
- Incomplete Baluster-Shafts – two with vestiges of paint.
- Part of a Frieze with flat-moulding, two incomplete figures confronting each other in combat.

PHOTO 697. Monkwearmouth 18.

WEST END OF NAVE INTERNALLY:
- Stonework removed from decorated exterior frieze above the western archway into the porch – the decoration is now almost impossible to see.

DISPLAY CASE IN CORRIDOR LEADING TO "BEDE'S BAKEHOUSE" INTERNALLY.
- Round-Headed Window: arched head cut out of a monolithic lintel.
- Incomplete Grave-Cover in four pieces with grooved-moulding and a cross in relief.

163.   TASBURGH, Norfolk – St Mary's Church.
ROUND TOWER:
- Coursed Rubble Walling with Flints.
- Round-Headed Single-Splayed Windows: arched heads constructed with individual stones placed on end and formed into a discernible arch; jambs and sills constructed with rubble and flints similar to the stonework in the adjoining walling.
- One row of seven Round-Headed Sunken Blind Arcading of Pilaster-Strips constructed with rubble and flints similar to the fabric of the adjoining walling, with above, another row of seven Headless (removed in building work in 1385) Sunken Blind Arcading of Pilaster-Strips constructed with rubble and flints similar to the fabric of the adjoining walling.

Anglo-Saxon Church Architecture & Stone Sculpture — 421

The two rows of arcades of Pilaster-Strips provide an alternating pattern.
- Internally. Very tall Round-Headed Tower Archway partially blocked with a later archway and doorway, not Anglo-Saxon, inserted below – the pointed late-14th century arch is roughly half the height of the Anglo-Saxon original. Although plaster obscures construction details, apparently, the voussoirs and square jambs are of rubble similar to the rubble fabric of the adjacent walling and the imposts are square stones.
- Second Floor Internally. Round-Headed Doorway reused as a window; plaster obscures construction details.

NAVE:
- Coursed Rubble Walling with Flints.
- The north-west and south-west corners of the original Nave extend buttress-like from each side of the Tower. Above the tops of these buttress-like features is faint scaring indicating the roofline of the earlier Nave.

164.   THORNHILL (NEAR DEWSBURY), West Yorkshire – St Michael and All Angels Church.
- Part of the lower vertical arm from a Free-Arm Cross-Head and part of its attached Angular Cross-Shaft with irregular-shaped interlace designs.
- Part of the end of an arm from a Free-Arm Cross-Head with flat-moulding, knot-work design and ring-knot design.
- Parts and Fragments of Angular Cross-Shafts with designs and patterns including: bush-scroll design, roll-moulding, meander-pattern design, plait-work design, plant-scroll design, stepped-pattern design, vertical incised lines forming narrow and wide bands.
- Part of Angular Cross-Shaft used as a grave-memorial to a named individual with designs and patterns including: flat-moulding, interlace design and stopped plait-work design. Incomplete Runic Inscription interpreted as "Gilswith raised up, in memory of Berhtswith, a beacon on a hill. Pray for her soul" - both personal names are feminine.
- Fragment of Angular Cross-Shaft used as a grave-memorial to a named individual with flat-moulding and incised with an incomplete Inscription in Letters interpreted as "in memory of Osberht, a monument" - Osberht is a masculine name.
- Incomplete Angular Cross-Shaft with designs and patterns including: flat-moulding, incised linear designs forming incomplete panels, plant-scroll design. Runic Inscription interpreted as "Ethelbercht set up (this memorial) in memory of Ethelwini" - both personal names are masculine .
- Incomplete Angular Cross-Shaft with designs and patterns including: flat-moulding, incised linear designs forming complete and incomplete panels, a mixture of an inhabited interlace and plant designs with beasts. Runic Inscription interpreted as "Eadred set up (this monument) in memory of Eateinne (probably a form of Eadthegn)" - both personal names are masculine.

165.   THORNTON STEWARD, North Yorkshire – St Oswald's Church.
NAVE includes the following which may be of Anglo-Saxon origin:
- Vestiges of Coursed Rubble Walling including Side Alternate Quoins.
- Vestiges of jambs of Doorway.
- Vestiges of the arches of Round-Headed Windows.
- Vestiges of Chancel Archway.
- Incomplete Plate-Ring Cross-Head with designs and patterns including: flat-moulding, grooved-moulding, pellets, roll-moulding. Crucifixion Scene.
- Part of a Ring-Head Cross-Head with flat-moulding, meander-pattern design. Incomplete Crucifixion Scene. Incomplete seated Christ in Majesty. See Page 422: PHOTO 698.

Thornton Steward, showing the west face with Christ in Majesty.
- ✠ Vestiges of a Ring-Head Cross-Head and part of its attached Angular Cross-Shaft with flat-moulding, plait-work design, central triangle design.
- ✠ Arm with indications of ring from a Ring-Head Cross-Head with free-arm cross, pellets, plait-work design.
- ✠ Fragments of Angular Cross-Shafts with pellets, spiral-scroll design; incomplete human figures, row of heads.

PHOTO 698. *Thornton Steward.*

166. THORPE-NEXT-HADDISCOE, Norfolk – St Matthias Church.
ROUND TOWER:
- ❖ Coursed Rubble Walling with Flints.
- ❖ Round-Headed Single-Splayed Windows at first and second floor levels – blocked apart from west and north: arched heads cut out of square through-stone lintels; jambs each comprise four stones of similar size – eastern jamb of north-west window at second floor level has five stones; sills constructed of coursed rubble and flints similar to the adjoining walling. The lintels of the south and west windows, at first floor level, have two semi-circular grooves concentric with the arch of the head of the window.
- ❖ Prokrossi.
- ❖ Row of Headless (removed by later building work, not Anglo-Saxon,) Sunken Blind Arcading of Pilaster-Strips constructed with rubble and flints similar to the adjoining walling.

NAVE:
- ❖ Coursed Rubble Walling with Flints.
- ❖ Side Alternate Quoins comprising small, dressed, stones – not rubble or flint.
- ❖ Internally: Circular Double-Splayed Window: constructed with rubble and flints similar to the stonework in the adjoining walling – now enclosed within tower.

167. THURSLEY, Surrey – St Michael's Church.
NAVE:
- ❖ Incomplete Round-Headed Single-Splayed Window (plaster obscures the construction details) - possibly Anglo-Saxon.

CHANCEL:
- ❖ Square Single Plinth of rubble.
- ❖ Round-Headed Double-Splayed Windows - they retain their mid-wall wooden frames; plaster obscures construction details both internally and externally.
- ❖ Internally, along the north wall and above the heads of the windows, the wall appears to be set-back. This could indicate the provisions for supporting an upper floor.

168. TITCHFIELD, Hampshire – St Peter's Church.
WEST PORCH now incorporated into Square Tower:
- ❖ Coursed Rubble Walling.
- ❖ Megalithic Side Alternate Quoining.
- ❖ Round-Headed Archway: through-stone voussoirs; no imposts; through-stone, including half-through-stone, square jambs.
- ❖ South wall: indications of blocked round-headed window: sill below external horizontal iron bar attached to the walling, above, break in the four horizontal courses of reused Roman tile-like bricks indicates positions of jambs, and above, arched head indicated by individual stones placed on end and formed into a discernible arch.

- First Floor: Little material of Anglo-Saxon origin survives.

NAVE:
- Coursed Rubble Walling.
- Megalithic Side Alternate Quoining – only south-west corner can now be identified.
- West wall survives to its full height but little original material can now be seen: vestiges above the roof of 12th century north aisle – now shaped like an oblong triangle. Internally: vestiges of coursed rubble walling at west and east ends of south wall; plaster obscures.

169.   WARDEN, Northumberland – St Michael's and All Angels Church.

SQUARE TOWER:
- Coursed Stone Walling.
- Side Alternate and Face Alternate including Megalithic Quoining.
- Round-Headed Single-Splayed West Window: arched head cut out of a single stone providing the shape of a free-arm cross; jambs laid horizontally, a single large stone with one (north jamb)/two (south jamb) additional horizontal stones above; sill provided by the top of the coursed stonework directly below.
- Round-Headed Single-Splayed Window in lower south wall: arched head of an irregular shape cut out of a monolithic lintel; jambs laid horizontally with stonework similar to the adjoining coursed stone walling; sill provided by the top of the coursed stonework directly below.
- Round-Headed Single-Splayed Window in upper south wall: arched head cut out of a monolithic lintel; vertical monolithic jambs; sill provided by the top of the coursed stonework directly below.
- Internally: Round-Headed Tower Archway of uncertain date: voussoirs; moulded imposts of likely Roman origin; square jambs.
- Internally: First Floor: Indications of Blocked Round-Headed Doorway linking the Tower and Nave.

CHURCHYARD – close to the south wall of the tower:
- Saxo-Norman Hammer-Head Cross-Head with attached Angular Cross-Shaft; the cross-head is decorated with a free-arm cross in relief and a pellet off-centre. See adjacent: PHOTO 699. Warden, showing the south wall of the tower with hammer-head cross-head and angular cross-shaft arrowed red.

PHOTO 699. Warden.

NAVE:
- Vestiges of Coursed Stone Walling.
- Part of Square Single Plinth.
- Possible indications of the base of the north-west quoins.

SOUTH PORCH INTERNALLY:
- Grave-Slab reusing part of Roman Altar with cable-moulding, extended loops, round-ended on left-had side, triangular-ended on right-hand side, combined with interlace design, plait-work design, free-ring designs and pellets; large standing human figure in portrait.
- Grave-Marker reusing part of a Roman Column incised with a free-arm cross within a circle.
- Anglo-Saxon Grave-Marker reusing part of a Roman Column cut down with a centrally placed vertical band of flat-moulding in relief on its front face.
- Anglo-Saxon Grave-Marker decorated in relief with a free-arm cross with central roundel with fan-shaped arms.

CHANCEL INTERNALLY:
- ✠ Possibly part of a Saxo-Norman Grave-Cover reminiscent of a hogback grave-cover: recumbent, triangular-shaped, with tegulations and roll-moulding.

170.   WHITCHURCH, Hampshire – All Hallows Church.
NAVE INTERNALLY:
- ✠ Round-Headed Grave-Memorial to a named individual with designs and patterns including: flat-moulding, scroll design, tree-scroll design. Half-figure of Christ in a stepped recess with the right arm giving a blessing and the left arm holding a book. Inscription which has been interpreted as "Here rests the body of Friðburg or Frioburga (a feminine name) buried into peace".

171.   WHITHORN, Dumfriesshire & Galloway – Priory Museum.
INTERNALLY:
- ✠ Pillar-Stone Memorials including "Latinus Stone" with Latin inscription to Latinus, aged 35, and his daughter, aged 4; "Peter Stone" incised with a free-arm cross with fan-shaped arms surrounded by concentric circles with inscription interpreted as "the place of Peter".
- ✠ Slab known as "Golgotha Stone" representing the central cross of Christ with a cross on each side representing the two thieves "Dismas" and "Gestas". Incised long-stemmed free-arm crosses, roll-moulding.
- ✠ Cross-Head and nearly all of Cross-Shaft known as "The Monreith Cross" comprising a Disc-Head Cross-Head and an Angular Cross-Shaft. Cross-Head with distinctive grooves, pellet-like features in the "eyelets", roll-moulding. Cross-Shaft with figure-of-eight ring-knot design and roll-moulding.
- ✠ Plate-Ring Cross-Head with grooved-moulding, pellet-like features in the "eyelets", stopped plait-work design, and part of its attached Angular Cross-Shaft with cable-moulding, stopped plait-work design; vestiges of runic inscription.
- ✠ Plate-Ring Cross-Head with roll-moulding, Part of Disc-Head Cross-Head – not decorated.
- ✠ Part of Angular Cross-Shafts with designs and patterns including: cable-moulding, diamond-pattern design, flat-moulding, interlace design, plait-work design; two haloed figures.
- ✠ Slabs incised with complete and incomplete Disc-Head Cross-Heads, Free-Arm Cross-Heads, Plate-Ring Cross-Heads, Ring-Head Cross-Heads and Cross-Shafts with designs and patterns including: cable-moulding, flat-moulding, free-arm crosses with fan-shaped arms surrounded by a circle, distinctive grooves, interlace design, key-pattern design, knot-work design, pellet and pellet-like features in the "eyelets", plait-work design, ring-chain design, ring-knot design, roll-moulding, scroll design, stepped-pattern moulding, stopped plait-work design. One inscription in runes including the feminine name "Hwitu", another slab with an incomplete runic inscription including representations of the letters "f", "e", "r", "th".
- ✠ Cross-Base and what is described as a "Stone Collar" for securing the base of the shaft; neither is decorated.
- ✠ Stone Pillars incised and decorated with designs and patterns including: disc-head cross-head with pellet-like features in the eyelets, free-arm crosses, linear and circular designs; beasts; human figures.

172.   WHITTINGHAM, Northumberland – St Bartholomew's Church.
SQUARE TOWER:
- ❖ Coursed Rubble Walling.
- ❖ Chamfered Single Plinth.

- Side Alternate Quoining in the lower three (south-west corner)/four (north-west corner) courses, and with Long and Short Quoining (some in "Sussex" fashion) in the upper fourteen (south-west corner)/thirteen (north-west corner – some restoration) courses.
- Internally: Restored Megalithic Round-Headed Tower Archway: with original voussoirs, above the imposts, which on the south side of the archway comprise two voussoirs on the east face and four on the west face, and on the north side of the archway comprise four voussoirs on both the east and west faces; chamfered imposts decorated horizontally in the centre with a row of horizontal pellets in a groove; through-stone square Escomb-like jambs; whole archway supported by a protruding chamfered single square plinth.

NAVE:
- Coursed Rubble Walling.
- Chamfered Single Plinth.
- Side Alternate Quoining in the lower three (south-west corner)/seven (north-west corner – some restoration) courses, and with Long and Short Quoining (some in "Sussex" fashion) in the upper seven (south-west corner)/six (north-west corner) courses.
- Internally: incomplete Blocked Round-Headed Opening possibly to a northern Porticus. Three voussoirs survive from the western arm of its arched head, along with the western impost, and ten stones from the western jamb.

CHURCHYARD WALL:
- Almost complete Free-Arm Cross-Head placed on trapezoid-shaped Cross-Base; neither are decorated.

173. WICKHAM, Berkshire – St Swithun's Church.
SQUARE TOWER - See adjacent: PHOTO 700. Wickham, showing the north wall on the left and the west wall on the right.

- Coursed Rubble Walling with Flints.
- Long and Short Quoining.
- South Wall: Restored Blocked Round-Headed Doorway above ground level for external access – no distinctive Anglo-Saxon features surviving.
- West Wall, lower window, Round-Headed Double-Splayed Window: arched head constructed with individual stones, possibly Roman tile-like bricks, placed on end and formed into a discernible arch; jambs and sill are a mixture of rubble, flints and reused Roman tile-like bricks all obscured by rendering from the 1845 restoration.
- West Wall, upper window, Round-Headed Double-Splayed Window: appears to have been cut out of a single slab (there is some cracking and damage); splay has been rendered.

PHOTO 700. Wickham.

- Below the current, top, belfry stage: North and South Walls: Restored Round-Headed Double-Belfry Openings: arched heads constructed with voussoirs; north opening square imposts protruding into the central void only, no imposts in restored south opening; north opening jambs include facing stones laid in side alternate fashion, jambs dating from 1845 restoration south opening; mid-wall, possibly reused Roman, shafts; to support the centre of the head of each of the double-openings a rectangular through-stone slab has been placed horizontally on top of the mid-wall shaft so that its sides overhang the mid-wall shaft. The through-stone slabs support the junction of both of the arched heads above; monolithic sills but they may date from 1845 restoration.

174. WILSFORD, Lincolnshire – St Mary's Church.
NAVE:
- Coursed Rubble Walling.
- Megalithic Long and Short Quoining.

CHANCEL:
- Coursed Rubble Walling.

NORTH AISLE:
✠ Fragment of Grave-Cover with part of an arm of a centrally placed free-arm cross.
✠ Fragment of Grave-Marker with gridiron design and linear designs.

175. WING, Buckinghamshire - All Saints Church.
NAVE:
- Coursed Rubble Walling.
- Vestiges of Side Alternate Quoining.
- Internally. Arcade of Interlocking Megalithic Round-Headed Archways: north wall two-stepped imposts, south wall three-stepped imposts; square jambs. Construction details are covered by plaster. These archways originally providing access into Anglo-Saxon north and south aisles which have been demolished and replaced with existing aisles.
- Internally: Restored Round-Headed Chancel Archway with hood-moulding placed on top of the voussoirs. Construction details hidden by plaster.
- Internally above Chancel Archway. Restored Round-Headed Double-Windows with interlocking arched heads each with radially placed reused Roman tile-like bricks placed on their ends; two-stepped, imposts protruding from the faces of the walls and overhang the central void; jambs constructed of coursed rubble walling – see externally, plastered internally; mid-wall baluster-shaft with a bulbous base and square capital. Stonework above mid-wall baluster shaft re-shaped at a later, not Anglo-Saxon, date. See adjacent: PHOTO 701. Wing 5.
- Internally First Floor. Round-Headed Doorways for external access to Western Gallery. Much of their construction details are hidden by plaster, one is partially blocked. However the north doorway has an arched head formed with voussoirs, and the south doorway, although partially blocked, has some stones exposed which form the upper parts of its jambs and the bottom voussoirs of the western arm of its arched head.

PHOTO 701. Wing 5.

NORTH AISLE part of east wall:
- Coursed Rubble Walling.
- Square Single Plinth.
- Blocked Round-Headed Doorway whose arched head is formed with voussoirs; both the voussoirs and the jambs similar to the coursed rubble stonework in the adjoining walling.

SEVEN SIDED APSIDAL CHANCEL:
- Coursed Rubble Walling.

CHANCEL EXTERNALLY:
- Vestiges of possible Double-Splayed Windows: arched heads constructed with individual stones placed on end and formed into a discernible arch which is incomplete. These can be identified above 14th century windows, but below arched heads of the arcade of round-headed pilaster-strips in north and south walls.
- Incomplete blind arcade of Round-Headed Pilaster-Strips: arched heads constructed with

individual stones placed on end and formed into a discernible arch; rectangular imposts; the individual stones forming the vertical pilaster-strips are fairly uniform in size and in their square shape (their length is hidden within the depth of the walling). Above the intersection of the arched heads these pilaster-strips continue vertically towards the roof.
- Incomplete blind arcade of Triangular-Headed Pilaster-Strips. These can be identified high above the blind arcade of round-headed pilaster-strips and extending up towards the roof.
- Complete and incomplete blocked Round-Headed Recesses - below apex of blind arcade of triangular-headed pilaster-strips. These recesses are similar to round-headed windows but not splayed. It is thought they were always blocked. Arched heads constructed with individual stones placed on end and formed into a discernible arch; rubble jambs and sills similar to the coursed rubble stonework in the adjoining walling.

CRYPT
- Coursed Rubble Walling.
- Central Octagonal Chamber with a barrel-vaulted roof supported by piers which enable the roof to extend over an outer ambulatory and also support the archways in the north, south and east side walls. These archways, with voussoirs and jambs all constructed with rubble similar to the stonework in the adjoining walling, provided access between the ambulatory and the central chamber. (Entrance to the ambulatory was from the east end of the Nave.)

176. WINTERBOURNE STEEPLETON, Dorset – St Michael's Church.
NAVE:
- Coursed Rubble Walling.
- Megalithic Side Alternate Quoining.
- Possible Saxo-Norman Flat-Headed Doorways (south is blocked): large half-round tympana outlined with hood-moulding – the horizontal bases of the tympana provide the flat-heads for the doorways; no imposts; megalithic square jambs rebated for doors.

CHANCEL INTERNALLY:
- Panel with most of a flying, haloed, winged, angel in profile to the right. The head of the angel is half-turned in portrait and looks backwards over its horizontal body with upturned legs and feet; the halo and the wings are incomplete.

SOUTH WALL OF NAVE EXTERNALLY:
- Stone with incomplete Inscription – the surviving letters are very faint and difficult to identify, they provide no obvious wording.

177. WIRKSWORTH, Derbyshire – St Mary's Church.
NORTH AISLE INTERNALLY:
- Almost complete coped Sarcophagus known as the "Wirksworth Stone", a "Tomb Lid" for the 7th century Northumbrian missionary "Betti". A horizontal band of roll-moulding separates the upper, surviving part, of the coped lid, from the lower, surviving, part of the side of the sarcophagus. Both parts are richly decorated in relief with figures depicting Biblical scenes. There are four surviving horizontal scenes in the upper row (the coped lid): Christ washing the feet of the feet of the disciples; a Crucifixion scene; the funeral procession of the Virgin Mary, and the Presentation of Christ in the Temple. There are four surviving horizontal scenes in the lower row (the side/wall): The Descent into Hell; The Ascension of Christ; The Annunciation, and the Presentation of Christ in a ceremony which took place outside the temple and not

another similar ceremony which took place inside the temple.

NORTH TRANSEPT INTERNALLY:
- ✠ Fragment from an Angular Cross-Shaft with flat-moulding, interlace design, roll-moulding.

SOUTH TRANSEPT INTERNALLY:
- ✠ Fragments possibly from an Angular Cross-Shaft with indications of plant-scroll design, and vertical bands of moulding including possibly roll-moulding.
- ✠ Fragment from an Angular Cross-Shaft with cable-moulding and a rather irregular, angled, interlace design.

178.   WITTERING, Cambridgeshire – All Saints Church.

NAVE:
- ❖ Coursed Rubble Walling.
- ❖ Square Single Plinth.
- ❖ Megalithic "Cut-Back" Long and Short Quoining.
- ❖ Internally. Megalithic Through-Stone Round-Headed Chancel Archway: voussoirs subdivided into three moulded shapes – half-roll, half-square and half "U" shaped curve; below a soffit-roll. Large inverted trapezoid-shaped imposts which extend beyond the hood-moulding on the west face of the wall; each impost divided into two by a central horizontal groove. Imposts protrude from all three faces of the walls including overhanging the central void between the opposing jambs. Through-Stone square jambs complemented on three sides by "half-round" cylindrical shafts – those on the west and east faces "angle-shafts" and those on the north and south sides in line with the soffit-roll above, "soffit-shafts". Between the angle-shafts and soffit shafts the jambs display a vertical square edge. Both angle-shafts and soffit-shafts have expanding capitals which taper upwards to the imposts and expanding bases which taper downwards. Accompanying half-square pilaster-strips and hood-moulding. Pilaster-Strips have square bases standing on same square single plinth protruding from the faces of the walls as the bases of the angle-shafts, soffit-shafts and jambs.

CHANCEL:
- ❖ Coursed Rubble Walling.
- ❖ Square Single Plinth (now hidden).
- ❖ Megalithic "Cut-Back" Long and Short Quoining.
- ❖ East Wall: evidence of gable on walling indicates earlier Roofline.

179.   WOLVERHAMPTON, Staffordshire. St Peter's Church.
- ✠ Circular Cross-Shaft from bottom to top and described as a "column". There are six, possibly seven, horizontal panels of different sizes extending around the circumference separated by horizontal bands of cable-moulding and roll-moulding. Decoration is very weathered and includes: cable-moulding, flat-moulding, plant design, plant-scroll design, roll-moulding, interlinked triangular shapes; inhabited plant-scroll design with a beast or a bird, affronted large beasts, bird-like creatures. The lower part of the column is not decorated. The round, convex, cap-stone on the top of the column appears to be decorated with slight indications of roll-moulding and interlace design.

180.   WOOTTON WAWEN, Warwickshire – St Peter's Church. Former Cruciform Church.

CENTRAL CROSSING WITH SQUARE TOWER ABOVE. Most of the walling is plastered internally.
- ❖ Coursed Rubble Walling.
- ❖ Internally. Long and Short Quoining – only west face of north-west and south-west, and east face of north-east and south-east quoining, can now be seen.

- Internally. Megalithic Round-Headed Archways: north and south archways are similar in size to each other but smaller in size than the west (nave) and east (chancel) archways. Voussoirs comprising: one band west and east archways, two bands south and north archways, the lower band is thinner than the upper band with plaster obscuring some of the details; voussoirs project from the face of the wall and vary in shape and size towards the centre. Through-Stone megalithic square imposts – some restoration; through-stones jambs laid in a similar way to Escomb jambs. Hood-Moulding on the west face of the east (chancel) archway on top of the voussoirs. Northern Archway is blocked and a window inserted (not Anglo-Saxon) – also view externally. See above right: PHOTO 702. Wootton Wawen 4, showing the west face of the east (chancel) archway.

PHOTO 702. Wootton Wawen 4.

- Externally. Indications of blocked Round-Headed Single-Belfry Openings in the north and south walls.
- Internally. Off-set, in the centre of the east face of the east (chancel) archway, is a stone shaped in the form of a Free-Arm Cross with short arms – the south arm is missing.

NAVE:
- Coursed Rubble Walling.
- Internally, North Wall: Possible Anglo-Saxon stonework survives in and around the blocked former north doorway adjacent to the west side of the current north doorway.
- Internally, West Wall: Possible Anglo-Saxon stonework survives in and around the blocked flat-headed doorway.

181. WORTH, West Sussex – St Nicholas Church. Restored Cruciform Church with only three, not four, archways in central crossing.

NAVE:
- Coursed Rubble Walling.
- Square Single Plinth.
- Long and Short Quoining some with "Sussex Variation" and some "cut-back".
- Pilaster-Strips constructed in long and short fashion – some "cut-back" – which rises to join the Chamfered String-Course.
- Chamfered String-Course, which in parts is "cut-back", also provides the sills for the Round-Headed Double-Windows.
- Round-Headed Double-Windows, not splayed – some 19th century restoration: through-stone voussoirs; through-stone square imposts flush with faces of the walls but protrude into the central void. Jambs comprise two rectangular through-stones placed vertically on top of each other (north wall windows)/a single middle, horizontally placed, through-stone, separating a vertically placed through-stone below with a square through-stone above (south wall window). Jambs in both walls have through-stone bases similar in shape and size to imposts – they protrude into the central void. Mid-wall cylindrical shafts support a rectangular through-stone slab, placed horizontally, and extending through the

entire depth of the walling of the window so that its sides overhang the mid-wall shaft. This slab supports above the junction of the heads of both windows. The mid-wall shafts stand on through-stone square bases which also protrude into the central void opposite both jambs. Bases of jambs and mid-wall shafts stand on the chamfered string-course around the nave externally/plaster obscures the construction details internally.
- Megalithic Round-Headed Doorways - south doorway with 14th century adaptations and blocked north doorway surviving in its original form: through-stone voussoirs; through-stone square imposts protruding into void between through-stone "Escomb-like" jambs. North doorway, externally, with most of the voussoirs of the arched head and some of the hood-moulding placed on top surviving – now flush with the face of the wall; there is also some indication of the jambs and adjacent strip-work. Doorways probably rebated for the hanging of doors. See above right: PHOTO 703. Worth 6, showing the south face of the north doorway.

PHOTO 703. Worth 6.

TRANSEPTS:
- Coursed Rubble Walling.
- Square Single Plinth.
- Pilaster-Strips constructed in long and short fashion.
- Long and Short Quoins some with "Sussex Variation" and some "cut-back".
- Square String Course.
- Internally. Round-Headed Archways (South Archway restored): through-stone voussoirs; large through-stone two-stepped imposts; through-stone square jambs. Hood-Moulding placed on top of the voussoirs. Pilaster-Strips aligned with the outer edges of the facing stonework of the jambs.

APSIDAL CHANCEL:
- Coursed Rubble Walling.
- Square Two-Stepped Plinth.
- Pilaster-Strips constructed in long and short fashion.
- Square String-Course.
- Internally: Chancel Archway: arched head with through-stone voussoirs; through-stone two-stepped imposts comprising two square slabs separated by a quarter-round band of roll-moulding – the lower slab has a rounded profile towards its base. Square jambs with large half-round cylindrical soffit-shafts. Both faces of the archway with hood-moulding placed on top of the voussoirs. Both faces of archway with pilaster-strips aligned with the outer edges of the facing stonework of the jambs.

182.   WROXETER, Shropshire – St Andrew's Church.
NAVE:
- North Wall: Coursed Stone Walling including megalithic work from reused Roman Stonework.
- Megalithic Side Alternate Quoining.
- Square String-Course.
- Blocked Flat-Headed Window with a monolithic lintel head, a single monolithic stone forms its east jamb and its west jamb comprises a large horizontal stone with a large square stone above.

NAVE INTERNALLY:
- Part of a Decorative Panel with geese-like birds and S-shaped worms.
- Anglo-Saxon Font cut from a reused Roman column base.

NAVE SOUTH WALL EXTERNALLY:
- Incomplete Collared Cross-Shaft with designs and patterns including: cable-moulding, flat-moulding, pellet-like features, plant-scroll design; inhabited ring-twist design with an upright (now horizontal) beast. Undecorated tenon.
- Parts of two Panels from the Collar of the same Collared Cross-Shaft identified above. Each is decorated with a dog-like beast in profile.

183.   YORK, North Yorkshire - The Yorkshire Museum.
- Part of a Grave-Cover with cable-moulding, flat-moulding, free-rings, interlace design, knot-work design, plait-work design. It is decorated with scenes including: S-shaped dragon, above a standing figure in profile to the left with a hand raised to their mouth, a headless figure opposite the standing figure, above the standing figure a beast in profile to the left, and above all another standing figure in portrait; two beasts engaged in combat with a bear-like beast beside them; a human figure in profile to the right holding an upright sword, with a dragon-like beast on each side, with, by their feet, a severed dragon's head. This tells the story of Sigurd killing Fafnir the dragon, the roasting of Fafnir's heart, the decapitation of Reginn the Smith, and the loading of the treasure on the horse Grani.
- Part of a Stele in two joining pieces tapering from bottom to top. Bordered vertically by two adjacent bands of flat-moulding forming a panel enclosing a centrally placed, incomplete, cross-shaft. It too tapers from bottom to top and is bordered vertically by two adjacent bands of flat-moulding. The cross-shaft stands on a semi-circular cross-base which is decorated with what may be a floriated design.
- Part of an Angular Cross-Shaft with two secular figures one wearing a sword and the other a horn at their waists; flat-moulding, plant-scroll design, ribbon beast within an interlace design.
- Most of a Dedication Stone with writing in both Old English and Latin recording the foundation of the church by Efrard. Aesc and Grim in 1020. See adjacent: PHOTO 704. York 2, showing the dedication stone from the former St Mary's Church, Castlegate, York.

PHOTO 704. York 2.

- Two parts of an Abbot's Chair with a modern intersection between. Top part comprises a three-dimensional head of a beast - the featured sides of the head are flat. Beast has distinctive eyes and open jaws - upper jaw with large fang, lower jaw smaller fang. Irregular linear designs on cheeks and neck, and top of its head with leaf-like design. A separate lower part, not adjoining, decorated with flat-moulding, interlace design, vertically placed leaf-like designs, and plant-scroll design.
- Part of an arm from a Free-Arm Cross-Head or Grave-Marker with a helmeted warrior with battle axe and sword on one face, and on the other face a warrior holding a sword with a female figure and with knot-work design below these figures.

INDEX OF CHURCHES AND MUSEUMS INCLUDED IN THE TEXT

ACTON BEAUCHAMP, Herefordshire. St Giles's Church.
254, PHOTO 523. Acton Beauchamp; 317.

ALDBROUGH, East Yorkshire. St Bartholomew's Church.
308, PHOTO 625. Aldbrough; 317.

APPLETON-LE-STREET, North Yorkshire. All Saints Church.
48, PHOTO 9. Appleton-le-Street 1; 139; 142, PHOTO 266. Appleton-le-Street 2; 145, PHOTO 277. Appleton-le-Street 3; 147, PHOTO 285. Appleton-le-Street 4; 149, PHOTO 294. Appleton-le-Street 5; 158, PHOTO 320. Appleton-le-Street 6, PHOTO 321. Appleton-le-Street 7; 317 to 318.

AYCLIFFE, County Durham. St Andrew's Church.
318 to 319, PHOTO 635, Aycliffe.

BAKEWELL, All Saints Church, Derbyshire.
239, PHOTO 495. Bakewell 1; 253, PHOTO 520. Bakewell 2; 265 to 266, PHOTO 544. Bakewell 3; 293 to 294, PHOTO 591. Bakewell 4; 319 to 320, PHOTO 636. Bakewell 5.

BARDNEY, Lincolnshire, St Lawrence's Church.
320, PHOTO 637. Bardney.

BARDSEY, West Yorkshire. All Hallows Church.
113, PHOTO 166. Bardsey 1, PHOTO 167. Bardsey 2; 117, PHOTO 182. Bardsey 3, PHOTO 183. Bardsey 4; 119 to 120, PHOTO 196. Bardsey 5, PHOTO 197. Bardsey 6; 141 to 142, PHOTO 265. Bardsey 7; 143, PHOTO 270. Bardsey 8; 150, PHOTO 297. Bardsey 9; 153, PHOTO 309. Bardsey 10; 158 to 159, PHOTO 322. Bardsey 11, PHOTO 323. Bardsey 12; 320 to 321, PHOTO 638. Bardsey 13.

BARNACK, Cambridgeshire. St John the Baptist Church.
55, PHOTO 30. Barnack 1; 58; 62, PHOTO 46. Barnack 2; 67, PHOTO 65. Barnack 3; 71 to 72, PHOTO 77. Barnack 4; 92 to 93, PHOTO 116. Barnack 5; 103; 108; 109; 115, PHOTO 174. Barnack 6, PHOTO 175. Barnack 7; 127 to 129, PHOTO 232. Barnack 8, PHOTO 233. Barnack 9, PHOTO 234. Barnack 10, PHOTO 235. Barnack 11, PHOTO 236. Barnack 12, PHOTO 237. Barnack 13; 153, PHOTO 310. Barnack 14, PHOTO 311. Barnack 15; 169 to 170, PHOTO 346. Barnack 16, PHOTO 347. Barnack 17; 171, PHOTO 351. Barnack 18; 175; 177, PHOTO 363. Barnack 18; 192 to 193, PHOTO 395. Barnack 19, PHOTO 396. Barnack 20, PHOTO 397. Barnack 21; 212; 321 to 322.

BARTON-UPON-HUMBER, Lincolnshire. St Peter's Church.
74, PHOTO 81. Barton-upon-Humber 1; 95 to 96, PHOTO 120. Barton-upon-Humber 2, PHOTO 121. Barton-upon-Humber 3; 121, PHOTO 202. Barton-upon-Humber 4, PHOTO 203. Barton-upon-Humber 5; 123, PHOTO 212. Barton-upon-Humber 6, PHOTO 213. Barton-upon-Humber 7; 135 to 136, PHOTO 259. Barton-upon-Humber 8; 139; 144, PHOTO 274. Barton-upon-Humber 9; 165 to 166, PHOTO 336. Barton-upon-Humber 10, PHOTO 337. Barton-upon-Humber 11; 174, PHOTO 357. Barton-upon-Humber 12; 209, PHOTO 427. Barton-upon-Humber 13; 323 to 324, PHOTO 639, Barton-upon-Humber 14.

BECKERMET, Cumbria. St Bridget's Church.
271, PHOTO 554. Beckermet; 324 to 325.

BEVERLEY MINSTER, East Yorkshire.
211, PHOTO 433. Beverley; 325.

BEWCASTLE, Cumbria. St Cuthbert's Church.
226, PHOTO 466. Bewcastle 1; 234 to 235, PHOTO 486. Bewcastle 2; 252, PHOTO 519. Bewcastle 3; 264 to 265, PHOTO 542. Bewcastle 4; 311, PHOTO 630. Bewcastle 5, PHOTO 631. Bewcastle 6; 325.

BILLINGHAM, County Durham. St Cuthbert's Church.
93 to 94, PHOTO 117. Billingham 1; 99, PHOTO 129. Billingham 2, PHOTO 130. Billingham 3; 139; 146, PHOTO 281. Billingham 4; 147, PHOTO 286. Billingham 5; 149, PHOTO 293. Billingham 6; 163 to 164, PHOTO 333. Billingham 7; 325 to 326.

BILTON-IN-AINSTY, North Yorkshire. St Helen's Church.
326 to 327, PHOTO 640. Bilton-in-Ainsty.

BISHOP AUCKLAND, County Durham. St Andrew's Church.
219, PHOTO 447. Bishop Auckland 1; 228; 229, PHOTO 471. Bishop Auckland 2; 238 to 239, PHOTO 494. Bishop Auckland 3; 242; 275 to 276, PHOTO 561. Bishop Auckland 4; 327.

BISHOPSTONE, East Sussex. St Andrew's Church.
308, PHOTO 626. Bishopstone; 327.

BLYBOROUGH, Lincolnshire. St Alkmund's Church.
220, PHOTO 448. Blyborough; 227; 327 to 328.

BOLAM, Northumberland. St Andrew's Church.
131, PHOTO 246. Bolam 1; 140; 147, PHOTO 284. Bolam 2; 152 to 153, PHOTO 307. Bolam 3, PHOTO 308. Bolam 4; 157 to 158, PHOTO 319. Bolam 5; 170, PHOTO 349. Bolam 6; 328. PHOTO 641. Bolam 7.

BOSHAM, West Sussex. Holy Trinity Church.
56 to 57, PHOTO 33. Bosham 1; 87 to 88, PHOTO 108. Bosham 2, PHOTO 109. Bosham 3; 103, PHOTO 141. Bosham 4; 106, PHOTO 154. Bosham 5; 328 to 329.

BRACEBRIDGE, Lincolnshire. All Saints Church.
329 to 330, PHOTO 642. Bracebridge.

BRADFORD-ON-AVON, Wiltshire. St Laurence Church.
51, PHOTO 19. Bradford-on-Avon 1; 211; 330 to 331, PHOTO 643. Bradford-upon-Avon 2.

BRADWELL-ON-SEA, Essex. Church of St Peter-on-the-Wall.
85, PHOTO 104. Bradwell-on-Sea 1; 179, PHOTO 369. Bradwell-on-Sea 2; 331 to 332, PHOTO 644. Bradwell-on-Sea 3.

BRAILSFORD, Derbyshire. All Saints Church.
249, PHOTO 514. Brailsford; 332.

BREAMORE, Hampshire. St Mary's Church.
46; 97; 98, PHOTO 127. Breamore 1; 188 to 190, PHOTO 389. Breamore 2, PHOTO 390. Breamore 3, PHOTO 391. Breamore 4; 210, PHOTO 429. Breamore 5; 211; 332.

BREEDON-ON-THE-HILL, Leicestershire. St Mary and St Hardulph's Church.
295, PHOTO 593. Breedon 1; 303, PHOTO 613. Breedon 2; 332 to 333.

BRIGHAM, Cumbria. St Bridget's Church.
225, PHOTO 462. Brigham 1; 257, PHOTO 528. Brigham 2; 261, PHOTO 537. Brigham 3; 333, PHOTO 645. Brigham 4.

BRIGSTOCK, Northamptonshire. St Andrew's Church.
51, PHOTO 20. Brigstock 1; 59 to 60, PHOTO 36. Brigstock 2; 71, PHOTO 76. Brigstock 3; 95, PHOTO 119. Brigstock 4; 103, PHOTO 143. Brigstock 5; 116, PHOTO 179. Brigstock 6; 120 to 121, PHOTO 200. Brigstock 7, PHOTO 201. Brigstock 8; 131, PHOTO 244. Brigstock 9, PHOTO 245. Brigstock 10; 179; 184 to 185, PHOTO 382. Brigstock 11, PHOTO 383. Brigstock 12; 333 to 334.

BRISTOL CATHEDRAL, Gloucestershire.
299, PHOTO 603. Bristol; 334.

BRITFORD, Wiltshire. St Peter's Church.
187 to 188, PHOTO 386. Britford 1, PHOTO 387. Britford 2, PHOTO 388. Britford 3; 334 to 335.

BRIXWORTH, Northamptonshire. All Saints Church.
44, PHOTO 4. Brixworth 1; 45; 53; 64; 69 to 70, PHOTO 72. Brixworth 2; 75; 76 to 77, PHOTO 85. Brixworth 3, PHOTO 86. Brixworth 4; 98, PHOTO 128. Brixworth 5; 104 to 105, PHOTO 146. Brixworth 6, PHOTO 148, Brixworth 7; 106; 114, PHOTO 170. Brixworth 8, PHOTO 171. Brixworth 9; 116, PHOTO 180. Brixworth 10; 122, PHOTO 206. Brixworth 11, PHOTO 207. Brixworth 12; 127, PHOTO 230. Brixworth 13, PHOTO 231. Brixworth 14; 136 to 137, PHOTO 260. Brixworth 15, PHOTO 261. Brixworth 16; 168 to 169, PHOTO 343. Brixworth 17; 179 to 180; 182 to 183, PHOTO 376. Brixworth 18, PHOTO 377. Brixworth 19, PHOTO 378. Brixworth 20; 184; 207 to 208, PHOTO 423. Brixworth 21, PHOTO 424. Brixworth 22, PHOTO 425. Brixworth 23; 235, PHOTO 487. Brixworth 24; 335 to 337.

BROMPTON-IN-ALLERTONSHIRE, North Yorkshire. St Thomas's Church.
225, PHOTO 463. Brompton 1; 285 to 286, PHOTO 580. Brompton 2; 337 to 338.

BROUGHTON, Lincolnshire. St Mary's Church.
49 to 50, PHOTO 15, Broughton 1; 51; 65, PHOTO 57. Broughton 2; 74 to 75, PHOTO 82. Broughton 3; 179 to 181, PHOTO 370. Broughton 4, PHOTO 371. Broughton 5, PHOTO 372. Broughton 6; 227; 338 to 339.

BURGWALLIS, South Yorkshire. St Helen's Church.
339.

BURTON-IN-KENDAL, Cumbria. St James's Church.
220, PHOTO 451. Burton-in-Kendal 1; 230, PHOTO 474. Burton-in-Kendal 2; 339.

BURTON PEDWARDINE, Lincolnshire. St Andrew's Church.
282, PHOTO 576. Burton Pedwardine; 339 to 340.

BYWELL, Northumberland. St Andrew's Church.
54, PHOTO 27, Bywell 1; 107 to 108, PHOTO 157. Bywell 2; 116, PHOTO 178. Bywell 3; 144, PHOTO 276. Bywell 4; 152, PHOTO 304. Bywell 5; 163, PHOTO 332. Bywell 6; 340.

CAMBRIDGE, St Bene't's Church.
60, PHOTO 38. Cambridge 1, PHOTO 39. Cambridge 2, PHOTO 40. Cambridge 3; 68, PHOTO 69. Cambridge 4; 72, PHOTO 78. Cambridge 5; 139; 142, PHOTO 268. Cambridge 6; 146, PHOTO 282. Cambridge 7; 149 to 150, PHOTO 295. Cambridge 8; 151, PHOTO 300. Cambridge 9; 164, PHOTO 334. Cambridge 10; 169, PHOTO 344. Cambridge 11; 171, PHOTO 352. Cambridge 12; 174; 210, PHOTO 431. Cambridge 13; 340 to 341, PHOTO 646. Cambridge 14.

CARLISLE CATHEDRAL, Cumbria.
258 to 259, PHOTO 532. Carlisle; 341 to 342.

CASTOR, Cambridgeshire. St Kyneburgha's Church.
294 to 295, PHOTO 592. Castor 1; 342, PHOTO 647. Castor 2.

CAWTHORNE, West Yorkshire. All Saints Church.
256, PHOTO 525. Cawthorne; 342.

CHESTER-LE-STREET, County Durham. St Mary and St Cuthbert's Church (The Anchorage).
274, PHOTO 558. Chester-le-Street; 342 to 343.

CHOLLERTON, Northumberland. St Giles Church.
261, PHOTO 538. Chollerton; 343.

CODFORD ST PETER, Wiltshire. St Peter's Church.
220, PHOTO 449. Codford St Peter 1; 243, PHOTO 503. Codford St Peter 2; 343.

COLCHESTER, Essex. Holy Trinity Church.
51, PHOTO 18. Colchester 1; 53; 61 to 62, PHOTO 45. Colchester 2; 96 to 97, PHOTO 122. Colchester 3; 100, PHOTO 134. Colchester 4; 143, PHOTO 272. Colchester 5; 147 to 148, PHOTO 288. Colchester 6; 151, PHOTO 303. Colchester 7; 154 to 155, PHOTO 312. Colchester 8, PHOTO 314. Colchester 9, PHOTO 315. Colchester 10; 172, PHOTO 356. Colchester 11; 177, PHOTO 362. Colchester 12; 343 to 344.

COLLINGHAM, West Yorkshire. St Oswald's Church.
344 to 345, PHOTO 648. Collingham 1, PHOTO 649. Collingham 2.

COLSTERWORTH, Lincolnshire. St John the Baptist Church.
224, PHOTO 457. Colsterworth; 345.

COLYTON, Devon. St Andrew's Church.
219, PHOTO 445. Colyton 1; 226, PHOTO 465. Colyton 2; 345.

COPPLESTONE, Devon. Cross-Shaft.
266 to 267, PHOTO 545. Copplestone; 345.

CORBRIDGE, Northumberland, St Andrew's Church.
111 to 112, PHOTO 160. Corbridge 1, PHOTO 161. Corbridge 2; 118, PHOTO 190. Corbridge 3, PHOTO 191. Corbridge 4; 345 to 347, PHOTO 650. Corbridge 5.

CORHAMPTON CHURCH, Hampshire.
63, PHOTO 51. Corhampton 1; 85 to 86, PHOTO 105. Corhampton 2; 311, PHOTO 632. Corhampton 3; 347.

CREETON, Lincolnshire. St Peter's Church.
268, PHOTO 548. Creeton 1; 347 to 348, PHOTO 651. Creeton 2.

CROPTHORNE, Worcestershire. St Michael's Church.
256 to 257, PHOTO 527. Cropthorne; 348.

DACRE, Cumbria. St Andrew's Church.
232 to 233, PHOTO 480. Dacre; 348.

DAGLINGWORTH, Gloucestershire. Church of the Holy Rood.
301 to 302, PHOTO 608. Daglingworth 1, PHOTO 609. Daglingworth 2, PHOTO 610. Daglingworth 3, PHOTO 611. Daglingworth 4; 307 to 308, PHOTO 624. Daglingworth 5; 348 to 349, PHOTO 652. Daglingworth 6.

DEARHAM, Cumbria. St Mungo's Church.
220; 227, PHOTO 468. Dearham 1; 252, PHOTO 518. Dearham 2; 260, PHOTO 535. Dearham 3; 349.

DEERHURST, Gloucestershire. St Mary's Church.
46, PHOTO 8. Deerhurst 1; 61, PHOTO 41. Deerhurst 2, PHOTO 42. Deerhurst 3, PHOTO 43. Deerhurst 4; 97 to 98, PHOTO 125. Deerhurst 5, PHOTO 126. Deerhurst 6; 100, PHOTO 133. Deerhurst 7; 103, PHOTO 142. Deerhurst 8; 105 to 106, PHOTO 151. Deerhurst 9, PHOTO 152. Deerhurst 10, PHOTO 153. Deerhurst 11; 106 to 107, PHOTO 155. Deerhurst 12; 108, PHOTO 158. Deerhurst 13; 137 to 139, PHOTO 262. Deerhurst 14, PHOTO 263. Deerhurst 15, PHOTO 264. Deerhurst 16; 174; 190 to 192, PHOTO 392. Deerhurst 17, PHOTO 393. Deerhurst 18, PHOTO 394. Deerhurst 19; 193, PHOTO 398. Deerhurst 20, PHOTO 399. Deerhurst 21; 209 to 210, PHOTO 428. Deerhurst 22; 212; 302 to 303, PHOTO 612. Deerhurst 23; 304 to 305, PHOTO 619. Deerhurst 24; 350 to 353, PHOTO 653. Deerhurst 25, PHOTO 654. Deerhurst 26.

DERBY, Derbyshire. Museum & Art Gallery.
247 to 248, PHOTO 511. Derby 1; 289 to 290, PHOTO 587. Derby 2; 353 to 354, PHOTO 655. Derby 3.

DESBOROUGH, Northamptonshire. St Giles's Church.
245 to 246, PHOTO 508. Desborough; 354.

DEWSBURY, West Yorkshire. Minster. All Saints Church.
234, PHOTO 484. Dewsbury 1; 238, PHOTO 493. Dewsbury 2; 239 to 240, PHOTO 496. Dewsbury 3; 283, PHOTO 578. Dewsbury 4; 354 to 355.

Anglo-Saxon Church Architecture & Stone Sculpture   435

DIDDLEBURY, Shropshire. St Peter's Church.
52, PHOTO 23. Diddlebury 1; 117, PHOTO 184. Diddlebury 2, PHOTO 185. Diddlebury 3; 119, PHOTO 194. Diddlebury 4, PHOTO 195. Diddlebury 5; 355.

DOLTON, Devon. Church of St Edmund King and Martyr.
306 to 307, PHOTO 622. Dolton 1, PHOTO 623. Dolton 2; 355 to 356.

DOVER, Kent. St Mary-in-the-Castle Church.
356 to 357, PHOTO 656. Dover 1, PHOTO 657. Dover 2.

DURHAM CATHEDRAL, County Durham. The Monks' Dormitory.
357 to 358.

EARLS BARTON, Northamptonshire. All Saints Church.
45; 101, PHOTO 137, Earls Barton 1; 103; 104, PHOTO 147. Earls Barton 2; 107, PHOTO 156. Earls Barton 3; 133 to 134, PHOTO 254. Earls Barton 4, PHOTO 255. Earls Barton 5; 152, PHOTO 305. Earls Barton 6; 156 to 157, PHOTO 318. Earls Barton 7; 169; 174 to 175, PHOTO 358. Earls Barton 8; 358 to 360, PHOTO 658. Earls Barton 9.

EDINBURGH, Lothian. National Museum of Scotland.
360.

ESCOMB CHURCH, County Durham.
40, PHOTO 1. Escomb 1; 45; 68, PHOTO 68. Escomb 2; 94, PHOTO 118. Escomb 3; 99, PHOTO 131. Escomb 4; 105; 115, PHOTO 172. Escomb 4, PHOTO 173. Escomb 5; 115 to 116, PHOTO 176. Escomb 6; 117 to 118, PHOTO 186. Escomb 7, PHOTO 187. Escomb 8, PHOTO 188. Escomb 9, PHOTO 189. Escomb 10; 130; 185 to 186, PHOTO 383. Escomb 11, PHOTO 384. Escomb 12; 211; 311 to 312, PHOTO 633. Escomb 13; 360 to 361.

EYAM, Derbyshire. St Lawrence's Church.
257, PHOTO 529. Eyam 1; 265, PHOTO 543. Eyam 2; 304, PHOTO 618. Eyam 3; 361 to 362, PHOTO 659. Eyam 4.

FLETTON, Cambridgeshire. St Margaret's Church.
295 to 296, PHOTO 594. Fletton 1, PHOTO 595. Fletton 2; 303 to 304, PHOTO 615. Fletton 3, PHOTO 616. Fletton 4; 362.

FORNCETT ST PETER, Norfolk. St Peter's Church.
45, PHOTO 6. Forncett St Peter 1; 70 to 71, PHOTO 74. Forncett St Peter 2; 124, PHOTO 216. Forncett St Peter 2; 144, PHOTO 275. Forncett St Peter 3; 145, PHOTO 280. Forncett St Peter 4; 147, PHOTO 287. Forncett St Peter 5; 148, PHOTO 290. Forncett St Peter 6; 150, PHOTO 296. Forncett St Peter 7, PHOTO 299. Forncett St Peter 8; 160, PHOTO 326. Forncett St Peter 9; 362 to 363.

GEDDINGTON, Northamptonshire. St Mary Magdalene Church.
131 to 132, PHOTO 247. Geddington 1. PHOTO 248. Geddington 2; 178 to 179, PHOTO 368. Geddington 3; 363.

GLENTWORTH, Lincolnshire. St Michael's Church.
109; 114, PHOTO 169. Glentworth 1; 124 to 125, PHOTO 218. Glentworth 2, PHOTO 219. Glentworth 3; 142, PHOTO 269. Glentworth 4; 145, PHOTO 278. Glentworth 5; 148, PHOTO 291. Glentworth 6; 151, PHOTO 301. Glentworth 7; 159, PHOTO 324. Glentworth 8; 169, PHOTO 345. Glentworth 9; 229; 363 to 364.

GOSFORTH, Cumbria. St Mary's Church.
243 to 244, PHOTO 504. Gosforth 1; 245, PHOTO 507. Gosforth 2; 247; 251 to 252, PHOTO 517. Gosforth 3; 259, PHOTO 533. Gosforth 4; 273, PHOTO 556. Gosforth 5; 284; 287 to 288, PHOTO 583. Gosforth 6, PHOTO 584. Gosforth 7, PHOTO 585. Gosforth 8; 364 to 365.

GREAT DUNHAM, Norfolk. Holy Trinity Church.
84 to 85, PHOTO 102. Great Dunham 1, PHOTO 103. Great Dunham 2; 121, PHOTO 204. Great Dunham 3, PHOTO 205. Great Dunham 4; 152, PHOTO 306. Great Dunham 5; 160 to 161, PHOTO 327. Great Dunham 6; 178, PHOTO 367. Great Dunham 7; 365 to 366.

GREAT PAXTON, Cambridgeshire. Holy Trinity Church.
65, PHOTO 55. Great Paxton 1, PHOTO 56. Great Paxton 2; 66, PHOTO 59. Great Paxton 3, PHOTO 61. Great Paxton 4, PHOTO 62. Great Paxton 5; 77, PHOTO 87. Great Paxton 6; 80, PHOTO 93. Great Paxton 7, PHOTO 94. Great Paxton 8; 122, PHOTO 208. Great Paxton 9, PHOTO 209. Great Paxton 10; 171 to 172, PHOTO 353. Great Paxton 11, PHOTO 354. Great Paxton 12; 366 to 367, PHOTO 660. Great Paxton 13.

GREAT URSWICK, Cumbria. St Michael's Church.
278, PHOTO 567. Great Urswick; 368.

GREATHAM, County Durham. St John the Baptist Church.
168, PHOTO 342. Greatham; 368.

HACKTHORN, Lincolnshire. St Michael's Church.
276, PHOTO 563. Hackthorn; 368.

HADSTOCK, Essex. St Botolph's Church.
92, PHOTO 115. Hadstock 1; 97, PHOTO 124. Hadstock 2; 101, PHOTO 136. Hadstock 3; 102; 130, PHOTO 242. Hadstock 4, PHOTO 243. Hadstock 5; 229; 368 to 369, PHOTO 661. Hadstock 6, PHOTO 662. Hadstock 7.

HALTON, Lancashire. St Wilfrid's Church.
273, PHOTO 557. Halton 1; 369 to 370, PHOTO 663. Halton 2, PHOTO 664, Halton 3, PHOTO 665. Halton 4.

HARPSWELL, Lincolnshire. St Chad's Church.
143, PHOTO 273. Harpswell 1; 166 to 167, PHOTO 338. Harpswell 2, PHOTO 339. Harpswell 3; 370.

HARTLEPOOL, County Durham. St Hilda's Church.
277, PHOTO 566. Hartlepool; 371.

HARTSHEAD, West Yorkshire. Walton Cross.
274 to 275, PHOTO 559. Hartshead; 371.

HAUGHTON-LE-SKERNE, County Durham. St Andrew's Church.
276, PHOTO 562. Haughton-le-Skerne; 371.

HAWKESWORTH, Nottinghamshire. St Mary and All Saints Church.
280, PHOTO 573. Hawkesworth; 371.

HEXHAM ABBEY, Northumberland.
43; 103 to 104, PHOTO 144. Hexham 1; 198 to 202, PHOTO 410. Hexham 2, PHOTO 411. Hexham 3, PHOTO 412. Hexham 4, PHOTO 413. Hexham 5, PHOTO 414. Hexham 6, PHOTO 415. Hexham 7, PHOTO 416. Hexham 8, PHOTO 417. Hexham 9; 211, PHOTO 432. Hexham 10; 220 to 221, PHOTO 452. Hexham 11; 224, PHOTO 459. Hexham 12; 227; 279 to 280, PHOTO 570. Hexham 13, PHOTO 571. Hexham 14, PHOTO 572. Hexham 15; 296 to 297, PHOTO 596. Hexham 16, PHOTO 597. Hexham 17; 371 to 373, PHOTO 666. Hexham 18.

HEYSHAM, Lancashire. St Peter's Church.
286 to 287, PHOTO 581. Heysham 1; 374 to 375, PHOTO 667. Heysham 2, PHOTO 668. Heysham 3.

HICKLING, Nottinghamshire. St Luke's Church.
220, PHOTO 450. Hickling 1; 227 to 228, PHOTO 469. Hickling 2; 284; 288 to 289, PHOTO 586. Hickling 3; 375.

HOLY ISLAND (LINDISFARNE). Northumberland. The Priory Museum.
375.

HOPE, Derbyshire. St Peter's Church.
223, PHOTO 456. Hope 1; 375 to 376, PHOTO 669. Hope 2.

HOUGH-ON-THE-HILL, Lincolnshire. All Saints Church.
99 to 100, PHOTO 132. Hough-on-the-Hill 1; 105, PHOTO 149. Hough-on-the-Hill 2, PHOTO 150. Hough-on-the-Hill 3; 108, PHOTO 159. Hough-on-the-Hill 4; 126 to 127, PHOTO 224. Hough-on-the-Hill 5, PHOTO 225. Hough-on-the-Hill 6, PHOTO 226. Hough-on-the-Hill 7, PHOTO 227. Hough-on-the-Hill 8, PHOTO 228. Hough-on-the-Hill 9, PHOTO 229. Hough-on-the-Hill 10; 130; 179 to 180; 181 to 182, PHOTO 373. Hough-on-the-Hill 11, PHOTO 374. Hough-on-the-Hill 12, PHOTO 375. Hough-on-the-Hill 13; 376 to 377.

HOUGHAM, Lincolnshire. All Saints Church.
282 to 283, PHOTO 577. Hougham; 377.

HOVINGHAM, North Yorkshire. All Saints Church.
377 to 379, PHOTO 670. Hovingham 1, PHOTO 671. Hovingham 2, PHOTO 672. Hovingham 3.

HOWE, Norfolk. St Mary's Church.
123, PHOTO 215. Howe 1; 379, PHOTO 673. Howe 2.

ILKLEY, West Yorkshire. All Saints Church.
233, PHOTO 481. Ilkley; 379 to 380.

IRTON, Cumbria. St Paul's Church.
229 to 230, PHOTO 472. Irton 1; 250 to 251, PHOTO 516. Irton 2; 380.

JARROW, County Durham. Jarrow Hall, Bede Museum.
211, PHOTO 434. Jarrow 8; 380.

JARROW, County Durham. St Paul's Church.
113 to 114, PHOTO 168. Jarrow 1; 116, PHOTO 177. Jarrow 2; 125 to 126, PHOTO 220. Jarrow 3, PHOTO 221. Jarrow 4, PHOTO 222. Jarrow 5, PHOTO 223. Jarrow 6; 167 to 168, PHOTO 341. Jarrow 7; 212, PHOTO 434. Jarrow 8; 297 to 298, PHOTO 598. Jarrow 9, PHOTO 599. Jarrow 10, PHOTO 600. Jarrow 11; 380 to 382.

JEDBURGH, Borders. Jedburgh Abbey.
382 to 383, PHOTO 674. Jedburgh.

KIRKBY STEPHEN, Cumbria. St John's Church.
244 to 245, PHOTO 506. Kirkby Stephen; 383.

KIRKBY WHARFE, North Yorkshire. St John's Church.
223, PHOTO 455. Kirkby Wharfe 1; 227, PHOTO 467. Kirkby Wharfe 2; 230, PHOTO 473. Kirkby Wharfe 3; 237, PHOTO 490. Kirkby Wharfe 4; 383.

KIRKDALE, North Yorkshire. St Gregory's Minster
65 to 67, PHOTO 58. Kirkdale 1, PHOTO 63. Kirkdale 2; 253 to 254, PHOTO 521. Kirkdale 3; 308 to 309, PHOTO 627. Kirkdale 4; 383 to 384, PHOTO 675. Kirkdale 5.

KIRK HAMMERTON, North Yorkshire. St John the Baptist Church.
41, PHOTO 2. Kirk Hammerton 1; 59, PHOTO 35. Kirk Hammerton 2; 384 to 385.

LANGFORD, Oxfordshire. St Matthew's Church.
46; 55, PHOTO 29. Langford 1; 62, PHOTO 48. Langford 2; 64, PHOTO 53. Langford 3; 66 to 67, PHOTO 60. Langford 4, PHOTO 64. Langford 5, PHOTO 66. Langford 6; 82 to 84, PHOTO 99. Langford 7, PHOTO 100. Langford 8, PHOTO 101. Langford 9; 102, PHOTO 140. Langford 10; 147; 156, PHOTO 317. Langford 11; 209, PHOTO 426. Langford 12; 300 to 301, PHOTO 606. Langford 13, PHOTO 607. Langford 14; 312, PHOTO 634. Langford 15; 385 to 386.

LAUGHTON-EN-LE-MORTHEN, South Yorkshire. All Saints Church.
386 to 387, PHOTO 676. Laughton-en-le-Morthen.

LEDSHAM, West Yorkshire. All Saints Church.
132, PHOTO 249. Ledsham 1, PHOTO 250. Ledsham 2; 387 to 388, PHOTO 677. Ledsham 3.

LEEK, Staffordshire. The Church of St Edward the Confessor.
270 to 271, PHOTO 553. Leek; 388.

LICHFIELD CATHEDRAL, Staffordshire.
293, PHOTO 590. Lichfield; 388.

LINCOLN, Lincolnshire. St Peter-at-Gowts Church.
53, PHOTO 24. Lincoln 1; 141; 145, PHOTO 279. Lincoln St Peter-At—Gowts 2; 146, PHOTO 283. Lincoln St Peter-At-Gowts 3; 159 to 160, PHOTO 325. Lincoln St Peter-At-Gowts 4; 388 to 389, PHOTO 678. Lincoln St Peter-at-Gowts 5, PHOTO 679. Lincoln St Peter-at-Gowts 6.

LITTLE BARDFIELD, Essex. St Katherine's Church.
48. PHOTO 10. Little Bardfield 1; 52, PHOTO 21. Little Bardfield 2; 53, PHOTO 26. Little Bardfield 3; 132 to 133, PHOTO 252. Little Bardfield 4, PHOTO 253. Little Bardfield 5; 140; 154 to 155, PHOTO 313. Little Bardfield 6; 172, PHOTO 355, Little Bardfield 7; 389 to 390.

LONDON. Victoria and Albert Museum.
390.

LOW DINSDALE, County Durham. St John the Baptist Church.
217 to 218, PHOTO 441. Low Dinsdale 1, PHOTO 443. Low Dinsdale 2, PHOTO 444. Low Dinsdale 3; 223, PHOTO 453. Low Dinsdale 4, PHOTO 454. Low Dinsdale 5; 390.

LOWTHER, Cumbria. St Michael's Church.
390 to 391.

LYTHE, North Yorkshire. St Oswald's Church.
242 to 243, PHOTO 502. Lythe 1; 276, PHOTO 564. Lythe 2; 284 to 285, PHOTO 579. Lythe 3; 391, PHOTO 680. Lythe 4.

MARTON, Lincolnshire. St Margaret's Church.
391 to 392.

MELBURY BUBB, Dorset. St Mary's Church.
305 to 306, PHOTO 620. Melbury Bubb 1, PHOTO 621. Melbury Bubb 2; 392 to 393.

MELSONBY, North Yorkshire. St James's Church.
212 to 213, PHOTO 435. Melsonby 1, PHOTO 436. Melsonby 2. 393.

MIDDLESMOOR, North Yorkshire. St Chad's Church.
258, PHOTO 531. Middlesmoor; 393.

MIDDLETON, North Yorkshire. St Andrew's Church.
217 to 218, PHOTO 442. Middleton 1; 224. PHOTO 458. Middleton 2; 230 to 231, PHOTO 475. Middleton 3, PHOTO 476. Middleton 4; 246, PHOTO 509. Middleton 5; 248, PHOTO 512. Middleton 6; 258, PHOTO 530. Middleton 7; 260, PHOTO 534. Middleton 8; 393 to 394.

MONKWEARMOUTH, (Sunderland), County Durham. St Peter's Church. See SUNDERLAND

NASSINGTON, Northamptonshire. St Mary & All Saints Church.
225, PHOTO 461. Nassington 1; 236 to 237, PHOTO 489. Nassington 2; 394.

NESTON, Cheshire. St Mary and St Helen's Church.
241 to 242, PHOTO 500. Neston 1; 246 to 247, PHOTO 510. Neston 2; 395.

NEWCASTLE-UPON-TYNE, Northumberland. Great North Museum.
219, PHOTO 446. Newcastle 1; 233 to 234, PHOTO 483. Newcastle 2; 240 to 241, PHOTO 497. Newcastle 3, PHOTO 498. Newcastle 4; 395 to 396.

NEWENT, Gloucestershire. St Mary's Church.
267 , PHOTO 546. Newent; 396.

NEWTON-BY-CASTLE ACRE, Norfolk. St Mary and All Saints Church.
129, PHOTO 238. Newton-by-Castle Acre 1; 396 to 397, PHOTO 681. Newton-by-Castle Acre 2.

NORTH ELMHAM, Norfolk. Ruins of Anglo-Saxon Cathedral and Bishops Palace
180; 183 to 184, PHOTO 379. North Elmham 1, PHOTO 380. North Elmham 2, PHOTO 381. North Elmham 3; 397.

NORTH WITHAM, Lincolnshire. St Mary's Church.
225, PHOTO 460. North Witham; 397.

NORTON, County Durham. St Mary's Church.
61, PHOTO 44. Norton 1; 78 to 79, PHOTO 90. Norton 2; 397 to 398, PHOTO 682. Norton 3, PHOTO 683. Norton 4.

NUNBURNHOLME, East Yorkshire. St James Church.
248 to 249, PHOTO 513. Nunburnholme; 398 to 399.

OLD CLEE, Lincolnshire. Holy Trinity and St Mary the Virgin Church.
71, PHOTO 75. Old Clee 1; 124, PHOTO 217. Old Clee 2; 399, PHOTO 684. Old Clee 3.

ORPINGTON, Kent. All Saints Church.
309 to 310, PHOTO 628. Orpington; 399 to 400.

OTLEY, West Yorkshire. All Saints Church.
233, PHOTO 482. Otley 1; 241, PHOTO 499. Otley 2; 400.

OVINGHAM, Northumberland. St Mary the Virgin Church.
141; 148, PHOTO 289. Ovingham 1; 151, PHOTO 302. Ovingham 2; 162 to 163, PHOTO 331. Ovingham 3; 256, PHOTO 526. Ovingham 4; 400 to 402, PHOTO 685. Ovingham 5, PHOTO 686. Ovingham 6.

OXFORD, Oxfordshire. St Michael's Church.
48 to 49, PHOTO 11. Oxford 1; 111; 122, PHOTO 210. Oxford 2, PHOTO 211. Oxford 3; 143, PHOTO 271. Oxford 4; 149, PHOTO 292. Oxford 5; 150, PHOTO 298. Oxford 6; 161 to 162, PHOTO 329. Oxford 7, PHOTO 330. Oxford 8; 167; 193 to 194, PHOTO 400. Oxford 9; 402.

PETERBOROUGH CATHEDRAL, Cambridgeshire.
292 to 293, PHOTO 589. Peterborough; 402 to 403.

POTTERNE, Wiltshire. St Mary's Church.
304. PHOTO 617. Potterne; 403.

RAMSBURY, Wiltshire. Holy Cross Church.
226, PHOTO 464. Ramsbury 1; 231, PHOTO 477. Ramsbury 2; 280 to 281, PHOTO 574. Ramsbury 3; 403 to 404, PHOTO 687. Ramsbury 4.

RASTRICK, West Yorkshire. St Matthew's Church.
228, PHOTO 470. Rastrick 1; 275, PHOTO 560. Rastrick 2; 404.

REED, Hertfordshire. St Mary's Church.
404, PHOTO 688. Reed.

REPTON, Derbyshire. St Wystan's Church.
82, PHOTO 97. Repton 1, PHOTO 98. Repton 2; 170; 196 to 198, PHOTO 403. Repton 3, PHOTO 404. Repton 4, PHOTO 405. Repton 5, PHOTO 406. Repton 6, PHOTO 407. Repton 7, PHOTO 408. Repton 8, PHOTO 409. Repton 9; 404 to 406.

RIPON CATHEDRAL, North Yorkshire.
104, PHOTO 145. Ripon 1; 198; 202 to 205, PHOTO 418. Ripon 2, PHOTO 419. Ripon 3, PHOTO 420. Ripon 4; 406 to 407.

ROCKCLIFFE, Cumbria. St Mary's Church.
267 to 268, PHOTO 547. Rockcliffe; 407.

ROLLESTON-ON-DOVE, Staffordshire. St Mary's Church.
260 to 261, PHOTO 536. Rolleston-on-Dove; 407.

ROMSEY ABBEY, Hampshire.
299 to 300, PHOTO 604. Romsey 1, PHOTO 605. Romsey 2; 407.

ROTHWELL, Lincolnshire. St Mary Magdalen's Church.
63, PHOTO 50. Rothwell 1; 170 to 171, PHOTO 350. Rothwell 2; 407 to 408, PHOTO 689. Rothwell 3.

ROTHWELL, West Yorkshire. Holy Trinity Church.
298 to 299, PHOTO 601. Rothwell 1, PHOTO 602. Rothwell 2; 408.

RUTHWELL, Dumfries & Galloway. Ruthwell and Mount Kedar Church.
234, PHOTO 485. Ruthwell 1; 409, PHOTO 690. Ruthwell 2.

SANDBACH, Cheshire. Market Square.
235 to 236, PHOTO 488. Sandbach 1; 254 to 255, PHOTO 524. Sandbach 2; 409.

SEAHAM, County Durham. St Mary's Church.
50, PHOTO 16. Seaham 1, PHOTO 17. Seaham 2; 112, PHOTO 162. Seaham 3, PHOTO 163. Seaham 4; 118 to 119, PHOTO 192. Seaham 5, PHOTO 193. Seaham 6; 130; 409 to 410.

SELHAM, West Sussex. St James Church.
49, PHOTO 13. Selham 1; 88 to 89, PHOTO 110. Selham 2, PHOTO 111. Selham 3, PHOTO 112. Selham 4; 227; 410.

SHELFORD, Nottinghamshire. St Peter and St Paul's Church.
237 to 238, PHOTO 491. Shelford 1, PHOTO 492. Shelford 2; 410.

SINNINGTON, North Yorkshire. All Saints Church.
254, PHOTO 522. Sinnington; 410.

SKELTON-IN-CLEVELAND, North Yorkshire. All Saints Church - the "new" church.
310 to 311, PHOTO 629. Skelton-in-Cleveland; 411.

SKIPWITH, North Yorkshire. St Helen's Church.
49, PHOTO 14. Skipwith 1; 52, PHOTO 22. Skipwith 2; 63 to 64, PHOTO 52. Skipwith 3; 72 to 73, PHOTO 79. Skipwith 4; 178, PHOTO 365. Skipwith 5; 194 to 195, PHOTO 401. Skipwith 6, PHOTO 402. Skipwith 7; 411 to 412.

SOCKBURN, County Durham. All Saints Church.
231 to 232, PHOTO 478. Sockburn 1, PHOTO 479. Sockburn 2; 244, PHOTO 505. Sockburn 3; 287, PHOTO 582. Sockburn 4; 412.

SOMPTING, West Sussex. St Mary the Virgin Church.
155 to 156, PHOTO 316. Sompting 1; 161, PHOTO 328. Sompting 2; 210, PHOTO 430. Sompting 3; 412 to 414.

SPROXTON, Leicestershire. St Bartholomew's Church.
414, PHOTO 691. Sproxton.

STANTON LACY, Shropshire. St Peter's Church.
175 to 176, PHOTO 359. Stanton Lacy 1; 414, PHOTO 692. Stanton Lacy 2.

STAPLEFORD, Nottinghamshire. St Helen's Church.
269 to 270, PHOTO 552. Stapleford; 414 to 415.

STONEGRAVE, North Yorkshire. Holy Trinity Church.
242, PHOTO 501. Stonegrave 1; 415, PHOTO 693. Stonegrave 2.

STOW-IN-LINDSEY, Lincolnshire. St Mary's Church.
42, PHOTO 3. Stow in Lindsey 1; 53 to 54, PHOTO 28. Stow-in-Lindsey 2; 68, PHOTO 67. Stow-in-Lindsey 3; 81 to 82, PHOTO 95. Stow-in-Lindsey 4, PHOTO 96. Stow-in-Lindsey 5; 101, PHOTO 135. Stow-in-Lindsey 6; 102, PHOTO 139. Stow-in-Lindsey 7; 109; 111; 112 to 113, PHOTO 164. Stow-in-Lindsey 8, PHOTO 165. Stow-in-Lindsey 9; 116, PHOTO 181. Stow-in-Lindsey 10; 120, PHOTO 198. Stow-in-Lindsey 11, PHOTO 199. Stow-in-Lindsey 12; 130, PHOTO 239. Stow-in-Lindsey 13; 173; 178, PHOTO 366. Stow-in-Lindsey 14; 229; 415 to 417, PHOTO 694. Stow-in-Lindsey 15.

STRETHALL, Essex. St Mary the Virgin Church.
62 to 63, PHOTO 49. Strethall 1; 64; 86 to 87, PHOTO 106. Strethall 2; 417, PHOTO 695. Strethall 3, PHOTO 696. Strethall 4.

SUNDERLAND, County Durham, Sunderland Museum.
214, PHOTO 440. Sunderland; 417 to 418.

SUNDERLAND, (Monkwearmouth), County Durham. St Peter's Church.
45, PHOTO 5. Monkwearmouth 1; 46, PHOTO 7. Monkwearmouth 2; 47; 69, PHOTO 70. Monkwearmouth 3, PHOTO 71. Monkwearmouth 4; 91, PHOTO 113. Monkwearmouth 5, PHOTO 114. Monkwearmouth 6; 97, PHOTO 123. Monkwearmouth 7; 102, PHOTO 138. Monkwearmouth 8; 142, PHOTO 267. Monkwearmouth 9; 164 to 165, PHOTO 335. Monkwearmouth 10; 167 to 168, PHOTO 340. Monkwearmouth 11; 186 to 187, PHOTO 385. Monkwearmouth 12; 192; 211; 213, PHOTO 437. Monkwearmouth 13, PHOTO 438. Monkwearmouth 14; 249, PHOTO 515. Monkwearmouth 15; 262, PHOTO 539. Monkwearmouth 16; 281, PHOTO 575. Monkwearmouth 17; 295; 418 to 420, PHOTO 697. Monkwearmouth 18.

TASBURGH, Norfolk. St Mary's Church.
176, PHOTO 360. Tasburgh; 420 to 421.

THORNHILL, West Yorkshire. St Michael & All Angels Church.
223; 278, PHOTO 568. Thornhill; 421.

THORNTON STEWARD, North Yorkshire. St Oswald's Church.
421 to 422, PHOTO 698. Thornton Steward.

THORPE-NEXT-HADDISCOE, Norfolk. St Mary's Church.
123, PHOTO 214. Thorpe-next-Haddiscoe 1; 132, PHOTO 251. Thorpe-next-Haddiscoe 2; 176, PHOTO 361, Thorpe-Next-Haddiscoe 3; 422.

THURSLEY, Surrey. St Michael's Church.
130, PHOTO 240. Thursley 1, PHOTO 241. Thursley 2; 422.

TITCHFIELD, Hampshire. St Peter's Church.
70, PHOTO 73. Titchfield; 422 to 423.

WARDEN, Northumberland. St Michael and All Angels Church.
423 to 424, PHOTO 699. Warden.

WHITCHURCH, Hampshire. All Hallows Church.
277; 279, PHOTO 569. Whitchurch; 424.

WHITHORN PRIORY MUSEUM, Wigtownshire.
262 to 263, PHOTO 540. Whithorn 1, PHOTO 541. Whithorn 2; 277, PHOTO 565. Whithorn 3; 424.

WHITTINGHAM, Northumberland. St Bartholomew's Church.
53, PHOTO 25. Whittingham 1; 70; 73, PHOTO 80. Whittingham 2; 424 to 425.

WICKHAM, Berkshire. St Swithun's Church.
425, PHOTO 700. Wickham.

WILSFORD, Lincolnshire. St Mary's Church.
55 to 56, PHOTO 31. Wilsford; 426.

WING, Buckinghamshire. All Saints Church.
43; 45; 75 to 76, PHOTO 83. Wing 1. PHOTO 84. Wing 2; 205 to 207, PHOTO 421. Wing 3, PHOTO 422. Wing 4; 426 to 427, PHOTO 701. Wing 5.

WINTERBOURNE STEEPLETON, Dorset. St Michael's Church.
303, PHOTO 614. Winterbourne Steepleton; 427.

WIRKSWORTH, Derbyshire. St Mary's Church.
290 to 292, PHOTO 588. Wirksworth; 427 to 428.

WITTERING, Cambridgeshire. All Saints Church.
54; 55 to 56, PHOTO 32. Wittering 1; 59; 60, PHOTO 37. Wittering 2; 62, PHOTO 47. Wittering 3; 64, PHOTO 54. Wittering 4; 87, PHOTO 107. Wittering 5; 177, PHOTO 364. Wittering 6; 428.

WOLVERHAMPTON, Staffordshire. St Peter's Church.
271 to 272, PHOTO 555. Wolverhampton; 428.

WOOTTON WAWEN, Warkwickshire. St Peter's Church.
59, PHOTO 34. Wootton Wawen 1; 78, PHOTO 88. Wootton Wawen 2, PHOTO 89. Wootton Wawen 3; 428 to 429, PHOTO 702, Wootton Wawen 4.

WORTH, West Sussex. St Nicholas's Church.
79 to 80, PHOTO 91. Worth 1, PHOTO 92. Worth 2; 134 to 135, PHOTO 256. Worth 3, PHOTO 257. Worth 4, PHOTO 258. Worth 5; 169; 429 to 430, PHOTO 703. Worth 6.

WROXETER, Shropshire. St Andrew's Church.
49, PHOTO 12. Wroxeter 1; 51; 170, PHOTO 348. Wroxeter 2; 268 to 269, PHOTO 549. Wroxeter 3, PHOTO 550. Wroxeter 4, PHOTO 551. Wroxeter 5; 430 to 431.

YORK, North Yorkshire. The Yorkshire Museum.
213 to 214, PHOTO 439. York 1; 431, PHOTO 704. York 2.